## KENT SERIES IN MANAGEMENT

Barnett/Wilsted, *Cases for Strategic Management*
Barnett/Wilsted, *Strategic Management: Concepts and Cases*
Barnett/Wilsted, *Strategic Management: Text and Concepts*
Berkman/Neider, *The Human Relations of Organizations*
Carland/Carland, *Small Business Management: Tools for Success*
Crane, *Personnel: The Management of Human Resources*, Fourth Edition
Davis/Cosenza, *Business Research for Decision Making*, Second Edition
Finley, *Entrepreneurial Strategies: Text and Cases*
Kirkpatrick, *Supervision: A Situational Approach*
Mitchell, *Human Resource Management: An Economic Approach*
Nkomo/Fottler/McAfee, *Applications in Personnel/Human Resource Management: Cases, Exercises, and Skill Builders*
Plunkett/Attner, *Introduction to Management*, Third Edition
Punnett, *Experiencing International Management*
Scarpello/Ledvinka, *Personnel/Human Resource Management: Environments and Functions*
Singer, *Human Resource Management*
Starling, *The Changing Environment of Business*, Third Edition
Steers/Ungson/Mowday, *Managing Effective Organizations: An Introduction*

## KENT INTERNATIONAL DIMENSIONS OF BUSINESS SERIES

Adler, *International Dimensions of Organizational Behavior*, Second Edition
AlHashim/Arpan, *International Dimensions of Accounting*, Second Edition
Dowling/Schuler, *International Dimensions of Human Resource Management*
Folks/Aggarwal, *International Dimensions of Financial Management*
Garland/Farmer, *International Dimensions of Business Policy and Strategy*
Litka, *International Dimensions of the Legal Environment of Business*
Phatak, *International Dimensions of Management*, Second Edition
Terpstra, *International Dimensions of Marketing*, Second Edition

## KENT SERIES IN HUMAN RESOURCE MANAGEMENT

Series Consulting Editor, Richard W. Beatty

Bernardin/Kane, *Performance Appraisal*, Second Edition

Cascio, *Costing Human Resources: The Financial Impact of Behavior in Organizations*, Second Edition

Kavanagh/Gueutal/Tannenbaum, *Human Resource Information and Decision Support Systems: Development and Application*

Ledvinka/Scarpello, *Federal Regulation of Personnel and Human Resource Management*, Second Edition

McCaffery, *Employee Benefit Programs: A Total Compensation Perspective*

Wallace/Fay, *Compensation Theory and Practice*, Second Edition

# SMALL BUSINESS MANAGEMENT

## TOOLS FOR SUCCESS

**Jim Carland • JoAnn Carland**
Western Carolina University

PWS-KENT PUBLISHING COMPANY
BOSTON

**To Trey and Jay for their patience and understanding.**

PWS-KENT
Publishing Company

*Acquisitions Editor:* Rolf Janke
*Production Editor:* Eve B. Mendelsohn
*Interior Designer:* Eve B. Mendelsohn
*Cover Designer:* Jean Hammond
*Manufacturing Coordinator:* Margaret Sullivan Higgins
*Compositor:* Progressive Typographers
*Text Printer and Binder:* R. R. Donnelley & Sons Company
*Cover Printer:* New England Book Components

PWS-KENT Publishing Company is a division of Wadsworth, Inc.



Printed in the United States of America.
1 2 3 4 5 6 7—94 93 92 91 90

**Library of Congress Cataloging-in-Publication Data**

Carland, Jim.
Small business management : tools for success / Jim Carland, JoAnn Carland.
p. cm.
ISBN 0-534-92036-5
1. Small business—Management. I. Carland, JoAnn. II. Title.
HD62.7.C357 1990 89-16135
658.02′2—dc20 CIP

# About the Authors

Jim and JoAnn Carland are ideally suited to author a text on small business. Their academic, business, research, consulting, and teaching backgrounds combine to give them unique insight into the problems and opportunities of small firms. The authors are entrepreneurs themselves; they have started two small businesses, one of which was a tremendous success and one of which was not. Consequently, they have experienced the challenges of entrepreneurship and learned how the storm is weathered. They speak as doers as well as teachers, and their text is founded on pragmatism.

**Jim Carland** holds a Ph.D. in management policy and systems with minors in finance, accounting, and economics from the University of Georgia. His baccalaureate is in mathematics from the University of North Carolina at Asheville and his masters in business is from Western Carolina University. He is a Certified Management Accountant and a Certified Public Accountant and has ten years of business experience. As a result of his work as a bank lending officer in commercial, consumer, and dealer loans, he has been involved in the approval process for loans to small businesses as well as the preparation and approval of SBA loans. His ten years of teaching experience include courses in small business, accounting, finance, and management policy. He has taught in both small schools and large community colleges and universities. An established author of more than sixty articles and papers, he is a recognized expert in small business.

**JoAnn Carland** holds a Ph.D. in educational psychology with minors in social dynamics, statistics, and computer systems from the University of Georgia. She also has a baccalaureate in French and Latin from Meredith College and a masters in education from Western Carolina University. She is a Certified Data Processing Professional and has five years of business experience. A prolific researcher, she has published more than sixty articles and papers and is a recognized expert in small business. She has taught computer information systems and small business at the college level for seven years. She has taught at every level from the fourth grade through graduate school and has been recognized for superior teaching by students, peers, and supervisors.

Frequent co-authors, Jim and JoAnn Carland have published in such prestigious journals as the *Academy of Management Review,* the *International Journal of Management,* the *International Journal of Small Business,* the *Journal of Small Business Management,* the *American Journal of Small Business,* the *Wisconsin Small Business Forum,* and the *Journal of Business Strategies.* Jim Carland's depth and breadth of knowledge in planning and management tools is complemented by JoAnn Carland's skills in teaching methodology, social dynamics, personality, and computerized systems. They have consulted with more than 300 small firms on a variety of topics ranging from computer systems to management processes. They have seen the inside of business in large and small firms and have experienced the thrill of success and the heartbreak of failure in their own firms. Their longtime collaborative efforts are culminated in this text, which reflects an exceptional depth of insight into small business.

# Preface

You have deeply ventured;
But all must do so who would greatly win.
Lord Byron
*Marino Faliero*
Act 1, Scene 2

Small business has become a fixture in the curricula of colleges nationwide. The interest that has developed in this topic is gratifying in light of the significance small business has for national and world economies and the challenging and rewarding careers it makes possible. We are pleased to offer this text for a first course in small business management.

The subtitle of this text, *Tools for Success,* reveals the primary focus that has been pursued in its development. As active teachers and consultants in small business and as former owners of two small businesses, we are convinced that a primary factor in the failure of many firms is the absence of management skills and planning. The fundamental objective of this book is the development of those skills.

The text is divided into six parts. Part I is an introduction to the subject of small business management. It describes the importance of the field from an economic and innovative perspective and examines personal considerations of importance to a prospective small business owner. Personality characteristics, life experiences, and their role in the establishment and success of small firms are discussed. The sacrifices required for success in a small venture are explored in depth.

Part II examines the tools required for the successful start up and management of a small business. Each chapter in this section has been designed as a "stand alone" so that any segments that are deemed unnecessary can be omitted. In fact, this entire part of the text can be skipped or sections of it can be used for review without impairing the remainder of the book.

The first chapter explains the principles of marketing that are pertinent to small firms. It establishes the knowledge that will be required to complete the marketing segments of the business plan and maintain successful operations. The next two chapters explain financial and managerial accounting and taxation. The focus is on the accounting knowledge the chief executive of a small firm should master rather than the processes an accountant will perform. Despite the fact that many readers of this book will have been exposed to basic accounting principles, experience teaches that few will have a real understanding of the relevant issues required for the successful start up and management of a small firm. Chapter 6 explores cost-volume-profit relationships and explains in great detail how break-even analyses and target sales analyses are conducted. Budgeting techniques with special emphasis on cash flow budgets and their role in strategic planning is the subject of Chapter 7. Chapter 8 on financial analysis focuses on the establishment of the analytical tools required for effective planning and evaluation in a small business setting. The final chapter in Part II is on computer systems and discusses the strategies required for the effective acquisition and operation of a management information system. In addition to establishing a level of computer literacy, this chapter details how a small firm should evaluate computer hardware and software.

Part III presents the business plan. A step-by-step approach to the initiation of a small business is explained from a strategic perspective. From the establishment of goals and objectives through market identification, feasibility assessment, development of financing, and the timing of the opening of a firm, the chapters in this section reinforce the value of planning as a key factor in the success of a small business venture. Because of their relative importance to a successful start-up, separate chapters on marketing and financial planning are included.

A special supplementary section called "Starting a Small Business Venture: Summary and Illustration" follows Part III. This section is an important and unique part of the text. It provides a detailed review of the business plan and an in-depth illustration of the actual preparation of such a plan. Because the contents of the plan have been presented in individual segments, this section serves to pull together all that has gone before. It shows "the forest" rather than "the trees."

Part IV is called "The New Venture." Legal organization and structuring and the pros and cons associated with alternative forms of business are covered in the first chapter. Income tax considerations and concerns are explored in depth. Chapter 14 covers purchasing an on-going business with a special emphasis on establishing the value of a firm. The final chapter of this unit explores franchising. Pertinent factors from the perspective of both a franchisee and a franchisor are discussed as are the pros and cons of franchising.

Part V is devoted to the management of an on-going small business. Strategic management and planning techniques are stressed throughout this section. The first chapter introduces strategic management and focuses on the functions of top management in a small enterprise. The second chapter examines the management of human resources and the third chapter explains marketing management. Chapter 19 deals with risk management and insurance issues and discusses the effective control of risks and hazards in operating a small business. The next four chapters treat special problems for chief executives of small firms. The effective use, control, and management of inventory, receivables, and production are explored in detail. A separate chapter on financial planning focuses on the acquisition and maintenance of adequate physical and financial resources for the operation of a small business.

The final unit in the text, Part VI, covers special topics. Any chapter in this section may be omitted without sacrificing the integrity of the text. The chapters cover international markets and opportunities for small firms (Chapter 24), business law issues (Chapter 25), ethical issues for owners and managers of small ventures (Chapter 26), and planning for management succession, bequeathing a small business, and the potentially catastrophic effects of divorce on small firms (Chapter 27).

The text stresses the importance of a strategic competency for a successful venture. The emphasis on tools and planning sets this book apart from its competitors. We believe that the key to success is planning, planning, and more planning. The tools we present are actually tools of planning. This text has been designed for individuals who will actually put its precepts into practice. The depth of material in the "tools" chapters will permit anyone to actually apply these tools in the start-up and operation of a small business. The detail in the planning chapters will enable an individual to systematically assess the feasibility of a business concept and to prepare a start-up plan. The managing chapters make the strategic issues clear and will facilitate the organization and maintenance of an effective management team in a small business.

The text has been written for individuals without experience or knowledge in small business. Those concepts from other disciplines that are mandatory for success in a small business are covered in detail; they include marketing, accounting, finance, economics, and management. A cursory reading of the contents might lead one to conclude that redundant material is included in the text. A closer examination will show that the depth and orientation of coverage is well planned and purposeful. Important concepts are intentionally reinforced throughout the text and discussed in relation to other topics so that all the many aspects of small business management fit together to form a more meaningful and applicable whole. For those whose knowledge of marketing, finance, accounting, and economics is oriented toward large firms, this text focuses on the aspects of those subjects that are pertinent and crucial to success in a small firm. In addition, the exposition of these subjects is precise and complete so that understanding will be facilitated.

The text is liberally supported with illustrations of concepts and approaches. Real-life examples and anecdotes are used to exemplify, reinforce, and illustrate important points. These are all actual cases, taken largely from our own consulting experiences. The abundance of these illustrations is one of the things that makes this text unique. The stories not only support the learning process, they add readability and interest. Short-answer questions, more in-depth projects, and brief cases at the end of each chapter allow the reader to apply and further understand the concepts covered in the chapter.

Our primary strategy in developing this text has been aimed at producing a book that will be both enjoyable to read and useful for small business owners. This, we believe, will lead to the achievement of our fundamental objective: a book that will aid the development of management and planning skills in small business owners.

The text is written simply and clearly and is well supported with examples. The book has a practical orientation and a real-world focus. We discuss all the subjects a small business owner needs to know about, and we talk about them from the perspective of a small enterprise. Our primary focus is on planning: we show the reader how to plan, we teach the tools required for planning, and we demonstrate how they are applied to produce a plan. Along the way, we have some fun, but we never lose sight of the objectives. We think that the result is a book that is readable and useful. We invite you to put us to the test.

This text would not exist were it not for the efforts of our Editor, Rolf Janke. His vision and support have been instrumental in the development of the book and in our development as writers. We owe him a tremendous debt. To Eve Mendelsohn, our Production Editor, we owe great thanks. The text would not be readable, well organized, and consistent without her efforts. To reviewers of the manuscript, Michael Cicero (Highline Community College), Renee Cohen (Southwestern Community College), and Paula Funkhouser (Truckee Meadows Community College), we offer our gratitude for their insight and support. To Nick Sarantakes (Austin Community College) we owe a special debt. His continuing efforts are largely responsible for the completeness of the text. The list of contributors to this work is long and distinguished. To them all we say, thank you.

Jim Carland
JoAnn Carland

# Brief Contents

# Contents

## PART III: THE BUSINESS PLAN

## PART VI: SPECIAL TOPICS

# PART I

# INTRODUCTION TO SMALL BUSINESS MANAGEMENT

# CHAPTER 1

# Small Business and Entrepreneurship

## LEARNING OBJECTIVES

After completing this chapter, you should be able to

- Define the term *entrepreneurship* and describe the impact of entrepreneurs on the economy of a nation.
- Define the term *small business* and describe the impact of small business owners on the economy of a nation.
- Describe the impact that business size has on the operations of the business.
- Describe the impact and importance of small businesses on innovation.
- Understand the personal goals and objectives involved in starting a small business and why they are important.

Small business had its origins when humans first began to live in groups, domesticate animals, and perform specialized tasks. Today a popular definition of **business** is, "the activities of individuals or groups who are involved in developing, producing, and distributing the goods and services needed to satisfy other people's needs or desires."[1] With a little imagination, we can visualize how business was born at the dawn of history.

One individual who was especially skilled at making a particular object was pressed by other members of the tribe to manufacture this item for them. Think about one of the earliest weapons, the sling. Making a good sling is truly an art. An individual who had mastered that art would be constantly besieged by peers to make slings for them. Surely these individuals would have been paid for the slings by meat or other items: the first barter. As the size of the tribe grew, the amount of time required to manufacture slings for other people grew. Soon the sling maker became an artisan specializing in the craft and dependent on the trade of the slings for food and other items. The sling maker was the first business owner, but was soon joined by other businesspeople who were adept at making spears and other weapons, clothing, and so on.

When primitive people began to specialize and produce goods or services for others, they were in effect participating in business, and because such ventures involved small numbers of people, they were small businesses. In fact, one of the earliest known writings, which dates from 2500 B.C., is a document concerning "money" loaned at interest.[2] As the size of the tribe increased and the demand for goods and services increased, these businesses grew. As tribes grew into nations and states, they developed laws and rules for living, some of which had to address business. The conduct of business was important to the well-being of every member of the society because each member increasingly was dependent on the producers for food, clothing, shelter, and luxuries. Each nation put its mark upon the activities that we call business and enhanced the means with which business was performed, while seeking to protect people from unscrupulous business activities. One of the earliest and best known examples of such laws is a code drafted by the King of Babylon in 2100 B.C. It contains 300 laws that were designed to protect both consumers and small businesspeople from fraud and other unscrupulous acts.[3]

As civilizations advanced, several factors caused the number, size, and complexity of businesses to increase:

1. More complex goods being manufactured.
2. Problems related to shipping goods.
3. Risks associated with collecting monies for goods sold on credit.

---

[1] All references appear at the end of the book.

4. The growing difficulty of communicating, frequently over long distances, with present and potential customers.
5. The increasing burden of compliance with the laws.

More and more skill in management was necessary to succeed in the enterprise of providing goods and services to others for a profit. The skill of the artisan was no longer sufficient for success. In today's business world, sling makers require capable managers in order to be successful in producing and selling their product.

## THE IMPORTANCE OF MODERN SMALL BUSINESS

Despite the rise in complexity of business operations, not all businesses became large; many remained small. In the United States, small businesses dominate the marketplace for many items. The U.S. government compiled a list of statistics that dramatically demonstrates the scope of the small business sector in this country. In 1978, the government defined a business as small if it "is independently owned and operated and is not dominant in its field of operation".[4] This definition was used to establish whether a business could qualify for assistance under the U.S. Small Business Administration (SBA) program, which was established in 1953 to aid small businesses. The Small Business Administration reports that

> There are some 18.1 million nonfarm businesses in the United States. Over 99 percent of these are considered small by the SBA.
>
> Approximately 98.8 percent of all businesses have less than 100 employees; 91.3 percent less than 20 employees [see Exhibit 1-1]. These small businesses account for approximately 56.7% of the gross product originated by businesses in the United States, and 56.5 percent of total business employment [see Exhibit 1-2]. The small business sector accounted for virtually all of the net new jobs created by business between 1969 and 1976. That pattern has continued to date [1987]. In 1986, civilian nonfarm employment reached an all time high of 101.3 million. Small business created jobs at 8 times the rate of large firms. Small business employment gained 1 million jobs while large businesses gained 97,000 jobs.[5]

It is not surprising that the president of the U.S. Chamber of Commerce stated that small business had been the backbone of the American economy since colonial days.[6]

There is still no clear consensus as to a definition for small business. The 1978 SBA guidelines were difficult, if not impossible, to apply. Some quantifiable guidelines were required. Consequently, in 1984 the SBA established a lengthy document, covering some 750 different industries, that delineated size classifications for firms industry by industry. These size classifications were based on sales in some industries and number of employees in others. Some

**EXHIBIT 1-1** *Business Size by Number of Employees*

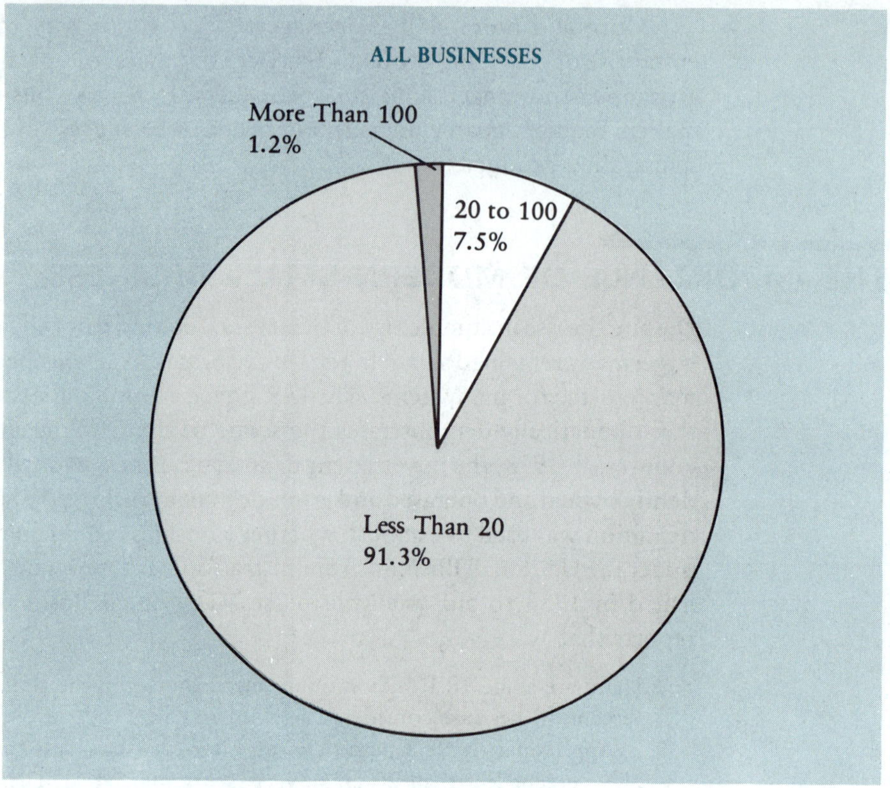


firms that would frequently be considered quite large still fall within the small business classification. For example,

- Service firms are considered small if their sales are below a maximum level ranging from $3.5 million to $14.5 million.
- Retail firms are considered small if their sales are below a maximum level ranging from $3.5 million to $13.5 million, depending on the industry.
- Wholesaling firms are considered small if their firms have a maximum of 500 employees.
- Manufacturing firms are considered small if the number of their employees is below a level ranging from 500 to 1500, depending on the industry in which they are primarily engaged.
- General construction firms are considered small if their average annual receipts did not exceed $17 million for the past three years.[7]

**EXHIBIT 1-2** *The Role of Small Businesses in Production and Employment*

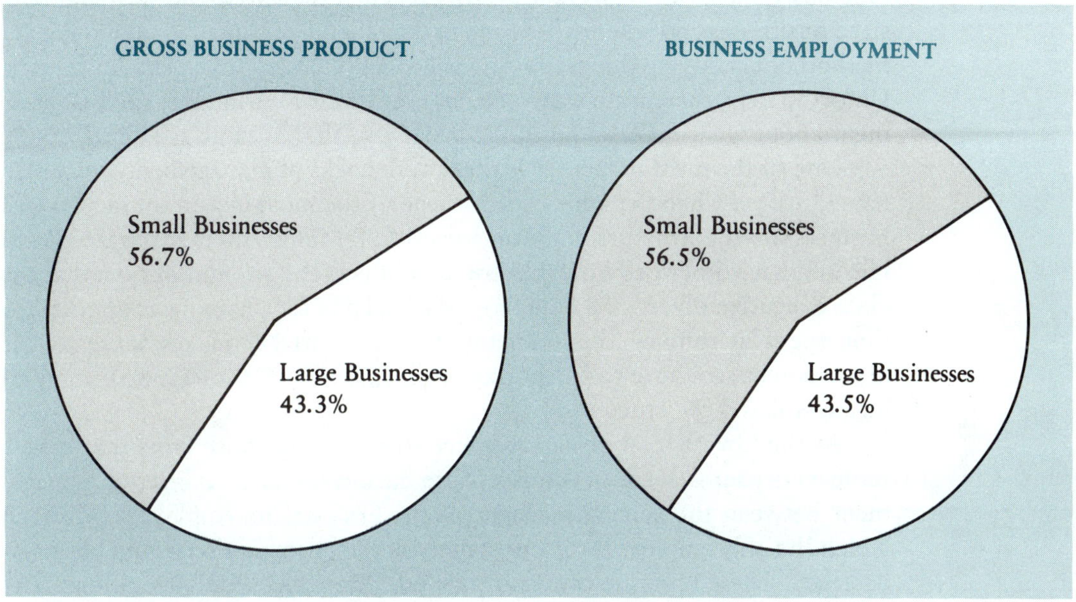


The specified levels vary by industry within the categories outlined. Many writers have embraced the SBA definitions, but others have criticized the wide range that the definitions permit. Despite any weaknesses in the SBA definitions, the statistics show that the impact of small business is real.

Frequently a writer in the area of small business will establish other definitions that generally require independent ownership and management and that select some arbitrary level of sales or assets or employees to qualify as small. Even if we choose another level such as number of employees, for example, the number of small businesses will still be impressive. A study by the U.S. Department of Commerce indicated that only one-tenth of 1 percent of firms in the United States employ more than 500 people and that 99 percent of all businesses employed 100 or fewer employees.[8] Regardless of the definition one uses, it is clear that U.S. business will be characterized by small firms. In fact, this is true for most of the nations of the world. The President's Task Force on International Private Enterprise declared in its 1984 report that "small and medium-sized businesses are the heart of the private sector in most of the countries in which the Agency for International Development operates."[9]

## A Taxonomy of Business

So far we have talked about businesses as if they were simply small or large. Obviously, businesses can come in any size. How then do we deal with middle-sized businesses and where do they fit in the scheme of things? A **taxonomy** is a method of classifying things; thus, we need a taxonomy to classify businesses. Unfortunately, there is no established taxonomy for businesses, and no agreement about what makes a business small-, middle-, or large-sized.

One of the most influential writers in the field of management was a man named Alfred Chandler who said that one of the most important factors in a business was the structure of the organization.[10] Many writers have agreed with him and have described how the structure affects the amount of time that the chief executive officer of a company has available for planning as opposed to time spent in running the company. Consequently, it makes sense to use management structure to categorize firms. Exhibit 1-3 shows a taxonomy of business based on structure.

At the lowest level of management structure are those firms that have a **unilevel organizational structure.** These businesses have no layer of management between the general manager of the firm and its employees. Firms in which the only employees are the owners of the business also would be in this category. These firms are frequently called "Mom and Pop" operations. The term is somewhat disparaging, but it is descriptive of firms in which everything is done by the owners. The general management in such a firm has no time to plan; in fact, it has no time for anything except day-to-day operations.

Those firms that have a **duolevel organizational structure** are businesses with only a single layer of management between the general manager of the firm and its employees. In such businesses, the general management is removed from the direct supervision of employees but still must devote the majority of time to operational details. More time is allocated to planning activities than in the unilevel firm but less than in the multilevel organization.

**Multilevel firms** can have a general management that devotes the majority of its time to planning concerns because a level of management above the direct supervisory level can handle the operational issues of the firm. Such firms may have more than one level of management above the supervisory level and below the general manager. The difference in such firms is the ability to delegate operational issues to lower management levels.

**Multidimensional firms** have more than one business unit, each of which is structured as a multilevel organization. Top management in such firms must devote the majority of its time to planning issues because the complexity of the overall operation is such that it cannot function effectively without strategic planning.

We could consider multidimensional firms to be large businesses and the

**EXHIBIT 1-3** *A Taxonomy of Business*

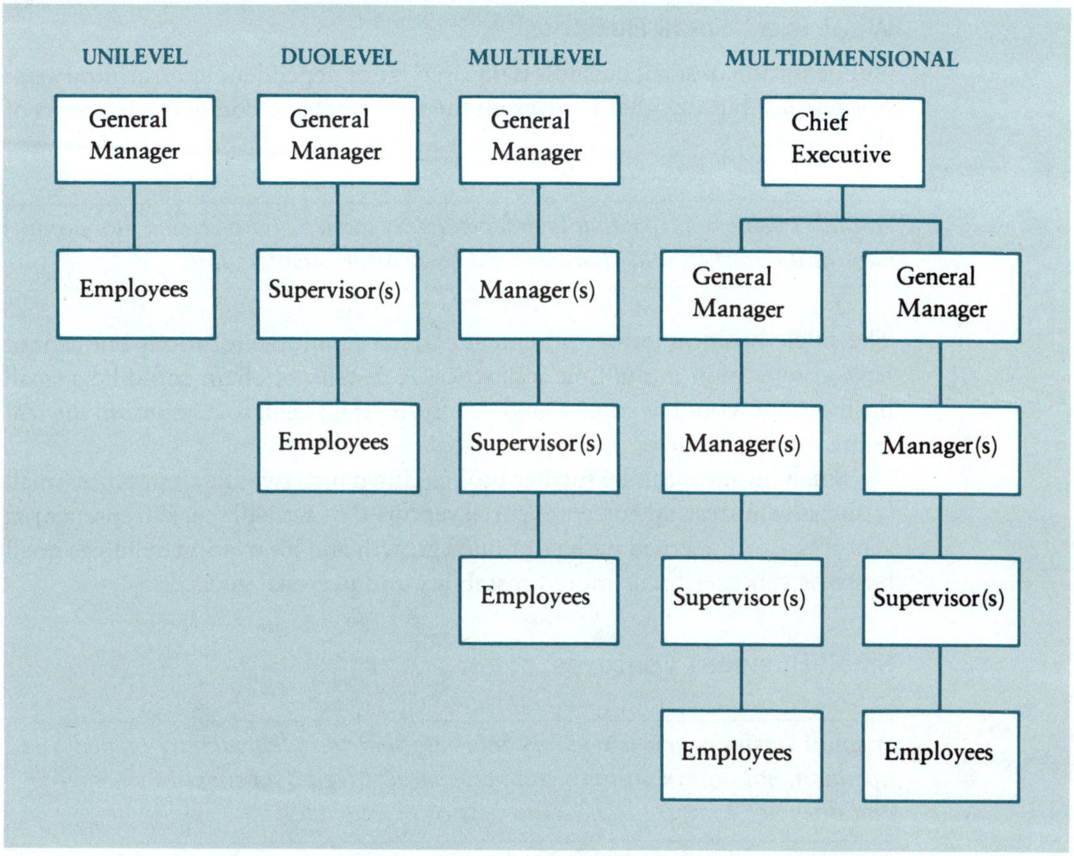


three remaining types of organizations in the taxonomy to be small businesses. It is these types of businesses that we will address in this book. It should be noted that a firm will not necessarily begin in the lowest level and pass through the other levels as it grows. In addition, the level in which a firm is located does not dictate the number of employees in the organization or its sales volume. A business can be started in any of the levels, including the multidimensional level, and it can stay where it is structurally or move up or down. The time available for top management to devote to planning activities does not guarantee that such planning will occur. The personalities of the top managers will dictate what is done. The important point is that management in the unilevel and duolevel firms *cannot* divorce itself from operational issues regardless of personal preferences. The taxonomy is a useful way of thinking about differences in business organizations that affect the way those businesses can and do behave in the marketplace.

## What Is a "Small Business"?

Our definition of small business is one that is not dependent upon arbitrary size restrictions, but one that focuses on the structural and competitive aspects of the operation.

*A **small business** is one that is independently owned and operated, not dominant in its market, and characterized by a single business unit.*

The single business unit requirement can have multiple locations but cannot have competition in multiple industries. A restaurant chain could be a small business but would become a large enterprise if it began to compete in the real estate market as well.

Small business can be further broken down into two different types: small business ventures and entrepreneurial ventures. As we will see, entrepreneurial ventures are concerned with continued growth and innovation, whereas small business ventures focus more on stability and personal goals.

## Small Business Ventures

*A **small business venture** is any business that is independently owned and operated, not dominant in its market, characterized by a single business unit, and does not compete in new markets or in new ways.*

Because they concentrate their activities in a single market, small business ventures have the greatest impact on the United States economy in the area of competition. Laws cannot truly regulate the business world because of the difficulty in discovering violations of rules. We cannot simply pass a law that makes businesses charge a fair price for their goods and services. If there were such a law, how would it be enforced? How could we know when a violation occurred? The existence of effective competition makes such laws unnecessary. Economists have long preached the values of economic competition in which the self-interest of a business owner will cause that individual to behave in a socially desirable manner.

Small businesses are particularly effective in the area of competition because they frequently have lower overhead levels, are more willing to cut prices to gain sales, and their owners are closer to the competitive picture than are the managers of a large business. The larger the number of firms competing with one another, the more effective that competition is and the less likely it is that businesses can conspire to hold up profits. The great trusts (e.g., Standard Oil) of the last century and the early part of this century were possible because a small number of firms controlled the market. The efforts of the oil producing nations of the world in establishing OPEC (Oil Producing and Exporting Countries) reflect their efforts to control the price of their product. As recent history has shown, the OPEC committee has been less effective than during its early years. Even the small number of member nations cannot agree consistently on a production and sales policy. Cartels, formal or informal, cannot exist when large numbers of competitors wield power. The large number of small firms in the United States and the substantial share that they have of the market collectively ensures that consumers receive lower prices, higher quality, and better service than if the economy were dominated by large firms.

## Entrepreneurial Ventures

The effect of small business is more pronounced in some industries than in others. As one might expect, small businesses play the least visible role in manufacturing ventures because of the immense capital investment they require. Small businesses dominate in the services industries where capital investment is smaller. But one aspect of the impact of small businesses comes through clearly in all industries: the role of small businesses in innovation. According to studies made by the U.S. Department of Commerce and by the Office of Management and Budget, small businesses have produced half of the major inventions in the United States since 1953.[11] Another study by the National Science Foundation supported those findings and further indicated that small firms produce inventions far more cheaply than larger firms.[12] This disproportionate role that small firms play in the area of innovation is highly important to the nation's economy. It shows up not only in new inventions but in the pioneering of new markets and new products and in the establishment of new and better means of production and distribution. Writers frequently call these pioneering actions **entrepreneurial activities.** Consider the following examples.

### From Carts to Cars

In 1885, William C. Durant, founder of the General Motors Corporation, was a twenty-four-year-old insurance salesman. That year he purchased a patent to manufacture two-wheel carts for $50 and went into business with Dallas Dort, a young hardware salesman. The company was very successful, based in part upon the marketing expertise of Durant. Yet in 1904, horse-drawn carts were about to become obsolete and replaced by the horseless carriage or the automobile. Durant saw the handwriting on the wall and reacted by purchasing the Buick Company, using the same practices of marketing hype and vertical integration (the practice of also purchasing companies to supply the raw materials and parts for his automobile industry). By 1908 he had become the largest automobile producer in the United States. He began with sixteen cars in 1905 and produced a total of 8,487 in 1908 to win that claim. Of course, today General Motors is one of the largest firms in the world.[13]

**The Apple Seed**

In 1976, a twenty-five-year-old technical genius who got his highs from integrated circuitry got together with a flashy twenty-year-old salesman to create a high-tech marketing scheme. The genius behind the microcomputer was Steve Wozniak, who could see sonnets in those circuits. Wozniak developed a way to scale down existing technology to make it smaller and affordable to consumers as well as businesses. Nevertheless, he never thought about selling his inventions until he met Steven Jobs, who had tried dropping out, commune living, the drug scene, and ascetic religious experiences. Even after a short stint with Atari computers, Jobs was not into the technical aspects of the machine but recognized an immense opportunity and was eager to "hold them up in the air and sell a few."

Both of our protagonists had some business experience prior to branching out on their own. Jobs had worked for a number of months with Atari under its original founder, Nolan Bushnell, and Wozniak worked for Hewlett-Packard. Both attended sessions of the Homebrew Computer Club, but Jobs was less interested in the technical aspects of the computers.

With capital raised by Jobs and Wozniak and some investment from friends, Apple, Inc., was on its way. The company was a product of the enthusiasm and talent of two individuals who worked together to develop a new product and a new market niche. From producing their first computers in the garage in 1976, the company was able to go public in 1980. Sales have now surpassed $2 billion. No company has ever grown so large so fast.[14]

Clearly, there was something about the people in these stories that was different from others who have started businesses. Whatever that nebulous difference is, researchers in the field of small business frequently call it *entrepreneurship*. The term *entrepreneur* has been around since the mid-1800s, and like the term *small business,* there is no clear-cut definition. Many writers consider entrepreneurial activity to simply be the establishment of a business. Such writers make no distinction among small businesses, terming the owners of any small business, entrepreneurs. One of the most famous of writers in the field of management is Peter Drucker. His definition of an *entrepreneur* is "somebody who endows resources with new wealth producing capacity."[15] In the recent writings in the field, differences among types of small businesses have been recognized, although there is no consensus as to what those differences are. In addition, it has come to be recognized that entrepreneurial activities can take place in large firms as well as small, although such activities may not be encountered as frequently in large firms. Our earlier definition of a small business venture was established with this problem in mind. We now can define another type of small business and have a clearer understanding of the actions of the two types of ventures.

*An* ***entrepreneurial venture*** *is a business created to introduce* new *goods or* new *methods of production or to open a* new *market or source of supply. The business will pursue growth and profitability and will be characterized by innovative strategic practices.*

Obviously, entrepreneurial ventures play a role in the establishment of the competitive environment which we discussed earlier, but they are different from other types of small businesses and will behave differently as well. This is not to say that one type of venture is superior to another. Actually, the nation's economy needs both types of firms because the small business ventures will provide stability and the entrepreneurial ventures will provide growth impetus. One of the sad facts about entrepreneurial ventures is that they frequently fail. Not all new ideas work! Clearly, the economy needs a group of stable competitors to maintain the balance required for larger firms. Entrepreneurial ventures would make a poor choice for this role for the same reasons that they are so vital to the health of the economy: they are unstable, always seeking new ways to do things and new markets in which to do them.

### McDonald's Origins

Ray Kroc spent seventeen years as a salesman for the Lily Tulip Cup Company selling paper cups and another seventeen years selling multiple-milkshake mixers for his own company. His mixers, invented by Earl Prince, made five milkshakes at a time and were selling for $150 each in 1954, which was expensive in those days. Ray learned that the McDonald Brothers, Maurice and Richard, were using eight of these multi-mixers in their shop in San Bernardino, California. He couldn't imagine how a restaurant could need to make forty shakes at a time, so he went to see for himself.

He was amazed at what he found. The McDonald Brothers really needed the production capacity because of the volume of customers they served. They had refined a system of production with a minimum of steps and had made french fries a fine art. Ray knew he was looking at a potential gold mine.

Ray tried to convince the brothers that they should open a chain of restaurants all across the country. He thought that he could sell thousands of mixers to such a chain. The brothers weren't interested. They were successful and satisfied and didn't want to take on the problems that a large business would entail. Ray suggested that they get someone else to run the business; they agreed and Ray decided to do it himself. Their agreement gave Ray 1.9 percent of gross sales from each franchise, of which the McDonalds would get .5 percent. The initial ten-year term of the contract was soon extended to 99 years.[16]

Note that our definition of an entrepreneurial venture does not require it to be a small business. Large firms can be entrepreneurial ventures as well. Many large firms spend a great deal of planning time and effort in an attempt to make themselves more entrepreneurial. Such activities will not be discussed in this book; we will focus on entrepreneurial ventures that are also small businesses.

## The Entrepreneur and the Owner of a Small Business Venture

What is an entrepreneur? We usually hear the term in context as the individual who owns or starts a small business. Do different types of people run the two classes of business ventures or are the people the same in both types of firms? We think that the people are as different as the business ventures they run. Small businesses do not have the depth of management that larger firms have; consequently, the businesses tend to reflect their owners. That is, the actions of the firms are a direct result of the desires, needs, and intentions of the owner. Because entrepreneurial ventures behave differently than small business ventures, their owners must be different also. We define an entrepreneur as an individual who owns an entrepreneurial venture.

*An **entrepreneur** is an individual who establishes and manages a business for the principal purposes of profit and growth. The entrepreneur is characterized principally by innovative behavior and will employ strategic management practices in the business.*[17]

**Strategic management** practices refer to the planning process. Our definition indicates that an entrepreneur can be expected to be more concerned with the future than with the day-to-day operations of a firm and consequently will spend a great deal of time planning for that future. This also means that few entrepreneurial ventures can be expected to have unilevel organizational structures.

Now what about the owners of small business ventures? Earlier in this chapter we introduced a definition for such ventures. We describe the individuals who own them as follows:

*The* ***owner of a small business venture*** *is an individual who establishes and manages a business for the principal purpose of furthering personal goals. The owner perceives the business as an extension of his or her personality, intricately bound with personal and family needs and desires.*[18]

Clearly there will be major differences in the way the two types of individuals manage their firms and the way the two types of firms will compete in the marketplace. Before we begin to outline the issues involved in these differences, let's look at the characteristics of persons who engage in small business successfully.

## PERSONALITY CHARACTERISTICS

Many researchers have sought to describe people who are business owners and entrepreneurs. Several characteristics have been alternately accepted and rejected as completing the profile of these types of people. Could anyone hope to start and maintain a successful small business? It seems to be the American dream to be your own boss. But what is required for this to happen? Studies show that people who start businesses successfully tend to be moderate risk takers, hard working, self-starters who plan their ventures.

Opening a business is risky at best, but when one must be able to meet one's personal or family financial needs based upon one's own ability to make a profit, the risk may seem even greater. The consequences of failure are certainly greater. The risk-taking propensity was examined by several researchers in an effort to ascertain whether it was indeed a characteristic of small business owners. The latest studies reveal that everyone has some risk-taking propensity and that people who start business ventures may not be any more or less averse to risk than the general population.[19] Every chance one takes to better oneself has risk inherent, whether a new business venture is involved or not. Nevertheless, everyone who starts a business is a risk taker and should be aware of the risks involved in the decision. Knowledge of the consequences of one's actions will allow the decision at least to be made rationally.

The popular press would have us believe that people who start businesses are gamblers who succeed in the face of great odds. This is patently untrue. Businesses created under conditions of great risk frequently fail. Some types of business ventures have more inherent risk than others. If there is an established market for a product, the requirements for success in a business providing that product are vastly different than the requirements for success when a business enters a new field or a new area.

If, for example, there are a half dozen successful pizza restaurants in town, then a new pizzeria will be successful in that town if it does a better job than the established competition. Location, hours, prices, food quality, menu, and service will be the factors of competition for the new restaurant. Success will be a function of doing better than the competition in some or all of these areas and in successfully convincing the population through marketing efforts that the restaurant, in fact, is better. In other words, success requires taking market share away from the established firms.

The requirements for success are quite different if no market exists. When Jobs and Wozniak started Apple there was no market for personal computers. Success for them required that they create such a market. They not only had to develop and produce a product, they had to convince people that the product was useful, affordable, and desirable. The fact that they were successful in this was not just a function of their brilliance. Had the population of the United States had lower educational and socioeconomic levels, they would not have been successful. Imagine their business being started in 1975 in Chile or in Argentina or in any of dozens of other nations in which the populations are more concerned with the necessities of life than luxuries. Imagine their business being started in the United States in 1965 rather than 1975. The venture would clearly have been a failure. Does this mean that Jobs and Wozniak were huge risk takers? The important point is that they were among the first to recognize that conditions were right for such a venture to be successful. We do not wish to minimize their accomplishment. Clearly, they were hard-working visionaries who merit their positions in history, but they were not starry-eyed gamblers. Many of the famous ventures of the past that deal with the creations of new markets are really examples of individuals who recognized conditions that favored the establishment of a new industry. Risk always is present in a new venture, but successful people recognize the risk and plan ways to overcome the barriers to success.

Studies have found that entrepreneurs have a stronger preference for *innovation* than owners of small business ventures. There are various types of innovation. If the product or service being offered were new, as in the case of Jobs and Wozniak, it might be classified as an *innovation.* If the method of marketing or production were new, as in the Ray Kroc example, it would also be an innovation. In fact, any new approach to any aspect of business could constitute an innovative venture. Entrepreneurs tend to prefer doing things in an innovative fashion and tend to spend a great deal of their time in determining new and different ways to do things. Owners of small business ventures, on the other hand, tend to prefer tried and true methods and spend more of their time in trying to make established processes more efficient. Both approaches are valuable, but the innovative approach tends to attract more attention. Entrepreneurs certainly are valuable to the economy because they find new markets, create new products, and generally keep the business world vibrant. However, our research indicates that entrepreneurs tend to have a distaste for detail; they tend to enjoy learning a new skill more than using it; and they dislike taking time for precision. Owners of small business ventures, on the other hand, are patient with routine details, tend to work more steadily, and have more realistic ideas about how long tasks take. They are good at precise work. Entrepreneurs also tend not to get along with other people as well as owners of small business ventures and therefore generally do not make good bosses. Perhaps these characteristics explain why entrepreneurs so frequently either choose or are forced to leave their businesses when they grow larger and become more bureaucratic. The management literature is filled with examples of businesses that became more profitable after the entrepreneur left the firm, the market settled down, and professional managers took over. Exhibit 1-4 compares the personality characteristics of entrepreneurs and owners of small business ventures.

The personalities of the two types of people we have described would seem excellent complements to each other. Unfortunately, they tend to have difficulty getting along with each other. Education can help make people more aware of the contributions that different kinds of people can bring to a business venture and understand the potential causes for friction.

## FAMILY BUSINESSES

Owners of small business ventures are a valued and valuable part of the business community. Personal aspirations to start or take over a family-owned business are as worthy as aspirations to invent a new product. The required skills for success in a small business venture are the same as those for an entrepreneurial venture. As we have seen, there generally is a difference in the personality characteristics of the people involved, but success will still involve a tremendous amount of work and will require the personal attributes discussed in the previous section.

A great deal of personal reward can be gained from establishing and running a family-owned small business. Such businesses can be either entrepreneurial ventures or small business ventures. The opportunity for spouses and family members to work together in the business is reward enough for many people. Modern society seems to place little emphasis on the family unit, but this has not always been the case. Pioneers in the American frontier required strong family units to survive. All of the members of a family worked together on the family farm in order to make it capable of supporting the family needs. Children were expected to succeed to the farm and were trained accordingly

**EXHIBIT 1-4** *Personality Characteristics of Entrepreneurs and Owners of Small Business Ventures*

| ENTREPRENEURS | OWNERS OF SMALL BUSINESS VENTURES |
|---|---|
| • Like solving new problems | • Dislike new problems and use standard ways to solve them |
| • Dislike doing the same thing over and over again | • Like an established routine |
| • Enjoy learning a new skill more than using it | • Enjoy using known skills more than learning new ones |
| • Work in bursts of energy powered by enthusiasm, with slack periods in between | • Work more steadily with a realistic idea of how long a task will take |
| • Frequently jump to conclusions | • Must usually work all the way through to reach conclusion |
| • Patient with complicated situations and impatient with routine details | • Impatient when the details get complicated and patient with routine details |
| • Follow their inspirations, good or bad | • Rarely trust inspiration and usually don't get inspired |
| • Often tend to make errors of fact | • Seldom make errors of fact |
| • Dislike taking time for precision | • Tend to be good at precise work |
| • Relatively unemotional and uninterested in people's feelings | • Generally very aware of other people and their feelings |
| • May hurt people's feelings without knowing it | • Enjoy pleasing people even in unimportant things |
| • Like analysis and putting things into logical order | • Like harmony |
| • Can get along without harmony | • Efficiency may be badly disturbed by office feuds |
| • Tend to make impersonal decisions, sometimes ignoring people's wishes | • Often let decisions be influenced by their own or other people's likes and wishes |
| • Need to be treated fairly | • Need occasional praise |
| • Able to reprimand people or fire them when necessary | • Dislike telling people unpleasant things |
| • Tend to relate well only to those with similar, logic-oriented personalities | • Relate well to most people |
| • May seem hard hearted | • Tend to be sympathetic |

*Source:* Hellriegel, D., Slocum, J., and Woodman, R. *Organizational Behavior: Contingency Views,* Third Edition (St. Paul: West Publishing Company, 1983). Use with permission.

during their youth. Growth beyond what was required to support the family comfortably was seldom considered or desired. A large number of families in the United States today pursue similar goals with businesses as well as farms. In addition, modern farms have become agribusinesses out of necessity. People involved in small farms place a great deal of emphasis on the family and keep the pioneer spirit alive. In other nations of the world, family businesses are a way of life. In China and Hong Kong, in Japan, in India and in numerous nations, family members are expected to enter family businesses and are groomed and trained accordingly. We tend to hear only about the huge foreign businesses, but small businesses are as important in other nations as they are in the United States and equally as prevalent.

Family businesses have been the backbone of economic development in the United States and continue to be a vital and energetic force in our economy. Individuals wishing to start a family business have all of the same trials and tribulations to endure as individuals starting other types of businesses, but may have the additional advantage of strong family support (financial and otherwise) for the venture. One aspect that concerns such ventures is the problem of succession. We will discuss planning for family succession in Chapter 27. The financial advantages of entering a family business may help avoid much of the pain involved in a business start-up plan. That is not to say that planning is unimportant. A new manager succeeding to a family-owned business should perform an in-depth assessment of the firm's strengths and weaknesses and should prepare a business plan that will reinforce the strengths and eliminate the weaknesses.

## SUMMARY

Small business had its origins centuries ago. Even though innovation and technology have spurred us to progress by boundless leaps through time, we still find that small business is the backbone of every free nation's economy. We have evolved using the technology of our day and enhanced our achievements through time. We have learned from our errors and benefitted from our strengths, made laws for our protection and enforced them with zeal, and used our imagination to dream dreams and create new worlds for the future generations to explore and expand.

The type of person who serves as the backbone of the nation's economy and maintains the stability of its growth is the small business owner who is willing to take the risk and strive for success in an increasingly competitive environment. The owner of a small business venture is that individual who goes into business to satisfy personal goals and often family needs, whereas the entrepreneur is the dynamic force who reaches out for growth, profit, and innovation. Although the two types differ in personalities and cognitive traits, they complement each other in the business environment.

Just as the individuals who own small businesses are different, so too is the organizational structure of those businesses. The taxonomy illustrates graphically the impact that structure can have on the functioning of the company. The majority of small businesses are unilevel in structure. Because of the involvement of the manager-owner in the day-to-day operation of these companies, much vital planning may be lost. Strategic planning involves those plans that can mean the life or death of the company and should not be left to chance. But many very small businesses or family-owned businesses find that the day is too short to accomplish everything, and planning typically suffers. Where the structure permits planning, the result is more often success.

## QUESTIONS

1. Define the following terms:
   a. entrepreneur
   b. owner of a small business venture
   c. strategic planning
   d. entrepreneurial activities
   e. family business
2. How do both personality or cognitive traits influence the success of a small business?
3. What are several personal considerations one might have when thinking about starting a small business?
4. In all planning in business, whether small or large, what are the primary considerations in a company? Why is this the necessary first step in the planning process?
5. Why is strategic planning necessary for success in small business enterprises?
6. What is the Small Business Administration's definition of small business? What are the implications for the future of small businesses without the guidance of the SBA?
7. Do you feel that innovation really is a characteristic inherent in successful small businesses? Explain why or why not.
8. Where did family business begin?
9. Discuss why it was necessary to have different definitions for different types of businesses.
10. Discuss the levels of the organizational structure (called the taxonomy) and their implications with regard to planning.
11. Must one always start on the unilevel tier when starting a business? Explain why or why not.
12. Strictly speaking, why is it impossible for laws to regulate the business world?

13. Describe a situation in which you may have witnessed the two personality types of an entrepreneur and an owner of a small business venture and describe how they interacted.
14. Which personality type do you feel is yours and why?

## PROJECTS

1. Find several examples of profiles of entrepreneurs or owners of small business ventures and discuss their characteristics and their long-term prospects for success.
2. To be one's own boss seems to be the American dream for a large number of people. If you could open your own business, what would be your service or product? The text should give you some pointers about how to start your own business, so you may want to continue this activity throughout the text as it explains about competitive strategies, strategic postures, and business plans.
3. If you are the employer in a small business, what types of personnel do you feel that you should hire, with what skills and what salaries? You have limited resources at present but cannot do all the work alone. Who would you hire and why?
4. After discussing this topic in class, several groups might like to visit some relatively new businesses in the area and ask them some of the following questions. After returning, these students should make a presentation of their findings. Based upon the answers to the questions, the students might then determine if the business owner could be classified as an entrepreneur or owner of a small business venture and discuss whether the company will be successful based upon those factors they deem important. Some questions that might be asked are
    - When you established this company, how did you plan to make money or what did you think would make your company successful?
    - Why did you start this company? What were your reasons and motivations?
    - What are your present plans for making money, or what do you think will make the company continue to be successful?
    - What is your company's greatest advantage over the competition?
    - What is your company's greatest weakness from a competitive view?
    - Who or what kinds of firms do you believe are your competition?
    - What are your long-range plans for growth or diversification of the company?
    - What are your personal goals and aspirations?
    - What have you done to make your company stand out from its competition, or what makes your company different from its competitors?
    - Do you feel that there are any external factors that could limit your success? If so, what are they and how do you plan to overcome them?
    - How much time do you spend in strategic planning? How much in day-to-day planning?
    - What are your long-term plans for the company—to make a living for your children or to go public or just to make a nice profit for yourself and your family?

# Case

Jim Reecer was a man with a dream. He had always wanted to go into business for himself. He had watched his mom and dad spend their lives slaving away in factories, just getting by but not happy in their jobs, waiting impatiently for retirement. At a very young age, Jim was determined that such was not going to happen to him. He was going to depend upon his own skills to get ahead and reap his own rewards. Enough of working and making others rich by his labor.

Jim was very good with his hands. He not only could fix what was broken, he could create masterpieces out of seemingly worthless junk. Locally he had made quite a reputation for himself, both as a handyman and as a source for unique gifts. Having worked at odd jobs to support himself through school and having made spending money working on his hobbies, he decided that perhaps he ought to concentrate on his assets and go into business for himself.

Jim was young but not naive. He knew that, to make his business a success, he would need more than just his hands. He would need a good business head, too. Jim's parents, who were quite proud of their son and his ideas, helped him get a loan at the local bank and find an inexpensive building not far from Main Street where he could set up shop. With the help of friends, Jim did most of the renovation of the shop and painted it in brilliant shades not only to brighten the gloom but also to draw attention to the "artwork" displayed there.

Just before opening his doors, Jim was beset by fear. How could he meet the public? He knew that people liked his work, but he had seldom sold any of his artwork or made any repairs for anyone except his friends or acquaintances and these people had come to him. He was basically a shy person and didn't like talking to strangers. He also knew that when he was working on his projects, he was totally oblivious to what was happening around him. He did not like interruptions even for such basics as eating or sleeping. What would he do? His friend Charles, who had been enthusiastically helping him get started, had been bubbling for the last two hours about how he should handle the opening of his shop with a party atmosphere. He had mentioned door prizes and balloons for the kids. Charles had thought the shop should open with a bang and Jim had imagined folks would just wander in from time to time, browse, and buy.

### Questions

1. What could Jim do at this eleventh hour? He wanted the shop to be a success but was beginning to see that perhaps talent was not enough. Discuss what you would do if you were he.
2. What does this case reveal to you about starting a business of your own? Is having a competence in one area enough for success? Why or why not?
3. From what you have learned in this chapter about personality types and small business ventures or entrepreneurship, what would be a reasonable solution to Jim's dilemma?

# CHAPTER 2

# Personal Considerations in Small Business

**LEARNING OBJECTIVES**

After completing this chapter, you should be able to

- Describe the personal considerations that influence people to go into business for themselves.
- Discuss the personality characteristics that frequently are attributed to entrepreneurs and owners of small business ventures.
- Discuss the influence of life experiences, parental influence, career displacement, and education on the development of personal values and the impact these values have on entry into small business.
- Understand the requirements for success in the small business environment.
- Be aware of the reasons why many small businesses fail.

Beyond a simple desire to be one's own boss, what makes people go into business for themselves? In 1971, Peter Kilby likened the search for an entrepreneur to the search for the "heffalump" that Winnie the Pooh conducted in A. A. Milne's famous book.[1] The heffalump was a large and important animal that everyone had seen. The problem was that each person who reported seeing the creature described it differently and no one wanted to admit not knowing what it was. People who start businesses are very like the heffalump: everyone has seen them, but no one agrees on their description.

A. A. Milne in his 1926 children's classic, *Winnie the Pooh,* featured a small boy named Christopher Robin and his teddy bear, Pooh, and their friends, including a small pig named Piglet. One chapter deals with Piglet's encounter with a Heffalump.

One day, when Christopher Robin and Winnie-the-Pooh and Piglet were all talking together, Christopher Robin finished the mouthful he was eating and said carelessly: "I saw a Heffalump today, Piglet."

"What was it doing?" asked Piglet.

"Just lumping along," said Christopher Robin. "I don't think it saw me."

"I saw one once," said Piglet. "At least, I think I did," he said. "Only perhaps it wasn't."

"So did I," said Pooh, wondering what a Heffalump was like.

"You don't often see them," said Christopher Robin carelessly.

"Not now," said Piglet.

"Not at this time of year," said Pooh.

In this chapter, we will examine some of the personality characteristics frequently attributed to entrepreneurs and owners of small business ventures. We also will examine the personal considerations involved in the decision to go into business and the characteristics associated with success. These attributes include the need for achievement, appropriate locus of control, personal values, and life experiences.

## THE NEED FOR ACHIEVEMENT

In a highly acclaimed work during the early 1960s, a Harvard psychologist, David McClelland, demonstrated that a high **need for personal achievement** was the primary factor in an individual's decision to become an entrepreneur. In several books and numerous articles, he demonstrated his precepts empirically.[2] However, in recent years the definition he used for entrepreneurship has come under attack. His definition permitted officers of large companies and salespersons, among others, to be defined as entrepreneurs. Many recent researchers disagree with his definition and, therefore, with his conclusions. More recent writers, attempting to duplicate his findings with a more rigorous definition, have found that the need for achievement is a weak indicator of the tendency to actually start a business.[3] We must conclude that a link between a high need for achievement and the desire to start a business is not proven. This means that people who go into business for themselves do not necessarily have a higher need for personal achievement than other people, and we must look to other personality characteristics to better understand venturers.

## LOCUS OF CONTROL

Other writers have attempted to demonstrate that an internal **locus of control** is the key factor in an individual's decision to start a business.[4] According to the locus of control theory, the outcome of an event is perceived to be within an individual's ability to control it or not. People with internal locus of control believe that they can and do control their own destinies and that luck or other external factors have no bearing.[5] Researchers have examined samples of entrepreneurs and declared them to have an internal locus of control.[6] However, recent writers, attempting to duplicate the earlier results, have disagreed with the findings.[7] Definitional issues again may be at fault. At any rate, a link between an internal locus of control and the initiation of a business has not been demonstrated, although there may be a link between successful people, both inside and outside entrepreneurial ranks, and an internal locus of control. This means that researchers think, but have not proven, that successful people in all walks of life have a belief in their ability to control their own destinies. Such a personality characteristic seems logical for success, but we still have no further information concerning the psychology of venturers.

## RESEARCH ON PERSONAL VALUES

One of the first major studies of personal values among people who start businesses was conducted in 1971, using objective tests to identify and measure a variety of personality characteristics. This study found that venturers scored higher on scales of **independence** and effectiveness of **leadership** than the general population, and lower on a scale measuring the need for support.[8] This would lead us to conclude that people who start businesses have more independent minds, prefer individual action, and display effective leadership. They also seem not to need support from other people for their actions or activities.

These findings are very attractive, because they tend to fit the stereotype many people have of venturers. However, the research was conducted with a small group of forty individuals, who had been in business for at least five years and demonstrated some success. The same study disclosed a high need for achievement among the individuals making up the businesses. In short, the findings cannot be extrapolated to the general population. Regardless of what we would like to believe about people who start businesses, very little can be demonstrated to be believable and dependable.

A great deal of research has been conducted in an attempt to better understand the personal values of people who start businesses. Unfortunately, all of it suffers from possible criticism of definitions employed. It is very difficult to study a group of people if no one fully understands who belongs to that group and who does not.

## THE ROLE OF LIFE EXPERIENCES

By this point it must be clear that no one really knows what the personal considerations in starting a business are! Even though our knowledge of personality characteristics is thin, we do know some things. It is clear that **life experiences** play an important role in the decision to start a new business. We will examine some of the aspects of those experiences in the following paragraphs.

### Parental Influence

Several researchers have shown that the children of people who started their own businesses are more likely to go into business than those whose parents work at regular jobs.[9] The record is clear that **parental encouragement** and support is an important factor in the decision to start one's own business whether there is a family business or not. Parents clearly impart a value system that can make a business venture seem more or less attractive, depending upon their perspective. This long has been true for virtually every profession; venturing is no exception. Several famous and successful people made references to the effects which their parents had had on their decisions to start businesses during a survey conducted by Babson College of its Academy of Distinguished Entrepreneurs.[10]

John Johnson, founder of Johnson Publishing Company, Inc., said: "My mother was one of the most intelligent people I have ever known. She is responsible for any success which I might have had over the years."

Mary Hudson, founder of Hudson Oil Company, said: "My mother and father firmly believed in the golden rule. They wanted for their children a good education, regular church, and success."

Mary Wells Lawrence, founder of Wells, Rich, Greene, Inc., said: "My mother used to whisper in my ear every night, 'You can do anything you want to, Mary, if you'll work hard enough.'"

Franklin P. Perdue of Perdue Farms, Inc., said: "My father established a rock solid foundation on which I could build."

## Career Displacement

Several researchers in the field have examined **career displacement** factors, such as the sudden loss of a job or a growing dissatisfaction with one's position; the impact of support from family, friends, and associates; and the existence of a mentor.[11] Most writers agree that dramatic changes in a person's life are closely linked with the decision to go into business. These range from the loss of an argument with one's superior to the loss of a country and forced immigration. It seems a sad statement on entrepreneurship that starting a business in the United States appears to be more the result of negative factors than positive ones. The loss of one's present position appears more likely to trigger a business start-up than the recognition of an untapped market or the discovery of a fantastic new product.

## Mentors

A positive factor with a major impact on the decision to start a business is the existence of a mentor. A **mentor** is a person one respects and looks up to who plays the role of convincing, assuring, and instructing. Such an individual, be it family member, friend, or teacher, exerts a powerful positive influence on potential ventures.[12] This is a well-known fact in other cultures, especially in the Far East. Immigrants from China brought a custom called **hui** with them to the United States. Japanese immigrants brought the same custom, called **tanomoshiko,** with them. In these customs, a pool of money is made up of regular contributions from the incomes of the members of the group. The funds are loaned to new immigrants or other poor members of the group for use in the establishment of business ventures.[13] American-Jewish communities have formed associations to provide free loans to help new immigrants, and Greek business owners frequently hire new immigrants and help them to start their own businesses.[14] These illustrations show that the American dream of owning one's own business is not restricted to America! They also demonstrate that positive influences can trigger the business start-up process and point educators to a role that can be assumed to foster business development and growth: that of mentor to students in small business and entrepreneurship programs.

## The Impact of Education

We cannot even be sure that education has any significant impact on the entrepreneurial spirit. Some researchers say that entrepreneurial abilities cannot be learned, whereas others say the opposite. Peter Drucker believes that entrepreneurship is a discipline and can be learned like any other.[15] Research on the impact of education on the decision to start a business demonstrates mixed results. In a 1975 study of fifty-six people who had started their own firms, it was found that 62 percent had graduated from college, and 59 percent reported that they had been "serious" about school.[16] All of the people in that study had businesses that survived at least five years and had at least eight employees; therefore, they had demonstrated at least some degree of success. Earlier studies tended to show that people starting nontechnical businesses had modest educational qualifications and often left school at an early age, though they did tend to have higher educational levels than the general population.[17] People starting technical businesses typically have college degrees and many have graduate degrees.[18] Successful business people, like researchers in the field, do not agree on the value or impact of education.

Education and its value to a person starting a business was discussed by the people surveyed by Babson College in its Academy of Distinguished Entrepreneurs.[19]

An Wang, founder of Wang Laboratories, Inc., said: "I was fortunate to have a good education."

John H. Johnson, founder of Johnson Publishing Company, Inc., said: "Education is important if you want to get ahead. I worked hard to get a good education though I never finished my last year of college. It was best for me; I went to college to get a good job."

Mary Wells Lawrence, founder of Wells, Rich, Greene, Inc., said: "My parents expected me to go to college. They wanted me to succeed."

Mary Hudson, founder of Hudson Oil Company, said: "My parents valued a good education."

Gustavo A. Cisneros, of Organizacion Diego Cisneros, said: "I am grateful for my . . . education."

Others surveyed were less sure of the value of education, as these comments indicate:

Wally Amos, founder of Famous Amos Chocolate Chip Cookie Corporation, said in a speech to a group of college students: "If I had your opportunity I maybe would have started Famous Amos cookies at 25. Then again, I might not have started it at all."

Franklin Perdue, who took over Perdue Farms, Inc., from his father, said, speaking of his father: "As I got older he seemed to get smarter, and after a couple of years of exposure to college professors I decided that the best teacher I'd seen in 14 years of education was back on the farm, so back I went to finish my education."

We can be sure about some aspects of the impact of education: the **requirements for success** in a business venture. If the business originators of the past have not been well educated, then the high failure rate of business start ups is more understandable. We will talk more about the problem of failure of business ventures and the impact education can have on that problem. Perhaps we do not understand the psychology of a person who starts a new business, but we do understand what is required for that new business to be successful. That knowledge can be imparted by education.

## REQUIREMENTS FOR SUCCESS

The majority of new business start ups do not succeed. Statistics kept by a variety of sources point to alarming **failure rates.** Dun and Bradstreet reports that 50 percent of all new ventures fail during the first five years, with as few as two businesses out of ten surviving for ten years.[20] The overwhelming majority of these failures are caused by poor management. Almost half of the failures are attributed to managerial incompetence, such as initial undercapitalization. We will talk more about the undercapitalization problem in Chapter 12. Over 90 percent of the failures are attributed to management errors and/or inexperience. Exhibit 2-1 outlines these statistics.

On the plus side, not all of the failures are bankruptcies. Many businesses are simply closed for a variety of reasons: boredom, absence of heirs, changing competitive environments, and so forth. Also, failure in a business venture does not preclude trying again. Many successful business owners have had business failures before finally becoming successful.

Henry Ford was credited with putting the country on wheels, but he was a loser before that. In 1899, Ford, together with a group of associates, started a company to build custom cars. He left that business, which later failed, to start another business in 1901, which manufactured racing cars. He personally raced 90 miles per hour in one of his cars, which brought him instant notoriety, but the market for racing cars was too small. That company failed. In 1903, at the age of 40, Ford began the Ford Motor Company with the express intention of building a car for the masses.[22]

Education can play an important role in reducing the failure rate of business ventures. Because managerial problems are the primary culprit, colleges and universities can attempt to provide management skills for its students. The primary purpose of this book and the college courses in this area is to provide those skills. Far too many people who start businesses think that all they need is a knowledge of the product or service to be offered—nothing could be farther from the truth. It would be closer to the truth to say that they need know nothing about a product or service to be successful in selling it. The knowledge required for success is managerial. The owner of a small business must wear many managerial hats. Large firms employ specialists in finance, marketing, accounting, production, personnel and planning; the owners of small firms must perform those tasks themselves.

**EXHIBIT 2-1** *Causes of Business Failure*

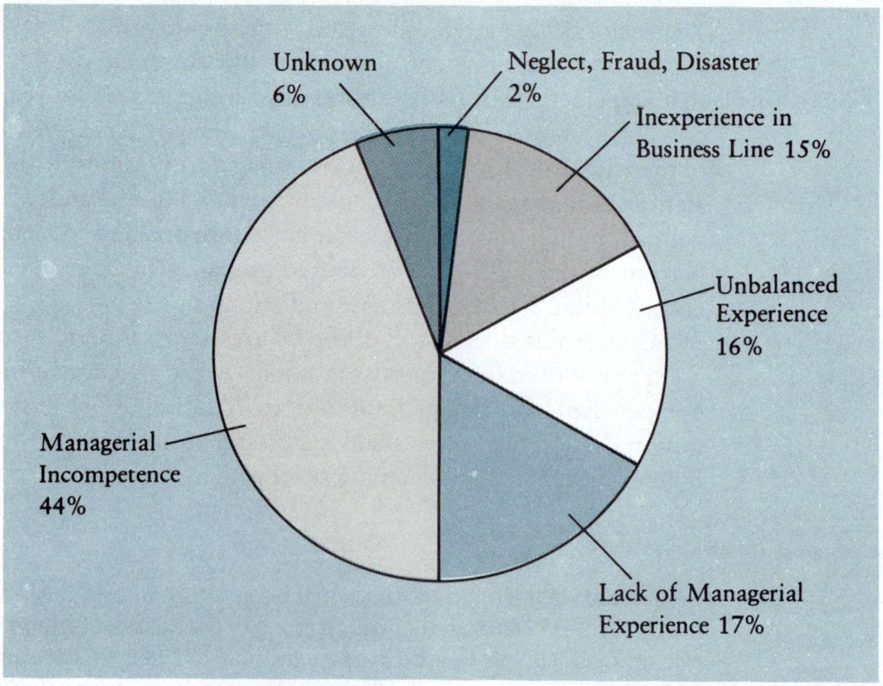

## Managerial Expertise

The first requirement for success in starting a business venture is knowledge of a variety of managerial functions and **managerial expertise** or a plan to acquire them. One need not be a specialist in all areas, but one must have an understanding of a variety of areas. Such knowledge is best obtained through a combination of education and experience. This experience is gained from working for someone else. Statistics show, and most writers agree, that work experience is a tremendous advantage in successfully launching a new enterprise. Obviously, this experience is best if it can be gained working in a business similar to that which one is going to launch. Even if this is not possible, some kind of work experience is an asset.

The second requirement for success in a new venture is the application of managerial knowledge before a business actually is begun. **Start-up planning** is crucial. Various sources show inadequate initial capitalization, poor initial marketing, bad site selection, misunderstanding of customer requirements, underestimation of competitive forces, overestimation of market size, and other such factors are prime ingredients in business failure. All of these and a host of other potential problems in a new business venture could be avoided with proper prior planning. The first step in starting a new business should be the preparation of a formal, written plan. In later chapters we will talk about what should go into such a plan and how it is prepared. This step is so important that some writers say it should precede the decision of what business to enter. That is, some writers say that an individual who wishes to go into business should first study various potential businesses and select the one that a start-up plan shows to have the greatest potential. Most people choose a business first and then prepare a start-up plan. Either way, a start-up plan is a must for success in any business venture.

## Ability and Willingness to Work

The third requirement for success in a business venture is the honest **appraisal of one's abilities.** Starting a business is hard work. A Gallup poll conducted for the *Wall Street Journal* in 1980 showed that 24 percent of the managers of small businesses worked 70 or more hours per week, whereas only 19 percent of those managers worked less than 50 hours per week.[23] These data are pictured in Exhibit 2-2.

These were managers of existing businesses. During the start-up phase of a business venture, one should expect to work much harder and much longer hours than will be required later. If an individual is unwilling or unable to devote such time and energy to a business venture, then it should not be undertaken. In short, it may not be necessary to be a workaholic to be successful in a business venture, but it helps.

**EXHIBIT 2-2** *Working Hours of Small Business Owners As Compared to Those in Medium-Sized and Large Firms*

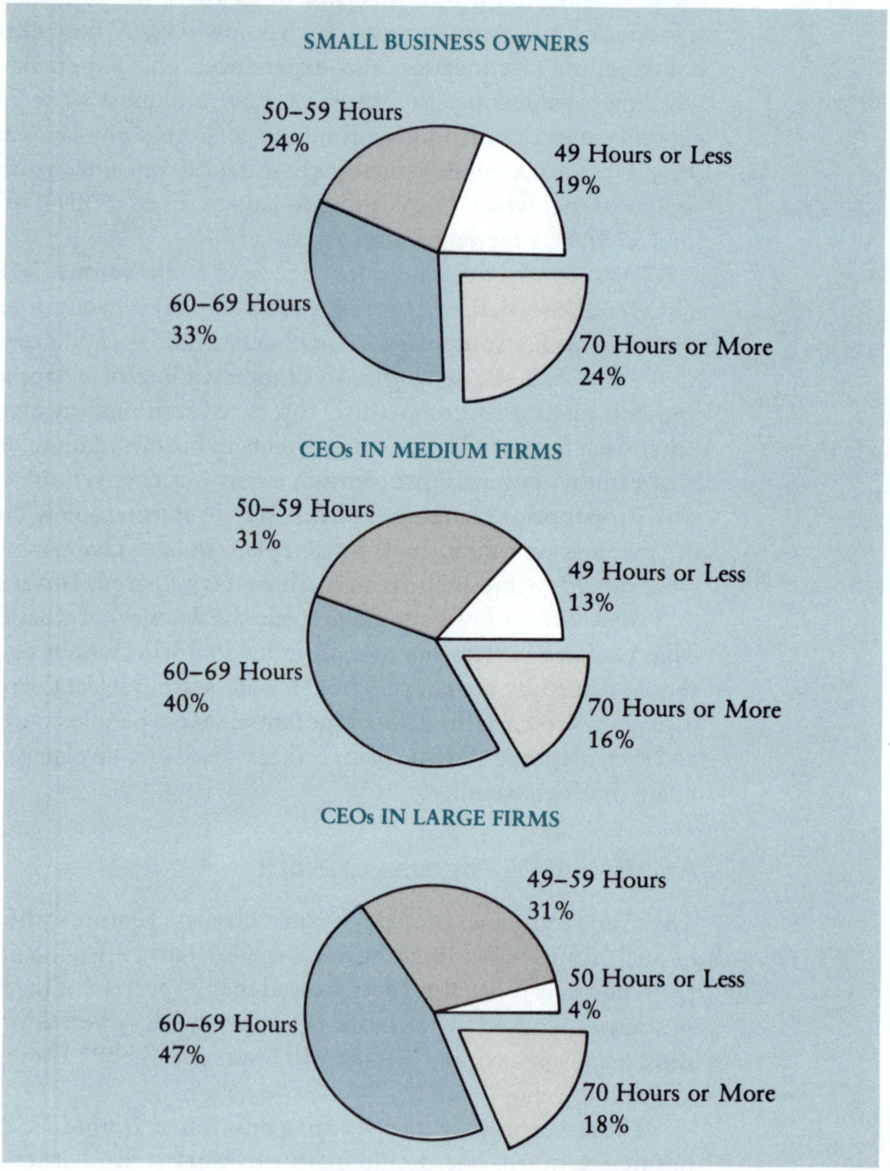

Self-appraisal should go beyond examining one's willingness to work. In a new business venture, no one will push, pull or persuade the boss. The owner must be a self-starter and self-motivator. Typically, self-motivation requires the establishment of **personal goals** and objectives and the acknowledgement of their relationship to the business goals and objectives. The written statement of these goals serves as a ruler for oneself as well as the others in a business. One's own goals and those of one's employees must support each other in order to ensure a successful work environment. This is called **goal congruence.** One also should monitor one's progress toward meeting those goals. Goals for the business will be a part of the start-up plan we talked about earlier. The personal goals may encompass those, go beyond them, or be entirely different. If you intend to start a business, then your personal goals should express what you expect for yourself at various points in the future: at the end of one year; at the end of five years; at the end of ten years. Such goals are not necessarily monetary in nature. They may include early retirement, more free time, careers for children, going public with the firm, and so on. The establishment of such goals, preferably in writing, will give you something to work toward and make continual self-motivation easier. It also will make it easier for you to be a finisher as well as a starter. Equally important for a prospective entrepreneur is to be an individual who finishes projects and undertakings as well as one who starts such projects.

Because of the long hours and hard work that will result from a decision to go into business, health is an important personal consideration. Poor health may make it impossible for one to follow through on the commitments made in a new venture.

Perhaps the best way to perform a self-evaluation is to consider oneself an applicant for the job of manager of the proposed business. What kinds of skills, education, experience, aptitudes, attitudes, and ability would you expect of a manager for your business? An honest evaluation of oneself as applicant for that job can be enlightening.

## Financial Requirements

One final attribute we need to discuss is wealth. Statistics show and researchers agree that the **primary source of capital** in a new venture is personal savings and loans from family sources. One step required in the business plan mentioned earlier will be the determination of start-up capital. A prospective entrepreneur should plan to have available a substantial proportion of the start-up capital required for a planned business venture before considering the plunge. Banks and creditors can and will provide some capital. In a later chapter we will discuss credit and financing of a new venture at great length. At this juncture, keep in mind a general rule of thumb: no one is going to be willing to risk more money in a new venture than the owner is risking. In general this translates into a requirement for personally having at least half of the start-up capital for a new business.

It should be clear by now that two planning phases are involved in starting a new venture. The start-up planning for the business itself is something we have touched upon in this chapter, but it is so important that we will devote an entire chapter to it later. The other planning phase that should be undertaken is personal planning. An individual who wishes to start a business would do well to plan for that action by establishing personal goals for the acquisition of knowledge and skill through education and work experience and for the accumulation of capital for the start-up phase.

## SUMMARY

To become a successful owner of a small business venture or entrepreneur requires more than just knowledge of a product or service; it requires tools and planning combined with hard work and ability. If owning your own business is your special dream, then be aware of the tools necessary, perhaps of the need for further education, and of the requirements for success. Don't be one of those who jumps into a business and flounders, risking family, health, and resources before finally closing in defeat. Be prepared and ready to spend the time and effort to be successful.

Personality attributes ascribed to small business owners include the intense need to achieve, a risk-taking attitude, an internal locus of control, and greater levels of independence and leadership effectiveness, and yet these characteristics are not definitive. Success is like the "heffalump": everyone knows what it is but has a difficult time labeling it or deciding how to reach that state.

Life experience, parental influence, career displacement, mentors, and education have been identified by successful entrepreneurs as factors that had a great impact upon their success, so perhaps inferences could be drawn in parallel. If you have had experiences such as those enumerated in this chapter, does that mean that you, too, will be successful? If you are able to heed the warnings, *plan,* and meet the requirements of success, no matter how difficult they may seem, success can be yours. Education is very important to your success, because it gives you the tools with which to work. Managerial expertise is essential. If you lack it, you must be aware of your limitations and get it for yourself or hire someone with it. You must be ready to work hard for long hours to accomplish your goals and come up with the capital requirements to get you started on your way to success.

Sounds easy, doesn't it! If you follow the prescription to success, it will be yours. Perhaps so, but remember four out of five small businesses have to close their doors in the first five years. Remember the secret of success is always *planning*. In the following chapters, we will help you to understand the important considerations in starting a small business and how each component is planned for success.

## QUESTIONS

1. If you were about to make the decision to go into business for yourself, what personal characteristics do you have that might make you successful?
2. What difficulties might you encounter or have to overcome because of your expectations or personal values?
3. Explain why or why not the following personality attributes are necessary for success in a small business:
   a. the need for achievement
   b. locus of control
   c. independence
   d. leadership
4. How might the following characteristics have an impact on success in small business:
   a. life experiences
   b. parental influence
   c. career displacement
   d. education
5. List and elaborate on the elements required for success.
6. What is the principal cause of failure in small business?
7. Discuss the failure statistics cited and state how one might learn from these statistics.
8. Why do you suppose being a workaholic is important?
9. Why is capital an important requirement for start up in the small business environment?
10. What two planning phases are important in starting a new venture?
11. Name several personal considerations for starting your own business.
12. Discuss the causes of business failures listed in your text.
13. Do you personally know of such a failure?
14. What can one do to reduce the risk of failure in a small business?

## PROJECT

Read the following profile of a start up and list those attributes that you feel made it successful. Are there any weaknesses in the situation that might have spelled doom if not handled adequately?

### The Apple Seed Revisited

The Homebrew Computer Club, located in Silicon Valley, was a prime factor in the beginnings of the Apple microcomputer. Stephen Wozniak claimed that the Apple I and II were designed strictly for fun, to be brought to the club and demonstrated. The club was a loose organization in early 1975; one of the first organizations of its kind. Stephen Wozniak and Steve Jobs, friends since high school, were members. The leader of the club was Lee Felsenstein, who later designed the Osborne microcomputer. The members would meet, trade parts, discuss projects and problems, and help each other. Wozniak passed out copies of the circuit schematics of the Apple I to members of the club and helped several members build their own machines. During the design phase of the machine, the computers were shown off every two weeks at the club meetings. Wozniak received tremendous positive feedback from the members during this time, which he found a highly motivating factor.

After a joint venture with "blue boxes" in college, Jobs and Wozniak found jobs with computer firms. Wozniak went to work for Hewlett Packard and Jobs for Atari. Jobs had long wanted to start his own company. Wozniak was more interested in the technical aspects of building computers. Jobs' experience at Atari led him to believe a fabulous market existed in inexpensive personal computers that no one was tapping. At that time there was only one personal computer in existence: the Altair 8800, which was based on the Intel 8080 microprocessor. That microprocessor sold for $370. Another microprocessor, the 6502, which sold for $20, was readily available. The Intel processor was available only through distributors. The 6502 chip seemed a natural for the processor in an inexpensive personal computer. Wozniak demonstrated this idea and designed a circuit that had the fewest chips of any microcomputer board built at that time.

Jobs developed a friendship with Nolan Bushnell, the founder of Atari, and several other key people in that organization. He developed a tremendous respect for Bushnell, who advised and coached him during the early start-up phase of Apple. Bushnell, himself a successful entrepreneur, may well have been the key factor in Jobs' decision to push Wozniak to start a company to produce and sell their hobby machine. It was an uphill battle. Wozniak enjoyed his work at Hewlett Packard and did not want to leave. In addition, he was concerned about the risk involved in starting a new venture. Jobs was relentless. He persuaded all of Wozniak's friends and relatives to call Woz up and tell him he was making a mistake. Woz finally was persuaded, and he and Jobs made the leap from a garage project to manufacturing.

They faced numerous problems, not the least of which was financial. Jobs persuaded a parts supplier to supply them on 30-day payment terms. They planned carefully. Production and sale prior to the parts bill due date was a must in the early days!

Jobs was as meticulous as he was brilliant at marketing. He not only sold machines, he sold people on the idea that the machines were useful and necessary. Nevertheless, a great deal more money was required for the firm to really get started.

Nolan Bushnell and Regis McKenna, of the McKenna advertising agency, referred Jobs to a venture capitalist, Don Valentine. The investor was repelled by the appearance of the principals: Jobs was wearing cut off jeans and sandals and sporting a Ho Chi Minh beard and shoulder length hair the day that Valentine came to see the machine. Valentine mentioned the visit to Mike Markkula, a thirty-five-year-old marketing manager at Intel. Markkula was intrigued. He ultimately left Intel and brought $250,000 and his not inconsiderable talents to the firm. Within months, Markkula had arranged for investments by venture capitalists totaling $377,000. With the required capital on hand, the company incorporated and began full scale operations.[24]

# CASE

Joan McCoy was a very good cook who loved making gourmet meals for friends and neighbors. Many times she would be asked to make her specialties for showers and weddings and felt quite good about what she was doing. Her husband, although he wanted to encourage his wife's enjoyment, felt that, when she counted her time and the massive storehouse of ingredients required by her hobby, she was getting very little in return for her effort.

Jim McCoy worked as an accountant in a large textile plant and was concerned about his job. The textile industry was facing enormous cutbacks, and even though he had been with the firm since graduation, he knew that he would be the first to go in a cutback in his department. Because of his job concerns, Jim also was upset about the personal expenditures at home. Joan was having a ball cooking for others and eating up the praise that came her way when her wares were displayed and tasted. When the McCoys were financially secure, there was no problem, but with Jim's job at risk, the extra expenses incurred by Joan were straining their already tenuous relationship.

One evening, in an effort to return their relationship to an even keel, Jim and Joan discussed frankly what was happening to their marriage and to their lives and how to improve the situation. Jim was worried about losing his job, even though he had been at it for a number of years. His job represented stability; it was nonthreatening. Joan wanted to work but her greatest asset seemed to be in feeding others. A friend, a local businessman who was aware of the strain Joan and Jim were under, suggested that the two open a bakery or sandwich shop. The McCoys immediately were interested. Working together in a business of their own might be the perfect solution.

After discussing what was necessary for start up with their friend, they decided to invest their savings in beginning a bakery. Because of his background in accounting and business, Jim knew some of the aspects of management and marketing. Therefore, he would handle the managerial functions of the bakery and Joan would produce the goods. If the business grew, they could hire some people to help out in the cooking area. The McCoys were ready to go. They began to plan the opening of their business.

## Questions

1. What personal considerations make it reasonable to assume that, if they plan wisely, the McCoys might make a success of their bakery?
2. What obstacles might they need to overcome to ensure their successful venture?
3. If you were the McCoys would you engage in this new venture?
4. List other alternatives to actually going into business that the McCoys might pursue initially if capital were a problem.
5. How might the McCoys raise the capital for their venture?

# PART II

# TOOLS FOR SUCCESS

# CHAPTER 3

# Marketing Tools for Success

**LEARNING OBJECTIVES**

After completing this chapter, you should be able to

- Understand the dynamics involved in marketing a product or service.
- Understand the considerations involved in marketing a product or service by examining the who, what, when, where, how, and why of purchasing products or services.
- Understand the factors involved in the marketing effort, such as seasonality, frequency, durability, location, and buying methodology.
- Be able to explain the three approaches to marketing — push, pull, and piggyback — and explain the advantages and disadvantages of each.
- Be familiar with the requirements for doing marketing research.

This chapter will focus on the marketing tools required for success in a small business. We will examine why people buy things, how things are sold, and the principles of marketing research. Finally, we will address the image of small businesses and the need for consistency in approach.

Early in the process of starting a small business a decision must be made as to the product or service to be offered. Many people choose a product or service based on past situations or experience. Others discover a product or service that they think no one is addressing and for which they believe a large market exists. Both approaches have value. It always is valuable to have experience with the product or service you intend to sell. This helps you to understand what is required in producing and selling the items. Tom Land, the founder of Land Pyrometers, one of the largest producers of industrial thermometers, avows, "Business is founded on knowledge."[1]

New products and services are valuable as are innovative ways of making, packaging, or offering existing items. If you plan to start a small business, you must be very careful during the start-up phase. All too often potential entrepreneurs take Ralph Waldo Emerson's words to heart: "If a man can write a better book, preach a better sermon, or make a better mouse trap than his neighbor, though he builds his house in the woods, the world will make a beaten path to his door."[2]

Many enterprises seem to bear out the truth of Emerson's words. Consider the case of Win Schuler, a millionaire restauranteur.

> Located in Marshall, Michigan, a town of only 6,000 people, Win Schuler built a restaurant which served more than 500,000 patrons in 1959. Many patrons commuted 100 miles, each way, to eat at Schuler's. Another half million people ate in the three newer units in Jackson, Grand Rapids, and St. Joseph, Michigan. One patron, when interviewed, explained, "this is the place to go. The food is excellent, the atmosphere unusual, and they know how to take care of people." Such attitudes among his customers has propelled Mr. Schuler's net worth to $3 million.[3]

Before you take Emerson too seriously, please note that Win Schuler took over the restaurant from his father in 1936. From then until 1946, it had a lackluster history and mediocre success. In 1946, the building was redesigned to give it the appearance of a European inn. The new decor, coupled with the 15-hour, seven-day weeks that Schuler worked, transformed it into the marvel it was in 1960. The truth is that Emerson was a bit naive. He failed to take the time factor into consideration in his advice to would-be business owners. Today we know that the world may beat a path to our door because of our superior offerings, but without a little help from the science of marketing, we may be out of business before the world gets there! It would be closer to the truth to accept the old adage: "nothing happens until somebody sells something."

Harley Procter, a salesman for Procter and Gamble, the family candle, lard, and soap company, realized the truth of that statement in 1878. When his firm developed a new, hard, white soap, he was given the job of selling it to America. His efforts laid the groundwork for much of the consumer advertising, merchandising, and marketing techniques in use today. Procter and Gamble remains one of the largest advertisers in the world, constantly renewing its faith in the sales process pioneered by Harley, despite the original reluctance the firm displayed when he proposed national advertising for what he dubbed "ivory" soap.[4] This is the point to keep in mind in selecting a product or service for a new business. Regardless of what the item is or what its appeal may be, it must still be sold! This means that the first thing we need to do is examine the sales process to better understand buyer motivation.

People buy things for complex, poorly understood reasons. Marketers attempt to examine those reasons by looking at consumer demand from the perspective of the who, what, when, where, how, and why of purchasing decisions. Exhibit 3-1 outlines the purchasing decision.

## WHO BUYS THINGS?

The **who** refers to the people making the purchase, which is not as simplistic as it sounds. Identification of the "who" in the purchasing decision is the first step in identifying a target market. The **target market** refers to the subgroup of the population to whom a particular product or service is sold. It is one of the most important concepts in marketing because it serves to focus marketing activities and planning.

Few items have universal appeal. This means that purchasers of a product or service generally can be classified as to age, sex, educational attainment,

**EXHIBIT 3-1** *The Purchasing Decision*

- *Who* buys things?
- *What* do people buy?
- *When* do people buy?
- *Where* do people buy?
- *How* do people buy?
- *Why* do people buy?

occupation or profession, family income, social status, and a host of other factors. Understanding those factors makes it easier to design marketing activities that will appeal to the appropriate group. Did you ever wonder why beer producers so frequently use professional athletes to promote their products? It is because marketing research shows that the primary consumers of beer are men, aged eighteen to forty, with blue-collar occupations and a strong identification with physical prowess. This is not to say that all beer drinkers have those characteristics nor that such characteristics are in any way undesirable. It simply means that a large proportion of the demand for beer comes from consumers who can be impressed and influenced by the use of professional athletes.

Few people can be expected to start a new beer brewery but the process of identification of the target market is just as important for any other type of business. If you plan to open a small hardware store in a small town, you must know to whom you will be selling in order to assess the prospects for success. Who buys hardware? If we determine by marketing research that the target market is men, aged twenty to fifty, homeowners, with middle-level family incomes and strong identification with hobbies, crafts, and do-it-yourself repairs, then finding the best location for the hardware store is a function of finding a community with a large proportion of those kinds of people. It almost seems so trivial and obvious when you look at it that way that you might wonder why anyone would fail to consider the "who" in the purchasing decision. People make such mistakes frequently! The obvious easily can be overlooked in the excitement of starting a new business. Consider the experience of a lounge owner.

---

We were called in as consultants by the owner of a small lounge in coastal Alabama. The owner, who was operating the lounge as a proprietorship, had been open for six months and had been losing money steadily during that time. The lounge was located in a small town located 50 miles from the nearest city and dominated by the shrimp fishing industry. We went to see the owner at the lounge on a Friday night. It was situated on the main drag, 3 or 4 miles from the center of the little town. We passed by another lounge on the way out that had a parking lot filled with cars.

When we got there we were really impressed with the place. It was beautiful! The owner said he had invested $20,000 in leasehold improvements in the place, and I don't doubt it. The building was well done, both inside and outside. It had a long padded bar, a carpeted floor space with circular tables and padded chairs, a hardwood dance floor, and a raised stage for musicians. Live music was featured on Friday and Saturday nights. No big names, but good players who featured contemporary pop music. The bar served several kinds of beer on tap, wine, mixed drinks, and snacks. No food was served except for a weekly oyster bash on Tuesday nights featuring fresh oysters and shrimp. Prices seemed to us to be reasonable. Not cheap, but not too expensive either. He had a bartender and two waitresses who were clean, well dressed, and polite. They were all young. The bartender was wearing a tie. The few customers in the lounge all seemed to be enjoying themselves. They were young, couples mostly and were all dressed nicely.

The owner said that this lounge had been a dream of his for years. He had always wanted to own a really nice place, not what he called a honky tonk. He had finally saved enough money to make the venture, but he was not a wealthy man and could not continue to put money into the business. He had tried all kinds of specials and all kinds of advertising, but he couldn't seem to make a profit. He had talked to customers at great length, but all of them said they loved the place and wouldn't change a thing. That's why he had called us. He was on the verge of losing the place.

We talked to him and the employees, looked at the books, watched the customers for a while and left. We told him we'd get back to him soon. On the way out of town we stopped by that other lounge we had passed to look at his competition. The place was jumping! It had a juke box, blaring so loud you couldn't hear a thing. It was packed with people, most of whom were wearing work clothes. The place wasn't nearly as nice as our client's and honestly wasn't terribly clean. Our client's problem suddenly became crystal clear.

Is it clear to you why the lounge owner was having problems? He had simply failed to consider the target market when he started the business. His lounge probably would have been a smashing success had he located it in a larger city. But the people in the small coastal town in which he did locate the business never considered his lounge for anything other than a place to go on special occasions, and there simply weren't enough people for him to be successful based on such an infrequent patronage. His competition was successful because it was perceived as an everyday place to go, and therefore had people coming frequently. Sadly, the stuff that dreams are made of may not sell at a given time or place.

We need to discuss one more aspect of the "who" issue. The person who buys an item is not necessarily the person who will use that item. Earlier we talked about who drank beer and we identified the consumers as predominantly men. That is true, but the purchasers of beer are predominantly women, because the major sales of the beverage are in grocery stores to women who buy it for their husbands. If you think about it you can see how the issue of who is going to buy an item is as important as who is going to use it. Most toys are used by children but purchased by adults. Therefore success in toy sales is a function of offering toys that will appeal to both the users and the buyers. Marketing efforts need to be oriented toward both groups. Frequently, this requires different marketing approaches. Saturday morning television is saturated with toy commercials aimed at children, but marketing efforts aimed at parents and grandparents must be timed and designed differently because they normally do not watch Saturday morning cartoons.

Of course, it is possible to rely totally on the demand created in the primary consumer without concern for the purchaser. Such a strategy would mean that a toy maker would depend on children communicating to their parents which toys they preferred. Toys that create a high level of desire in children probably need no other marketing effort. In recent years the He Man and Nintendo toys are a good example. Toys with a somewhat lower demand level or designed for children who cannot communicate well must have some marketing aimed at parents.

It also is possible to depend totally on marketing aimed at the purchaser rather than the consumer. In the toy example, a company that makes educational toys might decide to direct all of its marketing at parents and ignore the children completely. The point is that a firm needs to know who buys as well as who uses its products in order to market effectively.

## WHAT DO PEOPLE BUY?

The **what** of marketing may or may not be the product or service that people buy. Consider the case of a restaurant in a college town. Most college towns have no scarcity of restaurants from which students may choose. What makes the students select one restaurant frequently enough to make that business successful? Obviously food is not the only factor. A location convenient to the students clearly will be a major factor, but is there anything else? What makes you choose a restaurant when you decide to go out? Would it make any difference to your decision if you knew that you would see other students who were friends at a particular place? If you plan to open a restaurant, it may well be that what you will be selling is entertainment as much or more than food. If so, then the atmosphere of the restaurant will be as important as the menu and the food preparation. Remember, Win Schuler's restaurant did not begin growing until he changed the atmosphere.

Consider a hamburger franchise restaurant located on an expressway. Does such a place sell food or convenience? Does it make a difference? It certainly will! Speed of service will be more important to a restaurant selling to people in a hurry whereas food quality will be more important to a restaurant selling a taste treat.

Think about what is required for a national fast food restaurant to be successful. Food quality is obviously a factor, but how strong a factor and in what fashion? When travelers from out of town stop in at a McDonald's restaurant, what is it that they expect? If you think about that for a bit, you might see that food consistency is more important than any other aspect of quality. Travelers have eaten at other McDonald's restaurants, so they know what the sandwiches are supposed to taste like. So long as they are not unpleasantly surprised, the food quality will not be a factor in their decision to stop at another McDonald's in the next town or state. Some analysts think that the problems that the Kentucky Fried Chicken restaurants encountered a few years ago was the absence of consistency. Because the majority of the restaurants were franchised, the company exerted little control over them and the food ranged all over the scale in terms of taste and quality. The firm has since begun a program of acquiring more of the outlets and exerting more control over the remaining franchises. Its performance has improved since those changes were implemented.

The "what" that a business sells must be clearly understood to market effectively. If convenience, service, speed, or other factors are more important than the merchandise, then that is to be promoted in the marketing efforts, and also that is most important in the daily management of the enterprise.

## WHEN DO PEOPLE BUY?

The issue of **when** people buy a particular product or service includes but is not limited to the time of day. A major problem restaurants face is that people predominantly eat at set times each day. This means that the capacity of a restaurant must be adequate to handle the load during those times, and yet it will have excess capacity and therefore unnecessary expense most other times. The timing issue is closely related to the target market to which a business appeals. For instance, if a business appeals primarily to middle-income, working people, its hours must accommodate the times those people have available for shopping. The issue is much broader than that. Most businesses have seasonal patterns. This means that they sell more at certain times of the year than at other times. Consider a novelty and gift shop located in a vacation resort. Such businesses frequently close after the tourist season to save money, because they know that the sales volume at other times of the year is too low to cover the cost of staying open. Even when seasonality is less pronounced, it still has an effect; and marketing activities need to be closely meshed with the seasonality of a business.

Timing the opening date of a new business cannot be accomplished without knowledge of the seasonality factor. One restaurant with which we were familiar opened its doors in June after most of the students in town had gone home for the summer. The summer school population of the town was dramatically lower than at other times of the year, as is the case in most college towns, and the restaurant sustained extreme losses throughout its first summer of operations. The business was never able to recover and closed its doors within six months.

Another aspect of the "when" issue is the frequency of purchase. People buy soap more frequently than they buy cars. That means that you sell soap differently than cars. Soap is a **consumable** item: it is used up frequently and more must be purchased. Cars are **durable** items: they are used up over a longer period of time and therefore replaced infrequently. The development of **brand loyalty** is a frequent strategy in the consumables industry. Pepsi wants you to always buy a Pepsi instead of a Coke, and so their marketing efforts are aimed at developing that loyalty. It is much more difficult to develop brand loyalty in durables, so the producers of such items tend to concentrate on the characteristics that make their products superior in price, quality, or performance when compared to their competitors. The same holds true for services. Tax preparation services are sold differently than real estate listing services. The marketing approach and the timing of the opening of a business both are affected by the frequency of the purchase decision.

## WHERE DO PEOPLE BUY?

Did you ever stop to consider why retail stores tend to group themselves together? The issue of **where** people buy is one of the factors behind the development of shopping centers and malls. The grouping is largely a matter of finding a location convenient to shoppers. As recently as twenty years ago, the downtown area was the most convenient available, so retailers tended to congregate there. Suburban living patterns, two-income households, and changing life-styles changed all that. Now, a major social problem facing American cities is the decay of downtown shopping areas caused by the flight of retailers to malls and shopping centers located on the periphery.

Another factor, which plays a role in the development of malls and shopping centers, is **derived traffic.** That means that smaller retailers tend to group themselves near large stores that draw large numbers of people. In a shopping center or mall, such stores are called **anchors.** In a shopping center, the anchor store is frequently a grocery store. They make good anchors because people use them so frequently. Location of other retailers close to a grocery store enhances the convenience and also provides higher visibility. In malls the anchors tend to be major department stores. Such stores tend to have larger volumes of customer traffic because of their marketing efforts and the broad product lines they offer. Location of other retailers close to such stores enhances their convenience and visibility and also frequently aids sales when those retailers offer products and services complementary or competitive with those of the anchors.

Location and occupancy expense are interrelated. In general, the more desirable a location, the higher is the rent or purchase price of the site. Consequently, new businesses frequently choose lower rent areas in an effort to save money. This is not always wise. Although a lower occupancy expense is desirable for a new business, without established traffic patterns of consumers that business can tap, it will have to expend more marketing dollars to draw the necessary volume of people than otherwise. Marketing costs may well consume the occupancy savings. We will have a great deal to say about this problem in Chapter 11.

So far we have discussed the "where" issue as though it affected only retail businesses. This is not true; it also affects service businesses, wholesalers, manufacturers, and construction firms. In fact it affects every business to a greater or lesser degree. Consider a wholesaler: location of the business itself is important because of shipping patterns and costs, but the issue of where people buy the products is still real. The difference is that now the business is one step removed from the ultimate location of the purchase. The considerations for the wholesaler revolve around the kinds of retailers that will be approached. Marketing efforts must now include the retailer.

Services must be easily available to customers. Many times professionals will locate in parks with other professionals to attract their own and their competitors' customers. Although the reputation of a profession or service may be a draw after a few years, many times new businesses must compete for their clients with the existing market. Services must be convenient to the customers, so they must be easy to reach with sufficient parking for the clientele. Notice the increase of small financial institutions and photo kiosks in the parking areas of supermarkets. A small local bank has a branch with all the traditional services of the large banks actually in the grocery store. The location of service companies also can be important, because of its effect on their image. Consider the potential success of a young accountant or lawyer setting up shop in a strip shopping center versus one setting up shop in a professional park.

Manufacturers and construction firms have different needs. They typically sell their goods or products to wholesalers or dealers, so their main concern is sufficient space for manufacture or storage. They may have the advantage of more inexpensive facilities and location, but they must consider access to expressways, railways, and airports, to ensure the movement of their products to others. A neat, clean image although important is less important than good trade routes and space.

## HOW DO PEOPLE BUY?

When we talk about the **how** issue, people frequently say, "why with money, of course!" and laugh. Unfortunately, it is not that simple. People frequently do not buy with money but frequently charge items on credit cards or company accounts receivable. Sometimes they use layaway plans. Sometimes they borrow money. It is important to the marketing effort to understand how people will buy the product or service you intend to offer.

One client with whom we worked sold satellite receiving dish antennas. The dishes ranged in cost from $1,500 to $4,000 including installation. When we visited the owner of the business and asked him how people bought his antennas, he declared that he did not know. If any financing was needed, then the customers were arranging their own, because our client required cash. He refused to examine the issue or consider any alternatives. As you might guess, new competitors began to spring up who offered a variety of financing arrangements for their antennas and our client was forced to sell his business when his sales volume fell off. Obviously, the lack of success was not solely a function of the client's failure to offer financing, but that failure was a major factor; and it provided his competitors with a marketing approach that damaged his sales. Frequently in the business arena, competitors have used financing techniques to enhance their performance at the expense of a firm that demands cash.

Many merchants detest credit cards, not just because they require special handling but because they also cost money. The credit card firms charge merchants a fee for permitting them to accept the cards. This fee may run from 2 percent to as high as 6 percent, depending on the annual volume the merchant is expected to generate. A recent phenomenon in gasoline sales involves the discounting of sales when cash is used in lieu of credit cards. At least one major gasoline distributor currently is running ads that decry the practice and avow no differences in charges regardless of the payment methodology. It will be interesting to see which approach is successful over the long run.

It certainly is true that selling on credit or arranging financing for sales introduces complexity into a business's operations. Additional records must be kept and collection efforts have to be instituted. This does not mean that credit arrangements should not be considered. On the contrary, it is important to know how the consumers of a product or service will buy. Marketing activities and plans are affected by that knowledge.

## WHY DO PEOPLE BUY?

In a larger sense this entire section of the chapter deals with the issue of why people buy an item. In examining the **why** we want to focus on the specific motivation of an individual purchaser rather than the characteristics of the general target market group.

You are accustomed to considering items as falling into the categories of necessities and luxuries, but if you examine an individual's purchasing pattern, such classifications are of little value in understanding the pattern. Food is a necessity, but why does an individual shop at one grocery store rather than another? Why does an individual purchase one brand of bread rather than another? Jewelry and gift shops sell luxuries, but the same questions apply. The answers are not simplistic nor are they well known. The actual purchase decision of an individual is a psychological and sociological phenomenon.

Have you ever noticed how different producers of a product have different marketing approaches? Think about toothpaste. One producer of toothpaste touts its ability to prevent cavities. Another toothpaste producer touts its ability to whiten teeth and freshen breath. The first producer believes that people buy its toothpaste because they want to protect their teeth from decay. The second producer believes that people buy its toothpaste to enhance their sex appeal. Both producers are successful, so that must mean that they are both right!

The apparent inconsistency among the toothpaste companies can exist because there are two basic approaches to take when incorporating the "why" of the buying decision into a marketing strategy. The first is to attempt to discover, through market research, the primary motivations people have for buying a product and appeal to those motivations with the marketing effort. This is what the first toothpaste company has done. It attempts to appeal to the cavity prevention goal, which it believes is the primary motivation for people to purchase toothpaste. Its success means that a significant portion of the population has been swayed by its marketing efforts.

The second approach to developing a market strategy is to attempt to create a reason for people to want to purchase a product. That means that the marketing efforts are aimed at creating consumer demand rather than tapping an existing demand. This is what the second toothpaste company has done. It has decided that a marketing campaign could be effective in making people consider toothpaste in the same light as cosmetics. Its success means that a large enough portion of the population has been swayed by the marketing efforts to produce profits for the company.

Understanding why people buy things is difficult, perhaps impossible. About all that we can do is to attempt to gain an understanding of the motivations through research. This is what the first toothpaste company did. The best understanding comes from experience. We can attempt to sell an item using a market strategy we think appeals to the correct motivations. If it doesn't work, we can try something else. Gradually we learn about our target market and how best to appeal to it. The first toothpaste company developed and ran a variety of ads over the years, constantly changing and tuning its approach while monitoring the success of its various marketing approaches. Unfortunately, during the start-up phase of a new venture, there is no experience upon which to draw, unless familiarity has been developed through working with similar items in another company prior to the start up. This is the major reason that prior experience with a product or service is valuable for a new business owner.

Attempting to create a demand for an item with marketing can be effective. This is the route the second toothpaste company took. However, creating demand tends to be more costly from a marketing perspective, and it is definitely more risky. A much greater level of marketing is required to convince people that they will want to buy a product than to inform people who want to buy a product where they can get it. If the effort to convince is not effective or fails to convince a large enough portion of the target market, the new business can fail before it has an opportunity to try anything else.

## HOW THINGS ARE SOLD

There are three basic approaches that can be taken to the marketing of an item:

1. Push marketing.
2. Pull marketing.
3. Piggyback marketing.

Most marketing strategies represent one of these approaches or a combination of them. We might say another approach can be taken as well: the absence of a marketing plan. A business that does no marketing has made a selection of a marketing approach, even though no conscious decision may have been made. If the demand for an item is sufficiently great and competition is sufficiently small, then marketing may not be required for success. Markets like that are exceedingly rare. For many years professionals such as physicians, dentists, and attorneys believed that such was the case for their businesses. Professional association rules prevented marketing in many cases. Now professionals are coming to realize, as most business people have known for years, that marketing is a necessary process for a successful business.

### Push Marketing

**Push marketing** refers to the attempt to push an item through the market. It can be visualized best from the wholesale perspective. Consider a wholesaler calling on a retailer. The wholesaler can attempt to persuade the retailer to buy its products by offering price and discount concessions that will make it lucrative for the retailer to sell the items. Such a strategy is a "push" strategy, in which the wholesaler is dependent upon the retailer to ultimately sell the items to the consumer. The focus of the marketing is the intermediary rather than the ultimate consumer. Consider the use of private or generic labels in grocery stores. Pricing makes them attractive to the retailer and such discounts may be passed on to the consumer, thus creating a demand. These strategies frequently employ pricing policies, resupply agreements, and similar steps aimed at making the intermediary desirous of selling the items. One popular ploy has been gifts, trips and premiums for the individuals in the retail outlet who are responsible for buying from the wholesaler. Push marketing is inexpensive when compared to alternative marketing strategies and can be quite effective. It may be a more viable option for a new venture than "pull" marketing.

## Pull Marketing

**Pull marketing** refers to the attempt to pull a product through the market. This is done by creating demand in the ultimate consumers for an item. It also can be understood best by considering a wholesaler. As in the preceding section, consider a wholesaler selling to a retailer. An option that can be used as a marketing strategy is to create a demand in the retailer's customers for an item so that the retailer will wish to purchase it to satisfy its customers' needs. The focus is on the ultimate consumer rather than the intermediary. Consider the amazing success of Nintendo. Two years ago, no one had heard of their electronic games, and now consumers are purchasing them almost faster than the retailer can stock them. The demand for these electronic toys is causing the retailers to purchase them for their customers, many of whom are children and adolescents. This demand was created by television advertisements that were artfully done and created a sensation in the minds of the children, who demanded Nintendo and Nintendo cartridges for Christmas. This strategy is effective if the marketing is successful, but tends to be more expensive and time consuming than push marketing. It is attractive because it permits higher prices to intermediaries and thereby enhances profit margins. However, it may not be a viable strategy for a new venture because of the time and expense involved.

## Piggyback Marketing

One of the most frequently used marketing strategies for a new business venture is **piggyback marketing.** This refers to the identification of a successful competitor and "piggybacking" its marketing efforts. This can be visualized easily by considering the motel industry. The market research that goes into the identification of a site for a motel is extensive and expensive. Location is the prime factor in the ultimate success of such a venture. You probably can remember several occasions when you have seen a small motel built close to a large chain such as a Holiday Inn. Such firms attempt to succeed by competing with the larger motel on the basis of price. They pursue a piggyback strategy. The smaller inn does not expend the money for market research in site location or advertising. It tries to garner a section of the market attracted by its larger competitor and allows that business to do the marketing.

Piggyback marketing is one of the most viable alternatives for a new business venture. It involves building on the marketing efforts of competitors and attempting to perform some aspect of the sales process more effectively. It can be used in most industries and works equally well with services as with products. It is a conscious recognition of the adage that, "It is easier to take business away from an established firm than to create that business in the first place." It also is the reason why many inventors and innovators do not do as well as the firms that follow them into the new markets they have created.

## MARKETING RESEARCH

**Marketing research** refers to the exploration of the who, what, when, where, how, and why discussed in the first part of the chapter. It is not a simplistic area. In many schools, entire curriculums are devoted to marketing research, with multiple courses devoted to the development of understanding and skills. Our purpose here will be to familiarize you with the basic tenets of the science. The research can include the kind of library research with which most students are familiar and the preparation and use of surveys. Finally, it may involve direct exploration of pertinent facts. Exhibit 3-2 outlines methods of marketing research.

### Library Research

For almost all existing products or services, published sources contain great quantities of information. Virtually all established industries have magazines

**EXHIBIT 3-2** *Methods of Marketing Research*

I. Library research
   A. Industry publications
   B. General business publications
   C. Reporting services
   D. Government publications

II. Marketing surveys
   A. Rough and ready survey
   B. Counting surveys

III. Footwork

and journals that contain information of value to the businesses in that industry. Your library probably has many of these journals and, through interlibrary loan, can obtain others that might be needed. These journals are a priceless source of information about the markets that have been examined and identified for products or services in the industry, as well as specific articles and advice about marketing and other aspects of the industry. Don't overlook general business publications or books. *The Wall Street Journal, Business Week, Fortune, Inc., Advertising Age, Venture,* and other journals also are a valuable source of information. In addition, you may be surprised at the number of books written about markets and industries. Scholarly journals often are goldmines of information that may be of value to a marketing effort. Reporting services analyze industries and sell those reports. Your library probably subscribes to several of those, such as Value Line, Standard and Poors, Moody's, and others.

Additionally, information from government agencies will be included in the library, which can help with the more quantifiable aspects of a market. Census tract data not only describe populations, but family size, number of households, family incomes, retail sales, disposable income, and other information of value in marketing. A census tract is an area of 4,000 to 5,000 people that the Bureau of the Census uses to report the results of its studies. There also is a Census of Business, which reports information about businesses by census tract. Publications from government agencies and many local chambers of commerce offer sales data for various industries and areas, which can be of great value in investigating a market. Finally, published surveys that contain valuable information may be available. If these exist they frequently can be discovered through discussions with librarians, bankers, government assistance agencies, chambers of commerce, industry associations, and business school faculty members.

## Marketing Surveys

When most people think of marketing research they think of **surveys.** Surveys can be invaluable, but they are expensive and time consuming. The preparation and conduct of a survey is an exercise in statistical sampling, which means that it can be quite complex. Entire courses in market research curricula are devoted to surveys. It is possible for a prospective small business owner to conduct an inexpensive, "rough and ready" survey to gain an understanding of some aspect of the market. Simply stopping people on the street and asking questions can provide some insight, so long as you are careful to ask questions in such a way that the listener is not led to an answer. Other surveys involve measuring or counting items and activities of interest. Such attempts can be valuable but may not be reliable. The best use of such an approach is in the exploration of simple, straightforward issues such as automobile or foot traffic flows at a particular location.

## Footwork

One of the best and least expensive ways to conduct market research is **footwork.** By this we mean the personal investigation of a market and an area. Few people actually do much footwork when planning to start a business. Perhaps it is overlooked because it is so obvious. At any rate, there is no substitution for going out to look for and at a market. If you plan to start a business in an area, you should visit the local chamber of commerce. Not only will they have published information that may be of use, conversations with the people will provide insights and further contacts that can be explored. Discussions with bankers in the area can shed light on the market and its viability and be useful in establishing contacts that will be valuable later on in the business' life. Personal or telephone conversations with industry associations can be useful, as can discussions with salespeople. Few people have a better insight into the market for an item than those involved in selling to businesses in the area. Discussions with the representatives of government assistance agencies also can be invaluable. If there is an office of the Small Business Development Center in your state, it would be a serious mistake not to discuss a business start up with them. Other assistance agencies also exist including the Service Core of Retired Executives, Economic Development Centers, and various business development and assistance programs of state and federal agencies.

One final point about footwork deserves special mention. The existing competition for a new venture well may be the most valuable source of information from a marketing perspective available. Walk or drive through the area in which you plan to do business. Look at the yellow pages in the phone book. Talk to as many businesses as you can. Many potential competitors may be prepared to meet with you and discuss their businesses; others may be reluctant to talk to a potential direct competitor. In either case, close observation of competitors can reveal the existence and size of a market. Observation of marketing practices of competitors can reveal how they attract and keep customers. Additionally, such observation may reveal gaps or chinks in the marketing a new business can tap to make itself more competitive. If there are no direct competitors in an area under consideration, then examine similar businesses in other areas. Their experiences may not mirror those of a different area but certainly will be useful. People in business in other areas probably will be more amenable to meetings and discussions than potential competitors. They can be a goldmine of information about start-up marketing approaches and problems as well as a host of other aspects.

## THE BUSINESS IMAGE

Nothing is more important to the success of a business venture than the **image** it will portray to its customers. You should think long and hard about how you wish your customers to perceive your business. What do you want them to think of when they think of your business? What do you want them to think of when they see your business? You want to be distinct from your competition. What do you intend to do to make your business distinctive? You want your business to be as unique as your own personality. What do you wish your business' personality to be?

Whatever image you decide to portray, you must be consistent, as with everything else involved in the business. You cannot send conflicting signals to your customers. Consider the following case from our files.

The business was a small gift shop located in a rather expensive section of suburban Atlanta. The owner had called us in because she was losing money steadily and was at a loss as to the basis of the problem. The shop was beautiful. It had been in business for less than six months and was located in a shopping center with a good anchor store and excellent traffic patterns. The shop was tastefully decorated, and the inventory was artfully displayed. There were plenty of indirect competitors, but no direct competitors within 10 or 15 miles of the shop. When we walked in we were really impressed. The outside of the shop, its sign, and the shopping center in general were attractive, and it was clear that there was an adequate population base to make the store successful.

At first we asked to look at advertising records and mockups. When the program looked fine, we looked at the accounting records. One thing was puzzling: the gross profit margin had been stable at 20 percent. We thought that a bit low for a gift and novelty shop, so we asked about markup policy. The owner said the policy was a 25 percent markup based on selling price, but occasional sales held the margin down a bit. Then we looked more closely at the inventory in the store and the prices.

We couldn't believe the bargains! The items were beautiful, including many glass pieces and art objects at prices well below the prices you would expect in Atlanta.

Can you guess what the store's problem was? It was inconsistency in image. The prices were those of a discount, bargain store, whereas the decor, stock, and location were those of an exclusive gift shop. Our advice to the owner was to raise prices across the board by 25 percent. After considerable discussion and reluctance, she complied; and sales went up dramatically within a month, doubling within three months. The shop is now profitable. The point to remember is that all aspects of an image must be in harmony or your customers will be confused.

## SUMMARY

Your own judgment as to the value of a product or service is not necessarily valid. Nor is demand for a product or service an automatic guarantee for success. If the demand is present, effective marketing must be planned.

An early step in starting a new business is selecting the product or service to be sold. Whether the choice is based on experience or the fulfillment of a recognized niche in the marketplace, those items must be sold before a business can succeed. Customers seldom beat a path to the door of the new venture, so strategies must be designed to attract public attention.

To focus marketing activities and planning, examine the reasons people buy by considering the who, what, when, where, how, and why they purchase. Marketing efforts need to be oriented toward both users or buyers ("who"), and seasonality ("when"). Frequency of purchase is another consideration in marketing. When the product is consumed quickly, brand loyalty is a frequent strategy; whereas in a durables industry, concentration tends to be on the characteristics that make the product superior to competitors in price, quality, or performance. Location ("where") is another important factor in setting up a business. To be successful one must be aware of traffic patterns as well as convenience. "How" a customer pays is an important consideration: payment can be made in cash or on credit. The "why" of the buying decisions explores the primary motivations for buying a product or creates a reason for people to want to purchase a product.

The three basic approaches used to market an item are: push, pull, and piggyback. In the push method, the focus of marketing may be to the intermediary rather than the ultimate consumer and may well be a viable option for a new venture. Pull marketing depends upon consumer demand. It is quite effective when the marketing is successful, but tends to be more expensive and time consuming. Perhaps the most viable alternative for a new venture is the piggyback approach. This method tries to garner a section of the market attracted by its larger competition and allows its competitors to do the marketing.

Marketing research is a science whose tenets offer much to the small business owner. It is a method used to aid those interested in starting new ventures to discover the who, what, when, where, how, and why of business. Marketing research includes a literature search of newspapers, journals, periodicals, books, indexes, and census data. Surveys also render valuable data but may be complex and time consuming. A good, inexpensive method of conducting research is through footwork. There is no substitute for observing for oneself.

## QUESTIONS

1. Define the following terms:

| | |
|---|---|
| **a.** push | **e.** seasonality |
| **b.** pull | **f.** durables |
| **c.** piggyback | **g.** consumables |
| **d.** viability | **h.** image |

2. What factors are involved in the selection of a product or service for a new business?
3. Examine the who, what, when, where, how, and why of purchasing a satellite dish antenna? Notebook paper? Science fiction novels?
4. Why is brand loyalty less important a consideration in the durables industry? In what cases may brand loyalty be considered? Explain why.
5. List the three basic approaches to marketing and give an example of each.
6. What source would be good for finding industry averages for comparison purposes?
7. What are some advantages and disadvantages in library research? Footwork?
8. Why is area selection important to the marketing plan?
9. Why should marketing be included in the budget initially?
10. Why are image and timing so important in marketing?
11. Why is the marketing plan so important in the initial stage of small business management?
12. Can you foresee any problems that people like John Sculley might have when he went from the presidency of Pepsico to Apple Computers? Or Nolan Bushnell, who went from Atari Computers to pizza? How are the industries different? If you were on the board of directors of a durables industry, would you hire personnel from a consumables industry or vice versa? Explain why or why not. Sculley appears to have been successful whereas Bushnell has not. What are some of the adjustments each would have had to make? What do you feel made one successful in the transition and the other not?
13. Why must marketing attempts be designed to appeal to both users and purchasers? Give several examples other than those listed in the text.
14. Why are timing and image so important to a new venture? Can you give examples from your own knowledge that were either successful or unsuccessful because of the issues of timing and image?

## PROJECTS

1. You are about to set up your own business in VCR machine and tape rental and sales. Do some of the footwork involved in setting up your own business. Find a good location available locally, find out the rental or sales price of several sites, and compare them. Then go to the library and see if any industry averages are available on your product or if other information is available in periodicals about the industry into which you are about to venture.
2. Choose an area in which you are interested and develop a marketing plan.

# Case

The Ultimate opened its doors early last year. It was the ultimate college hangout. The place for good food, fun, friends, and variety. It had a menu of pizza, subs, steaks, lasagna, spaghetti, hamburgers, and chili. The manager was a local college-age student who knew everyone. He was in heaven about his new venture.

Opening week had its share of problems. Everyone wanted burgers when Todd expected the Italian cuisine to be the best seller based on his prior experience with a local competitor. He had to suggest alternatives. The help was slow, because they weren't trained, and frustrated diners with class schedules to keep had to bolt their food when it came.

The decor was romantic with red and white checkered table cloths for the booths and low lighting. Actually, there was a problem with the lighting. It was either off or on. On was very bright and off was dark. Todd wanted a romantic atmosphere for dates and dinners, so he placed filters in the light panels allowing only a very small amount of light to come through. Some of the customers were heard to remark to the waitresses that the food was very good but they wished that they could have seen it. Ordering from the menu was an adventure, too. Many customers were seen striking matches to see. When several of the older customers asked Todd about candles, he claimed that they were too expensive and the students would swipe them.

The food was delicious and the prices were reasonable for the quantity served. The portions were large but many diners were surprised by the low bill. The variety had something to please everyone; and there were specials from time to time, usually lasagna or all-you-can-eat spaghetti. Occasionally there was ribeye steak. The only difficulty for the patrons was that they didn't know when the specials were coming. The advertisement was on the chalkboard inside the restaurant.

Newcomers were told of this great place to eat just off campus, but most couldn't find it and ended up at the Pizza Hut a few feet down the road. The Ultimate was parallel to the main drag, but you had to know it was there. It was connected to a service station and not readily differentiated from the garage. The gas pumps and tow truck parked nearby fooled potential customers.

Too soon, the school year was over. Todd was in a quandary about whether to close down or stay open. He didn't have the same number of customers but many of the locals were hoping that he would stay open. Professors and students with late classes went there for a while, only to discover that Todd was closing early. There was no way to know the hours. Soon he was closing at lunch and open only from 4 P.M. to 10 P.M. Many of his best customers were no longer coming in. What could he do?

## Questions

1. What are some obvious problems you can deduct from the case?
2. Describe the location. Why would Todd have chosen it? What are potential advantages and disadvantages for such a location?
3. Were there any obvious or subtle inconsistencies in image?
4. What was Todd's target market, and how was he planning to compete?
5. Is this enterprise headed toward success or failure? Explain why or why not.
6. Why is marketing more than just advertising? What else is involved?

# CHAPTER 4

# Financial Accounting and Taxation Issues

**LEARNING OBJECTIVES**

After completing this chapter, you should be able to

- Understand the concept of accounting and its importance.
- Understand the hows and whys of record keeping.
- Know why the general ledger is called the heart of the accounting system.
- Define assets, liabilities, capital, revenues, and expenses.
- Understand when journals and subsidiary ledgers and adjusting entries are used.
- Understand the importance of the internal control guidelines.
- Discuss the four parts of a financial statement, the importance of each part, and how it is prepared.
- Explain the role of a CPA in a small business.

**Accounting** has been called the *language of business.* In reality, it is the language of trust. The transactions recorded in accounting are called **debits** and **credits.** These words are derived from Latin and developed from the Roman practice of accounting. That practice, which predates the birth of Christ, used the term **credere** to describe bookkeeping entries that represented obligations of people. The interesting point is that *credere* means "to trust." The Romans obviously thought that the transactions they recorded were supported by trust in the people who were to repay the debts. Today, people still trust one another to honor financial obligations, and accounting has become a science in which trust is paramount.

People trust the outcome of accounting: **financial statements.** People expect the financial statements to reflect the true financial condition of the firm. People outside and inside the firm trust the statements and use them to make decisions about the firm: decisions about investing in the firm and lending to the firm; decisions about buying from and selling to the firm; taxes due from the firm; decisions about pricing, cost control, expansion, and growth; decisions about the performance of managers and employees. In fact, every decision made in the business world is affected by financial statements.

The problem with financial statements is that they are not automatically trustworthy. People have confidence in accounting but that confidence is misplaced. In reality, accounting, like everything else in the business world, is a reflection of management. If management has designed a sound accounting system and installed sound accounting practices and controls, then the financial statements will be dependable and trustworthy. If management has not done these things, then the financial statements will be misleading and erroneous.

In this chapter we will present an overview of the accounting process in a small firm. Most of the information will be a review of the topics covered in accounting courses. Our purpose is to provide you with an appreciation of the accounting principles and processes required to effectively manage a small business. The pursuit of any business is profit. Plautus said some 2,400 years ago that profit cannot exist if the outlay is too great. Accounting is the tool used to control that outlay.

Remember, the purpose of this chapter is to give you an appreciation of accounting, not to make you an accountant. We will briefly review the process of capturing financial information and then we will provide a comprehensive illustration. The actual process is far more involved than this overview; consequently, we don't expect you to be able to do the accounting, just to understand the basic steps.

## RECORD KEEPING

The success of John D. Rockefeller often is ascribed to his "training in the points of scientific accounting at Folsom's Business College in Cleveland."[1] Rockefeller was quoted as saying, "I knew where I stood at the close of every business day. I charted my course in figures, nothing but figures."[2] It is clear that "figures" become increasingly important as a business grows. The larger a business becomes, the more removed its owners and managers are from the daily happenings and the more important numbers become in making management decisions. If a business is very small, then the owner or manager is intricately involved in everything. That person makes every sale, knows every customer, writes every check, and handles every piece of merchandise. Record keeping is unimportant because the owner personally feels the results of each day's business. This is possible only for extremely small ventures. As employees are added and as they take over the work, the manager begins to lose touch with the pulse of the business. Record keeping then becomes the source of the information that has been lost: the information about what happens each day.

**Record keeping** simply is the process of capturing every transaction that affects a business. We generally think of these transactions in financial terms, but they are not all financial. The hiring of people, recording of personnel evaluations, entering into contracts to buy or sell, capturing of names and addresses of customers, all are examples of records that must be kept. All of these things eventually will have a financial impact on the firm, but initially many records are not financial in nature. Management's responsibility is to decide what information is to be captured, when and how it is to be recorded, who is responsible for its capture and maintenance, and how and to whom it is to be reported. These decisions will establish the record keeping system for the business. Because the business will change constantly, the record-keeping system also must change. Consequently, management must always be cognizant of what is currently flowing into the record-keeping system, constantly compare that to desired information, and alter the system on an on-going basis. It is impossible for us to detail every type of information that should be captured, because this is likely to be different in every business. We will explore records that every business will require, but you should remember that the list will not be exhaustive. Any information you think would be of value in the decision making of the firm should be captured.

The proverbial "shoe box" of papers is all too common in small businesses. Consider the following case from our files.

Like most of the small firms who called us for help, this client was having "cash flow problems." Of course, inadequate cash flow is not a problem, rather it is a symptom of a problem. So it cannot be corrected without discovering the underlying cause.

We asked the client for specifics about his "cash flow problem" and he told us that he could not meet the payroll on a regular basis. We went out to take a look at the business.

It was one of the few times that we were completely stymied! There was absolutely nothing we could do to even begin to help the poor guy. When we asked to see his records, he pulled out a desk drawer literally overflowing with papers. He said all of his bills, receipts, invoices, and such were in there. He simply had not gotten around to arranging them in any order. We asked about accountants, tax returns, and the like. He had not gotten around to any of those things yet. He had been in business for a year and a half and knew that he was going to have to do "something soon." Right now he was more worried about not being able to meet payroll again this coming Friday.

We had seen "shoe boxes" before, of course. Everyone who works with small businesses sees those. But this was ridiculous! We explained to him how much it would cost to have us dig through that paper morass and he quickly decided that he had better make time for a little paperwork himself.

We showed the client how to set up a simple record-keeping system and got him started, then we left. At that point all we could do was hope that he could survive long enough to be able to generate some financial information to use in examining the company. The saddest part of the story is that he never called us back. The business doesn't exist anymore.

The small business owner in this illustration simply did not see the value in record keeping. He was probably like many other small business owners who think that record keeping is something that must be done for tax purposes, a common misconception. Owners who hold this opinion are apt to use shoe boxes and wait until tax time to have an accountant sift through the papers and put together enough information to prepare a tax return. Such people never stop to think how much more it costs to have an accountant wade through a box of papers than to use clear, clean reports from an accounting system. It is true that record keeping is required for tax purposes, but that is a minor aspect. The more important use of records is to aid management in making decisions about the company. All of the chapters in this section are "tools chapters." They explain how to use record keeping in managing a small business more effectively. Records and reports from those records are the primary tools of management. A good manager, like a good worker, keeps the tools of the trade sharp, clean, and well organized.

## General Ledger

The **general ledger** is the storehouse for all financial transactions that take place in a business. It is a collection of accounts, which are simply pages in a manual system devoted to particular kinds of transactions. A business will have as many or as few accounts as the management deems necessary. If you want separate information about cash, there must be a cash account in the general ledger. If you have multiple checking accounts and you want to keep information about each of them separately, then you must have a general ledger account for each. If the individual detail is unimportant, then a single cash account is sufficient. Examples of accounts are shown in Exhibit 4-2 (page 74) as part of a comprehensive illustration.

Accounts can be classified by the sections of the financial statement they will affect. Financial statements have sections for assets, liabilities, capital, revenues, and expenses. Accounts can be classified as one of those five types.

**Assets** are accounts that represent things of value to a business. The obvious ones are cash, accounts receivable, inventory, and plant equipment, buildings, and land. Less obvious assets include prepaid expenses like insurance premiums paid in advance. Those are assets because they prevent a company from having to pay monies in the future. Assets generally are subdivided into current and noncurrent asset categories. **Current assets** are those that are held in cash or are expected to be consumed in the business within one accounting cycle or one year, whichever is longer. For the vast majority of firms the time period used is one year. The **accounting cycle** refers to the length of time required for cash to be converted to inventory, which is then sold and converted to accounts receivable, which are then collected and converted back into cash. For most firms this process takes less than a year, hence the general period for recognition of current items is one year.

**Liabilities** are accounts that represent obligations of the firm to pay money in the future. The most obvious ones are accounts payable, notes and loans payable, accrued payroll, and mortgages. Less obvious liabilities include customer deposits that represent obligations to refund money in the event a product is not delivered, accruals for all types of expenses, and reserves for warranties and guarantees, which represent obligations to perform services for customers in the future. Liabilities also are subdivided into current and noncurrent categories. The distinction is the same as that used for recognizing current assets. Items payable within one year or one accounting cycle are considered **current liabilities,** and all others are **noncurrent liabilities.**

**Capital accounts** represent the investment of the owner (or owners) in the business. For a proprietorship, **capital** consists of an owner's account. In a partnership, each partner will have a capital account. For a corporation, capital accounts will consist of common stock and retained earnings. The **stock ac-**

**count** shows how much money has been invested in the corporation since its creation. The **retained earnings** account will show the sum total of all profits less all losses recorded since the firm's creation. The concept of retained earnings is not well understood. Many people think of it as money kept in the business for future investment. This misconception comes from the understanding that dividends to shareholders are paid out of retained earnings. In actuality, **dividends** are paid from cash but represent a reduction of retained earnings. Retained earnings represent the total of all profits and losses that have occurred in the entire history of the business. The total amount of dividends paid in the firm's history are subtracted from that total. The result is the balance in retained earnings that shows on the company's balance sheet. So you see, any money involved has already been spent!

The total of the capital accounts plus the total of the liability accounts must always equal the total of the asset accounts. These three categories of accounts make up the portion of the financial statement called a **balance sheet.** It gets this name from the fact that assets balance liabilities and capital. These three categories are also **permanent accounts,** which means that they always are a part of the business' records. The accounts represent the financial condition of the firm at any given point in time.

Revenue and expense accounts are **temporary accounts,** which means that they are used to accumulate transactions during the year. At the end of the year, the accounts are zeroed out and the net balance is transferred to capital. This way the accounts are clear and ready to begin accumulating transactions for the new year. **Revenue accounts** contain information about the sales or other income transactions in the firm. **Expense accounts** contain information about costs that have been expended to produce revenues; typically the costs of goods sold, salaries and wages, selling and advertising, office supplies, professional fees, and so on. Revenue and expense accounts do not represent the financial condition of the firm as do the previous categories, but rather show the totals of the transactions over a period of time. The difference between the two is called **profit,** or **loss** if expenses exceed revenues.

Profit is not well understood. Many people think of it as the money left over from revenues after expenses are paid, which is true, but only in the long term or for a company that uses the cash method of accounting. Very few businesses can use cash basis accounting, because it causes problems in generating financial information that is useful for decision making.

## Cash Versus Accrual Basis Accounting

Most businesses must use **accrual basis accounting.** Under accrual accounting, after a company has gone out of business, the totals of revenues and expenses will be the same as the cash that has been received and distributed. At any point in time for an on-going business, cash may have little relationship to profit. Revenues and expenses are recorded based on obligations to receive and pay money. The recording of the transactions is not dependent upon money changing hands. That means that **cash flow,** money moving through a business, and **profit,** the difference between revenues and expenses, are both important concepts but not the same thing.

**Cash basis accounting** systems record transactions only when money actually changes hands. This means that there are no accounts for receivables or for payables, because purchase and sales transactions will not be recorded until cash flows. This can be a problem for a business. Additional records have to be kept outside the accounting system to know about receivables or payables. If the records are outside the accounting system, then they are not subject to the same controls and accuracy can be a problem. In addition, revenues and expenses will be recognized when cash flows rather than when the transaction takes place. This will cause a distortion in the amount of income that results, especially toward the end of the accounting period. It is simply a matter of timing; the timing of when transactions are recognized. In turn, this timing problem will distort information used for decision-making purposes. You cannot decide that costs for inventory have been too high in any given month because you will not know how much was spent in that month, only what cash actually flowed out during that month.

Many small businesses use cash basis accounting despite the problems it creates. Many do it for income tax purposes because they think it results in lower taxes, which is not necessarily true. Only an accountant can examine a company's operations and determine whether cash basis tax reporting is desirable. If it is, then tax reports can be prepared on a cash basis and the company's records are kept on an accrual basis. Perhaps the primary reason for the prevalence of cash basis systems is that most small business owners think accounting is hard and accrual based accounting even harder. This is really not true but, even if it were, the prevalence of microcomputer-based accounting systems and their ease of use brings accrual basis accounting within reach of every small firm. We strongly recommend that all firms use accrual systems because of the improved decision-making information that results. The tools we present in this section of the text really require an accrual basis system in order to be effective. Every owner should learn enough about accounting to rise above the initial phobic reaction and establish a sound, accrual basis system in order to improve the prospects of the operation.

## Journals

**Journals** record transactions temporarily. The word comes from the use of daily journals kept on mercantile ships, which detailed shipments of goods. In a manual accounting system, journals are simply pages used to record transactions of a similar nature. For example, cash receipts might be recorded in one journal, and cash disbursements in another. Inventory purchases might be recorded in one journal, and sales in another. A business will have as many or as few journals as the management desires. All journals ultimately must be posted to the general ledger, which means posting the transactions recorded in the journals. Often, this information can be posted in summary form, a whole page in the journal can be totaled and the totals posted to the ledger, which saves bookkeeping work. An example of a general journal that does not separate types of transactions is shown in Exhibit 4-1 (page 73) as part of our comprehensive illustration.

## Subsidiary Ledgers

**Subsidiary ledgers** are records containing details about a general ledger account that management thinks are important. For example, **accounts receivable** is a single account in the general ledger but represents the obligations of many customers. The information about who owes what is contained in the accounts receivable subsidiary ledger. Names, addresses, credit lines, and any other information desired about customers also can be kept in the accounts receivable ledger. Each customer will have an account, a page in a manual system, in the receivables ledger. The total of all accounts in the receivables ledger will be equal to the balance in the general ledger account for receivables. This means double posting of receivables. Every transaction ultimately will have to be posted to a customer's account as well as to the general ledger account. Subsidiary ledgers also can be kept for **accounts payable,** the money the company owes for equipment or for any item in the general ledger. Each subsidiary ledger is said to be "controlled" by the account in the general ledger that summarizes the subsidiary.

## Transactions Flow

As transactions occur during the course of business, they must be captured by recording them in journals. The transactions are recorded as debits and credits: **debits** *increase* asset and expense accounts and *decrease* liability, capital, and revenue accounts; **credits** *decrease* asset and expense accounts and *increase* liability, capital, and revenue accounts. It is the use of debits and credits that gives the process the name "double-entry accounting." Examples of journal entries are shown in Exhibit 4-1 (page 73) as part of our comprehensive illustration. The journals must be posted to the general ledger (see Exhibit 4-2, page 74) and to any subsidiary ledgers that are appropriate.

A **trial balance** is taken to ensure that transactions have been properly recorded. A trial balance is simply a listing of the balances of each account in the general ledger. The total of the debit balances must equal the total of the credit balances. This ensures that the relationship between accounts is appropriate. An example of a trial balance is displayed in Exhibit 4-3 (page 76).

The financial statements, such as the income statement and balance sheet, and other reports, such as delinquency lists, are prepared from the general ledger and subsidiary ledger. The reports are really summaries of the information in the accounts. This is the process we call *record keeping* or *bookkeeping*. Because the financial statements and reports are used in managing the business and by outsiders to the business to support their decision making, the record keeping is crucial. If transactions are not captured when they should be, captured in the correct amounts, posted to the correct accounts, or summarized properly, the reports will be inaccurate. The steps management takes to ensure that all of these actions occur properly are collectively called **internal controls.**

## Comprehensive Illustration, Part One

The example that follows illustrates the process of transaction capturing, journalization, posting to the general ledger, and preparing the trial balance. The illustration uses an extremely simple operation, the running of a concession stand at the high school football games, but the processes are the same for any company. The difference in complexity simply means more transactions and more accounts. Remember, the purpose of this example is to display the process. Do not expect to be able to replicate the steps without further study.

A local church has been given permission to operate a concession stand at the high school football games. You have agreed to manage it for the church on as profitable a basis as possible. Your time will be donated, but any other labor must be paid. The finance committee at the church would like to see operating statements after each game so that they can see how much money can be withdrawn without damaging the operation. Here are the transactions for the first game.

- *September 5*. The church entrusts you with $200 as start-up funding.
- *September 6*. You sign a contract with the school for renting the concession stand. The rent will be 10 percent of the sales, but a minimum fee of $100 will be charged for the season, which is five home games. You investigate the product lines and prices of the competition and decide to charge $.50 for a hot dog and $.50 for a coke, which is the same as the other two stands.
- *September 7*. You purchase an ice chest for $45 and food-handling utensils for $37.50. You interview and hire two high school students to work the stand with you at $3.50 per hour.

- *September 9*. You open an account with the Acme Restaurant Supply Company and purchase paper supplies, cups, napkins, straws, lids, etc., for $35.54; condiments, mustard, ketchup, etc., for $29.44; 200 franks for $32.00; 200 buns for $20.00; and cokes enough to serve 200 drinks for $72.00.
- *September 11*. The first home game is tonight. You buy ice for $8.50 on the way to the stadium and discover when you get there that you forgot to get change or a box to put it in. You dash out and grab $20.00 worth of change and an empty cigar box at the drug store.
- *September 12*. You were so tired last night after the game that you just picked up the cigar box, tossed the leftover franks into the ice chest, told the students you would pay them on Monday for the 4 hours they worked, and went home. You took inventory today and discovered that 20 franks and buns were left over, half the condiments and paper goods were gone, and enough cokes were left to serve 10 drinks.
- *September 14*. You pay the students and prepare the records. You post the transactions to a journal (Exhibit 4-1), post the journal to a ledger (Exhibit 4-2), and prepare a trial balance from the general ledger (Exhibit 4-3).

The trial balance doesn't tell us whether or not the concession stand made a profit. However, these data provide the information necessary to assess profitability. We will return to this illustration in the section on financial statements where we will see how profitable the business was.

## INTERNAL CONTROLS

**Internal controls** are procedures designed to ensure that transactions are properly captured and handled. There are six general rules of internal control that should be followed. These guidelines are indications of work arrangements that enhance control.

### Guidelines for Internal Controls

1. *Use competent, well-trained people.* Hiring and retaining competent, capable people probably is the most important step in internal controls. This is accomplished through the firm's recruitment, compensation, and supervision policies. These people must be well trained and their training must be maintained as duties and responsibilities change.
2. *Separate custody from record keeping.* An individual who has custody of an asset should not have access to the records concerning that asset.

**EXHIBIT 4-1** *General Journal*

GENERAL JOURNAL — PAGE J1

| *Date* | *Description* | *Ref* | *Debit* | *Credit* |
|---|---|---|---|---|
| 9/5 | Cash | 100 | 200.00 | |
| | Capital (investment by church) | 400 | | 200.00 |
| 9/7 | Equipment—ice chest | 200 | 45.00 | |
| | Equipment—utensils | 200 | 37.50 | |
| | Cash | 100 | | 82.50 |
| 9/9 | Supplies—paper | 120 | 35.54 | |
| | Supplies—condiments | 120 | 29.44 | |
| | Inventory—franks (200) | 110 | 32.00 | |
| | Inventory—buns (200) | 110 | 20.00 | |
| | Inventory—drinks (200) | 110 | 72.00 | |
| | Accounts payable | 300 | | 188.98 |
| 9/11 | Ice expense | 660 | 8.50 | |
| | Cash | 100 | | 8.50 |
| 9/11 | Cash | 100 | 185.00 | |
| | Sales—hot dogs (180 @ .50) | 510 | | 90.00 |
| | Sales—drinks (190 @ .50) | 520 | | 95.00 |
| | Cost of goods sold—hot dogs | 610 | 46.80 | |
| | Inventory—franks (180 @ .16) (32/200) | 110 | | 28.80 |
| | Inventory—buns (180 @ .10) (20/200) | 110 | | 18.00 |
| | Cost of goods sold—drinks | 620 | 68.40 | |
| | Inventory—drinks (190 @ .36) (72/200) | 110 | | 68.40 |
| | Supply expense | 630 | 32.49 | |
| | Supplies—paper (1/2 × 35.54) | 120 | | 17.77 |
| | Supplies—condiments (1/2 × 29.44) | 120 | | 14.72 |
| | Rent expense (10% of 185, 20 minimum) | 640 | 20.00 | |
| | Accounts payable (100/5 games = 20) | 300 | | 20.00 |
| 9/14 | Wage expense (2 × 3.50 × 4 hours) | 650 | 28.00 | |
| | Cash | 100 | | 28.00 |

A person who is assigned an automobile should not have access to the records of that automobile and its supporting expenses; a person who has access to cash, or makes deposits in the bank, should not have access to the bank statement.

3. *Separate record-keeping duties.* Record keeping should be partitioned into components that support each other, and those components

**EXHIBIT 4-2** *General Ledger*

Account: CASH — Account # 100

| *Date* | *Item* | *Ref* | *Debit* | *Credit* | *Debit* | *Credit* |
|---|---|---|---|---|---|---|
| 9/14 | | J1 | 200.00 | | | |
| | | J1 | | 82.50 | | |
| | | J1 | | 8.50 | | |
| | | J1 | 185.00 | | | |
| | | J1 | | 28.00 | 266.00 | |

Account: INVENTORY — Account # 110

| *Date* | *Item* | *Ref* | *Debit* | *Credit* | *Debit* | *Credit* |
|---|---|---|---|---|---|---|
| 9/14 | | J1 | 32.00 | | | |
| | | J1 | 20.00 | | | |
| | | J1 | 72.00 | | | |
| | | J1 | | 28.80 | | |
| | | J1 | | 18.00 | | |
| | | J1 | | 68.40 | 8.80 | |

Account: SUPPLIES — Account # 120

| *Date* | *Item* | *Ref* | *Debit* | *Credit* | *Debit* | *Credit* |
|---|---|---|---|---|---|---|
| 9/14 | | J1 | 35.54 | | | |
| | | J1 | 29.44 | | | |
| | | J1 | | 17.77 | | |
| | | J1 | | 14.72 | 32.49 | |

Account: EQUIPMENT — Account # 200

| *Date* | *Item* | *Ref* | *Debit* | *Credit* | *Debit* | *Credit* |
|---|---|---|---|---|---|---|
| 9/14 | | J1 | 45.00 | | | |
| | | J1 | 37.50 | | 82.50 | |

Account: ACCOUNTS PAYABLE — Account # 300

| *Date* | *Item* | *Ref* | *Debit* | *Credit* | *Debit* | *Credit* |
|---|---|---|---|---|---|---|
| 9/14 | | J1 | | 188.98 | | |
| | | J1 | | 20.00 | | 208.98 |

*continued*

**EXHIBIT 4-2 continued**

Account: CAPITAL — Account # 400

| Date | Item | Ref | Debit | Credit | Debit | Credit |
|---|---|---|---|---|---|---|
| 9/14 | | J1 | | 200.00 | | 200.00 |

Account: SALES—HOT DOGS — Account # 510

| Date | Item | Ref | Debit | Credit | Debit | Credit |
|---|---|---|---|---|---|---|
| 9/14 | | J1 | | 90.00 | | 90.00 |

Account: SALES—DRINKS — Account # 520

| Date | Item | Ref | Debit | Credit | Debit | Credit |
|---|---|---|---|---|---|---|
| 9/14 | | J1 | | 95.00 | | 95.00 |

Account: COST OF GOODS SOLD—HOT DOGS — Account # 610

| Date | Item | Ref | Debit | Credit | Debit | Credit |
|---|---|---|---|---|---|---|
| 9/14 | | J1 | 46.80 | | 46.80 | |

Account: COST OF GOODS SOLD—DRINKS — Account # 620

| Date | Item | Ref | Debit | Credit | Debit | Credit |
|---|---|---|---|---|---|---|
| 9/14 | | J1 | 68.40 | | 68.40 | |

Account: SUPPLY EXPENSE — Account # 630

| Date | Item | Ref | Debit | Credit | Debit | Credit |
|---|---|---|---|---|---|---|
| 9/14 | | J1 | 32.49 | | 32.49 | |

Account: RENT EXPENSE — Account # 640

| Date | Item | Ref | Debit | Credit | Debit | Credit |
|---|---|---|---|---|---|---|
| 9/14 | | J1 | 20.00 | | 20.00 | |

Account: WAGE EXPENSE — Account # 650

| Date | Item | Ref | Debit | Credit | Debit | Credit |
|---|---|---|---|---|---|---|
| 9/14 | | J1 | 28.00 | | 28.00 | |

Account: ICE EXPENSE — Account # 660

| Date | Item | Ref | Debit | Credit | Debit | Credit |
|---|---|---|---|---|---|---|
| 9/14 | | J1 | 8.50 | | 8.50 | |

**EXHIBIT 4-3** *Trial Balance*

TRIAL BALANCE

| *Acc#* | *Account* | *Debit* | *Credit* |
|---|---|---|---|
| 100 | Cash | $266.00 | |
| 110 | Inventory | 8.80 | |
| 120 | Supplies | 32.49 | |
| 200 | Equipment | 82.50 | |
| 300 | Accounts payable | | $208.98 |
| 400 | Capital | | 200.00 |
| 510 | Sales—hot dogs | | 90.00 |
| 520 | Sales—drinks | | 95.00 |
| 610 | Cost of franks sold | 46.80 | |
| 620 | Cost of drinks sold | 68.40 | |
| 630 | Supply expense | 32.49 | |
| 640 | Rent expense | 20.00 | |
| 650 | Wage expense | 28.00 | |
| 660 | Ice expense | 8.50 | |
| | Totals | $593.98 | $593.98 |

should be handled by different people. Cash receipts should be recorded by a person who does not have access to cash disbursements and who does not prepare bank deposits. Accounts receivable posting should be handled by a person who does not have access to the general ledger or the bank statement.

4. *Rotate duties.* Every person performing record keeping activities should be cross trained and should be rotated between jobs periodically. Not only will this make it impossible for an individual to hide incorrect procedures, it will ensure that everyone follows the established record-keeping policy and encourage people to do better work. All employees will know that their work will be seen by others as jobs rotate. This will encourage them to follow established practices carefully because of the pending peer review of their work.
5. *Use proofs and security measures.* Proofs are checks and verifications used to ensure accuracy. They include such things as trial balances, summary totals, cross totals, and verification by others. Such devices are of particular importance in automated systems. Security measures refer to physical protection for records, restricted access to records, and back-up provisions for information systems.

6. *Conduct an independent review.* Every department should have a review or audit performed by an independent person at least once each year. The auditor should be totally independent and must report to the owner in order to maintain that independence. People will develop their own practices and fail to follow established systems and procedures if they know that no one ever checks! In addition, the independent review will give people the feeling that their work is important to the company.

Internal controls are the key to a successful record-keeping system. They are so important, that the first step a CPA firm performs in conducting an audit of a company's books is the review and assessment of internal control. Under established auditing standards, a CPA cannot testify to the fairness of the financial statements unless first satisfied with the adequacy of internal controls. In small businesses, internal controls must be established by the owner. No one else has enough influence in the business to make employees believe that such controls are important. This means that it is particularly important for a small business owner to understand internal controls and be aware of them at all times. Consider the following cases from our files.

You want to know about people who learned about controls the hard way? We've had a few of those. Most folks have. They're all sad stories.

- A client called us in after her head bookkeeper had been missing for two weeks. The bookkeeper had disappeared and no one knew where she had gone—not her neighbors, not her friends, no one. Our client feared the worst! The first thing we did was to check the role that the bookkeeper played in handling cash. It was an absolute disaster! This single person not only prepared the bank deposits, she reconciled the checking account statement! We couldn't believe it, but the client said she thought everything was all right because no one in the company could sign checks except herself. Besides, she had known the bookkeeper for fifteen years. They were good friends! It took several days to find out how much money was missing, but when we finished the owner was sick! The company did recover, but it took more than two years to get back to the position it had before the embezzlement.

- In another case, another trusted employee was involved. This person was the chief of purchasing and had no access to any of the records, so the owner thought he was safe. What happened was a lot of fictitious purchases to a fictitious company. Because no one else had to approve purchase orders, the cash disbursements clerk routinely cut checks to pay for things that were never delivered. That problem also was discovered when the purchasing agent left town.

• One client was especially upset because he was convinced that he had strong controls. His mistake was in assigning one employee to handle the mail. We found out later that she had opened accounts at several banks in nearby towns under the same names as many of the company's suppliers. Then she deposited the checks to her own accounts, instead of mailing them! To set up a business account, the banks just asked for a corporate resolution, which was easy to supply; and the mail clerk was able to deposit checks in the business name of those accounts. Because she opened the mail as well as took it to the post office, she just threw away the delinquency notices. When she heard about the owner getting upset about collection calls for accounts that he had paid, she cut and run. By that time she had taken over $100,000.

• Another client got suspicious because of one employee who didn't want to take his vacation. When the owner insisted, he left for two weeks but managed to find some excuse to come back in almost every day. Our client called us in and we checked over the workaholic's assignments. He was a bookkeeping clerk with responsibilities for accounts receivable. Every day he dropped by, he asked the woman filling in for him whether so and so, one of the delinquent accounts, had paid yet. When she said no, he just left. It wasn't hard for us to discover that he had been taking some of the accounts off the books through the normal charge off procedure, yet continuing to call those people for payment. When they made payments, they sent the checks to him, and he just pocketed it. Because the accounts were no longer on the books, there was no way the payments showed up anywhere. As for cashing the checks, he had a bank account in a neighboring town under the same business name. Simple! He was just afraid that the clerk filling in would receive a payment, try to post it, and find no record of the account. There was a sad aspect to this story. The bookkeeper had been with the firm a long time and was well liked and respected. He had always been honest and hard working, but his wife had come down with a horrible disease and the medical bills were killing him. The insurance only paid 80 percent and the other 20 percent was more than his entire salary. He broke down when we confronted him and swore that he intended to pay the money back. He just had to have more money now to pay for treatments. It was really a sad story and the guy was really basically honest.

Internal controls are the same for small companies as for large ones. The difference is that large companies have an accounting staff who worries about such things whereas the small business has only the owner. Some people think that controls mean a lack of trust in employees and so are hesitant to use them. But controls are for the benefit of employees, too. In the first place, strong controls protect them from being accused of an improper behavior. In the second place, they help keep honest people honest during times of extreme temptation. They also give employees a sense of importance and value. Controls mean that their work is vital enough to merit special procedures and attention. Controls are for everyone, employee and owner.

# FINANCIAL STATEMENTS

The primary output of an accounting system is the **financial statement.** This document can be prepared for any period but must be prepared at least annually, at the end of the firm's fiscal year. It portrays the financial condition of the firm and details the results of its operations. An effective manager will require at least an abbreviated financial statement every month in order to evaluate and guide the firm. These are called **interim** financial statements because they cover less than a full year of operations. Whenever the term *financial statement* is used, it generally means a year-end financial statement. By convention, one year is the established time period for a company's report on its performance. This is called the **fiscal year.** The fiscal year can begin and end on any date a firm desires, it need not correspond to the calendar year. Many companies choose a fiscal year that corresponds to the natural business year. This means that the fiscal year is matched to the seasonality of the industry. The low point in the cycle, the point at which inventories and receivables are at their lowest, is the fiscal year end. The advantage to this plan is that the physical inventory is less of a problem because inventories are at a minimum and year-end close out requirements, which include the preparation of the financial statements and tax returns, fall at a time when normal business activities are at their lowest. In 1987 the Internal Revenue Service instituted a new rule that makes it more difficult for small businesses to use a fiscal year that is different from the calendar year. The IRS wanted to standardize reporting periods, which probably is beneficial to the service, but their actions have forced a mismatch of fiscal and natural business years on many small firms.

## Income Statement

The **income statement** shows the aggregate of all revenues and expenses that have occurred during the year and nets these to determine profit or loss. The **cost of goods sold** section details all the expenses of acquiring or producing inventory and subtracts that from sales to produce **gross profit.** Service firms will not include this section in their statements. The remainder of the statement organizes and subtotals expenses to highlight important costs and subtracts those to find **net income.** Note that there is no account in the general ledger for net profit because it doesn't exist until the income statement is prepared!

## Balance Sheet

The financial statement consists of four parts. A complete statement is displayed in this chapter's Appendix. The **balance sheet** shows the dollar value of all assets, the present value of all liabilities, and the historic value of capital.

Assets are divided into current and noncurrent categories. As indicated earlier, current assets, in general, are those that are in cash or are expected to be converted into cash within one year. Liabilities also are separated into current and noncurrent categories, with the current liabilities generally being those that are expected to be paid within one year, and noncurrent liabilities being those that extend beyond one year. This separation usually requires long-term installment loans to be separated. The part of the principal of the loan that will be repaid during the next year is called **current portion of long-term debt,** whereas the remainder of the loan is called **long-term debt.** Of course, assets must balance liabilities plus capital or else an error has been made. That is why the statement is called a balance sheet.

## Comprehensive Illustration, Part Two

We can now return to our example of the concession stand. You remember that we had captured all of the information in the general journal, posted it to the general ledger, and ensured that it balanced with a trial balance. Now we can pull out the balances for revenue and expense accounts from the ledger and arrange them into an income statement. Exhibit 4-4 shows the result. Arranging the rest of the accounts and picking up the total from the income statement allows us to prepare the balance sheet, as pictured in Exhibit 4-5.

As you can see, the concession stand lost money on the first game. The

**EXHIBIT 4-4** *Income Statement*

INCOME STATEMENT

| | | |
|---|---|---|
| Sales of hot dogs | $90.00 | |
| Cost of franks sold | 46.80 | |
| Gross profit—hot dogs | | 43.20 |
| Sales of drinks | 95.00 | |
| Cost of drinks sold | 68.40 | |
| Gross profit—drinks | | 26.20 |
| Total gross profit | | 69.40 |
| Expenses: | | |
| Supply expense | 32.49 | |
| Rent expense | 20.00 | |
| Wage expense | 28.00 | |
| Ice expense | 8.50 | |
| Total expenses | | 88.99 |
| Net income (loss) | | $(10.19) |

**EXHIBIT 4-5** *Balance Sheet*

BALANCE SHEET

| | |
|---|---|
| Assets: | |
| Cash | $266.00 |
| Inventory | 8.80 |
| Supplies | 32.49 |
| Equipment | 82.50 |
| Total assets | $389.79 |
| Liabilities: | |
| Accounts payable | $208.98 |
| Capital: | |
| Church's capital | 200.00 |
| Loss to date | (10.19) |
| Total liabilities and capital | $389.79 |

records provide the manager with the information necessary to analyze the problem. Without the record keeping, steps to correct the problem would have to be made on a trial-and-error basis. The point is that the information is a tool of management and record keeping makes it possible to use that tool.

## Reconciliation of Net Worth

The **reconciliation of net worth** shows the beginning balances in capital accounts for the year, the changes that have taken place during the year, and the effect of profit or loss on the capital. The reconciliation shows the effect of the income statement on the balance sheet. You know that all profit or loss belongs to the owner. That means that at the end of the year, those profits or losses must be transferred to the owner's account. Then, any draws that the owners have taken, or dividends they have paid in the case of a corporation, must be deducted.

## Statement of Changes in Financial Position

The **statement of changes in financial position** shows the flow of funds through the business during the course of the year. The statement of changes shows flows affecting the balance sheet that otherwise would be a static statement of position. In the past the statement of changes could be based on cash or on working capital, as a company desired. **Working capital,** defined as the difference between current assets and current liabilities, is a representation of financial resources that can support daily operations. Recently, the **Finan-**

cial **Accounting Standards Board,** which sets rules for preparing financial statements, has decreed that all firms must use the cash basis in preparing the statement of changes.

### Interim Financial Statements

**Interim financial statements** generally do not include a statement of changes and require estimates of some liabilities, such as income tax, that the company will incur. Interim financial statements also generally are not supported by physical inventory counts. Because of the estimates, interim statements are less accurate than year-end statements. Nevertheless, interim statements are of extreme importance to the management of a firm. Because financial statements are historic in nature, showing what has happened, no action can be taken to change the results. By monitoring interim statements, a manager can identify actions that can correct developing problems during the year. In order to be of value, interim statements must be current. This means that the system needs to be designed to generate month-end statements as quickly as possible after a month is over.

## FINANCIAL STATEMENT PREPARATION

The preparation of the financial statements is principally a matter of arranging the account balances from the general ledger in the proper format. Accountants use a worksheet for this process. Most of the work involves arranging information in the proper format.

### Adjusting Entries

As we indicated earlier, the financial statements are prepared from the general ledger. Before this can be done, the general ledger must be balanced and adjusted. **Adjusting entries** are transactions posted to correct account balances that are misstated and to record transactions that have not been captured. Some transactions are posted on a cash basis during the year because it is simpler to do so. For example, salaries and wages generally are easier to post as payroll checks are prepared. Nevertheless, salaries and wages, as well as everything else, must be adjusted to reflect the accrual basis. This means that salaries and wages owed to employees but not yet paid must be posted as an expense and as an unpaid liability. In addition, such items as insurance premiums, generally posted on the cash basis, must be adjusted to reflect the actual amount of expense that relates to insurance coverage during the period with any remaining disbursements to insurance companies shown as a "prepaid expense," which will be an asset.

## Depreciation

Other types of transactions generally are not posted until it is time to prepare the financial statements because it takes too long to calculate and make the entries. Notable among these is depreciation expense. **Depreciation** is a method of allocating the cost of long-lived assets over their useful lives. If a building is expected to last fifteen years, then its cost should be allocated over that fifteen-year period. As you may know, there are several different methods of calculating depreciation. The method currently most popular, because of Internal Revenue rules, is called the ACRS, or **accelerated cost recovery system.** We will not go into the various methods of calculating depreciation here because of space restrictions and because our intention is not to make you an accountant. Nevertheless, you need to understand how depreciation affects the financial statements.

The depreciation we calculate for any period is only an estimate of the amount of cost of assets that should be allocated. Consequently, accounting principles say that we should show the results of those calculations separately from the cost of the assets that are being depreciated. This is done through the use of two accounts. One account is called **depreciation expense,** and as its name indicates, it is an expense account. The balance in the depreciation expense account will be shown on the income statement and will be subtracted along with other expenses to generate profit. Like other expense accounts, depreciation expense is a temporary account and will contain the depreciation for only the current year. It will be closed out at the end of the year to start out the next year with a zero balance. The second account is called **accumulated depreciation.** This account is a permanent account and shows on the balance sheet. Accumulated depreciation will be subtracted from the asset accounts depreciated to show **book value** of the assets. The asset accounts will contain the original cost information for the asset dating back to when the asset was first purchased. Accumulated depreciation contains the total of all depreciation expense that has been recognized on the asset since that time. The difference between the two, called the *book value,* represents the remaining amount of assets that has not been depreciated. That means that book value has nothing to do with the market value of assets.

In fact, the market value of assets does not show on the balance sheet at all. Accounting principles require the historic treatment of assets, which means that they will be shown at their purchase prices when they were acquired. By the same token, depreciation expense has nothing to do with cash outflow.

The cash required to purchase the assets had to be paid at the time the asset was acquired. Otherwise, the cost could have been paid over the life of an installment loan. In either case, the depreciation expense has nothing to do with the amount of cash that has been disbursed. Consequently, the depreciation expense represents an entry that does not have a cash outlay associated with itself.

## Preparation of the Statement of Changes

The statement of changes in financial position is the last portion of the financial statement to be prepared and the only one in which account balances are not used. Instead, it lists aggregate transactions that occurred during the year. This statement confuses many small business owners, so we will go into some detail to make it more clear. Let's focus on the cash basis because it is the only one now acceptable.

The first item on the statement is net profit because it is a source of funds. The net profit is adjusted for revenues and expenses that may have been recorded but that do not affect cash. Principal among these is depreciation, which is an expense which does not consume cash. That means that depreciation must be added back to net income. Note that depreciation is not added back because it is a source of cash, but because it originally was subtracted in finding income and should not be subtracted if we want to determine cash income.

Changes in the balances in current asset and current liability accounts are added or subtracted depending upon how they affect cash. All current asset accounts except cash generally will be used. Accounts receivable that go up during the year represent a higher investment of cash. Accounts receivable that go down during the year result in throwing off more cash. Consequently, increases in current assets will be subtracted and decreases in current assets will be added to arrive at cash generated from operations.

Exactly the reverse situation exists for current liabilities. Accounts payable that go down during the year represent cash used to retire the debt. Accounts payable that go up during the year represent cash that has not yet been disbursed to cover those expenses. Consequently, increases in current liability accounts will be added and decreases in current liabilities will be subtracted to arrive at cash generated from operations. Virtually all current liability accounts will be examined in this manner.

After the net cash generated by operations has been determined, every noncurrent asset account, every noncurrent liability account, and every capital account is examined. The gross amounts of additions to each of the accounts is calculated, as are the gross amounts of subtractions from the accounts. These sums will be reported as **sources or uses of funds** depending upon their impact on cash: if long-term debt goes up, it must have added to the cash position; if equipment or property has been purchased, it must have consumed cash; if dividends have been paid, cash must have been used. Finally, a reconciliation of funds will show the change in cash position and should balance to the net change in cash that results from the previous calculations.

### Notes to the Statement

In the last part of the financial statement, a section is included to explain the major accounting practices followed in the preparation of the financial statements and to disclose additional details about statement items deemed to be of value to users of the statement. These are called **footnotes.** Remember, the Appendix at the end of this chapter contains an illustration of a complete financial statement, including footnote disclosures.

## THE ROLE OF THE CPA

Most people think of CPAs as auditors, and most of the revenues of CPA firms comes from performing audits on financial statements. An **audit** is an investigation of the internal controls and record-keeping processes of a business and the evaluation, testing, and confirmation of the assets and liabilities of a firm. Most small businesses do not employ CPA firms to perform audits of their statements because the undertaking generally is expensive. Every **publicly owned business,** that is a corporation whose stock is subject to control by the Securities and Exchange Commission, is required by law to have an audit performed by an independent CPA firm each year. The word **independent** means that the CPA should not be involved financially or personally with the firm being audited. Contrary to popular belief, an audit is not designed to catch fraud. Its real purpose is to ensure that the financial statement has been prepared in accordance with the accounting principles that the profession has established. The testing, evaluation, and confirmation steps are based on samples and are designed to indicate only the reasonableness of the numbers. The review of internal controls is the key to the audit. This step is designed to ensure that the proper accounting principles are being followed and that the records are dependable. Also, this last step can be of value to a small business. An independent review of the internal controls can be revealing and result in a better record-keeping system and more dependable records.

CPAs perform other services as well as audits. They can prepare financial statements for a business without audit, the most frequently encountered use of CPAs by small businesses. This task simply involves taking the records maintained by employees of the firm and converting them into the correct format for financial statements. Sadly, this is one of the least valuable tasks a

CPA can perform for a small business. Any good microcomputer package can do the same thing faster and cheaper than a CPA or even an outside accountant. The use of CPAs to prepare statements continues because most small business owners know little about accounting and are convinced that the statements are some sort of mystical, magical creation. The truth is that CPAs do not actually prepare the financial statements either! Clerks and assistants in the CPA's office will prepare the statement, after which the CPA will look it over for completeness and any obvious mistakes. This, called a **review,** simply is a matter of examining the statement to determine whether it appears reasonable given the business and its background. Using a CPA for this purpose once a year should be enough! You would do better engaging a CPA to help you find a microcomputer accounting package than in preparing your monthly statements.

The best use of a CPA in a small business is as a partner to management in structuring the record-keeping systems necessary to provide the decision-making information required for effective control. CPAs call this kind of activity **management advisory services.** These services actually are less expensive than audits; and when compared to the benefits to be derived in the form of faster, more accurate and useful information, management advisory services can be an extremely good buy.

A CPA can be extremely important to your business, so you should select one carefully. You need to discuss your business with a CPA and get to know each other. You need a CPA who is knowledgeable about your industry, approachable when you need advice and help, and interested in working with you and helping the business. That kind of person should not be wasted on preparing financial statements, but used as a resource to develop and improve control and reporting systems of all kinds.

Another valuable role CPAs can perform is in the area of taxation. In Chapter 17, we talk about the complexity of preparing fringe benefit packages that could minimize taxes for employees and for the firm. A CPA is necessary for that kind of activity. Tax planning does not mean having a CPA prepare your tax returns once each year. Effective tax planning goes on throughout the year, not after the year is over. You need to involve your CPA in tax planning; you need to discuss the tax implications of any changes in the business you are considering; you need tax advice on an ongoing basis.

## Tax Planning

Tax issues in selecting the form of business will be presented in Chapter 13. In this section we will examine some of the other aspects of tax planning you should discuss with your CPA. Few people think about the need for involving a CPA in the day-to-day decision-making activities of a business. Small business owners need to recognize the potential tax consequences associated with everyday business transactions. However, it is important not to let tax issues overshadow other factors in a business decision. Tax laws change frequently and therefore are uncertain. Furthermore, taxes are only one variable in any business decision. It frequently is more important to examine effects on personnel, market position, image, and so on, rather than to focus solely on taxes.

One aspect of tax planning that will be important to small business owners is the alternative minimum tax (AMT). Prior to 1986, AMT usually was no problem for small firms. However, new rules mean that almost any action that affects the amount of income tax paid also can have an impact on AMT. The AMT prevents a firm or individual from using special treatment items to avoid paying income taxes. In formulating it, Congress was reacting to claims that wealthy individuals were able to avoid taxes by investing in particular areas. Unfortunately, the cure has far-reaching implications for small firms. For example, accelerated depreciation creates a faster write off of assets but can cause AMT to rise. The issue is complex and requires professional advice.

Tax issues frequently require a separate set of records. Not only are there differences in the way transactions should be handled for accounting vs tax purposes, a business may decide to handle some transactions in a way that can reduce taxes. Needless to say, professional advice is required to achieve that!

## Taxes and Fixed Assets

Tax laws concerning fixed assets and tax laws in general have changed rapidly in recent years. Congress uses tax legislation to manipulate the economy. For example, in the past an investment tax credit was used to encourage people to acquire long-lived assets. That credit has been replaced by a major increase in depreciation deductions for small firms. If fixed assets purchased for the year total less than $200,000, then the firm can deduct a maximum of $10,000 of the costs immediately. This can be extremely lucrative; however, the write off can affect the AMT just discussed, so professional advice is required.

New tax changes require particular accounting methods to be employed for various types of assets. For example, the IRS prescribes the way that a company can charge off bad debts, the way it calculates depreciation expense, the way it values inventory, and so forth. As we indicate so frequently in this section, a professional tax advisor is required.

Leasing can have tax implications because the entire amount of lease payments can be deductible if the lease is properly structured. However, leasing can be more expensive than buying, at least on a before-tax basis. We will examine the lease-buy question in more depth in Chapter 7 under capital budgeting, because taxes are only one of the issues that must be considered.

### The Importance of Choosing a CPA

Whether you need an audited financial statement each year or not, a CPA can be a valuable asset in managing the business, simply because few small firms can afford to employ a CPA or other qualified accountant as a full-time employee. Assistance in tax planning and management advisory services of all types easily can be justified by the benefits they produce. One final comment about CPAs is pertinent. The largest accounting firms in the United States are collectively called the *Big 8*. These eight firms control over 80 percent of the dollar value of accounting audits in the country even though there are thousands of CPA firms in the United States. Many people tend to think of size as indicative of competence or knowledge of accounting. Nothing could be farther from the truth. Just as your business can be a viable part of the economy and provide a superior product or service in the face of competition from giants, so can CPA firms. Many of them are small businesses as well. The CPA who will be working with you is far more important than the name of the firm.

## SUMMARY

Accounting was established by the early Romans, based on the trust that businesses felt in the honesty of people who owed them. Today that trust is still implicit in the accounting function. People expect financial statements to reflect the true financial condition of a company.

In reality, accounting is a reflection of management. If management has designed a sound accounting system and installed sound accounting practices and controls, then the financial statements will be dependable and trustworthy.

In extremely small businesses, record keeping is not as vital because the owner is aware of money flowing in and out of the business. However, with the addition of employees, the record-keeping process becomes essential to help management stay knowledgeable and provide a basis for decisions.

Two types of accounting techniques discussed here are cash basis accounting and accrual basis accounting. Small businesses should use the accrual methodology because of the demand for the generation of financial information necessary for decision making. Under the cash method, revenues and expenses are recorded only when cash changes hands. Under the accrual method, revenues and expenses are recorded whenever an obligation to receive or pay money arises, regardless of whether the money changes hands. This method results in a more systematic and accurate measurement of a firm's activities over time and is the preferred approach. However, under accrual accounting, a company can show a profit but have serious cash flow problems.

Guidelines were given for forming internal controls. These are techniques used to safeguard assets and records and ensure that transactions are properly recorded and the accounting process properly managed.

Also discussed in some detail in this chapter are the components of the financial statement and each of their benefits. The preparation of these financial statements and the information revealed for decision making is explained.

The role of the CPA is to be a partner in management, not simply a preparer of financial reports. That role involves tax consultation, management advisory services, tax planning, fringe benefit preparation, and advice about internal controls whether from a manual or automated perspective.

The purpose of this chapter is *not* to make you an accountant but to give you knowledge with which to *plan*. Planning record-keeping activities is the responsibility of small business owners, and knowing what is needed and from whom is a step toward success. Use this tool wisely and plan accordingly.

## QUESTIONS

1. Define the following terms:
   a. accounting
   b. profit
   c. cash flow
   d. auditing
2. Why is accounting called the *language of trust*?
3. Why is record keeping so important to a business?
4. Why would the general ledger be called the *heart* of the accounting system?
5. Explain when journals and subsidiary ledgers are used.
6. How would you set up internal controls in a small business? Explain and give specific examples.
7. Explain the four parts of the financial statement and what constitutes each part.
8. What task do CPAs usually perform for a small business, and what service would be better done for the business?
9. What is the purpose of an audit?

## PROJECTS

1. Visit a small, local, accounting firm and ask about the types of work performed for small business clients. What does the accountant consider to be the major problem in handling small business accounts? Does the firm do counseling or tax planning for

small businesses? What proportion of the firm's work is made up of small businesses? What kinds of businesses are these? Visit the local office of a large regional or national accounting firm and ask the same questions. Are there differences in the responses? Present your findings to the class.

2. Visit a small business owner and ask about accounting systems. Does the firm have a bookkeeper or accountant or is all work done outside by an accounting firm? Is the owner happy with the services of the accounting firm? How was the firm chosen? Does the business use accrual or cash accounting? Is there a complete set of records in the business? How often are interim financial statements prepared? When is the annual financial statement finished? Make a list of weaknesses that you see in the accounting system. Compare notes with the other members of the class.

# Case

Geraldine Franks was relieved. She had made a decision about her accounting situation. When she had decided to open her own small office supply company, she consulted a CPA and found that record keeping could be an expensive proposition. The CPA had suggested that he could do more for her than just preparation of financial statements, but she wasn't interested at that time. Now Geraldine had the answer. Yesterday, she had been approached by a computer salesman who claimed to specialize in accounting packages for small companies. The computer could handle all the accounting needs of the company and there would be no need for a CPA, claimed the salesman.

The computer system was installed and Geraldine felt that all five of her employees should know how to operate it, but she, herself, was too busy to find time for the training. After all, she had employees because she couldn't do everything!

The system was a success. The employees loved it. She had chuckled about all the game playing that had occurred after hours on the system because the salesman had thrown in a couple of games with the purchase. He claimed that the games would overcome resistance in the employees in learning to use the computer—and that it had!

All the employees had access to the system and Geraldine wondered what she had done without it. Bob Grant especially seemed to enjoy it. Although Susan Winters was the bookkeeper, every time she had a problem, she called Bob to help her. He was much more technically oriented than she, she insisted. Bob had even come in on nights and weekends to work on the computer.

Two years went by and Geraldine's future didn't look as rosy. She knew that business had picked up. Even an idiot could see that now more customers were dropping in and she had several large clients, which she didn't have last year. What was wrong? The cash flow wasn't there. Then the bank called and said that she was overdrawn. This couldn't be happening to her. What could she do?

### Questions

1. What do you think might be happening? What could be done to discover what was happening?
2. What internal controls may have been violated?
3. What common sense control was violated?
4. What should Geraldine do?
5. What could the CPA have done for her had she consulted him even after the purchase of the computer system?

# APPENDIX
# Financial Statements

The financial statement contained in this appendix is an actual representation of the annual report prepared by a CPA for a small business. The names of the business and the CPA have been disguised. The statements are unaudited. We selected this approach because it is the most frequently encountered type of statement in the small business arena.

Professional accounting regulations permit two types of unaudited financial statements to be prepared for a small business: the compilation and a review. In the compilation, an accountant does not express any assurance that the statements are accurate, complete, or properly prepared. A review is a higher level of service and requires an accountant to evaluate internal controls and confirm the existence of inventories and receivables. A review is not as high a level as an audit. The two types of financial statements will look the same, but the accountant's cover letter or opinion letter must spell out the level of involvement that the accountant had in the preparation of the financial statements. The appendix shows an example of each type of cover letter when no problems are discovered by the CPA. If the CPA had discovered any improper or unusual situations, then the opinion letter would have to disclose them.

## Example of a Compilation Letter

ADAMS AND POWERS
CERTIFIED PUBLIC ACCOUNTANTS
1 MAIN STREET
ATLANTA, GEORGIA 30000

February 15, 199C

Board of Directors
ABC Chemical Company, Inc.
Route 1
Southtown, Georgia

We have compiled the accompanying balance sheet of ABC Chemical Company, Inc., as of December 31, 199B, and the related statements of income, retained earnings and changes in financial position for the year then ended, in accordance with standards established by the American Institute of Certified Public Accountants.

A compilation is limited to presenting, in the form of financial statements, information that is the representation of management. We have not audited or reviewed the accompanying financial statements and, accordingly, do not express an opinion or any other form of assurance on them.

Adams and Powers
Certified Public Accountants

## Example of a Review Letter

ADAMS AND POWERS
CERTIFIED PUBLIC ACCOUNTANTS
1 MAIN STREET
ATLANTA, GEORGIA 30000

February 15, 199C

Board of Directors
ABC Chemical Company, Inc.
Route 1
Southtown, Georgia

We have reviewed the accompanying balance sheet of ABC Chemical Company, Inc., as of December 31, 199B, and the related statements of income, retained earnings and changes in financial position for the year then ended, in accordance with standards established by the American Institute of Certified Public Accountants. All information included in these financial statements is the representation of ABC Chemical Company, Inc.

A review consists principally of inquiries of company personnel and analytical procedures applied to financial data. It is substantially less in scope than an examination in accordance with generally accepted auditing standards, the objective of which is the expression of an opinion regarding the financial statements taken as a whole. Accordingly, we do not express such an opinion. On the basis of our review, we are not aware of any material modifications that should be made to the accompanying financial statements in order for them to be in conformity with generally accepted accounting principles.

Adams and Powers
Certified Public Accountants

ABC CHEMICAL COMPANY, INC.

**Balance Sheet**

ASSETS

| | December 31, 199B | December 31, 199A |
|---|---|---|
| Current assets: | | |
| Cash in banks | $ (4,902) | $ 204 |
| Accounts receivable (Note 3) (net of allowance for bad debts of $1,171 and $982 respectively) | 37,876 | 18,662 |
| Receivables from officers | 3,291 | 8,957 |
| Inventory (Note 1) | 27,629 | 18,849 |
| Prepaid expenses | 12,922 | 2,159 |
| Total current assets | 76,816 | 48,831 |
| Plant, property, and equipment (Notes 1 and 2): | | |
| Land | 10,500 | 10,500 |
| Building | 74,399 | 74,399 |
| Machinery and equipment | 28,527 | 28,527 |
| Leasehold improvements | 21,937 | 20,672 |
| Furniture and fixtures | 3,972 | 3,972 |
| Vehicles | 12,750 | 11,850 |
| Total | 152,085 | 149,920 |
| Less accumulated depreciation | (57,004) | (40,862) |
| Net book value | 95,081 | 109,058 |
| Other assets | 770 | 50 |
| Total assets | $172,667 | $157,939 |

LIABILITIES AND STOCKHOLDERS' EQUITY

| | 199B | 199A |
|---|---|---|
| Current liabilities: | | |
| Accounts payable | $ 95,762 | $ 93,237 |
| Accrued items | 9,382 | 7,113 |
| Current portion, long-term debt | 35,445 | 25,286 |
| Total current liabilities | 140,589 | 125,636 |
| Notes and mortgages payable (Note 2): | | |
| Mortgage on building | 37,745 | 52,186 |
| Notes due to banks | 44,789 | 13,651 |
| Total | 82,534 | 65,837 |
| Less current portion | (35,445) | (25,286) |
| Total long-term debt | 47,089 | 40,551 |
| Stockholders' equity: | | |
| Capital stock | 15,300 | 15,300 |
| Paid-in capital | 20,573 | 20,573 |
| Retained earnings | (50,884) | (44,121) |
| Total stockholders' equity | (15,011) | (8,248) |
| Total liabilities and stockholders' equity | $172,667 | $157,939 |

**ABC CHEMICAL COMPANY**
**Statement of Income (Loss)**
**for the Years Ended December 31**

| | *199B* | *199A* |
|---|---|---|
| Sales | $328,590 | $391,352 |
| Cost of goods sold: | | |
| Beginning inventory | 18,849 | 38,104 |
| Purchases | 184,645 | 203,340 |
| Plant labor | 22,541 | 21,301 |
| Total | 226,035 | 262,745 |
| Less ending inventory | 27,629 | 18,849 |
| Total cost of goods sold | 198,406 | 243,896 |
| Gross profit on sales | 130,184 | 147,456 |
| Operating expenses: | | |
| Salaries—officer | 16,090 | 28,250 |
| Other salaries | 12,482 | 14,642 |
| Payroll taxes | 3,860 | 8,854 |
| Freight out | 16,636 | 29,724 |
| Insurance | 8,011 | 7,191 |
| Utilities | 1,417 | 1,436 |
| Telephone | 4,737 | 5,281 |
| Auto and truck | 6,665 | 8,613 |
| Travel and entertainment | 9,597 | 6,002 |
| Bad debts | 1,305 | 1,759 |
| Depreciation | 16,141 | 14,018 |
| Miscellaneous | 21,457 | 12,731 |
| Total operating expenses | 118,398 | 138,501 |
| Operating income (loss) | 11,786 | 8,955 |
| Other expenses: | | |
| Interest | 14,549 | 6,885 |
| Income (loss) before taxes | (2,763) | 2,070 |
| Income tax provision | -0- | -0- |
| Net income (loss) | $ (2,763) | $ 2,070 |
| Retained earnings—beginning | (44,121) | (46,191) |
| Prior period adjustment | (4,000) | -0- |
| Retained earnings—ending | $ (50,884) | $ (44,121) |

## Cash Basis Example

**ABC CHEMICAL COMPANY, INC.**
**Statement of Changes in Cash Position**
**for the Year Ended December 31, 199B**

| | | |
|---|---|---|
| Cash flow from operations: | | |
| Net income (loss) | $ (2,763) | |
| Add items not requiring cash: | | |
| Depreciation | 16,141 | |
| Changes in current assets: | | |
| Accounts receivable | (19,214) | |
| Receivables from officers | 5,666 | |
| Inventory | (8,780) | |
| Prepaid expenses | (10,763) | |
| Changes in current liabilities: | | |
| Accounts payable | 2,525 | |
| Accrued items | 2,269 | |
| Current portion of long-term debt | 10,159 | |
| Total cash consumed by operations | | $ (4,760) |
| Cash from financing: | | |
| Bank notes payable | | 41,825 |
| Total cash provided | | $37,065 |
| Applications of cash: | | |
| Acquire leasehold improvements | 1,265 | |
| Acquire vehicle | 900 | |
| Acquire other assets | 720 | |
| Prior period adjustment | 4,000 | |
| Pay long-term debt | 35,286 | |
| Total applications of cash | | $42,171 |
| Net change in cash position | | $ (5,106) |
| Change in cash balance | | $ (5,106) |

## Working Capital Basis Example

**ABC CHEMICAL COMPANY, INC.**
**Statement of Changes in Financial Position**
**for the Year Ended December 31, 199B**

| | | |
|---|---|---|
| Sources of working capital: | | |
| Net income (loss) | $ (2,763) | |
| Add items not requiring working capital | | |
| Depreciation | 16,141 | |
| Total working capital provided by operations | | $13,378 |
| Other sources of working capital: | | |
| Bank notes payable | | 41,825 |
| Total sources of working capital | | $55,203 |
| Applications of working capital: | | |
| Acquire leasehold improvements | 1,265 | |
| Acquire vehicle | 900 | |
| Acquire other assets | 720 | |
| Prior period adjustment | 4,000 | |
| Pay long-term debt | 35,286 | |
| Total applications of working capital | | $42,171 |
| Net change in working capital | | $13,032 |
| Increase (decrease) in working capital: | | |
| Cash in banks | $ (5,106) | |
| Accounts receivable | 19,214 | |
| Receivables from officers | (5,666) | |
| Inventory | 8,780 | |
| Prepaid expenses | 10,763 | |
| Accounts payable | (2,525) | |
| Accrued items | (2,269) | |
| Current portion, long-term debt | (10,159) | |
| Net change in working capital | | $13,032 |

**ABC CHEMICAL COMPANY, INC.**
**Notes to Financial Statements**
**for the Years Ended December 31, 199A and 199B**

**1. SUMMARY OF SIGNIFICANT ACCOUNTING POLICIES**

Plant assets are stated at cost and are depreciated principally on the straight line method over the following useful lives:

| | |
|---|---|
| Building | 5–25 years |
| Machinery and equipment | 3–7 years |
| Automotive equipment | 3 years |
| Furniture and fixtures | 8 years |

Maintenance, repairs, and minor renewals are charged against earnings when incurred. Additions and major renewals are capitalized.

Inventories are valued at the lower of first-in, first-out cost or market and consist principally of merchandise held for resale.

Investment tax credits available for carry forward to offset future income taxes are approximately $2,500.

**2. LONG-TERM DEBT**

Mortgage note payable in monthly installments of $1,453, including interest at 9% through January 199F. Secured by land and building valued at $84,900.

One bank note payable is an installment note in the amount of $3,789 payable in monthly installments of $117 including interest at 18% through January 199D. Secured by a vehicle with an original cost of $4,350.

The remaining bank notes payable are secured by liens on accounts receivable and have various maturities from 90 days to 2 years. Interest rates vary from 11% to 13%.

**3. ACCOUNTS RECEIVABLE**

Substantially all of the company's accounts receivable are pledged as collateral for bank notes payable.

# CHAPTER 5

# Managerial Accounting Tools for Success

**LEARNING OBJECTIVES**

After completing this chapter, you should be able to

- Distinguish between financial accounting and managerial accounting.
- Define contribution margin and understand its significance in decision making.
- Explain the value of contribution margin reports and what managerial information can be learned from them.
- Calculate operating cash flow and net cash flow and understand the difference.
- Prepare a cash flow report and explain its importance in managerial decision making.

As we learned in the last chapter, **financial accounting** refers to the activities that result in the production of the financial statement. Accounting principles dictate how those statements must be prepared. Over the years, the accounting profession has developed such principles to generate statements that can be used by outsiders to support a broad range of decision-making activities: investment, buying, selling, taxing, lending, and so on. Also, because every firm must use the same rules in preparing financial statements, the statements of the various firms can be compared for a better understanding of how one firm compares to its competitors and other small businesses.

**Managerial accounting** uses the record-keeping tools developed in financial accounting, but it is not hampered with any rules or principles other than those of common sense. The outcome of managerial accounting is intended solely for internal use. Managerial reports are prepared by the owner and other managers in the business and can report on any area and in any format believed important. The only purpose of managerial statements is to support the decision making process. If they provide valuable information on a timely basis, then they are valuable; otherwise, they should not be prepared. In this chapter, we will explore several types of managerial statements and reports including contribution margin income statements and cash flow statements.

As we indicated earlier, **managerial statements** are financial reports designed for use inside the business. There is an almost unlimited variety of such reports. Some are well known, such as delinquency reports on accounts receivable, projected payments reports on accounts payable, and various kinds of inventory status and turnover reports. The variance reports discussed in Chapter 23, "Production Management," are another example as are sales by agent reports, mentioned in Chapter 17, "Human Resource Management." In fact, many of the things we talk about in this book are examples of the application of managerial accounting to small businesses. We cannot possibly examine all of the variety of reports possible. Consequently, we have selected two types of reports that can be of value to any kind of small business and that are not used with the frequency they deserve. We will concentrate on managerial reports dealing with contribution margins and cash flow reports. Remember that there are numerous other types of reports that can be of value to a small business owner. Many of these are specific to a particular industry, such as inventory movement by size in the garment and shoe industry. Others are unique to a particular small business or developed by an individual manager to serve specific needs.

These reports can be ongoing—generated on a regular basis—or they can result from a special study. Time and motion studies in a manufacturing business may be performed infrequently or customer arrival patterns may be studied in a bank. Special records might be kept to monitor the results of a marketing or advertising campaign or a sale of some kind. Whenever you think that you would like to know something about a particular aspect of the business or the results of some activity, a report can be designed to capture that information. In fact, managerial reports do not have to be historic in nature. Forecasts, analyses, and budgets all are examples of managerial reports. Reports can cover virtually any topic. The only risk is that the cost to accumulate the data might be more than the information is worth. To constantly guard against this, always consider the use that a particular piece of information will have and the potential value of that information. Comparing the yield to the effort required to capture and compile the data will give you insight as to whether such effort is worthwhile.

## CONTRIBUTION MARGIN STATEMENTS

**Contribution margin** is defined as the difference between sales and variable costs. Variable costs are not limited to those involved in the production or acquisition of inventory; they include any business costs that go up and down with changes in sales. Subtracting such costs from revenues will indicate the monies sales generate for support of the business. Contribution margin concepts are used in break-even analysis and target sales forecasting, but there are many other uses, as we will see in this chapter. Contribution margin can be converted to a percentage, thus eliminating dollar amounts, to allow comparison of various products, departments, and divisions in a business. Use of percentages also permits examination of marginal profits and can point out weaknesses and strengths. Contribution margin even can be calculated on the basis of a scarce resource to aid in selecting the best application of those resources.

A **scarce resource** is one that limits the ability of the firm to generate revenues. If, for example, a service company depends upon the expertise of its employees to generate sales, then employee time is a scarce resource; for example, in a law, CPA, or consulting firm. If a firm uses machines to fabricate a product, the scarce resource could be machine time. Money frequently is a scarce resource for new businesses. Whatever the scarce resource is, a firm cannot expand its sales and profit generation without increasing the amounts of the resource that it possesses.

One of the best applications of contribution margin is in income and expense statements, reflecting margins and prepared by product, department, division, or other business segment. These contribution margin statements demonstrate the relative role the segments play in a company's profits. They work equally well for service companies, retailers, wholesalers, manufacturers, construction firms, or other types of businesses. Exhibit 5-1 displays a contribution margin statement for a business that leases buses to musicians and other touring groups. In this small business, the age, condition, and appearance of each bus is a major factor in success; consequently, the statement reflects margin by vehicle.

You may have noticed that the income statement for Mountain Coach in Exhibit 5-1 does not follow the traditional format. The statement is designed

**EXHIBIT 5-1** *Income and Expense Statement for Mountain Coach, Inc. for the Period 7/1/XX–8/31/XX*

| | BUS 1 | | BUS 2 | | BUS 3 | | TOTAL | |
|---|---|---|---|---|---|---|---|---|
| Revenues | $13,020 | 100% | $14,130 | 100% | 16,200 | 100% | $43,350 | 100% |
| Daily average | $310 | | $307 | | $300 | | $305 | |
| Revenue percentage | 30% | | 33% | | 37% | | 100% | |
| Days up, (down), or idle | 42 (4) 14 | | 46 (7) 7 | | 54 (1) 5 | | 142 (12) 26 | |
| Variable expenses: | | | | | | | | |
| Commissions | $ 1,302 | 10% | $ 1,413 | 10% | $ 1,620 | 10% | $ 4,335 | 10% |
| Repairs | 335 | 3% | 1,169 | 8% | 1,967 | 12% | 3,471 | 8% |
| Other | 537 | 4% | 1,156 | 8% | 168 | 1% | 1,861 | 4% |
| Totals | 2,174 | 17% | 3,738 | 26% | 3,755 | 23% | 9,667 | 22% |
| Contribution margin | $10,846 | 83% | $10,392 | 74% | $12,445 | 77% | $33,683 | 78% |
| Fixed expenses: | | | | | | | | |
| Insurance | 1,306 | 10% | 1,305 | 9% | 1,305 | 10% | 3,916 | 9% |
| Depreciation | 4,688 | 36% | 5,625 | 40% | 4,688 | 29% | 15,001 | 35% |
| Interest | 5,868 | 45% | 7,043 | 50% | 5,868 | 36% | 18,779 | 43% |
| Profit margin | ($1,016) | 8% | ($3,581) | 25% | $ 584 | 4% | ($4,013) | 9% |
| Cash flow | $ 9,540 | 73% | $ 9,087 | 64% | $11,140 | 69% | $29,767 | 69% |
| Loan payments | 9,375 | 72% | 11,250 | 80% | 9,375 | 58% | 30,000 | 69% |
| Unallocated expenses: | | | | | | | | |
| Tags and taxes | | | | | | | 985 | 2% |
| Travel and entertainment | | | | | | | 150 | — |
| Miscellaneous | | | | | | | 40 | — |
| Professional fees | | | | | | | 500 | 1% |
| Totals | | | | | | | 1,675 | 4% |
| Profit (Loss) | | | | | | | ($5,688) | 13% |

to provide information of value to the management of the firm, not to those outside the company. The company is heavily in debt because of loans against the buses; consequently, the ability to cover loan payments is more important than profit. Therefore, the statement highlights loan coverage ability. Notice that the contribution margin by bus, as well as overall, is extremely high, which is normal in a service industry. Nevertheless, the contribution margins vary by bus. Can you see from the statement areas that need management attention? Is the relative value of each bus to overall operations highlighted? One important area to note is that not all expenses were allocated to the buses. This will almost always be the case for any business preparing a contribution margin statement. Some expenses cannot be traced to the products or segments of the operation. These expenses are correctly treated as expenses of the firm rather than allocated on some arbitrary basis.

Compare the service company statement in Exhibit 5-1 to the statement for a convenience food store displayed in Exhibit 5-2. The statement focuses on the sales and cost of sales by product groups within the business, because that is the key factor for monitoring performance in a convenience store. The income statement displays the results for December and the nine-month period ending in December as well.

Note that the percentages for the sales portion display the makeup of gross sales, whereas the percentage in the cost of sales and gross profit sections are based on the sales for the product group. The expense section percentages are based on gross sales. The gross profit displayed for this firm is equivalent to the contribution margin that we have been discussing because the only variable costs in the firm are product costs. Can you see any items that appear to need attention based on the statement? Why do you think the gross profit margin on tobacco changed so much during the last month as compared to the year to date? Could it be that a big price increase on tobacco items was implemented? That might explain the slight drop in tobacco sales as a percentage of overall sales. If there has been a price increase, then the sales bear watching!

Do you see any areas in which increased sales could improve the firm's performance? How about the **sundries?** These are items such as novelties that have a much higher markup than most of the items in a convenience store. The income statement makes that obvious! A small increase in sales of sundries could have a marked impact on gross profit, because the contribution margin for sundries is so much higher than for the other items. Consider, a $1,000 increase in the sales of sundries will produce $576 in profits (57.6%). Groceries have the next highest contribution margin at 21.1%, but it would take an increase in grocery sales of $2,730 in order to produce $576 in profits ($576/21.1% = $2,730). Gasoline has the lowest margin of all at 6.9%. It would take an increase in gasoline sales of $8,348 in order to produce that same $576 in profits ($576/6.9% = $8,348). The other side of that coin also is true. A

**EXHIBIT 5-2** *Income and Expense Statement for Convenience Food Stores, Inc. for the Nine Months Ended 12/31/XX*

| | THIS MONTH | | YEAR TO DATE | |
|---|---|---|---|---|
| | | *Percentage* | | *Percentage* |
| Sales: | | *of Total* | | *of Total* |
| Gasoline | $ 82,927 | 61.7% | $ 730,932 | 60.5% |
| Groceries | 16,136 | 12.0 | 150,778 | 12.5 |
| Tobacco | 19,922 | 14.8 | 189,224 | 15.7 |
| Beer and wine | 11,567 | 8.6 | 107,617 | 8.9 |
| Sundries | 3,747 | 2.8 | 29,412 | 2.4 |
| Gross Sales | $134,299 | 100.0 | $1,207,963 | 100.0 |
| | | *Percentage* | | *Percentage* |
| Cost of sales: | | *of Sales* | | *of Sales* |
| Gasoline | $ 76,493 | 92.2% | $ 680,585 | 93.1% |
| Groceries | 12,456 | 77.2 | 118,915 | 78.9 |
| Tobacco | 16,124 | 80.9 | 164,679 | 87.0 |
| Beer and wine | 9,652 | 83.4 | 91,224 | 84.8 |
| Sundries | 1,401 | 37.4 | 12,471 | 42.4 |
| Total | $116,126 | 86.5 | $1,067,874 | 88.4 |
| | | *Percentage* | | *Percentage* |
| Gross profit: | | *of Sales* | | *of Sales* |
| Gasoline | $ 6,434 | 7.8% | $ 50,347 | 6.9% |
| Groceries | 3,680 | 22.8 | 31,863 | 21.1 |
| Tobacco | 3,798 | 19.1 | 24,545 | 13.0 |
| Beer and wine | 1,915 | 16.6 | 16,393 | 15.2 |
| Sundries | 2,346 | 62.6 | 16,941 | 57.6 |
| Total | $ 18,173 | 13.5 | $ 140,089 | 11.6 |
| | | *Percentage* | | *Percentage* |
| Expenses: | | *of Gross* | | *of Gross* |
| Salaries | $ 6,783 | 5.1% | $ 51,397 | 4.3% |
| Payroll taxes | 508 | .4 | 1,748 | .1 |
| Employee benefits | 460 | .3 | 1,843 | .2 |
| Rent | 800 | .6 | 7,240 | .6 |
| Repairs | 892 | .7 | 10,312 | .9 |
| Utilities | 1,557 | 1.2 | 13,166 | 1.1 |
| Supplies | 305 | .2 | 4,126 | .3 |
| Insurance | — | — | 4,027 | .3 |
| Travel and entertainment | 279 | .2 | 4,397 | .4 |
| Professional fees | — | — | 2,169 | .2 |
| Management fees | 2,352 | 1.8 | 9,674 | .8 |
| Interest expense | 204 | .2 | 1,869 | .2 |
| Miscellaneous | 56 | — | 2,217 | .2 |
| Depreciation | 4,471 | 3.3 | 15,034 | 1.2 |
| Total | $ 18,667 | 13.9 | $ 129,219 | 10.7 |
| Net Income Before Taxes | ($494) | .4% | $ 10,870 | .9% |
| Cash Flow | $ 3,977 | 2.9% | $ 25,904 | 2.1% |

decline in sales of $1,000 in sundries would reduce profits by $576 whereas gasoline sales could drop by $8,348 before losing that much.

The contribution margin can demonstrate aggregate values, too. For example, gasoline sales had a 6.9% margin on total sales of $680,000. If prices could be increased enough to provide a 1% increase in the margin without losing sales, then the effect would be to increase profits by $6,800 — well over half the $10,870 profit the firm currently is generating. It may be hard to raise those prices without losing sales however, even though we are talking about only a 1% increase. Remember that the contribution margin ratio is directly affected by selling price. This means that an increase in selling price will produce an increase in contribution margin if the variable costs remain the same. Gasoline sales through convenience stores tend to be highly competitive. Consider the impact of raising the price and losing sales. As we saw earlier, a loss in gasoline sales will not have a pronounced effect on profits until a major loss occurs. However, if people stop coming to buy gas, they may stop coming to buy other things. How much of our sales of other items might we lose if we have a decline in gasoline business? Unfortunately, that potential cannot be calculated, it can be only estimated subjectively.

Quantitative techniques can provide only so much information. The owner-manager constantly must be aware of the nonquantifiable elements in any situation. Nevertheless, the contribution margin can be a useful tool. It can be used with historic numbers, forecasts, or a combination. It can monitor progress toward objectives and trends in performance. It also can provide the information useful for planning marketing, pricing, inventory stocking, and a host of other activities. Finally, the contribution margin can provide the information for comparing products or business segments as well as break-even analysis and target sales analysis. Consider the following case from our files.

---

The client, a building contractor, had called us in because he was "working himself to death and not making any money." He wanted to see if we could discover what he was doing wrong. He had plenty of jobs, won most of the bids he entered, and lacked the capacity to handle any more work. Nevertheless, his profits were never more than modest.

The comment about winning almost all of his bids made us very nervous. First, we asked to see his books and records. Even though he had been in business for nine years and was considered a successful and competent builder in the area, all he could show us were the financial statements prepared by his accountant for each of the previous year ends. He had no interim statements.

We explained that we had to see something to evaluate his bidding process and get some feel for his profit margins. He showed us a drawer full of file folders. He had one for each job he was working and one for each job he had finished since last year.

These were the records he gave to the accountant once each year to prepare his financial statements. As bills came in, he filed them in the folder for the appropriate job. The system worked pretty well for material expenses, but there was absolutely no record of how much labor was expended on a particular job. This meant that we could not determine the contribution margin of any given contract.

We asked how he prepared the labor portion of his construction bids. He explained that he ''spected'' the material and then added 25% to that number to arrive at labor estimates. The material was relatively easy to estimate and the records he had kept indicated that he had been doing an admirable job of estimating material costs in the past. He added that he was sure that the labor was being covered or else he wouldn't be making any money! His overhead was virtually nil; his own time being the primary component. The firm was profitable, but not in the same profit league as its competitors.

Because the client's records were of no value, we needed access to the bidding records of a state agency that our client and his competitors frequently serviced. Fortunately, those bids were a matter of public record. Our client was absolutely appalled to learn that he had won his last three bids with that agency by a 25% to 40% margin. In every case his bid was substantially lower than his competitors'. The solution to his problem was now obvious.

Do you see the solution to the contractor's problem? Clearly, his bids had been much too low. Because he had not been capturing labor costs by job despite properly estimating material requirements, he was underbidding labor expenses. By instituting a managerial accounting system that captures all costs by job, the contractor will be able to gain the expertise in estimating labor costs that will allow him to increase his profits. The consultants were nervous about his winning too high a percentage of his bids. That fact would indicate that the contractor was "leaving a lot of money on the table." If he had been generating cost estimates similar to his competitors', then he would be expected to win some bids and to lose others, depending on the inconsistencies of the estimation process. This small business owner apparently was consistently underbidding the real cost of construction.

## CASH FLOW STATEMENTS

Both of the income statements discussed in the previous section displayed cash flow numbers as well as profits. This was no accident. We mentioned the value cash flow has for a business several times. If you simply remember that **profit** always is a historic indication of the difference between revenues and expenses over some arbitrary period of time, then you will understand that profit cannot be used to pay bills or purchase items because *there is no cash there*! Only cash can be used to purchase items or pay bills. Profit is valuable for only two reasons: profit enhances a small business' borrowing power and financial strength because analysts use it as a major factor in evaluating firms, and profit is valuable because it is a source of cash flow. The first of these we will discuss at greater length in Chapter 22, "Financial Management." The second we will address in this chapter.

## Operating Cash Flow

What is the difference between profit and cash? The difference is in timing. Remember that to achieve a consistent evaluation of performance over time we recognize revenues and expenses at times other than when cash changes hands. This means that cash flow and profit will not be the same thing. Consequently, we must examine the cash flow of the business as closely as profit.

Think about revenues first. Accounts receivable are created as sales are made, unless the sale is made for cash. Of course, that portion of sales made for cash represents **cash inflow.** In some businesses virtually all sales may be for cash whereas in other businesses virtually all sales may be on credit. The rules of recognizing revenue say that an entry for sales must be made whether the cash is collected or not because an **account receivable** is a valuable asset given in return for the product or service delivered. Except for a small portion of accounts receivable that will be lost in the form of bad debts, the accounts represent cash that will be collected in the future.

When the accounts are collected, they will represent **cash inflow.** This means that we can convert the revenues for a given period of time to cash inflow by adjusting for accounts receivable. The beginning and ending balances of accounts receivable is the key. If the beginning value of accounts receivable is larger than the amount of accounts receivable outstanding at the end of the period, then there must have been more cash inflows than there were sales. For example, assume that accounts receivable at the first of the month were $1,500; sales during the month were $4,000; and receivables at the end of the month were $1,000. There were no charge-offs of bad debts during the month. Total cash inflows for that month must have been the entire $4,000 in sales plus $500 of the receivables outstanding at the beginning of the month. Because there were no charge-offs of bad debts, the decline in the balance of receivables must mean that we collected more money than was charged. It doesn't matter whether the sales were all for cash or all on credit, the total amount of money collected had to be $4,500. If all of the sales were on credit, then the initial accounts receivable of $1,500 would have been increased by the $4,000 in charges, which would have been a total of $5,500 in receivables. The only way that the $5,500 of receivables could have been reduced to $1,000 at the end of the month would be if $4,500 worth of payments were received. Had there been any charge-offs, we would have removed them from consideration because they were not collected. Now, the rule is add any decrease in accounts receivable to sales to arrive at cash inflow. Reverse the direction of change of receivables and you will see that an increase in receivables during a period must be subtracted from sales to arrive at cash inflow.

Cost of goods sold represents an expense but not a **cash outflow,** or the cash flowing out of the business. Cash is involved in the purchase of inventory. If any inventory items are acquired on credit, then **accounts payable** will be involved, just as accounts receivable were involved in sales. Cost of goods also is affected by changes in inventory levels. If we buy more than we sell, then inventory will go up. This must mean that more cash was expended than the cost of goods would indicate. If we sell more than we buy, then inventory will go down. This means that we used less cash than the cost of sales would indicate because part of the expense is coming from inventory that had been bought in a previous period. All this means that we must adjust cost of sales for both accounts payable and inventory changes. To convert cost of goods sold to cash outflow, we must add any decreases in accounts payable and add any increase in inventory during the period. Increases in accounts payable or decreases in inventory are subtracted.

The remaining expenses are converted to cash outflow by examining any accrued items that relate to the expense. For example, insurance expense is converted to cash outlay by examining the prepaid insurance account. Prepaid insurance is an asset. If the prepaid account has increased, then the amount of that increase must be added to insurance expense to arrive at cash outflow. A decrease must be subtracted. If there is an accrued liability, then it will behave opposite to assets. For example, if there is an accrued wages account, then any increase in that account must be subtracted from wage expense to arrive at cash outflow. A decrease is added. Liabilities behave in an opposite direction from assets because they are opposite in nature. If an asset increases, it means that cash has been expended to invest in the asset. If a liability increases, it means that cash has not yet been expended.

As you can see, the process of item-by-item inspection can become tedious. The solution is to begin with income and convert it directly into cash flow. We will focus on operating income first. **Operating income** is the profit that results from the day-to-day operations of the business. Any unusual items, money made or lost on sales of plant assets, or money from investments should not be included. Include only those revenues and expenses related directly to the operation of the business in the calculation of operating income. In this way, we will arrive at a number that represents the earnings power of the firm. The important thing about **earnings power** is that it represents performance that can be expected to continue in the future.

To find operating income we subtract from sales the cost of sales, selling expenses, and general and administrative expenses. Any items of "other revenues" or "other expenses" are ignored. Remember that interest expense is not an operating expense either. **Interest expense** results from debts the management has decided to undertake, and therefore, they are not a function of operations. Consequently, the operating income will be before taxes and interest expense, sometimes referred to as **EBIT** (earnings before interest and taxes). After operating income has been determined, we will convert it to operating cash flow by adjusting for the timing differences talked about earlier and adjusting for any items of expense that do not consume cash, principally depreciation expense. We already have discussed how depreciation expense reduces profit but does not affect cash. Amortization is another such expense. In reality, it is a type of depreciation. We generally term the depreciation of such assets as leasehold improvements and other intangibles, **amortization.** An **intangible** is an asset that is not a visible part of the business. For example, leasehold improvements really belong to the landlord, not to the business. Exhibit 5-3 displays the adjustments.

**EXHIBIT 5-3** *Operating Cash Flow*

I. Find operating income
   A. Operating Revenues
   B. Less cost of sales
   C. Less selling expenses
   D. Less general and administrative expenses

II. Adjust operating income for noncash expenses
   A. Add depreciation expenses
   B. Add amortization expenses

III. Adjust operating income for changes in current liabilities
   A. Add increases in accounts payable
   B. Add increases in any accrued liabilities
   C. Subtract decreases in accounts payable
   D. Subtract decreases in any accrued liabilities

IV. Adjust operating income for changes in current assets
   A. Add decreases in accounts receivable
   B. Add decreases in inventory
   C. Add decreases in prepaid expense items
   D. Subtract increases in accounts receivable
   E. Subtract increases in inventory
   F. Subtract increases in prepaid expense items

V. The result is operating cash flow

**Operating cash flow** may well be the most important number in a business. It reveals how much cash is generated by the ongoing activities of the business. This is the cash that must be used to pay bills, purchase assets, make loan payments, and so forth. The process of generating operating cash flow appears involved, but it actually is simplistic. Most people find that this is an excellent application of a computerized spreadsheet program. At any rate, operating cash flow should be calculated every time profit is calculated, which means at least monthly!

The changes in the items that affect operating cash flow from month to month frequently are minor. Accounts receivable and payable, inventory, prepaids, and accruals frequently change only a small amount. Consequently, many firms use a shortcut to approximate the operating cash flow. This method is to simply add depreciation back to operating income. That is what really was done in Exhibits 5-1 and 5-2 to arrive at the number called *cash flow*. This shortcut is acceptable if the amount of error is small. If there are large changes in any of the other components, then the longer version should be used.

One of the best uses of operating cash flow is a comparison to loan payments. Only the interest portion of loan payments shows on the income statement as an expense, but both the principal and interest portions of the payment consume cash. Examination of the operating cash flow demonstrates how easily, or with how much difficulty, a firm can meet its loan payments. The financial statement in Exhibit 5-1 made that comparison. While the **operating income** is an indication of future earnings power, the **operating cash flow** is an indication of the future cash generation capabilities of the firm.

## Net Cash Flow from Operations

Just as net profit is different from operating profit, net cash flow from operations is different from operating cash flow. To find this number we must adjust the net profit for any items that do not affect cash. Exhibit 5-4 displays the process.

As you can see, the process is very similar. The difference is that we do not restrict adjustments to items associated with ongoing operations. The **net cash flow from operations** is a valuable indication of the liquidity of a firm. **Liquidity** is the ease with which a firm can meet its obligations. This number is a historic one and will not be as representative of the future as the operating cash flow was, but it is a better indication of the performance of the firm during the time period under review.

**EXHIBIT 5-4** *Net Cash Flow from Operations*

I. Find net profit
   A. Total revenues
   B. Less total expenses
   C. Less income taxes
   D. Less unusual and nonrecurring items

II. Adjust net profit for Noncash Expenses
   A. Add depreciation expenses
   B. Add amortization expenses
   C. Add any other expenses that did not consume cash, such as loss on sale of noncurrent assets
   D. Subtract any revenues that did not generate cash, such as gain on sale of fixed assets

III. Adjust net profit for changes in current liabilities
   A. Add increases in any current liabilities
   B. Subtract decreases in any current liabilities

IV. Adjust net profit for changes in current assets
   A. Add decreases in any current asset except cash
   B. Subtract increases in any current asset except cash

V. The result is net cash flow from operations

## Net Cash Flow

You may have noticed that the process of generating net cash flow from operations is the same as would be followed in preparing a statement of changes in financial position on the cash basis. The process is identical and the conversion of the net cash flow from operations into net cash flow is simply the process of completing the statement of changes. Exhibit 5-5 displays that process.

**Net cash flow** always should equal the difference in the cash balance at the beginning and end of the period. If it does not, an error has been made in calculation. Of course, if there should be a net loss instead of a net profit, then the very first number in the exhibit will be negative and must be subtracted to arrive at total sources of cash.

The net cash flow calculations show where every dollar that flowed into a firm over a given time period came from, what every dollar that flowed out was used for, and the effect on cash of these flows. This can be a powerful tool in evaluating the effectiveness of the management of cash. It also demonstrates

**EXHIBIT 5-5** *Net Cash Flow*

I. Find net cash flow from operations

II. Find other sources of cash
  A. Any increase in a noncurrent liability
  B. Any increase in investments by owners
  C. Any decrease in a noncurrent asset

III. Add these to arrive at total sources of cash

IV. Find applications of cash
  A. Any decrease in a noncurrent liability
  B. Any decrease in investments by owners
    Withdrawals
    Dividends
  C. Any increase in a noncurrent asset

V. Add these to arrive at total applications of cash

VI. The difference is net cash flow

the role played by capital investment and debt in financing the firm's activities during the period. Finally, the schedule shows the acquisition, disposition, and financing sources for productive assets. Lenders are particularly interested in such information because it can indicate the ability of the firm to repay credit. Net cash flow is a historic representation and as such is not a good tool for judging future cash flow potential. Nevertheless, it is a good report card for management. Lenders are fond of saying that managers are like leopards and seldom change their spots. This means that a good manager probably will remain a good manager in the future, whereas a poor manager probably will remain a poor manager. The net cash flow schedule is one device for determining the category in which a manager should be placed. By monitoring the cash flows month to month, an owner can make adjustments that will result in being considered a good manager. If you wait until the year is ended before calculating the flows, it will be too late to change anything.

The effective management of cash is one of the most important management functions, because cash flow is the life blood of any business. In a later chapter we will discuss forecasting cash flows and talk about how it can be managed in a more **proactive** manner. This means making adjustments before something happens rather than after it happens. The continual monitoring of all three types of cash flow discussed is the best approach to self-evaluation. You will find that cash flows frequently are quite different from profits at any level. The continual monitoring of cash flow will prevent profits from obscuring the cash resources so important to your firm's survival.

## SUMMARY

*Financial accounting* refers to the activities that result in the generation of the financial statement. Accounting principles dictate how these statements should be prepared and are sufficiently general that different companies may be compared along appropriate lines.

Managerial accounting uses the record-keeping tools developed in financial accounting to generate reports for use internally in decision making: for example, delinquency reports, projected payment reports, and inventory turnover and status reports.

Two such reports of real value to a small business are contribution margin reports and cash flow reports. One of the best applications of the contribution margin is in the form of income and expense statements, reflecting margins and prepared by product, department, division, or other segment. This contribution margin statement demonstrates the relative role the segment plays in the company. The contribution margin report can help monitor progress toward objectives, aid in planning, and be used for comparing product and development as well as break-even analysis and target sales analysis.

A scarce resource is anything that limits a firm's ability to generate sales and profits. It frequently is money for a new small business, but it just as easily can be the time of expert employees, machine time, or any other factor. A firm cannot expand its sales and profits without increasing the amount of the scarce resource that it possesses.

Cash flow reports demonstrate the amount of cash available to the company to pay bills or purchase items. Involved in cash flow statements are operating cash flows and net cash flows.

The effective management of cash is one of the most important management functions because cash flow is the life blood of any small business. The continual monitoring of cash flow will prevent profits from obscuring the cash resources so important to the firm's survival.

## QUESTIONS

1. What is the difference between financial accounting and managerial accounting?
2. What is one of the best applications for the contribution margin?
3. How are the income and expense statements in Exhibits 5-1 and 5-2 different and why?

4. Why is cash flow more important to the survival of a company than profit?
5. How does one find operating cash flow and net cash flow?
6. What is a scarce resource, and what is its significance to management?

## PROJECT

Refer to the financial statement located in the appendix for Chapter 4. Calculate the net cash flow for that company and write an evaluation of what you find. The evaluation should include suggestions for improving any problems you found and describe points of interest if you found no problems.

# Case

Jason Trevor, a potter, was a true artisan. He had shown his work all over the country and gained acclaim for his unique designs. He had taken up the art of pottery from his grandfather, watching the old man lovingly create works of art with his hands. His grandfather could make the most simple, utilitarian object a masterpiece in Jason's eyes. The old potter taught his craft to his grandson, mostly because he loved having the boy around, not to preserve his skill for posterity.

Jason went to art school and studied other techniques, but he still preferred to use the one learned at his grandfather's wheel. After college and much recognition of his talent, Jason decided to go into business with his pottery. His work seemed to be in great demand, and he had been offered some sizeable dollar figures for his pots — or so he thought. What could be simpler? He had a wheel, a storage area, and his own talent. He was willing to work hard, and the business would indeed be a success.

A year into his business, frustration took its toll on Jason. He seemed to have hundreds of orders, more than he could possibly fill in the time allotted. Yet, he had just received notice from the bank that his account was overdrawn by his last order from his supplier, and he was exhausted. What was he going to do?

## Questions

1. What was the scarce resource that bounded the firm's ability to generate income?
2. What kinds of managerial reports would have been valuable in controlling the firm? When could they have been generated and how?
3. What problems can you foresee for Jason's company and why? What can he do about them?

# CHAPTER 6

# Break-Even Analysis

**LEARNING OBJECTIVES**

After completing this chapter, you should be able to

- Understand the principles of cost-volume-profit analysis.
- Perform break-even analysis for a new venture.
- Perform target sales analysis.
- Examine the relationship among cost, volume, and profit.

The financial planning required in starting up a new venture includes an assessment of the feasibility of the business, a major factor of which is the prospect for financial success. **Break-even analysis,** which is a cost-volume-profit (CVP) tool, permits the examination of financial feasibility. This concept is applicable to many more situations than a business start up. CVP analysis can aid in assessing the relative importance of various aspects of a business to its profitability. These aspects range from a product or market area to a plant, division, or department. CVP is one of the most versatile and useful tools available to a business owner. In this chapter, we will examine CVP assessment with particular emphasis on break-even analysis.

## WHAT IS BREAK-EVEN ANALYSIS?

No business should ever be started without a break-even analysis. It really is impossible to determine the viability of a new venture without assessing how much business will be required for the venture to survive and what is the probability of obtaining that level of business. Three steps are involved in break-even analysis: estimating the fixed costs that will occur; estimating the variable costs as a percentage of sales; calculating the break-even point.

### Fixed Costs

A **fixed cost** is not expected to fluctuate with changes in sales volume over a relevant range of activity. Consider, for example, the salary for a line supervisor, which would be a fixed expense because it will not vary as sales vary. Now, the aggregate of salaries for all line supervisors also will be a fixed cost, but only so long as sales do not drop below the point at which one of the shifts would be shut down to save money or rise above the point at which another shift would have to be added to produce the volume necessary. All fixed costs are like this. If we think about fixed costs in the form of a graph in which the costs are related to the volume of output, it would look like Exhibit 6-1. The graph shows a step function, so called because of its appearance, and demonstrates that fixed costs cannot be added or subtracted in small pieces, but only in chunks. We cannot hire one-quarter of a supervisor or buy one-half of a machine.

The range of expected sales activity usually is not a large change from the established sales level. That is, we do not normally face a situation in which we expect to lose a large percentage of sales, nor one in which we expect our sales to double or triple. Therefore, the expected activity frequently falls on a single stair step of the fixed cost function and the rest of the graph can be ignored. This expected level of activity is called the **relevant range.** Exhibit 6-2 shows

**EXHIBIT 6-1** *Fixed Costs*

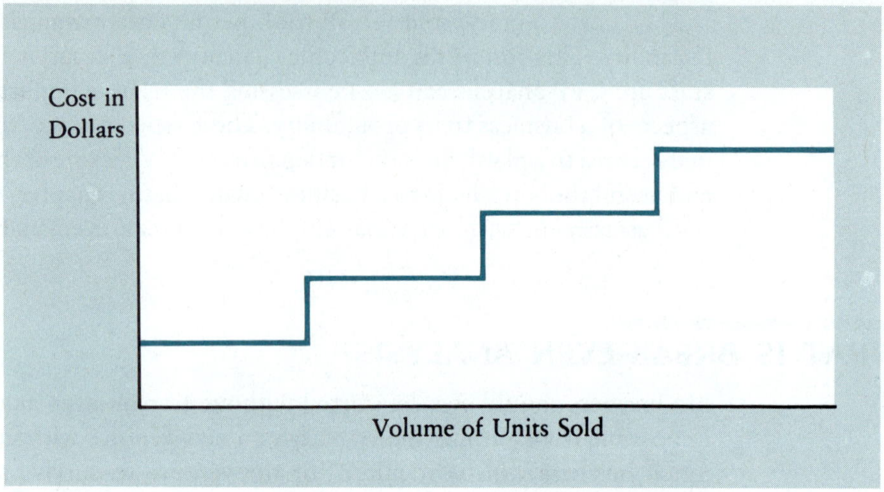


**EXHIBIT 6-2** *Relevant Range of Fixed Costs*

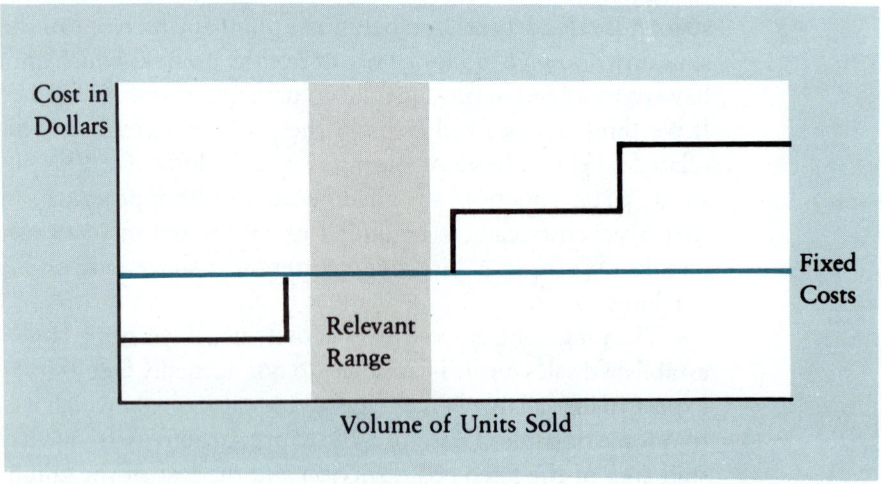

how the relevant range can be used to make fixed costs look like a straight line. This is done for simplicity; but remember, if the assumption of activity within the range is invalid or if the relevant range of activity falls across a step in the fixed cost function, then much of the break-even analysis must be changed to reflect the real expectations.

The fixed costs of a business could include salaries for officers, office workers, and others paid on a straight salary basis; rent or mortgage payments on buildings or equipment, unless the lease is tied to sales volume; depreciation expense on buildings and equipment, unless it is tied to units of production; supplies and materials used to support office, sales, and production efforts; utilities, unless much of utility consumption in the business is based on volume of production; insurance premiums; property taxes; and fringe benefits. Note that a lot of expenses can be fixed but are not automatically so for every business. To determine fixed costs, an owner must examine every possible cost and consider whether it will vary as sales do. Imagining every cost before a business actually begins can be difficult. Most people add a hedge factor, because they would rather overestimate fixed costs than underestimate them for break-even purposes. Probably the best approach is to generate a range of fixed cost forecasts for use in the analysis.

## Variable Costs

**Variable costs** are tied directly to sales levels. For a retailer or wholesaler, these can be easy to identify because they will be costs of the inventory, freight expenses for the inventory, sales commissions, and the like. For a service firm, there may be very little in the way of variable costs if the people providing the services are paid on a salary basis. If they are paid hourly, or by the job, then most of the expenses may be variable. For a manufacturing firm, the variable costs may be more difficult to identify. These costs generally will not be perfectly proportionate to sales because of **economies of scale** as volume increases. Remember that there will be price breaks for purchasing larger quantities of items. Exhibit 6-3 displays a graph of variable costs.

Note that, generally, the cost curve changes so gradually that, over the relevant range of activity, it is practically a straight line. This allows us to pretend that the line is straight, just as we did for fixed costs as a simplifying step. Exhibit 6-4 displays that assumption. As was the case for fixed costs, each expense a business experiences must be analyzed to identity the variable elements.

In many cases, a cost behaves as a variable cost, but the amount is so low that it is not worth the effort of tracing the cost to sales or keeping the records necessary to treat the cost as variable over time. An example of such a cost might be the cost of lubricants for the machines in a manufacturing company.

**EXHIBIT 6-3** *Variable Costs*

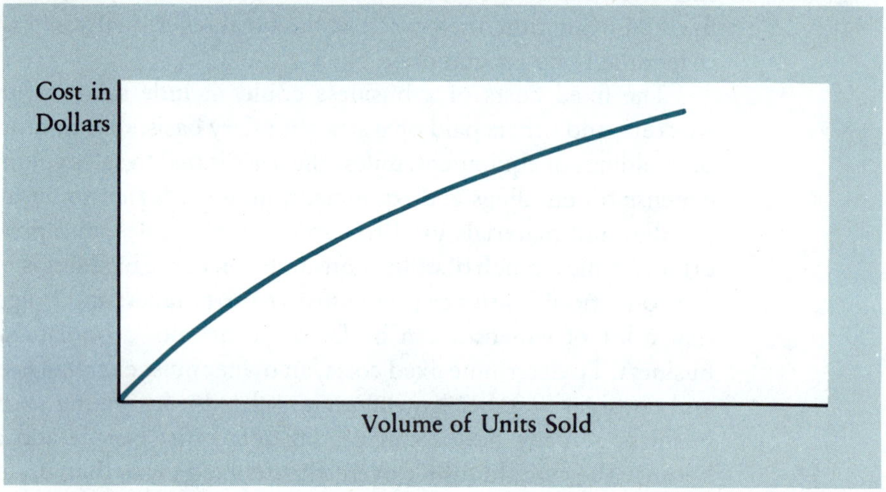


**EXHIBIT 6-4** *Relevant Range of Variable Costs*

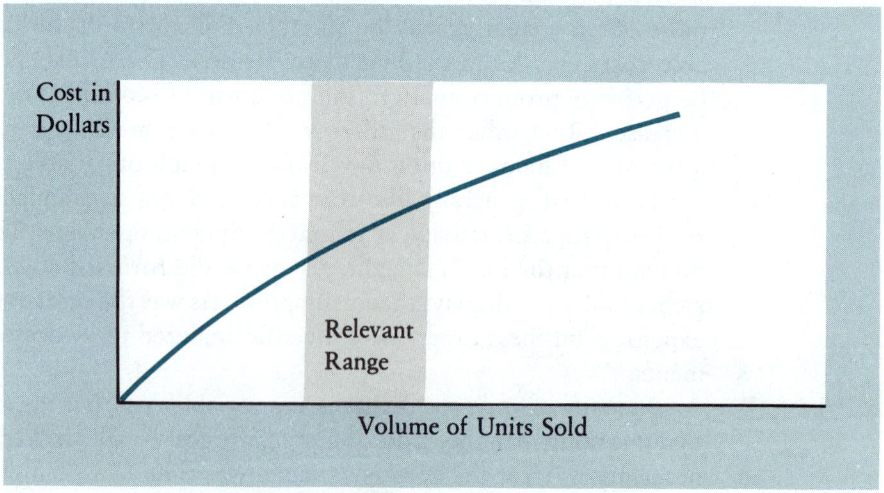

Clearly, such costs will be affected by the run time of the machines, which is a function of sales. Nevertheless, if the fluctuation in the cost is extremely low relative to other variable costs, then little value will accrue to its capture and treatment as a variable cost. In such cases, it is generally wiser to treat the cost as though it were fixed.

## Mixed Costs

Many costs really have elements of both a fixed and variable nature. These costs are called **mixed costs** and examples include rent when it consists of a minimum amount plus a percentage of sales, utilities when composed of a minimum fee and a usage charge, and other expenses of that nature. Mixed costs will be especially hard to allocate to either the fixed or variable cost pools when reviewing the cost categories of a business.

There are two ways to handle mixed costs. The first method requires the costs to be decomposed into a fixed portion and a variable portion. This method should be used when the mixed costs are significant compared to other costs in the business. The second method is to simply classify the cost as fixed or variable. This method should be used when the cost is insignificant compared to other costs. The choice of fixed or variable classification is purely arbitrary and will have little impact on the break-even amounts, if the costs are truly insignificant. Remember that the significance is not decided in terms of dollars, but in relation to other expenses. For example, the mixed cost of electricity could be quite high relative to other expenses in a manufacturing company that uses a great deal of electrical machinery and equipment. The same cost could be quite low relative to other expenses for a retailer whose only use of electricity is to provide lighting for the store. In the former case, decomposition of the expense would be wise; whereas in the latter case, treatment of the cost as a fixed expense would be appropriate.

## Revenues

**Revenues** are a function of sales volume, but like variable costs, the relationship is not perfect. Just as economies of scale result in lower variable costs as volume increases, lower unit prices accrue as volume goes up and purchasers receive volume discounts and economies of scale. This means that the true relationship when plotted on the cost-volume graph is a curve that is slightly concave in a downward direction. Exhibit 6-5 displays a graph for revenue.

Using the same reasoning as applied to variable costs, we can treat the revenue function as though it were a straight line, because it virtually is straight over the relevant range of activity. This simplifying assumption can permit the graphing of all three curves on a single chart.

**EXHIBIT 6-5** *Revenues*

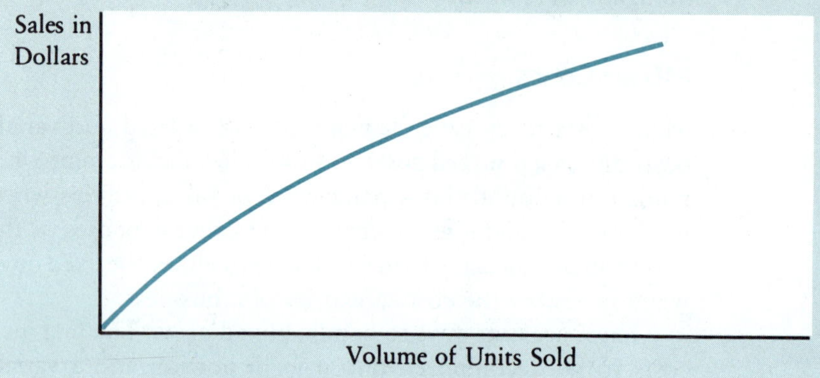


## Break-Even Chart

Exhibit 6-6 shows the three lines superimposed. Note that the variable cost line begins at the point at which the fixed cost line intersects the cost axis. This means that the total costs appear on one line and total revenue appears on another. The point of intersection between the two is the **break-even point** (BEP) for a company.

The area between the total revenue line and the total cost line is the amount of profit to the right of the break-even point and the amount of loss to the left of the break-even point. The slope of the two lines will dictate the amount of space between them. This, called **operating leverage,** displays how fast profits or losses will occur and how large the effect a change in volume will have on profits or losses.

In general, the larger the proportion of variable costs a firm has, the lower will be its operating leverage. The higher the proportion of fixed costs a firm has, the higher will be its operating leverage. A business with a high operating leverage will reap substantially greater benefit from an increase in volume than a firm with a low operating leverage. There is a down side to this relationship because high operating leverage also will create larger losses faster if volume decreases. The reverse situation holds for businesses with lower operating

**EXHIBIT 6-6** *Break-Even Chart*

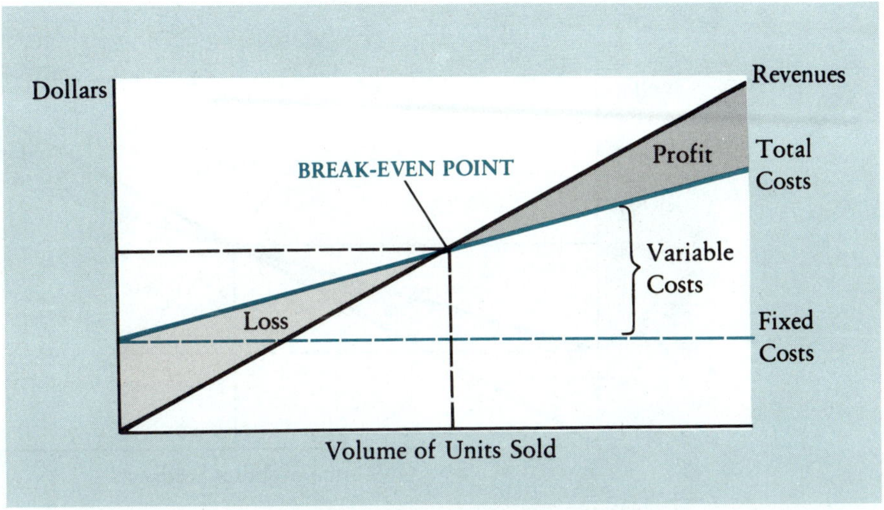


leverage. Exhibit 6-7 shows a comparison between the two cost structures. The two types of firms frequently are referred to as **capital intensive** and **labor intensive,** because labor tends to be a variable cost and capital a fixed cost.

A lower operating leverage carries less risk. Of course, risk and return usually are trade-offs; that is, higher risks are associated with higher returns whereas lower risks are associated with lower returns. This is the case with operating leverage. The higher leveraged firm has more risk because its fixed costs must be covered whether or not sales are made and it will incur greater losses if sales fall below the break-even point. However, after the break-even point has been reached, the higher leveraged firm will produce more profits, faster. Nevertheless, for a new business venture, lower risk and more flexibility are desirable. Consequently, most small businesses starting up should choose to structure themselves with a relatively low operating leverage. This is accomplished by committing to as small a level of fixed costs as possible, even though the resulting variable costs are higher as a result. After a business is firmly established, it can always increase its operating leverage.

Remember that the break-even chart contains simplifying assumptions about cost and revenue behavior over the relevant range of activity. If those assumptions are not valid or if the actual volume of the firm moves outside the predicted relevant range, then the chart is invalid.

**EXHIBIT 6-7** *Break-Even Charts for Two Cost Structures*

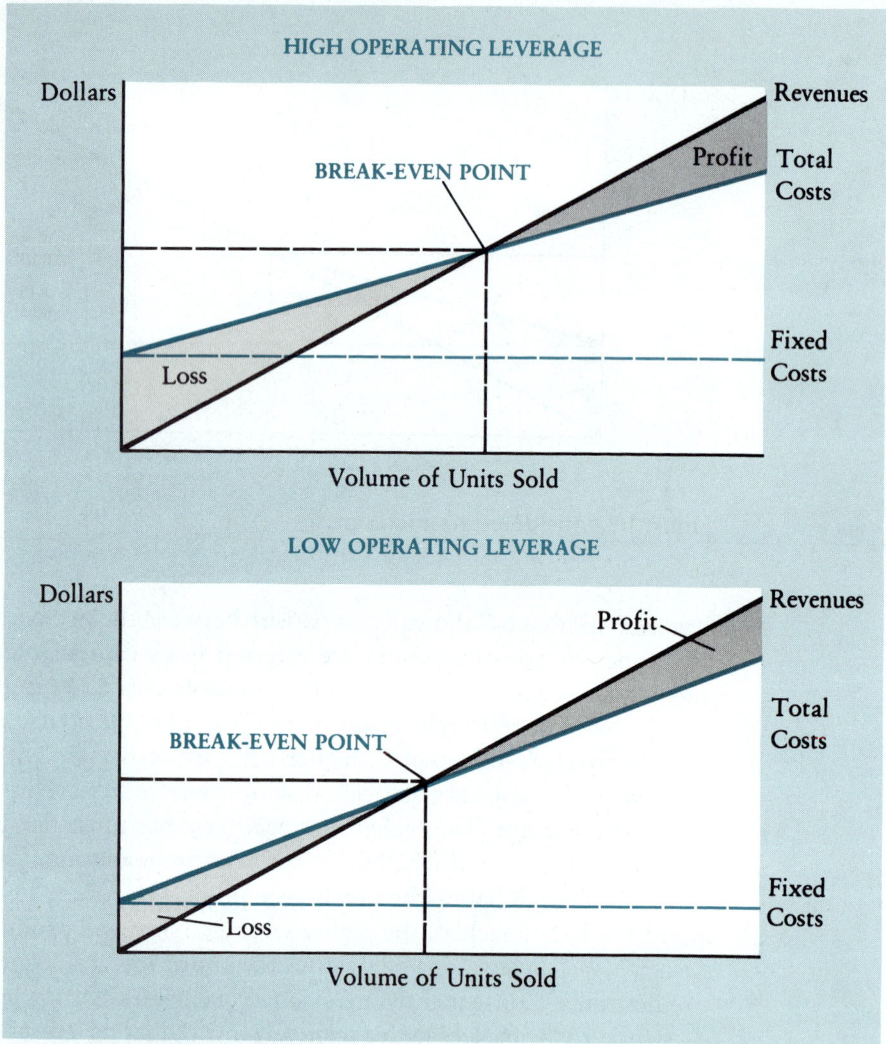


## Break-Even Formulas

The break-even point can be found mathematically as well as graphically. The calculations are straightforward and can be derived from the relationship of costs, revenues, and profits in a firm. Remember that *profit* is defined as the difference between revenues and expenses. Therefore, the break-even point, or the point at which profit is equal to 0, must be the point at which revenues equal expenses.

$$\text{Revenue} - \text{Variable expense} - \text{Fixed expense} = \text{Profit}$$

*Break-even point:*

$$\text{Revenue} - \text{Variable expense} - \text{Fixed expense} = 0$$

*or*

$$\text{Revenue} - \text{Variable expense} = \text{Fixed expense}$$

The left side of the equation is defined as the **contribution margin,** which is the amount of sales dollars left over to cover fixed expenses and provide profits after variable expenses are covered. The contribution margin is an extremely valuable concept because it makes break-even analysis, forecasting, and profit planning much easier. We discussed contribution margins in Chapter 5 in greater detail. Remember that gross margin, or the sales less cost of goods sold, is not necessarily the same thing. If a retailer or wholesaler has no other variable costs in the business, then gross margin and contribution margin will be the same. If there are variable expenses, like sales commissions, then these also must be considered to find contribution margin. In a service company there is no cost of goods sold, so contribution margins are much higher; in some service companies, they are 100%!

Look what happens if we convert the contribution margin equation to a contribution margin ratio by dividing both sides by revenues.

$$\text{Contribution margin} = \text{Revenue} - \text{Variable expense}$$

$$\frac{\text{Contribution margin}}{\text{Revenue}} = \frac{(\text{Revenue} - \text{Variable expense})}{\text{Revenue}}$$

$$\text{Contribution margin ratio} = \frac{(\text{Revenue} - \text{Variable expense})}{\text{Revenue}}$$

This means that revenues multiplied by the contribution margin ratio will always equal the contribution margin or the difference between revenues and variable expenses. Keeping this in mind, we can substitute contribution margin in the break-even equation and solve for the break-even revenues.

$$\text{Revenue} - \text{Variable} = \text{Fixed expense}$$

$$\text{Contribution margin} = \text{Revenue} - \text{Variable expense}$$

$$\text{Contribution margin} = \text{Fixed expense}$$

$$\begin{matrix}\text{Break-even} \\ \text{revenues}\end{matrix} \times \begin{matrix}\text{Contribution} \\ \text{margin ratio}\end{matrix} = \text{Fixed expense}$$

$$\text{Break-even revenues} = \frac{\text{Fixed expense}}{\text{Contribution margin ratio}}$$

This can be written as

$$BEP_{\$} = \frac{\text{Fixed costs}}{\text{CMR}}$$

*where:*

$BEP_{\$}$ = Break-even point in sales or revenues
CMR = Contribution margin ratio

Usually, expressing the break-even point in terms of sales or revenues is preferred, because most firms have a mix of products. However, a break-even point in terms of units sometimes is desired. A firm may deal in a single product or a calculation may be needed for one division or department that deals in one product. The break-even point can be converted to units by dividing by the price per unit or by direct calculation with a slightly different formula. Remember that the contribution margin is equal to fixed costs at the break-even point. If we convert to the contribution margin per unit, then the equation looks like this:

$$\text{Contribution margin} = \text{Fixed cost}$$

$$\text{Sales in Units} \times \text{Contribution Margin per Unit} = \text{Fixed Cost}$$

$$\text{Break-Even Sales in Units} = \frac{\text{Fixed Cost}}{\text{Contribution Margin per Unit}}$$

This can be written as

$$BEP_{\#} = \frac{\text{Fixed costs}}{\text{CM}}$$

*where:*

$BEP_{\#}$ = Break-even point in units of sales
CM = Contribution margin per unit

Actually, either break-even point can be converted into the other. Break-even sales can be found by multiplying break-even units by the selling price per unit, or break-even units can be found by dividing break-even sales by the selling price per unit.

## TARGET SALES

Frequently in cost-volume-profit analysis, we are not interested in the point at which an operation will break even. Rather, we are interested in the volume required to produce a particular profit. If we remember that the break-even points are simply the points at which profits equal 0, then the formulas can be generalized to include such profits. Remember the equations with which we started:

$$\text{Profit} = \text{Revenue} - \text{Variable expense} - \text{Fixed expense}$$

*Break-even point:*

$$\text{Revenue} - \text{Variable expense} - \text{Fixed expense} = 0$$

*or*

$$\text{Revenue} - \text{Variable expense} = \text{Fixed expense}$$

If profit is not assumed to be 0,

$$\text{Profit} = \text{Revenue} - \text{Variable expense} - \text{Fixed expense}$$

$$\text{Revenue} - \text{Variable expense} = \text{Fixed expense} + \text{Profit}$$

Break-even occurs where profit equals 0; consequently, the break-even formulas can be written as follows:

$$BEP_{\$} = \frac{\text{Fixed cost } + 0}{\text{CMR}} \qquad BEP_{\#} = \frac{\text{Fixed cost} + 0}{\text{CM}}$$

We can rewrite those formulas for target sales required to produce a target income like this:

$$TS_{\$} = \frac{\text{Fixed cost} + \text{TI}}{\text{CMR}} \qquad TS_{\#} = \frac{\text{Fixed cost} + \text{TI}}{\text{CM}}$$

*where:*

$TS_{\$}$ = Target sales in dollars
$TS_{\#}$ = Target sales in units
TI = Target income or profit desired
CMR = Contribution margin ratio
CM = Contribution margin per unit

The formulas for target sales are exactly like the ones for break-even points. There is no need to memorize two sets, because the break-even calculations are a special case of the target equations in which the desired profit is 0. The advantage of the more general formulas is that they can be used to find a break-even point or determine the amount of sales required to achieve any level of profit desired.

## COST-VOLUME-PROFIT FLEXIBILITY

Before we talk about applications of the formulas, we need to talk about their flexibility. The equations we have derived for break-even and target sales actually are functions of the relationships among cost, volume, and profit. These relationships can be for an entire small business, for a division of a business, for a department of a business, for a product of a business, or for a territory. All that is required is the capture or estimation of revenues and costs for the entity, area, or division under analysis. The CVP relationships can be based on forecasts for planning or calculated using historic results to analyze and evaluate performance. The difference is simply in whether the numbers used are actual or forecasted. The relationships can be calculated for any time period by simply ensuring that the numbers fit into the appropriate time horizon. In short, cost-volume-profit analysis, of which break-even analysis is a special case, is a powerful planning and management model available to any business regardless of its size.

## Assumptions of the Model

We already discussed the fact that break-even or CVP analysis assumes that revenue and cost curves are linear; that is, that the curves are straight lines. The amount of error that results from this assumption generally is small so long as the curves approximate a linear function over the relevant range of activity and activity remains within that range. The formulas will yield answers even if these assumptions are violated. This is the problem! Unless the numbers and forecasts are examined carefully, an owner may never realize that the results of analysis are invalid!

Other assumptions are incorporated into the CVP models, foremost among them is the assumption that the product mix will be constant. **Product mix** refers to the proportions of sales represented by the various products or services a business offers. Because few companies offer only a single product or service, product mix assumptions are a major limiting factor on CVP analysis. Specifically, the models assume that if three products make up the sales, then the percentage of the total sales volume that each product constitutes will remain constant over time and over changes in aggregate sales. This assumption almost always will be invalid. Nevertheless, as long as there are no major shifts in product mix over the period under analysis, the results of CVP analysis will be valuable, as the amount of error will not be major.

Additional assumptions of the model are that sales prices per unit will be constant over time and over changes in volume, as will variable costs per unit. This seldom, if ever, is true for any business. Also, the models assume completeness; that is, the analysis assumes that all costs and all revenues have been captured and measured accurately or, if forecasts are used, that the forecasts are accurate and complete. From a practical perspective, this assumption also frequently is invalid.

## Use of the Model

The solution to problems with erroneous assumptions is twofold. First, multiple calculations should be made using a variety of bases and estimates for the revenues and costs. The range of answers that results will not only indicate the area into which actual performance is likely to fall, but show the sensitivity of the model.

Understanding sensitivity is particularly important. If a large change in the

CVP answer occurs when a small change is made in one of the inputs, then the model is particularly sensitive to that item. Determining which numbers have the greatest impact on the results is called **sensitivity analysis.** Owners of small businesses must be especially careful of errors in items or estimates to which the model is sensitive.

The second approach to minimizing problems with erroneous assumptions is so simple that it frequently is overlooked—simply be aware of the limitations of the model. One should never say, "My break-even is . . ." but, rather, "My break-even appears to lie between . . . and . . ." By continually keeping the limitations of CVP models in mind, owners are less likely to make mistakes in using the results of the models. Actually, this is a good idea regardless of the tool being used. There are very few "facts" in business. Almost everything involves estimates of one type or another. For this reason, a business cannot be run quantitatively. The way small businesses operate, little can be expected to be perfectly accurate or perfectly representative. Consequently, a healthy dose of doubt can make the numbers from quantitative tools less likely to be followed blindly.

## CVP ANALYSIS FOR THE NEW VENTURE

One of the pre-venture planning steps is to forecast expenses. To perform break-even analysis for the start up, those expenses must not only be identified and forecasted, but classified as fixed or variable. Any mixed expenses must be disposed of, and selling prices must be developed. Once this is done, break-even analysis and the more general CVP analysis can be performed for the new venture.

Variable expenses can be predicted either on a per unit basis or in the aggregate based on total expected sales. Both approaches permit the calculation of the contribution margin ratio. Fixed expenses always must be predicted in the aggregate because they can never occur on a per unit basis. Aggregate sales can be predicted or average unit selling prices, whichever is preferred. If unit selling prices and unit variable costs are used, then we must be careful of sales mix problems. When more than one product or service is involved, we must calculate an average unit contribution margin that takes into consideration the sales mix. We also can use an industry average contribution margin if data is not available. This can be especially valuable when planning a start up. We will have a great deal to say about industry averages and their sources in Chapter 8.

The following cases are four different examples of break-even analysis. In the first example, a manufacturing firm handles a single product. The second example illustrates a retailer, who uses the industry average gross profit margin as a proxy for the contribution margin. In the third example, a manufacturer produces three products under an established sales mix. The fourth example shows a service company. For each situation, the steps in break-even analysis are outlined.

## Break-Even Analysis, Example 1

The starting up of a small manufacturing firm that will produce a single product is considered here. Engineering specifications have been prepared for the production of the product. The requirements for operation have been determined, and feasibility is being investigated. Planning and budgeting efforts have resulted in estimates for the various costs of operation and production. Those costs for the first year are as follows.

| | | |
|---|---|---|
| Fixed costs | | $125,000 |
| Variable costs per unit: | | |
| Direct labor | $ 4.95 | |
| Raw material | 2.35 | |
| Variable overhead | 2.20 | |
| Total variable costs | $ 9.50 | |
| Selling price per unit | $12.50 | |
| Contribution margin: | | |
| Selling price | | $12.50 |
| Variable costs | | −9.50 |
| Contribution margin | | $ 3.00 |

Contribution margin ratio: $3.00/$12.50 = .24 or 24%

Break-even points:

$$BEP_{\$} = \frac{FC}{CMR} \qquad BEP_{\#} = \frac{FC}{CM}$$

$$BEP_{\$} = \frac{\$125{,}000}{.24} \qquad BEP_{\#} = \frac{\$125{,}000}{\$3.00}$$

$$BEP_{\$} = \$520{,}833 \qquad BEP_{\#} = 41{,}667 \text{ Units}$$

Target sales for $25,000 profit:

$$TS_{\$} = \frac{(FC + Profit)}{CMR} \qquad TS_{\#} = \frac{(FC + Profit)}{CM}$$

$$TS_{\$} = \frac{(\$125{,}000 + \$25{,}000)}{.24} \qquad TS_{\#} = \frac{(\$125{,}000 + \$25{,}000)}{\$3.00}$$

$$TS_{\$} = \$625{,}000 \qquad TS_{\#} = 50{,}000 \text{ Units}$$

### Break-Even Analysis, Example 2

A retailer is starting up a small hardware store. A small retailer of this type has insignificant variable costs outside the cost of sales because there are no sales commissions. That means that the gross profit margin is virtually the same as the contribution margin. Further, because the hardware industry is well established, pricing and inventory costs can be expected to be outside the control of management. This means that gross profits should be virtually the same for most small hardware stores. Consequently, the industry average gross profit margin ratio will be used as a proxy for the contribution margin ratio in break-even analysis. This industry average was obtained from *Robert Morris Associates Statement Studies,* which is only one of the many references available in most libraries that contain averages for various financial ratios for small businesses. Planning and budgeting have resulted in the following estimates for the first year.

| | |
|---|---|
| Fixed costs | \$72,000 |
| Industry average gross profit margin | 35% |

Break-even point:

$$BEP_{\$} = \frac{FC}{CMR}$$

$$BEP_{\$} = \frac{\$72{,}000}{.35}$$

$$BEP_{\$} = \$205{,}714$$

Target sales for \$20,000 profits:

$$TS_{\$} = \frac{(FC + Profit)}{CMR}$$

$$TS_{\$} = \frac{(\$72{,}000 + \$20{,}000)}{.35}$$

$$TS_{\$} = \$262{,}857$$

### Break-Even Analysis, Example 3

A small manufacturing firm is starting up that will produce three different products. Engineering specifications have been prepared for the production of each product and the operating requirements have been determined. Planning and budgeting have resulted in estimates of the various costs of operation and production. Those costs for the first year are as follows.

| | | | |
|---|---|---|---|
| Fixed costs | | | $250,000 |
| Variable costs: | *Product 1* | *Product 2* | *Product 3* |
| Direct labor | $5.25 | $4.00 | $4.75 |
| Raw material | 2.46 | 2.03 | 2.19 |
| Variable overhead | 2.00 | 1.75 | 1.90 |
| Total variable costs: | $9.71 | $7.78 | $8.84 |
| Selling price per unit | $14.50 | $12.75 | $13.00 |
| Contribution margin | $14.50 | $12.75 | $13.00 |
| | −9.71 | −7.78 | −8.84 |
| | $ 4.79 | $ 4.97 | $ 4.16 |
| Percentage of sales | 40% | 30% | 30% |
| Contribution margin ratios: | $\frac{4.79}{14.50}$ | $\frac{4.97}{12.75}$ | $\frac{4.16}{13.00}$ |
| | 33% | 39% | 32% |

Weighted average contribution margin

$(.33 \times .40) + (.39 \times .30) + (.32 \times .30) = .345 = 34.5\%$

Break-even point:

$$BEP_{\$} = \frac{FC}{CMR}$$

$$BEP_{\$} = \frac{\$250{,}000}{.345}$$

$$BEP_{\$} = \$724{,}638$$

Target sales for $30,000 profit:

$$TS_{\$} = \frac{(FC + Profit)}{CMR}$$

$$TS_{\$} = \frac{(\$250{,}000 + \$30{,}000)}{.345}$$

$$TS_{\$} = \$811{,}594$$

## Break-Even Analysis, Example 4

A real estate broker is proposing to start up a small company. The firm will earn commissions of 6% of selling prices, but those constitute gross sales for the business. The firm's agents will receive one-half of the sales commission and there are no other significant variable costs, consequently the contribution margin ratio will be 50%. The broker forecasts rent, utilities, advertising, and clerical salaries totalling $57,000, and wants to be able to take a $30,000 draw out of the business.

Break-even point:

$$BEP_{\$} = \frac{FC}{CMR}$$

$$BEP_{\$} = \frac{\$57{,}000}{.50}$$

$$BEP_{\$} = \$114{,}000$$

Target sales for $30,000 draw:

$$TS_{\$} = \frac{(FC + Profit)}{CMR}$$

$$TS_{\$} = \frac{(\$57{,}000 + \$30{,}000)}{.50}$$

$$TS_{\$} = \$174{,}000$$

Property sales required at 6% commissions:

$$\text{Break-even point } \frac{\$114{,}000}{.06} = \$1{,}900{,}000$$

$$\text{Target sales point } \frac{\$174{,}000}{.06} = \$2{,}900{,}000$$

CVP analysis for a new venture involves the calculation of the range of break-even points deemed possible as a result of the planning, determining whether the target market area will support the required level of sales, and deciding whether the firm will be able to garner the required sales. The last decision frequently is subjective, but the proportion of the market that must be captured certainly will influence any lenders who may be approached. The best situation is one in which only a very small percentage of the potential market is required to break even. If a substantial proportion is needed, the risk is higher because it will be more difficult to wrest away the business from entrenched competition.

One question that frequently comes up during break-even analysis is how to determine the size of the market for a brand new product or service. Actually, this happens very infrequently because most products and services will have near substitutes if not direct competitors, and the market for the substitutes can be used as a proxy. In the rare situation where the offering is completely new and without substitutes, the evaluation becomes completely subjective. Nevertheless, the higher the break-even point, the more difficult it will be to convince a lender or investor that the venture is viable. This will be true in every situation. The lower the break-even point, the less risk is involved in the venture.

## CVP ANALYSIS AS AN ONGOING PLANNING AID

CVP analysis is useful not just for assessing the viability of a new business venture but can be an aspect of planning in an ongoing operation. It can be used to evaluate ideas and plans for new market areas, products, departments, divisions, plants, or services. It can be used in budgeting because target sales can be generated from desired profit levels and fixed costs can be anticipated. Further, it plays a role in pricing decisions, in monitoring and evaluating performance, and in supporting credit requests or investment proposals. Finally, it can be used to identify the effects of price and cost change on a firm's profitability. Consider the following examples.

### CVP Analysis, Example 1

A firm is setting prices in a market in which the sales volume in units can be predicted with a high level of confidence. Planning and budgeting efforts have produced estimates for the various costs of operation and prices for the product. Fixed costs are $175,000 and variable costs per unit are $125. The firm believes that 5,000 units of the product can be sold if the price does not exceed the level established by its competitors, which is $250. The firm desires a profit of $200,000. What should be its selling price?

$$TS_{\#} = \frac{(FC + TI)}{CM}$$

$$CM = SP - VC$$

$$TS_{\#} = \frac{(FC + TI)}{(SP - VC)}$$

Substituting the estimated factors:

$$5{,}000 = \frac{(\$175{,}000 + \$200{,}000)}{(SP - \$125)}$$

$$5{,}000 = \frac{\$375{,}000}{(SP - \$125)}$$

$$5{,}000(SP - \$125) = \$375{,}000$$

$$SP - \$125 = \frac{\$375{,}000}{5{,}000}$$

$$SP - \$125 = \$75$$

$$SP = \$75 + \$125$$

$$SP = \$200$$

CVP analysis indicates that the firm can undercut the established price substantially and still achieve its profit goal. Before finalizing a price, a range of values for the selling price should be calculated using the best, worst, and most probable estimates for fixed and variable costs.

### CVP Analysis, Example 2

A firm with established fixed and variable costs expects an increase in both over the next year. The firm is considering a price increase to offset those increases. The established costs and selling prices are as follows:

| | |
|---|---|
| Fixed costs | \$225,000 |
| Variable costs per unit | \$215 |
| Selling price per unit | \$330 |
| Established sales volume | 3,000 units |

Fixed costs are expected to rise by \$5,500 and variable costs are expected to increase by \$5 per unit. What price increase will be required in order to maintain the established profit level?

Established contribution margin:

Contribution margin per unit $\$330 - \$215 = \$115$

Total contribution margin $3{,}000(\$115) = \$345{,}000$

Established profit $\$345{,}000 - \$225{,}000 = \$120{,}000$

New fixed costs $\$225{,}000 + \$5{,}500 = \$230{,}500$

New variable costs $\$215 + \$5 = \$220$

$$TS_{\#} = \frac{(FC + TI)}{(SP - VC)}$$

$$3{,}000 = \frac{(\$230{,}500 + \$120{,}000)}{(SP - \$220)}$$

$$SP - \$220 = \frac{\$350{,}500}{3{,}000}$$

$$SP = \$116.83 + \$220$$

$$SP = \$336.83$$

### CVP Analysis, Example 3

A small business stocks an inventory that includes many items. Its contribution margin ratio has held stable at 30%. Its fixed costs are $325,000 per year. If it wishes to make a profit equal to 10% of its sales, how much must it sell?

$$TS_\$ = \frac{(FC + TI)}{CMR}$$

$$TS_\$ = \frac{(FC + .10TS_\$)}{CMR}$$

$$TS_\$ = \frac{(\$325{,}000 + .10TS_\$)}{.30}$$

$$.30TS_\$ = \$325{,}000 + .10TS_\$$$

$$.30TS_\$ - .10TS_\$ = \$325{,}000$$

$$.20TS_\$ = \$325{,}000$$

$$TS_\$ = \frac{\$325{,}000}{.20}$$

$$TS_\$ = \$1{,}625{,}000$$

CVP analysis is built around the concept of the contribution margin ratio that, from a small business perspective, is one of the most important concepts which we can identify. Given a properly structured accounting system, a regular, monthly report can be prepared that depicts the contribution margin ratio for a firm. Few tools can be as useful for monitoring performance, for giving advance warning of impending problems, or for comparing products, departments, and divisions to each other. A strong business is one in which the contribution margin ratio grows slowly over time. A stable business is one in which the ratio is constant. A declining ratio indicates potentially serious problems unless action is taken. Few financial tools are as versatile as cost-volume-profit analysis. A prospective small business owner would be well advised to master the techniques.

## SUMMARY

Three steps are involved in break-even analysis: estimating the fixed costs; estimating the variable costs; and calculating the break-even point. Fixed costs are those that are not expected to fluctuate over the relevant range of activity. They include such items as salaries, rent or lease payments, utilities, supplies, insurance, property taxes, and so on. Variable costs vary directly with sales volume and include such items as inventory expense, freight expense, and sales commissions. Mixed costs have elements of both fixed and variable nature. These may be treated as fixed or variable costs or broken into their fixed and variable components.

The relevant range of activity is established by the upper and lower levels of expected sales volume. One limiting assumption of CVP analysis is that revenues, variable costs, and fixed costs are linear functions within the relevant range. Revenue is a function of sales volume.

Cost-volume-profit analysis, of which break-even and target sales analyses are special cases, is a powerful financial and planning tool available to the management of any business regardless of its size. It is especially valuable to a small business in which mistakes in judgment can be disastrous. The CVP model assumes that revenue and cost curves are linear, that the product mix is constant, and that sales prices per unit will be constant over time as will variable costs per unit. However, these assumptions may be false.

The solution to the problem of erroneous assumptions is twofold. First, we should prepare multiple calculations, employing a variety of bases and estimates for revenues and costs. This will result in a range of solutions and reveal the sensitivity of the model to changes in the various inputs. Recognition of the relative sensitivity of factors will give owners a better understanding of the potential effects of such errors and pinpoint areas needing close scrutiny. The second approach to minimizing problems with erroneous assumptions is so simple that it is frequently overlooked—being aware of the limitations of the model. Such awareness will prevent blind dependence on the solutions to equations that are meant only as aids to decision making not decision values.

CVP analysis has applications beyond assessing feasibility in a new venture start up. In an ongoing operation, it can help evaluate ideas and plans for new market areas, products, departments, divisions, plants, or services. It can be used in budgeting, pricing, monitoring and evaluating performance, supporting credit and investment proposals, and in identifying effects of price, cost and volume changes on profitability. CVP perhaps is the most important tool available to your small business, so incorporate it into the planning process at start up and continue to use this valuable tool throughout the life of your business.

## QUESTIONS

1. What are the steps in break-even analysis?
2. Distinguish among fixed, variable, and mixed costs.
3. How would you handle a mixed cost?

4. What is *operating leverage,* and what is its significance for a small business?
5. How are target sales predicted?
6. What are some applications of CVP analysis?
7. What are the assumptions of CVP models?
8. What is *sensitivity analysis,* and why is it valuable?

## PROJECTS

1. Consider starting up a small boutique. Virtually no variable costs are expected beyond those associated with the inventory. Planning has resulted in the following estimates:

   Fixed costs for the first year: $40,000
   Industry average gross profit margin: 50%

   Calculate the break-even point in sales dollars. Calculate the target sales necessary to produce a profit of $20,000.

2. Consider starting up a manufacturing firm that will produce three products. Planning has resulted in the following estimates for the first year:

| | | | | |
|---|---|---|---|---|
| Fixed costs | | | | $350,000 |
| Variable costs: | *Product 1* | *Product 2* | *Product 3* | |
| Direct labor | $5.25 | $6.00 | $4.75 | |
| Raw material | 2.46 | 3.03 | 2.19 | |
| Variable overhead | 2.00 | 3.75 | 1.90 | |
| Selling price | $15.50 | $22.75 | $13.00 | |

   What is the contribution margin per unit? If the firm expects an equal proportion of each product to be sold, what will be the break-even point in sales dollars? What will be the break-even point in units? How many units of each product will be sold? If the sales mix is expected to be 25% of product 1, 40% of product 2, and 35% of product 3, what sales level will be required to produce a target profit of $30,000?

# Case

A case taken from our files illustrates how important a break-even analysis can be and why it should be done in the start-up phase. Several physicians decided that it would be a wonderful time to create a luxurious "fat farm" for discriminating individuals who wanted a beautiful mountain hideaway and a medically supervised diet and weight loss program. They discussed their plans and contacted colleagues who found the concept interesting and the area appealing. A mountaintop apartment complex was available with an honest-to-goodness castle to house the exercise facilities. The whole package could be had for $2 million. What could be better!

The list of doctors who wanted to participate was long and distinguished. Lots of money already had been spent on travel and entertainment to present the concept to the interested parties, and commitments of time had been made by those who felt that the concept was viable. Several preliminary approaches had been made to bankers to establish required funding, but none were interested. The primary participant in the concept was becoming disenchanted with several self-appointed backers, who had promised to obtain financing but had not been able to provide it.

Finally, we were asked to evaluate the concept and provide a break-even analysis for this project and present the findings. Of course, no statistics or industry averages existed specifically for weight loss clinics, either in terms of market size or financial ratios. However, the plan was to operate very much like a hospital, and several physicians would be on staff. Furthermore, an initial operating expense budget had been developed. We decided that some hospital averages could be expected to apply, and this gave us enough information with which to work. The results of our research are displayed in the following table. After analyzing the results, what do you feel we should have recommended to our client?

HOSPITAL EXPENSE STATISTICS

| | *Salaries as Percentage of Total Expense* | *Fringe Benefits as Percentage of Salaries* | *Total Expense per Patient Day* | *Nonsalary Expense per Patient Day* |
|---|---|---|---|---|
| Rehabilitation hospitals | 63.7% | 22.6% | $121 | $ 44 |
| Psychiatric hospitals | 68.6 | 17.9 | 138 | 43 |
| For-profit hospitals | 46.4 | 15.5 | 312 | 153 |
| Short-term and special | 51.0 | 16.2 | 290 | 142 |
| All hospitals | 56.6 | 16.5 | $284 | $123 |

HOSPITAL REVENUE STATISTICS

| | *Revenue per Patient Day* | *Revenue per Patient Visit* | *Outpatient Revenue as Percentage of Inpatient Revenue* |
|---|---|---|---|
| Community hospitals | $322 | $69 | 15.1% |
| South Atlantic hospitals | 310 | 67 | 13.6 |

ANNUAL DEBT SERVICING FORECAST

Based on Interviews with Commercial Lenders
for a Commercial Mortgage, 20-Year Amortization,
5-Year Balloon Maturity, at 3% over Prime Rate (13%)

| | |
|---|---|
| Castle plus improvements | $ 500,000 total cost |
| With no down payment | 70,295 per year |
| With $50,000 down payment | 63,265 per year |
| With $100,000 down payment | 56,236 per year |
| Apartment building | $1,500,000 total cost |
| With no down payment | 210,884 per year |
| With $150,000 down payment | 189,796 per year |
| With $300,000 down payment | 168,708 per year |
| Revenue forecast | |
| Proposed fees for inpatients | $150 per patient day |
| Outpatient revenues projected at 14% of inpatient fees | 21 per patient day |
| Total Revenue | $171 per patient day |
| Start-up Marketing Expense Forecast | $300,000 |

*Normal advertising budgets run 3% to 5% of revenues annually with start-up marketing costs expected to range from five to ten times the annual budget. If revenues are expected in the $1 million range, annual expenditures can be expected to range between $30,000 and $50,000. Therefore, initial campaign expenses can be expected to range between $150,000 and $500,000. Using a midpoint range, the start-up marketing budget should be $300,000.*

SALARY EXPENSE FORECAST

Based on Data Provided by Client

| | |
|---|---|
| Director | $ 60,000 |
| Medical director | 90,000 |
| Business manager | 40,000 |
| Nutritionist | 50,000 |
| Psychologist | 30,000 |
| Patient coordinator | 20,000 |

| | |
|---|---|
| Registered nurse | 24,000 |
| Secretary | 14,000 |
| Receptionist | 12,000 |
| Bookkeeper | 15,000 |
| Medical assistant | 10,000 |
| Activities director | 12,000 |
| Therapist | 12,000 |
| Janitor | 10,000 |
| Kitchen staff | 100,000 |
| Consultants | 24,000 |
| Total salaries | $ 523,000 |
| Fringe benefits | 73,220 (14%) |
| Total expense | $ 596,220 |

TOTAL COST FORECAST

| | |
|---|---|
| Total salary expense | $ 596,220 |
| Debt service | 63,265 |
| Initial marketing | 300,000 |
| Subtotal | 959,485 |
| Other costs | 280,575 |
| Total costs | $1,240,060 |

*Other costs based on a 68% ratio of salaries to total costs. The higher ratio is used in the interests of conservatism. (Note that the lower the salary ratio to expense, the higher must be other expenses.) These costs are fixed and do not include food.*

HISTORIC APARTMENT BUILDING REVENUES AND PROJECTED EXPENSES

| | | |
|---|---|---|
| 12 Efficiency apartments | $215/month | $ 30,960 |
| 36 One bedroom apartments | $265/month | 114,480 |
| 24 Two bedroom apartments | $325/month | 93,600 |
| Total revenue at 100% occupancy | | $239,040 |
| Debt service | | 189,796 |
| Operating expenses | | 87,700 |
| Total | | $277,496 |
| Cash deficit | | $ 38,456 |

*The apartment building cannot generate sufficient cash flow to cover its debt service and operating expenses using historic fees. Furthermore, the operating expenses forecasts do not contain provisions for managerial expenses or for janitorial services, both of which will be higher using the building for patient occupancy because of the more rapid turnover of renters. Added managerial and janitorial expenses are expected to total $90,000, bringing the total costs to $367,496.*

**BREAK-EVEN ANALYSIS FROM A CASH FLOW PERSPECTIVE**

| | |
|---|---|
| Revenue per inpatient day | $171 |
| Less food cost per inpatient day | 20 |
| Contribution Margin per inpatient day | 151 |
| Costs: | |
| Hospital operation | $1,240,060 |
| Apartment building operation | 367,496 |
| Total Costs: | $1,607,556 |
| Break-even in inpatient days | 10,646 days |
| Average inpatients per day | 30 |
| Capacity | 72 |

*Cash flow break-even operation requires a 42% average capacity assuming a year-round operation (365 days). Should winter prove an off season, the operation must still produce 10,646 inpatient days of service. If the average stay is 14 days per patient, 761 patients will be required to produce required revenues, with the maximum service capacity being 72 at any one time. Note that a stay of 14 days would result in a patient cost of just under $2,400.*

---

*Source:* Data for hospital expense statistics and hospital revenue statistics are from *American Hospital Association Annual Survey* (Chicago: American Hospital Association, 1981).

# CHAPTER 7

# Budgeting for Success

**LEARNING OBJECTIVES**

After completing this chapter, you should be able to

- Know the value of budgeting.
- Identify the key aspects of financial performance.
- Explain how budgets serve as objectives and controls.
- Know why continuous budgeting is important.
- Understand the concept of sensitivity analysis and its role in budgeting.
- Know how to generate a sales, purchases, production, expense, cash flow, and capital budget.
- Know the value of pro forma income statements.
- Understand the tools used to reveal return on investment: payback, present value, and internal rate of return.
- Realize that many important factors in the budgeting decision are nonquantifiable.
- Understand the factors involved in buying or leasing for capital investment.

The process of predicting costs, expenses, revenues, cash flows, or investments is called **budgeting.** It requires looking into the future, guessing what we expect to happen and then making plans accordingly. The architect who is building a house must first predict what the house will look like based on the land available for its construction. The land will constrain the house both in size and appearance as the architect strives to make the house complement the site. After the house has been visualized, then the requirements for its construction are laid out: this is the model. Finally, the costs of construction are estimated. There is an additional step that is seldom included because it is so obvious. The costs have to be examined to determine whether we can afford to build the house. When we apply this process to business, all of the financial flows that are being budgeted must be subjected to evaluation. The owner of a small business will be especially interested in whether the budget is feasible and viable given the financial position of the business. One of the most useful applications of a budget is the determination of whether a business can absorb the costs and cash outflows required in the plan. Advance knowledge of inadequate funds is invaluable. It permits a manager to change the plans or raise the necessary capital. In this chapter we will examine the process of budgeting in a small business with emphasis on operating budgets, cash flow forecasting, and capital budgets.

## THE BUDGETING PROCESS

Budgeting is the process of predicting and planning for the future. A budget is both a forecast of what you expect to happen and a goal toward which you will work: it is both a planning tool and a control tool. Budgets are not used as widely in small businesses as they should be, because many people consider them complex and difficult. They are neither; although they can be time consuming. Every large business in the country uses budgets extensively. The usefulness of the budgeting process is not limited to large businesses; budgeting certainly merits the attention of anyone who intends to own a successful small business.

The key aspects of **financial performance** are cash flow and profitability, both of which can be estimated in preparing the supporting budgets for a cash flow forecast. The process is to prepare a sales budget, purchases or production budget, and expense budget. The information on these budgets can then be combined to yield a cash flow forecast and a pro forma income statement. **Pro forma** simply means a forecast or estimate. If we add last year's financial statements to the information, then a pro forma balance sheet can be prepared as well.

Another major aspect of financial performance is the acquisition and use of long-lived assets. Managing this process is facilitated by capital budgeting techniques. Under **capital budgeting,** long-lived assets or plant assets are examined in terms of their return on investment to determine which assets will be most valuable to the firm.

## Budgets as Objectives

The numbers used in a budget are predicted for the future; therefore, those numbers form objectives of our desires for that time. For example, when a **sales budget** is prepared, it includes a forecast of sales for some specified period in the future. Those sales are an objective for the firm. Their prediction should be based on a realistic assessment of what is reasonable and obtainable. Every budget should be prepared the same way. The **expense budget** will form objectives for the various costs in the firm, just as the **purchases budget** will form an objective for the cash outlay associated with inventory.

Because every budget forms objectives for the firm, the owner must be intimately involved in their preparation. In this book we talk a great deal about strategic planning and how the owner must prepare ongoing goals and objectives for the firm. We indicate that those objectives should be quantified whenever possible. Budgets are a sound way of preparing quantified objectives. However, be careful to be realistic and reasonable. A budget cannot simply be plucked out of the air, it must be based on reality. This means involving everyone who has any knowledge that may be of value in the preparation of the budget. Input should be solicited from the lowest levels in the firm as well as from all managers. The final choice of budgets to be used is the decision of the owner. Those prepared without participation by the staff will be less accurate and less useful.

## Budgets as a Control

Budgets constitute benchmarks for comparison. The actual sales achieved in a given month can be compared to the budgeted sales for that month to determine how well the firm is progressing toward its objectives. The budgets for expenses can be compared to actual numbers to calculate variances. **Variances** frequently are used when talking about manufacturing firms, but variances can be calculated for any type of business. In essence, they are simply deviations from budgeted figures.

For budgets to be useful control devices, there needs to be input from everyone who will be expected to conform to the budget. As we said earlier, this participation helps to ensure a reasonable budget. In addition, participation in the preparation of the budget makes people more willing to accept the budget as a control device. People who have no input into the budget can more easily dismiss it as unrealistic. Those who assisted in its preparation are more willing to accept the budget as attainable and gear their efforts toward fulfilling its expectations.

There is one danger in preparation of the budget by lower level employees: the risk of incorporating "slack" into the budget. People can overestimate costs and underestimate revenues to ensure that the budget will be met. Such deliberate misstatements are called **slack.** This is a particular problem when budgets are used as a control, because people naturally may try to influence their future evaluation by making the budget easy to achieve. However, if no input to the budget is sought from lower levels, people may feel antagonistic and refuse to accept the budget as realistic. The result is an extreme lowering of morale. The best solution to this problem is the proper use of budgets in a control mode. Budgets should never be used as a club. Everyone should recognize that striving toward the objectives established by the budget is what is important, and that achievement of the budget is not an absolute necessity. It is far more important to put forth a determined effort and have it fail than not to budget at all. After all, budgets are forecasts and therefore cannot be achieved consistently over time. Deviations from the budget can occur due to a variety of factors, both inside and outside the firm. Consistent failure to achieve a budget signals serious problems, either in control or in budget preparation, but isolated variances are not automatically bad.

## Continuous Budgeting

**Forecasting** is a difficult process, initially, for a small business. As experience in the business grows and experience in forecasting develops, the process becomes easier and more accurate. For this reason, the strongest approach to budgeting is to continuously prepare forecasts. A **continuous budget** is prepared for twelve months, month by month. As each month goes by, the corresponding month of the budget is compared to actual results. Then, the remaining eleven months of the forecast are revised to incorporate what has been learned. Finally, a twelfth month is added to the forecast. The result is a constant focus on the budget and a continuous forecast of a full year of operations. You will find that, the closer an event is, the more accurate you can be in the forecast. Thus, the next three or four months of the budget will be more accurate than will be the eleventh and twelfth months of the forecast, because they are closer to the present. Revising the budget each month will provide you with a continuous planning horizon of several months of strong data and several months of weaker data.

Over time your forecasting skills will increase. In addition, the continuous emphasis on budgeting will keep management attention focused on the budget and its achievement, rather than day-to-day management. From this perspective, a budget can help make managers into planners and allow a firm to "proact" rather than "react" to changing conditions. **Proact** means to act before an event occurs, and it is the strongest type of management action. It is much easier to walk into a bank and arrange for a short-term loan to cover a cash deficiency three months hence than to obtain a loan to cover a cash shortage which has just been discovered. It is simply good management to anticipate the future.

### Sensitivity Analysis

Every budget is an estimate of future events, which means that every budget will contain some error. Consequently, it makes sense to analyze a budget to determine which factors have a major influence. **Sensitivity analysis** is the process of examining the effects changes in various components of a budget will have on the overall budget. The process involves calculating the budget using a range of estimates for the various factors. For example, various estimates of sales and variable and fixed expenses could be used to determine the effect of each on profit. Understanding what are the major components of a budget will help in examining the source of deviations from the budget and also identify the important areas for management's attention.

The preparation of multiple budgets can be laborious and time consuming. Consequently, an automated approach can be a valuable aid. Spreadsheet programs for microcomputers were designed with sensitivity analysis in mind. They permit a forecast to be prepared and then subjected to a series of "what if" questions to determine sensitivity. With a few keystrokes, you can examine the results of a 10% decrease in sales on profits or the impact of a 5% increase in fixed expenses on cash flow. In addition, such programs make continuous budgeting and budget revision a simple process. In fact, most businesses probably could justify a microcomputer for use in budgeting, even if it were not used for record keeping or other activities.

## THE SALES BUDGET

As indicated earlier, the first step in the budget process is the preparation of a sales budget. This means that sales for the next year must be forecast, month by month. This is not only the first step in the budget process, it is the most difficult. Sales forecasting can be complex, especially for a young firm with little history. Predicting the seasonal patterns that will affect the monthly sales also can be difficult. Many large firms have complicated computer simulation models that are used to predict sales. Most small businesses cannot afford such devices and, consequently, use an arbitrary growth percentage to predict sales: "Sales will increase by 10% next year!" This is not a good method!

## Sales Forecasting

A company with an established sales history can base its forecast on that history and any expected changes. Historic sales, by month, should be converted to percentages of the yearly sales. This will show the seasonality of sales. Now the sales trends from year to year can be examined and used to forecast sales for the next twelve months. Remember, don't simply add a percentage. Look at the change in sales over the years and consider what happened to affect those sales. Was there a change in competition or the opening of a new store or market that influenced sales? What caused the sales to grow each year? Then think about what you expect to happen this year. Are you opening new markets or stores? Will there be new products or a change in the competition? Are there any economic conditions or other factors that will affect sales? Will sales go up or will they go down? Do you plan any changes in marketing: new sales people, higher commissions, advertising campaigns. The human brain is a remarkable model builder. If you consciously examine past trends and expected changes in your business, you will be amazed at how well you will be able to forecast sales. The secret is to ensure that you don't overlook important factors that will affect performance.

After you have made a forecast of the dollar volume of sales for the next year, you must convert it to monthly figures. This is done by examining the historic monthly percentages and changes that may affect them over the next year: the same process as predicting sales. What were the trends in monthly sales over the years? What caused those trends? What do you expect to happen next year that will affect them? The result should be a forecast of the percentage of sales you expect to occur each month. The monthly sales forecast is now found by simply multiplying the percentages by the forecast for the year. Exhibit 7-1 displays an example of the process.

The sales forecast will be adjusted at the end of each month under continuous budgeting principles. At the end of January 1990, the actual sales for January will be compared to the budget, $10,350 in the example. Now, if the sales were higher than the budget and we expect that trend to continue, we would increase the sales forecast for the remaining eleven months. We also might decrease the sales forecast if the experience for January indicated that we should, or we might change the forecast for February and March and leave the rest intact. After we have made the adjustments necessary, sales for January 1991 would be forecast using the principles just discussed, and again we would have a full twelve months of sales predictions.

**EXHIBIT 7-1** *Sales Forecast Using Historic Results*

| | 1986 | 1987 | 1988 | 1989 | Projected 1990 |
|---|---|---|---|---|---|
| Total sales | $155,000 | $180,000 | $175,000 | $225,000 | $258,750 |
| Percentage change | — | 25% | (3%) | 29% | 15% |

*Using actual sales for 1986 through 1989 and expectations for changes during 1990, sales for that year are forecast to be 15% higher than 1989 sales.*

| Sales percentages: | 1986 | 1987 | 1988 | 1989 | Projected 1990 |
|---|---|---|---|---|---|
| January | 2% | 4% | 4% | 4% | 4% |
| February | 4 | 4 | 4 | 4 | 4 |
| March | 4 | 4 | 4 | 3 | 3 |
| Total | 10 | 12 | 12 | 11 | 11 |
| April | 3 | 3 | 2 | 2 | 1 |
| May | 3 | 3 | 3 | 2 | 2 |
| June | 4 | 3 | 3 | 4 | 5 |
| Total | 10 | 9 | 8 | 8 | 8 |
| July | 5 | 4 | 5 | 6 | 7 |
| August | 7 | 9 | 11 | 13 | 15 |
| September | 13 | 14 | 14 | 16 | 17 |
| Total | 25 | 27 | 30 | 35 | 39 |
| October | 14 | 14 | 15 | 16 | 16 |
| November | 25 | 24 | 22 | 20 | 19 |
| December | 16 | 14 | 13 | 10 | 7 |
| Total | 55 | 52 | 50 | 46 | 42 |

*Using actual percentages for monthly sales for 1986 through 1989, and expectations for changes during 1990, monthly percentages are forecast for 1990.*

*The 1990 Sales Forecast of $258,750 can be converted into a monthly sales forecast by applying the percentage forecast. The following numbers have been rounded to the nearest $10.*

| | | | | | |
|---|---|---|---|---|---|
| January | $10,350 | May | $ 5,180 | September | $43,990 |
| February | 10,350 | June | 12,940 | October | 41,400 |
| March | 7,760 | July | 18,110 | November | 49,160 |
| April | 2,590 | August | 38,810 | December | 18,110 |

## Sales Forecasting for a New Business

How do we prepare a sales forecast if we have no historic results to examine, if the history is too short to see any trends, or if the economic or other conditions have changed so much that historic results no longer are valid? In such cases, the sales forecast must be based totally on expectations. In some retail industries, industry averages for sales per square foot of display space are available. *Dollars and Cents,* a guide to shopping center averages, is published triannually by the U.S. Urban Land Institute. Your reference librarian can guide you to other publications that include such data. Sales forecasts then can be prepared using the industry averages and the square footage of your store. If such data is not available for your industry, a good approach is to examine inventory turnover averages for the industry. These also are available from many published sources. Using the industry average and your initial inventory stock level, you can predict sales for the year. Don't forget to adjust for the markup. For example, assume that the industry average is an inventory turnover of 3.5 times and that you will be using a markup of 50% of cost. A cost markup of 50% is equivalent to a markup based on selling price of 33%, 50%/(100% + 50%).* You should compare your markup plans to industry averages for gross profit to be sure that they are reasonable. If your initial inventory investment is $100,000, then an inventory turn of 3.5 would yield a sales forecast of $525,000 ($100,000 × 3.5 = $350,000; $350,000 × 50% = $175,000; $175,000 + $350,000 = $525,000).

After the sales forecast for the year has been prepared, you must convert it to a monthly forecast. Again, this is best done using industry averages for seasonality. Frequently, such numbers are available only on a quarterly basis. If that be the case, you should make a guess about how each month of the quarter will fall and expect to have to make significant adjustments to the forecast as actual results are accumulated for comparison purposes.

If no industry averages are available that you can use for sales forecasting, then the initial sales budget will be largely guesswork and therefore subject to great error. In such a case, you should make an initial forecast based on your best guess and monitor the actual results closely with the intention of making major adjustments to the forecast during the course of the year.

## Credit Sales

Once the sales forecast has been prepared, the next step is to predict the percentage of sales that will be made on credit. In many industries this is simple, because virtually all sales will be for cash, as in the case of a restaurant, or all will

*It is important to be able to convert markups based on cost into retail markups and vice versa. Markup based on retail is an important number because it is equivalent to the gross profit percentage. The process is simple if you remember that cost + markup = sales. Let MC be markup based on cost, MR be markup based on retail, and C stand for cost. Now, $MR = MC/(C + MC)$, or markup based on cost divided by cost plus markup based on cost will equal markup based on retail. You can solve in the other direction, too: Solving the equation $MR = MC/(C + MC)$ for MC yields $MC = (MR \times C)/(1 - MR)$.

be on credit, as in the case of a wholesale supplier to other firms. In most industries, sales will be a mix of cash and credit. It is important to isolate credit sales because we are going to want to predict the cash inflows that will result from sales. That means that we must predict cash collections from accounts receivable and add that to cash sales to determine the cash inflows in any given month.

If we have a history to draw upon, then credit sales percentage can be expected to continue its historic trends unless there are conditions or changes that will affect it. We will want to examine historic sales to determine both the percentage of sales made on credit and when those accounts receivable actually were collected. The historic collection experience plus the credit sales percentage is then applied to the sales forecast to arrive at a forecast of cash inflows from sales month by month. Exhibit 7-2 illustrates an example of the process using the sales forecast developed in Exhibit 7-1.

Notice in Exhibit 7-2 how the cash inflows exceed sales significantly in January, declining to just slightly over sales in March. This is an illustration of the cash to cash cycle: that is, the process of converting cash into assets, which are converted back into cash. Because sales on credit must be collected before the cash is available, cash inflows lag behind sales. This can be a significant effect and can cause great difficulty because stocking for major sales months frequently must take place at a time when cash inflow is at a low point.

## Credit Sales Forecasting for a New Business

Lacking reliable historic data to use in predicting credit sales and collection periods, we must fall back on industry averages. The percentage of credit sales generally is available from industry averages, but collection experience is not. However, accounts receivable turnover rates generally are available and these can be used to forecast collections. Consider an example in which the industry average for accounts receivable turnover was eight times. This is equivalent to 45 days (360 days/8 = 45 days). If the turnover is 45 days, the average account is paid within 45 days or roughly half the accounts are paid prior to 45 days and half are paid after 45 days. If the normal credit terms in the industry are 30-day terms, then we can assume that the accounts are paid evenly over the days prior to and after 45 days. This means that about half of the accounts can be expected to pay in the first 15 days of the month following the month of sale. The other half can be expected to pay during the last 15 days of that month and into the second month following the sale. Therefore, the majority of accounts are collected during the month following the sale. To be conservative, we can allow for a loss percentage and spread a portion of accounts over into the second and third month following the sale. This will provide a beginning point for the collection forecast, and we will anticipate the need to make adjustments

**EXHIBIT 7-2** *Cash Inflow Forecast Using Historic Results*

| | *1986* | *1987* | *1988* | *1989* | *Projected 1990* |
|---|---|---|---|---|---|
| Cash sales percentage | 45% | 38% | 37% | 36% | 35% |
| Credit sales percentage | 55 | 62 | 63 | 64 | 65 |
| *Collection experience* | | | | | |
| Percentage of credit sales: | | | | | |
| Paid within 30 days | 50% | 52% | 50% | 51% | 50% |
| Paid within 60 days | 40 | 36 | 40 | 39 | 40 |
| Paid within 90 days | 9 | 10 | 8 | 9 | 8 |
| Uncollectible | 1 | 2 | 2 | 1 | 2 |

CASH INFLOW PROJECTIONS FOR 1990 (ROUNDED TO NEAREST $10)

| | ACTUAL FROM 1989 | | | PROJECTED FOR 1990 | | |
|---|---|---|---|---|---|---|
| | *October* | *November* | *December* | *January* | *February* | *March* |
| Sales | $36,000 | $45,000 | $22,500 | $10,350 | $10,350 | $7,760 |
| Credit sales: | | | | | | |
| 64% | 23,040 | 28,800 | 14,400 | | | |
| 65% | | | | 6,730 | 6,730 | 5,040 |
| Cash sales (35%) | | | | 3,620 | 3,620 | 2,720 |
| Collections: | | | | | | |
| 50% within 30 days (.5 × last month) | | | | 7,200 | 3,365 | 3,365 |
| 40% within 60 days (.4 × 1 month ago) | | | | 11,520 | 5,760 | 2,690 |
| 8% within 90 days (.08 × 2 months ago) | | | | 1,840 | 2,300 | 1,150 |
| Total cash inflows (Cash sales + collections) | | | | $24,180 | $15,045 | $9,925 |

*The remainder of 1990 would be forecast in the same fashion.*

as experience is gained over time. The process is the same no matter what the turnover rate is. If the industry average was a 60-day collection period (six turns in a year), then we could expect half the accounts to pay prior to 60 days and half after 60 days. If they were evenly spread, that would mean half in the month following the sale and half in the second month following the sale.

If there is absolutely no experience or industry averages, then a good starting point is to assume that collections will be slightly longer than the terms being offered. If you will be offering 30-day terms on the accounts, then collections will probably be somewhat longer than 30 days. In that instance, a 45-day collection period would make a good starting point, and we would expect to make adjustments to the forecast as experience is accumulated.

## Accounts Receivable

In addition to predicting sales for the year and sales by month, the sales budget also contains the information needed to predict accounts receivable at any point in time. The balance in receivables will simply be credit sales that have not yet been collected. Exhibit 7-3 uses the data from the previous example to demonstrate the calculation of receivables at March 31, 1990.

**EXHIBIT 7-3** *Accounts Receivable Calculations*

| | PROJECTED FOR 1990 | | | |
|---|---|---|---|---|
| | *January* | *February* | *March* | *Total* |
| Sales | $10,350 | $10,350 | $7,760 | $28,460 |
| For cash | 3,620 | 3,620 | 2,720 | 9,960 |
| On credit | 6,730 | 6,730 | 5,040 | 18,500 |
| Collections: | | | | |
| 50% within 30 days (.5 × last month) | $ 7,200 | $3,365 | $ 3,365 | |
| 40% within 60 days (.4 × 1 month ago) | 11,520 | 5,760 | 2,690 | |
| 8% within 90 days (.08 × 2 months ago) | 1,840 | 2,300 | 1,150 | |
| Total collections | | | $39,190 | |

*By March 31, all receivables will have been collected except those related to sales in March, February, and January because experience shows 98% of sales being collected within 90 days. Examining the calculations, remove collections that come from months prior to January.*

| | | | |
|---|---|---|---|
| Collections: | | | |
| 50% within 30 days (.5 × last month) | — | $3,365 | $ 3,365 |
| 40% within 60 days (.4 × 1 month ago) | — | — | 2,690 |
| 8% within 90 days (.08 × 2 months ago) | — | — | — |
| Total collections | | | $ 9,420 |

*To calculate the receivables balance at March 31, add the credit sales for January through March, add the collections of those sales, and subtract.*

| | |
|---|---|
| Credit sales for January–March | $18,500 |
| *Less* collections during January–March | 9,420 |
| Accounts receivable at March 31 | $ 9,080 |

*Another approach is to use beginning accounts receivable, total credit sales, and total collections to arrive at ending accounts receivable. The beginning receivables balance can be found from the general ledger or a previous forecast. It simply is uncollected receivables.*

| | |
|---|---|
| Accounts receivable at December 31, 1989 | $29,770 |
| *Plus* credit sales for January–March | 18,500 |
| Total | 48,270 |
| *Less* collections during January–March | 39,190 |
| Accounts receivable at March 31, 1990 | $ 9,080 |

**EXHIBIT 7-4** *Sales Budget for 1990*

| | *January* | *February* | *March* | *April* | *May* | *June* | *July* | *August* | *September* | *October* | *November* | *December* | *Total* |
|---|---|---|---|---|---|---|---|---|---|---|---|---|---|
| Sales | $10,350 | $10,350 | $7,760 | $2,590 | $5,180 | $12,940 | $18,110 | $38,810 | $43,990 | $41,400 | $49,160 | $18,110 | $258,750 |
| Cash | 3,620 | 3,620 | 2,720 | 910 | 1,810 | 4,530 | 6,340 | 13,580 | 15,400 | 14,490 | 17,210 | 6,340 | 90,570 |
| Credit | 6,730 | 6,730 | 5,040 | 1,680 | 3,370 | 8,410 | 11,770 | 25,230 | 28,590 | 26,910 | 31,950 | 11,770 | 168,180 |
| Collections: | | | | | | | | | | | | | |
| 50% | 7,200 | 3,365 | 3,365 | 2,520 | 840 | 1,685 | 4,205 | 5,885 | 12,615 | 14,295 | 13,455 | 15,975 | |
| 40% | 11,520 | 5,760 | 2,690 | 2,690 | 2,020 | 670 | 1,350 | 3,360 | 4,710 | 10,090 | 11,440 | 10,760 | |
| 8% | 1,840 | 2,300 | 1,150 | 540 | 540 | 400 | 135 | 270 | 670 | 940 | 2,020 | 2,290 | |
| Total | 20,560 | 11,425 | 7,205 | 5,750 | 3,400 | 2,755 | 5,690 | 9,515 | 17,995 | 25,325 | 26,915 | 29,025 | 165,560 |
| Total cash inflow | $24,180 | $15,045 | $9,925 | $6,660 | $5,210 | $ 7,285 | $12,030 | $23,095 | $33,395 | $39,815 | $44,125 | $35,365 | $256,130 |

| | |
|---|---|
| Accounts receivable at December 31, 1989 | $ 29,770 |
| Credit sales during 1990 | 168,180 |
| Total | 197,950 |
| Collections during 1990 | 165,560 |
| Accounts receivable at December 31, 1990 | $ 32,390 |

The process illustrated in Exhibit 7-3 is used to estimate the receivables balance at any point in time. Notice that the percentage of uncollectible accounts, 2% in our example, will remain in accounts receivable. If we wish, an adjustment can be made to remove the uncollectible accounts from the receivables balance by subtracting the percentage of loss expected from the receivables. Generally, the loss percentage is so low that the error is insignificant; especially when we remember that the numbers are forecasts and estimates that will be subjected to adjustment at the end of every month. Exhibit 7-4 displays the finished sales budget.

## THE PURCHASES BUDGET

The **purchases budget** is based on inventory. We use the inventory turnover ratio and the gross profit margin along with a sales forecast to predict desired inventory levels. For example, assume that the inventory is expected to turn over eight times in one year. That will mean that the inventory at the end of each month should be sufficient to cover the next 45 days or 1.5 months' sales (360 days/8 = 45 days). Now the ending inventory for any month is simply the cost of goods sold for the next 1.5 months. If the gross profit percentage is 30%, then the cost of goods sold must be 70%. Using the sales numbers from the previous example, it looks like this:

| | *January* | *February* | *March* |
|---|---|---|---|
| Sales | $10,350 | $10,350 | $7,760 |
| Ending inventory | 9,960 | | |

*February Sales $10,350 plus 1/2 of March Sales, $3,880 = $14,230*
*70% of $14,230 = $9,960*

Using this approach we can estimate the necessary ending inventory balance for any month end. All we need are the sales forecast, the gross profit percentage, and the inventory turnover. Sales forecasts come from the sales budget; the gross profit and inventory turnover figures can be estimated based on historic averages or can come from industry averages. If we use historic averages, we must remember to adjust for any conditions or changes expected to affect the numbers during the coming year. Because the inventory budget also will be used for control purposes, the numbers we select for gross profit and inventory turns also should reflect our desires for the year. Be careful to ensure that the resulting ratios are reasonable and attainable. If you have averaged an inventory turnover of six times and you wish to increase it, it may not be reasonable to expect it to double. An increase to seven or eight turns may be more attainable. Gross profits are a result of both cost and price, so be sure to take into consideration expected changes in your merchandise or production costs as well as any changes you plan for your selling prices.

## Purchases

Once an inventory budget has been prepared, the forecast of purchases follows from the following relationship:

Beginning inventory + Purchases = Cost of goods available for sale − Ending inventory = Cost of goods sold

*In equation form:*

$$BI + P - EI = CofG$$

*Solving for purchases:*

$$P = CofG - BI + EI$$

*or,*

Cost of goods sold − Beginning inventory + Ending inventory = Purchases

If we use the numbers from the previous examples, the purchases forecast is calculated as displayed in Exhibit 7-5. The example assumes an inventory turnover of 1.5 months or eight times and a gross profit percentage of 30%. The beginning balance for January comes from the general ledger or previous forecasts. The beginning balance in inventory for all of the other months is the ending inventory of the preceding month.

The remaining months of the forecast are estimated in the same fashion as

**EXHIBIT 7-5** *Purchases Forecast*

| | *January* | *February* | *March* | *April* | *May* | *June* |
|---|---|---|---|---|---|---|
| Sales | $10,350 | $10,350 | $7,760 | $2,590 | $5,180 | $12,940 |
| Cost of goods sold (70%) | 7,245 | 7,245 | 5,430 | 1,810 | 3,630 | 9,060 |
| Ending inventory | 9,960 | 6,335 | 3,625 | 8,160 | — | — |
| Beginning inventory | 10,870 | 9,960 | 6,335 | 3,625 | 8,160 | — |
| Cost of goods sold | 7,245 | 7,245 | 5,430 | 1,810 | | |
| *Less* beginning inventory | 10,870 | 9,960 | 6,335 | 3,625 | | |
| *Plus* ending inventory | 9,960 | 6,335 | 3,625 | 8,160 | | |
| Purchases | $ 6,335 | $ 3,620 | 2,720 | 6,345 | | |

shown for January through April in the exhibit. The purchases budget is not yet finished, however, because the cash disbursements must be added to provide an estimate of cash outflows associated with merchandise purchases.

## Cash Disbursements

Cash disbursements are simple to forecast. We need know only the terms our suppliers require for payment. If our suppliers require 30-day terms, then the purchases for any given month must be paid during the following month. If our suppliers offer 2/10, net 30 terms, that means that a 2% discount will be available for payment within 10 days. In that case, the payment of purchases must be made within 10 days of receipt to get the discount. If we intend to take all discounts, then the disbursement for any month will be equal to two-thirds of that month's purchases plus one-third of the previous month's purchases. That is, assuming that purchases are made evenly throughout the month. The two-thirds comes from an assumption that those purchases made during the first 20 days, or two-thirds, of the month must be paid during that month. Those purchases made during the last 10 days, or one-third, of the month will be paid during the following month. By the same reasoning, terms of 2/15, net 30 would result in the payment of one-half of each month's purchases during the month plus one-half of the preceding month's purchases.

## Accounts Payable

Accounts payable also can be predicted using the purchases budget in the same manner as accounts receivable were predicted using the sales budget. Payables simply are purchases that have not yet been paid. Therefore, the balance of accounts payable at any point in time is the total of beginning payables plus purchases less payments. If we put it all together, the final purchases budget will look like the one displayed in Exhibit 7-6. The budget uses the sales data from the previous examples of sales budgets and assumes that the disbursement for purchases will be made on 30-day terms. This means that cash outflow will follow purchases by one month. The budget also assumes a gross profit level of 30% and an inventory turnover rate of eight times per year or 45 days.

The purchases budget is now complete. Note that it shows the total for cost of goods sold for the year and the ending inventory value for the year as well as purchases and payables. Note also that sales forecasts were required for January and February of 1991 in order to complete the inventory budget for December. That is because December's ending inventory is a function of January and February sales.

**EXHIBIT 7-6** *Purchases Budget for 1990*

| | *January* | *February* | *March* | *April* | *May* | *June* | *July* | *August* | *September* | *October* | *November* | *December* | *Total* |
|---|---|---|---|---|---|---|---|---|---|---|---|---|---|
| Sales | $10,350 | $10,350 | $7,760 | $2,590 | $5,180 | $12,940 | $18,110 | $38,810 | $43,990 | $41,400 | $49,160 | $18,110 | $258,750 |
| Cost of goods sold | 7,245 | 7,245 | 5,430 | 1,810 | 3,630 | 9,060 | 12,680 | 27,170 | 30,790 | 28,980 | 34,410 | 12,680 | 181,130 |
| Ending inventory | 9,960 | 6,335 | 3,625 | 8,160 | 15,400 | 26,265 | 42,565 | 45,280 | 46,185 | 40,750 | 16,845 | 12,495 | — |
| Beginning inventory | 10,870 | 9,960 | 6,335 | 3,625 | 8,160 | 15,400 | 26,265 | 42,565 | 45,280 | 46,185 | 40,750 | 16,845 | — |
| Cost of goods sold | 7,245 | 7,245 | 5,430 | 1,810 | 3,630 | 9,060 | 12,680 | 27,170 | 30,790 | 28,980 | 34,410 | 12,680 | 181,130 |
| *Less* beginning inventory | 10,870 | 9,960 | 6,335 | 3,625 | 8,160 | 15,400 | 26,265 | 42,565 | 45,280 | 46,185 | 40,750 | 16,845 | — |
| *Plus* ending inventory | 9,960 | 6,335 | 3,625 | 8,160 | 15,400 | 26,265 | 42,565 | 45,280 | 46,185 | 40,750 | 16,845 | 12,495 | — |
| Purchases | 6,335 | 3,620 | 2,720 | 6,345 | 10,870 | 19,925 | 28,980 | 29,885 | 31,695 | 23,545 | 10,505 | 8,330 | 182,755 |
| Disbursements | $ 7,250 | $ 6,335 | $3,620 | $2,720 | $ 6,345 | $10,870 | $19,925 | $28,980 | $29,885 | $31,695 | $23,545 | $10,505 | $181,675 |

| | *January 1991* | *February 1991* |
|---|---|---|
| Sales | $11,900 | $11,900 |
| Cost of goods sold | 8,330 | 8,330 |

| | |
|---|---|
| Accounts payable at January 31, 1990 | $ 7,250 |
| *Plus* purchases during 1990 | 182,755 |
| *Less* payments during 1990 | 181,675 |
| Accounts payable at December 31, 1990 | $ 8,330 |
| Alternatively | |
| Accounts payable at December 31, 1990: | |
| December purchases | $ 8,330 |

## THE PRODUCTION BUDGET

The purchases budget works for retailers and wholesalers, but what about manufacturers? If a firm produces a product, then its production must be budgeted instead of its merchandise purchases. There are three components of production: raw materials, labor, and overhead. Each of these must be budgeted, but each is dependent upon the quantity of goods to be produced. Consequently, the first step in **production budgeting** is the forecast of the number of units required.

### Production Forecast

The number of units to be produced can be derived from the sales budget. The difference is that the sales budget must be prepared in numbers of units rather than in dollars, as was the case for retailers and wholesalers; otherwise, the process is the same. Also, an individual sales forecast must be prepared for each product produced.

Once a sales forecast in units has been prepared for each product to be manufactured, we must establish inventory policies. If we intend to ship all goods upon completion, then the number of units that must be produced in any month is equal to the sales forecast for that month. If we intend to hold any finished goods inventory on hand, then we must prepare an inventory budget for finished goods just as we did for retailers. The process is exactly the same, but again the budget is prepared in units rather than dollars and a separate budget will be required for every product produced. The outcome of that process will be the number of units that must be produced rather than purchases. Exhibit 7-7 illustrates the process.

After the production forecast has been prepared, the requirements for raw materials, labor, and overhead must be calculated. This information comes from the design specifications in which the requirements for each unit were established.

### Raw Materials

The design specifications for each product to be manufactured includes a list of all raw materials required to produce a single unit and the quantities of those materials needed. Each raw material required must have a separate forecast prepared in units rather than in dollars, a process identical to the production forecast. If a "just in time" system is used for delivery of materials, then the numbers of units of raw material required is found by multiplying production for each month by quantities required in the design specs. **Just in time (JIT) inventory** practices mean that purchases of raw material are timed so that they

**EXHIBIT 7-7** *Production Forecast*

**SALES FORECAST IN NUMBERS OF UNITS FOR PRODUCT A**

| | *January* | *February* | *March* | *April* | *May* | *June* |
|---|---|---|---|---|---|---|
| Sales | 5,175 | 5,430 | 3,880 | 1,295 | 2,590 | 6,470 |

*Under immediate shipping, the production forecast would be the same.*

*Assuming an inventory policy geared toward an inventory turnover of finished goods of 8 times per year, ending inventory in units must always equal sales in units for the next month and one half. Beginning inventory for January comes from the actual count or a previous forecast.*

| | *January* | *February* | *March* | *April* | *May* | *June* |
|---|---|---|---|---|---|---|
| Ending inventory | 7,370 | 4,530 | 2,590 | 5,825 | — | — |
| Beginning inventory | 7,890 | 7,370 | 4,530 | 2,590 | 5,825 | — |
| Number of units sold | 5,175 | 5,430 | 3,880 | 1,295 | | |
| *Less* beginning inventory | 7,890 | 7,370 | 4,530 | 2,590 | | |
| *Plus* ending inventory | 7,370 | 4,530 | 2,590 | 5,825 | | |
| Units to be produced | 4,655 | 2,590 | 1,940 | 4,530 | | |

arrive at the factory just in time to be placed into production; no raw materials are kept on hand. If JIT is not used, an inventory turnover is used to estimate the requirements. Exhibit 7-8 illustrates the process.

The forecast for raw materials now can be converted to a budget with the addition of the expected cost factors for each unit, which comes from the design specifications and establishing when disbursements for purchases will be made.

## Labor

The **labor forecast** is handled exactly like the materials forecast in terms of hours required for production. Then the forecast is converted into a budget by the addition of labor cost estimates from the design specifications. Exhibit 7-9 displays a labor budget.

Labor costs generally are disbursed in the month in which they are incurred. If the payroll scheme crosses a month, then the disbursement forecast must consider this practice. For example, if the payroll is monthly on the fifteenth of the month, then payroll disbursement for any given month will be equal to one-half of the previous month's labor costs plus one-half of this month's labor costs.

**EXHIBIT 7-8** *Raw Materials Forecast*

PRODUCTION FORECAST

(in numbers of units for product A)

| | *January* | *February* | *March* | *April* |
|---|---|---|---|---|
| Units to be produced | 4,655 | 2,590 | 1,940 | 4,530 |

*Design specifications for one unit of Product A*

| | |
|---|---|
| Raw material X | 2 units at $9.50 each |
| Raw material Y | 5 units at $2.50 each |
| Direct labor hours | 2 hours at $10.00 per hour |

MATERIALS FORECAST

*Under JIT, the materials forecast is straightforward.*

| | *January* | *February* | *March* | *April* | |
|---|---|---|---|---|---|
| Units of material X | 9,310 | 5,180 | 3,880 | 9,060 | (2 × Production) |
| Units of material Y | 23,275 | 12,950 | 9,700 | 22,650 | (5 × Production) |

*Assuming an inventory policy geared toward an inventory turnover of raw materials of eight times per year, ending inventory in units must always equal production in units for the next month and one-half. Beginning inventory for January comes from the actual count or a previous forecast.*

| | *January* | *February* | *March* | *April* |
|---|---|---|---|---|
| *Material X* | | | | |
| Ending inventory | 7,120[a] | 8,410 | — | — |
| Beginning inventory | 11,900 | 7,120 | 8,410 | — |
| Number of units required | 9,310 | 5,180 | 3,880 | 9,060 |
| *Less* beginning inventory | 11,900 | 7,120 | 8,410 | — |
| *Plus* ending inventory | 7,120 | 8,410 | — | — |
| Units to be purchased | 4,530 | 6,470 | — | — |
| *Material Y* | | | | |
| Ending inventory | 17,800[b] | 21,025 | — | — |
| Beginning inventory | 29,750 | 17,800 | 21,025 | — |
| Number units required | 23,275 | 12,950 | 9,700 | 22,650 |
| *Less* beginning inventory | 29,750 | 17,800 | 21,025 | — |
| *Plus* ending inventory | 17,800 | 21,025 | — | — |
| Units to be purchased | 11,325 | 16,175 | — | — |

[a] (1,940/2 + 2,590) × 2 = 7,120
[b] (1,940/2 + 2,590) × 5 = 17,800

**EXHIBIT 7-9** *Labor Budget*

PRODUCTION FORECAST

(in numbers of units for product A)

| | *January* | *February* | *March* | *April* |
|---|---|---|---|---|
| Units to be produced | 4,655 | 2,590 | 1,940 | 4,530 |

*Design specifications for one unit of product A*

| | |
|---|---|
| Raw material X | 2 units @ $ 9.50 |
| Raw material Y | 5 units @ $ 2.50 |
| Direct labor hours | 2 hours @ $10.00 |

| | *January* | *February* | *March* | *April* | |
|---|---|---|---|---|---|
| Hours of labor | 9,310 | 5,180 | 3,880 | 9,060 | (2 × Production) |
| Labor costs | $93,100 | $51,800 | $38,800 | $90,600 | |

## Overhead

The only items remaining to be considered in the production budget are variable and fixed overhead costs. **Fixed overhead** is budgeted for the month or year independent of production planned, because fixed costs do not vary with production. Variable costs are handled in the same fashion as labor costs. A standard variable cost per unit of production is established and then multiplied by the production forecasted. Disbursement for fixed expenses is based on the actual timing of those expenses, which generally is in the month in which they are incurred. Disbursement of variable expenses also generally is in the month in which incurred. If either of the overhead costs include depreciation or other noncash components, then those items must be removed when estimating the disbursement.

Exhibit 7-10 displays a finished production budget assuming a JIT inventory policy and disbursement of all costs in the month incurred.

The completed production budget in the exhibit takes the place of the purchases budget for a manufacturing firm. If we applied the same processes, the balance in inventory of raw material, inventory of finished goods, and balance of accounts payable would be available from the budget.

# THE EXPENSE BUDGET

The expenses of a firm can be classified as either fixed or variable, as we discussed in the preceding chapter. Variable expenses are budgeted as a percentage of sales. Using historic averages or industry averages adjusted for

**EXHIBIT 7-10** *Production Budget for the First Six Months of 1990*

| | *Design specifications for one unit of product A* |
|---|---|
| Raw material X | 2 units @ $ 9.50 |
| Raw material Y | 5 units @ $ 2.50 |
| Direct labor hours | 2 hours @ $10.00 |
| Variable overhead | $5.00 per direct labor hour/$10 per unit |
| Fixed overhead | $5,400 per month (includes depreciation of $2,400) |

PRODUCTION FORECASTS

| | *January* | *February* | *March* | *April* | *May* | *June* |
|---|---|---|---|---|---|---|
| Sales in units | 5,175 | 5,430 | 3,880 | 1,295 | 2,590 | 6,470 |
| Units of production | 5,175 | 5,430 | 3,880 | 1,295 | 2,590 | 6,470 |
| Units of material X | 10,350 | 10,860 | 7,760 | 2,590 | 5,180 | 12,940 |
| Units of material Y | 25,875 | 27,150 | 19,400 | 6,475 | 12,950 | 32,350 |
| Direct labor hours | 10,350 | 10,860 | 7,760 | 2,590 | 5,180 | 12,940 |

COSTS OF PRODUCTION

| | *January* | *February* | *March* | *April* | *May* | *June* |
|---|---|---|---|---|---|---|
| Production (units) | 5,175 | 5,430 | 3,880 | 1,295 | 2,590 | 6,470 |
| Material X (units) | 10,350 | 10,860 | 7,760 | 2,590 | 5,180 | 12,940 |
| Cost | $98,325 | $103,170 | $73,720 | $24,605 | $49,210 | $122,930 |
| Material Y (units) | 25,875 | 27,150 | 19,400 | 6,475 | 12,950 | 32,350 |
| Cost | $64,688 | $67,875 | $48,500 | $16,188 | $32,375 | $80,875 |
| Direct labor (hours) | 10,350 | 10,860 | 7,760 | 2,590 | 5,180 | 12,940 |
| Cost | $103,500 | $108,600 | $77,600 | $25,900 | $51,800 | $129,400 |
| Variable overhead | $51,750 | $54,300 | $38,800 | $12,950 | $25,900 | $64,700 |
| Fixed overhead | $5,400 | $5,400 | $5,400 | $5,400 | $5,400 | $5,400 |
| Total costs | $323,663 | $339,345 | $243,020 | $85,043 | $164,685 | $403,305 |
| Disbursement | $321,263 | $336,945 | $240,620 | $82,643 | $162,285 | $400,905 |

changing conditions expected in the coming year, a percentage is developed for every variable expense in the firm. This percentage is applied to the sales forecast to estimate variable costs month by month. Disbursement for these expenses generally is in the month in which they are incurred. Any deviations from this practice should be incorporated into the budget. For example, advertising expense is frequently a variable cost. Advertising may require quarterly payments to an advertising agency. In that case, disbursement should not be forecast in the month in which the expense is incurred.

Fixed expenses are budgeted month by month and are derived from the estimates made for each individual fixed cost. Because these costs frequently follow a disbursement pattern that is different from the month in which they occur, care must be taken to estimate the disbursement properly. For example, property taxes frequently are shown as a monthly expense but paid annually; insurance expense generally is shown as a monthly expense but disbursement occurs in semiannual payments. In addition, some types of fixed costs do not involve cash and therefore should not be shown in the disbursements sections at all. Depreciation is the major cost of this type. Be sure to pay particular attention to taxes. Income taxes frequently are paid on a quarterly basis but because of accounting differences, tax expense may not be the same as cash outflow for taxes. In addition, payroll taxes on employees must be paid quarterly, but are withheld from employee salaries with a matching contribution by the employer on social security taxes. The withholdings generally are shown on a monthly basis, even though the deposit is made quarterly.

Finally, some cash requirements are not expenses and, therefore, have not been budgeted in any of the previous sections. For example, loan payments include interest expense and principal. The interest is an expense, but the principal portion of the payment is not an expense although it does require cash to be paid. The interest expense should have been included in the fixed expense section of the budget. Adjustment for disbursement requires that the interest expense be added back and the full amount of the payment be deducted. If we purchase a long-lived asset of any type, its cost will be spread over a period of years by charging depreciation expense. However, cash outflow will be required at the time of purchase. This obligation has not been captured. Consequently, a final section in the budget is needed to take into consideration transactions that are not expenses but that require cash.

If we prepare a budget that takes all of this into consideration, it will look like Exhibit 7-11. The example assumes known percentages for variable expenses and disbursement for all variable expenses in the month in which they are incurred.

If we total the rows of expense data, then, in addition to showing monthly expense, we will have an estimate of expenses for the year. This information can be used to prepare an income statement for the entire year or any period desired.

## THE CASH FLOW BUDGET

Each of the budgets we discussed has contained a section dealing with cash inflows or cash outflows, because **cash flow** is a vital factor in the life of a business. By combining all of the cash flow data from the previous budgets, we can forecast cash flows for the business on a month-by-month basis. Exhibit 7-12 illustrates a cash flow forecast.

**EXHIBIT 7-11** *Expense Budget for the First Six Months of 1990*

| | *January* | *February* | *March* | *April* | *May* | *June* |
|---|---|---|---|---|---|---|
| Sales forecast | $10,350 | $10,350 | $7,760 | $2,590 | $5,180 | $12,940 |
| Variable expenses: | | | | | | |
| Commissions (3%) | 310 | 310 | 230 | 80 | 155 | 390 |
| Advertising (3%) | 310 | 310 | 230 | 80 | 155 | 390 |
| Freight (1%) | 100 | 100 | 80 | 25 | 50 | 130 |
| Total | 720 | 720 | 540 | 185 | 360 | 910 |
| Disbursements: | | | | | | |
| Advertising | 850 | — | — | 625 | — | — |
| Other variables | 410 | 410 | 310 | 105 | 205 | 520 |
| Total | 1,260 | 410 | 310 | 730 | 205 | 520 |
| Fixed expenses: | | | | | | |
| Salaries | 2,100 | 2,100 | 2,100 | 2,100 | 2,100 | 2,100 |
| Rent | 800 | 800 | 800 | 800 | 800 | 800 |
| Utilities | 300 | 300 | 250 | 250 | 200 | 200 |
| Insurance | 150 | 150 | 150 | 150 | 150 | 150 |
| Depreciation | 500 | 500 | 500 | 500 | 500 | 500 |
| Interest expense | 100 | 100 | 100 | 100 | 100 | 100 |
| Other | 200 | 200 | 200 | 200 | 200 | 200 |
| Total | 4,150 | 4,150 | 4,100 | 4,100 | 4,050 | 4,050 |
| Disbursements: | | | | | | |
| Insurance | 900 | — | — | — | — | — |
| Other fixed | 3,400 | 3,400 | 3,350 | 3,350 | 3,300 | 3,300 |
| (omit depreciation) | | | | | | |
| (omit interest) | | | | | | |
| Cash requirements: | | | | | | |
| Purchase fixtures | — | — | 250 | — | — | — |
| Purchase equipment | — | 2,000 | — | — | — | — |
| Pay income taxes | — | — | — | 3,100 | — | — |
| Loan payments | 180 | 180 | 180 | 180 | 180 | 180 |
| Total | 180 | 2,180 | 430 | 3,280 | 180 | 180 |

The information contained in the cash flow forecast also can be used to generate a pro forma income statement—more about that in a minute. Note how the cash flows are highlighted for both operations and overall. This is because the **operating cash flow** is the cash generated by the day-to-day business. By examining this number separately from the **net cash flow,** which

**EXHIBIT 7-12** *Cash Flow Forecast*

| | *January* | *February* | *March* | *April* | *May* | *June* | *July* | *August* | *September* | *October* | *November* | *December* | *Total* |
|---|---|---|---|---|---|---|---|---|---|---|---|---|---|
| Sales | $10,350 | $10,350 | $7,760 | $2,590 | $ 5,180 | $12,940 | $18,110 | $38,810 | $43,990 | $41,400 | $49,160 | $18,110 | $258,750 |
| Cash sales | 3,620 | 3,620 | 2,720 | 910 | 1,810 | 4,530 | 6,340 | 13,580 | 15,400 | 14,490 | 17,210 | 6,340 | 90,570 |
| Credit sales | 6,730 | 6,730 | 5,040 | 1,680 | 3,370 | 8,410 | 11,770 | 25,230 | 28,590 | 26,910 | 31,950 | 11,770 | 168,180 |
| Collections | 20,560 | 11,425 | 7,205 | 5,750 | 3,400 | 2,755 | 5,690 | 9,515 | 17,995 | 25,325 | 26,915 | 29,025 | 165,560 |
| Cash inflows | 24,180 | 15,045 | 9,925 | 6,660 | 5,210 | 7,285 | 12,030 | 23,095 | 33,395 | 39,815 | 44,125 | 35,365 | $256,130 |
| Cost of goods sold | 7,245 | 7,245 | 5,430 | 1,810 | 3,630 | 9,060 | 12,680 | 27,170 | 30,790 | 28,980 | 34,410 | 12,680 | 181,130 |
| Ending inventory | 9,960 | 6,335 | 3,625 | 8,160 | 15,400 | 26,265 | 42,565 | 45,280 | 46,185 | 40,750 | 16,845 | 12,495 | — |
| Beginning inventory | 10,870 | 9,960 | 6,335 | 3,625 | 8,160 | 15,400 | 26,265 | 42,565 | 45,280 | 46,185 | 40,750 | 16,845 | — |
| Purchases | 6,335 | 3,620 | 2,720 | 6,345 | 10,870 | 19,925 | 28,980 | 29,885 | 31,695 | 23,545 | 10,505 | 8,330 | 182,755 |
| Cash outflows | 7,250 | 6,335 | 3,620 | 2,720 | 6,345 | 10,870 | 19,925 | 28,980 | 29,885 | 31,695 | 23,545 | 10,505 | 181,675 |
| Variable expense | 720 | 720 | 540 | 185 | 360 | 910 | 1,265 | 2,715 | 3,080 | 2,900 | 3,440 | 1,265 | 18,100 |
| Cash outflows | 1,260 | 410 | 310 | 730 | 205 | 520 | 3,750 | 1,550 | 1,760 | 4,915 | 1,965 | 725 | 18,100 |
| Fixed expenses | 4,150 | 4,150 | 4,100 | 4,100 | 4,050 | 4,050 | 4,000 | 4,050 | 4,050 | 4,100 | 4,100 | 4,100 | 49,000 |
| Cash outflows | 4,300 | 3,400 | 3,350 | 3,350 | 3,300 | 3,300 | 4,150 | 3,300 | 3,300 | 3,350 | 3,350 | 3,350 | 41,800 |
| Total cash out | 12,810 | 10,145 | 7,280 | 6,800 | 9,850 | 14,690 | 27,825 | 33,830 | 34,945 | 39,960 | 28,860 | 14,580 | 241,575 |
| Operating cash flow | 11,370 | 4,900 | 2,645 | (140) | (4,640) | (7,405) | (15,795) | (10,735) | (1,550) | (145) | 15,265 | 20,785 | 14,555 |
| Other cash needs | 180 | 2,180 | 430 | 3,280 | 180 | 180 | 180 | 180 | 180 | 230 | 230 | 230 | 7,660 |
| Net cash flow | $11,190 | $2,720 | $2,215 | $(3,420) | $(4,820) | $(7,585) | $(15,975) | $(10,915) | $(1,730) | $(375) | $15,035 | $20,555 | $ 6,895 |

includes all cash transactions, we get a feel for the firm's ability to support itself.

The forecast also showed negative cash flows for a significant period. Negative cash flows are not unusual. In fact, almost every business with any seasonality in its sales pattern will have negative cash flows. How can a business survive such flows? Obviously, it must obtain the cash necessary to continue functioning until the positive flows begin. The only source for such funds is money the firm has saved to cover its needs or money borrowed from a bank on a short-term basis. Because of limited capital, most small businesses try to cover their negative flows with bank loans.

To the cash flow forecast we must add information about the cash held in the business. Cash is held in the form of checking accounts, cash drawers, or savings accounts. A minimum level of cash should always be maintained. Cash must be held to cover the operational needs of the business and provide a safety cushion in the event of unforeseen problems. Some businesses also hold a certain level of cash for speculative purposes; an opportunity to make a large purchase of inventory at favorable prices might occur if cash is available. Every business should establish a minimum level of cash to keep on hand at all times. Once this is done a cash budget can be prepared using the cash flow forecast.

If we assume that cash shortages will be made up by advances against a line of credit at the bank and that the credit will be repaid out of excess cash, then we can proceed. The beginning cash on hand figure comes from the records or from a previous forecast. Exhibit 7-13 displays an example of a cash budget using the data from the cash flow forecast in the previous example. Interest on the line of credit is assumed to be 12% per year or 1% per month and the desired minimum cash level is $5,000.

The cash budget shows not only coverage of negative cash flows but when large excess cash flows will occur. This permits a manager to plan for the investment of excess funds as well as arrange coverage for cash shortfalls. The **cash budget** is an outstanding device to support loans and lines of credit with your bank. Bankers are much more inclined to handle the short-term needs of a business when a cash budget has been prepared to show when those needs will occur and when the advances can be repaid. In addition, the cash budget permits a manager to proact: plan in advance, rather than to react to a situation when it occurs. All of the effort expended in the budgetary process is easily justified by the cash budget, which is an essential managerial tool.

## PRO FORMA STATEMENTS

The budgets discussed contain all the information required to prepare a pro forma income statement and balance sheet for the business. All that is needed in addition is the preceding year's financial statement.

**EXHIBIT 7-13** *Cash Budget*

| | *January* | *February* | *March* | *April* | *May* | *June* | *July* | *August* | *September* | *October* | *November* | *December* |
|---|---|---|---|---|---|---|---|---|---|---|---|---|
| Net cash flow | $11,190 | $ 2,720 | $ 2,215 | $(3,420) | $(4,820) | $(7,585) | $(15,975) | $(10,915) | $(1,730) | $(375) | $15,035 | $20,555 |
| Beginning cash | 5,900 | 17,090 | 19,810 | 22,025 | 18,605 | 13,785 | 6,200 | 5,025 | 5,010 | 5,080 | 5,005 | 5,004 |
| *Plus* net cash flow | 11,190 | 2,720 | 2,215 | (3,420) | (4,820) | (7,585) | (15,975) | (10,915) | (1,730) | (375) | 15,035 | 20,555 |
| Subtotal | 17,090 | 19,810 | 22,025 | 18,605 | 13,785 | 6,200 | (9,775) | (5,890) | 3,280 | 4,705 | 20,040 | 25,559 |
| Loans | — | — | — | — | — | — | 14,800 | 10,900 | 1,800 | 300 | — | — |
| Repayments | — | — | — | — | — | — | — | — | — | — | 13,800 | 14,000 |
| Interest | — | — | — | — | — | — | — | — | — | — | 1,236[a] | 686[b] |
| Ending cash | 17,090 | 19,810 | 22,025 | 18,605 | 13,785 | 6,200 | 5,025 | 5,010 | 5,080 | 5,005 | 5,004 | 10,873 |
| Loan balance | — | — | — | — | — | — | $14,800 | $25,700 | $27,500 | $27,800 | $14,000 | — |

[a] $14,800 × .01 × 5 months + $10,900 × .01 × 4 months + $1,800 × .01 × 3 months + $300 × .01 × 2 months = $1,236
[b] $1,000 × .01 × 6 months + $10,900 × .01 × 5 months + $1,800 × .01 × 4 months + $300 × .01 × 3 months = $686
Total $1,922

The **income statement** can be projected from the sales budget, the purchases or production budget, and the expense budget. The cash budget is needed for interest expense. The income statement in Exhibit 7-14 is a composite of the previous budgets.

Preparing a pro forma balance sheet requires last year's statement. The changes made in asset and liability accounts will show on the various budgets. Every budget will be involved and numbers from each will be required to complete the balance sheet. Exhibit 7-15 shows a balance sheet incorporating information from the operating budgets displayed in previous examples. The balance sheet for 1989 is the actual historic statement from the firm's records. The balance sheet for 1990 is a pro forma statement.

We now have completed the coverage of all the operational budgets. At this point, the process of preparing these budgets and reviewing and modifying

**EXHIBIT 7-14** *Pro Forma Income Statement for 1990*

| | | | |
|---|---|---|---|
| Sales | | | $258,750 |
| Cost of goods sold | | | 181,130 |
| Gross profit | | | 77,620 |
| Selling expenses: | | | |
| Commissions | 7,760 | | |
| Advertising | 7,760 | | |
| Freight | 2,580 | | |
| Total | | 18,100 | |
| Administrative expenses: | | | |
| Salaries | 25,200 | | |
| Rent | 9,600 | | |
| Utilities | 2,800 | | |
| Insurance | 1,800 | | |
| Depreciation | 6,000 | | |
| Interest expense | 1,200 | | |
| Other | 2,400 | | |
| Total | | 49,000 | |
| Interest on line of credit | | 1,922 | |
| Total expenses | | | 69,022 |
| Income before taxes | | | $ 8,598 |
| Income taxes | | | 3,100 |
| Net income | | | $ 5,498 |

**EXHIBIT 7-15** *Pro Forma Balance Sheet*

| | 12/31/89 | 12/31/90 |
|---|---|---|
| Assets: | | |
| Cash[a] | $ 5,900 | $10,873 |
| Accounts receivable[b] | 29,770 | 32,390 |
| Inventory[c] | 10,870 | 12,495 |
| Total current assets | 46,540 | 55,758 |
| Equipment and fixtures[d] | 19,000 | 21,400 |
| Accumulated depreciation[e] | (6,500) | (12,500) |
| Net investment in equipment | 12,500 | 8,750 |
| Total assets | $59,040 | $64,658 |
| Liabilities: | | |
| Accounts payable[f] | 7,250 | 8,330 |
| Notes payable[g] | 13,200 | 12,240 |
| Total liabilities | 20,450 | 20,570 |
| Stockholders' equity: | | |
| Capital stock | 15,000 | 15,000 |
| Retained earnings | 23,590 | 23,590 |
| 1990 income[h] | — | 5,498 |
| Total stockholders' equity | 38,590 | 44,088 |
| Total liabilities and net worth | $59,040 | $64,658 |

[a] Ending cash balance for December from cash budget.
[b] Accounts receivable balance from sales budget.
[c] Ending inventory balance for December from purchases budget.
[d] Equipment of $2,000 and fixtures of $250 shown purchased on expense budget during the first half of 1990; $150 of fixtures purchased in the second half of 1990 as shown by the increase in other cash requirements on cash budget.
[e] Depreciation of $6,000 from pro forma income statement.
[f] Accounts payable balance from purchases budget.
[g] Notes payable reduced by $80 principal payment each month for 12 months. The loan payments shown on expense budget were $180 per month; the interest expense was $100 per month; meaning that $80 per month was a principal payment.
[h] Income from pro forma income statement.

them each month probably seems like an overwhelming task—especially for the owner of a small business who also is beset with daily operational issues! True, the monthly maintenance can be time consuming, but these budgets constitute planning activities. Their use can make the difference between a business that fails or is only moderately successful and one that is dynamic and vibrant. There is no substitute for planning!

Fortunately, there are automated systems that can take much of the pain out of the budgeting process. Microcomputer spreadsheets are ideal for the preparation of the budgets discussed in this chapter. They can make modification each month a quick, easy task. In Chapter 9, we will discuss some of these spreadsheets and the benefits they can provide.

## CAPITAL BUDGETING

The final area of budgeting we need to discuss is **capital budgeting,** or planning for major purchases. The long-lived assets of a business, frequently referred to as plant assets, are a major factor in the health of the business. This especially is true for a manufacturing firm or other business that requires a large investment in plant assets. Service firms that have a minor investment in plant assets can use capital budgeting techniques to analyze projects or contracts. The principles are the same whether we are dealing with a machine or with a project. In each case, capital budgeting techniques are used to analyze cash inflows and outflows associated with a decision and to project the benefit a business can expect from an investment.

### Return on Investment

**Return on investment** (ROI) probably is the best-known phrase in the world of finance. It actually is a collection of tools used to compare the cash flows associated with a particular investment over time. The investment may be the purchase of a machine, the opening of a store or territory, production of a new product, agreement to perform certain services, or any of an almost unlimited variety of business decisions.

An easy ROI technique is the **payback method,** which simply requires that we add up all the costs associated with an investment and divide the total by the annual revenues associated with the investment. The result is the number of years required to recoup the initial investment. This method really is quite crude and limited. It can be used only with investments that require cash outlay at the beginning and it fails to take into consideration the time value of money. The **average rate of return** method cures the first problem but not the second. To find the average rate of return, we simply calculate the average cost or investment per year, calculate the average revenues or returns per year, and divide the first number by the second. This still ignores the time value issue, however. Money clearly has a time value; a dollar today is worth more than a dollar to be received next year, because if you had the dollar today you could invest it and earn a return during the year. Consequently, any really viable ROI tool should take time value into consideration.

## Present Value

Several ROI methods use present value techniques to allow for the time value of money. **Present value techniques** are simply methods that take into consideration the amount of interest money can earn over time. Exhibit 7-16 displays present values for a sum. The exhibit gives the present value of $1 received at the end of 1 year, 2 years, up to 5 years at various interest rates. For example, the exhibit indicates that $1 due at the end of 5 years is worth $.476 if money can be invested to earn 16% per year. The exhibit is prepared by finding the inverse of the future value. If $1 were invested at 16% per year for 5 years, it would earn $.16 the first year and be worth $1.16. It would earn $.186 the second year because of compounding and be worth $1.346; $.215 the third year; and so on. The exhibit is designed to show how much money would have to be invested now at a specified interest rate in order to accumulate $1 at the end of a given time.

Because the exhibit is set for $1, we can find the present value of any sum by multiplying by the number of dollars involved. The present value of $450 due in 2 years at 14% is $346.05, (.769 × $450 = $346.05). The exhibit shows periods; that is, the number of compounding periods. The interest rate must be expressed in the same terms. For example, if interest is compounded quarterly, then there will be four periods per year. An investment lasting 2 years will then take up eight periods. The interest rate must be expressed in quarters as well. If the annual rate is 12%, the quarterly rate is 3%.

If we have repeated payments of equal amounts, then we are dealing with an **annuity**. Loans and leases are examples of annuities. Any series of equal payments at equal time intervals is an annuity. Finding the present value of a series of payments using the present value exhibit would be laborious, but tables have been developed especially for annuities. Exhibit 7-17 is a present value table for annuities.

**EXHIBIT 7-16** *Present Value of One Dollar at Various Interest Rates*

| NO. OF PERIODS | 10% | 12% | 14% | 16% | 18% | 20% |
|---|---|---|---|---|---|---|
| 1 | .909 | .893 | .877 | .862 | .847 | .833 |
| 2 | .826 | .797 | .769 | .743 | .718 | .694 |
| 3 | .751 | .712 | .675 | .641 | .609 | .579 |
| 4 | .683 | .636 | .592 | .552 | .516 | .482 |
| 5 | .621 | .567 | .519 | .476 | .437 | .402 |

**EXHIBIT 7-17** *Present Value of an Annuity of One Dollar at Various Interest Rates*

| NO. OF PAYMENTS | 10% | 12% | 14% | 16% | 18% | 20% |
|---|---|---|---|---|---|---|
| 1 | .909 | .893 | .877 | .862 | .847 | .833 |
| 2 | 1.736 | 1.690 | 1.647 | 1.605 | 1.566 | 1.528 |
| 3 | 2.487 | 2.402 | 2.322 | 2.246 | 2.174 | 2.106 |
| 4 | 3.170 | 3.037 | 2.914 | 2.798 | 2.690 | 2.589 |
| 5 | 3.791 | 3.605 | 3.433 | 3.274 | 3.127 | 2.991 |

The annuity table is used by multiplying the amount of the payment by the appropriate factor for time and interest rate. For example, $1,250 due annually for 5 years at 12% would be worth $4,506, (3.605 × $1,250 = $4,506.25). In other words, an investment of $4,506 today at 12% would permit you to withdraw $1,250 each year for five years. The exhibit shows number of payments, which must be stated in the same terms as the interest rate. This means that for monthly payments we must convert the interest rate to a monthly basis. If the annual interest rate is 12%, then the monthly interest rate is 1%; if the annual rate is 18%, then the monthly rate is 1.5%.

Using tables for calculating present values is simple, but a book of tables large enough to cover all of the possibilities would be quite large indeed. A calculator can be used if it has the capability to do powers and the formulas that follow. It is just as easy to calculate future values, or the amounts that will accumulate over time at interest using formulas and a calculator. Note that each formula has an exponent, which means that the sum within parentheses must be raised to a power. When selecting a calculator, be sure it has the ability to handle powers.

*Present value formula:*

$$P = \frac{A}{(1 + i)^n}$$

*where:*

P = Present value
A = Amount to be received
i = Interest rate per compounding period
n = Number of compounding periods

*Future value formula:*

$$A = P(1 + i)^n$$

*where:*

$P$ = Present value
$A$ = Amount to be received or future value
$i$ = Interest rate per compounding period
$n$ = Number of compounding periods

*Present value of an annuity formula:*

$$P_a = R\left[\frac{1 - 1/(1+i)^n}{i}\right]$$

*where:*

$P_a$ = Present value of the annuity
$R$ = Amount of periodic payment
$i$ = Interest rate per period
$n$ = Number of compounding periods

*Future value of an annuity formula:*

$$A_a = R\left[\frac{(1+i)^n - 1}{i}\right]$$

*where:*

$A_a$ = Future value of the annuity
$R$ = Amount of periodic payment
$i$ = Interest rate per period
$n$ = Number of compounding periods

Using the formulas is simple: simply plug the numbers into a calculator. Just remember always to express the interest rate in the same terms as the periods. If *n* is expressed in years, then *i* should be an annual rate; if *n* is months, then *i* should be a monthly rate; and so forth. Exhibit 7-18 displays an example of the use of present values in a capital budgeting decision.

The example calculates a net present value (NPV), which is the difference between the present value of the inflows and the present value of the outflows. Because the outflow in this example takes place at the beginning, it is already in the correct time frame and therefore a present value. The inflows take place over a 5 year period and form an annuity. We need to calculate a present value for the inflows. The NPV is the difference between the two numbers. The NPV is negative; therefore, the machine should not be purchased. Had the NPV been positive, purchasing the machine would have been advisable, at least from a financial perspective.

Note that the example in Exhibit 7-18 does not consider income taxes. If we reexamine the purchase decision after tax, it might change our viewpoint. The machine not only will save salary expenses, it will create depreciation charges that reduce income taxes. If the machine is depreciated on a straight-line basis over 5 years with no salvage value, then it will produce \$5,000 per year

**EXHIBIT 7-18** *Present Value Illustration*

*Consider the purchase of a machine with a cost of \$25,000 and a life of 5 years. It will save \$6,000 per year in labor costs. Money is worth 15%. Cash inflow of \$6,000 per year for 5 years is an annuity.*

$$P_a = R\left[\frac{1 - 1/(1+i)^n}{i}\right]$$

$$P_a = \$6{,}000\left[\frac{1 - 1/(1+.15)^5}{.15}\right]$$

$$P_a = \$6{,}000 \times 3.352$$

$$P_a = \$20{,}112$$

*The cash outflow is \$25,000 payable at purchase. The net present value, or the difference between outflows and inflows, is as follows.*

$$NPV = \$20{,}112 - \$25{,}000$$

$$NPV = (\$4{,}888)$$

in depreciation charges. If we are paying 25% in taxes, then the depreciation will save \$1,250 in taxes each year (\$5,000 × .25 = \$1,250). Unfortunately, this is not enough. We currently are paying \$6,000 per year in wages, which save us \$1,500 in taxes (\$6,000 × .25), and this will disappear if we buy the machine. Consequently, the after-tax savings of the machine will be \$6,000 + \$1,250 − \$1,500 or \$5,750. Clearly, the NPV will be even less after tax. Nevertheless, taxes can make a difference in capital budgeting decisions and should always be taken into consideration.

The NPV calculation is sensitive to the estimates for interest rates as well as term and cash flows. Errors in any of these will affect the NPV. For any significant investment decision, you should calculate a range of NPVs using various estimates for interest rate, cash flow, and term. This will demonstrate how sensitive the NPV is to changes in any of the factors and provide a range of estimates for use in the decision.

## Internal Rate of Return

Another ROI method that takes into consideration the time value of money is the **internal rate of return** (IRR). In essence, the present value formulas are used to find an interest rate that will produce an NPV of zero. To make the calculation, a trial-and-error process is used. You calculate the NPV using various interest rates, raising or lowering the rate each time, until you find the rate at which the NPV is zero. This rate is called the *IRR*. It can be a laborious process if performed manually, but many of the more sophisticated calculators and most microcomputer spreadsheets are capable of making the calculations for you. Once an IRR has been determined, the decision to go ahead with the investment is based on whether the return is acceptable to the firm. Obviously, the higher the rate, the higher the benefit to the firm from a financial perspective.

## Nonquantifiable Factors

Whether you use the NPV or IRR method to evaluate a capital budgeting problem, you should be aware that many factors will not be quantifiable; that is, a dollar value cannot be calculated to show the impact on the firm. For example, a machine being considered may show a negative NPV or an extremely low IRR but might have the capacity to increase the quality of goods produced. How can you value an increase in quality? You cannot, but clearly there will be some influence! There are many such factors for any capital investment decision, and they always must be taken into consideration on a subjective basis. Otherwise, computers could replace managers! These factors do not mean that NPVs and IRRs should not be calculated, but simply that these methods are only one aspect of the decision.

Sometimes certain factors can force a project to be undertaken regardless of its NPV. Governmental regulations a few years ago were frequently applied to firms accused of polluting the environment. Those firms were forced to acquire expensive equipment to reduce pollution. Other firms voluntarily acquired pollution control devices out of a sense of civic duty.

Risk is a very real, but difficult to assess, aspect of any capital budgeting decision. What are the probabilities that the projected revenues or cost savings actually will materialize? Will shifts in the marketplace or in competitive situations make an investment worthless? Not only are the probabilities for identifiable risks impossible to calculate, it is difficult to even list all of the factors that can go wrong in a particular investment. Many large firms use sophisticated models to forecast probabilities in an attempt to quantify risk elements. Regardless of their sophistication, all such models require a large portion of human judgement. No one has ever developed a method of assessing risk objectively. Nevertheless, it is real, and you must take it into consideration on any capital investment decision. The only aid we can offer is the old cliche "risk and return are related." If you are examining an investment with a large return, chances are that its risk is higher than would be the case for an investment with a lower return. Does that sound like common sense? Most things in business come down to that.

## LEASE OR BUY?

The final topic we want to discuss is the lease or purchase decision. In capital budgeting decisions, the lease or buy issue is an important one. In general, it costs more to lease or rent an asset than to buy it, because the owner of the asset is making a profit on the lease. Because the entirety of lease payments can be tax deductible, it is possible for individuals or firms in high tax brackets to come out better with a lease than a purchase. Small businesses seldom are in such tax brackets. Consequently, for the vast majority of small firms, leasing is a more expensive option.

That doesn't mean that leasing should not be considered for a small business. It can have major advantages, such as the reduction or elimination of initial costs. Almost anything you buy must have a down payment, frequently 20% or more, in order for a bank to consider financing. Most leasing plans require, at most, two payments in advance. For a small business with limited resources this can be a major factor!

Another factor that favors leasing is the credit strength of the firm. Leasing companies, because they are obtaining larger returns, frequently have lower standards than a bank for a loan of the same amount: they are willing to accept a higher risk. This means that it is possible for a small business to obtain a lease for an asset when a bank would refuse to loan the money to buy it.

The term of a lease can be an advantage. This is especially true when a building is involved. If you buy a building and the location turns out to be less favorable than you thought, you may have a difficult time selling it. If you lease a building, you are locked in for the term of the lease, but moving at the end of the lease is a simple process. Term advantage may not exist for equipment and machinery. Most firms offering leases on these assets desire terms that will ensure that they recoup their investment in the asset fully. This means that lease terms are frequently similar to loan terms and are noncancelable. This is especially true for equipment that has limited sales appeal such as heavy machinery or machines that are subject to technological obsolescence such as computers.

Finally, if a lease is properly structured, it will not show on the balance sheet of a business. This is called **off balance sheet financing** and permits a business to acquire assets without damaging its ability to borrow in the future. This is a sensitive issue and many leases will not qualify for such treatment. Many leases, called **financing leases,** are structured in such a fashion that the transaction is closer to a loan than a lease. Accounting principles require leases of this type to be shown on the balance sheet exactly as though they were loans. Consequently, if you are considering a lease for this reason, it is mandatory to obtain advice from a CPA before entering into the lease.

While we have been dealing primarily with the lease or buy decision as it relates to capital budgeting, we might also mention that operating leases are also a consideration for small businesses. As we have indicated, capital budgeting addresses the purchase of a building, equipment, fixtures, or other major acquisition. Leases can also be important when smaller purchases are made or in short-term need situations. For example, copiers are generally leased to avoid maintenance problems. In addition, a lease may be useful to obtain a specialized machine that will only be required for a single job. In such instances, leasing may well be the only viable option.

The tremendous range of types and terms of leases can confuse the decision. Therefore, any major purchase should be carefully evaluated by a professional in order to obtain the most beneficial structure. Your CPA should be consulted on any transaction of significant size before you enter into a contract.

Breaking a lease can be a serious problem. In general, there is no way out of a lease prior to its expiration except through contractually permitted means without seriously damaging the firm or risking litigation. This means that you should never enter into a lease agreement without a clear understanding of the terms of the contract, especially those terms that relate to early termination. Always be sure that the term is reasonable given your plans for the business.

## SUMMARY

Budgeting is the process of predicting costs, expenses, revenues, cash flows, or investments. Because budgeting is the process of predicting and planning for the future, it is a tool vital to the success of small businesses. Yet, it is one frequently not used because of the time it can consume. The key aspects of financial performance are cash flow and profitability and acquisition and use of long-lived assets. Budgets should be prepared to support the prediction of cash flow, and that information used to produce a pro forma income statement.

Budgets have many other uses. They can be used to formulate the objectives of the company. Based upon a realistic assessment of what objectives are possible, the budget can be designed as a method of quantifying those objectives. Budgets also may serve as controls for comparison purposes. The amount of deviation from a budget is an important bit of information in controlling the assets of a company. Participation in generating the input for a budget is important in itself. People feel "ownership" of those ideas they developed. Beware, however, that slack is not introduced into the budget so that it always will be met. Because a budget is a prediction, it may not always come true. Isolated variances are not automatically bad, however; but continued deviations from the budget should denote problems in budgeting either in the preparation or control and suggest reevaluation.

Forecasting is difficult initially but experience makes the process easier. A continuous budget with month by month evaluation is best. This enables a business to anticipate rather than react to changing conditions.

Sensitivity analysis is the process of examining the effects changes in various components of a budget will have on the overall budget. The process involves calculating the budget using a range of estimates for various factors.

Because the preparation of multiple budgets can be time consuming, an automated approach can be valuable. Spreadsheet programs for microcomputers were designed with sensitivity analysis in mind, so that one quickly can examine the effects various changes can have on the budget.

Sample budgets for sales were introduced, including sales forecasting, credit sales, and accounts receivable and budgets for purchases, production, expense, cash flow, and capital.

Return on investment is a method of comparing the cash flows associated with a particular investment over time. The techniques involved include the payback method, present value, and internal rate of return, each of which has strengths and weaknesses. Nonquantifiable factors and the lease or buy decision also are discussed.

Budgeting is a time consuming task but the value gained by planning for the future cannot be equaled. If you do not want to do the work yourself, hire an accountant with microcomputer knowledge. However, as the owner/manager, you must know what factors are in the budget and be able to evaluate the output. Management truly makes or breaks the business through its decisions. Each manager must plan, staff, direct, control, and supervise the business—and do all these jobs effectively. Budgeting gives a manager the most knowledge, and with knowledge comes success.

## QUESTIONS

1. Why is budgeting important?
2. What are the key aspects of financial performance?
3. How are budgets both objectives and controls?
4. Why is continuous budgeting important?
5. What is *sensitivity analysis,* and when is it used?
6. How are budgets best generated?
7. What is the first step in the budgeting process?
8. Why is the prediction of cash inflow so important to a small business?
9. How does one generate a sales forecast for a new business?
10. What must be captured to generate a sales budget?
11. Why is the knowledge of credit sales important?

12. What must be prepared before a forecast of purchases can be calculated?
13. Why are discounts important to the success of a company?
14. What must be captured to generate a purchases budget?
15. For whom is a production budget important?
16. What are the three components of production?
17. What factors exist for any capital investment decision?
18. Why are some cash disbursements not considered expenses?
19. Can a company ever have a negative cash flow and survive? If so, how?
20. What do pro forma income statements tell you?
21. Which ROI method is the best predictor, and why?
22. Why is budgeting important even to a new business?
23. What are the advantages of buying capital improvements?
24. What are the advantages of leasing capital improvements?
25. Who is ultimately responsible for the success of a small business, and why?

## PROJECT

We have prepared a sales forecast for next year for the Second Venture. Credit is extended on 30-day terms; 10% of sales are for cash; 50% of credit sales are collected in the month following the sale; 30% are collected during the second month following the sale; and 10% are received in the third month following the sale. Prepare a cash collections forecast for the first six months of the new year.

| | | |
|---|---|---|
| October Sales | | $ 13,000 |
| November Sales | | 25,500 |
| December Sales | | 37,000 |
| Sales Forecast: | | |
| January | 5.0% | $ 12,500 |
| February | 4.0 | 10,000 |
| March | 4.5 | 11,250 |
| April | 6.5 | 16,250 |
| May | 9.5 | 23,750 |
| June | 10.0 | 25,000 |
| July | 11.5 | 28,750 |
| August | 8.5 | 21,250 |
| September | 7.5 | 18,750 |
| October | 6.0 | 15,000 |
| November | 11.5 | 28,750 |
| December | 15.5 | 38,750 |
| Total | 100.0 | $250,000 |

36,000 PPE

Inventory is purchased on 30-day terms and generally is paid for in the month following the month of purchase. The gross profit margin is expected to average 30% next year, and we plan to have enough inventory on hand at all times to cover the next two months' sales. Ending inventory at 12/31 last year was $15,500. Prepare a forecast of cash outflows for purchases for the first six months of the new year.

Advertising is planned to be 3% of sales and will be paid for in the month incurred. ~~Salaries and wages are fixed at $5,000 per month. Rent is $500 per month and utilities are expected to be fixed at $150 per month.~~ Insurance payments of $250 will be due in March and June and income tax deposits of $400 must be made in January and April. Depreciation of $300 will be charged each month and loan payments of $290 will be due each month. Prepare a forecast of cash outflows for expenses for the first six months.

60/40 prin/int 20,000 init. 3600 In. 2000 will be interest 10%

We plan to keep a minimum of $5,000 in the bank account at all times and the balance at the end of December last year was $5,500. Prepare a complete cash flow forecast predicting amounts of excess cash and cash needs for each of the first six months of the new year.

# CASE

Dan Merchant of Merchant's Office Furniture was upset. He had just talked with the bank again this morning and they were getting more and more adamant about his financial difficulties. The young banker that he had talked with was fairly new with the bank and not his usual contact. Bud Rice had been a friend of Dan's family for years and had handled many potential disasters, but he had retired six months ago and now Dan was really getting tired of the business.

Orville Merchant, Dan's father, had also retired but was keeping a hand in by doing much of the inventory ordering. This in itself was a problem because Orville's taste ran to the much older styles popular thirty years ago, and so much of the inventory on hand was not what customers desired. In order to satisfy customers' needs, merchandise had to be specially ordered while the store accumulated more inventory than it could handle and it was not able to sell.

Dan had been uneasy for the last six months. He knew that although the warehouse and store were full, more inventory was arriving monthly. The difficulty was that he was unable to meet the floor-plan agreement with the bank. Floor-plan agreements usually involve a fixed-term loan in which the bank loans 100 percent of the money needed for purchasing inventory, but the bank expects the loans to be repaid in some stated period such as 90 days. This is the methodology used by retailers of large expensive items such as cars, mobile homes, trucks, boats, and furniture. This was a method that was good for both the bank and the retailer as a rule unless the retailer failed to turn over the inventory purchased under such a plan. Banks can even understand that retailers might have trouble occasionally in meeting their requirements, but when the failure is consistent, the bank stands to lose as well.

With Bud, Orville had just called up the bank and asked for a signature loan for 30 days and had covered the floor-plan agreement when he experienced what he called a "short fall." But with both men retired, it had fallen to Dan to handle the financial end of the business and "cronyism" was no longer possible. Even Bud, before his retirement, had tried to talk to Dan about the issue of curtailments. Curtailments are floor-plan repayments that result when inventory does not sell within the specified period. If the furniture sells, then the proceeds of the sale usually cover a reduction of the floor plan and include some profit as well. Yet when the sale does not occur, the payment must be made anyway, and the money comes from another source within the company or is borrowed.

This is the problem Dan is facing now. Far too many items are requiring curtailment, and this is placing a growing burden on the company and driving up fears in the bank. The young banker has offered to work with Dan or to help him find a financial consultant to help him to eliminate his curtailments before it is too late. What can be done?

## Questions

1. What are the financial difficulties faced by the Merchant Office Furniture company?
2. What are the personal difficulties faced by Dan Merchant? What can he do about them?
3. What tools can Dan use to help him get a better financial picture of just how the company is doing?
4. What specific methods might be used to help Dan resolve the issue of excessive inventory?
5. In what ways does Dan's problem relate to the tools explained in this or other chapters?

# CHAPTER 8

# Financial Analysis for Success

**LEARNING OBJECTIVES**

After completing this chapter, you should be able to

- Explain what financial analysis is and why it is valuable to small business management.
- Describe the techniques of financial analysis, their strengths and weaknesses.
- List the areas of financial performance that financial analysis is used to evaluate.
- Explain how financial analysis fits into the month-end planning and budgeting process.
- Perform a financial analysis.
- Use financial analysis to evaluate the effectiveness of past decisions and actions.
- Use financial analysis to guide development of changes in operations and policies.
- Use financial analysis in the development of new budgets, forecasts, and plans.

One of the best and least understood tools of management is financial **analysis.** The **financial position** of a firm at any point in time is a result of the actions and decisions made by its owners/managers. Consequently, financial analysis provides a "report card" for management, a method for evaluating how well or poorly management has performed. Perhaps the primary reason that financial analysis is used so infrequently by small business owners is the difficulty of self-evaluation. None of us likes to hear criticism or to admit failure. But management, like medicine, is not an exact science. In actuality, there are no right or wrong decisions: some decisions are simply better than others. **Financial analysis** is a tool for evaluating the results of decisions. It provides a device for determining what was done well in the past and what to do differently in the future. It can demonstrate strengths and weaknesses in a firm.

Financial analysis should be an underlying support for planning activities. Planning that does not take into consideration financial strengths and weaknesses, that does not incorporate the effects of past planning activities, is not really planning at all. It is simply hoping: hoping that things will proceed as desired, which is a poor substitute for the truth.

Financial analysis is a device for determining the truth about the firm. That truth is found by examining things as they really are, not by believing what we would prefer things to be or what they appear to be. In this chapter we will discuss the basics of financial analysis. We will present the processes of ratio analysis and trend analysis and talk about industry averages. The focus will be on using financial analysis to support management decision making.

## TECHNIQUES OF FINANCIAL ANALYSIS

The **financial statement,** as we discussed in Chapter 4, consists of the income statement, balance sheet, reconciliation of net worth, and statement of changes in financial position. These reports are the chief indicators of financial performance over the past year. In addition, interim income statements and interim balance sheets should be prepared at the end of each month, because they are valuable additions to financial feedback. These statements can tell a great deal about the financial well-being of a company. However, much of the information contained in the statements is not readily visible. Analysis is required to learn the maximum amount from them. This is what financial analysis is all about.

In Chapter 5, we displayed various managerial statements that contain percentages for the various items on the statement. This avoids the confusion that typically follows when dollar levels are examined. It is called **component percentage analysis** and provides a methodology for examining the relative relationship among items on a statement and over time. Generally, this is the starting place for financial analysis.

The best-known technique for detailed examination of the financial statements is **ratio analysis.** Various items from various statements are divided by one another to yield a ratio, which may be expressed as numbers or percentages. These numbers can then be used to evaluate various aspects of financial position, by showing the relative relationships among items and over time.

An aspect of financial analysis frequently overlooked because it is so obvious is **trend analysis.** This simply involves comparing component percentages and ratios to those for previous periods. The longer the time period, the better the trends in items can be identified. Trend analysis is a particularly revealing analytic tool, but it requires a greater understanding of the relationship among the items on the statements.

**Industry comparison,** another well-known aspect of financial analysis, involves comparing ratios and component percentages to averages compiled from other firms in the same industry. It is a very dangerous tool in financial analysis because it leads to absolute conclusions: either a number is better or worse than the industry average and therefore good or bad. In fact, the term **industry norm** frequently is heard when talking about industry averages. Actually, there is no normal or standard ratio for any business. Furthermore, there is no way to obtain true averages of ratios and percentages. For 2 years, one of the authors served on the Robert Morris Associates Statement Studies Committee, an association of commercial banking officers that publishes a book of industry averages each year. The financial statements used to prepare the averages were obtained from member banks in the association. Unfortunately, human nature affects the process. Specifically, some banks submit statements only from the financially strong customers because the officers do not want to admit that they have made loans to weak firms. Some people think that the vast majority of the statements submitted for compilation have been subjected to such screening either deliberately or unconsciously by the officers. Also, only firms who were borrowing from the banks were included in the sample, and you can see how the averages would be skewed.

Many industry associations also compile averages. These, too, are beset with problems because the source of data is from members. Not only is the membership of the association not necessarily representative of all of the firms in that industry, but financial statements are obtained from the members on a voluntary basis. Again, human nature will prevent most of the weaker firms from submitting their statements. Dun and Bradstreet industry averages are similarly skewed because the sample from which the averages are prepared tend to be the stronger firms. Another problem with the averages is the classification of the firms themselves. In reality few firms are identical to others classified in the same industry. The firms differ in size as well as markets, products, and strategic postures. We have talked at great length about the differences in firms that result from the posture chosen by their managements. Industry averages attempt to incorporate these postures into the classification scheme but, due to the great variety of approaches, the averages are flawed.

All of this is not to say that industry averages should not be used in financial analysis. They should be used whenever possible, because they add more information. However, they should not be considered the only tool in the analysis or the most important. They are simply another piece of evidence. So long as you keep in mind that a deviation from an industry average is not automatically good or bad, they can be quite useful. They can give you a feel for how the stronger firms with similar competitive environments are performing and how your company compares.

The techniques of component percentages, ratio analysis, trend analysis, and industry comparison are collectively called **financial analysis.** None is used in isolation. As we discuss analysis, we will talk about information gleaned from all of those sources at once because they support each other during evaluation. In other words, the evaluation of financial data involves examining the results of all these techniques.

## FINANCIAL PERFORMANCE

Generally four areas of financial performance are of interest when examining the financial well-being of a firm:

1. *Liquidity:* The ability of a firm to meet its maturing obligations.
2. *Activity:* The effective utilization of a firm's assets.
3. *Leverage:* The appropriateness of a firm's debt level and its ability to handle that debt.
4. *Profitability:* The cost-revenue relationships of a firm.

We will talk about each of these areas separately and then discuss the overall evaluation of a business.

### Liquidity

**Liquidity** refers to a firm's ability to meet its maturing obligations. These are the debts that must be paid within the next year. We say that a firm is liquid if it can handle its short-term debts without difficulty. The best-known measure of liquidity is the **current ratio,** which is calculated by dividing the current assets by the current liabilities. Remember that current liabilities are those that must be paid within 1 year, and current assets consist of cash and other assets that are expected to be converted to cash within 1 year, such as accounts receivable and inventory. If we had $10,000 in current assets and $5,000 in current liabilities, the current ratio would be 2, (10,000/5,000 = 2). This ratio tells us that the firm has twice as many current assets as are normally required to cover existing current liabilities. Another ratio, sometimes used by firms with high inventory levels to measure liquidity, is the **quick ratio,** which is calculated by subtracting inventory from total current assets and dividing the result by current liabilities. This ratio, sometimes called the **acid test,** is an indication of how easily a firm can meet its existing obligations if it is unable to sell any of its inventory.

Numerous ratios can be used in the evaluation of liquidity. For example, the **inventory liquidation ratio** can be calculated for firms with high inventory levels. It is found by subtracting "quick assets," such as cash and accounts receivable, from current liabilities. The result is divided by inventory and expressed as a percentage. It tells us what proportion of inventory must be sold to cover maturing obligations. It can be especially useful when compared to an activity ratio for inventory movement.

Many ratios are specific to one industry; that is, special ratios are developed for particular industries. This is true for liquidity as for all other categories. For example, banks and finance companies are dependent upon the collection of their loan portfolios for liquidity. Consequently, the **loan liquidation ratio** is an important one. This ratio represents the average collection period of various categories of loans. It is calculated from information not included in the financial statements and represents the ratio between the total amount of principal payments received during a period to the average amount of loans outstanding during that period.

## Activity

**Activity** refers to the utilization of a firm's assets. A firm that normally extends 30-day terms to its customers would expect its accounts receivable to turn over twelve times per year if all of its customers paid their bills on time. Of course, all the bills are not paid on time, and having a large part of a firm's resources tied up in accounts receivable is expensive. A measure of how effectively accounts receivable are being managed is the calculation of the actual **accounts receivable turnover.** Dividing total credit sales by the average amount of accounts receivable yields the ratio. If a firm had $100,000 of sales on credit and an average of $10,000 in accounts receivable, then the accounts receivable turnover would be 10, (100,000/10,000 = 10). If we wished to examine the turnover in terms of days, we could divide the factor into 360, (360/10 = 36) and find that on the average our customers pay their bills in 36 days. That would be a fantastic collection rate if our terms were 30-days, but a poor collection rate if our terms were to require payment within 7 days. Consequently, the **accounts receivable collection period** must be compared to a firm's credit terms in order to be of value.

Another asset of extreme importance to many firms is inventory. The turnover period for inventory can be calculated to aid in measuring how well this asset is being managed. The **inventory turnover** can be found by dividing the total cost of goods sold by the average inventory. If a firm has $50,000 in cost of goods sold and an average of $10,000 in inventory, then it has an inventory turnover of 5, (50,000/10,000 = 5). Like the accounts receivable turnover, this ratio can be converted into days by dividing it into 360. In this example, the inventory turnover period would be 72 days (360/5 = 72), which would be a poor turnover rate if we were dealing with perishable goods, but a fantastic one for new cars.

Turnover rates can be calculated for any asset. Firms with high levels of fixed assets, such as manufacturing firms, would be interested in how well those assets are supporting sales. The fixed asset turnover could be calculated by dividing sales by the average investment in plant, property, and equipment.

Assets exist to support sales. Consequently, their effective management should be reflected in sales. The overall performance, measured by the **total asset turnover,** is found by dividing sales by the average total assets owned. Later on, we will discuss how this ratio can be coupled with a profitability ratio to better evaluate the firm.

One note of caution is due here. All these ratios have used average asset levels. Frequently, this is a difficult number to find. Most people simply take the beginning and ending balances of the assets from two balance sheets and find the average by adding the two together, then dividing by two. Some error is included in this amount, but it is the method used for most industry averages and so using another method will impair comparison. If there is a major shift in asset levels during the period, then the average will not be representative. In such cases, it may be wiser to use the ending value for the asset rather than an average. There are no hard and fast rules about financial analysis. The approach to use is the one that works best in your situation.

## Leverage

**Leverage** has to do with the debt level of a firm. From a simplistic point of view, there are only two kinds of money in the world: ours and everyone else's. Leverage is an indication of the proportion of assets and resources acquired by a firm using money contributed by owners compared to money contributed by others. One measure of leverage is the **debt to assets ratio,** found by dividing total liabilities by total assets and normally expressed as a percentage. If total assets for a firm are $250,000 and total liabilities are $175,000, then 70% (250,000/175,000 = .70) of the firm's assets are provided by debt and 30% (100% − 70%) by the firm's owners or its own capital. The higher the debt ratio, the greater is the risk to which the firm is exposed.

Alternately, debt can be divided by net worth to yield the **debt to worth ratio.** In this example, the ratio would be 2.33 (175,000/(25,000 − 175,000) = 2.33). This ratio indicates that 2.33 times as much debt as capital has been used to acquire the firm's assets.

Other ratios that are important when evaluating debt are indicators of coverage. The **interest coverage ratio** is calculated by dividing the income before interest expense and taxes by the total interest expense. This tells us how well the interest charges on debt are being covered by the firm's profits. Because obligations can take the form of leases as well as loans, the **fixed charge coverage** is a valuable ratio. It is calculated by dividing the income before interest, lease payments, and taxes by the sum of interest expense and lease payments. These ratios can be calculated on a cash basis to yield more information. Operating cash flow before loan payments and taxes is divided by total loan payments. Leases can be included by dividing the operating cash flow before loan and lease payments and taxes by the sum of loan and lease payments. The larger these coverage ratios are, the stronger is the debt position.

### Profitability

**Profitability** measures include the **gross profit ratio** and the **contribution margin.** Other ratios of importance include the **net profit ratio,** calculated by dividing net income by sales, and the **return on investment ratio** (ROI), found by dividing net income by net worth or total capital. One item of caution is required when examining the ROI: leverage affects the ratio. Actually the area of analysis called *leverage* takes its name from the impact of debt on the ROI. In Chapter 7, we discussed the impact of debt on the ROI.

**Component percentages** are another device for evaluating profitability. The ratios of the various expenses to sales can display the effectiveness of cost control measures as well as reveal the proportion of sales required to support the various activities within the firm.

Some of the strongest profitability evaluation processes involve more than simply ratios. Dozens, perhaps hundreds, of different ratios can be calculated in the analysis of a firm's financial well-being. Many are industry specific, as mentioned earlier. Regardless of the number or kinds of ratios calculated, examination of the ratios in isolation is weak. A better analysis involves examining the ratios and percentages over time.

## TREND ANALYSIS

When we examine the financial statements of a firm, we use historic data in the analysis. However, our focus really is on the future: how a firm can be expected to behave in the future; what income levels and ROIs can be expected next year. Although we cannot predict the future, we can examine **trends** in the ratios over time as an indication of what to expect. For example, we could calculate key ratios in each of the four areas for the financial statements prepared at each of the last three year ends. It would be more revealing to see that the current ratio has moved from 1.0 to 1.5 to 2.0 over the last three years than to know that the current ratio was 2.0 on December 31, 1990.

Trend analysis also aids in evaluating past performance and financial condition. If we instituted a new policy of inventory control at the beginning of last year, then we should see an improvement in the inventory turnover ratios for that year compared to the previous ones. If the improvement did not materialize, then the changes may not be working as they should. If we changed pricing policies, then we should see a difference in the component percentages on the income statement.

Trends can reveal just how strong or weak our financial health is. A poor liquidity position would be of less concern if it were an unusual case; but, if the firm consistently has poor liquidity, then it may be weaker than the ratios reveal. A strong gross profit margin would reflect an even stronger business if it were consistently strong over time. If we have had a poor gross profit margin in every year but the last, then chances are that the firm has changed its pricing and cost control policies to correct such a weakness.

Trend analysis can be useful because potential problems might be revealed before they become problems. If the accounts receivable collection period for the last three years has been 45 days, 50 days, and 55 days, respectively, then we could conclude that a problem is developing in that area—and a cash flow problem could develop subsequently. If the gross profit margin has declined from 25% to 24% to 23% over the last three years, then it would be wise to examine pricing and product cost patterns now to ward off a more serious problem in the future. Trend analysis can highlight such potential problem areas.

Trend analysis also can demonstrate patterns that can be expected to prevail in the future. The longer the trend, the more reliable it can be expected to be, within certain limits. If the contribution margin has been constant for several years, then we probably can count on its being constant in the future. Of course, we must take economic factors and other conditions into consideration, both those of the past and those expected in the future. A trend line that includes years of economic hardship or economic booms is less valuable for prediction of the future. We would expect, for example, housing starts or new construction to suffer during a recession and jump considerably at the end of a national recession. Obviously, a downward trend in the ratios of a construction company is less revealing if those trends occur during times of economic recession than they would be if housing starts had been growing. Other factors that might have a bearing must be considered as well. We would expect an American firm that has been competing heavily against a Japanese firm to experience more favorable financial performance after a strict import policy has been adopted by the U.S. Congress. Trend analysis requires considerable knowledge about the industry and the economy in which a firm operates as well as the policies and practices of the firm in order to be as effective as possible.

## INDUSTRY AVERAGES

Another step in determining a firm's well-being is comparison of the ratios to averages of other firms engaged in the same general business. As discussed earlier, such industry averages are available from a variety of sources. Trade associations frequently compile average statistics for key ratios from financial statements of its members. These averages are then made available to its members. It is more revealing to know that the average current ratio in our industry is 2.0, whereas our current ratio is 1.5, than to be totally ignorant of the industry's pattern.

Dun and Bradstreet and Robert Morris Associates calculate average ratios for various industries and sell publications of industry averages. Some government agencies also publish industry averages. For example, the Urban Land Institute publishes a triannual survey of shopping malls that contains a wealth of average ratios compiled from stores located in the nation's shopping centers and malls.

As mentioned earlier, whatever source of industry averages is used, you must be aware that they are simply averages and not indications of desired or proper ratio levels. For example, economic fluctuations can occur regionally without a great deal of effect on national compilations. We discussed other types of bias that can creep into the calculations. If an organization depends upon voluntary submissions of financial statements for the averaging process, then firms with less desirable operating results are likely to be underrepresented. Consequently, industry averages are useful only as one of several tools to be applied in the analysis process, and never should be considered benchmarks or desired ratio levels.

A word of caution is important concerning industry averages. Conditions change from year to year. Consequently, the results of a year's operations must be compared to industry averages compiled for that specific year. This is especially important if significant economic or other factors have changed.

Another evaluation technique is the comparison of percentages and ratios to those of a specific competing firm or firms. This is a popular technique for evaluating publicly held companies, but it is less valuable in the small business arena. Publicly held firms are required by the Securities and Exchange Commission to publish their financial statements, and so they are available to anyone who wishes to review them. Most small businesses are privately owned and publish no financial statements. Bankers use this approach to compare customers within the same industry, but it can be difficult for you to obtain the information on a competitor. If a firm has cooperated with Dun and Bradstreet while it conducted a credit review, then financial statements can be obtained for a fee from that source. Otherwise, direct comparison may not be possible.

Trend analysis can be conducted with industry average ratios and percentages to determine how a firm compares over time. This can be a valuable technique, especially when you consider that the bias in industry averages probably makes them higher than is really the case. With this in mind, it would be more valuable to know that the current ratio started out below industry averages three years ago and climbed to equal the average for last year than to look at last year alone.

## PUTTING FINANCIAL ANALYSIS TO WORK

Now that we have talked about the various techniques, how can they be used to evaluate your firm's progress and financial position? The best approach is to evaluate the various aspects of your firm's performance at each month end. The budget process requires you to review each month's results and modify the remaining months of forecast under continuous budgeting. This is the time for financial analysis. Don't just look at the month's performance—analyze it, then adjust the forecasts and budgets and make whatever policy changes or decisions seem appropriate. In the following sections we will illustrate how this process can function. The secret is consistency. You must make the monthly review of your business a habit. It must become a part of the planning activities. If you view those planning activities as the most important part of your function as the owner of a small firm, you will find yourself miles ahead of the competition and able to set and achieve goals.

It will be hard work. Often it seems impossible to find the time. Just think about all the firms that have failed and all the firms that eke out a subsistence income. The difference between those firms and a strong healthy business is good management. Good management means planning. Planning requires financial analysis.

### Sales and Expenses

Because sales or revenues are the basis for everything in a business, it makes sense to start our analysis there. The first step is to calculate vertical and horizontal component percentages. **Vertical percentages** are found by simply dividing every item on the income statement by net sales or sales less returns and allowances. **Horizontal percentages** are found by dividing each item on the income statement by the same item on last year's statement. If you are looking at a monthly interim statement, then you should use last month's figures. If your business has seasonal factors, then you should use the same month in last year rather than last month. For example, January should be compared to January rather than to December. This displays how things have changed since the last statement in real terms rather than in dollar amounts. For example, if sales were $50,000 last period and are $55,000 this period, then the horizontal percentage would be 110%, ($55,000/$50,000). This says that sales are 10% higher this period than they were last. If salaries this period are 97% of last period's salaries, then salary expense was down by 3%. Do this for each item on the statement. Now examine the horizontal percentages over time. If you have kept the prior analyses, this simply means adding another column of data. Incidentally, spreadsheet programs are ideal for this process. If you have an accounting package that can generate a file readable by a spreadsheet package, then you won't even have to rekey the data. After the horizontal percentages have been prepared, consider why the changes took place. What happened to make sales go up or down? What did you do last month or last year that is reflected in the changes? Are the changes good or bad? What are the trends like? Is the seasonal factor the same? Were any marketing or advertising programs in effect last period? Did those programs work? Do you need to change your advertising approach? Did you make any price changes? What were their effects? Do you need to make price changes? Are things moving in the direction of your goals and objectives? What changes in operations need to be made?

Consider the vertical percentages and compare them to the last period's percentages. Remember the effect of pricing. If you sold the same number of ball bearings this period as you did last, but sold them at a higher price, then sales will have gone up, but the increase will be only in dollars. Remember that every item on the statement will be affected because each is divided by sales. The variable expense percentages, especially the gross profit margin, should stay constant over time unless there has been some change in the relationship. If the gross profit margin has gone down, then it can result only from a decrease in costs of sales or an increase in prices. Which was it? Look at all the variable expense items. What are their trends over time? Is the contribution margin flat? What have you done over the last month or last year that should have affected the numbers? Did your actions have the expected effect? Do you need to make changes in the future? If variable cost items go up and prices stay the same, then the percentages will go up and the contribution margin will decrease. This trend cannot be tolerated for long. Obviously, the desirable result is for all variable expense percentages to stay flat or decrease over time. Is this happening?

Examine the fixed cost percentages. Fixed costs should stay the same in dollar amounts over time unless changes are made. That means that an increase in sales should result in a decrease in the fixed cost percentage. Did that happen? Did you take any actions last month or last year that should have affected the fixed costs? Did the desired result occur? Are there changes you need to make? A major problem of small businesses during periods of rapid growth is control over fixed costs. Frequently, they act like variable costs; that is, the fixed cost percentage stays flat. If that happens, then the firm eventually will find itself in serious trouble. Should sales growth slow down, the rising fixed costs will consume the firm's cash flow at an alarming rate. Fixed costs must behave like fixed costs. Look at the changes from a horizontal basis. What caused the changes you see? Are the changes permanent? Have they resulted in increased capacity, or are you simply paying more for the same thing?

Compare results to the budget. What did you forecast for sales, variable expenses, and fixed expenses? How far off were the forecasts? What caused the deviation? Do you need to make changes? What will happen next month? Are any of the relationships in the budget different? If the variable costs have changed their relationship to sales, then the budget will have to be changed to reflect the new percentages. If fixed costs have changed, that will have to be reflected. Do you plan any changes in marketing, pricing, cost control, or other areas that will affect the forecasts? What objectives or goals should you set for next month and for the future?

Compare the component percentages and ratios to industry averages. Are you stronger or weaker than the average? Are there factors in your strategic posture that explain the difference? For example, if your quality is consistently higher than your competitors that could explain a higher cost of goods sold ratio. What have been the trends in the averages? Have your trends been moving in the same direction? Are you satisfied with your position relative to the averages? Will your banker be satisfied with your position? Are there any factors that the banker should understand as supporting detail for the financial data?

## Profits and ROI

The gross profit, contribution margin, operating profit, and net profit margins have been calculated as part of the component percentages. Now, calculate the return on investment (net profit divided by net worth) and the total asset turnover (sales divided by total assets). The latter ratio is used to calculate the return on total investment under the **DuPont method,** which multiplies the total asset turnover by the net profit margin. The result is the net profit divided by total assets, which represents the total investment in the firm. It can be calculated directly; however, that would cloud the components of the ratio because return on total investment is a combination of an activity and a profitability ratio. It looks like this:

$$\text{Return on total investment} = \text{Total asset turns} \times \text{Net profit margin}$$

$$\text{ROTI} = \frac{\text{Sales}}{\text{Total assets}} \times \frac{\text{Net profit}}{\text{Sales}}$$

Using both ratios in the calculation will reveal which part of the operations are weak or strong. Pricing and cost control actions will be reflected in the profit margin. The effective use of assets will be reflected in the asset turns. Even if the profit margin is strong, the return on total investment can be weak because of poor asset management. The DuPont evaluation will disclose any such problems.

After the numbers are calculated, look at the trends. Gross profit and contribution margin should be constant unless variable cost increases have not been reflected in pricing or a change in the pricing policy. Operating profit reflects the effect of fixed costs on the contribution margin. Net profit reflects the impact of interest expense and other revenue or expense items on the operating profit. The operating profit is more important because it is the profit that can be expected to continue in the future. What happened? Were the results as you anticipated? How did they compare to the budget? Were there any unusual items that affected net profit? Will these recur in the future? How do the numbers compare to the budget? Are there changes you need to make in operations? Were the returns on investment and total investment acceptable? Were they within your goals or objectives? Did debt leveraging affect the ROI? Was the asset turnover satisfactory? How do the returns look over time? Are they going up or down? Why are they moving? What can you do to make the returns better?

Compare the numbers to industry averages. Are you satisfied with your comparison? Are your trends comparable to the trends in the averages? Are differences between your ratios and the averages reasonable when you consider the unique aspects of your business? Will your banker think so?

## Cash Flow

In Chapter 5 we discussed cash flow and how it can be calculated from an income statement and balance sheets. Operating cash flow, net cash flow from operations, and net cash flow should be calculated and converted to percentages of net sales like all of the components of the income statement. Horizontal analysis should be conducted for each number. Now, examine the trends. Cash flow tends to be much more volatile than profit because the accrual accounting methods used to calculate income smooth out much of the timing problems. This means that you should not expect cash flow to follow profit or reflect smooth percentage relationships. Nevertheless, if there are significant deviations from the cash flow forecast, you should determine the cause.

Cash flow is the life blood of any business. Consequently, no analysis is complete without a detailed consideration of cash flows. Were they higher or lower than expected? What caused the deviations from budget? Calculate the accounts receivable turnover ratio, and look for any changes in the collection rate. Does this change account for the deviation in cash flows? Have you changed the process of paying accounts payable? Were there any significant accrual items in revenues or expenses that affected the cash flows? Were there any unexpected inflows or outflows of cash? What about debt? Did you borrow any additional funds or repay any loans not anticipated on the forecast? Is the cash flow acceptable? Do you need to make any changes in operations? What modifications need to be made to the cash flow forecast?

If industry averages exist for cash flow, then you should definitely compare your results to them. The analysis should proceed just as for the previous areas. Unfortunately, such averages frequently are not available, although sometimes sufficient detail will be given to allow estimates of the industry average cash flow. For example, net profit plus depreciation can be a close approximation to cash flow from operations in a stable industry.

## Activity and Liquidity Levels

Calculate the component percentages for the balance sheet. This means that each item on the balance sheet should be divided by total assets to yield a percentage. In addition, horizontal analysis should be performed on each item. Calculate the turnover rates for receivables, inventory, fixed assets, and total assets. Calculate the current ratio and if inventory is present, calculate the quick ratio and the inventory liquidation ratio. Calculate **working capital,** which simply is the difference between current assets and current liabilities. Convert working capital to a percentage of total assets. Examine the trends and compare the balance sheet to the pro forma balance sheet developed in the master budget.

Have the components of current assets or liabilities changed? What do these changes mean? An inventory that moved from 40% to 45% to 50% over a three-year period could be disturbing, especially if horizontal analysis showed total assets to be rising during the same time period. Why would the inventory percentage go up? Has the inventory turnover ratio changed? If the investment in inventory goes up without a corresponding increase in sales, then the turnover ratio can be expected to go down. The same is true for all the asset turnover items. The desired results are flat or increasing turnover rates.

The investment levels will change in horizontal terms as sales grow. They must to support higher levels of sales. In terms of component percentages, however, the relative investment in the various assets should remain basically level. Any shifts in investment should occur only as a result of changes in policies or procedures. If you change the inventory policy, then its ratio to total assets can be expected to change. If you make a significant new investment in fixed assets, then its ratio to total assets can be expected to change. If you make no investments in fixed assets at all, then its ratio will still change because of the effects of depreciation. As more depreciation expense is recorded on existing assets, the investment level in fixed assets will shrink. This should show in both the horizontal and vertical percentages. New purchases are required to keep the investment level. Because fixed assets are acquired in large chunks, the ratio of fixed to total assets can be expected to be more volatile. Therefore, you must determine whether the changes in the investment level are in accord with your plans.

Are the trends in activity levels and liquidity levels good? What actions did you take last month or last year that affected those trends? Were your efforts successful or do you need to try something else? Are there any seasonal factors? Were there any changes in the credit card sales or collection periods? How about credit sales as a percentage of total sales, were there any changes there? Are these changes expected to prevail in the future? Did short-term loans go up due to cash flow deficits that are expected to reverse themselves next month? Do you need to make changes in the operations to improve the trends? Are there any problems developing? What about working capital—is it satisfactory? What trends have accounted for it? Have you borrowed any money that affects the current liabilities? Are there any maturing notes or loans that will affect it next year? Have there been any loan repayments that you had not anticipated during the budget? What adjustments do you need to make in the budget to bring it closer into line for the next period?

Do you have a revolving line of credit? How much of it have you drawn and how much is left? If unused credit exists, it can form a major portion of the liquidity of a firm. When must it be paid out and what is the renewal date? Will you be able to handle the pay out? Is your financial strength such that the renewal of the line will be approved by the bank?

Compare your percentages and ratios to the industry averages. How does your firm compare? Are the trends in your numbers consistent with those in the industry? Can you explain the differences in terms of differences in your operation? Are you satisfied with your position relative to the industry averages? Will your banker be satisfied?

## Debt Management

The debt ratio (debt to total assets) will have been calculated as part of the component percentages on the balance sheet. Now, calculate the debt to net worth ratio. If yours is a firm with a significant level of long-term debt, then it could make sense to calculate the ratio of long-term debt to net worth. In addition, interest and fixed charge coverage ratios should be calculated both normally and under the cash approach.

Now, examine the trends in ratios and percentages, both horizontal and vertical. How do the numbers compare to the pro forma balance sheet in the master budget? Are the trends consistent with your actions and objectives? Did you make any significant loans or loan repayments? Are these reflected in the trends? What are the upcoming maturity dates of the loans? Are you going to be able to handle them? Are the coverage ratios satisfactory? How about on the cash basis? Were you delinquent on any payables or lease or loan payments during the last period? Do you expect any changes that will affect the coverage in the future? Are any of the loans on a floating rate basis? Were there any changes in those rates that you had not anticipated? What do you think they will do in the future? Is the balance between short-term and long-term debt acceptable? Will any expansion plans for the future require more debt? Will the firm's financial position be such that the loan requests will be approved? Is the debt level unduly influencing the return on investment? Should you make any changes? What adjustments should you make to the budget for the next months? Do you have compensating balance requirements or other special requirements to support your loans? Compensating balances are deposit levels required by a bank as part of the loan agreement. In addition, all kinds of other requirements can be made part of a loan agreement, from minimum levels for current ratios to limitations on overall debt levels. If any such requirements exist, you should ensure that you are in compliance and that no circumstances will damage that compliance in the future. Finally, is your financial position such that you will be in a stronger bargaining position with respect to terms and rates on loans? Should you consider renegotiation with the bank now? Do you have room to add more debt? Will you be able to finance expected growth through debt? Should you consider seeking investors and searching for alternative debt sources?

Compare your ratios and percentages to the industry averages. How do you look? Are you satisfied with your debt trends when compared to debt trends in the industry? A fact of life is that bankers will compare your ratios to industry averages as part of their evaluation of any loan proposals. That means that you should be able to justify any significant deviations from industry averages before you make a loan application. Remember that the averages may be skewed high or represent firms that truly are not comparable to yours because of size, market, or other factors. They also may fail to reflect local or regional economic or competitive factors, and frequently the data are too old for real comparison to current data because of the lag time required for publication. Unfortunately, you may have to justify one or more of these factors to a lender unless you have cultivated a deep understanding of your business in that lender. Consequently, you should always be aware of significant deviations from industry averages and be prepared to explain them.

## Sources and Uses of Funds

In Chapter 4 we discussed the statement of changes in financial position. This statement details the sources and uses of funds during a period. The analysis needs to extend to this statement as well. Preparation of the statement of changes is part of the annual financial statement. Analysis involves converting all numbers on the statement to percentages of total sources of funds, which requires dividing each item on the statement by total sources of funds and comparing those percentages to the percentages from previous statements.

The statement of changes normally is not prepared as part of interim or month-end financial statements. An easy way to analyze sources and uses for month ends is simply to compare two balance sheets. Each item on the balance sheet for this month end is subtracted from the same item on last month's balance sheet. The difference shows the movement of funds through the balance sheet, sometimes called the *rough and ready approach* or **sources and uses of funds.** Every increase in a liability or capital account and every decrease in an asset account is a source of funds. Decreases in liability or capital accounts or increases in asset accounts are uses of funds. To separate sources of funds from operations, the changes in retained earnings or owners' capital accounts and the changes in accumulated depreciation are listed separately, because these changes will be equal to net profit plus depreciation for the month. As in the case of the statement of changes, the total sources must equal the total uses. The numbers on the sources and uses are converted to percentages of total sources, just as in the previous case, and compared to percentages from prior periods. Exhibit 8-1 illustrates the process and Exhibit 8-2 displays the report.

Once the percentages have been prepared, the analysis examines where money came from and where it went. Remember that short-term financing generally should be used for short-term assets and long-term financing should be used for long-lived assets. Is that what happened? Where did the majority of the funds come from? How much came from operations? What are the trends? Is this period consistent with previous sources and uses of funds? What happened to create the differences? Were any plans in effect that should have affected the results? Were the results as expected? A firm that consistently acquires funds from debt eventually will have problems. Operations should be

**EXHIBIT 8-1** *Sources and Uses of Funds Calculations*

| | THIS PERIOD | LAST PERIOD | DIFFERENCE SOURCES | DIFFERENCE USES |
|---|---|---|---|---|
| Current assets: | | | | |
| Cash in banks | $ ( 4,902) | $ 204 | 5,106 | |
| Accounts receivable | 37,876 | 18,662 | | 19,214 |
| Receivables from officers | 3,291 | 8,957 | 5,666 | |
| Inventory | 27,629 | 18,849 | | 8,780 |
| Prepaid expenses | 12,922 | 2,159 | | 10,763 |
| Total current assets[a] | 76,816 | 48,831 | | |
| Plant, Property, and Equipment: | | | | |
| Land[b] | 10,500 | 10,500 | | |
| Building[b] | 74,399 | 74,399 | | |
| Machinery and equipment[b] | 28,527 | 28,527 | | |
| Leasehold improvements | 21,937 | 20,672 | | 1,265 |
| Furniture and fixtures[b] | 3,972 | 3,972 | | |
| Vehicles | 12,750 | 11,850 | | 900 |
| Total[a] | 152,085 | 149,920 | | |
| Accumulated depreciation[c] | ( 57,004) | ( 40,862) | 16,142 | |
| Net book value[a] | 95,081 | 109,058 | | |
| Other assets | 770 | 50 | | 720 |
| Total assets[a] | $172,667 | $157,939 | | |
| Current liabilities: | | | | |
| Accounts payable | $ 95,762 | $ 93,237 | 2,525 | |
| Accrued items | 9,382 | 7,113 | 2,269 | |
| Current portion, long-term debt[d] | 35,445 | 25,286 | | |
| Total current liabilities[a] | 140,589 | 125,636 | | |
| Notes and mortgages payable: | | | | |
| Mortgage on building | 37,745 | 52,186 | | 14,441 |
| Notes due to banks | 44,789 | 13,651 | 31,138 | |
| Total[a] | 82,534 | 65,837 | | |
| Less current portion[d] | ( 35,445) | ( 25,286) | | |
| Total long-term debt[a] | 47,089 | 40,551 | | |
| Stockholders' equity: | | | | |
| Capital stock[b] | 15,300 | 15,300 | | |
| Paid in capital[b] | 20,573 | 20,573 | | |
| Retained earnings[e] | ( 50,884) | ( 44,121) | | 6,763 |
| Total equity[a] | ( 15,011) | ( 8,248) | | |
| Total Liabilities and Stockholders' Equity[a] | $172,667 | $157,939 | | |
| Total sources and uses | | | 62,846 | 62,846 |

[a] Sources and uses are not calculated for subtotals or totals.
[b] No change.
[c] An increase in accumulated depreciation is a source of funds.
[d] Current portion of long-term debt is ignored because it is included in long-term debt.
[e] Because there is a net loss, it is a use of funds.

**EXHIBIT 8-2** *Sources and Uses of Funds Statement*

| | SOURCES | | USES | |
|---|---|---|---|---|
| Operations: | | | | |
| Income | ( 6,763) | (12.1%) | | |
| Depreciation | 16,142 | 28.8 | | |
| Total from operations | 9,379 | 16.7 | | |
| Cash in banks | 5,106 | 9.1 | | |
| Accounts receivable | | | 19,214 | 34.3% |
| Receivables from officers | 5,666 | 10.1 | | |
| Inventory | | | 8,780 | 15.7 |
| Prepaid expenses | | | 10,763 | 19.2 |
| Accounts payable | 2,525 | 4.5 | | |
| Accrued items | 2,269 | 4.0 | | |
| Total current items | 15,566 | 27.8 | 38,757 | 69.1 |
| Leasehold improvements | | | 1,265 | 2.3 |
| Vehicles | | | 900 | 1.6 |
| Other assets | | | 720 | 1.3 |
| Mortgage on building | | | 14,441 | 25.7 |
| Notes due to banks | 31,138 | 55.5 | | |
| Total noncurrent items | 31,138 | 55.5 | 17,326 | 30.9 |
| Total | 56,083 | 100.0 | 56,083 | 100.0 |

a major source of funds most of the time. Was this the case for your firm? Do you need to make any changes in operations for the coming months?

The firm in the exhibit had some problems during the period under analysis. The majority of funds came from long-term debt (55.5%) and were used to acquire current assets (69.1%). If that were to develop into a trend, the company could find itself in trouble because the current assets would be consumed and the debt would still remain, thereby placing a burden on future operations.

## OVERVIEW OF FINANCIAL ANALYSIS

The steps of financial analysis are displayed in Exhibit 8-3. This process should be followed at the end of each month as part of the planning and budgeting activities.

The ratios in the exhibit are not an exhaustive list. Add any industry specific ratios important to your business or any other ratios you consider valuable. In addition, the contents of the income statement should be mana-

**EXHIBIT 8-3** *Steps in Financial Analysis*

I. Prepare month-end (or year-end) financial statement
   A. Income statement
   B. Balance sheet
   C. Statement of changes in financial position or sources and uses of funds statement

II. Convert each statement to component percentages
   A. Divide each item on income statement by net sales
   B. Divide each item on balance sheet by total assets
   C. Divide each item on changes or sources and uses statement by total sources

III. Calculate horizontal percentages
   A. Divide each item by itself for the last period
   B. Use last year's statement for year-end statements
   C. Use the same month from last year for monthly statements

IV. Calculate key ratios
   A. Liquidity

| | |
|---|---|
| 1. Current ratio: | Current assets/Current liabilities |
| 2. Quick ratio: | (Current assets − Inventory)/Current liabilities |
| 3. Inventory liquidation: | (Current liabilities − Quick assets)/Inventory |

   B. Activity

| | |
|---|---|
| 1. Receivables turnover: | Sales/Average accounts receivable |
| 2. Inventory turnover: | Sales/Average inventory |
| 3. Fixed asset turnover: | Sales/Average fixed assets |
| 4. Total asset turnover: | Sales/Average total assets |

   C. Leverage

| | |
|---|---|
| 1. Debt ratio: | Debt/Total assets |
| 2. Debt to worth: | Debt/Total net worth |
| 3. Interest coverage: | Profit before interest and taxes/Interest |
| 4. Fixed charge coverage | Profit before interest and lease/(Interest + Lease) |
| 5. Cash coverages: | Operating cash flow before loan payments/Payments |
| | Operating cash flow before loan and lease payments/Payments on loans and leases |

   D. Profitability and cash flow

| | |
|---|---|
| 1. Gross profit margin: | Gross profit/Sales |
| 2. Contribution margin: | Contribution margin/Sales |
| 3. Operating profit margin: | Operating profit/Sales |
| 4. Net profit margin: | Net profit/Sales |
| 5. Return on investment: | Net profit/Net worth |
| 6. DuPont ratio: | (Sales/Total assets)(Net profit/Sales) |
| 7. Operating cash flow: | Operating cash flow/Sales |
| 8. Cash flow from Operations: | Cash flow from operations/Sales |
| 9. Net cash flow: | Net cash flow/Sales |

*continued*

**EXHIBIT 8-3 continued**

V. Examine trends for all ratios and percentages

VI. Compare ratios and percentages to budgets and plans

VII. Consider the impact of past actions and need for future actions

VIII. Evaluate the firm and its strengths and weaknesses

IX. Make decisions about changes in operations and policies

X. Prepare new budgets and forecasts; make new plans

gerially oriented. This means that fixed and variable costs should be identified and separated, so that a contribution margin can be calculated on the face of the statement. Any items of particular interest to you on the income statement or balance sheet should be included.

Note the comparison with prior year-end statements when analyzing year-end statements. If a month-end or quarter-end statement is analyzed, then the comparison should be made to the same period in prior years to reflect the seasonality of the firm. Also make the comparisons directly to the previous month. This can be a valuable technique to evaluate decisions made last month at the earliest possible date. The only danger is that you must keep in mind the impact of seasonal factors on the numbers.

To develop and maintain good relations with a banker, it is helpful to furnish a copy of your month-end analysis to your lender. This not only will keep that individual up to date with your operations, you will have to do a complete job of analysis each month because someone outside the firm will be seeing it.

The results of analysis, budgeting, and planning should be communicated inside the firm. If you have managers in the firm, they should assist in the process, be aware of how the company stands, and what it needs to do for improvement. Staff and employees also need to be aware of the firm's position, although detailed knowledge generally is not important. It is important for the staff to understand the reasonableness of the plans and budgets so that they will support the firm's progress.

## SUMMARY

Financial analysis is one of the best and least understood tools of management. The financial condition of a firm at any given point results from the decisions and actions of its owner(s), consequently, financial analysis provides a report card for management.

Financial statements include the income statement, balance sheet, reconciliation of net worth and the statement of changes in financial position and are prepared at the end of each fiscal year. Interim statements are prepared at the end of each month and tend to be less complete than the annual statement. If interim statements are analyzed, they should be compared to the same month in the prior year as well as the preceding month.

The techniques used in financial analysis include component percentage analysis or vertical analysis and horizontal analysis. Ratio analysis, the best-known technique of financial analysis, involves dividing various items on the statement by other items to highlight and reveal relationships. Literally hundreds of ratios can be calculated, and many of these are useful only in specific industries.

Trend analysis involves comparing component percentages and ratios to those for previous periods. The longer the time period, the better trends can be identified. This useful financial analysis technique can highlight problems before they develop.

Ratios and percentages can be compared to industry averages. This is a well-known financial analysis technique, but it is less valuable than popularly believed. Industry averages tend not to be representative of the entire industry: they tend to represent stronger companies and therefore probably are skewed higher than the real average. Be very careful using industry averages because of these problems.

Financial performance is divided into four areas. *Liquidity* refers to a firm's ability to meet its maturing obligations. *Activity* refers to how well a firm is employing its assets. *Leverage* refers to the proportion of debt involved in a firm's financial structure. *Profitability* refers to pricing and cost control policies of a firm.

Before analysis, be sure that the statements are in a form that separates fixed and variable expenses and highlights the contribution margin. Then calculate the various cash flow figures, including operating cash flow, cash flow from operations, and net cash flow.

If you are examining an interim statement, the statement of changes in financial position normally is not a part of the package. The process of preparing a rough and ready sources and uses of funds statement is outlined in Exhibits 8-1 and 8-2. The financial analysis process is outlined in Exhibit 8-3.

A microcomputer with a good spreadsheet program can make the preparation of the numbers fast and simple. This will free time for thought and interpretation. Financial analysis is part of any sound planning program and cannot be overlooked if you wish to maintain a strong, vibrant company.

## QUESTIONS

1. What is *financial analysis?*
2. Why is it important to study and understand financial analysis for a small business owner/manager?
3. What are the techniques of financial analysis?
4. What are the areas of financial performance?
5. Which technique is the most useful? Which technique is the least valuable?
6. What are the disadvantages of industry averages?
7. Name at least two ratios in each of the four performance areas.
8. How many ratios are there? Which should you use for your business?
9. What do ratios reveal?
10. How does cash flow compare to profit?
11. What is the *DuPont ratio?*
12. How often should you perform financial analysis on your own business?

## PROJECT

The following statements are for a manufacturer of specialized machinery used in the textile industry. The firm has been in business for four years and the information covers the last three years of the company's operation. The machinery is built to order, consequently the inventory consists solely of raw materials and work in process. Analyze the financial position.

| | *199C* | *199B* | *199A* |
|---|---|---|---|
| Current assets: | | | |
| Cash | $ 3,362 | $ 394 | $ 14,686 |
| Accounts receivable | 69,199 | 36,913 | 5,138 |
| Inventory | 92,448 | 56,574 | 7,894 |
| Prepaid expenses | 1,386 | 1,990 | — |
| Total | 166,395 | 95,871 | 27,718 |
| Plant, property, and equipment: | | | |
| Furniture and fixtures | 9,972 | 3,584 | 3,717 |
| Shop Equipment | 26,344 | 18,660 | 12,081 |
| Trucks and autos | 7,465 | 1,000 | 10,592 |
| Leasehold Improvements | 3,219 | 2,229 | 1,099 |
| Total | 47,000 | 25,473 | 27,489 |
| Accumulated depreciation | ( 16,884) | ( 7,377) | ( 4,160) |
| Net plant, property, and equipment | 30,116 | 18,096 | 23,329 |

| | | | |
|---|---|---|---|
| Other assets: | | | |
| Patent (net) | 36,427 | — | — |
| Deposits | 1,600 | 800 | 800 |
| Organization expense (net) | — | 91 | 212 |
| Total | 38,027 | 891 | 1,012 |
| Total assets | $234,538 | $114,858 | $ 52,059 |
| Current liabilities: | | | |
| Accounts payable | $ 26,583 | $ 20,430 | $ 4,361 |
| Notes payable | — | 33,317 | — |
| Accruals | 3,631 | 3,606 | 4,086 |
| Deposits on sales | 89,674 | 22,516 | 4,083 |
| Current portion, long-term debt | 30,231 | — | 8,196 |
| Total | 150,119 | 79,869 | 20,726 |
| Long-term debt: | | | |
| Notes payable | 63,124 | — | — |
| Stockholder loans | 21,574 | 11,574 | 22,707 |
| Less current portion | ( 30,231) | — | ( 8,196) |
| Total | 54,467 | 11,574 | 14,511 |
| Total debt | 204,586 | 91,443 | 35,237 |
| Stockholders equity: | | | |
| Common stock | 1,570 | 1,570 | 1,310 |
| Paid in capital | 8,240 | 8,240 | — |
| Retained earnings | 23,142 | 16,605 | 18,512 |
| Less treasury stock at cost | ( 3,000) | ( 3,000) | ( 3,000) |
| Total | 29,952 | 23,415 | 16,822 |
| Total liabilities and equity | $234,538 | $114,858 | $ 52,059 |
| Gross sales | $363,740 | $144,584 | $126,868 |
| Returns and discounts | 895 | — | 1,211 |
| Net Sales | 362,845 | 144,584 | 125,657 |
| Cost of Goods Sold: | | | |
| Material | 103,571 | 37,587 | 33,831 |
| Labor | 57,553 | 36,175 | 18,394 |
| Engineering and other costs | 11,865 | 385 | 800 |
| Total | 172,989 | 74,147 | 53,025 |
| Gross profit | 189,856 | 70,437 | 72,632 |
| Selling expenses: | | | |
| Commissions | 14,136 | 222 | 150 |
| Advertising | 1,063 | 1,674 | 839 |
| Selling expenses | 14,354 | 3,610 | 2,832 |
| Postage and freight | 4,329 | 2,989 | 1,345 |
| Vehicle and travel expense | 3,201 | 1,502 | 946 |
| Total | 37,083 | 9,997 | 6,112 |

| | | | |
|---|---|---|---|
| General and administrative: | | | |
| Salaries | 50,880 | 18,360 | 15,598 |
| Fringe benefits | 4,447 | 755 | 976 |
| Insurance | 2,698 | 2,627 | 2,612 |
| Professional fees | 9,803 | 2,831 | 2,572 |
| Taxes and licenses | 12,266 | 4,237 | 3,326 |
| Utilities | 15,700 | 6,742 | 4,028 |
| Rent | 8,545 | 4,773 | 4,920 |
| Repairs, maintenance, tools | 2,727 | 3,771 | 500 |
| Research and development | 6,064 | — | — |
| Depreciation and amortization | 13,170 | 6,036 | 3,276 |
| Office expense | 8,712 | 1,414 | 1,740 |
| Laundry | 1,583 | 1,006 | 278 |
| Supplies | 8,127 | 9,005 | 4,012 |
| Miscellaneous | 630 | 145 | 1,050 |
| Total | 145,352 | 61,702 | 44,888 |
| Total expenses | 182,435 | 71,699 | 51,000 |
| Operating income | 7,421 | ( 1,262) | 21,632 |
| Other (income) and expense: | | | |
| Interest expense | 2,772 | 2,051 | 1,680 |
| Relocation expense | 1,210 | — | — |
| Gain on sale of equipment | — | ( 5,529) | — |
| Bad debts | — | — | 2,825 |
| Other income | ( 2,192) | ( 2,436) | ( 748) |
| Royalties | — | 2,150 | — |
| Total | 1,790 | ( 3,764) | 3,757 |
| Income before taxes | 5,631 | 2,502 | 17,875 |
| Provision for taxes | ( 906) | 810 | 3,300 |
| Net income | $ 6,537 | $ 1,692 | $ 14,575 |

# CASE

The following financial statements are for a retail card and gift shop. The business was begun four years ago and originally was located downtown but moved to a mall two years later. That move resulted in a tremendous increase in sales but also a major increase in rent expense. Rent went from $100 per month to $300 per month plus 2% of sales in excess of $25,000. As a result of the higher sales level, the owner began to take a small salary of $6,000 per year out of the business. Three months before the end of its last fiscal year, a new location became available and the company moved from its central location in the mall to a location at the end of a wing. This resulted in a decrease in rent, but sales dropped by one-half in the last three months compared to the same quarter last year. Rent dropped from the $300/2% level to $200 plus 2% of sales over $25,000. The following financial statements are for the first four years of the company's life. The owner needs to increase her salary to at least $12,000 and would like to go on up to $20,000 as soon as possible. Right now she is wondering whether the business will ever be able to support her. Analyze the financial position of the firm and make recommendations.

| | *199D* | *199C* | *199B* | *199A* |
|---|---|---|---|---|
| Cash | $ 762 | $ 830 | $ 159 | $ 202 |
| Receivables | 829 | 486 | 565 | 323 |
| Inventory | 17,556 | 24,063 | 6,474 | 5,031 |
| Total | 19,147 | 25,379 | 7,198 | 5,556 |
| Leasehold improvements | 4,991 | 4,991 | 4,991 | 4,991 |
| Equipment and fixtures | 10,890 | 10,890 | 8,108 | 8,108 |
| Accumulated depreciation | (10,593) | ( 8,869) | ( 5,642) | ( 2,488) |
| Net plant, property, and equipment | 5,288 | 7,012 | 7,457 | 10,611 |
| Notes receivable | 1,579 | 1,579 | — | — |
| Deferred interest | 3,921 | 4,192 | — | — |
| Other assets | 99 | 98 | 176 | 481 |
| Total assets | $30,034 | $38,260 | $14,831 | $16,468 |
| | | | | |
| Accounts payable | 9,952 | 13,705 | 4,313 | 1,055 |
| Notes payable | — | — | 3,074 | 1,901 |
| Accruals | 456 | 713 | 254 | 215 |
| Current portion, long-term debt | 5,456 | 4,264 | — | — |
| Total | 15,864 | 18,682 | 7,641 | 3,171 |
| Long-term debt | 23,212 | 22,919 | — | — |
| Due to shareholders | — | — | 19,611 | 19,611 |
| Current portion, long-term debt | ( 5,456) | ( 4,264) | — | — |
| Total | 17,756 | 18,655 | 19,611 | 19,611 |

| | | | | |
|---|---|---|---|---|
| Common stock | 4,500 | 4,500 | 4,250 | 4,250 |
| Retained earnings | ( 8,086) | ( 3,577) | (16,671) | (10,564) |
| Total | ( 3,586) | 923 | (12,421) | ( 6,314) |
| Total liabilities and net worth | $30,034 | $38,260 | $14,831 | $16,468 |
| Gross sales | 46,983 | 51,377 | 13,231 | 11,382 |
| Returns | 541 | 445 | — | — |
| Net sales | 46,442 | 50,932 | 13,231 | 11,382 |
| Beginning inventory | 24,063 | 6,474 | 5,031 | — |
| Purchases | 18,164 | 34,696 | 9,686 | 10,576 |
| Ending inventory | (17,556) | (24,063) | ( 6,474) | ( 5,031) |
| Cost of goods | 24,671 | 17,107 | 8,243 | 5,545 |
| Gross profit | 21,771 | 33,825 | 4,988 | 5,837 |
| Salaries | 12,458 | 6,926 | 2,292 | 6,505 |
| Rent | 3,740 | 4,164 | 1,200 | 1,000 |
| Advertising | 1,628 | 1,930 | 1,434 | 2,141 |
| Utilities | 1,117 | 1,212 | 1,563 | — |
| Taxes and licenses | 1,091 | 1,159 | 208 | 703 |
| Repairs and maintenance | 663 | 234 | 265 | 102 |
| Depreciation and amortization | 1,514 | 2,227 | 2,604 | 2,089 |
| Travel and auto | 689 | 373 | 261 | — |
| Supplies | 560 | 745 | 676 | — |
| Insurance | 304 | 236 | 246 | — |
| Other expenses[a] | 383 | 801 | 44 | 3,424 |
| Total | 24,147 | 20,007 | 10,793 | 15,964 |
| Interest expense | 2,133 | 699 | 301 | 437 |
| Income before tax | ( 4,509) | 13,119 | ( 6,106) | (10,564) |
| Income tax | — | — | — | — |
| Net income | ($4,509) | $13,119 | ($6,106) | ($10,564) |

[a]*Note:* Record keeping in the first year failed to separate many expense categories. Consequently, the "other" category of expense seems excessive.

# CHAPTER 9

# Computing for Success

**LEARNING OBJECTIVES**

After completing this chapter, you should be able to

- Understand the essence of computer literacy.
- Know the terminology used in computerization of small businesses.
- Understand the key aspects involved in acquiring computers for small businesses.
- Know why management must be involved in the whole computerization process.
- Know how to evaluate software for small businesses.
- Realize that the computer needs of small and large firms may be different.
- Distinguish the important components and their concepts from those of lesser importance.
- Explain the difference between top-down and bottom-up design and how it relates to small businesses.
- Understand the importance of adequate security measures in a small business.
- Understand the significance of disaster planning to a small business.

In 1645, Miyamoto Musashi listed in *Book of Five Rings* nine principles for the mastering of strategy. Miyamoto said that a successful student of strategy must become familiar with every art and must know the ways of all professions. Miyamoto is a legend in Japan. He is called *Kensei,* or "sword saint," and his book is required reading for every practitioner of *kendo,* the Japanese study of sword fighting. In recent years his book has been recognized as invaluable to the development of strategy in business and now is studied by every Japanese manager. Miyamoto's book has become popular in the United States and is studied in many prestigious business schools. Countless readers have discovered that Miyamoto's words ring as loudly today as they did 300 years ago. He tells us that the manager of an enterprise must become knowledgeable about every aspect of the business—including computers! As the owner of a small business, you *must* become computer literate. You cannot delegate the responsibility for gaining this knowledge if you wish to effectively employ computers in your business. You must become sufficiently knowledgeable to be able to evaluate the equipment and software you will purchase and oversee its use in the business. Frequently, managers concentrate on the managing of people in the enterprise. This truly is of paramount importance, but managing people is only one task of a chief executive. People-oriented work may be more enjoyable, but an owner must undertake control of all of the aspects of a small business and therefore needs a knowledge of all of the aspects, including automation. Miyamoto warns against having a favorite weapon. He said that to become overly familiar with one weapon was as much a fault as not knowing that weapon sufficiently well. Computer literacy can be an effective weapon in a business arsenal.

In this chapter we will present the basics of computer literacy. We will talk about the "buzz words" that the members of the computer industry use and explore their meanings. We will address the key aspects of computer systems, which should be known before attempting to acquire a system. We will talk about how computer systems can be of use in a small business and the security precautions that must be taken to protect records and equipment.

## FINDING THE MICRO SYSTEM FOR YOUR SMALL BUSINESS

In this era of high-tech automation, small business owners who have not purchased a microcomputer are being deluged with solicitations from computer companies; bombarded by microcomputer advertising; beset by competitive and peer pressure to automate; and nagged by feelings of inadequacy and archaism. On the other hand, small business owners who have purchased a microcomputer are baffled by the voluminous choice of software packages; deluged by advertising pointing out the deficiencies of their present software and the flexibility of new, more costly, packages; and plagued by problems of a non-computer literate staff trying to maintain daily routines while learning the new system.

It is well known that there has been an explosion in personal computers around the world. Nowhere has that explosion had more impact than the small business arena. Decreasing prices, technological breakthroughs, and advances in software development promise even more efficiency and less expense for small business users. We anticipate that by the mid-1990s virtually all small businesses will have one or more microcomputers in their firms. With this staggering growth rate predicted in the microcomputer field, what should the small business owner consider when assessing the need for automation? And what is the responsibility of the computer industry to small businesses?

First of all, don't be intimidated by the language. The microcomputer industry is rife with catch words and technical jargon that creep into any discussion about computers. Many of these esoteric terms describe computer hardware and software. We will talk about some of these, but you should never be embarrassed to demand explanations and clarifications of unusual terms when a computer specialist uses them. After all, the business world also has catch words and technical terms, many of which baffle computer jocks! Don't let a language barrier stop you from understanding a machine's features.

## AN INTRODUCTION TO MICROCOMPUTERS

Catch words and technical jargon creep into any discussion about computers. This terminology is the source of most of the confusion surrounding the field. If you become familiar with the language, computer literacy loses its mystery and becomes attainable.

As shown in Exhibit 9-1, a computer system consists of hardware and software, both of which need to be understood. **Software** refers to the instructions for operating a computer. These instructions usually will be prepared in one of the higher level or programming languages such as BASIC, COBOL, PASCAL, or any one of dozens of other languages that a computer can speak. All these programming languages are short, concise lists of commands and operations that the computer can understand. The instructions themselves are called **programs.** Programs control the response of a computer to an operator and dictate the way in which the machine will accept, store, and process data. **Operating systems** are programs that control the basic functions of the computer. Programs designed to handle specific tasks are called **applications programs.**

**EXHIBIT 9-1** *Components of a Computer System*

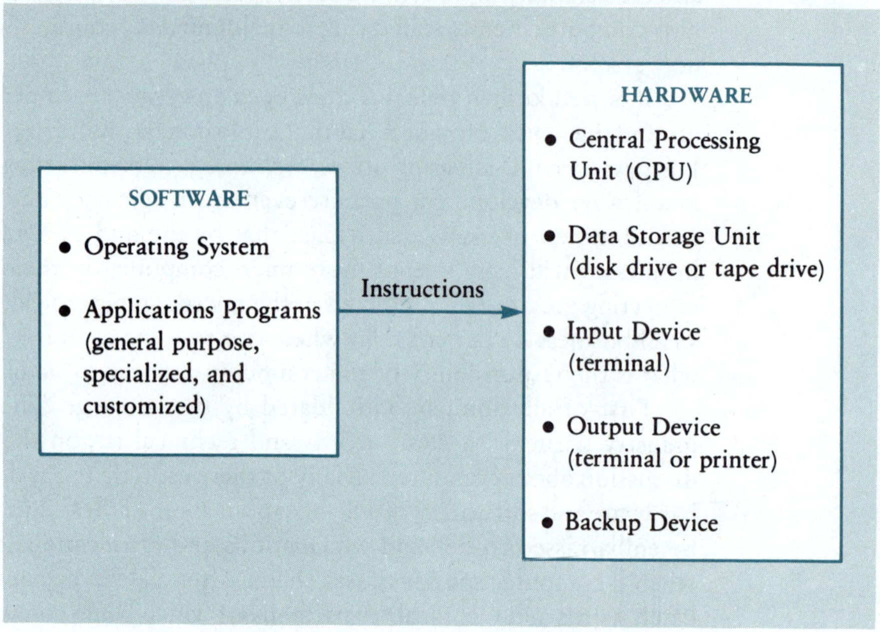


The computer itself, sometimes called a CPU or central processing unit, and all of its associated machinery collectively is called **hardware.** The associated machinery generally includes a data storage unit, a printer, and an input terminal or device. Data generally is stored by use of a disk drive or a tape drive, which can store and retrieve magnetic characters of data. Tape drives use spools of magnetic sensitive film much like that used by a tape recorder and generally are used only with large computer systems. Disk drives usually are much faster than tape drives and frequently are used with microcomputers.

## Bundling

A term coined by the computer industry to describe a concept of major importance to a small business owner is *unbundling.* To **unbundle** means to sell each item of hardware separately at additional cost to consumers, as opposed to **bundling,** in which a package of items is sold at a single price. Most microcomputer manufacturers today employ various levels of unbundling in their marketing. A popular advertising scheme pictures or displays all of the equipment and software possibilities of a system with a reasonable price displayed in large block letters. In small print, however, you find that the price quoted is only for the central processing unit, or CPU, and each additional item pictured, such as the disk drive, cables, printer, and software, are priced separately, thus adding to the figure quoted. The important price to a small business owner, of course, is the complete system price. This is not to say that the system price is prohibitive (because it may not be) but that you must be a wise consumer. You need to know both how much the hardware, the actual equipment, will cost and how much the software, the programs or packages that make the equipment do what we want it to do, will cost as well.

## Microcomputer Capacity

Perhaps the factor most frequently cited in microcomputer marketing is the capacity of the machine. Vendors of computer systems speak fondly of the capacity of their hardware, as though this were the major factor in the choice of a microcomputer system for a particular business. Such is not the case. **Capacity** refers to the memory limitations of the computer and its disk storage units. The computer itself will be described as having a certain level of RAM (**random access memory**) storage, such as 256K, 512K, 640K, or 1M. Such descriptions refer to the portion of computer memory available for use by the applications programmer. One K or **kilobyte** contains 1,024 bytes of memory. One **byte** holds one character of data. One M or **megabyte** contains 1,024,000 bytes. There is an additional capacity indicator that is important: the ROM (**read only memory**) storage. ROM refers to the portion of a computer's memory not accessible to the applications programmer. The ROM is used for programs (or **firmware**) written by the manufacturer of the computer or by manufacturers of computer accessories and enhancements. These programs are written on silicon ROM chips, or small wafers, and dictate the operations of the computer: the way it handles data and responds to the software.

The capacity issue can be confusing. Vendors insist that the capacity of their microcomputers determines the size of the software that can be accommodated. This is only partially true. The problem is this: some manufacturers design their computers so that part of the software is not stored in ROM but must be read into the computer from a disk drive. Such software usually is an **operating system** that controls the way the computer communicates with its disk drive and printer and the way the computer interprets the programs. The use of disk-based systems adds flexibility to a computer, but reduces the RAM available for use by programs because it must reside in the computer's memory in order to work. Limited capacity may not be a problem, however, because programs can be designed in components that are stored on a disk and loaded into the computer as required. In other words, segments of the program load other segments. In addition, RAM storage in most machines can be expanded, within limits, by simply plugging additional memory circuits into the computer. Clearly then, the memory capacity of the computer may not be the most important consideration in determining which system to buy.

## HARDWARE

*Hardware* refers to the physical machinery that makes up the computer system. It includes the central processing unit (which can be as large as a mainframe computer or as small as a microprocessor), disk drive, printer, terminal, backup device, and any other components.

### Microcomputer Architecture

The heart of a microcomputer is its microprocessor and **architecture** refers to the structure of the microprocessor. The small business owner needs to understand the basics of microprocessor architecture but does not need to be an expert in this area. A **microprocessor** looks like a small wafer of silicon. This "chip," or a memory circuit, directs the operations of the computer. The processor is the brain of the computer and has been miniaturized in microcomputers. Prior to 1981, almost all microcomputers had 8-bit processors, but with the introduction of the IBM PC, the Radio Shack Model 16, the Apple Macintosh, and others, the 16-bit processor became the standard. (A bit is a binary digit and comes from the acronym Binary digIT. Computers can only handle binary systems since electricity is either present or not, so base ten arithmetic is too complex.) A 16-bit processor produces greater speeds, more power, and greater accuracy than an 8-bit processor. Speed is measured in megahertz, or millions of cycles per second. The cycles refer to the movement of electrical impulses through the computer, so the larger the megahertz rating, the faster the machine will handle processing. Now, technological advances have brought the 32-bit processor into being and many microcomputers are equipped with it. Although the cost of some of these systems is still rather high when compared to 16-bit systems, competition is rapidly driving prices down.

One of the more important advantages of the 16-bit and 32-bit processors is multitasking, a potential not readily available on 8-bit machines. Multiprocessor boards can be installed on 8-bit machines that, in effect, can simulate 16-bit processing, but they add to the cost of the machine. **Multitasking** is the ability of the microcomputer to perform more than one task at a time. For example, payroll checks could be printed while a letter is typed, or data could be transmitted across telephone wires while items are posted to the general ledger. The greater capacity, wider range of software products, and broader price range of today's microcomputers allow small businesses to better meet their needs, but the situation creates an environment in which the user must become better educated or seek professional consultation. And, as is usually the case, the greater the flexibility, the more difficult the final selection may become.

An additional feature of the more advanced processors is **multi-user capability.** In such a system more than one person can work through terminals at a time. A terminal is simply an access device, keyboard and video screen, that allows an operator to use the equipment. If more than one person can use a system at a time, then multiple access points can be established for operators to work on the system doing different things. For example, one person could be using a terminal to handle charges to accounts receivable while another is processing the payroll. If single-user equipment were used, the records of the business would not be available to more than one person at a time. Even if you intend to use a single operator for a computer system initially, multi-user capability can be an advantage because you can expand the computer system to take advantage of that capability at some time in the future when the business size makes it more feasible.

A network is a series of microcomputers linked together so that they can share files, printers and other peripheral devices and communicate with each other. It is a step up from a multi-user system and is more powerful, but also more expensive. As in the case of multi-user systems, networks can be added at a later date. This allows a business to expand its computer support system as its needs dictate without losing the use of the initial machines acquired.

## Disk Drives

Disk drives can use hard or soft disks. **Hard disk drives** utilize a permanent, sealed unit enclosing a circular plate of magnetically sensitive material upon which data is stored. The disk spins like a phonograph record and data is read or written by a "head" suspended just above the surface of the disk. This head can read by sensing magnetic polarity changes in the disk or write by charging the surface of the disk with the correct magnetic polarity codes. A special system of codes defines the pattern of magnetic charges used to represent given letters or numbers. Because the head can be moved from edge to edge of the disk, data stored anywhere on the disk can be retrieved with equal speed. The unit is hermetically sealed, which permits extremely rapid rotation. Spin speeds of 10,000 revolutions per minute are possible, which means that positioning the head over a particular location on the disk is a matter of milliseconds.

**Soft disk drives** use removable floppy diskettes, which are thin wafers of magnetically sensitive material. The floppies come in $3\frac{1}{2}$-, $5\frac{1}{4}$-, 8-inch, and other diameters. Floppy disk drives function in much the same fashion as hard drives but cost less. Because floppy drives are not sealed and the read-write head actually contacts the diskette, they must spin at much slower speeds to avoid destruction by friction. Spin speeds are closer to 300 revolutions per minute. Consequently, data storage and retrieval with floppy drives is much slower.

The capacity of the disk drive is stated in K or M (1,024 or 1,024,000 byte increments). In addition to being 50-100 times faster than floppy disk drives, hard disk drives are capable of handling more data. They also cost a great deal more! A typical hard disk drive may have a capacity of 20 or 30 megabytes, but can range up to 100 megabytes or more. Floppy drives typically handle only 360 K to 1.44 megabytes of storage on each disk. A single drive handles only one diskette at a time and should never be considered for use in a business, unless the system also has a hard disk. With a dual disk drive, copies of data diskettes can be made quickly and simply, which is mandatory for a business whose major asset may well be its records.

Actually, the storage capacity of the disk drive is more important to a user than the capacity of the computer itself. Even though software can be designed to use multiple floppy diskettes for data storage, thereby leveraging the capacity of a system greatly, the more diskettes involved in the operation of a system, the more confusing the system becomes from an operator's perspective. In addition, there is greater danger of data loss by disk destruction because of increased handling. The best possible system is one that can store all records for a business on a single diskette, permitting all operations to take place without manipulating diskettes. Should a hard disk be required to achieve this, you should pay particular attention to data backup, which by necessity is more of a problem than in a floppy disk system that has two disk drives. (We discuss backup devices in a later section.)

## Printers

Printers are available with a wide variety of features. Printers usually are described as dot matrix, daisy wheel, or laser jet printers, although other types of print machines are available. The **dot matrix** machine uses an upright column of pins to form the character being printed. The column, called a *print head,* is moved across the paper while the printer extends various combinations of pins against an ink ribbon to form the letters by printing a pattern of dots. Such machines are capable of high speed, but have generally lower quality print than daisy wheel or laser printers. Print speeds can reach 200 cps (characters per second) on a relatively inexpensive dot matrix printer. Such speeds are accomplished by **bidirectional printing,** which simply means printing in both directions across the paper. The size of the print field for a dot matrix printer determines the readability of the print and is measured by the maximum number of dots appearing horizontally and vertically in a character. Head sizes of 9 × 9 are common and yield legible if not attractive print. Many dot matrix printers are capable of reducing the speed and increasing the number of dots printed per character to produce a higher quality of print. Such print is termed **correspondence quality.** The printer actually prints each character twice, or sometimes three times, with the print head shifted slightly on each printing. This places the dots closer together and thereby improves the type quality.

**Daisy wheel printers** use a wheel or disk with letters and characters appearing along the edge. The printer spins the wheel until the desired character falls into position and then drives the edge of the wheel against an inked ribbon above the paper with a "hammer." Such printers produce print exactly like a typewriter, which is considered high print quality. These printers have dramatically slower speeds than dot matrix or laser printers. Speeds of 55 cps are extremely fast for a daisy wheel printer. Such printers also are limited in the number of characters they can produce: only the characters engraved on the print wheel can be printed. Dot matrix printers generally allow graphics to be designed and printed by instructing the printer which pins to extend in the print head. Daisy wheel printers produce **letter quality** type and are generally more expensive than dot matrix machines.

**Laser jet printers** combine the speed of dot matrix printers and the letter quality of daisy wheel printers. These devices still are relatively expensive compared to other types of printers but promise future price drops as competition heats up. The actual printing is accomplished in the same fashion as a photocopying machine. An image is prepared for reproduction by the computer and ink is melted by a laser heating process to form the desired image. Print characteristics are outstanding and print speeds are so high that output is generally measured in pages per minute. A laser printer producing eight pages per minute can have print speeds as high as 500 cps, depending upon the number of characters on a page. Because of the printing methodology, there is no difference in printing a page filled with characters from margin to margin and a page with two lines of type. Faster speeds are available now with ten and twelve page-per-minute printers and interchangeable type fonts, which permit a broad range of type characteristics. Graphics also can be produced because no print head is involved. Laser printers are making major inroads in the printing industry because of their ability to produce virtually any type of image.

Desktop publishing has become a new buzz word. It really refers to the use of a microcomputer-based word processing and printing system to produce documents that used to have to be professionally prepared. The laser printer is the real reason that desktop publishing has arisen. Word processing packages have existed for some time that are capable of combining pictures, diagrams, figures, tables and text. However, only a laser printer can produce such a variety of output with high enough quality to use as a printing master. Any small business that has a high volume of advertising copy or other printing needs would be well advised to consider a desktop publishing system. One of its nicest features is that it uses the same microcomputer that is used for accounting. The real added expense will be a laser printer, and that may well be justifiable through other cost savings.

## Terminals

Access to the computer is usually afforded by a **terminal,** which consists of a typewriterlike keyboard and a display screen or CRT (cathode ray tube). Instructions, programs, and data are entered or **input** into the computer's memory by typing, while the screen displays both instructions to the machine and responses from the machine. **Output,** or the result of the execution of instructions, may be routed to the screen rather than to a printer. Other types of input devices were common in prior years, including punched card readers and teletype terminal machines, but most computer input is now entered through the screen-equipped terminals because of the ease of use of such devices.

Terminals can be monochrome, able to display only two colors, or color, able to display dozens of different colors. Color screens are more expensive than monochrome but may be desirable in some situations, such as engineering, in which designs will be displayed; also, some programs can be run only on a color screen. The quality of a screen is measured by the number of **pixels** or dots the screen can display. Screens are measured by the number of lines and columns they can display, the 80-column and 25-line display are the most common. Each line, however, is made up of tiny dots of light that are used to form characters and images. The smaller the dots or pixels and the more of them a screen has, the higher the quality of the picture. A high quality screen will be made up of a matrix of dots that has 720 pixels per row and 600 pixels per column ($720 \times 600$), or even greater. High quality image is not required in every type of installation, however, and the higher price such screens command may not be justifiable in every situation.

## Backup Devices

**Backup** simply means making duplicate copies of disks at designated times of the day, week, or month. To backup a disk on a dual floppy disk drive, you place the data disk in one drive and a blank disk in the other and tell the system to copy or "back up" the disk. To prevent the data from being accidentally destroyed during copying, simply place a small piece of tape called a **write protect tab** across the inset on the disk being copied (or flip the write protect switch on a $3\frac{1}{2}$-inch disk). The backup process for a hard disk drive is somewhat more complex because of the data capacity of the hard disk. To backup one hard disk with floppy disks might require as many as twenty floppies, creating more potential for error. However, special backup equipment for the hard disk allows duplication on cassette tape. Backup devices for hard disks generally use a tape cartridge much like a video cassette. The devices are still relatively expensive but may be a good investment, because the most valuable asset in your business may well be its records.

A new disk drive combines many of the better aspects of both floppy and hard disk drives. The device, called a **Bernoulli drive,** has removable rigid disks that operate at hard disk drive speeds, but with operating commands similar to floppy disk drives. The typical configuration of the device has dual drives, each capable of storing 10 megabytes on a removable diskette. The dual drive structure and floppy disk controls permit one drive to be copied to the other simply and quickly. The Bernoulli drive has great potential in the business market because it combines the ease of use and backup of a floppy drive with the speed and capacity of a hard disk drive. The Bernoulli drive generally is more expensive than a hard drive of comparable capacity but less expensive than the combination of a hard drive and a cassette tape backup.

## Change and Advancement in Microcomputers

Exhibit 9-2 compares a typical microcomputer-based system in 1978 and 1988. The chart shows how rapidly hardware has changed in a ten-year period. We can see what could be purchased for the same approximate cost at the beginning and end of the decade. In 1978 a typical microcomputer system with a price of $3,000 had a memory capacity of 32 kilobytes, and used a floppy disk drive with 180 kilobytes of storage. The system weighed about 50 pounds, operated at speeds of less than one megahertz, and was only capable of running proprietary software. As we will discuss in the software section, "proprietary"

**EXHIBIT 9-2** *Microcomputers Then and Now*

| 1978 | 1988 |
|---|---|
| • 32 kilobytes RAM | • 1 Megabyte RAM |
| • 180K floppy drive | • 1.44 M floppy drive |
| | • 20 M hard drive |
| • Less than 1 MHertz | • 12 MHertz |
| • 50 pounds | • 10 pounds |
| • Proprietary software | • Applications software |
| • Price: $3,000 | • Price: $3,000 |

means that only software designed specifically for a particular machine will run on that machine.

The same $3,000 investment in 1988 would have bought a machine with one megabyte of RAM memory, a hard disk drive with a 20 megabyte capacity, a floppy disk drive with 1.44 megabyte capacity, and an operating speed of 12 megahertz. The machine would have weighed about 10 pounds and been capable of running a variety of applications software packages. Microcomputer hardware has developed rapidly over the last 10 years and is continuing to develop at an incredible rate. Although the basic computer components and architecture have not changed significantly, the speed, capacity, and flexibility have grown dramatically. What this portends for the small business owner is an extremely powerful processing tool that can be acquired at reasonable cost.

## SOFTWARE

Software is the key to any microcomputer system. The software is what actually performs the tasks you want a computer to accomplish. The software cannot be divorced from the hardware because most microcomputer software is not entirely **portable.** Software that is portable will run on different kinds of computers: it can be moved from one kind of machine to another. Unfortunately, microcomputer manufacturers have not standardized these aspects of their hardware operating requirements, although there are some tentative steps in that direction. The "operating system" is the culprit.

### Operating Systems

An *operating system* actually is a kind of a program that stands between the software you purchase and the computer on which you run it. The operating system controls the way the computer stores data on the disk drive and other aspects of its internal functioning. Several attempts have been made to develop standardized operating systems that will work on different kinds of computers. For example, some software packages require a version of Control Program for Microcomputers (CP/M), an operating system designed by Digital Research, Inc.; the MS-DOS operating system (Microsoft Disk Operating System) handled by Microsoft, Inc.; OS/2, produced by IBM; or some other widely used operating system such as a Unix-based system.

These software packages are considered portable because microcomputers produced by different manufacturers include the requisite operating system as their software. Nevertheless, it is dangerous to consider micro software truly portable. There are several versions of most operating systems, and computer manufacturers also may add customizing features to the operating system that make it less than perfectly compatible with the same system on other machines. For example, IBM uses a version of MS-DOS called PC-DOS, which is slightly different from the original. This means that most software packages designed to run with MS-DOS will run on the IBM, but not every package. The reverse is also true: not every software package designed for the IBM and its PC-DOS will run on other machines under MS-DOS. Consequently, considerable confusion exists over what is or is not truly portable software. Many computers are referred to as **clones,** or copies, of major brands of machines, but they never are exact duplicates. To a small business about to buy a system, this means that a microcomputer system must be evaluated as a whole: hardware and software combined. A business cannot buy a computer, then search for suitable software or vice versa. It is a good idea to decide on what software you want before choosing a computer; just don't buy anything until you see software and hardware running together.

Software is the greatest problem facing the microcomputer industry. Technological advances in hardware have far outstripped the development of software, so that the state of the art and the practice of the art are years apart. Software makes a system functional and practical for a business. Development of good business software has been greatly hampered by the lack of understanding of the customer's needs. Most microcomputer software specialists do not understand business needs in general and small business needs in particular. Of course, there are exceptions, but the industry has been dominated by computer experts rather than business experts.

## Systems Design

Software for microcomputers all too frequently has been chopped down from software designed to operate on larger hardware systems or has been designed from the "bottom up." For example, when software originally designed for mainframe or minicomputer systems is adapted for use in smaller machines, features of the systems that would have been valuable to a small business user are often omitted. This practice can cause a mismatch of software to hardware capability.

**Bottom-up design** refers to the orientation of the programmer of a software package. In bottom-up design, computer specialists focus on the data in designing a software package or system. In this case, the data to be captured by the system is organized and structured into what in the industry is termed a *data base.* The software then is designed around the data base. The process is called *bottom-up* systems design because the design focus is on the bottom of the system: the data itself. This approach made sense in the days when computer equipment was so expensive that its effective use was the most important factor in cost justification.

A better approach to systems design is **top down,** which focuses on the top of the system: the user. For a computer system to be effective and provide more timely and accurate managerial information, it must communicate efficiently with the user. It doesn't matter what a system is capable of doing; it matters what a user can make a system do. If the process of data entry is foreign to the flow of information in a business, the system will not be as effective or as comfortable as it could be. If the reports and printouts generated by a system are not in an understandable or usable format or arrangement, or are not timely, then the system is practically worthless. And, if the output of a system does not contain the information needed by management for its decision-making processes, then the system *is* worthless!

All of these problems can exist in a bottom-up design. The bottom-up approach to systems work developed during the days of mainframe computers, when the operators of the system were computer specialists and computer costs were so high that it made sense to build an operation around the computer. The process has persisted because so few people in the microcomputer field understand business sufficiently to develop a top-down system and the costs of developing entirely new systems are extremely high.

## General Purpose Software

When we talk about software in general, we are interested in applications software, or programs that perform specific functions, in our case business functions. *Applications software* is available in off-the-shelf packages, designed to handle a particular business function. Accounting systems of all types are available that purport to handle the accounting needs of small businesses. These off-the-shelf packages have the advantage of price over customized alternatives, but can never be a perfect fit for any business. Because the packages are designed to fit a large market made up of a wide range of small firms, they will seldom fit any given firm perfectly.

There are several types of software packages that virtually any user of microcomputers can employ. These packages include word processing software, spreadsheet packages, and data base managers. Large numbers of each type have been developed and are available for virtually any microcomputer an individual might choose.

**Word Processing.** **Word processing** packages can do much more than simply produce letters and reports. Many of the more sophisticated packages can add columns of data, maintain mailing lists, produce individually addressed letters to selected portions of the mailing list, correct spelling errors, or provide expandable outlines for use in developing your ideas. Examples of popular word processing programs include WordStar, WordPerfect, Word, and Peachtext. Several of the newer packages, termed *integrated,* come with spreadsheet or data base systems or both. These packages are capable of sharing data files with other components so that you can use reports from one of the other systems in the word processor to prepare a written report including both data and narrative. Some word processing packages are more difficult to use than others. A potential purchaser of a microcomputer should insist on being shown how a particular word processor is used to produce the kinds of written documents anticipated.

**Spreadsheets.** **spreadsheet** package is a software program that allows the user to set up a matrix of data and manipulate the rows, columns, and elements of that matrix in virtually any fashion. Examples include the best selling Lotus 1-2-3 and the ever popular VisiCalc and its spinoffs. Spreadsheet programs have a vast range of usefulness, but can be difficult to use without considerable training. Many managers find it necessary to attend a seminar before mastering a spreadsheet program. The integrated spreadsheets may include a word processor and be capable of sharing data files with it. A spreadsheet program requires considerable internal processing capacity (RAM) to handle significant quantities of data, because the entire data base, or large portions of it, must be in memory in order to be manipulated. If truly large amounts of data must be manipulated, a data base manager may be more effective. Among the more useful applications of spreadsheets are the preparation of forecasts and budgets and summaries of more lengthy reports, because the system facilitates the manipulation of data. Forecasts, once prepared, easily can be changed to reflect a variety of "what if" scenarios, and reports can be quickly converted into charts, graphs, or other formats.

**Data Base Management.** **Data base management** systems, in essence, are spreadsheet programs that allow the user to set up a matrix of data on the disk drive. This means that the quantity of data that can be manipulated and stored is not a function of the computer memory but a function of the disk drive capacity. These systems are "relational" data bases, which are simpler to use and more powerful. Examples include DB Master, dBase IV, and R-Base System V. Many of the data base managers require considerable disk storage capacity for effective use with any significant quantity of data. A hard disk storage system may be required to achieve maximum benefit from the data base manager.

Some of the more powerful relational data base managers can be coupled with a **query language,** which permits the user to employ ordinary English in instructing the system about the contents of a particular report or data summary. Query languages generally permit the user to establish a vocabulary of several hundred words that will be used in presenting instructions to the system. Query languages can be a powerful tool and can permit a user to effectively program the data base system without knowing a programming language or understanding programming techniques.

Virtually any firm can make extended use of general purpose packages. Their role in simplifying the planning and budgeting process alone can justify their use. Because of their widespread use, virtually every leading package can be acquired for virtually any brand of microcomputer. Consequently, general purpose packages can be acquired independently of the decision concerning computer hardware and specialized software packages. We highly recommend that every prospective small business owner become familiar with general purpose packages.

## Specialized Software

In addition to general purpose software, packages are available to perform a wide variety of business functions, numerous recordkeeping tasks from accounting to project management, at very modest costs. In fact, too many such packages are available! It can be extremely confusing to try to determine which package is best for your business. Because they are developed for general sale, no package will fit your business exactly. Of course, this is also what makes the packages inexpensive. An accounting system that would require $200,000 in development costs can be acquired in general form for $200. Consequently, the gaps these packages leave in fulfilling your needs frequently can be justified on the basis of cost. The trick is to choose the best possible package for your needs. Keep in mind that you actually are choosing a system rather than a software package. The system must be evaluated as a whole.

## Customized Software

There are two types of customized software: **custom designed and programmed software** and **customized or modified packaged software.** The former refers to the preparation of a software system especially for an individual firm. Large businesses frequently employ such custom designed software. Such systems generally are written by internal data processing staffs and therefore fit the requirements of a particular organization better than any alternative. Custom designed software usually is not a feasible option for a small business. Although highly desirable, it is extremely expensive. Unless a firm has a data processing department with the requisite expertise and hardware, custom programming requires contracts with outside specialists. The systems design and programming process is not only complex but time consuming. A complete accounting system, for example, could easily require two to four personnel-years for completion. The expense associated with this kind of time is prohibitive for most small firms. More simplistic systems might be faster and less expensive, but they include potential problems. It is virtually impossible to debug a software system in a laboratory environment. That is, errors in a custom designed program will inevitably occur after the system is placed in operation. Without an internal data processing capacity to deal with such problems, system maintenance is expensive and unwieldy.

Customization or modification of an existing software package also can be a problem for a firm with no internal data processing department. This process involves making changes to the programs that make up an off-the-shelf software package. Frequently, such packages are protected by their originators to preclude such tampering. In addition, making changes to programs written by others without the programmer's documentation is extremely involved and difficult. The result is that customizing a software package generally is feasible only for the company supplying the software. Again, the process tends to be expensive. There also remains the problem with undiscovered errors in the system. Contracts with a software vendor should be explicit with respect to responsibility for and response to software problems occurring after purchase. A small business should approach software customizing very carefully.

## Selecting Software

The impact of any information system is in the area of decision making. It is reasonable, therefore, to design the software system to support decision-making activities. The output of the system should supply the information needed, when it is required, and in the most usable format. The remaining design steps involve identifying the source of the data required for information output and determining how and where this data is to be captured in an operation. Finally, the data base can be designed. This process is admittedly more complex than the bottom-up approach, but it is infinitely more useful. It is rarely practiced in microcomputer design, principally because expertise in business rather than computer expertise is required. One reason so many small business managers have trouble understanding and using microcomputer systems is now clear: many of those systems were not properly designed to communicate with and complement small business management!

For example, it is not enough to know that an inventory system must provide information about items in stock, on order, and sold to date. The systems designer must know what constitutes inventory management in a small business. Is "on order" information as important in larger businesses where management is not directly involved in the purchasing process? Does the small business benefit sufficiently from this information to justify the entry of such data? In fact, many small businesses keep no records of inventory items on order because the lag times and number of items involved are so small that management has an excellent grasp of out of stock and excess stock situations. In many small businesses the real inventory management problem is in determining the true cost of sales. Because physical inventory is so time consuming, it may be ignored until year end, when it is forced on management. In the meantime, obsolescence, loss, damage, theft, and so forth may have been eroding profits. An inventory management system might better serve small businesses if it focused on inactivity within the inventory and on improving partial inventory counts through its departmental physical inventory sheets. Such a system might be more valuable if it were capable of generating FIFO (first in, first out) and LIFO (last in, first out) cost assumption comparisons because so many small business owners really do not understand the significance of those accounting decisions. The point is that the inventory information needs of a small business do not necessarily mirror those of larger businesses.

Another major source of difficulty is the location, format, and timing of data entered into a software system. For a microcomputer to save time and money for a small business, it must not create problems in data input requirements. The data source, availability, and timing of the information flow in a small business frequently is quite different from that of a more structured, larger firm. The problem often is compounded by the lack of communication skills between computer specialists and small business managers. Even though they are speaking different languages, each group assumes the other understands more than actually is the case. This can be a source of surprise when a computer specialist designs a system for a small business owner. The communication problem makes the already expensive process of custom designed software that much more expensive, time consuming, and risky.

## EVALUATION OF COMPUTER SYSTEMS

So, how can a small business owner identify the right computer system? Actually, it is not hard to evaluate a system. Focus on the software and let the hardware decision follow its selection. First, a potential purchaser ought to ask the system vendor about the qualifications of the individual or firm that wrote the software. This question seems natural in other contexts but is almost never asked when off-the-shelf or packaged software is involved. In a contract custom design situation, the credentials of the specialist are examined, so why is this not the case in a software package? Actually, it is more difficult and complex to design and program a general purpose system than to do a custom job. Accordingly, a business should be more critical of the author of a software package than those of a custom programming job.

## In-House Evaluation

Evaluating the credentials of software writers should not be merely a function of asking how many systems have been sold. Shelved software is appallingly frequent in a small business; that is, software packages that have been purchased but are not used either because of mismatches of capabilities and needs or difficulty of operation. Satisfied customers are not necessarily a good checkpoint either. Small businesses are so diverse and so numerous that almost any software package is bound to fit someone. References from other users of a system can be useful only to reassure a potential purchaser that the software does operate and that there are no bugs or points of system failure. Unfortunately, that is all the other users can tell us. The final analysis and evaluation of a software package must be performed at the keyboard and by the managers of a small business. That's right, by the manager—especially, the owner! Professional advice can be sought, but only the owner can make the proper decisions.

Small business owners often have been heard to say, "I won't be operating the system so don't bore me with that stuff!" Whether or not a small business owner intends to actually enter data into a computer system, that individual will be responsible for seeing that the data is entered and for managing and supervising the people who are trained to use the system. In addition, the manager will be using the system output in decision making; and if the manager does not understand how the data was captured, crunched, and transformed into the information contained in the system reports, then use of the information is severely restricted.

If a small business owner is not willing personally to learn to operate a microcomputer system, then the system should not be purchased. A business reflects its owner in its organization, structure, and operating procedures. A microcomputer system will not be compatible with a business unless it, too, reflects its owner's needs and desires. Therefore, the only acceptable evaluation technique is for the owner to sit at the keyboard and insist on being shown how to operate every aspect of the system; to examine every report and printout that the system can generate; and to demand an explanation of how each element of information on each report got there and what happened to the data between entry and report. Such an evaluation will immediately indicate how easy or difficult it will be to enter data when the manual system is converted to the automated system and how useful the system will be. If the match between the computer and the business is not acceptable, then beware! Mismatches between systems and users can result in increased costs and information of little or no value to management.

A common cause of microcomputer system mismatch is the actual operating process. For example, software packages frequently are designed to use a transaction file in which data affecting all aspects of the system are accumulated. Typically, this process employs an updating routine for each component of the system. That is, at the end of a month or other selected period, an updating routine must be run to post transactions affecting the general ledger; a second updating routine, to post transactions affecting accounts receivable; a third, to post inventory; another, to post payables; and so forth. With a structure of this type, information on the business is available only after the updating is completed. For example, a simple question like How much cash do we have on hand? may not be answerable until the end of the month! The time required to update the relevant files may make the system impractical on a frequent update basis. This would damage one of the most valuable aspects of a computer system: availability of data. One of the major problems in manual systems is that it takes too long and is too much work to generate progress reports for frequent reports to be justified. If a computer cannot improve the timeliness of information, its only remaining value to a small business lies in cost savings from reduced personnel needs. And if the data-entry process does not conform to the information flows in a business, then an automated system may actually increase personnel requirements!

## Professional Assistance

Increasingly, small businesses are employing consultants to assist in the evaluation of software packages and the selection of microcomputers. CPAs as well as independent computer consultants can be valuable advisors during the process. If you feel a lack of understanding or knowledge about accounting or any other business function being automated, the use of a professional in that area can make good sense. The same is true if your feelings of inadequacy revolve around computers and systems. The fees involved for such assistance frequently are well justified in obtaining a better fit between system and firm.

A consulting engagement must be managed in order for it to be beneficial. You must keep in mind that you are buying advice and training, not hiring someone to make the selection for you! You and your business, not the consultant, will have to live with the system selected. In addition, regardless of the skill and knowledge of the consultant, no one can know your business as well as you do. This means that you must use the professional to gain knowledge about processes in the business and the pros and cons of various systems. You should view the consulting engagement as a training exercise. The goal is for you to gain the knowledge to make the necessary decisions personally.

Two types of decisions are involved: the computer system to be acquired and changes in the business processes that must be made to make the system fit the firm. The latter decision is caused by the lack of a perfect fit from software packages. The decisions made in both areas will have long-range effects on the firm and its efficiency. No one should make such decisions except the owner. In addition, decisions involving changes in operations should involve the people in the firm who will be affected by those changes. Frequently, operational changes mandated by automation can result in more streamlined and efficient functions, but the reverse can occur. Many firms have found that operational changes create extreme prejudice among employees against computer systems, cause more work, and damage morale. Getting the people affected by a computer system, directly and indirectly, involved in the decisions can help preclude such problems. As is always the case, the final decisions belong to the owner.

## COMPUTER BRANDS

One final point needs to be made about microcomputer system evaluation: the name on the computer is less important than popularly believed. Most microcomputer manufacturers do not produce the key components of their machines. The actual heart of the machine, the microprocessor, dictates the primary capabilities of the computer. The type of microprocessor around which a machine is built is frequently the same in competing computers. The heart of the IBM PC, for example, is a microprocessor built by Intel Corporation, which is also the heart of more than twenty competing brands. Only a handful of companies are involved in the design and manufacture of microprocessors, so their product shows up in many computers. In fact, other components of microcomputers also are frequently purchased rather than produced by manufacturers to provide flexibility for the company and reduce the risk of obsolescence. Many brands of microcomputers in reality are assembled rather than manufactured by the company whose label is displayed on the machine. That means that fears of potential hardware problems when a supplier goes out of business are not nearly as valid as they once were. Nevertheless, market share statistics indicate that brand name is a factor in most people's decision to buy a computer. Machines differ in structure, thus some brands of microcomputers run faster or perform better than competing brands that have the same architecture. However, as is the case with most technology, the cutting edge of innovation and development is not necessarily present in the giants of the industry. Small business owners are fond of saying that there are things they can do better and cheaper than large business, and they are correct. They should keep this in mind when they make purchases themselves.

Perhaps the primary benefit to be gained from choosing a system vended by a large company is the availability of service. Service, obviously, is of paramount importance. Because the initial contact for service calls traditionally has been the local dealer, the vendor firm usually is considered crucial to the continued availability of service. However, this is not so important with microcomputers. If a microcomputer or peripheral device requires service beyond the mere changing of components, it frequently requires highly sophisticated repair. Most dealers in microcomputers and peripherals do not have such expertise and must send the equipment to specialists for repair. Computer repair firms are springing up to fill this need. These firms repair a variety of brands of equipment and are available to dealers who find themselves unable to handle a repair problem. Consequently, the primary service needed by small business owners from the dealer is the provision of loaner equipment to avoid a business shutdown because of machine failure. The dealer's long-term capability to provide loaner equipment on short notice should be the first consideration of a potential purchaser when considering service.

### Maintaining Currency

Learning about microcomputer systems and software is facilitated by reading relevant periodicals. Before purchasing a system, a manager would be well advised to read several magazines, preferably over a period of several months. Among the better periodicals in the microcomputer field are *Infoworld, Byte,* and *PC Magazine.* Not only will such magazines review hardware and software, their articles will enhance the computer literacy of the reader and predict developments in the computer industry that may be relevant to a particular business. Reading such periodicals for a month or two before investing in a system is a must. Back issues can be examined in most libraries and may well prove worthwhile. Even after a microcomputer system is in use, continued reading is necessary to keep abreast of changes in the industry that may affect the business. New products will be announced and reviewed, new applications of old products discussed, and industry trends will be examined. Such information will keep a manager current to the use of the automated portion of the managerial arsenal.

## THE PROBLEM OF SECURITY

The recent growth in the use of computers and computer services in the small business arena mandates a review of the plans of such firms for disaster or theft. Computer-based information systems produce many benefits, however, along with the benefits come disadvantages. Among them are the need for tougher computer security and recovery planning. The industry is rife with horror stories of companies losing not only hardware but diskettes filled with irreplaceable records. One of the more famous cases is of the group of youngsters in Atlanta who broke into offices after hours and walked away with equipment and diskettes that they planned to recycle or use for games.[1] Another small business was forced into bankruptcy when an employee chose to steal from the company via program "diddling."[2] After a near loss of its facilities by tornado, still another company failed to update its disaster recovery plan and suffered a complete loss by fire.[3] The list grows.

Much has been written in the past few years about the concern for computer security. The concern is well placed: computer sabotage and spying have become a major problem. Large corporations tend to be more concerned with electronic security because their physical security issues have long been a concern and therefore are well planned. Are small businesses less well prepared in the area of computer security? With the increasing number of small businesses purchasing microcomputers, the need for security is of greater importance. The small box is easily accessible and many programs require no password. Often there may be no separation of duties or built-in controls. The lack of extra requirements for installation and maintenance may mean that plans for disaster recovery are not considered.

There are two aspects to computer security. Electronic security, the more flashy attention getter, involves protecting a firm from illegal data manipulation, information theft, and data sabotage. Disaster security deals with protection from physical mishaps. Although electronic crime can be expensive, physical accidents can totally destroy a company's operations. An electronic thief may access a system, steal information, and slip away: hardware and data remain intact. However, if a fire occurs, hardware is destroyed and data is lost, causing a major problem for a company without an adequate disaster plan.

Until the proliferation of mini- and microcomputers, little was written about security planning. Large businesses long had ensured against computer crime as best they could, and established contingency plans for recovery in the event of a natural catastrophe. Small business managers, although conscious of the benefits of computing resources, had little time to concern themselves with events they considered remote. However, with the sudden influx of articles detailing the damage done by young hackers or disgruntled employees, people are becoming more concerned.

The latest threats to surface are computer viruses. These are programs written by hackers that can transport themselves from machine to machine through telephone or modem links or through floppy disks that are read by more than one computer. These viruses can be benign; that is, harmless pranks. They can also be much more serious. Several viruses have damaged or destroyed files and data segments and even on occasion the hardware. Security precautions must now take into consideration potential problems from viruses.

With the furor following the movie *War Games,* the legal system has begun the slow, grinding process to evolve laws that deal with computer crime. Meanwhile, security measures to protect small businesses from such losses by necessity have become more complex as technological advances resulted in more data stored in fewer places, allowing greater access from remote locations.

Perhaps the most informative article concerning natural disaster and recovery planning was prepared by Stair.[4] Stair's proposed five-step disaster plan includes the following components:

1. A statement of the objectives for the plan; that is, what kinds of protection are desired from the plan, and what it is supposed to accomplish;
2. An analysis of the potential disasters; that is, a list of all the things that could happen to a computer system;
3. A formulation of a disaster plan; that is, a list of the actions to be taken for each potential disaster identified;
4. The documentation of the disaster plan, which simply means that the plan must be in writing;
5. The implementation of the plan, which means assigning responsibility for putting the plan into action.

In a recent telephone survey, we found that small businesses are not preparing disaster plans.

We surveyed 110 firms by telephone. Only the larger organizations, having larger computer configurations and more than ten data processing employees, had adequate disaster and backup plans. Those companies having microcomputers for processing and only one or two data processing employees typically never considered computer security as other than a natural precaution for regular office equipment. Most were aware of backup procedures and the necessity for them but were not concerned about access to hardware or software or the separation of functions.

Of the companies surveyed, 90% claimed that accounting functions, such as accounts receivable and payroll, were kept on their computer and yet only seventeen admitted any restriction of access to the computer, the programs, or the data. Only two companies claimed to limit the access to data and systems via passwords.

An issue of great concern to the researchers was the absence of vital and active top management involvement in computer security plans. Only twenty-six companies claimed that management was involved in planning for computer security, and when asked to what extent, all claimed that the top management supported the plans developed by other personnel.

The conclusions reached in this short study are less surprising than frustrating. Small business owners have realized the need for a management tool that can put vital strategic information at their fingertips, and yet they treat that tool as if it were a broom. Top management should be more involved with security measures that could affect the life of the company. Token support is better than a lack of interest but has far reaching implications for the company. Managing the information system security function can be a complex task.

An editorial in *Infoworld* a few years back claimed that small businesses, and businesses in general, were becoming too security conscious, that the computer should be available to any employee because it is a tool and should be used as such.[5] Unfortunately, the author was referring to a microcomputer in a mainframe environment, when many small businesses only have micro systems. He likened carrying home a diskette of data to carrying home a file folder. He should have likened it to carrying home an entire filing cabinet, which would be frowned upon by any management. When microcomputers are the sole means of automation in a business, that business must be security conscious. Computer security can mean the life or death of the company.

The relatively low level of security imposed over most companies' computer-based systems can be traced to two main reasons. First, and most important, is the lack of top management understanding of the vulnerability and importance of their computer- and information-related resources. Second, is the failure of most hardware manufacturers to develop system architectures that could make computer security simple. There is little we can do about the second problem, but self-education can cure the first one. Exhibit 9-3 offers some suggestions.

No one person or group should bear complete responsibility for protecting the computer system. The need for controls should be instilled in the entire organization, starting with the owner and extending to all personnel. It is most important that you be aware of the nature and implications of the risks associated with computer based systems. This is especially important in light of the growing level of computer literacy. The expansion of personal computing by the general public has greatly increased the group of potential abusers of computer systems. The simultaneous expansion of on-line and **networked systems,** which are computer systems with access by remote terminals, has increased the points of entry into a computer system. The two trends increase the risk dramatically.

The effectiveness of any security program ultimately is dependent on the significance attached to it by top management. Most important is the recognition by users of the significance of computer security to the overall well-being of the organization. With the growing level of computer use and access, the user increasingly will be responsible for computer security, but the responsibility for that security rests with the owner.

**EXHIBIT 9-3** *Disaster Planning and Security Precautions Dos and Don'ts*

DOS

1. Do protect yourself against unauthorized users, programs, and software.
2. Do use networks wisely and limit access to protected lines.
3. Do follow backup and copy procedures faithfully.
4. Do keep important records, files, programs, and documents in a safe place.
5. Do make provisions for disasters before they happen, such as loan of a system or the use of "site" experts.
6. Do use internal controls for access to the computer.
7. Do become the final authority on the use, change, or misuse of your system.
8. Do set up rules for the use of the system and follow those rules strictly.
9. Do plan and plan wisely to protect your company's greatest assets: its records.

DON'TS

1. Don't use diskettes other than those provided by the vendor to protect yourself against viruses.
2. Don't use bulletin boards from your business computer and only use designated lines for networking.
3. Don't forget to make periodic backups of your data and programs from your hard disks, because they can crash when you least need or expect a problem.
4. Don't forget to keep copies of important programs, data, and insurance papers off the business site in a safety deposit box or other protected location.
5. Don't forget to make arrangements with computer vendors for maintenance contracts or replacement systems.
6. Don't allow unlimited access to the microcomputer by all members of your staff.
7. Don't allow changes to be made to programs, data, or documentation without your understanding and authorization.
8. Don't allow employees access to the system after hours for personal activities.
9. Don't forget to plan because you have the most to lose.

## SUMMARY

In this era of high tech computerization, small businesses are finding that they must automate or be deemed hopelessly obsolete and noncompetitive. Actually, many businesses are so small that computerization would be a time consumer rather than a time saver. However, the trend across the country is more and more toward automation.

Managers who are making the decisions to automate should not be intimidated by the language. Terminology that is unclear should be explained. Don't be caught in the trap of pretending knowledge that doesn't exist. Ask questions about software (the programs that make the computer work) and hardware (the equipment upon which the programs run: the central processing unit, the keyboard, the monitor, the disk drive, and the printer)—their speeds, capacities, and advantages. Ask, too, about how these components are priced.

*Backup* refers to the duplication of records so that when accidents occur, the information so vital to the life of the company will not be lost.

The microprocessor is the brain of the computer and dictates whether the business can perform one or more applications at a time on the system, as well as how many different people can have access to the system at a given time.

Technological advances in hardware have far outstripped the development of software, so that the state of the art and the practice of the art are years apart. Software makes a system functional and practical from a business perspective. Development of good business software has been greatly hampered by the lack of understanding of business needs on the part of many system developers. The best method for ensuring that software meets the needs of businesses is to design the software from the perspective of the information needed for decision making or from the user; from the top down. Small businesses are distinct from large businesses and, although some of the functions of both are generic, their needs are different.

There are two types of software: off-the-shelf and customized software. Customized software may be custom designed and programmed software, or customized (or modified) packaged software.

A small business should probably acquire a good system, which has expansion capabilities, with a large amount of general packaged software available to run on it. With generalized software packages such as word processors, spreadsheets, and data base managers, a great deal of information quickly can be at the fingertips of the manager. Specialized software packages also are available.

A good consultant who understands the needs of small businesses could help in choosing the right system, but the manager must be involved in both the decision to purchase a computer system and its use. The name of the computer is less important than popularly believed. The microprocessor dictates what the computer can do, and it is the same in many of the most well-known computers. Decisions should be based on features and concepts rather than the name of the machine. Large computer vendors tend to sell service as well as machines, so if this is a primary concern, then it should be reflected in the decision. Make yourself knowledgeable. Read the journals and stay up to date.

Computer security is a topic of concern. Small businesses typically backup diskettes, but they do not always restrict access to the microcomputers or take the ordinary precautions they would without a computer. Disaster plans often are never formulated. To use this automated tool wisely and with knowledge, make written plans.

## QUESTIONS

1. Why is it not really necessary for all businesses to computerize?
2. If you were the manager of a small business, what would you do about computerization and why?
3. Why is management's continued involvement necessary in the computerization process?
4. Define the following terms:
   a. hardware
   b. software
   c. firmware
5. What is the difference between top-down and bottom-up design, and why should small businesses look for software with the top-down approach?
6. Describe the components necessary in a computer system. Which components are more important and why?
7. Why should a manager not pretend to know computer lingo if he or she doesn't?
8. How might small businesses and large businesses differ in their needs and decision-making activities?
9. Why is the brand name on a computer not important?
10. What are the several types of software, and how are they different?
11. Why do you think it would be safer to use a general purpose software package than hire someone to customize personalized software for small business usage? (Read several of the articles listed in the notes.)
12. Why is disaster planning important?
13. Why is computer security an issue?
14. How should a small business owner/manager evaluate a computer system?

## PROJECTS

1. Go to several microcomputer vendors and question them about the components they have for a small business computer system and their prices. Before you go, discuss with the class what the requirements for the system will be and what aspects of the business you wish to computerize. Think about whether you want multi-user capability and how many machines. Go to several vendors with your requirements and consider their responses to you and your questions. Compare these experiences when you return to class. You may have a feel for how the small business owner is treated when he or she goes to a computer vendor. What knowledge did you gain about computers from this venture? What knowledge did you gain about people?
2. If you know of several small businesses in your town who have micro- or minicomputers, interview them. Ask about how they decided to become computerized and why. Ask about their vendors: whether they are happy with the service and what kind of service they have. Ask if they had a consultant help them and, if not, do they now wish they had used one. Ask about whether they feel that automation has enhanced their decision making and in what manner. Ask if they have disaster plans and why or why not. Use your knowledge and imagination to gain further insight into small business computing.

# CASE

Jim Collins and Jeff Reid were software consultants for a microcomputer firm responsible for helping set up clients' computer systems and assuring that the implementation went smoothly. They were very good at their jobs and had a fine reputation in their business circles. Usually, from the first contact with their client, they worked with management to automate the business. But this case was difficult for them.

It started out badly and continued in that vein. Collins and Reid typically talked to the manager and discovered the business' needs, purchased the computer and software based on those needs, did some of the training on the system, and were in constant touch through the start-up phase. This time the manager already had decided which system he wanted, based on a friend's suggestion, and insisted the two consultants follow his wishes in the matter. This was easy, thought the consultants, a man who knows his own mind.

However, after purchasing the system, the manager was never available for any of the training. He said that as long as his staff knew how to work the computer, he was happy. After all, he was automating for them. He didn't have to know how the computer worked.

The staff, on the other hand, was belligerent. Why did they have to change to a computer? After all, they had been doing the same things all these years and were quite content. They didn't have time to learn all the new ways to do things and still get their work done. Besides, the boss felt he was too good to have to fool with a computer, so why should they?

Collins and Reid's trouble was just starting. No sooner were all the records converted to the new system than the consultants were called by an irate manager. It seems that his part-time bookkeeper, an elderly lady who came in twice a week to do the books, claimed that the computer was making mistakes. Because one of her tasks was to compute payroll, the payroll module was hers; and the first month, the payroll was wrong! What were Collins and Reid going to do about it?

As the consultants were familiar with the software being used, they asked the bookkeeper to send them her diskette and the supporting documentation for the employees who were in error. They would find the mistake and correct it. After looking at the program, manually calculating the payroll for each employee, and comparing that result to the bookkeeper's, it became very obvious where the problem lay.

Collins and Reid ascertained by phone who had entered the setup data on each employee (with such things as marital status, dependents, withholdings, etc.) and found that the bookkeeper would not touch the computer. All input had been done by a secretary who input data from the files and in some cases this data was different from that used by the bookkeeper, which accounted for those discrepancies. More serious, however, was another check that had been miscalculated. This check belonged to the bookkeeper, herself, and the amount paid to her by the computer was $100 less than when she wrote the checks. No amount of reconciliation of her data was able to identify the error. Each month, she was paying herself $100 more than she merited.

Collins and Reid double checked everything to ascertain that all other errors reported were errors made by the bookkeeper in not maintaining current files on the employees, but her problem could be explained by only one answer: embezzlement.

When Collins and Reid tactfully tried to explain the situation to the manager, he became angry. The computer had made a mistake. After all, this lady had been working for him for the last 5 years and had many years of experience before coming to him. The fact that the computer was correct on all the other occasions didn't matter. If Collins and Reid couldn't fix the computer, then he would just quit using it, which he did.

## Questions

1. Were you able to anticipate problems before they occurred in this situation?
2. Why do you think the manager felt as he did in this case and took such an action?
3. If you had been the consultants, what would you have done differently?
4. How could this situation have been avoided? What could make the system work?

# PART III

# THE BUSINESS PLAN

# CHAPTER 10

# Overview of the Business Plan

**LEARNING OBJECTIVES**

After completing this chapter, you should be able to

- Explain the importance of each step of the business plan.
- Understand why personal goals and objectives must be considered in business ventures.
- Understand the importance of establishing business objectives.
- Realize the significance of strategic issues and their impact on business.
- Explain the requirements for success as outlined by the planning stages.
- Identify the distinctive competency of a business.
- Plan for the physical and capital requirements of a business venture.

Julius Caesar's famous quotation, "Veni, vidi, vici," comes from his 47 B.C. report to the Roman Senate about his successful campaign against the Gauls. Caesar had crossed into what is now France with a force of troops vastly outnumbered by the fighting Gauls and was faced with a territory larger than Italy in which those forces were deployed. Through superior military strategy and tactics, Caesar was successful in subjugating the territory and adding it to the Roman Empire. His report of that success was vain and lacked details, but his letter expressed the desires of all individuals who start new businesses. He simply said, "I came, I saw, I conquered." That, in essence, is what a successful new business venture must do. It must establish a presence in the target market area, examine the characteristics of the market and competition in that area, and effectively employ strategies and tactics that will establish the venture as a permanent force in the area. The most important consideration for the success of a business is the plan it will follow in its campaign: its strategy. That plan is the subject of this chapter.

## OUTLINE OF THE BUSINESS PLAN

The first step in preparing a business plan is to establish business objectives. These objectives must not be vague or general. They must be concrete, specific, and quantifiable. The objectives will be used to measure the progress the company has made; therefore, they need to be as detailed as possible. The personal objectives of the owner may or may not be a part of the business objectives, but they, too, should have been examined and recorded as part of the evaluation process in the decision to start the business. Exhibit 10-1 outlines the entire process.

Although the steps in the business plan are listed in sequential order in the exhibit, many of them will be performed simultaneously. The important point to remember is that each step must be performed prior to actually starting the business, and the results of each step must be written down in the planning document. The location of the steps in Exhibit 10-1 simply indicates the point at which an absolute final determination of each aspect of the plan is required relative to the others.

Upon completion of the business plan, the prospective owner will have a written document to guide the business through its start-up phase and provide a tool to monitor the progress of the venture. Remember that the plan inevitably will require adjustment as the start up proceeds. Changes will have to be made as new knowledge is gained and plans prove untenable. This is to be expected and is not a sign of failure. Changes to the plan should be made in writing so that the document can continue to provide a benchmark for evaluating progress.

**EXHIBIT 10-1** *Outline of the Business Plan*

I. Establish your personal objectives
  1. Determine your present objectives
  2. Determine where you wish to be in 5 years
  3. Determine where you wish to be in 10 years

II. Choose a product or service
  1. Evaluate the marketability of the product or service
  2. Determine the feasibility of the product or service

III. Select a Market Area
  1. Evaluate the market area
  2. Determine the feasibility of the market area
  3. Evaluate the competition

IV. Establish your business objectives

V. Begin your strategy development

VI. Establish a timetable

VII. Determine your human resource requirements

VIII. Determine your physical resource and capacity requirements

IX. Select a site

X. Finalize your business strategies
  1. Determine your distinctive competency
  2. Prepare a marketing plan

XI. Determine your capital requirements

XII. Prepare forecasts and budgets
  1. Prepare a sales forecast
  2. Prepare a marketing budget
  3. Prepare an operating budget
  4. Prepare a capital budget
  5. Prepare an income statement
  6. Prepare a balance sheet

XIII. Perform a break-even analysis

XIV. Evaluate and modify your plan

XV. Locate and obtain capital

XVI. Implement the plan

XVII. Evaluate your progress

## FEASIBILITY

The first three steps of the business plan actually revolve around the feasibility of the venture. The examination of personal goals and objectives serves two purposes. It forces a prospective owner to examine whether he or she personally is willing to pay the price of success in this new business and forces a recognition of what that price will be. We talked about the long hours worked by successful business owners in the introductory chapters. We also discussed the characteristics required for success. Sadly, the personal price of success in a new venture can be quite high. It must be something one wants and wants greatly. The cover story in *Inc.* for March 1986 was "Divorce."[1] The upshot of the article was advice to business owners that to plan for a divorce may ruin a marriage, but not to plan for it may destroy a company. That the magazine publishers thought the story worthy of primary coverage is noteworthy. Starting a new business is a very serious step. No one should undertake that step without first carefully examining his or her personal goals and objectives.

Product or service viability is not synonymous with salability. For a product or service to be viable, there must be a demand for it and it must be feasible to produce and sell. This means that **viability** is a function of the market, the costs of production, and the sales price obtainable for the item. The first part of the question is answered through market research. The second part of the question involves break-even analysis. Break-even analysis is listed among the final steps in the business plan, because one of the last steps is the calculation of the final break-even characteristics of the organization, but a rough estimate of the break-even point is required at the stage when product or service viability is being examined.

The actual calculation of a break-even point is a simple arithmetic solution, as we saw in Chapter 6. If we are assessing the viability of a product or service, then we need a rough estimate of what the fixed and variable costs will be. The **fixed costs** are not hard to calculate; they include such things as rent, salaries, insurance, and utilities. **Variable costs** are the costs of actually producing the product or service. If the business is to be a retail store, then variable costs are the costs of inventory. However, estimates of the variable costs may be very difficult to make, especially in the case of a manufacturing company. Estimates of possible selling prices also may be difficult. The variable costs need to be expressed per unit or per dollar of sales to calculate the contribution margin. The **contribution margin** is simply the amount of money left over to cover fixed expenses after the variable costs have been paid. In terms of one unit of sales, the contribution margin is the amount of the sales price left over after paying for the unit. The contribution margin usually is expressed as a percentage of sales. Dividing projected fixed costs for the first year of operations by the contribution margin will yield an estimate of the dollar volume of sales that must be generated for the business to break even and avoid a loss. Because all of the numbers are estimates, it is wise to make several calculations for each variable, using a range of estimates from pessimistic to optimistic.

The final determination of viability of a product or service frequently comes down to a subjective determination of whether the sales level required to break even can be achieved in a given market area. At this point in the planning process, the prospective business owner must decide whether there is a high enough probability for success of a given product or service in a given market area to continue the planning process. If the decision is positive, then the remaining steps of the business plan should be addressed. The original rough estimates of break-even point and product or market viability should be reassessed continuously during the planning process as new and more accurate information is obtained.

Chapter 3, "Marketing Tools for Success," discusses the technical aspects of marketing in a small business enterprise. Because of the relative importance of marketing to a successful start up, we will dedicate Chapter 11 entirely to the issues of product or service selection and the preparation of the marketing plan. For now we assume that the prospective small business owner already has selected a product or service and market area.

## BUSINESS OBJECTIVES

As indicated earlier, the business objectives must be concrete and specific. They should address where the business should be in terms of sales, profits, and market share at the end of the start-up period and at the end of each of the next three to five years. Any other key aspects of the business' success should be included in the objectives as well. For example, the product mix might be considered important for a retailer or wholesaler who plans to expand the lines and number of products offered during the early years of the venture. If so, then objectives should be established for the product mix. If the number or skill mix of the employees is important, as in the case of a business offering professional services, then the personnel levels and skills should be part of the objectives. The point is that the objectives must address the key aspects that will determine the success or failure of the business. Such concerns are called **strategic issues.** Successful management of strategic issues will mean that the firm survives; unsuccessful management of strategic issues will spell doom for the business.

Setting objectives for the firm actually requires that the owner recognize the strategic issues for his or her business. What must the business do to ensure its survival? The issues will be different for different businesses. For example, in a restaurant that caters to a local market, a strategic issue will be to establish a high level of repeat patronage. Does this sound obvious? Most strategic issues are like this, but sometimes the most obvious things are the most difficult to see.

The determination of strategic issues for a business frequently revolves around the image a company wishes to portray: its marketing image. If, for example, a business is to have an image of high quality, then not only must the proper appearance be maintained in the business and in dealing with the market, but the owner must pay attention to competitors to ensure that no one usurps the image in the market area. If the image is to be one of low price, then the same rules hold true. Not only must everything in the business be consistent with the established image, but the business must continue to portray that image when compared to its competitors. This requires a close and continuous monitoring of competing firms in the market area. Consider an actual case of a small grocery store in southern Georgia as described by an independent consultant.

We were called in as consultants because the store was losing money. It was a small grocery store located in a predominantly rural area in southern Georgia. It had been in existence for almost twenty years and had been profitable until the last two years. The owner had inherited the place from his father five or six years ago.

We visited the store, talked to the owner, and looked at the financial statements. The statements showed a steady decline in sales starting about eighteen months prior to our visit. Losses had begun to be recorded about twelve months prior and the store looked like it might not survive.

The owner said that everything had been going fine until a Piggly Wiggly opened up down the street and killed his business. We checked on that, but the Piggly Wiggly was a bit higher priced than our client's store and it had been in existence for a little over two years. At least six months of that time our client had done all right, so that didn't make any sense. We checked for other competitors, but there really weren't any significant changes in the competitive picture during the eighteen months of the sales decline.

When we toured the store, we found the problem. But even then we couldn't get the client to see it. The first clue was a mess in the lower shelves of the pet food section. Several bags had apparently been torn because there was a lot of dog food on the floor and on the shelves between the bags. We didn't figure it out immediately, but when we got to the meat section, there wasn't a lot of meat on display in the coolers and several of the packages were torn and discolored. The store really wasn't dirty enough to explain the tears, although some packages were torn, too. We really were puzzled. Then we took a peek in a gap between the ice cream cooler and the adjoining shelving. That's when we saw it.

It was a rat trap! Not a mouse trap—a rat trap. You could have caught rabbits in that trap!

We asked several of the employees whether any customers had ever complained about rats. The response was that only one or two had ever reported actually seeing a rat and only one had ever left because of it. Apparently, one lady had left a full grocery cart sitting in the aisle and departed the store in a hurry.

We confronted the owner with the problem. However, he denied that this could be the source of his troubles, because he had about gotten rid of all the rats. It seems that a delivery truck had backed into the warehouse door one day a couple of years ago and the door had never closed completely since then. As soon as the rats were noticed, they had apparently come in the door crack from a nearby creek, he had fixed the door and started trapping the pests. Most were now gone, so the owner said. Besides, the health department hadn't noticed anything.

We asked about a professional exterminator service, but the owner said they were too expensive. Besides, the one firm he talked to had wanted to fumigate the place, which would have meant losing a fortune in meat and produce!

Can you believe it! In the interest of saving a few dollars in the short run, the owner was killing his business! And somehow, we just couldn't make him see it.

A true but sad story. The grocery store ultimately failed. Its owner had not paid attention to a strategic issue. Shoppers in a grocery store demand a clean facility—one that is not infested with rodents or insects. The moral of the story is that a business owner who would be a success must determine what the market demands and fulfill that demand consistently and constantly.

Business strategies are plans to achieve business objectives. As soon as the objectives have been established, you must begin to consider strategies. These cannot be finalized until a timetable has been established, human and physical resources determined, and a site selected; however, the strategies that you will pursue will affect every aspect of the plan. We will discuss the strategy development process in a later section, but be aware that your initial considerations should begin as soon as objectives have been set.

## TIMETABLE

The **timetable** refers to the establishment of dates for the beginning of the preventure advertising, the completion of all the opening requirements, the opening date, the end of the start-up marketing phase, the dates when key people will be placed on the payroll, starting dates for the remainder of the staff, and the date for the start of completely normal operations. Many new venturists neglect this phase of the plan because it is so difficult to complete. If there are construction aspects to the opening of the business, whether the building of a new facility or the completion of leasehold improvements, you quickly will learn that the estimate for completion of construction activities frequently is a complete guess. Many other time factors will be difficult to estimate as well. For example, the arrival date for the first inventory shipment, the installation date for telephone systems, the arrival of fixtures and furniture, and a host of other details will be difficult to estimate. Nevertheless, the timetable should not be neglected. The process of developing a timetable will be of immense value even if every date in it turns out to be wrong. Preparing the timetable will force you to make a written list of every aspect of the start-up phase of your business. Until you have actually prepared the list once, you will be amazed at how many details are involved in starting a new business and how easy it is to overlook them.

Other aspects of the timetable are less difficult to determine because they are planned. These include the duration of the start-up marketing program (its beginning and ending dates), personnel requirements, and the beginning of normal operations. You should give considerable thought to the establishment of this part of the timetable. Budgetary restraints will play a role, of course, but other factors like the level of established competition, the dispersion of the target market, and the difficulty of reaching that market also will affect the planning. A retail business with a small market area and a low level of established competition will not require an elaborate preopening marketing campaign nor will a wholesale business that will depend on sales calls to make its presence known to the market. On the other hand, a retailer or service firm facing deep, entrenched competition or a widely dispersed market area may well be better served by extensive preopening advertising and a lengthy period of specials or promotional activities after its opening. Personnel needs prior to opening will be a function of the amount of work that must be done prior to opening the doors and the amount of that work you can do personally. Staffing requirements at and after opening are largely determined by the human resource planning, which we will discuss more fully in the following sections.

After the timetable has been established, you must remember that it is a planning document and therefore subject to change. As new and better estimates of dates for the various activities are known, the timetable should be updated. If experiences during the opening make clear that the transition to normal operations should be postponed or accelerated, then those changes should be made. By the same token, as activities are discovered that were omitted from the original timetable, those items should be added. The timetable, like all planning documents, should be continuously updated as new knowledge and experience is gained.

## HUMAN RESOURCES

**Human resource requirements** refer to the number and skill levels of the personnel involved in the business. The planning for personnel needs should encompass the entire first year of operations for the venture. Thereafter, human resource planning should be a permanent part of the planning activities of the firm. We will discuss ongoing human resource needs in Chapter 17, but start-up needs are addressed in this section.

For most types of businesses, employees are the most valuable asset of the business. Competent, capable people are an absolute must for success in any venture. Remember that human resources means not only clerks and laborers but management people as well, including the top management. Your own skills and abilities should be assessed as part of this process. If there are managerial skills you lack, then plans should be made to acquire people who can shore up your inadequacies.

Don't forget to consider outsiders when you consider human resource requirements. Many small business ventures use an independent accountant to handle bookkeeping needs initially, and almost all ventures require an attorney. These people are part of the human resource requirements of the firm, as are the employees, and must be planned and budgeted for just as the employees are.

The first step in human resource planning is the preparation of an organization chart. You have doubtless been exposed to such charts previously and know that an **organization chart** simply is a diagram of all of the positions within a firm with lines connecting positions to others responsible for supervising their activities. The organization chart will simultaneously establish all of the positions that will exist in a business, identify all of the management functions that will require people, and establish the chain of command in the business. Be sure to specify numbers of people and salary levels as you build the chart. As management people are hired, reexamine the organization chart. Get their input and make changes. All of the employees will have to function within the organizational hierarchy, so it makes sense to gain their acceptance of what that hierarchy will be.

### Compensation

Few things are as difficult to plan in a new business start-up as salary levels. Because of the uncertainty surrounding the new venture, we are fearful of the effect of a large number of high salaries on the break-even point of the business. At the same time, we want the best people available for the jobs, and so we must offer compensation levels that will attract the best and most competent. One factor to keep in mind is that compensation includes things other than salaries. The compensation package needs to address fringe benefits such as life, health, and disability insurance; vacation and sick leave; and retirement plans. When Social Security payments are considered, currently running 7.5% of the salary, the fringe benefits easily can become a highly significant part of the compensation package. Costs of 30% and more for fringe benefits as a percentage of salaries are not uncommon. Nevertheless, such offerings will be demanded by the employees if you are to be able to attract and keep good people.

One aspect that can work to the benefit of the business is the establishment of a substantial portion of the compensation package in the form of profit-sharing or bonus plans. This is especially true for managerial positions, whose occupants will feel better able to affect the performance of the company. Bonuses can be established and keyed to performance levels of the business, which are expressed in the objectives of the firm. The payment of these bonuses then should be accompanied by performance levels that make the payment feasible. Bonuses also can be paid in stock, if the corporate form of business has been selected, or in the form of stock options. A portion of the bonus can be deferred for a period of time to encourage employees to stay with the company. Don't make the mistake of assuming that such deferrals can save the company cash outflows, however. To protect the employees and the firm, deferred compensation plans must be meticulously prepared and should be funded through a trustee. Discussions with an accountant or the trust officer of a bank can help to ensure that the plans are properly prepared and maintained and that they produce the best tax treatment possible for the firm.

Remember to include your own compensation when planning this phase of the business. Your own salary should be the minimum required for maintenance of your family until the business has established itself in the marketplace. You can provide substantial deferred compensation for yourself keyed to the performance of the firm, but you should be careful not to overburden the cash flow of the business. In addition, the compensation level you establish for yourself and any other owners of the firm will have a significant effect on the salaries that you pay to the other employees. In general, people will be more satisfied with less current salary and more deferred compensation if they see that you are leading the movement.

The actual level of salaries and other compensation you offer will be a function of the standard of living in the area in which your business is located. To determine what is acceptable for individuals with various skill levels, you may explore employment agencies, employment security commissions, or industry associations. Don't forget to look at job listings in the newspaper. You also may try to find out the salary levels of similar businesses or competitors in the area, but expect some people to be reluctant to talk to you. Employment agencies or commissions also can give you an idea of the people currently available with specified skills and what they are likely to request as starting salaries. These organizations can help you in recruiting, too.

## Recruiting

Where do you find the people you need? As we mentioned in the previous paragraph, employment agencies and security commissions can help. Ads in the newspaper also can be of value, but don't overlook your own contacts and those of the people going into the venture with you or already hired. A key aspect of the recruiting process is the determination of the responsible parties for hiring decisions. In a venture with a very small number of employees or one with few management positions, you may do all of the interviewing and hiring personally. In a venture with several management positions or a large number of people, the interviewing and hiring may be delegated to the other managers. In a very large venture, a personnel department may be planned. You should decide who will be hiring for each position before the interviews begin.

Interviewing is an art. How to determine in a short period, with a few questions and an employment application, which people will be best suited for the business is difficult and fraught with error. You should decide what questions will be asked on the employment application and prepare that document in advance. Examine the applications used by other firms in similar businesses or by your competitors. You might even interview with some of these yourself to determine how their interviews are conducted. You also should make a list of questions that will be asked during the interview. These may vary by the position involved. Such questions should go beyond qualifications and experience. You are going to be concerned with how well the people mesh into an effective force, how well they get along with each other, and the image they will portray to your customers. Questions concerning reactions to working with a new and as yet unproved business are not inappropriate nor are questions concerning reactions to deferred compensation plans. You should plan to have time during the interview for the applicant to ask questions as well. The kind of questions asked sometimes can be more revealing than the answers to your own questions. Remember, just because you decide that you want to hire a particular applicant does not guarantee that the individual will accept your offer. The applicant will be assessing you and the planned venture as well as considering the compensation package offered. With key positions, especially managerial positions, you may need to negotiate with an applicant. Such factors as degree of autonomy and authority as well as compensation may be negotiated. Remember that the people you hire will have a major effect on the ultimate success of the business. We will have more to say on this topic in Chapter 17, "Human Resources Management."

# PHYSICAL RESOURCES

The size of the facility which your business will require really is not decided in the sequential fashion indicated on the business plan. Everything discussed about the new venture to this point will affect the requirements. Site selection is properly considered during the marketing research phase. At this point a prospective business owner must make a conscious decision about the size and characteristics of the physical facility required. This decision will be affected by the amount and variety of inventory you intend to display and store, by the number of people who must be housed, and by the growth expectations for the business. Far too many new businesses simply go to real estate agents and find a place to rent they believe they can afford. This is absolutely the wrong way to go about obtaining physical resources. The first question that any real estate agent will ask is, How large a place do you need? Until you can answer this basic question, there is no need to begin looking for a facility.

## Prioritizing Needs

The first step in planning for physical resources is the determination of the relative importance of those resources. If the new venture is to be a retail store, for example, and it plans to piggyback its marketing by locating near a major competitor, then the physical resources will be of prime importance. In such cases, it is possible for a business to gear its size, number of employees, and inventory levels to a facility available in a mall or other prime location. However, the physical resources could be of lesser importance, as in the case of a wholesaler whose contact with customers will be in their places of business through sales personnel. Service businesses can experience both conditions, too. A construction firm may have a low level of importance attached to the physical resources, whereas a firm of attorneys may require a prestigious address in an established office building to support a desired image. Whether or not customers will be coming to the business is a major factor in the relative importance, as is the requirement for the physical handling of goods. In the former case, even though customers never frequent the business, location on or near major transportation arteries may be crucial.

If the physical resources are to be a crucial aspect of the business, then budgetary restraints may be the only other factor required for consideration before searching for a facility. Otherwise, consideration should be given to the area required to display and store inventory, to conduct the business, to house the staff, and for expected growth in all of those areas. Regardless of whether the facility is bought, built, or rented, expansion of the capacity of the physical resources will not be easy. Even with a rented facility, an increase in space will not be easily accomplished without moving, and lease terms can make moving prior to the expiration of a lease exceptionally expensive. Consequently, the initial facility should have room available for growth, even though that space is not used initially.

One of the more difficult spatial needs to determine is the area required to display inventory. Too much or too little inventory displayed in an area can damage the image of the business in the eyes of its customers. Without a great deal of experience, planning the right square footage for a given dollar value of inventory is challenging in the extreme. One approach is to use sales per square foot statistics and inventory turnover statistics from industry associations or government publications and work backwards to determine the space requirements. It works this way. Assume that the average sales per square foot in your industry is $400 per year and that the inventory turnover average is four times per year. If your markup is 50% based on selling price (100% based on cost) then you will be averaging $50 of inventory per square foot ($400/2 = $200; $200/4 = $50). Now you can use inventory stocking plans or sales forecasts to determine the display area requirements. Plans to sell $500,000 in the first year would require a display area of 5,000 square feet ($500,000/2 = $250,000; $250,000/$50 = 5,000). Sales per square foot averages are available from many industry associations or government publications like the *Dollars and Cents,* published by the Urban Land Institute and containing averages for shopping centers and malls for a variety of retailers. Assistance in finding such references is available from librarians or government assistance programs like the Small Business Development Centers.

Storage area needs for a retailer, wholesaler, or any type of business are much easier to estimate. The physical size of items to be stored dictates the overall size of the facility, but don't forget to consider handling requirements and storage weights. If mechanical equipment is to be used, the storage facility must accommodate it, and floors must be strong enough to handle the planned weight of the goods. In addition, if required for special types of inventory, air conditioning or heating must be considered as well.

Space requirements for a manufacturing firm can be extremely difficult to estimate. In essence, a production operation must be laid out on paper to obtain space requirements. This layout process is discussed in Chapter 23, "Production Management." Construction firms must consider storage space for tools and equipment. Repair facilities must allocate space for such storage as well as the repair operation itself. Motels must determine the size of the rooms to be offered and then calculate the number of rooms based on sales projections.

Restaurants have special problems in space estimates. Seating capacity in large measure will dictate the maximum sales volume possible and therefore is crucial to the operation. Plans for required seating capacity usually are estimated by calculating the turnover expected during each meal to be offered and working backward from sales forecasts with average tickets. The turnover expected will vary greatly depending upon the type of restaurant and the target market. Average sales tickets can be calculated from menu prices or using averages from industry associations and publications.

## Budgeting

The budget is a very real factor in the selection and acquisition of physical resources. The first issue is whether you will buy, build, or lease the facilities. The last choice generally is less expensive in the short run, whereas the others are less expensive in the long run. Many businesses cannot consider buying because of their location requirements; that is, the need to locate within a shopping center or mall. If there is a choice, you should recognize that financing the acquisition or construction of a facility for a new and unproven business can be difficult. We will talk more about this in Chapter 12, "The Financing Plan." Until then, be aware that the more money you have to borrow during the start-up phase of the business, the more difficult it will be to obtain that money.

There is an advantage to leasing beyond that of reduced up-front capital requirements: flexibility. Although you probably will have to sign a lease agreement, the term generally will be one to five years. At the end of the lease, or earlier in some lease agreements if you can find a replacement for your business, you have the option of moving. If location is not a critical issue for your particular type of business, this may not be a valuable advantage. If location is important, the flexibility may be a large advantage, because your early experience may well show that your initial location decision was not as good as it could have been. Also, if growth outstrips your expectations, it is possible for your business to outgrow the facility. It also is possible for a target market to shift its desires concerning location. In either of these instances, the ability to reevaluate the site, and change if necessary, could be valuable. Of course, it also is possible that a particular business has no choice but to build a facility because none is available with the desired features.

## Selecting a Site

Occupancy expense is a function of location as well as size of the facility. There are tradeoffs between cost and location. However, less expensive locations are not automatically better ones. A more expensive site might well be worth the difference in cost. This consideration is important and should be examined during the market research phase of the initial planning. These issues are covered in depth in the following chapter. Although it appears late in the business plan, the site selection may have been completed at a much earlier stage in the planning. If it has not been done, then now is the latest time possible for the final determination.

During the market research and earlier phases of the planning process, several alternative sites should have been selected and examined. Information about costs or lease terms and provisions and facility size and characteristics should have been developed and recorded. Demographic factors that will affect the business should have been examined. Now that the decisions concerning the physical resources required have been made, a final selection among those alternatives is possible. Recognizing that no site will be perfect, choose the one that has the best combination of factors among those available.

Site selection is more than the location of a building. It also involves the selection of the geographic region, city, or town in which the business will be located. Far too many small business owners simply choose to locate their businesses near their homes without giving any further thought to the process. Demographic and growth patterns may make location in your home town undesirable. Large firms spend a great deal of time and energy in selecting the locations for their operations. There is a good reason for this, and small business owners would be well advised to consider them. We will examine the site selection issue in greater depth in the following chapter.

## BUSINESS STRATEGIES

**Business strategies** are the plans made to obtain the business objectives. After the strategic issues have been identified and goals and objectives established, then an owner must begin to decide how to achieve the objectives. These strategies are statements about the image or other aspects of the business that will dictate how the firm is to be managed. When the timetable, human and physical resources, and site issues are settled, the strategies must be finalized. The day-to-day management of the enterprise will be conducted in accordance with the strategies. For example, our grocery store owner could have established, as one of his strategies, the maintenance of a clean store. From an operational perspective, daily management would have to ensure that attention was paid to that detail. The strategies actually become objectives for the operational management. Frequently, a strategy will dictate what must be done before a company can open its doors. Consider the case of Fred Smith, the founder of Federal Express.

Frederick W. Smith first proposed the idea of an airline that would carry small packages overnight from city to city in a term paper he wrote for an economics course in college. Although he got a C for the paper, he proved the validity of his concept by establishing the Federal Express company. The firm is based in Memphis and is now fifteen years old and highly successful. In 1986, the firm grossed $2.6 billion and showed profits of $132 million. A Vietnam veteran with 200 missions in forward-control aircraft, Smith knew that customers would demand the ability to ship anywhere in the United States. That meant that the entire delivery system had to be in place before he could begin operation. Smith did just that. He invested his family fortune of $8.5 million and armed with market research reports persuaded venture capitalists and lenders to invest another $90 million in his idea. The entire delivery system, which required a fleet of planes and a fleet of trucks, was in place before the firm began soliciting deliveries. After high initial losses and extreme problems with fuel costs during the 1973–1974 fuel crisis, Federal Express turned the corner. Since 1975, its revenues have been doubling biannually, outperforming projections. Smith now has extended the business to Europe.[2]

What do you think the strategic issue is for Federal Express? Smith felt that it was the ability to deliver on the promise of overnight delivery to virtually anywhere in the United States; something even the U.S. Post Office cannot guarantee. Did you also notice the statement that revenues outperformed projections? This indicates that objectives had been set for sales revenues. You can bet that other objectives for Federal Express include the number and locations of cities to be added to the delivery network each year. Smith's experiences may not seem applicable to your ideas to open a small business because so many dollars were involved in his venture. The fact is that the preventure planning that Smith conducted, the establishment of a viable market, the preparation of goals and objectives, and the determination of strategic issues and strategies is exactly what any would-be business owner would do. Here is another case in which the initial investment was $1,000.

Phil Knight, the co-founder of Nike, Inc., designs and sells shoes. His company became the top selling shoe producer in the United States in less than ten years. But things weren't always rosy. Like many other venturists, Knight got the idea for his business while in college. While a member of the track team, he became friends with Bill Bowerman, Oregon's famous track coach. Bowerman, who had done some shoe design, complained that American shoe companies produced products that were too heavy and clumsy for any serious runner to use. Knight remembered this and later while working on a graduate degree in business became convinced that a well-made Japanese shoe could gain a major share of the American market. Six years after his initial talks with Bowerman, a partnership was formed. Bowerman and Knight each put up $500 and bought 300 pairs of running shoes from Onitsuka of Japan. Before long, they were into national distribution. Knowing the value of a winning reputation, the partners designed a shoe and pushed it through production in time for the 1972 Olympic trials in Oregon. They persuaded marathoners to wear their shoes and were able to advertise that "four of the top seven" finishers were wearing Nikes. They did not mention that the top three finishers were wearing Adidas from West Germany. It was off and running from there. Knowing that they could not rest on their laurels, Bowerman and Knight continued new product development and the search for more and better suppliers. When the running craze hit in the mid-1970s, Nike was ready with new products for the amateur runner. Knight was convinced that the secret was to build shoes that professional athletes would wear and to even pay pros to use those shoes. It's called "trickle down" fashion. Nike has established plants in New Hampshire and Maine, but still gets most of its shoes from suppliers in China, South Korea, Taiwan, Japan, Malaysia, Thailand, and the Philippines.[3]

Knight and Bowerman recognized that the strategic issue for their firm was product design. Their marketing image was that of the producer of winning shoes. They have continued to maintain that image and push product design for changing market demands. Theirs is a prime example of the development of an image that is divorced from the supply of the product. Few wearers of Nike shoes probably know or care where their shoes were manufactured. They have confidence in the shoes because of the image of Nike, not that of the actual manufacturer of the product.

One side issue is raised in the Nike illustration: the timing of a business venture. In previous chapters we talked about the necessity for a would-be business owner to have the experience and knowledge to run a particular type of business. Knight waited six years and completed a graduate degree before he felt ready to make the leap. Even then he recognized the need to have an experienced shoe designer in the firm and went into partnership with Bowerman, who brought to the firm exactly that expertise.

## Distinctive Competency

Development of the business strategies essentially revolves around the establishment of a distinctive competency and plans to maintain that competency. A **distinctive competency** is the primary thing that makes a firm stand out from its competitors. You might think of it as the thing a business does best. As we discussed in the last chapter, every business must have something that distinguishes it from its competitors in the minds of the market. Without some distinguishing characteristic, a business then becomes just like its competitors and there is no reason for a consumer to select one firm over another. We remember one business owner who objected to advertising in the yellow pages of the telephone book. When we questioned him on that oversight, he replied that consumers had already made up their minds to buy before they went to the yellow pages. Consequently, he believed, they used the yellow pages to simply shop price. Because his business did not compete on the basis of price, he felt himself at a disadvantage when faced with such callers and preferred to spend his available advertising dollars in ways that would bring customers directly to his business before they decided to buy, or at least before they decided to shop prices. We had to admit that his approach made a lot of sense.

The distinctive competency that Federal Express developed was an extremely high level and speed of service. When the U.S. Post Office responded to pressure from Federal and other overnight delivery services by installing its own high speed service, Federal was able to survive despite its higher prices because of its image and its continuing efforts to maintain that image. The Post Office doesn't come to your door to pick up your packages: Federal does. Nike has a very different distinctive competency. It makes the best shoes for various sports. It has succeeded in maintaining this image even though it does not make the shoes it sells. The distinctive competency can be based on service, product, or any number of other factors including price, location, hours of operation, breadth or depth of product line, or simply the friendliness of the employees. A friend of ours remarked the other day that he frequented a restaurant in town because the people there all knew him by name and were so very friendly. He commented that he was fearful of taking any of his luncheons elsewhere because he did not want to damage the business of his friends. We can expect few customers to develop that high a degree of loyalty, but it illustrates how a simple thing like consistently cheerful, friendly employees can actually be a distinctive competency.

When developing the distinctive competency for your venture, be sure to consider the role of price. It is possible for the competency to be based on price. Charles Schwab founded a discount brokerage firm and quickly became the largest such firm in the United States with revenues of $42 million and profits of $5 million in 1981.[4] Even though you may decide not to compete on the basis of price, if your prices are not competitive, then the distinctive competency becomes even more important. Your customers must have something for which they will be willing to pay a higher price. That something may be service, convenience, or atmosphere, but it must exist. This points out the importance of knowing your competitors' prices and keeping apprised of their pricing policies. This is not to underestimate the value of added factors. We are familiar with a restaurant and inn whose distinctive competency actually is that it has the highest prices in town. It is located in a town with a high volume of tourist trade and has developed an image of an extremely luxurious inn with an exceptional restaurant. That image actually is at odds with the facts—as the inn is neither as new nor as luxurious as are several others in town—and the restaurant, although quite excellent, is seldom recognized by the local populace as among the finest. Nevertheless, the business is quite vibrant and consistently sells its patrons on the belief that they are frequenting the finest establishment of its type in the region.

## Marketing Plan

The marketing plan is a natural outgrowth of the prior steps of the business plan. In the following chapter we will talk about the preventure marketing research that must be conducted and discuss the development of a start-up marketing plan that will address the advertising prior and subsequent to opening a new venture. We will talk about marketing strategies for the opening period and steps that should be taken to ensure that the members of the target market are informed about the new business. In this chapter we will focus on the development of a marketing plan that will encompass the entire first year of a business' life. This plan must address the transition period to normal business operations as well as consider long-term marketing strategies. We simply cannot say too much about the need for careful planning in the marketing area. Consider the case of a young man with a fabulous product: a light bulb that lasts forever.

Kevin Keating thought that all he had to do was to let people know that he had produced a light bulb that would last fifty years under normal use—and his fortune would be made. It didn't work that way. After completing the engineering and searching for a manufacturer who would build the bulbs, Keating, the founder of DioLight Technology, Inc., offered the bulbs directly to the consumer. He reasoned that distributors would not want to handle the bulb that would cut into their replacement business. But consumers just weren't buying. In the first place the bulb cost seven times as much as a comparable GE product, even though it would last sixty times as long. In the second place, no one had ever heard of DioLight and simply didn't believe the firm's claims. Finally, no one really seemed to be interested.

After stacking up huge losses for a year and unsuccessfully attempting to sell bulbs to a variety of consumers including small businesses, large businesses, and state and county agencies, Keating was at his wits end. Finally, in desperation he looked up some distributors of light bulbs in the yellow pages and called fifteen of them on the phone. Twelve weren't interested; but three listened, and one bought. That was the beginning. The distributors recognized that the bulbs actually have a valid niche in the market place: to provide lights in hard to reach areas. Because it costs slightly more in electricity to burn the bulbs, they really are not as cost efficient as they sounded initially. But, in hard to reach installations, the cost of replacing bulbs can be greater than the added electric costs of long-lived bulbs.

Keating's early experience did reveal that the "forever" bulbs are a great gimmick. Capitalizing on the gimmick aspect, Keating has now appeared on over 300 radio stations, in over 50 newspaper articles, in 50 pieces in trade and consumer magazines, and had 7 television features. All of the publicity was free and it helped to reach distributors who could recognize the market niche that such bulbs could fill.

Apparently, no one really wants a bulb which lasts forever, but everyone likes a gimmick. Keating doesn't care, as long as the future seems bright.[5]

If special or promotional activities or prices are planned as part of a business' opening, then one sure problem must be dealt with in the plan. What happens when the special prizes or prices or features are discontinued? When should they be discontinued and what marketing strategies should be pursued thereafter? A new grocery opened recently in our town. Its opening was well promoted for several months in advance and its initial pricing was truly amazing. The early marketing efforts were an astounding success. Virtually everyone in the market area shopped at the store during its two week grand opening sale. But since then the parking lot has been sparsely occupied. Clearly a great deal of money was expended on the start-up marketing efforts in the form of prices well below costs and massive advertising, but the ongoing marketing has been lackluster and the prices rose to the highest level of any store in town. After several months it does not appear that the new store has garnered a significant share of the market. This failure is not simply due to price, although that has had an effect. The failure is primarily due to the assumption by the management that the initial marketing efforts were all that would be required. As soon as the marketplace recognized the store's existence and saw its facility, they were certain that success would be theirs. This has not been the case for the new grocery store, and it seldom is the case for any new venture.

The marketing plan must address the "postopening blues" and include steps to minimize the problem and smooth the transition to normal business operations. Such plans must focus heavily on the distinctive competency. Ideally, the start-up marketing has been prepared with the distinctive competency in mind so that those efforts will not damage the firm's strategies. Our new grocery store might have done better with less impressive sales prices during its grand opening, if it intended to offer consistently higher prices than those of its competitors. The contrast then would not have been as great when the sales prices were removed. If the start-up marketing has been well planned, then the transition to normal operations should be associated with continuing marketing and advertising efforts that focus on the firm's distinctive competency. The purpose of the start-up marketing is to let everyone in the target market know that you are there. The ongoing marketing is designed to make your market continue to do business with you over the long term.

Like the start-up marketing plan, this aspect of the overall business plan should have a budget. We will talk about all the budgets later on, but the actual preparation of the marketing inputs to the budget have to be associated with the marketing plan itself and so it is done as a part of the preparation of the plan.

## CAPITAL REQUIREMENTS

At this point in the preparation of the business plan, you will have finished the majority of the inputs required to determine the capital requirements for starting your business. You have determined how much the facility and physical resources are going to cost, what the personnel costs are going to be, prepared a start-up marketing budget, and explored the inventory costs and other expenses of operating the business.

In Chapter 12, "The Financing Plan," we will examine the preparation of the capital requirements and the acquisition of start-up funding. In general, the **capital requirements** will include all of the out of pocket costs of acquiring the physical resources of the business, the expenses that will be incurred prior to the opening of the business, initial advertising and marketing costs, and three to six months of operating expenses.

There are many sources of capital available. Sadly, your personal savings remain the most important single source. Few lenders or investors are willing to work with a venture that does not have a substantial investment by its owner. They want to know that the owner is willing to assume the risk and is highly committed to the venture. This problem, the sources of funding and plans for obtaining capital, will be explained in greater detail in Chapter 12.

## COMPLETING THE PLAN

The final steps in the business plan cover budgets, break-even analysis, and plan modification. The process of developing budgets is explained in depth in Chapter 7, and break-even analysis is presented in Chapter 6. Budgets must be prepared for marketing and operations. Forecasts must be prepared for sales and cash flows. Finally, a capital budget must be prepared that will detail the funds required for launching the new venture.

These steps are actually performed during the preparation of the earlier aspects of the plan. The forecasts and budgets are constantly revised as the plan develops and more information is gained. An initial break-even analysis is performed and then retested as the forecasts and budgets are updated. Consequently, the process is **iterative;** that is, repeated each time new and more accurate information is obtained. As the budgeting, forecasting, and financial analysis evolve, the business plan is evaluated and revised. The location of the steps at the end of the plan indicate that the revisions must be finalized before the plan is complete. Once this has been done, the start-up capital can be located and the plan implemented. However, the business plan is never actually finalized. As the plan is implemented and throughout the first year of operations, progress should be evaluated and the plan modified.

As you will learn in Part V of the text, planning is an ongoing aspect of any successful business. As soon as the time period covered by the start-up plan is over, a new plan must be developed. Although we will detail many tools and their uses as important to the success of small businesses, ***Planning* is absolutely the single most important task of a small business owner**. Planning involves using the tools for success consistently and well, both at start up and for the life of the business.

## A DIAGRAM OF THE BUSINESS PLAN

Exhibit 10-2 is a diagram or flowchart of the planning process for starting a small business. As you can see, the elements are the same as described in the previous sections, however, the diagram can show that many steps are performed simultaneously. Notice that the establishment of personal objectives, business objectives, and strategies are linked by a feedback loop. Plan modification and progress evaluation are also included in the loop. This means that the process is iterative or repetitive. It is obvious that if a break-even analysis shows the business failing, something must be changed in order to proceed. The same thing is true for every aspect of the plan. If the strategies developed are not acceptable to the owner, then either the personal or business objectives must be changed and all aspects of the planning revised.

The loop between business objectives and strategies is an extremely important segment of the process. The objectives, you remember, tell you where you want to be and the strategies say how you plan to get there. That means that both objectives and strategies must be well developed. It also means that the supporting aspects of timing, site, people and equipment must be able to support the strategies which you will pursue.

Every aspect of the plan is important, and all are interconnected. The exhibit makes it possible to visualize the process and also provides a way to manage it. The format of the exhibit is actually that of a PERT chart (Program Evaluation and Review Technique). That means that it shows the completion points of the steps that must be conducted in the start-up plan and it also shows which steps are dependent on others for completion. If you follow the diagram in completing a business plan and check off each item as it is completed, you

**EXHIBIT 10-2** *The Business Plan*

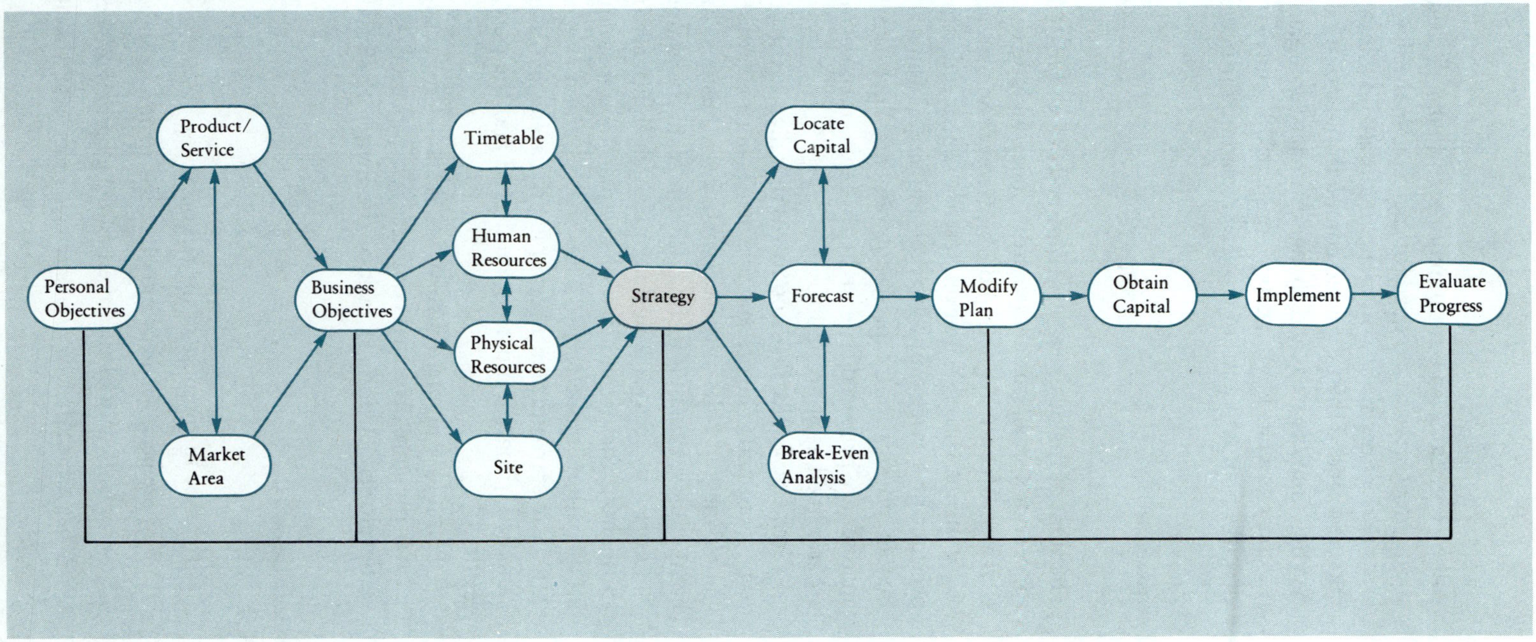

will be less likely to omit a major step that will slow down the process. You should keep a written record for each step in the diagram. Record your original ideas and all revisions you make. Estimate how long you think each step will take and record the estimated completion dates for each point in the diagram. As you complete steps and change estimated completion dates, record those on the chart as well. That means planning to use the plan! It will also mean a more effective plan and a more workable planning process.

## SUMMARY

The steps of the business plan, outlined in Exhibit 10-1, define strategies for the success of a small business venture. They include the statement of personal as well as professional goals and objectives. The plan addresses the feasibility of the concept through market research, proceeds through the selection of a product or service and a market and site. A timetable is specified as are the human, physical, and capital requirements. Forecasts, budgets, and break-even analyses are prepared repeatedly throughout the planning stage, and the plans are modified as appropriate.

Strategic issues, those concerns that dictate the life or death of a firm, need to be identified. The prospective owner must establish goals and objectives for the business in light of these issues. Every business must identify a distinctive competency, one that distinguishes it from its competitors.

Forecasts, budgets, and financial feasibility are iterative steps performed throughout the preparation of the plan, but they must be finalized and final modifications made to the plan before capital can be located and obtained. After the start-up plan is completed, capital is obtained, and the venture is launched, progress must be monitored and the plan revised to reflect actual results.

Planning is an ongoing process. A successful business always has a plan. As soon as the start-up plan is complete, a new plan for continued operations must be developed. A primary task of the owner of a small business is planning.

## QUESTIONS

1. Describe the purpose of the business plan.
2. Why are personal goals and objectives important in business ventures?
3. What is the importance of establishing business objectives?
4. What is the significance of strategic issues, and what is their impact on business?

5. What are the requirements for success in the planning stages?
6. What does *distinctive competency* mean? Give an example.
7. How does one plan the physical requirements of a business?
8. How does one plan the capital requirements of a business?
9. What is the most important consideration for success?
10. What are *business strategies*, and why are they important?
11. What is the purpose of the marketing plan after the initial phase of planning and opening the doors?
12. To what does the *timetable* refer?
13. What is the first step in human resource planning?
14. What is the difficulty in deciding on salary levels?
15. What is the first step in planning the physical resources?
16. Why is location of less importance to certain types of businesses?
17. What other considerations should be given to a location other than site?
18. How can one determine the space requirements for inventory?
19. What are three ways to obtain facilities?
20. What are the inputs required to determine the capital requirements for starting your business?
21. Define the following terms:
    a. break even
    b. fixed costs
    c. variable costs
    d. strategic issues

## PROJECTS

1. You have decided to open a small craft shop. Draw up a business plan for your new business. Include in this plan all the steps as required by the business plan outline. (This activity may best be done as a group project if only limited time is available, or it may be ongoing as more is learned about the process in later chapters.)
2. Visit a small business in your community and ask the owner how the venture came about, whether planning was conducted, how it was done, and by whom. Try to determine the strategic competency of the business. (You also might assign groups to various types of small businesses and have them present to the class the most important aspects of their planning, especially noting how the emphases may change according to industry. This activity will highlight the lack of planning that takes place in some small business.)

# CASE

Al Kitchen was excited. He was going to own his own business just as soon as he got all the paperwork squared away. He was young and enthusiastic, and his whole life was ahead of him. Just a few short weeks ago, he had said good bye to Uncle Sam. When he couldn't immediately find a job that appealed to him and for which he was qualified, he decided to start his own business and be his own boss.

He had always enjoyed cooking and his grandmother had passed down several recipes that were out of this world. This gave him the idea. One day when he came home early from job hunting some delicious home cooking was waiting to ease his troubled spirits. And it had! It gave Al a wonderful idea about what to do with his future. The job hunting was not going well and he had to do something soon, because he needed to support his wife and little boy.

He started making his plans. A new mall was going up outside of town and all the spaces had not yet been leased. He would go talk to them and see what he could do. After all, if he served only soup, it couldn't be too expensive a proposition — could it? And, too, there was no other place in town like this, so it was bound to be successful. He would start small and then grow.

Al decided to make his a family business. His sister and wife would help him out with the cooking and wait on tables. He also could cut down on expenses by using paper and plastic products rather than dishes that had to be washed. If things went really well, he would expand to sandwiches and hire someone to take over for his wife from time to time.

Al already had contacted the mall officials about leasing possibilities and learned that the only site he could afford leased for $10 per square foot and measured 500 square feet. It was in the shape of an ell in an interior corner of the mall. He had to sign the lease quickly if he was to get the space, because the mall manager was anxious to have all the floor spaces assigned within the next few weeks. Al was tempted to sign the lease right there on the spot rather than risk losing out to someone else. He had $5,000 mustering out pay from the service in the bank when he got home, but his wife had made him promise not to sign anything until they had had time to discuss it more fully.

When Al got home full of visions of grandeur and dreams of making this small area just the beginning, he and his wife started discussing how much money would be needed in addition to the lease payment. There was kitchen equipment to lease, paper products and supplies to buy, operating expenses, and leasehold improvements and furniture. Because this was a new mall, no other tenants had been in this space before and he needed to start from scratch.

At the bank, he was declined the $20,000 loan he requested. It seemed that the loan officer didn't share his dream of success. The loan officer had asked him some searching questions about things he had never considered. The one that bothered him most was about his break-even analysis. The banker asked how much soup Al had to sell to break even. This had him worried. The banker had suggested that he call an assistance agency that gave this kind of advice free.

Al called the Small Business Development Center (SBDC) and decided that before he gave up his savings, he would see those people. He would see whether they thought he could be successful and find out exactly what his break even was. Surely, they would see how great his idea was and maybe they would even help him get a loan.

## Questions

1. Should Al continue with his dream?
2. Look at the outline for the business plan and discuss which steps he has considered even informally.
3. Discuss which steps he needs to consider more fully.
4. Which steps has he left out altogether?

Al received help from the SBDC in developing estimates for the expenses the business would incur in its operation. They also established the following forecasts for prices and average ticket levels for the customers:

| | | |
|---|---|---|
| Average ticket per customer | | $2.50 |
| Fixed cost estimates for the first year: | | |
| Lease (store) | $ 5000.00 | |
| Lease (kitchen equipment) | 2400.00 | |
| All utilities | 2600.00 | |
| Insurance | 1500.00 | |
| Salaries (wife and sister) | 12000.00 | |
| Owner | 20000.00 | |
| Fringe benefits | | |
| 15% of salaries | 4800.00 | |
| Total fixed costs | | $48300.00 |
| Variable cost estimates for the first year: | | |
| Food (industry average) | 60% of sales | |
| Paper and utensils | $.10 per customer | |
| Variable cost ratio | $.10/$2.50 = 4% | |
| Total variable costs | 64% | |
| Contribution margin | 36% | |

Examine the information and prepare a break-even analysis for the operation. Be sure to calculate the break-even point in sales dollars and in number of customers. Also calculate the break-even point in sales and number of customers per day. This will help determine the reasonableness and attainability of the forecast.

5. On the basis of your analysis, do you think the venture is feasible?

# CHAPTER 11

# The Marketing Plan

**LEARNING OBJECTIVES**

After completing this chapter, you should be able to

- List the steps in starting a new venture.
- Understand the trade-offs in site selection.
- Understand the importance of image and timing in starting up a new venture.
- Prepare a start-up marketing budget.
- Frame the steps of the marketing plan into a viable program.

In this chapter we are going to assume that you are planning to go into business. We will examine the steps that should be taken to ensure that your product or service is viable from a marketing perspective. The marketing considerations covered in this chapter will be those involved in the start-up phase; ongoing marketing considerations will be discussed at greater length in Chapter 18. Here we focus on the steps to take to establish a market for a product or service and the initial marketing plan. One word of warning is valid at this point. Your own judgement as to the value of a product or service is not necessarily valid. Just because you would buy an item or service is no guarantee that your market area has enough other people in need of the item to make a business successful; market research is required to answer that question. Further, even if there is sufficient demand for that item in an area, the business will not automatically be successful. The manner in which the item is offered for sale will be a major factor in determining its success.

## THE FIRST STEP

As discussed in the last chapter, the first step in starting a new business is to establish personal goals and objectives. The prospective small business owner should determine why he or she wants to start a business and what outcome is desired. The prospective owner should evaluate his or her skills, strengths, and weaknesses and determine the price of the venture in terms of personal time, effort, and dedication. In the introductory chapters we discussed the characteristics of a successful venturist. If any of those are missing from your personality or if you are unwilling to pay the price in terms of time and effort, then the best decision may be not to start a new business, or to wait until required skills or abilities can be gained. Once the decision has been made and you have recorded your personal objectives, then you can proceed to the next step. The entire business plan was displayed in the last chapter. An excerpt of the marketing portion of the business plan is reproduced in Exhibit 11-1. The exhibit indicates that evaluating the product or service and evaluating the market area are separate steps. This is to emphasize the importance of evaluating both the offerings and the area in which the offerings are to be sold. In practice, however, the two aspects generally are evaluated at the same time. In the later sections of this chapter, we will discuss the evaluation simultaneously.

The first step in the marketing plan is to select the product or service that is to be sold. As discussed in Chapter 3, many people choose a product based on past situations or experience. Others discover a product or service they think no one is addressing and for which they believe a large market exists. Both approaches have value. Experience with the product or service you intend to sell helps you to understand what is required to produce the items and what is required to sell them.

**EXHIBIT 11-1** *The Marketing Plan*

II. Choose a product or service
  A. Evaluate the marketability of the product or service
  B. Determine the feasibility of the product or service

III. Select a market area
  A. Evaluate the market area
  B. Determine the feasibility of the market area
  C. Evaluate the competition

## DEVELOPING A MARKETING PLAN

The marketing process was outlined in Chapter 3 in great detail. We explored the importance of identifying *who* the consumers of the product or service are; *what* it is that they really are purchasing; *when* the purchase transactions take place; *where* the sale actually occurs; *how* the sales transaction is handled; and, *why* a consumer would wish to buy a product or service. We explored the three basic approaches to marketing: push marketing, pull marketing, and piggyback marketing. In *push* strategies, an intermediary supplier is encouraged to purchase goods rather than the ultimate consumer. In *pull* marketing, the ultimate consumer is persuaded to purchase the goods. In *piggyback* strategies, a competitor creates a market and attracts consumers who are then drawn away on the basis of price or some other factor. Other techniques discussed included marketing research and importance of the business image and the need for consistency. We discussed the concept of a distinctive competency to set a business apart from its competitors: a factor customers will think of when they think about our business. Now that we have a basic understanding of the marketing process, we can discuss the steps in developing a marketing plan for a new business venture. Those steps are outlined in Exhibit 11-2.

Steps 1 through 5 are iterative. This means that the venture should not be initiated nor the marketing plan finalized until products or services and the market area are deemed to be viable based upon the market research.

## SELECTION OF THE PRODUCT OR SERVICE

Most people select a product or service with which they have experience or for which they believe there is an untapped demand. Market research may be simpler in the former instance but is still required. In the latter instance, lack of

**EXHIBIT 11-2** *Steps in the Marketing Plan*

1. Select the products or services to be offered.
2. Select the area in which the business is to be located.
3. Conduct market research.
4. Examine products or services and areas for viability.
5. Change products, services, or areas as necessary.
6. Select alternative sites for the business.
7. Establish pricing strategies and policies.
8. Establish promotional strategies.
9. Establish the budget for start-up marketing.
10. Determine the image to be portrayed.
11. Make the final site selection.
12. Establish the marketing plan.

familiarity with the items to be offered presents potential difficulties. It is always better to have experience with an item when possible. If not, then the acquisition of people with appropriate experience should be a high priority. Starting off in a new venture with a product or service with which you have no experience and with no knowledge in the firm from other sources makes the venture more risky and success more difficult. If you intend to start such a venture, be especially sure that the market research has been well and thoroughly done!

Stories abound about fortunes made by the inventor or originator of new products. In truth, many inventors and innovators are not successful. We just don't hear about the failures very much. If your product or service is a new one for which a market does not really exist, then be forewarned that success in a business based on that item will not be achieved easily. The real success stories for new items frequently involve a venture that has been well funded and in which talented people in a variety of areas have been obtained. The days of a single inventor being able to start a million dollar business on a shoestring are gone forever—if they ever existed!

## AREA SELECTION

### Consumer Support

The **market area** is that geographic territory from which you can expect sales and is a part of the site selection process. Most people starting a new venture pay too little attention to the issue of area selection. All too often the area chosen is simply the one in which the originator lives at the time. The area chosen will have a profound impact on the ultimate success of the company. As the market research should show, the size and viability of demand for the offerings of a new business vary by geographic area.

We are familiar with a small business that failed in its first year because it located in an area without consideration of economic prospects in that area. Consider the facts.

The business was located in a rural county in North Carolina that had one major employer. The employer was a paper mill that had been in existence for more than forty years and had more than 5,000 employees. For more than ten years, the paper mill had been coming under attack because of water pollution claims. In fact, in the preceding year, the Environmental Protection Agency (EPA) had threatened to close the plant if it did not reduce the level of its discharges into the local river. Political pressure had been brought to bear; the plant spent considerable money in pollution control; and the EPA was appeased for the time being.

Our client decided to go into business in his hometown without consideration for any other details, never thinking about the potential impact of a failure of the paper mill. He had been in business less than six months when the EPA ax fell. Pressure from environmental groups had been building and the EPA required that the mill update its pollution controls even further. The management of the mill declared it was not economically feasible to upgrade such an old facility and dramatically reduced its operations to those that could meet EPA standards. The result of this cutback was a layoff of more than 3,000 workers. In a county with a population of 30,000 people and virtually no other industry to absorb this layoff, the effects were devastating. Our client was only one of many small firms to fail in the ripple effects.

Obviously, no prospective small business owner would start a business in an area experiencing such problems unless the business was proof against the ripple effect of a major upsurge in unemployment. Nevertheless, all the signs indicated that a negative ruling from the EPA was highly possible. In fact, one could say that the signs made it clear that some major change would be occurring, the unknown factor being timing. Our client simply failed to consider the possibility. In fact, he failed to consider any possible change in the local economy.

The story reinforces the need to examine an area in terms of its future as well as present economic and demographic characteristics. A host of publications are available that can provide insight into the area selection process. The Census Bureau publishes manuals that contain not only the basic demographic data about every area in the country but also a host of business factors. The Small Business Administration also produces publications designed to help in area and site selection. In fact, all states have a business development office whose function is to provide information to prospective business venturists starting up within the state. These offices collect business and demographic data that can be of assistance not only in choosing a state in which to locate, but a region within that state as well. Most of this information is available free or at a small charge. Contact your local SBA office, the SBA office or Census Bureau in Washington, or the office of business development in the respective state capital. Local chambers of commerce frequently collect data of interest to small businesses and are always happy to assist a prospective new business. One of the publications available from the SBA is a compilation of statistics that show the number of people needed in an area to support a particular kind of business. Combine this information with a population count from the Census Bureau and you will have a much better idea of the potential viability of an area.

To make maximum use of data about an area, you need to know the characteristics of your target market. In Chapter 3, we indicated that **target markets** are classified according to age, sex, income, occupation, family status, and so on. **Demographics** are more than population counts. Census data and data available from state and local sources also include income and other factors. This means that a firm understanding of target market will make the utilization of demographic data more effective. Remember the example of the lounge owner in Chapter 3. He had located a bar with an exclusive image in a small town that lacked the higher income people needed to support such a venture. The company failed, but it could well have been successful if located in a city with a larger population of more well-to-do people.

## Competition

One of the prime factors involved in area selection is competition. A **direct competitor** is one with whom you will be competing "head to head"; one who carries the same basic items or provides the same basic services as you. An **indirect competitor,** on the other hand, will offer competition for some items you carry but not all or will offer competition for the dollars your customers can spend. An example of the latter situation is the competition offered to a movie theater by an arcade. Both offer entertainment and therefore compete for the entertainment dollars of the market area, but they are not direct competitors because they offer different kinds of entertainment.

Contrary to the usual first impression, it is easier to start a business in an area that has direct competition than in one that does not. Piggyback marketing strategies are possible in such areas, but not in areas without direct competitors. To be successful in an area with direct competitors, you need only do a better job than the established firms. To be successful in an area with no direct competitors, you must create a market. That may be simple in the case of a product or service that a community has long desired, such as a theater in a small town whose people had to drive to the city. On the other hand, it may be quite difficult. The establishment of a microcomputer retail store in that same small town could be a risky venture!

A man wanted help in starting a new business. He had found a vacant lot on the edge of town that was available at a good price and had good access from a highway. He wanted to build a roller skating rink. Now, you must realize that this fellow was from an extremely small town in rural Mississippi. The town had a population of about 5,000 people, located some 60 miles from a city of 75,000. The city had two roller skating rinks, and both seemed to be surviving.

Our client was convinced that a skating rink would be successful in his home town because so many of the local high school kids drove to the city on weekends to skate. Not only would he be closer, he could undercut the prices charged in the city as well.

The man had done some research. He knew what it would cost to buy the lot, build a rink the size he desired, as well as pave the parking lot, put up a sign, and other costs. Together with the cost of the land, he needed $250,000. He wanted us to help him put together an SBA loan package to get the money because his local bank had refused the loan.

We didn't like the idea at all. In the first place, we just could not believe that the folks in that small town wanted a skating rink. The one big plant in town employed most of them and the local economy was not strong. In the second place, the client had no conception of breaking even. He was sure that he would have no problems because his wife and children were going to work in the rink, and he would run it on weekends when he was off work from the plant. That meant low overhead, plus he would be able to keep his job until the place was established. We forced him to do some cost estimation for operating the rink and to forecast his own salary and then we prepared a break-even analysis.

The major fixed cost was the loan payment. It was so high that he would have needed 250 skaters a week to cover it. We just didn't think that was feasible long term in his town. He wouldn't believe us. He got someone else to help him and now there is a nice new building with hardwood floors for sale.

Another case illustrates the right way to do things. These clients wanted to start a restaurant.

A young couple just out of college called to ask for help in starting a restaurant. They said they selected our town because it had a large university that was growing and would provide a steady source of new patrons. Plus, it was in the Sun Belt and had liberal liquor laws. We talked about what kind of restaurant they wanted. They said they hadn't decided yet. They wanted to look at the local competition and locations that might be available.

We found several good places located close to the university, several within walking distance of some of the larger dorms. We also found that there were eighteen pizzerias in town, that being the single largest type of restaurant. Our clients checked out every one of those, and all seemed to be doing fine. Our clients decided to go with pizza and beer. They settled on a place, leased it, and put $20,000 into leasehold improvements. The place was built for students! They had three different rooms set up, each with a juke box and lined with booths. The only tables were long ones down the center of two of the rooms. The third room had arcade games between the booths.

Inside three months, they had surpassed their sales forecast for the year! The place was a resounding success! That was three years ago, and now they have three restaurants and two arcades scattered about the edges of the campus. For two kids in their twenties they are an impressive pair!

The people in this example went about site selection the right way. They located in a different state from their home but spent several months locating the right spot. That effort and the other start-up planning they conducted was worthwhile. They easily were able to outdistance the established competition because they understood their target market and organized the business to attract it. The business actually was selling entertainment, but making money on pizza and beer.

## Suitability

The kind of business you intend to start has an effect on the area required. As you can see from the pizza example, access to the target market and a market of sufficient size were the primary criteria. For a manufacturing business, area requirements could include a ready supply of labor and access to transportation networks. For a construction company, area requirements might be major population growth that would drive up new home construction. For a wholesaler, access to manufacturers or jobbers and to retail customers could be the primary consideration. For other firms, the regulatory environment could be a key. One client selected the Atlanta, Georgia, area to start a local delivery trucking company. The city required trucks delivering within the city limits to have a permit, and the city was extremely reluctant to issue new permits. This meant that established firms held a strong competitive position. Our client located a small trucking company whose owner wished to retire, bought the firm to obtain access to the delivery permit, and established a highly successful operation.

In all cases the area to be considered must be researched to determine its suitability for the venture. We mentioned the use of Census Bureau, SBA, state business development offices, and local chambers of commerce as sources of information about an area. Don't overlook the possibility of personal research. In the pizza example, the owners surveyed the established competition by personally visiting every pizza restaurant in town. They looked the place over, bought dinner, watched the customers, evaluated the service, hours, location, and menu of every competitor. As a matter of fact, they continue to do this on a regular basis today! There is no substitute for personal investigation.

The process of market research to determine area suitability starts with an understanding of the venture which you will begin and the characteristics of the target market which you wish to tap. Once that has been determined, you know what kinds of information about an area you require. That makes your research more effective and improves your ability to interpret data in publications from various sources.

Don't overlook general information about an area. It is easy to get lost in demographic detail and overlook pertinent information such as number and stability of employers, economic conditions, and prospects for future growth. Strong insight into the viability of an area can be obtained by investigation through the local employment security commission. Not only can this agency help you find prospective employees, it can give you information about unemployment levels, skill levels of the work force, nature and number of employers in the area, and a host of other factors.

The local zoning board also can be a goldmine of information. It can show you where various types of industry can be located and concentrations of potential competitors. Of course, the zoning board also can give you insight into locations that may be suitable for your business. You can avoid problems like those of an owner who built a grocery store based on traffic count data and accessibility. After construction was underway, he learned that the city limits were about 1,000 feet short of his location, which meant that he must operate under county laws. The county prohibited the sale of beer and wine! This was a major setback because the other grocery stores in town could sell beer and wine giving them a competitive edge.

In Chapter 3 we talked about marketing strategies. One approach was piggybacking. If you intend to locate close to competitors to benefit from their draws, be sure that those competitors are strong. A company established an inexpensive motel across the street from a Holiday Inn in an attempt to siphon off business based on price competition. Less than a year later, the Holiday Inn was sold to a discount hotel chain, which changed its name and reduced its rates! Piggybacking is especially popular as a strategy for location within a shopping mall. Research is required in this instance to determine the viability of the mall and the traffic patterns within it. Some locations in malls have better traffic patterns than others.

## MARKET VIABILITY

The assessment of viability for a new venture entails evaluating the market for a product or service that has been identified in an area by market research and the comparison of that information with the financial requirements for the new venture. In simple terms, **market viability** means the ease with which a new company can sell enough to make a profit in a specific area and location. We discussed mathematical techniques of break-even analysis in Chapter 6. Those tools can be useful in determining viability, but they will not provide an ultimate answer. In essence, the assessment of viability is the judgement that there is sufficient market demand in the area for the offerings of a business to make that business successful. In the case of a business whose market area is not constrained by its location, such as a mail order business, the viability of an area will be based on other factors. These might include access to shipping, warehousing, or suppliers, or they could be such factors as regulatory environment or labor pool and conditions.

Viability often is a subjective evaluation: it cannot be computed mathematically but is a matter of judgement. Break-even analysis can tell you how much you have to sell, but the determination as to whether you can achieve that number remains a judgement call. Market research can help to make that judgement stronger. For example, if you know that a population base of a certain level is required to support your business, it is easy to determine whether such a population base exists in a given area and location. To do that you must accumulate the information.

The best approach to market research is to make a list of the factors that will be important in making your business successful. Be specific and make the list as complete as you possibly can. Then make a list of potential areas for location. You can base the initial list on areas in which you would like to live. Study each of the success factors for each area. Assess the market viability and eliminate areas. Once a viable area has been found, repeat the process with locations within the area. Remember that if an area is not deemed viable, then a new area or new products or services should be selected, and the process of market research and evaluation repeated. Until you feel comfortable with the probability of success in an area with a particular business configuration, you should not proceed with the business venture.

## SITE SELECTION

The selection of the actual location of a business within the market area has cost-benefit trade-offs. This means that some sites will cost more, but may be more valuable from the perspective of the amount of business expected to occur at that site. The business site is more important for some types of businesses than others. If customers will be expected to come to the business location, then the site obviously is more important than if salespeople called on customers at other locations. It is very difficult to make the evaluation as to a particular site, especially when funds are limited, as usually is the case in a new venture. Traffic patterns, both automobile and pedestrian, as well as public transport access, ease of access, visibility, makeup of the surrounding area, and a host of other factors play a role in the relative worth of a business site. A good starting point is to look at where the competition is located. As we indicated earlier, site selection can be piggybacked, just like marketing strategies. Footwork also should be used. Get out and look at alternative sites. Draw up a list of the sites you are considering and record their good and bad points. In other words, use the procedure we outlined earlier: list desirable factors, list alternative locations, and study the factors for each location. Remember, a more expensive location should not be eliminated automatically. Consider as many alternatives as you can before making a final selection. The site you finally select is going to be with you for a while; make sure it is the right one for your business.

One final point needs to be made about site selection. When we talk about the marketing plan, we will discuss the image you wish to portray to your customers. The site you finally select is a major part of that image. If you are opening a professional services business, then a prestigious address may be required to support such an image. If you are opening a discount retail business, an address in a shopping mall could carry with it the image of expensive stores. No final decision as to location can be made until you have finalized the image for your business.

The final site selection should include consideration of the image as well as the cost-benefit trade-offs you should have analyzed for each alternative site. If no site seems to fit, then more should be sought until you are pleased with the result. Relocating a business is expensive. Lease terms frequently make it impossible during the first year.

Be sure to allow for business change or growth in the site selection as well. Try to visualize what the business will be like in a year or two if it is successful. A liquor store had selected a fine site in a shopping center but located in an inner space, thereby eliminating the option of drive-up service. When the business grew and customers began to desire drive-up service, the business was forced to relocate. The landlord required a substantial sum for early release from a five-year lease. At the time of the original lease, a corner location was available for a small additional rental. The liquor store owner had tried to save a few dollars and ended up spending much more.

Exhibit 11-3 summarizes the steps in area and site selection. Note that the first step is an identification of the target market. As we have discussed, a location for a business cannot be established without a sound understanding of the market to which the business will be appealing.

## PRICING AND PROMOTIONAL STRATEGIES

How much is a product or service worth? There is no answer to this question. As we discussed in Chapter 3, we cannot even be sure we know what a customer is buying when they purchase goods and services from us. In the pizza example, the customers appeared to be buying entertainment rather than pizza. The restaurant was one in which all their friends hung out, consequently, it became the place to go. Obviously, this would not have happened if the customers felt that prices were too high. On the other hand, mink coats are not sold in nonluxury department stores. People who purchase such items expect a level of service from the sales staff that is inconsistent with department stores. Furthermore, they don't expect to find a discount mink coat. Clearly, a furrier can have a sale on furs and can have success with that sale, but the items are sold differently and price is less of a factor than with many other goods.

Cost really is not an important consideration in pricing, contrary to popular opinion. Prices can be perceived by customers as low even when mark ups are quite high. Consider the case of expensive jewelry. Mark ups of 300% are common, although customers may still perceive these as low. On the other hand, grocery store mark ups tend to be extremely low on staple goods, 10% to 15%, but customers still make price comparisons and may perceive these prices as high. As you can see, customer perceptions make prices high or low, not costs!

How many times have you heard people say that prices must be high enough to at least cover costs? In Chapter 5 we learned that there are many different types of costs. It is true that no business can sell for less than variable costs over the long term and be successful, but as long as variable costs are covered, fixed costs can be absorbed by volume sales. This may not even be as static as it sounds. When Texas Instruments was a young, entrepreneurial venture, it got into the calculator business. Competition was quite heavy. TI

**EXHIBIT 11-3** *Area and Site Selection*

**TARGET MARKET**

- Before an adequate area and site selection can be made, you must define the group of customers to which you intend to appeal.
- Identify the characteristics of the target market; that is, the age, sex, income, occupation, family status, etc.; for business customers, the types, sizes, and characteristics.
- Make sure you know what you are selling; not simply the product or service to be offered.

**AREA SELECTION**

- Select several geographic areas for examination.
- Consider economic prospects and socioeconomic factors including number and stability of employers, economic conditions, income levels and prospects for future growth.
- Examine demographic trends and expectations.
- Compare the population characteristics of the area to those of the target market.
- Examine labor supply, wage rates, transportation access and special requirements.
- Assess the legal environment, including licensing requirements and local laws that might restrict business locations, types of businesses, hours of operation, etc.
- Identify direct and indirect competitors: number, location, strength, etc.
- Consider marketing strategies that will be required to penetrate the target market and displace competitors.
- Determine the existence of suitable sites within the area, their costs, availability, and terms of acquisition or lease.
- Gather needed information from such sources as the Census Bureau, the Small Business Administration, the state business development office, local chambers of commerce, local employment security commissions, local zoning boards, and real estate brokers, as well as personal research.
- Establish the viability of the area; that is, are the prospective market demand, competitive environment, and other factors such that the business can be successful in this area.

**SITE SELECTION**

- Determine minimal site requirements and desirable factors.
- Select several alternative sites identified within the chosen area for further examination; each site should meet minimum size, structure, and location requirements.
- Profile each site in terms of costs and benefits; that is, cost of lease terms and conditions, renovation or repair requirements, availability and cost of signage, automotive and pedestrian traffic patterns, public transport access, ease of access, visibility, shipping and transportation access, position with respect to competitors, neighboring businesses, prospects for growth and expansion.
- Pay particular attention to the planned image of the business and consistency of alternative site and image.
- For each site being considered, list good points and bad points and cost considerations.
- Perform a cost-benefit analysis for each alternative location; remember that cost is only one factor and is relative to the potential benefits that a particular site can offer.

grossly undercut the prices of all of its competitors, who responded by cutting their prices as well. TI recognized that its labor force was becoming more proficient at manufacturing calculators, remarkably so, and decided to capitalize on that learning curve. They actually priced calculators below their own costs in anticipation that those costs would drop as volume of sales went up and labor continued to improve its efficiency. The strategy worked: competitors did not feel able to match the extremely low prices; volume grew and efficiency grew with it. TI was able to establish a major market share in calculators and become profitable as manufacturing costs dropped.

None of this helps in establishing initial prices or promotional strategies for a new venture, so how does one go about it? The first step is to assess the competition. There are three basic pricing strategies that we will discuss in more detail in Chapter 18:

1. *Pricing below the market* implies that a major aspect of your business will be price competition. That is, you will be attempting to win business based on a lower price.
2. *Pricing above the market* implies that you will strive to win business based on quality, image, location, service, or other factors.
3. *Pricing at the market* implies that you will strive to remove price considerations from the purchase decision. In other words, you will not want price to be a factor in the customer's purchase decision.

Each approach has advantages and disadvantages. However, pricing below the market can be dangerous for a new venture because established competitors can retaliate by lowering their prices in an attempt to force out the new company before it has a chance to get established. If the start up can weather such a storm — as TI did — then this could be a viable strategy. But, if a venture is weak financially, as most are, and cannot afford a battle with established competitors, pricing below the market can be risky.

Pricing above the market also carries significant risk. If the firm is unable to convince its customers that the higher price is justified by quality or other factors, the business may not be able to establish itself. Nevertheless, during the early months of a new venture, customers tend to be more cognizant of prices because they have no image of the business in their minds. Furthermore, all of the customers have been purchasing from other firms and therefore are aware of price discrepancies. An established business is more likely to be able to price itself slightly above the market without its clientele realizing that fact than a new venture.

As you can see, the least risky pricing strategy is to price at the market. This infers that competition will be based on features other than price. Be aware that within market price are fluctuations that result from image differences. In other words, there are multiple prices for a product or service in the marketplace. For example, men's suits have an established price range in department stores. They have another established price range in discount stores. Tax preparation services have an established price in CPA firms. They have another established price in accounting firms and still another in tax preparation chain stores.

When you set out to establish the market price for your goods or services, you must be sure to examine competitors with the same approach or image as the one you will be pursuing. Of course, this implies that the image of the business will be established before its pricing policies. This is the case with much of the marketing effort because consistency of price, location, hours, service, promotion, and so on can be obtained only if each is consistent with the image the business will portray.

One other point about pricing must be made. If you carry multiple products or services, all must be priced consistently. You cannot be lower than the market in some areas and higher in others, because your customers will be confused by the differences and unable to formulate an image of your business in their minds. This confusion may not be voiced, but it will exist and cause many customers to feel uncomfortable with your business.

Promotion strategies cannot be set until pricing strategies have been established, both of which must follow the image of the business. **Promotion** is more than advertising. We will talk about initial advertising in the next section and examine it in more detail in Chapter 18. At this point we need to focus on the nonadvertising aspects of promotion: signs; layout; point-of-sale promotional pieces; letters, notes, or cards to be mailed to customers periodically; special events and sales—to name a few. Every aspect of your business seen by customers is an aspect of promotion. It is no accident that salespeople in multiple industries send their customers birthday cards; retailers send customers private announcements of sales; and people in services businesses send newsletters. All of these are oriented at obtaining and maintaining visibility in the eyes of the customer. You want present and prospective customers to think of your business often and in a positive light. When they are ready to buy, you don't want them to shop! You want them to call you!

Effective promotion requires constant planning. Before the venture is established, you should consider various approaches to obtaining visibility, ensure that they are consistent with the image you want to portray, and establish a timetable for their execution. One locally owned furniture store has a sale every month. Each sale has a different name and each promises huge discounts off the manufacturer's retail price. Actually, the store is a discount furniture store and the prices offered are those the store would charge anyway. Nevertheless, the sales work! The store sells the vast majority of each month's volume in the week-long sale. Furthermore, the constant exposure from sales promotions makes the store's name a household word.

## MARKETING BUDGET

People frequently think of the start-up capital requirements for a new venture strictly in terms of the cost to acquire an initial inventory, equipment, supplies, and so forth, and the initial operating expenses for some period of time. This is not adequate. The start-up budget must include money for start-up marketing and the operating expenses must include an allowance for ongoing marketing expenditures as well. Obviously, funds will be limited, but inventory, equipment, supplies, leasehold improvements, and the like will not be valuable to a company with no customers. Marketing is expensive but vital.

Discussions with advertising agencies can be valuable. Such firms are expensive, which may be why few small businesses starting up use them, but you should at least investigate the possibility of employing an agency and discussing start-up advertising campaigns. Talk to more than one agency and discuss agencies with other business owners, bankers, the chamber of commerce, and others. The selection of a good agency could be a valuable step in the marketing plan. If you decide not to go with an advertising agency, let that decision result from conscious thought, not the failure to consider the alternative.

If you decide to handle your own marketing, then talk to the various media representatives in the area and get circulation or coverage data as well as prices. Don't overlook outdoor advertising or direct mail. You should explore the cost of mailing lists and printing of brochures. The chamber of commerce can give you ideas about sources of mailing lists, as can other businesses, bankers, and state and federal assistance offices. In addition, most larger communities have directories available that list the names and addresses of the population. The chamber of commerce can help you with that as well.

The start-up marketing budget really is the result of planning the initial advertising and estimating its cost. The start-up operating budget, which we will discuss in Chapter 12, recommends incorporating some "slack," in case any expenses have been overlooked or underestimated. This is a good idea for the marketing budget, too. Once you have estimated the requirements, add more in case you have overlooked something or in case a second advertising push is required to get the business rolling.

As mentioned repeatedly, nothing is more important to the success of a business venture than the image it portrays to its customers. Consider carefully how you wish your customers to perceive your business and how your business will be distinct from its direct and indirect competitors. Whatever image is chosen, you must be consistent with everything else, especially the advertising. In large measure, the advertising approach you take initially in a new venture will set the tone for the image the business will have in the minds of its customers.

## THE MARKETING PLAN

The start-up marketing plan includes much more than the initial advertising. The plan should address the opening date, the initial marketing budget, start-up advertising and its media, and beginning promotional plans. The purpose of the plan is to gain rapid recognition in the target market and persuade potential customers to examine your offerings. Frequently, an advertising campaign will be accompanied by sales prices, contests or prizes, or other attention gainers. The plan should include a timetable for the various aspects of the venture's start up. All aspects of the start up must be coordinated. Staffing concerns are not the least of these. A restaurant held its grand opening after much start-up advertising and promotional coupons, but neglected to train the temporary waiters and waitresses who were hired to handle the expected opening night crowds. The expected crowds appeared, but the staff confused the orders, forgot to replenish the salad bar, and became exasperated and distraught. Many of the customers left, vowing never to return. Everything had been done perfectly, and the advertising and promotions had attracted tremendous attention. One small detail, the training of six temporary staff members, turned the grand opening into a catastrophe from which the business may never recover.

The process described in this chapter for developing a start-up marketing plan applies to any type of venture. Owners of service businesses tend to overlook some aspects of the process, but their services, like products, must be marketed. In a particular type of business, some aspects of the start up may be less important than others. For example, site location may be less important to a firm whose customers never come to its offices. This does not mean that any step is unimportant or should be skipped. Only by systematically proceeding through the process can the pitfalls of starting a business be minimized. Just as in meeting people, first impressions are hard to change, the first impressions customers develop of a new business are hard to overcome. The only way to ensure that those impressions are positive is to plan.

## SUMMARY

The first step in starting a new business is selecting the product or service to be sold. The product or service can be chosen based upon experience or to fulfill a recognized niche in the marketplace. After a product or a service is chosen, strategies must be designed to attract public attention.

The steps in the marketing plan are outlined in Exhibit 11-2. These steps in the plan are generalizable to service and other types of businesses as well as the traditional retailer. Some steps will be more important for a specific business than others. Nevertheless, no step can be omitted or else the prospective business owners risk initial mistakes that can be costly and difficult to correct in the future.

## QUESTIONS

1. Why is your own personal judgement about the marketability of an item invalid?
2. List the steps in starting a new venture.
3. Why is the evaluation of personal goals and objectives the first step in starting a new business?
4. Discuss or review the who, what, when, where, and how of the marketing process.
5. Describe the three approaches to marketing.
6. How does market research affect the success of a new product or service in its selection?
7. What is *market area,* and why is its selection important?
8. What is the difference between *direct* and *indirect competition*?
9. Why is your choice of products or services and market area iterative?
10. What are some of the considerations in determining site selection for your business?
11. Why is a marketing budget important, and what areas should you examine in determining your marketing alternatives?
12. Explain the components of the marketing plan.
13. Define the following terms:
    a. market area
    b. direct competitor
    c. indirect competitor
    d. market viability
    e. image

## PROJECTS

1. Take a look in your neighborhood. Observe several businesses to see if they have an observable marketing plan. If they advertise, rate the methods used. In conjunction with deciding about marketing plans, evaluate the image, location, and product or service. Do these attributes indicate planning or happenstance?
2. Are any new businesses starting up in your town? What types of activities can you see that would indicate a marketing strategy? Do they have a market plan? What observations can you make about their activities? What would you do if you were they?

# CASE

Mark Davis was a conscientious young man who was determined to be successful. He wanted to set up a really neat bar in the university town he had adopted. He had gone to school there and was finishing up his MBA. This was where he wanted to stay. After nearly six years in the town as a student, he knew that there were few places where students could really go and have fun. The town was progressive in the sale of beer, wine, and liquor, but the only places in town where one could drink on the premises were "joints." Mark had visited some of these places with friends and found them to be a bit rough. The customers were serious drinkers, and they didn't much cater to the younger crowd who wanted music and fun.

Mark decided to approach this decision to open a pub realistically. He wanted to create an atmosphere where students could meet or date and dance, listen to music, and relax. Most of all, he wanted to be successful. He asked the nearest Small Business Development Center for their advice about starting his business. He needed to make a loan, acquire a site, hire people, and do marketing. He worked with the consultants assigned to him and everything was looking good. His case worker told him that his success would depend upon how well his initial marketing campaign was carried out and whether he could get some capital. So Mark began to do some planning.

**Questions**

1. What kind of site do you think Mark should find?
2. What external or legal constraints might Mark have in starting a bar? Would this consideration have been different a few years ago?
3. What kinds of planning should Mark do to see if a bar is a viable alternative?
4. Who would be Mark's competition?
5. How would Mark build an image for his bar, which would accommodate drinks, snacks, and dancing, that would be more pleasing to him?
6. What probably would be his target market?
7. Prepare an initial marketing plan for Mark's business.
8. Obtain cost estimates for the locations which you consider appropriate for such a business and estimate the cost for the promotion and advertising plans that you have prepared for the business.

# CHAPTER 12

# The Financing Plan

**LEARNING OBJECTIVES**

After completing this chapter, you should be able to

- Understand that financial planning includes consideration of risks to which firms will be exposed, the performance levels required for solvency, start-up capital requirements, and plans for obtaining that capital.
- Determine capital requirements for a new venture.
- Find sources of funding.
- Identify assistance agencies.
- Draw up a loan proposal.

The financial planning required in starting up a new venture includes determining the start-up capital requirements and plans for obtaining that capital. Each of these areas is addressed in this chapter. As these topics are discussed, remember that we are still in the planning phase and these considerations are part of the business plan discussed in this part of the text. These are the final considerations before embarking on a new venture start up, but they are no less important than the market considerations or other aspects of the business plan. In fact, determining capital needs and acquiring capital may be two of the most important aspects of starting a new business, because undercapitalization is a major problem contributing to business failures.

## CAPITAL REQUIREMENTS

If you were to conduct a poll of owners of small businesses and ask them to list the major mistakes they made during the start-up phase, the first item on that list would likely be starting with too little capital. Start-up capital is hard to get. When people have made their minds up to do something, they are hard to discourage. Consequently, the vast majority of small businesses are begun undercapitalized. Many ventures are unable to recover from this mistake and ultimately fail. Many others find their growth severely restricted and their prospects doomed to mediocrity because they lack enough capital to properly establish the business.

If the financial portion of the preventure planning is done properly, determining the capital required for start up is not difficult. Exhibit 12-1 is a checklist of some of the items to review and estimate in determining the capital requirements for a successful start up.

Note that several of the items required in the capital needs assessment come from the forecasts and budgets discussed in the business plan. This area frequently is overlooked in capital planning. It is not enough to have sufficient capital to open a new venture: enough capital is required to carry the operation until it becomes self-sustaining through its cash flow generation. In general, this means having between three and six months of operating expenses on hand in the form of cash at start up or set aside in committed lines of credit from a lender. The best determination comes from looking at the cash flow expected from the sales forecast and operating budget. This is why the first item on the list of determining capital requirements is a sales forecast! Until you assess your expectations for sales, you cannot determine the kinds of facilities, personnel, and other requirements you will need. The preparation of the initial sales forecast was discussed in detail in Chapter 7. Review that section to assure that you understand how to determine the monthly and annual sales estimates.

**EXHIBIT 12-1** *Determining Capital Requirements for a New Venture*

I. Prepare a sales forecast

II. Determine the cost of production and supporting assets
   A. Cost of land and building, if applicable
   B. Cost of machinery and equipment
   C. Cost of furniture and fixtures
   D. Cost of telephones and communications equipment
   E. Cost of computers and information systems
   F. Insure that all costs include delivery and installation
   G. Investigate the cost and availability of used equipment
   H. Investigate construction costs
   I. Investigate leasing costs

III. Determine the cost of inventory and supplies
   A. Initial inventory requirements and cost
      1. Initial inventory should be sufficient to support the inventory turnover expected
      2. Cost should include freight
   B. Initial supplies required
      1. Production supplies
      2. Office supplies
      3. Janitorial supplies

IV. Determine the start-up marketing costs
   A. Initial promotional expenses
      1. Signs, point-of-sale displays
      2. Promotional materials, premiums, gifts
      3. Special events and demonstrations
   B. Initial advertising costs
      1. Media costs
      2. Direct mail, mailing lists, printing, and postage
      3. Flyers and their distribution
   C. Initial price concessions, discounts, and sales

V. Determine operating requirements
   A. Fixed costs (estimate for a full year, using a monthly forecast)
      1. Occupancy expense
      2. Salary and personnel expense, including fringe benefits
      3. Insurance premiums
      4. Rental or lease expense, if any
      5. Maintenance of computers or information systems
      6. Communication expense: telephone, fax, etc.
      7. Repairs, maintenance, and upkeep expenses
      8. Property and other taxes
      9. Licenses and fees

*continued*

**EXHIBIT 12-1 continued**

10. Professional fees
    a. Accounting
    b. Legal
    c. Other
11. Franchise fees, if any

B. Variable costs (estimate as a percentage of sales)
1. Production costs
    a. Raw materials
    b. Direct labor
    c. Variable overhead
2. Inventory replacement expense
3. Commissions
4. Freight
5. Variable rent or lease expense, if any
6. Variable franchise fees, if any
7. Marketing and advertising expense

C. Cash on hand and in banks to support operations

VI. Calculate the required operating capital for start up
A. Minimum of three months of operating expenses
B. Preferably sufficient capital to carry firm until cash flow forecasts become self-supporting
C. Monthly payments on loans

VII. Add production and supporting assets, inventory, marketing, cash and operating capital to determine total start-up capital required

## Cost of Production and Supporting Assets

During the process of site selection discussed in the last chapter, a prospective business owner should be gathering information about costs of facilities. Comparing the costs of acquiring or leasing various facilities and equipment should be a routine part of site evaluation. The key here is to establish a complete list of specifications for the business. How large must the facility be? What kinds of machinery, equipment, furniture, fixtures, and so forth will be required? What kinds of computing equipment and software will be required? What other assets are needed? How much will it cost to deliver and install these assets? Should new or used items be acquired? Should they be purchased, constructed, or leased? Don't forget office equipment and initial supplies, telephones, supplies for the rest rooms, and so on. Preparation of a complete list makes the process of contacting real estate agents, equipment suppliers, and vendors more productive. The list of items in the exhibit is by no means complete. It is a sample of the kinds of considerations that must be made. The complete needs of a new venture are determined by the characteristics and plans for that venture in its specific product and market.

Cost estimates start at real estate agencies that specialize in commercial properties or agencies that handle the accounts of malls, shopping centers, office buildings, or specific sites of interest. From this point, contact suppliers or vendors of the types of equipment you need. A copy of the yellow pages and a few telephone calls should get you started. Be sure to ask vendors who handles items they do not carry. In smaller towns you may have to search for suppliers in nearby cities. Call several vendors for each item on your list and be sure to check on the availability and costs of used equipment at the same time. Watch for advertisements of sellouts of the fixtures and furniture you need. Equipment and furnishings are expensive. A little shopping around can save a great deal. Be sure to look into the possibility of construction. One restaurant owner hired a local contractor during the off season to build booths and tables. The result was an attractive alternative that cost 25% of the price of new tables and chairs.

## Initial Inventory and Supplies

One area in which initial cost estimation presents difficulties, especially for retailers and wholesalers, is the determination of initial inventory requirements. Industry averages for the percentage of total assets represented by inventory is a good starting place. Factors that influence the decision include lag time for receipt of inventory after purchasing, the risk of obsolescence, and the risk of stock outs. Obviously, if new inventory items can be acquired in a short time from a reliable vendor, then the amount of inventory to be carried at start up is less important than it would be if it took weeks to get the items. In the latter case, it could be dangerous to stock too little inventory. Also, if there is little risk that the inventory items purchased will become worthless if not sold, then the amount acquired is less important than if unsold inventory had to be written off as a complete loss. In that case, it could be dangerous to stock too much inventory. Stock out problems affect the decision in the same fashion. If you don't have the items a customer wants, will you lose that customer completely? Will you damage your ability to sell to that customer in the future? If the answer to these questions is no, then the risk associated with too little inventory or too narrow product lines is lessened. These factors must be balanced against a need to minimize the initial cash investment in inventory.

If little risk is associated with underestimating the start-up inventory, then the best strategy may be to acquire sufficient inventory to ensure that the facility looks good. In a retail business, if a store looks understocked, people will form an opinion about the store that may be detrimental to its image. Of course, the opposite can be true as well: a store that looks cluttered because it has too much inventory crowded into too small a space will give consumers a poor image of the business. To aid that problem, industry averages about inventory levels per square foot of space can help, but nothing is superior to planning the display of inventory. Part of the start-up planning should be determining how inventory is to be displayed and how much space it will take up in display.

If significant problems are associated with understocking or incomplete stocking of inventory, then deciding on the correct initial supply will be of major importance. The key factor will be determining an inventory policy to follow consistently and to use in budgeting purchases. The inventory policy should be stated in terms of sales. Assume, for example, that you decide to carry sufficient inventory for one and one-half month's sales at all times, because of the lag time for resupply and the risks of obsolescence and stock out. If the cost of goods sold percentage is expected to be 50%, then the initial and continuing inventory levels should always be equal to 50% of the sales forecast for the next month and a half. This approach makes the sales forecast even more important, but it will prevent unrestrained purchasing from depleting the resources of the firm. The inventory policy should be adjusted as experience is gained, but changes should be assessed carefully before being implemented. We will discuss this process at some length in Chapter 20, "Inventory Management."

Whatever the inventory requirements, most start ups will have to deal with initial supplies. As indicated in the previous section, you need to make a list; how about office supplies, janitorial supplies, and so on? Call several office supply firms and explain your needs. They will not only provide price quotes, but help you determine what items you will need and how much you should purchase initially.

## Start-up Marketing Costs

Most people think about the costs of the initial advertising campaign to announce the opening of a new business, but few people remember to budget for items like premiums to be given to customers. If you are going to provide pens, pencils, windshield scrapers, kitchen mitts, or lollipops to people during your grand opening, someone has to order and pay for them! What we need here is another list. It seems like we are "listing you to death," doesn't it? Unfortunately, no one can expect to remember all of the details associated with a business start up. You simply must make lists! The costs of signs, printing, and special events like radio shows on site or demonstrations are all readily available if you simply look. The secret is remembering to look. Lists help you remember.

In Chapter 11 we talked about the initial advertising you intend to pursue.

As you investigate advertising agencies and media availability, be sure to accumulate cost data as well. Your new venture will have trouble reaching customers if they don't know you exist.

One aspect of start-up marketing costs frequently overlooked is the cost of price concessions. If you will be offering special prices, discounts, or sale items during an opening period, be sure to include an estimate for this cost. Preparation of a sales and cash flow forecast generally is based on pricing policies that will be pursued in the business. Significant deviations from those prices will damage the forecasts unless you take those prices into consideration. This cost may not be an out-of-pocket expense unless your initial price is below variable cost, but it will affect forecasts and cash flow.

We need to make a point about initial sale prices while we are on this subject. If you start a business with a sale, when the prices go back to their real levels, your customers may react adversely. This is especially true if there is a major difference between sale prices and regular prices. Your customers then may decide that your prices are higher than the market, when in fact this is not so! In general, we discourage start-up sales for this reason. Customers generally will be curious about a new venture and attracted to it simply because it is new. This means that a sale may not be needed.

## Operating Requirements

The list of fixed and variable costs in Exhibit 12-1 represents the kinds of costs that must be considered in start-up planning. Some of these items more properly may be termed mixed costs, in that they have both fixed and variable components. We discussed these costs in Chapter 6 and described how they must be handled. Mixed costs must be classified either as fixed or variable if the amount of error from that treatment is not significant. Otherwise, they must be decomposed into fixed and variable components and budgeted in that fashion. For example, a part of the occupancy expense is cost of utilities. Heat, light, water, and so forth may be virtually fixed for some companies, like retailers and service firms, but variable for other companies, like manufacturing firms. Communication costs usually consist of a flat fee each month plus charges for long distance calls. If a company has few such calls, its communication expense should be treated as fixed. If it has many long distance calls, its communications may be better budgeted as variable.

As in the previous cases, the exhibit represents the kinds of operating costs that may occur, but each venture must establish for itself the costs it will face. If you lack experience in the kind of business you are starting, this can be a difficult job. The best approach is to think through every aspect of what the company will be doing each day. What is required to support those activities in terms of facilities, personnel, and supplies? How will the costs of those activities behave in relation to sales? Make another list! Now you can set about obtaining estimates for the costs.

Industry averages from published sources or industry trade associations may be helpful in making these cost estimates, but great variation between companies is the rule. That means that a lot of leg work will be required to obtain sound estimates for these expenses. Remember that it is better to estimate too high than too low. A pleasant surprise is better than an unpleasant one at the end of the month.

In Chapter 7 we described how these expense forecasts should be made monthly and yearly, with variable expenses set as a percentage of sales and fixed expenses as a set amount each month. We described the preparation of a monthly and annual expense forecast based on the sales forecast. We also talked about the minimum cash on hand required to support operations. We want enough cash at start up to cover at least three, and preferably six, months of operations. In fact, what we really need is enough cash to carry the business until the point at which cash flows are expected to become self-supporting. The preparation of a cash budget will predict when this point will be reached.

All this information ultimately will be used to prepare a loan request, so be sure to keep supporting estimates, quotes, and details to show to the lender. You also need to be careful not to overlook anything and prepare estimates properly. If a prospective lender discovers significant omissions or errors in any of these forecasts, then loan prospects will be dim. Consider the following case from our files.

We were called in to help obtain financing. Our client had done a fine job of start-up planning, but he had made one small mistake. The business was to be a service company selling advertising for the cable television stations in a 300-mile radius. The prospective owner was convinced that cable operators did not have the time, staff, or expertise to find advertisers for the slots reserved for local use. He proposed using a staff of sales people to locate advertisers and sell advertising contracts. He also would have facilities for filming commercials. It sounded like a fine idea to us.

He had decided that a computer printout from a spreadsheet would impress lenders. Unfortunately, he didn't know anything about computers, so he hired a student in computer science at the university to prepare spreadsheets for all of the income, expense, and cash flow forecasts.

When he presented his loan package to the bank, the loan officer asked several pointed questions about expenses that had been forecast. Apparently, she didn't like the answers she got, because the loan request was denied. We asked to see the forecasts.

The forecasts had been prepared on a month-by-month basis for three years. It was obvious that all of the expenses on the forecast had been classified as fixed, because none of them fluctuated as sales growth occurred. We found that hard to believe. In the first place, this meant that all sales people would be salaried and that no additional sales force was planned as growth occurred. In the second place, it assumed that most of the commercials were going to be prepared by advertising agencies or other outsiders, because there were no added costs in the firm to support growth.

Our client apparently thought that the student who prepared the forecasts had considered these questions. At any rate, no one had addressed them in the forecasts. We showed him how to fix the forecasts.

The mistake caused a real problem, because only one bank in town really was interested in lending to small firms with good ideas but limited capital—and that bank had already said no! It also refused to reconsider the loan. No other banks would give our client the time of day! Because the venture was entirely new to their experience and our client had little money, they weren't interested. We never did find debt financing for him. The client finally had to bring in some partners and ultimately lost control of the venture. We still believe that a mistake in the forecasts caused this!

### Total Start-up Capital

Addition of all of the elements discussed in the preceding sections will produce a forecast of the capital needs of the new venture. One further problem, however, complicates the forecast. If you intend to borrow funds, as most new ventures do, you will need to include loan payments for the first several months in the start-up capital needs. Obviously, this means that you need to know how much money to borrow, but the amount you borrow changes the amount you need. The solution is to accumulate all the capital requirements and then add the prospective loan payments for a variety of borrowing amounts. This will result in a range of estimates, of which you should take the largest as your capital forecast. As mentioned in the previous sections, it is better to err on the side of conservatism.

## SOURCES OF FUNDING

After you have determined how much capital will be required for the new venture you must find the necessary funding. For a new and untried business this can be a major problem, especially if the venture is initiated by a new and untried business owner.

### Personal Sources

The first place to look for funding is personal savings and assets. People are fond of telling stories about million dollar companies started on a shoestring and people who started with nothing and became rich. In truth, such stories tend to be greatly exaggerated. One successful business owner who seemed to typify the rags to riches stereotype once confided to us:

> I like to talk about immigrating to this country fifty years ago with two dollars in my pocket and a head full of dreams. Now I own a string of restaurants and everybody thinks I became rich overnight! They forget that I slaved for twenty years saving every dime until I got enough money to open my first restaurant! It took another ten years of eighteen-hour days for that to become successful enough for me to expand. I am very grateful for the opportunity that exists in this country, and I am proud to be a citizen, and I am proud to have my own business. But I worked for it!

Few lenders or investors will be willing to risk their funds in a new venture in which the owner/manager does not have a significant investment. The inescapable reasoning is that if times get tough, as they probably will, an owner without much to lose may be inclined to walk away. A person who stands to lose his or her life savings and family home is much more inclined to stay with the venture and make every effort to make it succeed. An unwritten rule of thumb that many lenders quote says never lend more than half of the start-up requirements to a new business. Whether or not such a rule is followed, clearly everyone you approach for funding is going to be deeply interested in how much of your own money is tied up in the venture. One word of caution is important here. If your own investment in the business is not cash from savings but cash from loans that must be repaid, then the amount of cash required for that repayment must be considered part of the operating requirements for the business, in addition to everything else. Otherwise, you can find yourself unable to meet payments on those debts because the business is not generating enough cash to cover your living requirements and also pay back the loans.

Another prime source of capital for a new venture is family, friends, and business contacts. If such people are willing to invest in the venture, it can decrease your ultimate borrowing requirements. Many potential business owners are reluctant to approach family and friends because they fear rejection or failing those close to themselves. If you intend to be successful in a business venture, then the first fear must be overcome. If you start a business, then you will be faced with rejection repeatedly. You might as well get some practice now! The latter fear may be very real. If you don't believe that your family or friends can afford to assume the risk involved in your new venture, then it may be better not to approach them. If you are going to be constantly concerned with the repercussions of failure for those close to you as well as its impact on your own situation, then your judgement and your ability to manage the business may be adversely affected. On the other hand, if you truly believe that the venture entails tremendous risk, then perhaps you should reconsider your decision to begin! If you obtain financing from family or friends, be sure to cover the arrangements in writing. Paul Margolis told a story about how loans from his family used to start his business became a nightmare in family squabbling after his business became successful. The fight was over how much of the business his family owned.[1] His experience was not unique.

## Investors

Before we talk about finding investors, we need to say a few words about investment instruments or securities. Securities need not necessarily be common stock. Securities may also be preferred stock, which has a specified dividend rate and may have conversion or repurchase provisions; bonds or debt instruments, which can have conversion features or can be secured by mortgages or liens on assets; partnership certificates, which may have risk limitations; or special classes of common stock, which may have special participation features or restricted voting rights. In general terms, a ***security*** simply is an instrument that outlines the details of an investor's interest in a business and the obligations of the business to the investor. Because they can be quite complex, most small business owners considering the use of securities as an investment vehicle should obtain legal and professional assistance at an early stage.

The regulations of the Securities and Exchange Commission have special provisions that permit small business to solicit investors. The SEC oversees the securities markets and has the power to regulate virtually all public offerings in the United States. Its rules are quite complex. No one should consider attempting a public offering, regardless of its size, without the aid of an attorney experienced in SEC matters. Frequently, the assistance of a CPA firm also will be required to prepare and certify forecasts. Because of the difficulty involved in skirting SEC registration and disclosure requirements for new businesses and the difficulty in complying with those rules and the expense involved, few small business ventures actually obtain funding from this source. There are added problems: after professional assistance has been obtained and an offering properly structured, it still must be sold. That means that a local stock brokerage firm or similar agency must be obtained to actually find investors in the securities. Needless to say, such assistance is not without expense. From a practical perspective, few small business ventures can expect to obtain capital from public offerings of securities. Data about small company public offerings, which is quoted in support of the rapid growth of such financing arrangements, generally includes data for all offerings, not just start ups, and frequently classifies businesses as small based on quite large net worth levels. If you plan to start a venture that you believe will be large enough to consider a public stock offering, then we recommend early exploration of the issues with an attorney.

Instead of a public offering, a private placement of securities may be a much more viable option for a small business. Numerous investment groups— some formal, some informal—exist to find investment opportunities for members. These groups generally are made up of well-to-do individuals looking for larger than average returns on their investments. The formal groups may hire professionals to seek out and screen investment opportunities or may use a local stock brokerage firm or bank for the same purpose. Informal groups may be nothing more than a group of friends or coworkers who meet to discuss a potential investment that has come to the attention of one of the members. Frequently, access to an investment group can be obtained from local stock brokerage firms, bankers, business consultants, or private financial planning firms. These groups may prefer to specialize in loans, in equity investments, or in a combination of the two. They may prefer investing in a particular industry or a particular kind of security, such as real estate. They may have minimum or maximum investment amounts that they like to consider. Generally, a successful approach to one of these groups will require professional assistance in preparing and structuring an investment proposal.

**Venture Capitalists.** **Venture capitalist** firms specialize in investing in new venture start ups. These firms frequently structure their own investments by specifying percentages of ownership required and taking a combination of equity and debt securities. Venture capitalists also frequently offer managerial assistance. Such firms may want to handle all the outside investment in a new venture to protect their position relative to other investors. The investment contract may have restrictive covenants to ensure this position. Frequently, venture capitalists will require as part of the deal stock options that can be exercised at a future date should the business become a major success. There have been cases in the past in which venture capitalists used options to take control of a business after it had survived its start-up problems. Venture capitalists also may be willing to provide funding on a continuing basis as a business grows and requires more capital. They frequently desire a voice in management to protect their interests.

The public library is the best place to find venture capitalists. Because there are over 500 such firms in the United States, numerous directories of investment capital firms are published. Your reference librarian can select the correct directory for your needs. Many venture capitalists specialize in a particular industry, market, or geographic territory. For example, some limit their investments to high technology industries, whereas others are interested only in ventures that will provide real estate as collateral. The directories will indicate such preferences and explain the minimum and maximum requirements of the firms.

Venture capitalists frequently have minimum and maximum investment amounts. The minimums may seem quite high. Many venture capitalists feel that an investment of less than $500,000 is not justifiable because of the expense of reviewing and analyzing the investment. Consequently, venture capitalists frequently are a viable option for only a small business that doesn't plan on being a small business for long! By this we mean, a new venture that consists of a local restaurant or retailer generally will not be able to approach a venture capitalist. Such firms are more interested in ventures that project tremendous growth in the short run and plan on rapidly becoming national in scope.

If you believe your venture would attract a venture capitalist, then be aware that the analysis of your venture or its business plan will focus heavily on you and your background. Venture capitalists will be interested in determining whether your venture is viable and whether you are qualified to manage it. We recommend that you communicate directly with a venture capitalist before preparing an investment proposal. You will find a wide range of requirements for the proposal; consequently, it is best to tailor the package to the specifications of the venture capital firm reviewing it. A word of caution is due here. According to an article in the *Wall Street Journal*, 95% of applicants for venture capital investment are declined.[2] This doesn't mean you should be discouraged from seeking the investment: just don't spend any of the money until you have it!

**Small Business Investment Companies.** **Small business investment companies** (SBICs) are public or private firms licensed and regulated by the U.S. Small Business Administration under the Small Business Investment Act of 1958 to provide capital for small businesses. In 1969 a new type of investment firm was created especially to aid minority-owned firms. The **Minority Enterprise Small Business Investment Companies** (MESBICs) also are licensed and regulated by the SBA, but generally require 51% ownership of any small business seeking assistance to be held by minority or socially or economically disadvantaged individuals. A list of SBICs and MESBICs can be obtained from the local office of the Small Business Administration or through the National Association of Small Business Investment Companies located in Washington, D.C. In 1985, SBICs invested $435 million in 2,400 businesses.[3] These firms are truly venture capitalists operating in a more regulated environment so you can expect much the same situation as discussed in the preceding section. One major difference is that SBICs and MESBICs typically have lower minimum investment levels, making them a more viable option for truly small start ups.

## Assistance Agencies

A variety of local, state and federal assistance agencies can be of value in obtaining start-up funding as well as continuing funding for small businesses. An example of local assistance is the **Local Development Company** (LDC) program. The federal government provides assistance in the form of loans to LDCs, who frequently have favorable lending terms and rates to aid small business start ups. Requirements for assistance vary greatly. To determine whether your community has established an LDC, contact your local bankers or city or county offices. Other forms of local assistance can come from loans or grants made to cities by the U.S. Department of Housing and Urban Development, which are used by the cities to finance small businesses that will aid the local economy. City offices are the source of information about the existence of such programs in your local area.

About twenty states have agencies that provide loans to small businesses. Some of these have special provisions, such as a requirement for matching funds from other sources. To determine whether your state has such a program, contact the bureau of commerce or office of business development or similar agency in the state capital. Such agencies also can identify other state assistance programs that may exist.

The federal government has numerous loan and assistance programs designed to aid small businesses. Many of these place special emphasis on start ups. In fact, there are some 350 assistance programs. The programs are offered through the departments of Commerce, the Interior, Housing and Urban Development, Farmer's Home Administration, the National Science Foundation, and the Small Business Administration. There is actually a bewildering array of programs, which is poorly publicized and consequently frequently underutilized. The government publishes a list of agencies and their programs. The *Catalog of Federal Domestic Assistance* is available from the U.S. Printing Office in Washington, D.C.

One of the best places to find a program that could help you in a particular venture is the local office of the **Small Business Development Center** (SBDC). SBDCs are an assistance program of the Small Business Administration and now exist in almost every state. They generally are established as joint programs with state university systems. SBDCs provide counseling and consulting services of all types for small businesses, generally without charge. If an SBDC exists in your state, you should definitely contact it for aid in preparing the business plan as well as information about loan and investment programs. The home office of the Small Business Administration in Washington maintains lists of SBDC offices around the country.

The **Economic Development Administration** (EDA) is a branch of the U.S. Commerce Department located in Washington, D.C. The EDA has a loan program to aid businesses in geographic areas of the country that have been identified as economically depressed. The loan process is highly complex and the application is quite involved. To determine whether your area qualifies and to obtain assistance in preparing loan packages, contact the nearest EDA office. The location of the offices can be obtained from the Washington headquarters of the EDA.

The **Farmer's Home Administration** (FmHA) has a loan program to aid the development of businesses in rural areas. Towns with populations of less than 25,000 generally qualify for FmHA assistance. The program is one of loan guarantees rather than direct loans and therefore requires a local bank's participation. Consequently, your best source of information about FmHA loans will be from local participating banks. You should contact several local banks to find one willing to participate in the guarantee program.

## Small Business Administration

The SBA is probably the best known assistance agency for small businesses in the United States. It offers a broad range of counseling and consulting programs through SBDCs, mentioned earlier, and the **Service Corps of Retired Executives** (SCORE) and other programs. These consulting activities generally are without cost to a qualifying small business. Information about such programs can be obtained through the nearest SBA office.

The loan assistance programs of the SBA have fallen under a great deal of criticism recently due to cost overruns and excessive losses. Consequently, the loan programs have been curtailed sharply. For all practical purposes, the direct loan program for small businesses has been eliminated. There remains a direct lending process, but it is restricted to disaster assistance and special programs. The SBA still has a loan guarantee program, although the amounts of the guarantee have been reduced. The guarantee will now generally be a maximum of 80 percent of a qualifying loan with the participating bank assuming 20 percent of the risk. The maximum loan amounts and maximum loan terms vary depending upon the use of loan proceeds and the collateral assigned. The application package is lengthy and involved.

The SBA loan guarantee program is designed to reduce the risk of default to a participating bank thereby encouraging banks to make loans they might not consider otherwise. Because the program now revolves around bank participation, the best source of information about SBA loans is your local banker. A **bank certification program** has been developed that permits selected banks to process the entire SBA loan guarantee package independently. Several hundred banks in the United States have been so certified. Noncertified banks can participate by routing an application package through the local SBA office for approval. You may need to check with several banks in your area to find one that has been certified or that is willing to participate in an SBA-guaranteed loan. A call to the local office of the SBA should help in finding certified or cooperative banks. Although the program has several attractive features from the perspective of a bank, some banks prefer not to participate due to the reporting requirements of the SBA. One word of caution is necessary at this point. SBA-guaranteed loans generally carry restrictions against the acquisition of additional debt prior to repayment and frequently require blanket liens on all assets. Consequently, you need to be especially careful that the start-up capital is sufficient before accepting an SBA loan. Future access to debt will be difficult!

### Banks and Other Finance Companies

Throughout the preceding sections we ignored local banks as a source of start-up capital. This is not because banks do not make start-up loans to small businesses; in fact, they make many such loans. Banks tend to be cautious in lending in a start-up situation. Finance companies and insurance companies also make business loans and may be more willing to accept a start-up loan than banks. Insurance companies, however, generally require stable collateral for a loan, such as real estate. Exhibit 12-2 recaps the potential sources of capital discussed in this chapter. The list is by no means exhaustive, but it does illustrate the range of funding sources that exists.

## LOAN PROPOSAL

Regardless of where you locate financing, you will need a **loan proposal** that spells out the total capital involved in the start up, the amount requested from the lender, the use of the funds, the terms of repayment, the collateral available, and the source of repayment. Exhibit 12-3 displays the contents of a typical loan proposal.

In essence, the information required in the loan proposal is a shortened version of the business plan. The proposal must be as short as possible without omitting pertinent information that may be of value to the lender in reaching a decision. Once the proposal has been completed, you should arrange to present it to the lender in person, if possible. Most lenders will have loan committees that actually make the decision; however, a lending officer generally will present your proposal to the committee and make a recommendation. A good presentation, displaying an open, confident attitude and a professional demeanor, can go a long way toward assuring that the lending decision is on your side.

**EXHIBIT 12-2** *Potential Sources of Capital*

1. Personal funds and savings
2. Family and friends—loans and investments
3. Partners—friends and business associates
4. Private investors—need professional assistance to find
5. Venture capitalists—more than 500 appear in published lists
6. Small business investment companies (SBICs) and minority enterprise SBICs—Both chartered by the SBA; check with the SBA for lists and addresses
7. State sources—check with business assistance office
   - Local development companies
   - Industrial development and business development agencies
8. Federal sources
   - Small Business Administration
   - Department of Housing and Urban Development
   - Department of Commerce—Economic Development Administration
   - Farmers Home Administration
   - More than 350 assistance programs
   - Published directory available from Printing Office
9. Banks—independent, SBA certified, SBA participating
10. Insurance companies
11. Finance companies
12. Public or private stock offerings—Require professional assistance

Whether or not you intend to obtain credit from a bank, it is a good idea to establish a banking relationship and discuss your venture with a banker. Even if you do not solicit bank loans for start-up purposes, you probably will have recurring needs for loans in the future. Obtaining lines of credit for operating purposes and loans for expansion will be enhanced if your banker is knowledgeable of the business from its inception. As discussed when describing the search for an attorney and accountant, selecting a banker should take some thought. The convenience of branch locations is of less importance than developing a relationship with lending officers who understand your business and are willing to assist it in its growth and development.

**EXHIBIT 12-3** *The Loan Proposal*

I. Amount of loan requested
   A. Total amount and sources of all capital
   B. Uses for loan proceeds
   C. Repayment terms desired for loan

II. Assets of the business
   A. Value of all assets presently owned
   B. Value of assets to be acquired
   C. Assets pledged as collateral to others
   D. Assets available and offered as collateral for loan

III. Personal assets of owners
   A. Listing of all owners of the business
   B. Personal financial statements for all owners
   C. Listing of managers of the business
   D. Resumes for all owners
   E. Personal guarantees offered by the owners

IV. Forecasts
   A. Sales forecast and supporting data
   B. Income statement forecast and supporting data
   C. Cash flow forecast and supporting data

V. A Summary of the business plan
   A. Description of the business and its products or services
   B. The target market and market research data
   C. The break-even analysis
   D. The distinctive competency and market strategy

## SUMMARY

The vast majority of small businesses are undercapitalized at start up. Many are unable to recover from this mistake and ultimately fail or find their growth severely restricted as a result.

If the financial portion of the preventure planning is done properly, determining the capital required for start up is not difficult. Exhibit 12-1 presents a list of some of the items that must be reviewed in determining the capital requirements for a successful start up. Note that, in addition to the capital required to open the doors of a new business, three to six months of operating expenses also should be on hand or set aside in committed lines of credit.

After determining capital requirements, finding funding can be a problem for a new and untried business. Prospective business owners should look first to personal sources: family, friends, and business associates. Investors, public or private, can be pursued, but professional assistance frequently is required to gain access to such funds. Venture capitalists, SBICs, MESBICs, and local, state, and federal assistance agencies can be explored. The federal government has more than 350 loan and assistance programs designed to aid small businesses.

Banks are a prime source of credit for small businesses, both initially and on a continuing basis. It is a good idea to establish a sound working relationship with a bank early in a new venture, whether or not start-up financing will be sought. The business plan, when completed, will yield the information necessary to prepare loan and investment applications and proposals, regardless of the source of funding sought.

## QUESTIONS

1. Why are capital needs determination and acquisition perhaps the most important aspects of starting a new business?
2. What does the acquisition of capital entail?
3. What are the capital considerations in determining the cost of production and supporting assets?
4. What are the capital considerations in determining the cost of inventory and supplies?
5. What are the capital considerations in determining operating requirements?
6. How much capital is required at start up and why?
7. What factors influence the initial inventory requirements?
8. What are the trade-offs between low initial inventory and initial cash investment?
9. Why should you plan your displays of inventory before purchase?
10. Discuss possible sources of funding and include the advantages and disadvantages of each source.
11. Why are public offerings not usually a good method for obtaining funding for a new venture?
12. What are the advantages and disadvantages of dealing with a venture capitalist?
13. How do you find a venture capitalist?
14. What are the major components of a loan proposal?
15. Why are relationships with attorneys, accountants, bankers, and other professionals important in starting a new business or maintaining an existing one?

16. Define the following terms:
    a. start-up capital
    b. undercapitalization
    c. securities
    d. preferred stock
    e. bonds and debt instruments
    f. partnership certificates
    g. common stock
    h. venture capitalists

## PROJECTS

1. Visit or call several of the assistance agencies listed in the text and determine the level of funding that might be received or determine if you qualify for any assistance.
2. Visit a venture capitalist and solicit the support of that group or individual for your potential enterprise.
3. Develop a loan proposal for a new start up and take it to your local bank. What does the lender feel are its strengths and weaknesses?

# CASE

Trax and Trux, a new skateboard and bicycle outlet, opened its doors two weeks before Christmas. Barb and Don were excited about their new venture. As in all small towns, they had had a great deal of drop in and see. The kids were all excited and started revamping their Christmas lists on hearing of the new enterprise. Skateboards were back in and free-style bikes were the most popular items on the lists that year.

Many parents, eager to finish their shopping and thrilled to find a place in town that sold such items, rushed to make purchases only to find that the store had been opened with a very modest inventory. The five free-style bikes in pink held sold signs and no skateboards were complete. The parents had to purchase the assembly, the deck, wheels, trucks, clouds, and decals separately, then put them together. Most parents were at a loss. They had written down specific details about the boards, knowing full well that only someone who knew boards could help them. Yet they remained unconvinced that their assembly would build the desired product.

Several annoyed customers asked the owners why they had decided to open a board and bike shop. They replied that there was a market in this area for replacement parts for such items. Don knew because he had spent a great deal of time and energy trying to find parts his son needed. The demand indeed was there but the frustration was also present.

Parents needing Christmas toys had to resort to a larger town 65 miles away because Trax and Trux was an almost empty building. They had replacement parts but the stock was not all that complete—a perfect nightmare for Christmas morning. Several months later, they carried an exceptional amount of inventory. So much that it was difficult to walk into the store without knocking against ice skates, jams, vans, and almost any part you could imagine. But, Christmas was over!

## Questions

1. What do you think customers felt at the lack of inventory at the opening?
2. Why do you think that the owners opened their doors when they did?
3. How well do you think the store is doing today and why?
4. Why do you suppose the situation ends with the statement "But, Christmas was over"?
5. Do you think that Trax and Trux might have had a problem with start-up capital? Or do you think the problem was entirely different?
6. What aspect of planning may have been short-circuited in this case?
7. What should have been done—and what might still be done—to cause the business to succeed?

# SUPPLEMENT

# Starting a Small Business Venture: Summary and Illustration

In Parts I through III of the text we discussed the aspects of a small business start up. In the last three parts, we address management issues and the concerns of ongoing businesses. Much of the preventure planning activities are similar to the ongoing planning activities of an existing venture. Consequently, it is wise to take a few moments and review these activities and tie together any loose ends. Because the areas are broken down into chapters and the aspects of a business start-up plan overlap a great deal, seeing the big picture is sometimes difficult. In this supplement, we review the major aspects of the business plan and project a picture of the final product. Then we provide a case for your practice in preparing a business plan.

## THE BUSINESS PLAN

In previous chapters we described the contents of a business plan. Exhibit 1 lists the contents of such a plan. Remember that even though the steps are arranged in sequential fashion, the actual completion of one step frequently overlaps the completion of another. Sometimes, the order in which the steps appear will be changed to fit specific circumstances. The steps of the plan frequently are iterative; that is, new knowledge developed in the completion of a later step makes us reevaluate an earlier step or change an earlier part of the plan. The important point is that no activity in the business plan can be omitted. In the following sections we will review the actions required to complete each step and try to make the timing of the process more clear.

### Evaluate the Personal Considerations

The first step of the business plan is to establish **personal objectives.** This process is integral to any business plan. It requires you consciously analyze yourself and your short- and long-term desires. Consider what you desire now, where you would like to be in five years—what you would like to be doing then—and where you want to be in ten years. Convert those desires into objectives, goals you intend to work toward. You should identify the actions required to achieve your objectives and decide whether the price you must pay, in terms of work and sacrifice, is too great. If so, modify your objectives and repeat the process of identifying actions required to achieve the goals. Ideally, while analyzing yourself, you will determine whether owning a business fits your objectives and whether you are willing to pay the price of success in self-employment. As discussed in an earlier chapter, people who own their own businesses generally work longer hours than people who are employed by others. In addition, a great deal of stress is involved in owning a business. As the preceding chapters have shown, the owner of a business has to wear many hats and perform a variety of planning and control activities. Many of the functions required to successfully start and manage a business are not pleasant. In addition, there is great risk in starting a business. A large proportion of new businesses fail. As discussed in the financing chapter, your personal assets will be deeply involved. You can expect liens against your home or other assets as collateral for business start-up loans. A client spent ten years repaying a loan taken out to start a business that failed. The loan had been secured by a second mortgage on the family residence and had to be repaid even though the business went bankrupt. If it sounds like we are trying to scare you, that's right! The decision to start a business should not be taken lightly. The work is hard; the

**EXHIBIT 1** *Outline of the Business Plan*

- I. Establish your personal objectives
  - A. Determine your present objectives
  - B. Determine where you wish to be in 5 years
  - C. Determine where you wish to be in 10 years
- II. Choose a product or service
  - A. Evaluate the marketability of the product or service
  - B. Determine the feasibility of the product or service
- III. Select a market area
  - A. Evaluate the market area
  - B. Determine the feasibility of the market area
  - C. Evaluate the competition
- IV. Establish your business objectives
- V. Begin your strategy development
- VI. Establish a timetable
- VII. Determine your human resource requirements
- VIII. Determine your physical resource and capacity requirements
- IX. Select a site
- X. Finalize your business strategies
  - A. Determine your distinctive competency
  - B. Prepare a marketing plan
- XI. Determine your capital requirements
- XII. Prepare forecasts and budgets
  - A. Prepare a sales forecast
  - B. Prepare a marketing budget – Same as Present +
  - C. Prepare an operating budget
  - D. Prepare a capital budget   Cash Flow Analysis
  - E. Prepare an income statement   Proj.
  - ~~F. Prepare a balance sheet~~
- XIII. Perform a break-even analysis
- XIV. Evaluate and modify your plan
- XV. Locate and obtain capital
- XVI. Implement the plan
- XVII. Evaluate your progress

hours are long; and the risk is real. The potential rewards are great; however, the quest is not for the faint hearted. A strong personal commitment to doing whatever is necessary to be successful is the all-important first step to starting a business. We want you to have a complete understanding of the risks and requirements so that you can determine whether you have the necessary personal commitment. There is no shame in opting not to start a business — only in closing your eyes to the consequences of your actions.

## Choose a Product or Service

Selecting the kind of business you intend to start seems so trivial that many people fail to give it the consideration it requires. For many, the decision to go into business and the decision of what business to go into are one and the same. They should not be! Getting into a business about which you know something and that has a chance to succeed in a given market may be one of the most important of the planning steps. It definitely merits careful consideration. Far too many people develop an idea for a business and then are unable to examine the idea critically because they are too closely involved. Criticism of the idea seems too much like criticism of themselves. A column in the *Wall Street Journal* devoted to the concept of choosing the right business included a checklist to guide a person considering the purchase or start up of a new business. The author emphasized that the business plan was the key to success.* This is the message of this text.

Choosing a product or service involves the market and market area in which you intend to compete as well as the competitive environment. You need some level of knowledge about the **product or service.** If you have no working experience in the industry, then serving an apprenticeship may be a good idea. Should that not be feasible, then knowledge must be acquired by recruiting competent managers with experience in the industry and who will fit well into the venture.

Much of the decision about the product or service to be offered is tied up in the personal issues discussed previously. A large body of research literature on small businesses explains that the decision to start a new venture stems from one's life experiences. Frequently, the loss of a job or some other displacement pushes a person into starting a business. When this happens, far too little thought or planning occurs. Pausing to make a detailed study and critical review can save pain later and prevent failure.

* Richards, B., "One Giant Step," *Wall Street Journal* (May 19, 1986), pp. 10D–12D.

As the business plan indicates, choosing a product or service entails assessing the viability of the selection in the specific market area under consideration. This means that selecting the market area, the next step in the plan, must be accomplished in general terms before the present step can be completed. You must select the city or area in which you intend to operate in order to evaluate the market for your product or service in that area. The final site selection can wait, but you must be able to identify the specific target market to which you intend to appeal. Once this is done, you must assess whether your product or service is salable in sufficient quantities to make the business viable. Determining the quantities required for survival is part of the break-even analysis. Here again, the steps overlap. Unless the market is determined to be huge, at least a cursory break-even analysis will be required to determine viability.

Identifying the size of the market can be quite difficult. Previously we discussed sources of data that could be used to estimate the market for an established product or service. We also indicated that competing in an established market is easier for a new firm than creating demand for a new product or service. We cautioned you to avoid allowing personal preferences and prejudices to influence the analysis. It doesn't matter what product or service you think is desirable; it matters what the market thinks is desirable. An unbiased assessment of the market is one of the most difficult things for a prospective business owner to perform.

## Select a Market Area

The next step of the plan overlaps the preceding one, as just indicated. Both must be completed together. Many people starting small businesses fail to consider the market selection by choosing to start in their home towns. This is included as a separate step in the plan to call attention to the fact that you don't have to start in any given location: you can choose the market area just as you choose any other aspect of the business. The area selected will have a major influence on the ultimate viability and growth prospects for the business. Far too many ventures have failed because there was not enough demand for their offerings in a given location, yet they may have survived had they been located in a different area. Whether you make the location decision consciously or unconsciously, the choice will follow the business all of its life and will have a marked influence on its every aspect.

The selection of the **market area** and the product or service to be offered can be an iterative process. That is, if a particular market area does not seem to support the business planned, another area can be considered until one is found in which the business is viable. Also, the choice of product or services can change to fit the area in which you wish to do business. Perhaps, minor changes are required, such as substituting a full service restaurant for a fast food restaurant or vice versa. The interaction between the market area and the product or service is the real reason for showing the two decisions as separate steps in the plan. The decisions are separate and treating them jointly limits flexibility.

In selecting the market area, remember to consider the competition. It often is easier to steal a slice of the market share than to create a demand where none now exists. Competition is a healthy phenomenon. It allows prospective consumers to feel that they have a choice, and it encourages businesses to do their best to gain that consumer support. An objective evaluation of the competition—what it has to offer and how you might differentiate from it—is a must in the planning process.

## Establish Business Objectives

Like the personal objectives established in the first step, **business objectives** must be concrete and specific and should cover the first year, five years, and ten years. From a broad perspective, business objectives are intricately tied up with personal objectives. That is, what you want for yourself may well dictate what you want for the business. Nevertheless, you cannot really quantify and specify objectives for the business until you know its market area, its products and services and their viability, and your competitive environment. General objectives for the business should be developed at the same time as personal objectives. After gaining knowledge of the market area and establishing what the business will be doing, you can make the business objectives more specific. Those objectives should be realistic in terms of the market area and the strength of demand expected in that area over the next ten years. Please note that the area and the products or services may be part of the objectives. That is, some of the business objectives may deal with an expansion into additional market areas or the development of additional or different products or services. If so, the objectives should be consistent with the business that realistically can be expected from the changes in area or product or service.

After the objectives are specified, compare them to the personal objectives recorded earlier. If the two groups of objectives are inconsistent, something must be changed. If the business is incapable of providing what you want, then it must be changed or the idea abandoned.

As soon as the objectives have been established, you must begin to consider strategies; however, they cannot be finalized until a timetable has been established, human and physical resources have been determined, and a site has been selected. Remember that the strategies you pursue will affect every aspect of the plan.

## Establish a Timetable

The **timetable** refers to the opening date for the business and the steps that must be completed before that date. A rough idea of the opening date generally is developed as soon as the products or services are selected and the market area determined. Thereafter, the actions that must be taken to open the business are cataloged and times estimated for their completion. The overall timetable, which will spell out completion dates for every aspect of the start up, is never really finished. We include it as a step in the planning process to call attention to the importance of timing on the new venture. Many businesses have failed because they opened during an off season in their market areas and were unable to survive long enough to reach the peak season.

It is important to understand how critical is the opening date for a new business and to work to achieving that date. It also is important to know when a date cannot be achieved so that alternative plans can be developed or new dates selected. The timetable can aid in the latter process because it lists the activities needed and estimates the time for their completion. It also should indicate which activities are constrained by others. For example, inventory cannot be acquired until the physical facility is prepared. If there is a long lead time for inventory acquisition, then knowing that lead time and the time estimated for facility completion can make for a more effective use of time in general.

The timetable would be a worthwhile addition to the business plan even if dates were never added because it forces consideration in great detail of all the things that must be completed to get the business started. In some ways the timetable can be considered a companion to the business plan. It is a tool used in completing the plan and coordinating the start-up activities. Begin developing it as soon as you begin developing the plan and add items as you think of them or learn of them. Make estimates for the times required for completion, the dates to be completed, and change them as new information arises. This process will ensure that you do not forget or overlook details and keep you on track for the accurate prediction of the opening date.

The timetable also should predict the conversion of the business from start up to a normal operation. That is, when opening specials, offers, premiums, special activities, and extra staffing will stop and regular prices, hours, procedures, and staffing will begin. Such a timetable is required for the completion of the marketing budget as well as facilitating the conversion process itself.

## Determine Human Resource Requirements

Determining the **human resource requirements** for a new venture is a twofold process: determining the skills required, and determining the number of people required with the various skills. Recruiting activities and hiring dates will be part of the timetable. You probably will begin thinking about people very early in the planning process. As soon as you determine the products or services to be offered, the skills required as part of the staff will begin to become clear. Part of the personal objectives you develop probably will be the role you intend to play in the business, which will give you an indication of the kinds of management positions you will have to fill. You will not be able to complete the determination of staffing requirements until the physical resources have been finalized and the budgetary process completed. Actually, both the physical resources and financial aspects of the business plan interact with the staffing plans. Consequently, the human resources will be planned on an iterative basis with rough numbers established early and adjusted as the overall plan nears completion.

## Estimate Physical Resources and Capacity

**Physical resources** include the facility the business will occupy; the machinery, fixtures, and equipment the business will require; and the inventories and supplies needed. Requirements in this area will affect the capital requirements for the business as well as most aspects of the budget and forecasts. **Capacity** refers to the business output or scale of operations; that is, the scales that can be supported by the physical resources. Capacity is measured differently for different industries. For example, in a restaurant, capacity refers to the number of people who can be served within a given time period, whereas for a manufacturing business capacity is the number of units that can be produced within a given time period. Consequently, capacity is a function of the size or amount of physical resources and human resources. An extra shift can be run in a given facility by just adding more people. Of course, the two interact as well: there are only so many people who can work in a given facility at one time.

Frequently the site selected for a business will be a constraint on the size of the facility, as will the capital available or that can be acquired. Consequently, the physical resources planning also is begun early and continues throughout the completion of the business plan. One key point to keep in mind about physical resources is that they must be at least adequate to support the break-even sales required for the business.

## Select a Site

The actual **site location** is more important for some kinds of businesses than for others. You should make sure you understand how critical the site is for your venture and then begin to develop several alternatives as soon as the market area has been determined. The advantages and disadvantages of each should be weighed to settle on the location to be used. Because the physical and human resource requirements as well as the capital available will influence the decision, the site generally cannot be finalized until the majority of the business plan is complete.

## Determine Business Strategies

After you have decided where the business is going, you must decide how it is going to get there. This is the essence of **business strategies.** A strategy is the plan for achieving some objective.

The most important strategy is how to set your business apart from its competition. This is called the **distinctive competency.** The thing your customers will remember about your business, the image they will develop of your business, the things that will come to mind when a customer thinks of your business — these are determined by the distinctive competency.

Distinctive competency may be tied up with your personal objectives. You may intend to portray a particular image in your business simply because that is what you want to do. In such cases, the distinctive competency is the leading business objective, and the others must follow from it. We described a bar owner whose up-scale business was unsuccessful because he was providing a service in a market area that lacked the people to support it. Unwilling to change the business to meet the desires of the market, he was forced to sell out. This is an important point. Far too many people develop an image of the business they want to run but fail to consider the impact of that image on the prospects for the business. If you wish to have a business that is considered to offer extremely high-quality products, for example, you must be sure that the products you will offer, the prices they will carry, and the market area in which you will operate are compatible.

A better way to choose competency is to examine what is required to meet the objectives you have set for the business and to develop an image that will advance the business along that route. It is not always a matter of price or quality, although those are important aspects. Perhaps, you wish your business to be known for the depth or breadth of its product line or services, its hours of operation, the friendliness or competency of its employees, the speediness of its response, or any of a host of other attributes or combination of attributes. The point is that you must consciously decide what image you want to portray and take steps to ensure that the image is reinforced consistently and constantly in every aspect of the business. This includes its site location, its hours, its staff, its product or service line, its decor, the dress of its people, the sign that hangs outside, and of course the advertising it does and the media it selects for that advertising.

The distinctive competency you select will constrain the marketing plan.

The purpose of a start-up marketing plan is to notify the members of the target market in your area that the business is open, to attract as many of those individuals to the business in as short a time as possible, and to effectively penetrate the market. By **penetrate** we mean establish the business as a viable competitor in its market area, one that will survive and become a major participant in the competitive scheme of the area. We have discussed a variety of ways of approaching the development of the market plan.

The budget for the marketing plan will influence the capital requirements, the break-even analysis, and the operating forecasts. In turn, it will be influenced by the overall budget for the business. Therefore, the marketing plan cannot be finalized until the budgetary process is completed. At this stage in the plan, the marketing plan should be drafted with estimates for expenses of the various parts of the plan. As the remainder of the plan is completed, the marketing plan can be modified to fit within the means of the venture.

## Determine Capital Requirements

By this point in the planning process, you have developed a rough idea of how much is required to actually start the business. The **capital requirements** also must include enough funding to cover operations for a period of time. This is called **working capital.** We indicated in the text that three to six months of working capital generally is recommended. This money can be in the form of cash or lines of credit, but is as critical to the success of the venture as the capital to acquire the physical resources. This means that the overall capital requirements cannot be finalized until all of the budgets have been completed. Like many of the other steps, capital planning actually starts with the inception of the idea to go into business and continues through the completion of the business plan. Along with planning the total amount of capital required to start a business is the need for planning to acquire the money. This may mean delaying the start of a business for several years while personal savings are accumulated. We indicated in the chapter that a substantial portion of any start-up funding will be expected to be provided by the owner of the business. Whatever the source of the start-up capital, remember that one of the most oft-quoted reasons for failure of business ventures is **undercapitalization.** Far too many people start a business using whatever capital they are able to acquire without consideration for the capital required to do a good job in starting the business.

## Prepare Forecasts and Budgets

Every dollar you intend to spend in start up and all aspects of the sales process must be well in hand to complete the **budgetary process.** You must determine selling prices and fixed and variable costs of operations as well as the cost of the start-up marketing and promotion, all physical resources including occupancy expense, and of all the human resources including salaries, wages, and fringe benefits. This information generally will not be complete until late in the planning process but you must begin early, using rough estimates to determine the viability of the venture. The budgetary process will culminate with **forecasts** of income and expense for the first two to three years of operation, forecasts of balance sheets for the same time period, and forecasts of the costs of physical resources to be acquired initially and over that time period. This step in the plan should include sources and justifications for all of the financial numbers used to develop the forecasts, because this information is required by lenders or investors. These forecasts should be started early in the planning process and adjusted regularly as more information is developed.

## Perform a Break-Even Analysis

As indicated earlier, a **break-even analysis** using rough data is part of the process of determining whether a given product, service, or market area is viable. Because the actual break-even point of a business is a function of all of its resources, expenses, and revenues, the final calculations cannot be made until the budgetary process is completed. This is why break-even analysis shows up in the business plan following forecasts. As indicated, break-even analysis is one of the most valuable tools in management. It should be used throughout the planning process to assess the viability of those plans as they unfold. It also should be used as a final check on all the plans before starting the business. In actuality, the final break-even analysis performed at this point in the planning process provides the last opportunity to change the plan, abandon the idea, or make any other adjustments before going ahead with the commitments. After you are satisfied with the last analysis, you will begin to make binding commitments to start the business.

## Evaluate and Modify the Plan

After the final break-even analysis is performed, review every aspect of the business plan and make modifications where necessary. This may mean changing your personal objectives or any other aspect of the plan. Be sure to restate all aspects of the plan affected by any changes in other parts. As shown here, most of the steps interact with each other. After all changes have been made, if the plan seems viable and the break-even analysis is acceptable, you are ready to make commitments to start the business.

Prior to this point the start-up plan can be abandoned, delayed, or changed in any fashion. After you begin to make commitments, changes cost money. This does not mean that no other changes will be made. The timetable will continue to change as you approach the opening date, and many other aspects of the plan may change as well. In fact, the business plan will follow you into your daily operations, as we will see, and will never stop changing.

## Locate and Obtain Capital

In all probability you will begin to search for capital long before this point in the business plan is reached. In fact, you probably will not reach this point in the plan without some idea that financing will be obtainable. Nevertheless, most of the foregoing steps will have to be finalized to some degree before you can actually obtain significant capital from outside sources. The previous steps in the business plan will form a lending or investment package that you can use to support requests for capital.

## Implement the Plan

There are two aspects to management: planning what is to be done, and doing it! The best plans in the world are worthless without sound execution. The reverse of the statement is equally true. No matter how effective you are at running the business, without a business plan, you won't know where you are going. You must carry through the plan for it to affect the prospects of the business, but you are not a slave to it. If some aspect needs changing in the light of new knowledge, then change it. However, if you do make changes, all steps affected by the change should be adjusted and the new plan followed. Never operate without a firm business plan that spells out the steps you intend to take.

## Evaluate the Progress

Upon completion, the business plan becomes a benchmark for comparison of results as well as a guide for actions. The principal source of changes to the plan should come from new knowledge obtained from comparing actual results to the predictions and forecasts. In this fashion, the business plan will evolve into a continuous planning and control document. It will become of paramount importance in the daily operation of the business, as well as the tool used to establish it. To ensure development and facilitate the execution of the start-up plan, evaluation should be made a formal activity. During the start-up phase, you should compare results to the plan on a daily basis. After start-up, results should be compared on a weekly or monthly basis. Initially, most changes will take place in the financial portions of the plan. As time goes by, changes will take place in the objectives sections. Consequently, you should not restrict your comparisons to financial matters, but review every aspect of the business plan. This also will help to keep all activities and operations consistent with the distinctive competency you have selected for the business.

## CONCLUDING COMMENTS

We reviewed the business plan as it has been outlined in the preceding chapters. Our intent has been to demonstrate how all of the pieces fit together now that you have studied them on an individual basis. This extra step is justified, we think, because the theme of this book is the value of planning. All of the tools presented and all of the time spent describing what seems to be laborious, time consuming busy work reinforces the basics of planning. Business counselors and specialists in small business believe that there is only one key to success—planning!

We have examined the overlap and interaction of the steps of the business plan. As you see, there is a great deal of both! Exhibit 2 is a diagram of the planning process that shows this interaction and overlap. Personal objectives, business objectives, and strategies are linked by a feedback loop that includes plan modification and progress evaluation. The process is iterative. If a break-even analysis shows the business failing, a change must be made to proceed. This is true for every aspect of the plan. The loop between business objectives and strategies is especially important because the objectives tell where you want to be and the strategies explain how you plan to get there.

In reality it is impossible to establish a chronological listing of the steps required to start a business. Consequently, the major value of the business plan in Exhibit 2 is to ensure that nothing is overlooked. The actual use of such a diagram should be to consider each item during each day of the planning process. The business plan actually will be a succession of documents and lists. You constantly will be making estimates and preparing tentative plans, then changing the estimates and plans as more information becomes available and new knowledge is gained. This is why it is so important to write down everything in every step. There is no such thing as effective informal planning!

Exhibit 2 visualizes the process and provides a tool to manage it. It shows the completion points of the steps in the start-up plan and their dependence on other steps. You should estimate completion dates for each point in the diagram and follow it in completing a business plan, checking off each item as it is completed. You should keep a written record for each step in the diagram and record original ideas and completion dates and all revisions you make. As

**EXHIBIT 10-2** *The Business Plan*

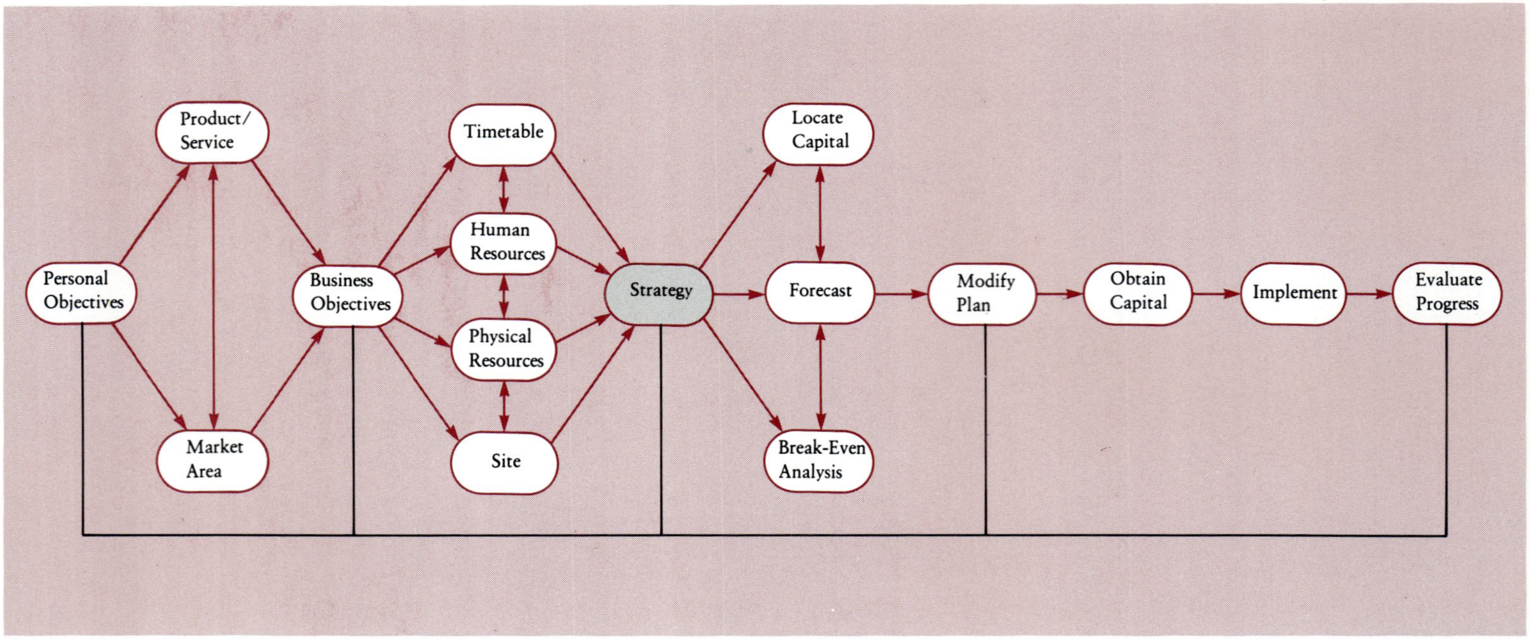

you complete steps and change estimated completion dates, record those on the chart as well. This will result in a more effective plan and a more workable planning process.

The illustrative case that follows represents an actual start up of a small business. The business was successfully launched and has survived, although under new ownership. We include this case, not as a device for saying this is the only way it can be done, but as a demonstration of how start-up planning can be done and how it can improve prospects for your business.

## PROFESSIONAL OFFICE SERVICES: AN ILLUSTRATIVE CASE

We first met Mary Adams three years ago, when she was a representative for a duplicating machine sales company selling Savin and Minolta copy machines. She had an excellent sales record with the company. Because of that record and the contacts she had made in the copier business, she had been offered a dealership for Royal duplicating machines and was considering going into business for herself. She was twenty-eight years old, single, and held a BBA from the university. She had been born and raised locally and was well known in the community. In addition to her sales experience, she had been a secretary, held various clerical jobs, and had three years of experience supervising the office workers in a local manufacturing firm.

We discussed her business opportunity with particular emphasis on break-even points, sales quotas, and leasing outlets. Royal had a quota of fifteen machines the first year. The machines would sell for around $4,000 but there was difficulty in obtaining leases or financing for the machines. Her present employer had a lease-financing arrangement with a lender on which recourse was required. *Recourse* means that the lender expects the dealer to guarantee the performance on all loans to customers. Mary's personal net worth was quite small, and it seemed unlikely that she would be able to obtain a similar arrangement. The town had three established sales companies that handled copy machines, and all used recourse financing. We recommended against the venture and she concurred.

Subsequently Mary returned with an idea to go into business on a broader scale of services, with the intention of expanding into duplicating machine sales at a later date. She thought that a temporary services company, employing university students and their spouses, could be successful, but she proposed to augment this with a host of professional and office services to the university and business markets. We recommended that she prepare a business plan and discussed its contents. She began the process and we assisted her with the research aspects. She produced the following plan:

## Business Plan for Professional Office Services

### 1. Personal Objectives

- To be my own boss
- To become financially comfortable
- To own and manage a business in my home town
- To own a business that will provide a needed service to the community
- To become well known and respected as a business person in the community
- To marry and have children

### 2. Products or Services

- Initially, temporary secretarial and bookkeeping services
- Typing, word processing, resume, thesis, dissertations, and photocopying services
- Mailing addresses, labels, and mailing services
- Answering services
- Meetings and conventions arranged
- Within two years of opening the business, sales of duplicating machines
- Sales of other office machines and equipment, after three to five years

### 3. Market Area

- A 50-mile radius of Athens, Georgia
- *Feasibility:* According to the city marshall's office, 1,100 businesses are in the area; there are 459 members of the chamber of commerce; use the chamber membership to forecast demand for temporary services; discount revenues from other services as being insignificant in the short run

A survey published in *Office Magazine* gave statistics for use of temporary personnel. Applying these numbers to her market resulted in the following:

| FREQUENCY OF USE | PERCENTAGE | NO. OF FIRMS |
|---|---|---|
| Continually | 5.0% | 22 |
| Frequently | 8.2 | 37 |
| Occasionally | 37.5 | 173 |
| Rarely | 33.1 | 152 |
| Never | 16.2 | 75 |
| Total | 100.0 | 459 |

She applied the frequency of use percentages to her population of 459 businesses to obtain the 384 businesses expected to use her services at some time.

| DAYS/HOURS USED | PERCENTAGE | NO. OF FIRMS | NO. OF HOURS |
|---|---|---|---|
| Over 1,000 days | 2.3% | 8 | 64,000 hrs |
| 500–999 days | .8 | 3 | 12,000 |
| 100–499 days | 19.7 | 75 | 60,000 |
| 50–99 days | 19.7 | 76 | 30,000 |
| Under 50 days | 57.5 | 222 | 24,640 |
| Total | 100.0 | 384 | 190,640 |

Then she applied the usage percentages to the 384 businesses to obtain the number of businesses in each use category. To find the hours of use, she multiplied the number of businesses in each category by the lowest level of use in each category. For the under 50-days category, she arbitrarily selected 14 days. Using 8 hours in each day, she calculated the hours of use.

She checked temporary services in Atlanta, the nearest such firms, and found that $6.55 per hour was the lowest rate charged for temporary services. Multiplying that rate times the total hours yielded an estimate of the market in her area.

Total market = 190,640 hours or $1.249 million per year

Discussions with temporary employment services in Atlanta indicated that a 20% market share was reasonable. For us, a 20% market share would amount to 730 hours per week. Currently, no temporary personnel services are available in her area. Businesses using such services obtain them from Atlanta, 60 to 70 miles from the center of her market area. Consequently, she believed that a 20% market share was a reasonable estimate for her venture. Information provided by the Kelly Girl franchise stated that the average growth rate for temporary services is 30% per year. She used a 20% growth rate for her venture to determine its second year's sales and held the market constant.

Sales forecast for year 1 = 20% of $1,249,000 = $249,800

Sales forecast for year 2 = 24% of $1,249,000 = $299,760

According to information in the Kelly Girl franchise kit, the industry average contribution margin is 30%. She downscaled that to 25% for the first year and 28% for the second year, to allow for added variable expenses from start up.

Contribution margin for year 1 = 25% of $249,800 = $62,450

Contribution margin for year 2 = 28% of $299,760 = $83,930

Fixed expenses are expected to be

| | | |
|---|---|---|
| Owner's salary | $15,000 | |
| Equipment rental | 6,000 | |
| Rent | 2,400 | |
| Telephone and utilities | 1,000 | |
| Insurance | 500 | |
| Advertising | 1,500 | |
| Supplies | 350 | |
| Licenses and permits | 100 | |
| Professional fees | 500 | |
| Miscellaneous | 500 | |
| Total | | $27,850 |

Projected income before taxes: $62,450 − 27,850 = $34,600

After she had completed the feasibility sections of the business plan, Mary decided to go forward with the venture and began work on the rest of the plan. Mary never really had considered seeking a franchise, due to limitations on other activities included in franchise contracts. In the absence of local direct competition, she decided that the franchise had little to offer. Although we used data from franchise averages, we agreed that no modification of the numbers was required to compensate for an independent firm.

**4. Business Objectives**

- To become known as a temporary employment services firm providing high-quality workers on short notice in the area
- To obtain a 20% market share of that business in the first year and to grow to a 50% share of that business within five years
- To develop the additional secretarial services within six months
- To obtain the majority of thesis and dissertation typing from the university within two years
- To expand into copy machine sales within three years
- To expand into other business machine sales within six years
- To open additional offices in other towns within ten years
- To reach $1 million in gross sales within five years and $5 million within ten years

### 5. Timetable

- Opening date, May 1, to be ready for vacation coverage
- Rent office, April 1
- Purchase office furniture and machines during April
- Secure business license, permits, and so on during March
- Charter the corporation during March
- Finalize financing, March 1
- Hire receptionist during April
- Have direct mail ready for mailing by April 15
- Have campus bulletin board posters advertising for temporary workers by April 1
- Run temporary workers ad in local and school newspapers, last week in March and first week in April
- Begin interviews with temporary workers, April 1
- If 100 workers not found by April 15, more newspaper ads and direct mail to students
- Have employment contract prepared by attorney during March

### 6. Human Resources

- Owner-manager at $15,000
- Receptionist-typist at $8,000
- 100 temporary workers to start
- 1,000 temporary workers by year end
- Second office worker-typist within six months at $8,000
- Phone workers for answering service within 6 months
- Four workers at 6 hours each per day at minimum wage
- Salesperson after 6 months: $15,000 plus bonus based on sales

### 7. Physical Resources

Office in inexpensive office building: 400 sq. ft. minimum

| | |
|---|---|
| Word processor | $6,000 |
| Typewriter | 1,500 |
| Photocopier | 4,000 |
| Two office desks | 1,400 |
| Sofa | 300 |
| Four chairs | 250 |
| Typing chair | 150 |

| | | |
|---|---|---|
| Filing cabinet | 300 | |
| Desk calculator | 100 | |
| Initial supplies | 500 | |
| Two telephones | 100 | |
| Telephone installation | 200 | |
| Miscellaneous | 500 | |
| Total | | $15,300 |

Will use personal car for sales calls (upgrade insurance)

## 8. Site

- Office available in office building on University Drive
- 80% filled, 10 years old
- Convenient to university
- Good access-egress, adequate parking
- Stable businesses in other offices
- Good appearance and repair
- One-year renewable lease
- Two month's rent deposit
- 600 sq. ft., two rooms—one L-shaped, closet
- Electricity included, bathroom down the hall
- $220 per month

## 9. Business Strategies

- *Distinctive competency:* The source of intelligent, competent, hard-working temporaries on extremely short notice
- Establish a personnel pool of university students and spouses (100 people to start; 1,000 by year end) and maintain a formal record of job performance for every placement
- Use the personnel search to find highly skilled typists, individuals to blanket the campus bulletin boards with literature, and a full-time receptionist-typist
- Use word processor for dissertations and theses with reduced fees for retyping
- Contact every member of the chamber of commerce by direct mail during the first month
- Contact every business in the area by direct mail during the second and third months
- Make a personal sales call on every member of the chamber of commerce

with 500 or more employees during the first month and every business with 250 or more employees during the second month
- Continue the personal calls, always calling on at least ten new businesses per week
- Ask for referrals on all sales calls
- Ask for referrals from all temporary workers
- Continue temporary worker solicitation through bulletin boards and newspapers every month
- During the third month begin solicitation for answering service
- Must have $2,500 in monthly fees to break even
- By the sixth month add a salesperson and a second office worker
- By the sixth month, bring answering service on line

## 10. Capital Requirements

| | | |
|---|---|---|
| Equipment | $15,300 | |
| Printing and brochures | 2,500 | |
| Postage | 200 | |
| Initial advertising | 500 | |
| Attorneys fees | 750 | |
| Licenses and permits | 130 | |
| Initial insurance | 250 | |
| Total | | $19,630 |

## 11. Forecasts and Budgets

MONTHLY OPERATING EXPENSES

| | | |
|---|---|---|
| Salaries | $1,900 | |
| Fringe benefits (12%) | 230 | |
| Advertising | 50 | |
| Printing and postage | 150 | |
| Rent | 220 | |
| Telephone | 100 | |
| Travel (2,500 miles @ $.20) | 500 | |
| Supplies | 50 | |
| Miscellaneous | 100 | |
| Total | | $ 3,300 |
| Three months working capital | | $ 9,900 |
| Total capital needs: | | $19,630 |
| | | 9,900 |
| | | $29,530 |

| | | |
|---|---|---|
| Savings available | | \$ 3,700 |
| Financing needed | | \$ 25,830 |

Loan payments on \$26,000 at 12% for 5 years: \$578/month. Need three payments in working capital

| | | |
|---|---|---|
| Capital needs | \$29,530 | |
| Working capital for payments | 1,800 | |
| Total | | \$ 31,330 |
| Less savings | | 3,700 |
| Financing needed | | \$ 27,630 |

BUDGET

| | | |
|---|---|---|
| Sales Forecast | | \$249,000 (100%) |
| Wages for temporaries | | 186,750 (75%) |
| Gross profit | | 62,250 (25%) |
| Salaries, fringe benefits | 25,560 (10%) | |
| Advertising, printing, postage | 2,400 (1%) | |
| Rent | 2,640 (1%) | |
| Telephone | 1,200 (—) | |
| Travel | 6,000 (2%) | |
| Supplies | 600 (—) | |
| Depreciation | 3,930 (2%) | |
| Interest expense | 3,090 (1%) | |
| Miscellaneous | 1,200 (—) | |
| Total | | 46,620 (19%) |
| Operating income | | 15,630 (6%) |
| Taxes (15%) | | 2,345 (1%) |
| Net income | | 13,285 (5%) |
| Cash flow | \$13,285 | |
| Depreciation | 3,930 | |
| Interest | 3,090 | |
| Cash flow for loan payments | | \$ 20,305 (8%) |
| Loan payments (\$615 per month) | | 7,380 (3%) |
| Net cash flow | | \$ 12,925 (5%) |

## 12. Break-Even Analysis

$$BEP_{\$} = \frac{\text{(Fixed Costs)}}{\text{(Contribution Margin)}}$$

$$BEP_{\$} = \$\ 46{,}620/.25$$

$$BEP_{\$} = \$186{,}480$$

*Cash Flow Break-Even Analysis:*

$$\text{CBEP}_{\$} = \frac{(\text{Cash Fixed Costs})}{(\text{Contribution Margin})}$$

$$\text{CBEP}_{\$} = (\$46{,}620 - 3930 - 3090 + 7380)/.25$$

$$\text{CBEP}_{\$} = \$187{,}920$$

### 13. Evaluation and Modification of Plan

- Because the temporary services are the key to success, during the first six months all efforts will be concentrated on developing that business. Until that portion has been developed, expansion into other services will be delayed. Comparison of results to forecasts will be made on a weekly basis during that time.

### 14. Locate Capital

- Seek bank loan with SBA guarantee

Mary's request for a bank loan was declined by two banks. We assisted Mary in the preparation of an SBA loan application. One bank agreed to participate if the SBA guarantee was approved. It was, although with a three-month wait, and the loan was made with Mary's personal guarantee required. The business was launched two months late.

Results exceeded forecasts during the first two months, so Mary decided to expand into typing services. She hired another person and began to concentrate on developing a market for typing theses and dissertations. She neglected the personal sales calls and stopped direct mail advertising. Her labor pool reached about 500 people and she slacked off on building that. Within six months the business was losing money. She began to reemphasize the temporary personnel services, but closed out the first year on a loss, well below the forecast for revenues.

The second year proved to be no better. Midway through the second year, she was unable to make payments on the loan. Thoroughly discouraged, she arranged to sell the business to a local business person and took a sales job in Atlanta. The new owner did not seek us out, but in an interview indicated that he had made a new business plan quite similar to the original and was following it carefully. Within six months of acquiring the business, he indicated that it was operating at break even. The business continues to survive.

## QUESTIONS

1. Do you think that the business planning activities prior to start up of this business were well done? Was the concept sound and feasible?
2. Why do you think that Mary failed?
3. Do you think that the business will survive long term?
4. Consider the steps you would take to evaluate the feasibility of starting a temporary manpower services in your own community.

# PART IV

# THE NEW VENTURE

# CHAPTER 13

# Tax Considerations and Business Formation

**LEARNING OBJECTIVES**

After completing this chapter, you should be able to

- Distinguish among the legal forms of business and know the advantages and disadvantages of each.
- Explain the alternatives to originating your own business.
- Explain the requirements for a Subchapter S form of corporation;
- Explain the tax differentiations between S Corporations and partnerships.
- Evaluate the organizational issues in establishing a new venture.
- Understand the federal income tax responsibilities of a small business enterprise.

In this chapter we address the legal form of business and the pros and cons of alternative forms. We also discuss options other than starting an independent business from scratch. The approach you take in initiating your new venture is important because it will follow you throughout the life of the business. Finally, we examine federal income tax issues of concern to any small business venture. Many of the topics discussed in this chapter are quite complex. Frequently, we will recommend retaining professional assistance to ensure that pertinent factors are considered before a decision is made. The expense of such assistance easily is justifiable because of the far-reaching implications of the decisions that must be made in starting a new venture.

## THE LEGAL FORM OF BUSINESS

There are three forms of business: a sole proprietorship, a partnership, and a corporation. It is important to understand how each is treated from a legal perspective and from an income tax perspective to properly choose the optimal form for your new venture. Laws, including tax laws, recognize entities and endow them with rights, obligations, and responsibilities. The entities recognized do not include businesses. **Entities** simply are natural persons or corporations. Complicating factors are involved, such as the existence of fiduciaries that can represent other entities and therefore have rights and obligations as well. Natural persons are simply people. **Corporations** include, but are not limited to, business corporations. Nonprofit organizations, charitable organizations, and foundations also are corporations. **Fiduciaries** include estates and trusts or individuals acting on behalf of others. Exhibit 13-1 is a graphical representation of the number of each type of business in the United States in 1986.

### Sole Proprietorship

The simplest and easiest business to form is a **sole proprietorship.** Its popularity rests with its simplicity. A sole proprietorship is simply an individual who conducts a business. If that individual uses his or her own name in the name of the business, then all that is required to start the venture is to open the doors for business. The owner who does not use his or her name for the business need only file a declaration of identity of ownership with the local court house. This document simply establishes a public record demonstrating who are the individuals behind the fictitious name of a business. Filing is simple and inexpensive. From a legal perspective or a tax perspective, sole proprietorships do not exist. The individual who owns the business is a natural person, and therefore,

**EXHIBIT 13-1** *Number of Sole Proprietorships, Partnerships, and Corporations*

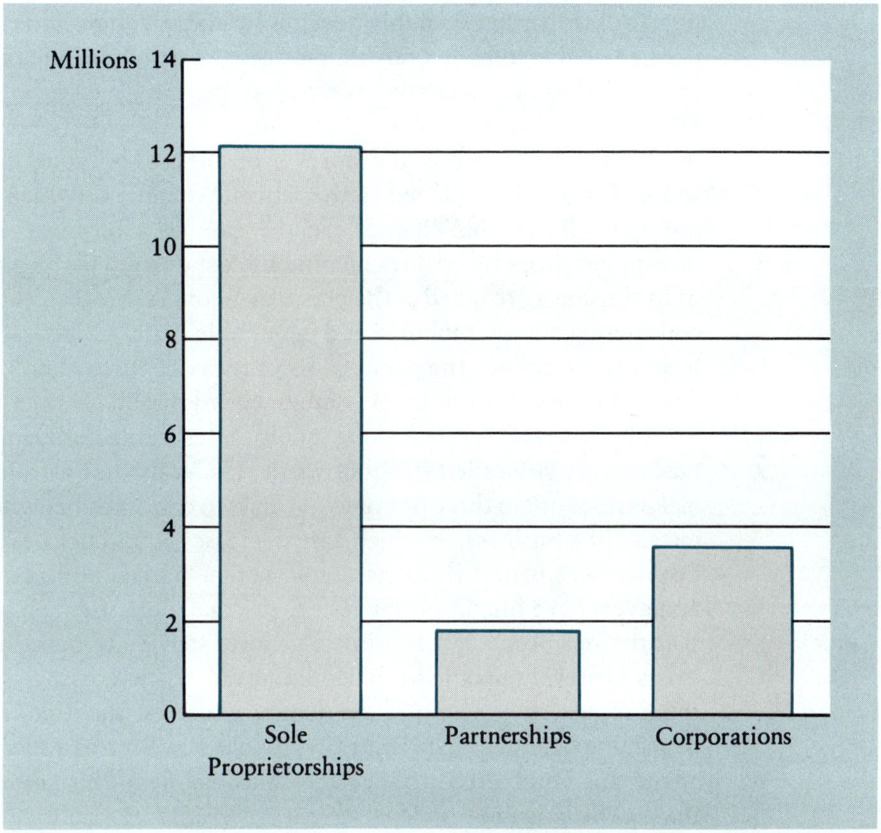


*Source: The State of Small Business: A Report of the President Transmitted to Congress 1987* (Washington, D.C.: U.S. Government Printing Office, 1987).

the business is simply treated as an extension of that person. This has far-reaching implications.

All entities have obligations under the law to behave in a rational manner and refrain from injuring other entities. In the event that another person or entity sustains injury, whether physical, mental, or financial, the law provides recourse to the injured party through litigation. The injured party can sue the responsible party for damages. If the injured party wins the suit, the court can award damages from the responsible party's property. Because there is no difference under the law between a sole proprietorship and its owner, if the business loses a suit, then the courts can award the property of the owner to the damaged party. Legally, personal assets do not exist separate from business assets.

From an income tax perspective, a sole proprietorship pays no tax. The owner of the business simply declares business income and expenses on his or her personal income tax return. Because the owner is the taxpayer, salaries or draws paid to the owner by the business are not expenses of the business. The taxpayer simply pays taxes on the amount of profit whether or not any of those funds have been removed from the business. The filing usually requires a special form to be attached to the return: **Schedule C** (which is reproduced in the appendix to this chapter), in the case of a business; other forms for investment property or farm income and expenses. This means that the profits of the business are taxed at the personal income tax rate in effect for the owner considering all other income and deductible items. Of course, losses from the business can reduce the personal income tax of the owner, but problems can develop if losses continue over an extended period.

The *Internal Revenue Code* incorporates a rule concerning losses from a business activity called the **hobby rule**. Under the hobby rule, a business that makes no profit in three out of five years is in danger of being adjudged a hobby instead of a business, in which case the losses would not be deductible on the taxpayer's return. It is not as simple as that statement makes it sound. Many taxpayers have fought hobby rulings in Tax Court and won by demonstrating that the business was a legitimate venture striving to make a profit. The rule exists to prevent people from deducting the expenses associated with activities that are not truly of a business nature. One test the Tax Court has used to determine whether the intent exists to make a venture profitable is whether its affairs are conducted in a businesslike manner. This means, among other things, the existence of separate bank accounts, accounting records, and the like. To take the step of incorporating a venture is definitely evidence of a businesslike manner.

We can find little to recommend the choice of the proprietorship form of business. As we will discuss later, the taxation issue is not really a problem because corporations can elect to be taxed in the same manner as the owners are taxed. Although no form of business is as easy to start as the proprietorship, that simplicity is more than offset by the problems involved. First is the lack of a legal liability limit. Some would argue that the liability issue can be resolved through insurance, but that is only partially true. In the event of a serious litigation, modern courts might well award damages far above the limits of insurance coverage. Not even a corporate veil can protect an owner's personal assets in the event of a truly flagrant act of negligence. We will talk more about this in a later section. Perhaps, the most important drawback to the proprietorship form of business is the requirement to pay personal taxes on all of the profit regardless of the amount of draw an owner makes. This can result in a penalty for the retention of profits in the business. In order for long-term success to be achieved, most businesses need to reinvest at least some portion of profits back into the business to fuel growth and enhance borrowing power, which is best achieved through the corporate form of business. Furthermore, the corporate form can provide opportunities for stock-funded profit sharing and ownership plans, which will be discussed in Chapter 17. In general, we believe the corporate form to be superior to the proprietorship.

## Partnerships

A **partnership** exists when two or more people go into business together without filing for a corporate charter. A contract should spell out the rights, powers, and participation of the partners in the firm. Although it is possible to start a partnership without such a written agreement, it is not wise.

We had worked with the business before it was established, helping to complete the business plan, finding financing, and setting up the business, so we had established a relationship with the two owners. For this reason they called us six months later to say that things weren't going so well. The business was owned by two young, very talented women, who produced stained glass art objects, lamp shades, and windows. Their work was exceptional. We knew of several churches and restaurants that used their work and several gift shops that carried their art objects. The business was strictly wholesale and work done under contract. No attempt was made to get into retailing.

We had tried to persuade the owners to incorporate the venture at the outset, but they refused. They wanted to share 50/50 in every aspect of the enterprise, and for some reason felt that a corporate form would damage that sharing. They were best friends and trusted each other implicitly, they said. Furthermore, they had the utmost respect for each other's talents and abilities. We tried to convince them that none of those facts was in dispute and that the managerial functions would proceed better under the corporate form, but they would have none of that. The cost of incorporating was not a deterrent either. Looking back on it, it seems that they were unwilling to assign the office of president to one and vice-president to the other.

Anyway, when we went to see them, we found that they were not being consistently profitable even though they had more work than they could handle. They had hired three people to assist with the work, but none was talented enough to handle a job alone. One of the partners had to design and lay out every piece. We looked at the books and found nothing terribly amiss, although expenses seemed to be running a little more than the projections and sales a little less. We asked them to be more precise about the problems they were having and the major factor appeared to be inadequate cash flow. They couldn't be more specific.

In the shop, we noticed that supplies and inventory seemed to be quite high. In fact, so much stuff had been bought that there wasn't room to store it all and glass and other supplies were stacked against the walls all around the production area. When we commented on that, the whole story came tumbling out.

It seems that the two partners who had had such a close and trusting relationship six months ago now couldn't stand each other. There had never been a decision made about who would be responsible for any particular aspect of the business, so one partner had taken it upon herself to acquire a large quantity of inventory when a "deal" surfaced. The other partner was angry, saying that the business did not have sufficient cash to handle that purchase. The second partner had incensed the first with a bid on a large church. The first partner was convinced that the bid was below cost and the size of the contract was such that the business could not sustain the loss. After that, things really got bad. They were even angry at each other over failures to take appropriate turns at posting the books and cleaning the workshop!

There was little we could do except point out how crucial it was for them to allocate responsibilities and reduce those to writing. One person had to have the ultimate responsibility for the various aspects of the business and had to be held accountable for her performance. We suggested that they consider incorporating the business and assigning offices, powers, and duties to each other. They said they would consider it, and we left feeling quite sure that they wouldn't.

Sadly, we were right. Less than three months later the business shut down. One of the partners had left town—with all the cash in the bank, according to the other partner. At any rate, what had great promise as a strong, viable business went down the tubes. The worst thing was that there was a market for the product and the people could penetrate that market. The cause of the failure had nothing to do with sales or business—it was all in not understanding the establishment of authority and responsibility.

When two or more people go into business together, it is an absolute certainty that problems will develop between them. The only unknown factor is when those problems will surface and how severe they will be. More than one business has been destroyed by disagreement among its owners. The only way to minimize the effect of future disagreements is to firmly establish at the outset what each owner's role will be in the organization. In a partnership, this can be accomplished only through a contract. Such a requirement makes the partnership virtually of equal difficulty in formation as a corporation. Therefore, simplicity of formation is not an advantage for the partnership form of business.

From a legal perspective, a partnership carries some special problems. If the contract establishes equal power in the organization, then any partner can bind the others. In fact, unless the partnership agreement explicitly restricts the powers of a partner, that partner can bind the others without their knowledge or consent. This means that if a partner enters into a contract with someone outside the firm, then the other partners are bound to live up to the terms of that contract. In the absence of a partnership agreement, all partners are considered equal and have this binding power. In fact, even if a partnership agreement expressly restricts a partner's power, that individual might still be able to bind the organization. Because outsiders are not privy to the contents of a partnership agreement, the courts have held that the actions of a firm are the important factor in dealings with the public. If a partner acts as though he has authority to bind the organization and the other partners permit that impression to exist in the minds of the public, then that partner can bind the others. This is called the **doctrine of ostensible authority** or **apparent authority**. If someone enters into an agreement with a partner in a firm and does so in good faith, assuming that the partner has the power to speak for the firm, then the courts may enforce the provisions of the contract even if the partner did not have the power to speak for the firm. If the courts believe that the partner consistently displayed apparent authority that a reasonable person would have interpreted as binding authority, then the contract will be considered valid. Clearly, such a possibility is not a recommendation for the partnership form.

Income taxes for the partnership form of business are similar to those for a proprietorship. The business pays no taxes, but the partners must declare on their personal returns their share of profits or losses and pay taxes on those sums personally. As in the case of a proprietorship, any salaries or draws made by a partner are not deductible by the business. Additionally, the owners must pay tax on all profits, whether or not they are withdrawn, resulting in the same penalty for accumulating profits in the firm as for a proprietorship. The partnership must file its own tax return, Form 1065 reproduced in the chapter appendix, but the return simply is an information return. The partnership filing simply declares who are the partners, what was the taxable income of the business, and what was the pro rata share of that income for each partner. The amount reported on the partnership return must agree with the amounts declared by each of the partners on their personal returns.

A partnership form of business tends to increase the friction between the owners, especially if the partnership is equal, simply because the issues of relative power of the individuals in the firm are not clearly resolved. For that reason alone, we cannot recommend the partnership form. For some types of **professional businesses**, such as physicians, lawyers, and accountants, the partnership form is the only one available. The rationale behind the rule is that a professional selling his or her advice, skills, or knowledge should not be able to avoid responsibility for that advice by hiding behind a corporate shield. All of the states have passed professional association acts that permit such firms to be taxed as though they were corporations. If the venture you intend to start is such a professional organization, then be aware of the potential problems in management that so often arise in partnerships. The best plan to prevent problems is to structure the business as though it were a corporation. This includes the establishment of individuals in the firm with specified powers and limitations, appointment of a chief executive officer, and establishment of a chain of authority and command. It also includes the establishment of a board, made up of the partners, who will act as a board of directors to oversee the chief executive officer and other members of management. Voting rights on that board for each partner should be part of the plan. This entire structure should be created by the partnership agreement and enforced through everyday management. Nothing short of an established and accepted chain of authority and command can forestall the managerial problems inherent in the partnership form of business.

## Corporations

It should be clear before we begin to discuss the corporate form of business, that it is our preference for any venture in which it is possible. As we mentioned in the prior section, some types of businesses legally cannot choose the corporate form. In addition, there are special cases in which the corporate form is not advisable. Most of these revolve around income tax issues and generally affect ventures expected to produce losses instead of profits. Consequently, we will not delve into such ventures in this book, because they involve highly technical issues and are more properly considered in the realm of investments rather than management.

**Corporations** are created by filing a charter with the Secretary of State's office in the state in which the business will be operated. If the business will operate across state lines, then the filing generally must be done in the state that the business will call home and that houses the headquarters of the venture. The charter is really not difficult to prepare and file. Most people starting a new venture engage attorneys for the purpose of preparing the charter and establishing the business. An attorney is not required, nor are legal skills necessary to prepare the charter or any of the other documents involved in setting up a corporation. Nevertheless, an attorney will be required from time to time during the business start up and later on during the business operations. Inevitably, contracts will be involved that an attorney should prepare or review for any business. Legal fees for chartering a corporation vary considerably, depending upon competition among attorneys in a particular area and the complexity of the corporation being established. Nevertheless, legal fees for chartering a corporation are not unreasonable considering the difficulty of the preparation of the filings by a novice. Consequently, we recommend that an attorney be engaged to prepare and file the charter and to handle such other needs as may arise. We do recommend that you talk to several attorneys before choosing one. You should ask not only about chartering fees, but legal specialties, background, and experience. Above all, determine whether the attorney truly is interested in you and in your business.

## TAX ISSUES IN BUSINESS FORMATION

Some people criticize the corporate form of business because of the income tax treatment of such entities. They claim that the corporate form leads to **double taxation**; that is, the corporation pays income taxes on its profits and the owners pay income taxes on the salaries they draw and any dividends they receive. This is true, but less of a problem for small ventures than it seems on the surface. First, a corporation pays income taxes on its profits. It must file Form 1120 (see the chapter appendix). The tax structure is similar to that of the personal income tax rules in that income is taxed on a sliding scale. Exhibit 13-2 displays that scale as well as the individual tax rates for comparison. Remember that salaries paid, including salaries paid to the owners of the business, are deductible expenses for the corporation and taxable income to the owner. This means that the income an owner derives from salaries for services rendered to the business will not be taxed twice, but will be taxed at personal income tax

**EXHIBIT 13-2** *Corporate and Individual Federal Income Tax Rates*

| TAXABLE INCOME | TAXATION RATE |
|---|---|
| *Corporate* | |
| $50,000 or less | 15% |
| $50,001 – 75,000 | 25 |
| $75,001 – 100,000 | 34 |
| $100,001 – 335,000 | 39 |
| $335,001 or more | 34 |

*Note: The 39% corporate rate for $100,000 to $335,000 includes a 5% surcharge designed to eliminate the lower tax rates that apply to income less than $75,000. In other words, if a corporation has taxable income of $335,000 or more, it will pay a flat 34% income tax on the full amount.*

| TAXABLE INCOME | TAXATION RATE |
|---|---|
| *Individual (Married, filing jointly)* | |
| $29,750 or less | 15 |
| $29,751 – 71,090 | 28 |
| $71,091 – 171,090 | 33 |
| $171,091 or more | 28 |

*The individual tax rates are those set for 1988 income and are scheduled to be indexed upward in future years to account for inflation. The 33% bracket eliminates the effect of the lower brackets for higher incomes. In other words, incomes of more than $171,090 will be taxed at a flat rate of 28%. The $171,090 figure is based on two personal exemptions. For each additional dependent, that number is raised by $10,920.*

rates when the money is received. Dividends paid by corporations are not deductible expenses and therefore are subject to double taxation; the corporation pays income tax at corporate rates, then the recipient pays taxes again at personal rates. Nevertheless, there are two approaches an owner can take to minimize the effects of double taxation.

The best-known tax saving step is the chartering of the corporation under a special provision in the Internal Revenue Code called **Subchapter S,** which permits a qualifying corporation to be taxed as though it were a proprietorship or partnership. We will talk about this in the next section. The other approach is to simply utilize the salaries, bonuses, and fringe benefits provided by the corporation to its employees as the sole source of income to the owners and thereby avoid dividends entirely. So long as an owner is careful about the structure and amounts of salaries, bonuses, and fringe benefits, all of the items will be deductible expenses to the corporation thereby eliminating double taxation. In fact, it is even possible for the owner to realize tax-free income that also is deductible for the corporation. Health insurance premiums and life insurance premiums, with certain restrictions, are an example of a fringe benefit which is tax deductible for the corporation and not taxable to the owner. In other situations, tax-deferred income can be provided. For example, qualifying pension plans are tax deductible to the corporation and not taxable to the owner until such time as the cash is received. It also is possible to minimize the overall tax bill by manipulating the amounts that will remain for corporate tax purposes and the amounts that will have to be taxed personally through a year-end bonus. Because personal income and corporate income are taxed at different rates as displayed in Exhibit 13-2, adjusting the amount that will fall into each category makes good sense.

Competent tax advice is required for success in maneuvering through the tax rules. The general rule is that an expense must be ordinary and necessary to the business in order to be deductible. Just what falls into those categories can be surprising. A good CPA or tax advisor is a must if a business owner expects to minimize taxes. As in the selection of an attorney, the selection of the tax advisor should be approached carefully and methodically. One final point must be made. Please don't construe our comments about taxation as being critical. We are not condoning tax evasion; that is illegal. We are recommending tax avoidance whenever possible. Justice Learned Hand, formerly of the U.S. Supreme Court, wrote in a dissenting opinion:

> Over and over again courts have said that there is nothing sinister in so arranging one's affairs as to keep taxes as low as possible. Everybody does so, rich or poor, and all do right, for nobody owes any public duty to pay more than the law demands: taxes are enforced exactions, not voluntary contributions. To demand more in the name of morals is mere cant.[1]

## SUBCHAPTER S CORPORATIONS

As mentioned earlier, one method of avoiding the double taxation issue is to charter a corporation under Subchapter S of the Internal Revenue Code. Such a corporation generally is exempt from taxation, except for certain tax preference items. For a corporation to qualify for Subchapter S status, it must be a **domestic corporation**; that is, chartered in the United States. It must also have thirty-five or fewer shareholders, none of whom can be a corporation or nonresident alien. It is important to note that married shareholders are treated as a single person regardless of their stock ownership proportions. The firm can only have one class of stock, although differences in stock voting rights are allowed. Certain types of firms are precluded from Subchapter S classification including financial institutions and most insurance companies and corporations that already enjoy another favorable tax treatment, such as DISC (Domestic International Sales Corporation) with tax-sheltered income. The firm's income must not be from passive sources. If more than 25% of the corporation's gross receipts are from rents, royalties, interest, dividends, annuities, or gains on sales of securities, it will not qualify for this status. All shareholders must agree to the election of Subchapter S status, which can be revoked in future years if a majority of shareholders desire.

S corporations generally pay no federal income taxes. Most states also recognize S corporations for state income tax purposes. The firm is required to file a tax return that details all corporate activities and identifies shareholders and their pro rata shares of corporate income. (Form 1120S is shown in the chapter appendix.) The shareholders must report their shares of corporate income on their personal returns and pay taxes on those amounts at their respective taxation rates. This is the same requirement for a partnership. The two types of organizations are treated similarly for tax purposes although there are significant differences. Exhibit 13-3 compares tax treatment of Subchapter S corporations and partnerships.

Subchapter S corporations carry most of the benefits of ordinary corporations. They are not treated differently under the law in any way except taxation. Consequently, they can be a viable vehicle for elimination of the double taxation problem caused by dividends paid to owners without having to resort to the partnership form.

## CHOOSING THE FORM OF BUSINESS

We believe that the corporate form of business is superior to proprietorships or partnerships. Consequently, we recommend that the corporate form be selected whenever possible. If Subchapter S status is being considered by the new

**EXHIBIT 13-3** *Tax Comparison of S Corporations and Partnerships*

| ITEM | S CORPORATION | PARTNERSHIP |
|---|---|---|
| Ownership restrictions | 35 shareholders, 1 class of stock, no corporate or nonresident alien owners | None |
| Income restrictions | Maximum of 25% passive income (royalties, rents, dividends, interest, annuities, gains on sales of stocks or securities) | None |
| Tax liability for firm | None, except possible tax on large capital gains, excess passive income, or special treatment items | None |
| Treatment of income or loss | Passed through to shareholders | Passed through to partners |
| Tax liability for owners | Personal income tax on pro rata share of income or loss | Same |
| Limitation on losses passed through | Cannot exceed basis of owner's investment in firm but can be carried forward indefinitely | Same |
| Fringe benefits available to owners | Same as partnership for 2% shareholders | Generally same as sole proprietor |
| Treatment of cash distributions to owners | Nontaxable, but excess over investment basis is treated as taxable gain from sale of property | Same |
| Determination of basis of owners' investment | Initial investment plus income less losses of firm less distributions | Same |

*Source: The Internal Revenue Code.*

venture, then that possibility should be discussed at length with the tax advisor. S status is not automatically superior. Issues such as desire to retain funds for future investment must be considered. Under S status, as in a partnership, all income will be taxed, whether received by the owner or not. Therefore, retaining funds is an S corporation can result in paying taxes on funds that have not been received. The issue can be quite complex and really requires expert assistance in weighing the pros and cons of the election.

## FEDERAL INCOME TAXATION ISSUES

Federal income tax laws apply to small businesses in two ways. First the business, its owner, or both are subject to taxation on income. Second, the business must collect income taxes for the federal government on all employees. In fact, all businesses except sole proprietorships must obtain from the IRS an **Employer Identification Number** (EIN). This number serves the same purpose as the Social Security number for individual tax payers and for sole proprietorships; that is, it provides the IRS with an identification device to ensure that all taxpayers are included on its rolls. Acquiring an EIN is simple; if you call, the IRS will send you an application form that, contrary to the typical IRS form, is not difficult to complete. Unfortunately, handling the tax paying and tax collection responsibilities is more complex.

### Estimated Taxes

Virtually all small businesses, regardless of type, must file a declaration of estimated income tax liability and pay toward that liability during the year. The **estimated tax payments** play the same role as withholding on employee paychecks. That is, it provides the government with progressive payments toward the tax liability during the year. A business must forecast its income, estimate its income tax liability and file a declaration by April 15 of each year. The taxes must be paid at the time of declaration or in four installments on April 15, June 15, September 15, and January 15 (December 15 for corporations). The business will settle up with the IRS at its normal tax time, usually March 15, because virtually all small businesses now must use calendar years for tax purposes.

If the estimated taxes paid are substantially less than the real tax liability, the business may be subject to penalties. If the tax payments are equal to the amount of last year's tax liability or are at least 80% of this year's tax liability (90% for corporations), then there will be no penalty.

## Determining Tax Liability

In general, small businesses must include income from all sources in their calculation of gross income. From this may be deducted expenses that are "ordinary and necessary to the operation of the business." Exhibit 13-4 lists typical income and expense items for a small business.

The list is by no means exhaustive, but representative of the approach to determining business income. If the business is a proprietorship, then these income and expense items will be shown on Schedule C of the owner's personal income tax return. If the business is a partnership, then these items will be reported on **Form 1065,** which also discloses the individual partner's names and shares of the income for reporting on their personal returns. If the business is an S corporation, these items are reported on **Form 1120S,** which also discloses owners and income shares. If the business is a corporation, these

**EXHIBIT 13-4** *Computation of Business Income*

**GROSS INCOME**

- Receipts from sale of products or services
- Interest, rents, royalties
- Gains from sale or exchange of property
- Other income

−

**EXPENSES AND DEDUCTIONS**

- Cost of goods sold
- Salaries and wages to employees
- Salaries to officers (for corporations)
- Professional fees
- Rents, repairs, and maintenance
- Bad debts (if accrual method is used)
- Advertising
- Pension and profit sharing contributions
- Employee benefit costs
- Taxes, interest, insurance
- Charitable contributions
- Losses from sale or exchange of property
- Depreciation, amortization
- Travel and entertainment expenses (limited)

=

**BUSINESS INCOME**

items are reported on **Form 1120**, and the corporation pays taxes on the income shown.

Most of the expenses of a business easily are justified as ordinary and necessary to the operation of the business. There are a few exceptions which we need to talk about. We will examine these in the following sections.

## Depreciation

Long-lived assets, those expected to last more than a year, must be deducted over several years, a practice called **depreciation**. The time period and amount no longer has any significant relationship to life expectancy, however, because the ACRS (**Accelerated Cost Recovery System**) must be used to calculate depreciation. There are four life-length categories: three, five, ten, and fifteen years. Exhibit 13-5 displays the depreciation charge that can be used for the first three lengths. Personal property items like automobiles, light trucks, and tools are in the three-year category. Personal property items like office furniture, fixtures, and equipment are in the five-year category. Real property like mobile homes are in the ten-year category. Real property items like buildings are in the fifteen-year category. Straight line depreciation can be used in lieu of the ACRS, but this seldom is desirable because it reduces the amount of the deduction in the early years. Because money has time value, the next best thing to tax deduction is tax deferral.

Total cost of the asset without regard to salvage value is multiplied by the percentage from Exhibit 13-4 for the respective year in which the asset has been owned to arrive at the depreciation amount. In Chapter 4 we discussed the excess depreciation charge instituted to replace the now expired investment tax credit. In general, a business can deduct the full cost of depreciable assets purchased each year up to $10,000. This applies only if the business purchases

**EXHIBIT 13-5** *Accelerated Cost Recovery System*

| | 3-YEAR PROPERTY | 5-YEAR PROPERTY | 10-YEAR PROPERTY |
|---|---|---|---|
| Year 1 | 25% | 15% | 8% |
| Year 2 | 38 | 22 | 14 |
| Year 3 | 37 | 21 | 12 |
| Year 4 | | 21 | 10 |
| Year 5 | | 21 | 10 |
| Year 6 | | | 10 |
| Years 7–10 | | | 9 |

less than $200,000 worth of depreciable assets during the year. This last exclusion is designed to prevent large firms from taking advantage of the deduction.

**Amortization** refers to the depreciation of an intangible asset. Small businesses most frequently have amortization for leasehold improvements. These costs generally are deductible over the term of the lease.

## Home Office Deduction

It has become extremely difficult to justify a tax deduction for an office in your home. Recent changes in the tax laws have closed what were considered "loopholes" in the tax code that permitted these deductions. To be able to claim a home office deduction, you must be able to demonstrate one of the following:

1. A portion of your home is used exclusively as your principal place of business.
2. A portion of your home is used exclusively and on a regular basis to see patients, clients, or customers in the normal course of business.

As you can see, the new rules are tough. There is virtually no way you can justify the part-time use of a portion of your home as a business expense. You can take a deduction for using a portion of your home to store business inventory items even if you cannot justify the home office deduction. It also may be possible to justify some other expenses, such as an office telephone, even if you do not get the home office deduction. Professional assistance is important in this area.

If you do qualify for the home office deduction, the amount you can claim is the pro rata portion of rent, interest or depreciation, utilities, cleaning, repairs and maintenance, insurance, property taxes, and so on. You can even deduct a pro rata share of termite inspections! These are basically the same kinds of deductions that would be permissible if the office were not in your home. The pro rata allocation generally is based on square footage of your home and the office portion.

## Travel and Entertainment Expenses

Travel must be reasonable in amount and required in the business. That means that you cannot fly first class unless you can demonstrate some business reason to justify the extra expense. All expenses associated with travel are deductible, including meals and lodging if you or your employees travel away from home overnight, although only 80% of the cost of meals is deductible.

Entertainment of business clients and customers is an area heavily criticized as a tax loophole. Consequently, new tax laws have significantly restricted what is deductible and when. Professional assistance is required in planning for entertainment deductions.

### Owner Compensation

The amount you choose to pay yourself in a corporation can present tax problems if the IRS considers the amount to be **excessive**. The IRS permits deductions for salaries that are **reasonable**, but it will treat compensation in excess of that as dividends and subject to double taxation. Large, unplanned year-end bonuses are especially suspect to the IRS. This means that you should plan early, set your salary and bonuses early in the year, and keep records to substantiate those decisions. Professional tax advice can help in this regard. With proper planning and record keeping you can justify large salaries.

## SMALL BUSINESS AS TAX COLLECTOR

As mentioned earlier, any business that has employees must calculate and withhold income taxes from their paychecks. These funds must then be paid to the government. This is an extremely important and sensitive area. Small business owners actually have gone to jail for failure to deposit tax withholdings from their employees! The government does not consider this to be tax evasion—it is theft! Proper planning and control are important in tax withholdings.

Calculating payroll tax withholdings is beyond the scope of this book. It is a lengthy and complex process and requires professional assistance to organize and plan for the proper calculation, record keeping, and report generation. Payroll withholdings involve federal, state, and sometimes local income taxes. Withholdings also are required for Social Security taxes, which must be matched by the employer. Furthermore, federal unemployment taxes must be withheld as well. In some states, state unemployment taxes must also be withheld, whereas in other states these taxes must be paid entirely by the employer.

A report must be prepared to detail the amounts withheld in each category for every employee and this report must be filed with the federal and state taxing authorities. In addition, payment of the amount of the withholdings plus the employer's share of social security must be paid to the federal and state departments of revenue. These reports and payments are required at least quarterly for most small businesses.

Numerous microcomputer-based payroll systems are available that can calculate payroll taxes, print checks, keep appropriate records, and print necessary reports and forms. Any business that has more than a few, stable employees, would be well advised to consider purchasing such a system. The record keeping rapidly can become an expensive, time-consuming problem. Of course, if you consider acquiring a system, it would be wise to have a professional examine the system to ensure that it will handle your needs and is justifiable.

## SUMMARY

There are three organization forms that a business may use: proprietorship, partnership, and corporation. Proprietorships and partnerships do not have a legal existence separate from their owner(s). They pay no taxes. Their assets are available to creditors and successful litigants as are the personal assets of their owners. Personal assets of owners of corporations are exposed only in the case of gross negligence.

Professional organizations cannot adopt the corporate form; however, all states recognize a professional corporation that has the same tax treatment as a corporation but is legally a partnership.

Corporations cannot deduct dividends when calculating taxable income whereas individuals receiving dividends must pay taxes on them. This results in double taxation. Using salaries, bonuses, or fringe benefits instead of dividends can help avoid this problem but professional assistance is required to avoid potential IRS claims of excess compensation.

Subchapter S corporations are taxed in the same fashion as partnerships but have all of the legal treatment of regular or C corporations.

Income taxation and tax withholding issues generally require professional assistance due to their complexity and potential impact. Therefore, the advice of your attorney or accountant can help you determine the most appropriate form for your small business and the best method for receiving the most benefits from that business. So plan ahead and take advice.

## QUESTIONS

1. Name the three forms of business and give a brief analysis of how each is treated.
2. What are the different types of corporations?
3. What is the simplest form of business to start?
4. In what ways can a proprietorship be dangerous? A partnership?
5. What is the primary cause of conflict in a partnership?
6. What form of business is available to professionals? Explain why.

7. Why is the corporate form of business preferred?
8. What is *double taxation* and how can it be minimized?
9. How is depreciation calculated?
10. In what way is a small business a tax collector?
11. What tests must be met to obtain a home office deduction?
12. Define the following terms:
    a. the hobby rule
    b. the doctrine of ostensible authority
    c. excess compensation

## PROJECTS

1. Ask a lawyer and a tax advisor to come to class or to a club meeting and discuss the options available for starting a real or contrived business.
2. In your community find owners of each of the types of businesses and ask them how they arrived at the decision to form a proprietorship, a partnership, or a corporation.

# Case 1

Bill and Diane ran a small photographic studio. It was run out of their apartment and they decided that they would share everything 50/50 in this partnership. They were reasonably successful and the business grew. They needed more space. The apartment was too small for themselves, their three cats, and the darkroom. Most of their business was outside. They handled school pictures, weddings, parties, and studio shots. They also liked to take nature shots for themselves, frame them, and give them to family and friends as gifts.

The couple were quite happy until a former roommate of Bill's moved in with them. He also was into photography and helped with the business. The extra hand increased business, but clear lines of responsibility and recompense had not been drawn, as happens with friends. The three shared the apartment, the work, and the recreation. Yet, Gene wanted more. Gene began to develop a relationship with Diane that Bill did not suspect. Diane fell for the attraction. She was thrilled with the attention of someone besides her husband, who found himself taking on more and more responsibilities at work.

Bill came home late one Friday night to discover that Diane had left him for Gene, taking all the money in the business checking account. Gene and she were going to set up a shop of their own.

### Questions

1. Breakups in partnerships can occur with regularity. Are there any more serious ramifications when the partners are married?
2. What should or could have been done to save this company and this relationship?

# Case 2

Bryan was a recent graduate of a regional university who decided to start his own business. He felt that there was a demand for a store in the town to sell computer hardware, software, peripherals, supplies, and customized work. To start his business, he was advised to do a marketing plan to see if the area really could support such an endeavor. He claimed to have done such a study, but his results never were available for perusal. He also was asked to do a break-even analysis on his products and services, to see again whether he could be successful in the area. He was asked to establish who formed his competition and how serious they were. Then it came to the capital.

Bryan had an original plan to secure his start-up capital. He identified ten professors, some of whom he knew well and some of whom only slightly.

According to his plan, each professor would invest $10,000 in his company. This would give him $100,000 in capital and eliminate the need for a loan. His pitch included the comment that, if the company failed, no one could lose more than 10% of his or her original investment.

## Questions

1. Would you invest in this business? Explain why or why not.
2. What type of organization would you select if you did invest?
3. Expound upon Bryan's business plan. What troubles you as a potential investor?

# APPENDIX
# Income Tax Forms for Small Businesses

The federal income tax forms most frequently used by small businesses are reproduced in this appendix. They are shown here primarily for reference purposes and so you can gain a general familiarity with their content. Careful analysis and understanding of each form is neither expected nor necessary. All forms shown were those used by filers for tax year 1988; forms will change slightly from year to year depending on the nature and extent of changes in the tax law. Four forms are reproduced as follows:

1. Schedule C: Profit or Loss from Business (Sole Proprietorship).
2. Form 1065: U.S. Partnership Return of Income.
3. Form 1120: U.S. Corporation Income Tax Return.
4. Form 1120S: U.S. Income Tax Return for an S Corporation.

**SCHEDULE C (Form 1040)**

Department of the Treasury
Internal Revenue Service

# Profit or Loss From Business

**(Sole Proprietorship)**

**Partnerships, Joint Ventures, Etc., Must File Form 1065.**

▶ Attach to Form 1040, Form 1041, or Form 1041S. ▶ See Instructions for Schedule C (Form 1040).

OMB No. 1545-0074

**1988**

Attachment Sequence No. **09**

Name of proprietor | **Social security number (SSN)**

**A** Principal business or profession, including product or service (see Instructions) | **B** Principal business code (from Part IV) ▶

**C** Business name and address ▶ | **D Employer ID number (Not SSN)**

**E** Method(s) used to value closing inventory:
(1) ☐ Cost (2) ☐ Lower of cost or market (3) ☐ Other (attach explanation)

**F** Accounting method: (1) ☐ Cash (2) ☐ Accrual (3) ☐ Other (specify) ▶

| | Yes | No |
|---|---|---|
| **G** Was there any change in determining quantities, costs, or valuations between opening and closing inventory? (If "Yes," attach explanation.) | | |
| **H** Are you deducting expenses for business use of your home? (If "Yes," see Instructions for limitations.) | | |
| **I** Did you "materially participate" in the operation of this business during 1988? (If "No," see Instructions for limitations on losses.) | | |

**J** If this schedule includes a loss, credit, deduction, income, or other tax benefit relating to a tax shelter required to be registered, check here ▶ ☐
If you check this box, you MUST attach **Form 8271**.

## Part I Income

| | | |
|---|---|---|
| **1a** Gross receipts or sales | 1a | |
| **b** Less: Returns and allowances | 1b | |
| **c** Subtract line 1b from line 1a. Enter the result here | 1c | |
| **2** Cost of goods sold and/or operations (from Part III, line 8) | 2 | |
| **3** Subtract line 2 from line 1c and enter the **gross profit** here | 3 | |
| **4** Other income (including windfall profit tax credit or refund received in 1988) | 4 | |
| **5** Add lines 3 and 4. This is the **gross income** ▶ | 5 | |

## Part II Deductions

| | | | | | |
|---|---|---|---|---|---|
| **6** Advertising | 6 | | **23** Repairs | 23 | |
| **7** Bad debts from sales or services (see Instructions) | 7 | | **24** Supplies (not included in Part III) | 24 | |
| **8** Bank service charges | 8 | | **25** Taxes | 25 | |
| **9** Car and truck expenses | 9 | | **26** Travel, meals, and entertainment: | | |
| **10** Commissions | 10 | | **a** Travel | 26a | |
| **11** Depletion | 11 | | **b** Meals and entertainment | | |
| **12** Depreciation and section 179 deduction from Form 4562 (not included in Part III) | 12 | | **c** Enter 20% of line 26b subject to limitations (see Instructions) | | |
| **13** Dues and publications | 13 | | **d** Subtract line 26c from 26b | 26d | |
| **14** Employee benefit programs | 14 | | **27** Utilities and telephone | 27 | |
| **15** Freight (not included in Part III) | 15 | | **28a** Wages | | |
| **16** Insurance | 16 | | **b** Jobs credit | | |
| **17** Interest: | | | **c** Subtract line 28b from 28a | 28c | |
| **a** Mortgage (paid to banks, etc.) | 17a | | **29** Other expenses (list type and amount): | | |
| **b** Other | 17b | | | | |
| **18** Laundry and cleaning | 18 | | | | |
| **19** Legal and professional services | 19 | | | | |
| **20** Office expense | 20 | | | | |
| **21** Pension and profit-sharing plans | 21 | | | | |
| **22** Rent on business property | 22 | | | 29 | |

| | | |
|---|---|---|
| **30** Add amounts in columns for lines 6 through 29. These are the **total deductions** ▶ | 30 | |
| **31** **Net profit or (loss).** Subtract line 30 from line 5. If a profit, enter here and on Form 1040, line 12, and on Schedule SE, line 2. If a loss, you MUST go on to line 32. (Fiduciaries, see instructions.) | 31 | |

**32** If you have a loss, you MUST check the box that describes your investment in this activity (see Instructions)
**32a** ☐ All investment is at risk.
**32b** ☐ Some investment is not at risk.

If you checked 32a, enter the loss on Form 1040, line 12, and Schedule SE, line 2. If you checked 32b, you MUST attach **Form 6198.**

**For Paperwork Reduction Act Notice, see Form 1040 Instructions.** **Schedule C (Form 1040) 1988**

Schedule C (Form 1040) 1988 Page **2**

## Part III Cost of Goods Sold and/or Operations (See Schedule C Instructions for Part III)

| | | | |
|---|---|---|---|
| 1 | Inventory at beginning of year. (If different from last year's closing inventory, attach explanation.) | 1 | |
| 2 | Purchases less cost of items withdrawn for personal use | 2 | |
| 3 | Cost of labor. (Do not include salary paid to yourself.) | 3 | |
| 4 | Materials and supplies | 4 | |
| 5 | Other costs | 5 | |
| 6 | Add lines 1 through 5 | 6 | |
| 7 | Less: Inventory at end of year | 7 | |
| 8 | **Cost of goods sold and/or operations.** Subtract line 7 from line 6. Enter the result here and in Part I, line 2. | 8 | |

## Part IV Codes for Principal Business or Professional Activity

Locate the major business category that best describes your activity (for example, Retail Trade, Services, etc.). Within the major category, select the activity code that identifies (or most closely identifies) the business or profession that is the principal source of your sales or receipts. **Enter this 4-digit code on line B on page 1 of Schedule C.** (**Note:** *If your principal source of income is from farming activities, you should file* **Schedule F** *(Form 1040), Farm Income and Expenses.*)

### Construction

*Code*

0018 Operative builders (building for own account)

**General contractors**

0034 Residential building
0059 Nonresidential building
0075 Highway and street construction
3889 Other heavy construction (pipe laying, bridge construction, etc.)

**Building trade contractors, including repairs**

0232 Plumbing, heating, air conditioning
0257 Painting and paper hanging
0273 Electrical work
0299 Masonry, dry wall, stone, tile
0414 Carpentering and flooring
0430 Roofing, siding, and sheet metal
0455 Concrete work
0471 Water well drilling
0885 Other building trade contractors (excavation, glazing, etc.)

### Manufacturing, Including Printing and Publishing

0612 Bakeries selling at retail
0638 Other food products and beverages
0653 Textile mill products
0679 Apparel and other textile products
0695 Leather, footware, handbags, etc.
0810 Furniture and fixtures
0836 Lumber and other wood products
0851 Printing and publishing
0877 Paper and allied products
0893 Chemicals and allied products
1016 Rubber and plastics products
1032 Stone, clay, and glass products
1057 Primary metal industries
1073 Fabricated metal products
1099 Machinery and machine shops
1115 Electric and electronic equipment
1313 Transportation equipment
1339 Instruments and related products
1883 Other manufacturing industries

### Mining and Mineral Extraction

1511 Metal mining
1537 Coal mining
1552 Oil and gas
1719 Quarrying and nonmetallic mining

### Agricultural Services, Forestry, and Fishing

1917 Soil preparation services
1933 Crop services
1958 Veterinary services, including pets
1974 Livestock breeding
1990 Other animal services
2113 Farm labor and management services
2212 Horticulture and landscaping
2238 Forestry, except logging
0836 Logging
2279 Fishing, hunting, and trapping

### Wholesale Trade—Selling Goods to Other Businesses, Government, or Institutions, Etc.

**Durable goods, including machinery, equipment, wood, metals, etc.**

2618 Selling for your own account

*Code*

2634 Agent or broker for other firms—more than 50% of gross sales on commission

**Nondurable goods, including food, fiber, chemicals, etc.**

2659 Selling for your own account
2675 Agent or broker for other firms—more than 50% of gross sales on commission

### Retail Trade—Selling Goods to Individuals and Households

3012 Selling door-to-door, by telephone or party plan, or from mobile unit
3038 Catalog or mail order
3053 Vending machine selling

**Selling From Store, Showroom, or Other Fixed Location**

**Food, beverages, and drugs**

3079 Eating places (meals or snacks)
3095 Drinking places (alcoholic beverages)
3210 Grocery stores (general line)
0612 Bakeries selling at retail
3236 Other food stores (meat, produce, candy, etc.)
3251 Liquor stores
3277 Drug stores

**Automotive and service stations**

3319 New car dealers (franchised)
3335 Used car dealers
3517 Other automotive dealers (motorcycles, recreational vehicles, etc.)
3533 Tires, accessories, and parts
3558 Gasoline service stations

**General merchandise, apparel, and furniture**

3715 Variety stores
3731 Other general merchandise stores
3756 Shoe stores
3772 Men's and boys' clothing stores
3913 Women's ready-to-wear stores
3921 Women's accessory and specialty stores and furriers
3939 Family clothing stores
3954 Other apparel and accessory stores
3970 Furniture stores
3996 TV, audio, and electronics
3988 Computer and software stores
4119 Household appliance stores
4317 Other home furnishing stores (china, floor coverings, drapes, etc.)
4333 Music and record stores

**Building, hardware, and garden supply**

4416 Building materials dealers
4432 Paint, glass, and wallpaper stores
4457 Hardware stores
4473 Nurseries and garden supply stores

**Other retail stores**

4614 Used merchandise and antique stores (except used motor vehicle parts)
4630 Gift, novelty, and souvenir shops
4655 Florists
4671 Jewelry stores

*Code*

4697 Sporting goods and bicycle shops
4812 Boat dealers
4838 Hobby, toy, and game shops
4853 Camera and photo supply stores
4879 Optical goods stores
4895 Luggage and leather goods stores
5017 Book stores, excluding newsstands
5033 Stationery stores
5058 Fabric and needlework stores
5074 Mobile home dealers
5090 Fuel dealers (except gasoline)
5884 Other retail stores

### Real Estate, Insurance, Finance, and Related Services

5512 Real estate agents and managers
5538 Operators and lessors of buildings (except developers)
5553 Operators and lessors of other real property (except developers)
5710 Subdividers and developers, except cemeteries
5736 Insurance agents and services
5751 Security and commodity brokers, dealers, and investment services
5777 Other real estate, insurance, and financial activities

### Transportation, Communications, Public Utilities, and Related Services

6114 Taxicabs
6312 Bus and limousine transportation
6338 Trucking (except trash collection)
6510 Trash collection without own dump
6536 Public warehousing
6551 Water transportation
6619 Air transportation
6635 Travel agents and tour operators
6650 Other transportation and related services
6676 Communication services
6692 Utilities, including dumps, snowplowing, road cleaning, etc.

### Services (Providing Personal, Professional, and Business Services)

**Hotels and other lodging places**

7096 Hotels, motels, and tourist homes
7211 Rooming and boarding houses
7237 Camps and camping parks

**Laundry and cleaning services**

7419 Coin-operated laundries and dry cleaning
7435 Other laundry, dry cleaning, and garment services
7450 Carpet and upholstery cleaning
7476 Janitorial and related services (building, house, and window cleaning)

**Business and/or personal services**

7617 Legal services (or lawyer)
7633 Income tax preparation
7658 Accounting and bookkeeping
7674 Engineering, surveying, and architectural

*Code*

7690 Management, consulting, and public relations
7716 Advertising, except direct mail
7732 Employment agencies and personnel supply
7757 Computer and data processing, including repair and leasing
7773 Equipment rental and leasing (except computer or automotive)
7914 Investigative and protective services
7880 Other business services

**Personal services**

8110 Beauty shops (or beautician)
8318 Barber shop (or barber)
8334 Photographic portrait studios
8516 Shoe repair and shine services
8532 Funeral services and crematories
8714 Child day care
8730 Teaching or tutoring
8755 Counseling (except health practitioners)
8771 Ministers and chaplains
6882 Other personal services

**Automotive services**

8813 Automotive rental or leasing, without driver
8839 Parking, except valet
8854 General automotive repairs
8870 Specialized automotive repairs (brake, body repairs, paint, etc.)
8896 Other automotive services (wash, towing, etc.)

**Miscellaneous repair, except computers**

9019 TV and audio equipment repair
9035 Other electrical equipment repair
9050 Reupholstery and furniture repair
2881 Other equipment repair

**Medical and health services**

9217 Offices and clinics of medical doctors (MDs)
9233 Offices and clinics of dentists
9258 Osteopathic physicians and surgeons
9274 Chiropractors
9290 Optometrists
9415 Registered and practical nurses
9431 Other licensed health practitioners
9456 Dental laboratories
9472 Nursing and personal care facilities
9886 Other health services

**Amusement and recreational services**

8557 Physical fitness facilities
9613 Videotape rental stores
9639 Motion picture theaters
9654 Other motion picture and TV film and tape activities
9670 Bowling alleys
9696 Professional sports and racing, including promoters and managers
9811 Theatrical performers, musicians, agents, producers, and related services
9837 Other amusement and recreational services

8888 Unable to classify

Form **1065**

Department of the Treasury
Internal Revenue Service

# U.S. Partnership Return of Income

▶ **For Paperwork Reduction Act Notice, see Form 1065 Instructions.**

For calendar year 1988, or fiscal year beginning ________________, 1988, and ending ______________, 19 ___.

OMB No. 1545-0099

**1988**

| | | | |
|---|---|---|---|
| A Principal business activity | Use IRS label. Otherwise, please print or type. | Name | D Employer identification number |
| B Principal product or service | | Number and street (or P.O. Box number if mail is not delivered to street address) | E Date business started |
| C Business code number | | City or town, state, and ZIP code | F Enter total assets at end of tax year $ |

G Check accounting method: (1) ☐ Cash (2) ☐ Accrual (3) ☐ Other

H Check applicable boxes: (1) ☐ Final return (2) ☐ Change in address (3) ☐ Amended return

| | Yes | No |
|---|---|---|
| I Number of partners in this partnership ▶ _____________ | | |
| J Is this partnership a limited partnership (see the Instructions)? | | |
| K Are any partners in this partnership also partnerships? | | |
| L Is this partnership a partner in another partnership? | | |
| M Does the partnership meet **all** the requirements shown in the Instructions for **Question M**? | | |
| N Was there a distribution of property or a transfer (for example, by sale or death) of a partnership interest during the tax year? If "Yes," see the Instructions concerning an election to adjust the basis of the partnership's assets under section 754 | | |
| O (1) Does the partnership have any foreign partners? | | |
| (2) If so, were any distributions made to foreign partners during the tax year? | | |

| | Yes | No |
|---|---|---|
| P At any time during the tax year, did the partnership have an interest in or a signature or other authority over a financial account in a foreign country (such as a bank account, securities account, or other financial account)? (See the Instructions for exceptions and filing requirements for Form TD F 90-22.1.) If "Yes," write the name of the foreign country. ▶ _______________ | | |
| Q Was the partnership the grantor of, or transferor to, a foreign trust which existed during the current tax year, whether or not the partnership or any partner has any beneficial interest in it? If "Yes," you may have to file Form 3520, 3520-A, or 926 | | |

R Check this box if the partnership has filed or is required to file Form 8264, Application for Registration of a Tax Shelter ☐

S Check this box if this is a partnership subject to the consolidated partnership audit procedures of TEFRA. (See the Instructions.) ☐

T Check this box if the partnership is a publicly traded partnership as defined in section 469(k)(2) ☐

**Caution:** *Include* **only** *trade or business income and expenses on lines 1a–21 below. See the instructions for more information.*

| | | | |
|---|---|---|---|
| **Income** | **1a** Gross receipts or sales $ ____________ **1b** Minus returns and allowances $ ___________ Balance ▶ | 1c | |
| | **2** Cost of goods sold and/or operations (Schedule A, line 7) | 2 | |
| | **3** Gross profit (subtract line 2 from line 1c) | 3 | |
| | **4** Ordinary income (loss) from other partnerships and fiduciaries (attach schedule) | 4 | |
| | **5** Net farm profit (loss) (attach Schedule F (Form 1040)) | 5 | |
| | **6** Net gain (loss) (Form 4797, line 18) | 6 | |
| | **7** Other income (loss) | 7 | |
| | **8** **TOTAL** income (loss) (combine lines 3 through 7) | 8 | |
| **Deductions** *(see instructions for limitations)* | **9a** Salaries and wages (other than to partners) $ __________ **9b** Minus jobs credit $ __________ Balance ▶ | 9c | |
| | **10** Guaranteed payments to partners | 10 | |
| | **11** Rent | 11 | |
| | **12** Deductible interest expense not claimed elsewhere on return (see Instructions) | 12 | |
| | **13** Taxes | 13 | |
| | **14** Bad debts | 14 | |
| | **15** Repairs | 15 | |
| | **16a** Depreciation from Form 4562 (attach Form 4562) $ ______________ **16b** Minus depreciation claimed on Schedule A and elsewhere on return $ ______________ Balance ▶ | 16c | |
| | **17** Depletion (***Do not deduct oil and gas depletion.***) | 17 | |
| | **18a** Retirement plans, etc. | 18a | |
| | **b** Employee benefit programs | 18b | |
| | **19** Other deductions (attach schedule) | 19 | |
| | **20** **TOTAL** deductions (add amounts in column for lines 9c through 19) | 20 | |
| | **21** Ordinary income (loss) from trade or business activity(ies) (subtract line 20 from line 8) | 21 | |

**Please Sign Here**

Under penalties of perjury, I declare that I have examined this return, including accompanying schedules and statements, and to the best of my knowledge and belief, it is true, correct, and complete. Declaration of preparer (other than taxpayer) is based on all information of which preparer has any knowledge.

▶ Signature of general partner ▶ Date

**Paid Preparer's Use Only**

| | | | |
|---|---|---|---|
| Preparer's signature ▶ | Date | Check if self-employed ▶ ☐ | Preparer's social security no. |
| Firm's name (or yours if self-employed) and address ▶ | | E.I. No. ▶ | |
| | | ZIP code ▶ | |

Form 1065 (1988) Page 2

## Schedule A Cost of Goods Sold and/or Operations

| | | | |
|---|---|---|---|
| 1 | Inventory at beginning of year | 1 | |
| 2 | Purchases minus cost of items withdrawn for personal use | 2 | |
| 3 | Cost of labor | 3 | |
| 4a | Additional section 263A costs (attach schedule) (see instructions) | 4a | |
| b | Other costs (attach schedule) | 4b | |
| 5 | Total (add lines 1 through 4b) | 5 | |
| 6 | Inventory at end of year | 6 | |
| 7 | Cost of goods sold (subtract line 6 from line 5). Enter here and on page 1, line 2 | 7 | |

**8a** Check all methods used for valuing closing inventory:

**(i)** ☐ Cost

**(ii)** ☐ Lower of cost or market as described in regulations section 1.471-4

**(iii)** ☐ Writedown of "subnormal" goods as described in regulations section 1.471-2(c)

**(iv)** ☐ Other (specify method used and attach explanation) ▶

**b** Check if the LIFO inventory method was adopted this tax year for any goods (if checked, attach Form 970) ☐

**c** Do the rules of section 263A (with respect to property produced or acquired for resale) apply to the partnership? ☐ **Yes** ☐ **No**

**d** Was there any change in determining quantities, cost, or valuations between opening and closing inventory? If "Yes," attach explanation ☐ **Yes** ☐ **No**

## Schedule H Income (Loss) From Rental Real Estate Activity(ies)

**1** In the space provided below, show the kind and location of each rental property. Attach a schedule if more space is needed.

Property A

Property B

Property C

| Rental Real Estate Income | | Properties A | Properties B | Properties C | Totals (Add columns A, B, C, and amounts from any attached schedule) | |
|---|---|---|---|---|---|---|
| **2** Gross Income | 2 | | | | 2 | |
| Rental Real Estate Expenses | | | | | | |
| **3** Advertising | 3 | | | | | |
| **4** Auto and travel | 4 | | | | | |
| **5** Cleaning and maintenance | 5 | | | | | |
| **6** Commissions | 6 | | | | | |
| **7** Insurance | 7 | | | | | |
| **8** Legal and other professional fees | 8 | | | | | |
| **9** Interest expense | 9 | | | | | |
| **10** Repairs | 10 | | | | | |
| **11** Taxes | 11 | | | | | |
| **12** Utilities | 12 | | | | | |
| **13** Wages and salaries | 13 | | | | | |
| **14** Depreciation from Form 4562 | 14 | | | | | |
| **15** Other (list) | | | | | | |
| | | | | | | |
| | | | | | | |
| **16** Total expenses. Add lines 3 through 15 | 16 | | | | 16 | |
| **17** Net income (loss) from rental real estate activity(ies). Subtract line 16 from line 2. Enter total net income (loss) from all properties on Schedule K, line 2 | 17 | | | | 17 | |

Form 1065 (1988) Page 3

**Schedule K** **Partners' Shares of Income, Credits, Deductions, etc.**

| | (a) Distributive share items | | (b) Total amount |
|---|---|---|---|
| Income (Loss) | 1 Ordinary income (loss) from trade or business activity(ies) (page 1, line 21) | 1 | |
| | 2 Net income (loss) from rental real estate activity(ies) (Schedule H, line 17) | 2 | |
| | 3a Gross income from other rental activity(ies) — 3a | | |
| | b Minus expenses (attach schedule) — 3b | | |
| | c Balance: net income (loss) from other rental activity(ies) ▶ | 3c | |
| | 4 Portfolio income (loss) (see instructions): | | |
| | a Interest income | 4a | |
| | b Dividend income | 4b | |
| | c Royalty income | 4c | |
| | d Net short-term capital gain (loss) (Schedule D, line 4) | 4d | |
| | e Net long-term capital gain (loss) (Schedule D, line 9) | 4e | |
| | f Other portfolio income (loss) (attach schedule) | 4f | |
| | 5 Guaranteed payments | 5 | |
| | 6 Net gain (loss) under section 1231 (other than due to casualty or theft) (see instructions) | 6 | |
| | 7 Other (attach schedule) | 7 | |
| Deductions | 8 Charitable contributions (attach list) | 8 | |
| | 9 Expense deduction for recovery property (section 179) (attach schedule) | 9 | |
| | 10 Deductions related to portfolio income (do not include investment interest expense) | 10 | |
| | 11 Other (attach schedule) | 11 | |
| Credits | 12a Credit for income tax withheld | 12a | |
| | b Low-income housing credit: (1) Partnerships to which section 42(j)(5) applies | 12b(1) | |
| | (2) Other | 12b(2) | |
| | c Qualified rehabilitation expenditures related to rental real estate activity(ies) (attach schedule) | 12c | |
| | d Credit(s) related to rental real estate activity(ies) other than 12b and 12c (attach schedule) | 12d | |
| | e Credit(s) related to other rental activity(ies) (see instructions) (attach schedule) | 12e | |
| | 13 Other (attach schedule) | 13 | |
| Self-Employment | 14a Net earnings (loss) from self-employment | 14a | |
| | b Gross farming or fishing income | 14b | |
| | c Gross nonfarm income | 14c | |
| Tax Preference Items | 15a Accelerated depreciation of real property placed in service before 1/1/87 | 15a | |
| | b Accelerated depreciation of leased personal property placed in service before 1/1/87 | 15b | |
| | c Depreciation adjustment on property placed in service after 12/31/86 | 15c | |
| | d Depletion (other than oil and gas) | 15d | |
| | e (1) Gross income from oil, gas, and geothermal properties | 15e(1) | |
| | (2) Deductions allocable to oil, gas, and geothermal properties | 15e(2) | |
| | f Other (attach schedule) | 15f | |
| Investment Interest | 16a Interest expense on investment debts | 16a | |
| | b (1) Investment income included on lines 4a through 4f, Schedule K | 16b(1) | |
| | (2) Investment expenses included on line 10, Schedule K | 16b(2) | |
| Foreign Taxes | 17a Type of income | | |
| | b Foreign country or U.S. possession | | |
| | c Total gross income from sources outside the U.S. (attach schedule) | 17c | |
| | d Total applicable deductions and losses (attach schedule) | 17d | |
| | e Total foreign taxes (check one): ▶ ☐ Paid ☐ Accrued | 17e | |
| | f Reduction in taxes available for credit (attach schedule) | 17f | |
| | g Other (attach schedule) | 17g | |
| Other | 18a Total expenditures to which a section 59(e) election may apply (attach schedule) | 18a | |
| | b Attach schedule for other items and amounts not reported above (see instructions) | | |
| Analysis | 19a Total distributive income/payment items (combine lines 1 through 5, above) | 19a | |
| | b Analysis by type of partner: | | |

| | (a) Corporate | (b) Individual | | (c) Partnership | (d) Exempt organization | (e) Nominee/Other |
|---|---|---|---|---|---|---|
| | | i. active | ii. passive | | | |
| 1. General partners | | | | | | |
| 2. Limited partners | | | | | | |

Form 1065 (1988) Page **4**

**Schedule L** **Balance Sheets**

(See the Instructions for Question M Before Completing Schedules L and M.)

| Assets | Beginning of tax year | | End of tax year | |
|---|---|---|---|---|
| | (a) | (b) | (c) | (d) |
| 1 Cash | | | | |
| 2 Trade notes and accounts receivable | | | | |
| a Minus allowance for bad debts | | | | |
| 3 Inventories | | | | |
| 4 Federal and state government obligations | | | | |
| 5 Other current assets (attach schedule) | | | | |
| 6 Mortgage and real estate loans | | | | |
| 7 Other investments (attach schedule) | | | | |
| 8 Buildings and other depreciable assets | | | | |
| a Minus accumulated depreciation | | | | |
| 9 Depletable assets | | | | |
| a Minus accumulated depletion | | | | |
| 10 Land (net of any amortization) | | | | |
| 11 Intangible assets (amortizable only) | | | | |
| a Minus accumulated amortization | | | | |
| 12 Other assets (attach schedule) | | | | |
| 13 **TOTAL** assets | | | | |
| **Liabilities and Capital** | | | | |
| 14 Accounts payable | | | | |
| 15 Mortgages, notes, bonds payable in less than 1 year | | | | |
| 16 Other current liabilities (attach schedule) | | | | |
| 17 All nonrecourse loans | | | | |
| 18 Mortgages, notes, bonds payable in 1 year or more | | | | |
| 19 Other liabilities (attach schedule) | | | | |
| 20 Partners' capital accounts | | | | |
| 21 **TOTAL** liabilities and capital | | | | |

**Schedule M** **Reconciliation of Partners' Capital Accounts**

(Show reconciliation of each partner's capital account on Schedule K-1 (Form 1065), Question K.)

| (a) Capital account at beginning of year | (b) Capital contributed during year | (c) Income (loss) from lines 1,2, 3c, and 4 of Sch. K | (d) Income not included in column (c), plus nontaxable income | (e) Losses not included in column (c), plus unallowable deductions | (f) Withdrawals and distributions | (g) Capital account at end of year |
|---|---|---|---|---|---|---|
| | | | | | | |

**Designation of Tax Matters Partner**

The following general partner is hereby designated as the tax matters partner (TMP) for the tax year for which this partnership return is filed:

Name of designated TMP ▶ Identifying number of TMP ▶

Address of designated TMP ▶

**SCHEDULE K-1 (Form 1065)**
Department of the Treasury
Internal Revenue Service

# Partner's Share of Income, Credits, Deductions, etc.

For calendar year 1988 or fiscal year
beginning , 1988, and ending , 19 .

OMB No. 1545-0099

**1988**

**Partner's identifying number ▶**

**Partnership's identifying number ▶**

Partner's name, address, and ZIP code

Partnership's name, address, and ZIP code

**A** Is this partner a general partner? . . . ☐ Yes ☐ No

**B** Partner's share of liabilities:
Nonrecourse. . . . . . . . . . $ ________
Other . . . . . . . . . . . . . $ ________

**C** What type of entity is this partner? ▶ ________

**D** Is this partner a ☐ domestic or a ☐ foreign partner?

**E** Enter partner's percentage of:

| | (i) Before decrease or termination | (ii) End of year |
|---|---|---|
| Profit sharing . . . . . | ____% | ____% |
| Loss sharing . . . . . | ____% | ____% |
| Ownership of capital . . . | ____% | ____% |

**F** IRS Center where partnership filed return ▶ ________

**G** Tax Shelter Registration Number ▶ ________

**H(1)** Did the partner's ownership interest in the partnership change after Oct. 22, 1986? . . . . . . . . . ☐ Yes ☐ No
If yes, attach statement. (See Form 1065 Instructions.)

**(2)** Did the partnership start or acquire a new activity after Oct. 22, 1986? . . . . . . . . . . ☐ Yes ☐ No
If yes, attach statement. (See Form 1065 Instructions.)

**I** Check here if this partnership is a publicly traded partnership as defined in section 469(k)(2) . . . . . . . . . . ☐

**J** Check here if this is an amended Schedule K-1. . . . . ☐

**K** Reconciliation of partner's capital account:

| (a) Capital account at beginning of year | (b) Capital contributed during year | (c) Income (loss) from lines 1, 2, 3, and 4 below | (d) Income not included in column (c), plus nontaxable income | (e) Losses not included in column (c), plus unallowable deductions | (f) Withdrawals and distributions | (g) Capital account at end of year |
|---|---|---|---|---|---|---|
| | | | | | | |

**Reminder:** If you received a 1987 Schedule K-1 that was for a short year and you chose to report the 1987 amounts over a 4-year period, be sure to include one-fourth of the short year amounts, in addition to the items reported on this Schedule K-1, on the appropriate lines of your 1988 Form 1040 and related schedules.

**Caution:** *Refer to attached Partner's Instructions for Schedule K-1 (Form 1065) before entering information from this schedule on your tax return.*

| | (a) Distributive share item | | (b) Amount | (c) 1040 filers enter the amount in column (b) on: |
|---|---|---|---|---|
| Income (Loss) | 1 Ordinary income (loss) from trade or business activity(ies) . . | 1 | | (See Partner's Instructions for Schedule K-1 (Form 1065)) |
| | 2 Net income or loss from rental real estate activity(ies) . . . . | 2 | | |
| | 3 Net income or loss from other rental activity(ies). . . . . . | 3 | | |
| | 4 Portfolio income (loss): | | | |
| | a Interest . . . . . . . . . . . . . . . . . | 4a | | Sch. B, Part I, line 2 |
| | b Dividends . . . . . . . . . . . . . . . . | 4b | | Sch. B, Part II, line 4 |
| | c Royalties . . . . . . . . . . . . . . . . | 4c | | Sch. E, Part I, line 5 |
| | d Net short-term capital gain (loss). . . . . . . . . . | 4d | | Sch. D, line 5, col. (f) or (g) |
| | e Net long-term capital gain (loss) . . . . . . . . . . | 4e | | Sch. D, line 12, col. (f) or (g) |
| | f Other portfolio income (loss) (attach schedule) . . . . . . | 4f | | (Enter on applicable lines of your return) |
| | 5 Guaranteed payments . . . . . . . . . . . . . | 5 | | (See Partner's Instructions for Schedule K-1 (Form 1065)) |
| | 6 Net gain (loss) under section 1231 (other than due to casualty or theft) . . | 6 | | |
| | 7 Other (attach schedule) . . . . . . . . . . . . . | 7 | | (Enter on applicable lines of your return) |
| Deductions | 8 Charitable contributions . . . . . . . . . . . . | 8 | | Sch. A, line 14 or 15 |
| | 9 Expense deduction for recovery property (section 179 ) (attach schedule) . . | 9 | | (See Partner's Instructions for Schedule K-1 (Form 1065)) |
| | 10 Deductions related to portfolio income . . . . . . . . | 10 | | |
| | 11 Other (attach schedule) . . . . . . . . . . . . . | 11 | | |
| Credits | 12a Credit for income tax withheld . . . . . . . . . . . | 12a | | See Partner's Instructions for Schedule K-1 (Form 1065) |
| | b Low-income housing credit: (1) Partnerships to which section 42(j)(5) applies | b(1) | | Form 8586, line 5 |
| | (2) Other . . . . . . . . . . . . . . . . . . | b(2) | | |
| | c Qualified rehabilitation expenditures related to rental real estate activity(ies) (attach schedule) . . . . . . . . . . | 12c | | (See Partner's Instructions for Schedule K-1 (Form 1065)) |
| | d Credit(s) related to rental real estate activity(ies) other than 12b and 12c (attach schedule) . . . . . . . . . . . | 12d | | |
| | e Credit(s) related to other rental activity(ies) (see instructions) (attach schedule) | 12e | | |
| | 13 Other credits (attach schedule) . . . . . . . . . . . | 13 | | |

Schedule K-1 (Form 1065) (1988) Page **2**

| | | (a) Distributive share item | | (b) Amount | (c) 1040 filers enter the amount in column (b) on: |
|---|---|---|---|---|---|
| Self-employment | 14a | Net earnings (loss) from self-employment | 14a | | Sch. SE, Section A or B |
| | b | Gross farming or fishing income | 14b | | (See Partner's Instructions for Schedule K-1 (Form 1065)) |
| | c | Gross nonfarm income | 14c | | |
| Tax Preference Items | 15a | Accelerated depreciation of real property placed in service before 1/1/87 | 15a | | Form 6251, line 5e |
| | b | Accelerated depreciation of leased personal property placed in service before 1/1/87 | 15b | | Form 6251, line 5f |
| | c | Depreciation adjustment on property placed in service after 12/31/86 | 15c | | Form 6251, line 4j |
| | d | Depletion (other than oil and gas) | 15d | | Form 6251, line 5c |
| | e | (1) Gross income from oil, gas, and geothermal properties | e(1) | | See Form 6251 Instructions |
| | | (2) Deductions allocable to oil, gas, and geothermal properties | e(2) | | See Form 6251 Instructions |
| | f | Other (attach schedule) | 15f | | (See Partner's Instructions for Schedule K-1 (Form 1065)) |
| Investment Interest | 16a | Interest expense on investment debts | 16a | | Form 4952, line 1 |
| | b | (1) Investment income included in Schedule K-1, lines 4a through 4f | b(1) | | (See Partner's Instructions for Schedule K-1 (Form 1065)) |
| | | (2) Investment expenses included in Schedule K-1, line 10 | b(2) | | |
| Foreign Taxes | 17a | Type of income ________ | | | Form 1116, Check boxes |
| | b | Name of foreign country or U.S. possession ________ | | | Form 1116, Part I |
| | c | Total gross income from sources outside the U.S. (attach schedule) | 17c | | Form 1116, Part I |
| | d | Total applicable deductions and losses (attach schedule) | 17d | | Form 1116, Part I |
| | e | Total foreign taxes (check one): ▶ ☐ Paid ☐ Accrued | 17e | | Form 1116, Part II |
| | f | Reduction in taxes available for credit (attach schedule) | 17f | | Form 1116, Part III |
| | g | Other (attach schedule) | 17g | | See Form 1116 Instructions |
| Other | 18a | Total expenditures to which a section 59(e) election (relating to the optional 10-year writeoff of certain tax preference items) may apply (attach schedule) | | | (See Partner's Instructions for Schedule K-1 (Form 1065)) |
| | b | Other items and amounts not reported on lines 1 through 17g, 19, and 20 that are required to be reported separately to you | | | |
| Recapture of Tax Credits | 19a | Low-income housing credit: Partnerships to which section 42(j)(5) applies | 19a | | Form 8611 |
| | b | Low-income housing credit: Other | 19b | | |

| | | 20 Investment Tax Credit Property: | A | B | C | |
|---|---|---|---|---|---|---|
| Recapture of Tax Credits | a | Description of property (State whether recovery or nonrecovery property. If recovery property, state whether regular percentage method or section 48(q) election used.) | | | | Form 4255, top |
| | b | Date placed in service | | | | Form 4255, line 2 |
| | c | Cost or other basis | | | | Form 4255, line 3 |
| | d | Class of recovery property or original estimated useful life | | | | Form 4255, line 4 |
| | e | Date item ceased to be investment credit property | | | | Form 4255, line 8 |

**Other Information Provided by Partnership:**

Form **1120**
Department of the Treasury
Internal Revenue Service

# U.S. Corporation Income Tax Return

For calendar year 1988 or tax year beginning ______________, 1988, ending ______________, 19 ____

▶ For Paperwork Reduction Act Notice, see page 1 of the instructions.

OMB No. 1545-0123

**1988**

Check if a—
A Consolidated return ☐
B Personal holding co. ☐
C Personal service corp.(as defined in Temp. Regs. sec. 1.441-4T—see instructions) ☐

Use IRS label. Otherwise, please print or type.

Name

Number and street (or P.O. box number if mail is not delivered to street address)

City or town, state, and ZIP code

D Employer identification number

E Date incorporated

F Total assets (See Specific Instructions.)
Dollars | Cents
$

G Check applicable boxes: (1) ☐ Initial return (2) ☐ Final return (3) ☐ Change in address

## Income

| | | | |
|---|---|---|---|
| 1a | Gross receipts or sales ____ b Less returns and allowances ____ c Bal ▶ | 1c | |
| 2 | Cost of goods sold and/or operations (Schedule A) | 2 | |
| 3 | Gross profit (line 1c less line 2) | 3 | |
| 4 | Dividends (Schedule C, line 19) | 4 | |
| 5 | Interest | 5 | |
| 6 | Gross rents | 6 | |
| 7 | Gross royalties | 7 | |
| 8 | Capital gain net income (attach separate Schedule D) | 8 | |
| 9 | Net gain or (loss) from Form 4797, Part II, line 18 (attach Form 4797) | 9 | |
| 10 | Other income (see instructions—attach schedule) | 10 | |
| 11 | **Total** income—Add lines 3 through 10 and enter here ▶ | 11 | |

## Deductions (See instructions for limitations on deductions.)

| | | | |
|---|---|---|---|
| 12 | Compensation of officers (Schedule E) | 12 | |
| 13a | Salaries and wages ____ b Less jobs credit ____ c Balance ▶ | 13c | |
| 14 | Repairs | 14 | |
| 15 | Bad debts | 15 | |
| 16 | Rents | 16 | |
| 17 | Taxes | 17 | |
| 18 | Interest | 18 | |
| 19 | Contributions (**see instructions for 10% limitation**) | 19 | |
| 20 | Depreciation (attach Form 4562) — 20 | | |
| 21 | Less depreciation claimed in Schedule A and elsewhere on return — 21a | 21b | |
| 22 | Depletion | 22 | |
| 23 | Advertising | 23 | |
| 24 | Pension, profit-sharing, etc., plans | 24 | |
| 25 | Employee benefit programs | 25 | |
| 26 | Other deductions (attach schedule) | 26 | |
| 27 | **Total** deductions—Add lines 12 through 26 and enter here ▶ | 27 | |
| 28 | Taxable income before net operating loss deduction and special deductions (line 11 less line 27) | 28 | |
| 29 | **Less: a** Net operating loss deduction (see instructions) — 29a | | |
| | b Special deductions (Schedule C, line 20) — 29b | 29c | |

## Tax and Payments

| | | | |
|---|---|---|---|
| 30 | Taxable income (line 28 less line 29c) | 30 | |
| 31 | **Total tax** (Schedule J) | 31 | |
| 32 | **Payments: a** 1987 overpayment credited to 1988 — 32a | | |
| | b 1988 estimated tax payments — 32b | | |
| | c Less 1988 refund applied for on Form 4466 — 32c ( ) d Bal ▶ 32d | | |
| | e Tax deposited with Form 7004 — 32e | | |
| | f Credit from regulated investment companies (attach Form 2439) — 32f | | |
| | g Credit for Federal tax on fuels (attach Form 4136) — 32g | 32h | |
| 33 | Enter any **penalty** for underpayment of estimated tax—check ▶ ☐ if Form 2220 is attached | 33 | |
| 34 | **Tax due**—If the total of lines 31 and 33 is larger than line 32h, enter amount owed | 34 | |
| 35 | **Overpayment**—If line 32h is larger than the total of lines 31 and 33, enter amount overpaid | 35 | |
| 36 | Enter amount of line 35 you want: **Credited to 1989 estimated tax** ▶ **Refunded** ▶ | 36 | |

**Please Sign Here**

Under penalties of perjury, I declare that I have examined this return, including accompanying schedules and statements, and to the best of my knowledge and belief, it is true, correct, and complete. Declaration of preparer (other than taxpayer) is based on all information of which preparer has any knowledge.

▶ Signature of officer | Date | ▶ Title

**Paid Preparer's Use Only**

Preparer's signature ▶ | Date | Check if self-employed ☐ | Preparer's social security number

Firm's name (or yours if self-employed) and address ▶ | E.I. No. ▶ | ZIP code ▶

Form 1120 (1988) Page 2

**Schedule A** **Cost of Goods Sold and/or Operations** (See instructions for line 2, page 1.)

| | | | |
|---|---|---|---|
| 1 | Inventory at beginning of year | 1 | |
| 2 | Purchases | 2 | |
| 3 | Cost of labor | 3 | |
| 4a | Additional section 263A costs (see instructions—attach schedule) | 4a | |
| b | Other costs (attach schedule) | 4b | |
| 5 | Total—Add lines 1 through 4b | 5 | |
| 6 | Inventory at end of year | 6 | |
| 7 | Cost of goods sold and/or operations—Line 5 less line 6. Enter here and on line 2, page 1 | 7 | |

8a Check all methods used for valuing closing inventory:

(i) ☐ Cost (ii) ☐ Lower of cost or market as described in Regulations section 1.471-4 (see instructions)

(iii) ☐ Writedown of "subnormal" goods as described in Regulations section 1.471-2(c) (see instructions)

(iv) ☐ Other (Specify method used and attach explanation.) ▶

b Check if the LIFO inventory method was adopted this tax year for any goods (if checked, attach Form 970) ☐

c If the LIFO inventory method was used for this tax year, enter percentage (or amounts) of closing inventory computed under LIFO 8c

d Do the rules of section 263A (with respect to property produced or acquired for resale) apply to the corporation? ☐ Yes ☐ No

e Was there any change in determining quantities, cost, or valuations between opening and closing inventory? If "Yes," attach explanation ☐ Yes ☐ No

**Schedule C** **Dividends and Special Deductions** (See Schedule C instructions.)

| | | (a) Dividends received | (b) % | (c) Special deductions: multiply (a) × (b) |
|---|---|---|---|---|
| 1 | Dividends from less-than-20%-owned domestic corporations that are subject to the 70% deduction (other than debt-financed stock) | | 70 | |
| 2 | Dividends from 20%-or-more-owned domestic corporations that are subject to the 80% deduction (other than debt-financed stock) | | 80 | |
| 3 | Dividends on debt-financed stock of domestic and foreign corporations (section 246A) | | see instructions | |
| 4 | Dividends on certain preferred stock of less-than-20%-owned public utilities | | 41.176 | |
| 5 | Dividends on certain preferred stock of 20%-or-more-owned public utilities | | 47.059 | |
| 6 | Dividends from less-than-20%-owned foreign corporations and certain FSCs that are subject to the 70% deduction | | 70 | |
| 7 | Dividends from 20%-or-more-owned foreign corporations and certain FSCs that are subject to the 80% deduction | | 80 | |
| 8 | Dividends from wholly owned foreign subsidiaries subject to the 100% deduction (section 245(b)) | | 100 | |
| 9 | **Total**—Add lines 1 through 8. See instructions for limitation | | | |
| 10 | Dividends from domestic corporations received by a small business investment company operating under the Small Business Investment Act of 1958 | | 100 | |
| 11 | Dividends from certain FSCs that are subject to the 100% deduction (section 245(c)(1)) | | 100 | |
| 12 | Dividends from affiliated group members subject to the 100% deduction (section 243(a)(3)) | | 100 | |
| 13 | Other dividends from foreign corporations not included in lines 3, 6, 7, 8, and 11 | | | |
| 14 | Income from controlled foreign corporations under subpart F (attach Forms 5471) | | | |
| 15 | Foreign dividend gross-up (section 78) | | | |
| 16 | IC-DISC and former DISC dividends not included in lines 1, 2, and/or 3 (section 246(d)) | | | |
| 17 | Other dividends | | | |
| 18 | Deduction for dividends paid on certain preferred stock of public utilities (see instructions) | | | |
| 19 | Total dividends—Add lines 1 through 17. Enter here and on line 4, page 1. ▶ | | | |
| 20 | Total deductions—Add lines 9, 10, 11, 12, and 18. Enter here and on line 29b, page 1 ▶ | | | |

**Schedule E** **Compensation of Officers** (See instructions for line 12, page 1.)

Complete Schedule E only if total receipts (line 1a, plus lines 4 through 10, of page 1, Form 1120) are $150,000 or more.

| (a) Name of officer | (b) Social security number | (c) Percent of time devoted to business | Percent of corporation stock owned (d) Common | (e) Preferred | (f) Amount of compensation |
|---|---|---|---|---|---|
| 1 | | % | % | % | |
| | | % | % | % | |
| | | % | % | % | |
| | | % | % | % | |
| | | % | % | % | |

| | | |
|---|---|---|
| 2 | Total compensation of officers | |
| 3 | Less: Compensation of officers claimed in Schedule A and elsewhere on return | ( ) |
| 4 | Compensation of officers deducted on line 12, page 1 | |

Form 1120 (1988) Page 3

## Schedule J Tax Computation (See instructions.)

| | | |
|---|---|---|
| **1** Check if you are a member of a controlled group (see sections 1561 and 1563) . . . . . . . . ▶ ☐ | | |
| **2** If line 1 is checked: | | |
| **a** Enter your share of the $50,000 and $25,000 taxable income bracket amounts (in that order): *(i)* $ *(ii)* $ | | |
| **b** Enter your share of the additional 5% tax (not to exceed $11,750) $ | | |
| **3** Income tax (See instructions to figure the tax). Check this box if the corporation is a qualified personal service corporation (see instructions) ▶ ☐ . . . | 3 | |
| **4a** Foreign tax credit (attach Form 1118) . . . | 4a | |
| **b** Possessions tax credit (attach Form 5735) . . . | 4b | |
| **c** Orphan drug credit (attach Form 6765) . . . | 4c | |
| **d** Credit for fuel produced from a nonconventional source (see instructions) . . . | 4d | |
| **e** General business credit. Enter here and check which forms are attached: ☐ Form 3800 ☐ Form 3468 ☐ Form 5884 ☐ Form 6478 ☐ Form 6765 ☐ Form 8586 . . . | 4e | |
| **f** Credit for prior year minimum tax (attach Form 8801) . . . | 4f | |
| **5** Total—Add lines 4a through 4f . . . | 5 | |
| **6** Line 3 less line 5 . . . | 6 | |
| **7** Personal holding company tax (attach Schedule PH (Form 1120)) . . . | 7 | |
| **8** Recapture taxes. Check if from: ☐ Form 4255 ☐ Form 8611 . . . | 8 | |
| **9a** Alternative minimum tax (see instructions—attach Form 4626) . . . | 9a | |
| **b** Environmental tax (see instructions—attach Form 4626) . . . | 9b | |
| **10** Total tax—Add lines 6 through 9b. Enter here and on line 31, page 1 . . . | 10 | |

**Additional Information** (See instruction F.) — Yes / No

**H** Refer to the list in the instructions and state the principal:

**(1)** Business activity code no. ▶ ____________

**(2)** Business activity ▶ ____________

**(3)** Product or service ▶ ____________

**I (1)** Did the corporation at the end of the tax year own, directly or indirectly, 50% or more of the voting stock of a domestic corporation? (For rules of attribution, see section 267(c).) . .

If "Yes," attach a schedule showing: (a) name, address, and identifying number; (b) percentage owned; and (c) taxable income or (loss) before NOL and special deductions of such corporation for the tax year ending with or within your tax year.

**(2)** Did any individual, partnership, corporation, estate, or trust at the end of the tax year own, directly or indirectly, 50% or more of the corporation's voting stock? (For rules of attribution, see section 267(c).) If "Yes," complete (a) through (c) . . . .

(a) Attach a schedule showing name, address, and identifying number.

(b) Enter percentage owned ▶ ____________

(c) Was the owner of such voting stock a person other than a U.S. person? (See instructions.) **Note:** *If "Yes," the corporation may have to file Form 5472.* . . . . . .

If "Yes," enter owner's country ▶ ____________

**J** Was the corporation a U.S. shareholder of any controlled foreign corporation? (See sections 951 and 957.) . . . . . . . .

If "Yes," attach Form 5471 for each such corporation.

**K** At any time during the tax year, did the corporation have an interest in or a signature or other authority over a financial account in a foreign country (such as a bank account, securities account, or other financial account)? . . . . . . . .

(See instruction F and filing requirements for form TD F 90-22.1.)

If "Yes," enter name of foreign country ▶ ____________

**L** Was the corporation the grantor of, or transferor to, a foreign trust which existed during the current tax year, whether or not the corporation has any beneficial interest in it? . . . . . . . .

If "Yes," the corporation may have to file Forms 3520, 3520-A, or 926.

**M** During this tax year, did the corporation pay dividends (other than stock dividends and distributions in exchange for stock) in excess of the corporation's current and accumulated earnings and profits? (See sections 301 and 316.) . . . . . . . . .

If "Yes," file Form 5452. If this is a consolidated return, answer here for parent corporation and on **Form 851**, Affiliations Schedule, for each subsidiary.

**N** During this tax year did the corporation maintain any part of its accounting/tax records on a computerized system? . . . . . .

**O** Check method of accounting:

**(1)** ☐ Cash

**(2)** ☐ Accrual

**(3)** ☐ Other (specify) ▶ ____________

**P** Check this box if the corporation issued publicly offered debt instruments with original issue discount . . . . . . . ☐

If so, the corporation may have to file Form 8281.

**Q** Enter the amount of tax-exempt interest received or accrued during the tax year ▶

**R** Enter the number of shareholders at the end of the tax year if there were 35 or fewer shareholders ▶

Form 1120 (1988) Page 4

**Schedule L Balance Sheets**

| Assets | Beginning of tax year (a) | (b) | End of tax year (c) | (d) |
|---|---|---|---|---|
| 1 Cash | | | | |
| 2 Trade notes and accounts receivable | | | | |
| a Less allowance for bad debts | | | | |
| 3 Inventories | | | | |
| 4 Federal and state government obligations | | | | |
| 5 Other current assets (attach schedule) | | | | |
| 6 Loans to stockholders | | | | |
| 7 Mortgage and real estate loans | | | | |
| 8 Other investments (attach schedule) | | | | |
| 9 Buildings and other depreciable assets | | | | |
| a Less accumulated depreciation | | | | |
| 10 Depletable assets | | | | |
| a Less accumulated depletion | | | | |
| 11 Land (net of any amortization) | | | | |
| 12 Intangible assets (amortizable only) | | | | |
| a Less accumulated amortization | | | | |
| 13 Other assets (attach schedule) | | | | |
| 14 Total assets | | | | |
| **Liabilities and Stockholders' Equity** | | | | |
| 15 Accounts payable | | | | |
| 16 Mortgages, notes, bonds payable in less than 1 year | | | | |
| 17 Other current liabilities (attach schedule) | | | | |
| 18 Loans from stockholders | | | | |
| 19 Mortgages, notes, bonds payable in 1 year or more | | | | |
| 20 Other liabilities (attach schedule) | | | | |
| 21 Capital stock: a Preferred stock | | | | |
| b Common stock | | | | |
| 22 Paid-in or capital surplus | | | | |
| 23 Retained earnings—Appropriated (attach schedule) | | | | |
| 24 Retained earnings—Unappropriated | | | | |
| 25 Less cost of treasury stock | | ( ) | | ( ) |
| 26 Total liabilities and stockholders' equity | | | | |

**Schedule M-1 Reconciliation of Income per Books With Income per Return** (You are not required to complete this schedule if the total assets on line 14, column (d), of Schedule L are less than $25,000.)

1 Net income per books

2 Federal income tax

3 Excess of capital losses over capital gains

4 Income subject to tax not recorded on books this year (itemize): ____________________

5 Expenses recorded on books this year not deducted in this return (itemize):

a Depreciation . . . $ ____________

b Contributions carryover $ ____________

c Travel and entertainment . $ ____________

6 Total of lines 1 through 5

7 Income recorded on books this year not included in this return (itemize):

a Tax-exempt interest $ ____________

8 Deductions in this tax return not charged against book income this year (itemize):

a Depreciation . . . $ ____________

b Contributions carryover $ ____________

9 Total of lines 7 and 8

10 Income (line 28, page 1)—line 6 less line 9

**Schedule M-2 Analysis of Unappropriated Retained Earnings per Books (line 24, Schedule L)** (You are not required to complete this schedule if the total assets on line 14, column (d), of Schedule L are less than $25,000.)

1 Balance at beginning of year

2 Net income per books

3 Other increases (itemize): ____________

4 Total of lines 1, 2, and 3

5 Distributions: a Cash

b Stock

c Property

6 Other decreases (itemize): ____________

7 Total of lines 5 and 6

8 Balance at end of year (line 4 less line 7)

Form **1120S**
Department of the Treasury
Internal Revenue Service

## U.S. Income Tax Return for an S Corporation

For the calendar year 1988 or tax year beginning ______________, 1988, ending ____________, 19____

▶ For Paperwork Reduction Act Notice, see page 1 of the instructions.

OMB No. 1545-0130

**1988**

A Date of election as an S corporation

B Business code no. (see Specific Instructions)

Use IRS label. Otherwise, please print or type.

Name

Number and street (P.O. Box number if mail is not delivered to street address)

City or town, state, and ZIP code

C Employer identification number

D Date incorporated

E Total assets (see Specific Instructions)
Dollars Cents
$

F Check applicable boxes: (1) ☐ Initial return (2) ☐ Final return (3) ☐ Change in address (4) ☐ Amended return

G Check this box if this is an S corporation subject to the consolidated audit procedures of sections 6241 through 6245 (see instructions) . . . . . ▶ ☐

H Enter number of shareholders in the corporation at end of the tax year . . . . . ▶

**Caution:** Include **only** trade or business income and expenses on lines 1a through 21. See the instructions for more information.

**Income**

| | | |
|---|---|---|
| 1a Gross receipts or sales ______ b Less returns and allowances ______ c Bal ▶ | 1c | |
| 2 Cost of goods sold and/or operations (Schedule A, line 7) | 2 | |
| 3 Gross profit (subtract line 2 from line 1c) | 3 | |
| 4 Net gain (or loss) from Form 4797, line 18 (see instructions) | 4 | |
| 5 Other income (see instructions—attach schedule) | 5 | |
| 6 **Total** income (loss)—Combine lines 3, 4, and 5 and enter here ▶ | 6 | |

**Deductions (See instructions for limitations.)**

| | | |
|---|---|---|
| 7 Compensation of officers | 7 | |
| 8a Salaries and wages ______ b Less jobs credit ______ c Bal ▶ | 8c | |
| 9 Repairs | 9 | |
| 10 Bad debts (see instructions) | 10 | |
| 11 Rents | 11 | |
| 12 Taxes | 12 | |
| 13 Deductible interest expense not claimed or reported elsewhere on return (see instructions) | 13 | |
| 14a Depreciation from Form 4562 (attach Form 4562) . . . 14a | | |
| b Depreciation reported on Schedule A and elsewhere on return . . 14b | | |
| c Subtract line 14b from line 14a | 14c | |
| 15 Depletion (**Do not deduct oil and gas depletion.** See instructions.) | 15 | |
| 16 Advertising | 16 | |
| 17 Pension, profit-sharing, etc. plans | 17 | |
| 18 Employee benefit programs | 18 | |
| 19 Other deductions (attach schedule) | 19 | |
| 20 **Total** deductions—Add lines 7 through 19 and enter here ▶ | 20 | |
| 21 Ordinary income (loss) from trade or business activity(ies)—Subtract line 20 from line 6 | 21 | |

**Tax and Payments**

| | | |
|---|---|---|
| 22 **Tax:** | | |
| a Excess net passive income tax (attach schedule) . . . 22a | | |
| b Tax from Schedule D (Form 1120S) . . . 22b | | |
| c Add lines 22a and 22b | 22c | |
| 23 **Payments:** | | |
| a Tax deposited with Form 7004 . . . 23a | | |
| b Credit for Federal tax on fuels (attach Form 4136) . . . 23b | | |
| c Add lines 23a and 23b | 23c | |
| 24 **Tax due** (subtract line 23c from line 22c). See instructions for Paying the Tax ▶ | 24 | |
| 25 **Overpayment** (subtract line 22c from line 23c) ▶ | 25 | |

**Please Sign Here**

Under penalties of perjury, I declare that I have examined this return, including accompanying schedules and statements, and to the best of my knowledge and belief, it is true, correct, and complete. Declaration of preparer (other than taxpayer) is based on all information of which preparer has any knowledge.

▶ Signature of officer  Date  ▶ Title

**Paid Preparer's Use Only**

Preparer's signature ▶  Date  Check if self-employed ▶ ☐  Preparer's social security number

Firm's name (or yours if self-employed) and address ▶  E.I. No. ▶  ZIP code ▶

Form 1120S (1988) Page **2**

**Schedule A** **Cost of Goods Sold and/or Operations** (See instructions for Schedule A.)

| | | | |
|---|---|---|---|
| **1** | Inventory at beginning of year | **1** | |
| **2** | Purchases | **2** | |
| **3** | Cost of labor | **3** | |
| **4a** | Additional section 263A costs (attach schedule) (see instructions) | **4a** | |
| **b** | Other costs (attach schedule) | **4b** | |
| **5** | Total—Add lines 1 through 4b | **5** | |
| **6** | Inventory at end of year | **6** | |
| **7** | Cost of goods sold and/or operations—Subtract line 6 from line 5. Enter here and on line 2, page 1 | **7** | |

**8a** Check all methods used for valuing closing inventory:

(i) ☐ Cost

(ii) ☐ Lower of cost or market as described in Regulations section 1.471-4

(iii) ☐ Writedown of "subnormal" goods as described in Regulations section 1.471-2(c)

(iv) ☐ Other (Specify method used and attach explanation) ▶

**b** Check this box if the LIFO inventory method was adopted this tax year for any goods (if checked, attach Form 970) ☐

**c** If the LIFO inventory method was used for this tax year, enter percentage (or amounts) of closing inventory computed under LIFO **8c**

**d** Do the rules of section 263A (with respect to property produced or acquired for resale) apply to the corporation? ☐ Yes ☐ No

**e** Was there any change in determining quantities, cost, or valuations between opening and closing inventory? (If "Yes," attach explanation.) ☐ Yes ☐ No

**Additional Information Required**

| | | Yes | No |
|---|---|---|---|
| **I** | Did you at the end of the tax year own, directly or indirectly, 50% or more of the voting stock of a domestic corporation? (For rules of attribution, see section 267(c).) If "Yes," attach a schedule showing: (1) name, address, and employer identification number; and (2) percentage owned. | | |
| **J** | Refer to the listing of business activity codes at the end of the Instructions for Form 1120S and state your principal: **(1)** Business activity ▶ ; (2) Product or service ▶ | | |
| **K** | Were you a member of a controlled group subject to the provisions of section 1561? | | |
| **L** | At any time during the tax year, did you have an interest in or a signature or other authority over a financial account in a foreign country (such as a bank account, securities account, or other financial account)? (See instructions for exceptions and filing requirements for form TD F 90-22.1.) If "Yes," enter the name of the foreign country ▶ | | |
| **M** | Were you the grantor of, or transferor to, a foreign trust which existed during the current tax year, whether or not you have any beneficial interest in it? If "Yes," you may have to file Forms 3520, 3520-A, or 926. | | |
| **N** | During this tax year did you maintain any part of your accounting/tax records on a computerized system? | | |
| **O** | Check method of accounting: **(1)** ☐ Cash **(2)** ☐ Accrual **(3)** ☐ Other (specify) ▶ | | |
| **P** | Check this box if the S corporation has filed or is required to file **Form 8264,** Application for Registration of a Tax Shelter ▶ ☐ | | |
| **Q** | Check this box if the corporation issued publicly offered debt instruments with original issue discount ▶ ☐ If so, the corporation may have to file **Form 8281,** Information Return for Publicly Offered Original Issue Discount Instruments. | | |
| **R** | If the corporation: (1) filed its election to be an S corporation after December 31, 1986, (2) was a C corporation prior to making the election, and (3) at the beginning of the tax year has net unrealized built-in gain as defined in section 1374(d)(1), enter the net unrealized built-in gain (see instructions) ▶ | | |

**Designation of Tax Matters Person** (See instructions.)

The following shareholder is hereby designated as the tax matters person (TMP) for the tax year for which this tax return is filed:

| | | | |
|---|---|---|---|
| Name of designated TMP ▶ | | Identifying number of TMP ▶ | |
| Address of designated TMP ▶ | | | |

Form 1120S (1988) Page 3

**Schedule K** **Shareholders' Shares of Income, Credits, Deductions, Etc.** (See Instructions.)

| (a) Distributive share items | | | | (b) Total amount |
|---|---|---|---|---|
| **Income (Loss) and Deductions** | | | | |
| 1 Ordinary income (loss) from trade or business activity(ies) (page 1, line 21) | | | 1 | |
| 2a Gross income from rental real estate activity(ies) | 2a | | | |
| b Minus expenses (attach schedule) | 2b | | | |
| c Balance: net income (loss) from rental real estate activity(ies) | | | 2c | |
| 3a Gross income from other rental activity(ies) | 3a | | | |
| b Minus expenses (attach schedule) | 3b | | | |
| c Balance: net income (loss) from other rental activity(ies) | | | 3c | |
| 4 Portfolio income (loss): | | | | |
| a Interest income | | | 4a | |
| b Dividend income | | | 4b | |
| c Royalty income | | | 4c | |
| d Net short-term capital gain (loss) (Schedule D (Form 1120S)) | | | 4d | |
| e Net long-term capital gain (loss) (Schedule D (Form 1120S)) | | | 4e | |
| f Other portfolio income (loss) (attach schedule) | | | 4f | |
| 5 Net gain (loss) under section 1231 (other than due to casualty or theft) (see instructions) | | | 5 | |
| 6 Other income (loss) (attach schedule) | | | 6 | |
| 7 Charitable contributions (attach list) | | | 7 | |
| 8 Section 179 expense deduction (attach schedule) | | | 8 | |
| 9 Expenses related to portfolio income (loss) (attach schedule) (see instructions) | | | 9 | |
| 10 Other deductions (attach schedule) | | | 10 | |
| **Credits** | | | | |
| 11a Jobs credit | | | 11a | |
| b Low-income housing credit: (1) Partnership to which section 42(j)(5) applies | | | 11b(1) | |
| (2) Other | | | 11b(2) | |
| c Qualified rehabilitation expenditures related to rental real estate activity(ies) (attach schedule) | | | 11c | |
| d Credits related to rental real estate activity(ies) other than on lines 11b and 11c (attach schedule) | | | 11d | |
| e Credit(s) related to other rental activity(ies) (see instructions) (attach schedule) | | | 11e | |
| 12 Other credits (attach schedule) | | | 12 | |
| **Investment Interest** | | | | |
| 13a Interest expense on investment debts | | | 13a | |
| b (1) Investment income included on lines 4a through 4f, Schedule K | | | 13b(1) | |
| (2) Investment expenses included on line 9, Schedule K | | | 13b(2) | |
| **Tax Preference and Adjustment Items** | | | | |
| 14a Accelerated depreciation of real property placed in service before 1987 | | | 14a | |
| b Accelerated depreciation of leased personal property placed in service before 1987 | | | 14b | |
| c Depreciation adjustment on property placed in service after 1986 | | | 14c | |
| d Depletion (other than oil and gas) | | | 14d | |
| e (1) Gross income from oil, gas, or geothermal properties | | | 14e(1) | |
| (2) Gross deductions allocable to oil, gas, or geothermal properties | | | 14e(2) | |
| f Other items (attach schedule) | | | 14f | |
| **Foreign Taxes** | | | | |
| 15a Type of income ........ | | | | |
| b Name of foreign country or U.S. possession ........ | | | | |
| c Total gross income from sources outside the U.S. (attach schedule) | | | 15c | |
| d Total applicable deductions and losses (attach schedule) | | | 15d | |
| e Total foreign taxes (check one): ▶ ☐ Paid ☐ Accrued | | | 15e | |
| f Reduction in taxes available for credit (attach schedule) | | | 15f | |
| g Other (attach schedule) | | | 15g | |
| **Other Items** | | | | |
| 16 Total property distributions (including cash) other than dividends reported on line 18, Schedule K | | | 16 | |
| 17 Other items and amounts not included in lines 1 through 16, Schedule K, that are required to be reported separately to shareholders (attach schedule). | | | | |
| 18 Total dividend distributions paid from accumulated earnings and profits contained in other retained earnings (line 26 of Schedule L) | | | 18 | |

Form 1120S (1988) Page 4

**Schedule L Balance Sheets**

| Assets | Beginning of tax year (a) | (b) | End of tax year (c) | (d) |
|---|---|---|---|---|
| 1 Cash | | | | |
| 2 Trade notes and accounts receivable | | | | |
| a Less allowance for bad debts | | | | |
| 3 Inventories | | | | |
| 4 Federal and state government obligations | | | | |
| 5 Other current assets (attach schedule) | | | | |
| 6 Loans to shareholders | | | | |
| 7 Mortgage and real estate loans | | | | |
| 8 Other investments (attach schedule) | | | | |
| 9 Buildings and other depreciable assets | | | | |
| a Less accumulated depreciation | | | | |
| 10 Depletable assets | | | | |
| a Less accumulated depletion | | | | |
| 11 Land (net of any amortization) | | | | |
| 12 Intangible assets (amortizable only) | | | | |
| a Less accumulated amortization | | | | |
| 13 Other assets (attach schedule) | | | | |
| 14 Total assets | | | | |
| **Liabilities and Shareholders' Equity** | | | | |
| 15 Accounts payable | | | | |
| 16 Mortgages, notes, bonds payable in less than 1 year | | | | |
| 17 Other current liabilities (attach schedule) | | | | |
| 18 Loans from shareholders | | | | |
| 19 Mortgages, notes, bonds payable in 1 year or more | | | | |
| 20 Other liabilities (attach schedule) | | | | |
| 21 Capital stock | | | | |
| 22 Paid-in or capital surplus | | | | |
| 23 Accumulated adjustments account | | | | |
| 24 Other adjustments account | | | | |
| 25 Shareholders' undistributed taxable income previously taxed | | | | |
| 26 Other retained earnings (see instructions) | | | | |
| Check this box if the corporation has subchapter C earnings and profits at the close of the tax year ▶ ☐ (see instructions) | | | | |
| 27 Total retained earnings per books—Combine amounts on lines 23 through 26, columns (a) and (c) (see instructions) | | | | |
| 28 Less cost of treasury stock | | ( ) | | ( ) |
| 29 Total liabilities and shareholders' equity | | | | |

**Schedule M Analysis of Accumulated Adjustments Account, Other Adjustments Account, and Shareholders' Undistributed Taxable Income Previously Taxed** (If Schedule L, column (c), amounts for lines 23, 24, or 25 are not the same as corresponding amounts on line 9 of Schedule M, attach a schedule explaining any differences. See instructions.)

| | Accumulated adjustments account | Other adjustments account | Shareholders' undistributed taxable income previously taxed |
|---|---|---|---|
| 1 Balance at beginning of year | | | |
| 2 Ordinary income from page 1, line 21 | | | |
| 3 Other additions | | | |
| 4 Total of lines 1, 2, and 3 | | | |
| 5 Distributions other than dividend distributions | | | |
| 6 Loss from page 1, line 21 | | | |
| 7 Other reductions | | | |
| 8 Add lines 5, 6, and 7 | | | |
| 9 Balance at end of tax year—Subtract line 8 from line 4 | | | |

# CHAPTER 14

# Buying a Venture

**LEARNING OBJECTIVES**

After completing this chapter, you should be able to

- Evaluate a small business venture.
- Calculate the three methods of valuing businesses: value of salable assets, gross profit multiplier, and discounted cash flow methods.
- Know the two ways to buy a business.

The alternative to starting a business from scratch is to purchase one. The business you purchase can be an independent venture or it can be a franchise. How do you decide which approach is the best? It may seem that most of what we have discussed in the prior chapters concerns starting a totally independent business from scratch. Actually, the planning steps we have discussed are relevant no matter what kind of business start up is contemplated. In this and the following chapter, we will address alternatives to the independent start up and how planning is important in those cases. In this chapter, we will address purchasing a business. The next chapter is devoted to franchising, because it is an option, whether a business is bought or started anew. Keep in mind that all of our comments in this chapter are relevant to the purchase of a franchise or an independent business.

## THE BUSINESS PURCHASE

Many people who start in business do so by buying an existing business, because an existing business has an established customer base and reputation in the market area. It also has survived the start-up phase and therefore is less risky than starting a new business from scratch. These things may or may not be true. All too often a small business is sold because its owners cannot make ends meet, and selling is the only alternative to bankruptcy. Consequently, one of the primary interests you should have when considering the purchase of a business is why the owner wants to sell. If the business is not doing well, then you may be better advised to start a duplicate business from scratch. Of course, if the business has some asset, franchise, or license you want, then you may have to purchase it anyway. In that case, however, the value of the business cannot be much more than the value of the asset you want.

If the business is doing well, why does the owner want to sell it? It may take some research to find out the answer to this question. Financial statements and statements made by sellers necessarily must be suspect. Talk to competitors, bankers, suppliers, and customers. Make sure you establish a satisfactory reason for the sale before you proceed.

The biggest disadvantage in buying a business is the tendency of the purchaser to overlook all or part of the start-up planning. Buying a business does not remove any of the requirements for preventure planning. In fact, buying a business adds an additional step to the process, in that the price for the business must be evaluated to determine its fairness.

In some industries, buying an existing business may be the only viable alternative. For example, local trucking permits may be extremely difficult to obtain in a city. There may be a territorial franchise restriction which prohibits entry into a particular market. In other cases, liquor licenses may be difficult to obtain. In such instances, buying an existing business is the only entry into the market, but these are not really purchases of ongoing ventures so much as purchases of selling rights. In other instances, the attraction of the business may be its location, and purchasing the business is the only way to obtain the location.

If you consider buying a business, you should be sure to carefully evaluate what you are buying. Outside of the situations just mentioned, the purchase of a small business may well provide little more than the physical assets of the business and any time left on a lease. Sellers of small businesses are fond of speaking of "goodwill" as a major asset of the business. **Goodwill** actually is an accounting term used to describe the portion of the purchase price of a business that exceeds the value of its assets. Sellers frequently use the term to refer to some nebulous level of market acceptance. Is there such a thing, and if so, is it transferable? Goodwill exists in the economic sense but it is a difficult concept to handle in small firms. In general, it refers to some sort of advantage a small business has over its competitors. Many people think of it as customer loyalty. But, in the case of a small business, any loyalty developed in a customer group is apt to be directed at the owner(s) of the firm rather than at the firm itself. In that case, transfer of the loyalty may not be possible. We will address the issue of goodwill in more depth in a few minutes.

## USE OF PROFESSIONALS IN BUYING A BUSINESS

There are two ways to buy a business. Its assets may be bought, or the business can be bought as a going concern. In the former case, the purchaser simply acquires the physical assets of the firm and starts a new business that owns those assets. In the latter case, the business continues under new ownership. The difference is that purchasing a going concern means assuming the liabilities of the business as well as its assets. As you can readily see, this could be dangerous because all of the liabilities of the business might not be disclosed, or even known, by the seller. Purchasing the assets of a business generally is a better idea because any debts to be assumed then must be spelled out contractually and any liens that exist against the assets can be readily determined. The differences between these two methods are outlined in Exhibit 14-1.

You should retain an attorney or a business broker to handle the actual sale itself. An attorney will collect the purchase price from the buyer and hold it in escrow for the seller until such time as clear ownership rights in the assets being

**EXHIBIT 14-1** *Methods of Buying a Business*

| PURCHASE OF THE ASSETS | PURCHASE OF THE BUSINESS |
|---|---|
| • Only identified liens assumed | • All assets and liabilities acquired |
| • Unknown liabilities excluded | • Unknown liabilities included |
| • A new business results | • The old business continues |

acquired can be transferred to the buyer. Both parties are protected in such a situation. No sale or purchase of a business should be considered without the use of an attorney or broker.

Many communities have business brokers who handle the listing and sales of businesses in the same manner as real estate agents handle the sale of homes. The involvement of a broker in a business purchase can bring substantial benefits. In the first place, the broker tends to be more knowledgeable about the competitive environment and can better advise a seller or buyer as to realistic values for a firm. Further, brokers must operate in a reputable fashion for their own firms to succeed, which means that a broker will be concerned about having a satisfied buyer as well as a satisfied seller. Of course, you should satisfy yourself that the broker indeed is reputable. Check with the Better Business Bureau, check with local bankers, and ask for references to other businesses sold. Most business brokers truly are ethical and responsible.

A broker can advise the buyer and seller of the proper procedures to follow whether the sale is for assets or a going concern. The broker can handle the sale through an escrow account or refer you to an attorney experienced in such matters. This is important to ensure that buyer, seller, suppliers, creditors, customers, and other parties are properly protected and the transfer of ownership is properly handled.

A consultant also can be a valuable asset when purchasing a business. An individual skilled in small business valuation can aid in determining whether a particular price is appropriate. Furthermore, a competent consultant can aid in determining whether the purchase is a good idea in general terms. The consultant can aid in identifying advantages and disadvantages of purchasing a particular business or of purchasing in general. As in the case of a broker, you should satisfy yourself that the consultant is knowledgeable and capable. Check with bankers, the Better Business Bureau, and former clients. If there are business brokers in the community, be sure to check with them as well.

Assistance programs such as the Small Business Development Center, sponsored by the SBA, also can be of value. In Chapter 16, assistance programs are discussed at some length: what are available, how they are located, what benefit they can serve, and so on. Refer to that chapter for more information about obtaining assistance from such programs.

## VALUING A SMALL BUSINESS

There are three basic ways to value a small business: the value of salable assets method; the gross profit multiplier method; and the discounted cash flow method.[1] The first two are simple, whereas the last may require the assistance of a professional or a consultant. If you intend to purchase a business, you should calculate the value using all three methods whenever possible. The actual purchase price then can be compared to the range of values to determine whether the transaction is fair. If you feel uncomfortable with the valuation techniques, be sure to use a business broker or a consultant. It is extremely unwise to proceed with a business purchase without having a sound idea as to the underlying worth of that business.

### The Salable Assets Method

The **value of salable assets** method simply involves an appraisal of all of the assets owned by the company and transferred to a new owner. Although this sounds simplistic, the determination of fair value for the assets is frequently difficult. You should be especially careful to ensure that the assets actually can be transferred. In the case of leased premises, for example, the leasehold improvements generally belong to the landlord and cannot be transferred to a new owner. The lease itself may not be transferrable if it has provisions prohibiting such. Inventory may have been provided on a consignment basis and still be owned by the supplier.

Even after transferrable assets have been identified, appraisal is not necessarily simplistic. Inventory replacement costs may be readily available, but just what is the value of the used furniture and fixtures? Specialized machinery, equipment, or facilities can be especially challenging. If such assets have little or no use outside a narrow industry, then they should not be valued highly in a sales transaction. Consider, for example, the specialized equipment used in a printing business. That equipment has little value to anyone not involved in printing. In addition, technological advances continue to make existing machinery obsolete. Consequently, printing equipment probably should not be valued highly in a sales situation despite the fact that it was expensive to acquire initially. For these reasons, it may be necessary to bring in a specialist to appraise the assets of a business.

Once the assets have been identified and appraised, liens that exist must be examined. A **lien** is evidence of the holding of an asset as collateral for the repayment of a loan. Ownership of an asset that has a lien against it can only be passed subject to the lien. This means that if you buy an asset being used by a bank as collateral on a loan, you will have to repay the loan or see that it is repaid to protect that asset from repossession in the event of nonpayment. Liens on any titled assets, such as trucks and cars, will be filed with the department of motor vehicles in the state in which the asset is titled. Liens on any untitled assets, such as inventory, equipment, and fixtures, or accounts receivable, will be filed with the Secretary of State's office in the state in which the firm does business. Both of these offices should be checked to determine the extent of claims against the assets.

If you are purchasing the assets of the business subject to liens, then the value of the business simply will be the difference between the value of the assets and the amount of liens. If you are buying the assets unencumbered by liens, then the value of the business is the value of its assets. But remember, the value is not necessarily a fair price for the business. It is simply a comparison figure to assist in evaluating the price. The process is outlined in Exhibit 14-2.

## The Gross Profit Multiplier Method

The **gross profit multiplier** method requires calculating the gross profit and gross profit ratio or margin for the business, determining the inventory turnover ratio of the business, and determining the industry averages for gross profit margins and inventory turns. Consequently, it is of little value for firms other than retailers or wholesalers. The method can be employed for manufac-

**EXHIBIT 14-2** *How to Calculate the Value of Salable Assets*

1. List and identify all assets to be acquired
2. Determine whether liens exist on any of these assets and establish the amounts of such liens; check with Secretary of State's office and county Register of Deeds or with state Department of Motor Vehicles
3. Ensure that the assets actually can be transferred and the present owner has valid title to them
4. Appraise the value of each asset; it may be necessary to use a professional to accomplish this
5. Net the value of assets against outstanding liens

turing firms, but may yield highly erroneous results due to the higher levels of overhead expense such firms generally have. The first step is to compare the ratios for the business to the industry averages. If the numbers are not consistent with each other, then you may want to use the more conservative of numbers in the calculation. Alternatively, you can calculate two values for the firm thereby providing a range of values.

A note of caution should be injected here. It is difficult to justify the use of a gross profit margin significantly higher than the industry average. Firms with this kind of performance are not sold everyday. After you have selected the ratios to be used in the calculation, then determine the sales that can be expected to occur during the next year. If the business has a history, then sales may be predicted consistent with the sales trend over the last few years. If it is a new business, then sales may be predicted to be the same as for the present year. Be sure that the resulting sales forecast is reasonable. The value is determined by multiplying the sales forecast by the gross profit ratio and then multiplying the resulting number by the inventory turnover. Exhibit 14-3 outlines the process.

Consider the following example:

STEPS 1 AND 2

| *Year* | *Sales* | *Sales Growth* | *Gross Profit* | *Inventory Turns* |
|---|---|---|---|---|
| 1983 | $250,000 | — | 34% | 3.2 times |
| 1984 | 275,000 | 10% | 34.5 | 3.1 times |
| 1985 | 300,000 | 9 | 35.6 | 3.3 times |
| 1986 | 325,000 | 8 | 37 | 3.5 times |
| 1987 (expected) | 347,750 | 7 | — | — |

STEPS 3 AND 4

*Industry averages from Robert Morris Statement Studies:*

| | |
|---|---|
| Gross profit ratio | 40% |
| Inventory turnover | 3.2 times |

*Average gross profit ratio:* (34 + 34.5 + 35.6 + 37)/4 = 35.3%

*Average inventory turnover:* (3.2 + 3.1 + 3.3 + 3.5)/4 = 3.3 times

STEPS 5 AND 6

Select 35.3% gross profit margin and 3.2 inventory turns:

| Predicted sales | × | Gross profit ratio | × | Inventory turns | = | Gross Profit Multiplier |
|---|---|---|---|---|---|---|
| $347,750 | × | .353 | × | 3.3 | = | $405,094 |

The gross profit multiple of the firm is approximately $405,100.

**EXHIBIT 14-3** *How to Calculate the Gross Profit Multiplier*

1. Determine the historic or average gross profit margin for the business
2. Determine the historic or average inventory turnover ratio
3. Determine the industry average gross profit margin and inventory turnover ratio
4. Use the smaller of the company average or industry average
5. Multiply the gross profit margin by projected sales
6. Multiply the resulting gross profit by inventory turnover

The rationale behind the valuation technique is that, in a retail or wholesale business, one exerts little control over the costs of inventory, and pricing largely is dictated by competition. The major aspect of the business is the sale of inventory; consequently, the use of measures involving the inventory turns and gross profit margins yields an estimate of the returns before overhead expenses that can be expected from a business during a year. If the calculation is considered too conservative, adjustments can be made by considering more than 1 year. If this is done, the values from future years should be discounted to the present using discounted cash flow techniques like those described in the following section. Remember that the value of the business is not necessarily its price; it is a comparison figure to evaluate the price.

## Discounted Cash Flow Method

The **discounted cash flow** method is based on the premise that cash flow is the life blood of every business and therefore should be the cornerstone of all business decisions. When one buys a business, the future cash flows truly are being purchased. Because it is somewhat more difficult than the other methods, it seldom is used in practice; but its accuracy and theoretical basis make it worthwhile and we highly recommend its use in any valuing situation. We think that the cost of a consultant can well be justified by the calculation of a value based on discounted cash flows.

Four steps are involved in the discounted cash flow method: estimating expected cash flows; determining an appropriate discount rate; determining a reasonable life; and calculating the value with present value techniques. We will look at each step individually.

Estimating expected cash flows involves predicting cash inflows, principally sales, and cash outflows, principally expenses other than depreciation; finding the net cash flow; and predicting any growth expected in the cash flow.

If a firm has been in existence long enough to have a history, then the calculations can be based on that history. Otherwise, predictions can assume that the present experience will continue or that cash flows will follow industry averages for the firm. It is possible for growth rates to change in the future. For example, many small businesses experience an extremely rapid growth rate for a short period, followed by a more normal growth rate thereafter. If this behavior is expected, the calculations can take both growth rates into consideration.

The starting point is the income statement. The net cash flows will be net income after tax plus depreciation and interest expense. If the income statement includes any extraordinary or unusual items that affect income, these should be removed, because we wish to predict future cash flows and unusual items can be expected not to recur. If debt is significant and expected to continue to be so, then the cash flows should be adjusted by subtracting loan payments. Remember that loan payments include both principal and interest. If you adjust cash flows in that fashion, then the growth rate probably should have a separate calculation for the period after the loan is repaid. Once the historic cash flows have been calculated, the growth rate can be determined. If cash flow for year 1 is $CF_1$ and cash flow for year 2 is $CF_2$, then the growth rate for year 1, $g_1$, is $(CF_2 - CF_1)/CF_1$. Growth rates for each year can be calculated in a similar manner and then averaged. We will want a single number for the growth rate, so the average generally is used. If there is a growth in the growth rate itself, then the geometric mean can be used instead of the arithmetic average. The geometric mean takes into consideration the increase in the growth rate and is calculated simply. It looks like this: assume that the growth rates for three years were 5%, 7%, and 10%; the geometric mean would be

$$[(1.05) \times (1.07) \times (1.10)]^{\frac{1}{3}} - 1 = 7.31\%$$

The exponent $\frac{1}{3}$ means that the cube root of the products is taken. The process involves multiplying together all the growth factors, say there are $n$ of them, then taking the $n$th root of the product and subtracting 1 to yield the geometric mean. After the mean has been calculated, it should be compared to the industry average growth rate to determine whether it seems reasonable.

Future cash flows are simply an extension of past flows. For example, the cash flow for years 1 and 2 in the future are a function of the present cash flow at year 0 and the growth rate:

$$CF_2 = CF_1(1 + g) = CF_0(1 + g)(1 + g) = CF_0(1 + g)^2$$

After the cash flows have been calculated, the discount rate must be selected. This involves determining the required rate of return of the investor or buyer of the business. Because risk and return are related, an investor who views the business as more risky than another investor will have a higher required rate of return than the second investor. Finance textbooks devote a great deal of attention to this subject. Because it is beyond the scope of this book, we suggest a simple rule of thumb for determining the discount rate. Compare the riskiness of the business with some alternative investment such as a certificate of deposit. If you believe that the business venture is twice as risky as the CD, then the discount rate should be twice the rate of the CD. This short-cut method relies totally on your subjective evaluation of the riskiness of the venture and therefore may not be highly accurate, but remember that a variety of discount rates can be selected and used to generate a range of values.

The life to be selected simply involves the determination of whether you expect the business to survive you. That is, do you expect that the business will be sold or liquidated at your retirement, or do you expect it to continue? By law, proprietorships and partnerships have lives that are restricted to the longevity of the owners. If a thirty-five-year-old individual buys a business that is expected to last only until retirement, then the life to be used should be thirty years, based on the assumption that retirement will take place at age sixty-five. On the other hand, the life expectancy of corporations generally is assumed to be infinite.

After the life has been determined, the discounted cash flows can be calculated. The general form of the model is:

$$PV_0 = \frac{CF_1}{(1 + R)} + \frac{CF_2}{(1 + R)^2} + \cdots + \frac{CF_n}{(1 + R)^n}$$

*where:*

$PV_0$ = Value of all future cash flows at the present
CF = Expected cash flows for the year of the subscript
R = The discount rate
$n$ = The number of years of life expected for the business

If the life of the business is expected to be infinite, then the model is

$$PV_0 = \frac{CF_1}{R - g}$$

*where:*

$PV_0$ = Value of all future cash flows at the present
$CF_1$ = Estimated cash flow for the next year
R = The discount rate
g = The expected growth rate of cash flows

The second model, called the *constant growth model,* can be used only if the expected growth rate is less than the discount rate. If this is not the case, then the model will yield erroneous results, and the general model must be used.

Consider this example of the application of the discounted cash flow method. This example includes a supernormal growth period followed by a normal growth period and an infinite life. In this situation, sales have shown tremendous growth over the three-year life of the firm and are expected to continue the rapid growth for five more years, after which a normal growth pattern can be expected. Because the firm has had profits for only the last year (losses for its first two years), the industry average cash flow percentage will be used on sales. In this case the industry average was obtained from *Robert Morris Associates Statement Studies*. The average ratio of net cash flow to sales for the last five years for the industry was 4.9%. The average growth rate of the net cash flows was 4.8% over the last five years. We will use the industry averages for net cash flow based on sales and the industry average growth rate for cash flows. Sales growth will be based on the geometric mean of historic sales growth for the next five years. The discount rate will be 20% and was based on the subjective determination of the buyer in this example.

---

**ILLUSTRATION OF DISCOUNTED CASH FLOW METHOD**

| | |
|---|---|
| Last year's sales growth | 69% |
| Prior year's sales growth | 18% |
| Prior year's sales growth | 39% |

Geometric mean growth $= [(1.39)(1.18)(1.69)]^{1/3} - 1 = 40.5\%$

Projected sales and cash flows for the next five years

| | *Year 1* | *Year 2* | *Year 3* | *Year 4* | *Year 5* |
|---|---|---|---|---|---|
| Sales | $335,100 | $470,800 | $661,500 | $929,400 | $1,305,800 |
| CF | 16,400 | 23,100 | 32,400 | 45,500 | 64,000 |

*Sales were found for year 1 by multiplying this year's sales of $238,500 by 1.405 and rounding to the nearest hundred; multiplying year 1 sales by 1.405 for year 2, and so forth.*

Cash flow was found by multiplying each year's sales by 4.9% and rounding to the nearest hundred.

$$PV_0 = \frac{16{,}400}{(1.20)} + \frac{23{,}100}{(1.20)^2} + \frac{32{,}400}{(1.20)^3} + \frac{45{,}500}{(1.20)^4} + \frac{64{,}000}{(1.20)^5}$$

$$PV_0 = \$\ 96{,}100$$

Normal growth expectations using constant growth model

$$PV_5 = \frac{\text{Cash flow for year 6}}{\text{Required return} - \text{Constant growth factor}}$$

$$PV_5 = \frac{64{,}000(1.048)}{.20 - .048} = \frac{67{,}100}{.152}$$

$$PV_5 = \$\ 441{,}400$$

Discounting to the present

$$PV_0 = PV_5/(1.20)^5$$
$$PV_0 = 441{,}400/(1.20)^5 = \$\ 177{,}400$$

Total value

$$\text{Value} = \$\ 96{,}100 + \$\ 177{,}400 = \$273{,}500$$

---

As in the earlier methods, the value of the firm is not necessarily the price, but a figure that can be used to determine the fairness of the price. The discounted cash flow method is preferable to the earlier more simplistic approaches because it yields a more accurate picture of the true worth of a business.

## THE ROLE OF GOODWILL IN SMALL BUSINESS VALUATION

Numerous articles and books have been written on the subject of valuation of the small business. The processes of determining values for assets or future income streams or cash flows as described in this chapter are well established in the literature; however, the issue of goodwill remains a problem. Goodwill is well established in the economic sense. It is defined as a **sustainable competitive advantage.** The practical application of this definition in a specific small business setting is not well established. From a valuation perspective, three significant problems surround goodwill in a small business. The first problem is ascertaining that a competitive advantage exists and identifying what it is. Second, the possibility of transferring the competitive advantage to a new owner-manager must be addressed. Finally, the economic value that the identified advantage creates must be determined.

Goodwill traditionally has been associated with a higher level of earnings than would have existed in the absence of the intangible resource.[2] This means that some aspect of a firm's reputation, location, or strategic posture causes it to experience higher earnings than a similar company in a similar market that does not possess the same advantage. Clearly, if a company possesses such a resource and if that resource is sustainable and transferable, the company should have a higher value. If the higher earnings are not expected to continue, then goodwill cannot be said to exist. If higher earnings are expected due to a temporary competitive example, like the printing company in the discounted cash flow section, then they can be considered in the valuation, but they are not truly goodwill in the economic sense.

If we accept the premise that goodwill constitutes a higher level of earnings, then the issue becomes the identification of a basis for the existence of goodwill. If excess earnings truly exist, they must result from a competitive advantage that is sustainable;[3] that is, the advantage will not disappear. The only way such an advantage can be expected to continue in the face of competitive pressure is if it results from a distinctive competency.[4] Otherwise, excess earnings will quickly evaporate as competitors move to copy the posture of a more successful firm. We have discussed distinctive competency at great length in previous chapters. It is an aspect of business that a firm performs in a manner superior to its competitors, that gives it a competitive edge, that increases its earnings potential.

Many categories of distinctive competency have been identified in small businesses,[5] from the knowledge or skill of the owner to reaching an untapped market niche. **Sustainability** is a function of the competitive environment. As such, it must be assessed case by case by examining the probability that competitors will not or cannot duplicate a specific competitive edge in a specific firm.

The source of a distinctive competency is a major factor in evaluating its goodwill. If the competency is not transferable to new owners, then it should not be considered in determining the firm's value. Consequently, in the case of a firm with excess earnings, goodwill should be assessed if a distinctive competency can be identified that accounts for the excess earnings, that is sustainable, and that is transferable to a new owner.

**Excess earnings** can be defined as those profits that exceed the industry average performance. The utilization of averages from trade associations or Robert Morris Associates or other sources permits identifying excess earnings by a firm as well as the value of those earnings.

Once the excess earnings have been demonstrated, the distinctive competency that is the source of those earnings must be identified. Finally, the sustainability and transferability of the distinctive competency must be investigated. The key is identifying the distinctive competency itself. If this can be done, then it is not difficult to determine whether that competency will disappear when the ownership changes. Identifying the competency may require the use of a professional.

If goodwill value exists for a firm, it should be capitalized separately and added to the value determined previously. The process simply involves using discounted cash flow techniques for the amount of excess earnings identified. The problem is complicated by concerns about how long the excess earnings are expected to last: for several years or forever. Furthermore, you must decide whether the earnings are expected to be constant in terms of dollars, constant as a ratio of earnings, or growing over time. As you can see, a consultant or professional can be a real asset in establishing a value for goodwill.

## DETERMINING THE PRICE

All three methods of valuing should be applied to a business whenever possible to yield a range of values. This approach will permit a better evaluation of the purchase price of a business. Remember that the actual sales price of a business will be a negotiated price agreed upon by the buyer and seller. Seldom will that price be the same as the value under any of the preceding methods. Nevertheless, the valuation techniques provide a starting point for the negotiation process.

A fair price for any business will be one with which both buyer and seller are pleased. The valuation techniques simply are tools to aid you in arriving at a range of selling prices you would be willing to accept. Another tool that can be of use in determining price is planning. As mentioned earlier, a major problem with purchasing a business is the tendency to overlook the need for planning. Consider how much better prepared you would be in evaluating a business purchase opportunity, if you knew what were the initial investment and expectations for a new venture. By preparing a business start-up plan as described in the planning section, you will be able to compare the purchase price with investment cost. Furthermore, you will be able to compare established sales and profit levels to projected levels. If you add to this information the range of values just generated, you will be an extremely well-informed buyer. There can be no better way to decide whether purchasing or starting from scratch is the preferable option.

## SUMMARY

The steps in the process of planning a new venture are equally applicable to purchase of an existing business or franchise. In addition to those steps, the business must be evaluated for comparison to the purchase price.

The purchase of a business may not be a wise decision despite relative value or price. A business often is sold because its owners are having difficulty. On the other hand, buying a business may be the only option available because of location, licenses, permits, franchise agreements, and so on. This simply means that planning is even more important than ordinarily.

A business may be purchased as a going concern or its assets may be acquired alone. The latter is preferable because no debts will be assumed beyond those spelled out in the purchase agreement. In any case, a professional, either a business broker or an attorney, should handle the transaction.

Three basic techniques are used in valuing a small business: the value of salable assets, the gross profit multiplier, and the discounted cash flow technique. All three methods should be employed when possible to yield a range of values for comparison to purchase price.

Goodwill in the economic sense is defined as excess earnings that result from a sustainable, competitive advantage. This means a distinctive competency. For goodwill to be an appropriate part of the valuation, the distinctive competency must be transferable to the new owner.

## QUESTIONS

1. Discuss the advantages and disadvantages of buying a business as opposed to starting one from scratch.
2. Define *goodwill* in the accounting sense.
3. Define *goodwill* in the economic sense.
4. When should goodwill be used in the valuation process?
5. What is the danger of purchasing a going concern?
6. Describe the three ways to value a small business.
7. Why is the value of the business not necessarily its price?
8. Explain why cash flow is the life blood of every business.
9. What steps are involved in the value of salable assets method? In the gross profit multiplier method? In the discounted cash flow method?
10. What is an easy rule of thumb for choosing a discount rate?
11. Why should you use all three methods for valuing a business?
12. What role does a business broker play?
13. What kinds of professional assistance can be valuable?

## PROJECTS

1. Using the financial statements for ABC Chemical Company from the appendix at the end of Chapter 4, apply the valuation techniques and determine a range of values for that business.
2. Assume that you are going to purchase an existing movie theater or other small business in your town. What is the distinctive competency? What would be the probable goodwill factor in that purchase?

# CASE

A local karate school seemed to be taking the town by storm. The sudden proliferation of martial arts movies and the wider goals of self-discipline and self-confidence provided a ground swell of appeal to not only future karatekas but to their parents as well. Riding this wave of sudden popularity, many schools sprang up. Many black belt students who had worked under other teachers suddenly decided to go out on their own. The needs were not great; a large empty room with mirrors would suffice. The *Kar Ren Dojo* opened its doors on just such a shoestring and began attracting students by the score.

The building had belonged to Randy's family and he was a second degree black belt. He had large numbers of students vying for his attention and no one was too young or too old to learn. Randy had a better rapport with the young kids than with his older students but soon the classes were so large that he had to break them apart in order to handle them. He handpicked several students for rapid promotion and began letting his senior students take on some of the responsibility for teaching the classes. The students were proud and a steady source of free labor.

The success of the studio was evidenced by Randy's new Porsche and the expansion of the dojo into a weight and exercise facility. A new dojo was opened in a town 20 miles away, as demands and dreams drove expansion. Yet suddenly, Randy was facing financial difficulties and decided to sell his business. One of his senior students, who had taken on some of the responsibilities of teaching, was interested in purchasing the studio. Jack had never seen the books but he knew that the school had been growing steadily since his first entry into the school. He was sure that success could be his. After all, he had become the primary instructor as Randy had turned more and more of the teaching responsibilities over to him. Should he buy the business?

## Things to Consider

The primary building belonged to Randy's father, who had owned it for more than twenty-five years; it was vacant for five years until Randy installed his school and fixed the place up. Randy's father was willing to lease it to the new owner for $500 per month as part of the sale of the business. Utilities for that building averaged $100 per month and it contained 2,400 square feet, with 1,000 feet in karate floor, 1,000 feet in weight training floor, and the rest in bathrooms and office. The parking lot, which was gravel, could accommodate twenty cars.

The secondary building was leased, with three years left to run on the lease at $600 per month. Utilities for that building averaged $200 per month. The building contained 2,200 square feet with 200 feet in changing rooms and bathroom and the rest equally divided between weight area and karate floor by a central partition. The building was ten years old, but in excellent condition and located on the main thoroughfare of town with room for fifteen cars in the paved lot.

Both sites had weight and exercise equipment, which was being paid for with a $25,000 loan from the bank in Randy's name. The equipment was less than one year old and had cost $35,000 initially. About half the equipment was located in each building. Monthly payments on the loan were $575. There were no employees.

Presently 150 karate students were paying $35 per month for three one-hour lessons per week. The students were divided into beginner and advanced classes: one group for children under sixteen, and one group for adults. Consequently, four classes per week were taught in each of the two facilities. Because all the karatekas were students or employed elsewhere, classes took place after 3:30 P.M. There were slightly more students in the older facility than in the newer one.

Fifteen weight students worked out an average of five times per week. These students paid a membership fee of $25 per month. Five students were in the newer building and ten were in the original location.

## Questions

1. Why do you think that Randy wants to sell his karate school?
2. What do you think that Randy's turning over his teaching duties indicates?
3. What is the impact on purchase of the leases held by the school?
4. What would a buyer of the business gain?
5. What do you think would be a fair selling price for the business?
6. How would your value for the business compare to the costs of starting such an operation from scratch?
7. What would be the competitive issues in beginning a new karate school in the same town as Randy's business?
8. Would you recommend that Jack buy the business?

Jack bought the business with very little forethought, convinced that he had to act fast before someone else snapped up the opportunity. He quickly discovered how hasty he had been. Randy had kept little or no records. Many of the students were behind in their payments for lessons. In light of the new knowledge, Jack thought that the initial decision to sell might have been encouraged by the threat of Randy's losing the Porsche to the bank. To top off his problems, Jack discovered that many of the young kids who had been the cornerstone of the school were dropping out. Even some of their parents seemed to have given up on the school.

## Questions

1. What do you think Jack should do now?
2. Was the original purchase of the business a good idea in retrospect?
3. Would the start up of a competing business have been preferable to purchasing this one?
4. Can the business be saved? How?

# CHAPTER 15

# Franchising

**LEARNING OBJECTIVES**

After completing this chapter, you should be able to

- Explain the pros and cons of franchising as an alternative to starting an independent business.
- Evaluate a franchise contract and know the prominent issues that should be included in it.
- Explain how the business plan must be modified to consider a franchise operation.
- Explain the benefits of franchising to the franchisor.

The alternative to starting a business from scratch or purchasing an independent venture is to acquire a franchise. Many prospective business owners believe that a franchised business is superior to an independent operation because of the advertising, managerial, financial, and accounting support provided by the franchisor. As we will discuss in the following sections, this is not automatically true. A great diversity of services is offered by firms to their franchisees, and a broad range of fees are charged for these services. In addition, the amount of freedom and independence of action permitted to franchisees varies. There can be advantages to franchising. It is certainly one of the most popular methods of beginning a business in the United States today, and its popularity is on the increase. However, there are no guarantees in a franchise just as there are none in an independent business. The prospective franchise owner must perform the same planning steps discussed in the planning section or risk failure in the new venture.

## FRANCHISING

A **franchise** is a business that has a contractual relationship with another business in which marketing and management services are provided in return for initial and ongoing fees. Franchises are independent businesses but the public tends not to be aware of that fact. This lack of recognition in large part is a function of the blurring of ownership that occurs in the national chains. For example, most of the fast food chains have both franchises and company-owned stores in the operation. The public generally cannot tell the difference between the two. The company-owned stores are simply additional outlets, managed and staffed by company employees. The franchises are independently owned and managed although they bear the same name as the company.

Franchises automatically are neither better nor worse than an independent business. Like most decisions in the business world, and in every other world, it is a matter of evaluating the best option for your individual situation. The franchising arrangement is spelled out in a **franchise contract** that establishes the rights and privileges of the **franchisee** (which is the independent business), and the **franchisor** (which is the sponsoring business). Franchise contracts can be established between any firms regardless of the type of firm or the industry.

## TYPES OF FRANCHISING ARRANGEMENTS

Manufacturers or producers can enter into franchising relationships with wholesalers. This frequently is done in the soft drink industry in which the bottlers of soft drinks are franchisees and the producers are franchisors. The overwhelming majority of soft drinks in the United States are bottled under franchise relationships.

The franchisor also can be a wholesaler and the franchisee, a retailer.

Hardware stores, supermarkets, convenience stores, and department stores frequently are set up under franchise contracts.

The manufacturer also can enter into relationships with retailers. The vast majority of gasoline and new automobile sales are handled under franchise arrangements. These two types of franchises are so prevalent that they account for the vast majority of total franchise sales of all types in the United States!

Service companies can enter into franchising relationships, too. Restaurants are an excellent example, as are hotels and motels. Printing services are a new and rapidly growing example of franchising in the services industries.

Regardless of the industry, franchising works in the same way. The franchisor charges a fee up front and collects a fee on a continuing basis, often called a **royalty fee** and frequently tied to sales volume, in return for marketing and management services. You must take the cost of start up plus the ongoing royalty into consideration when deciding upon the opportunity presented by the franchise. Can the costs be justified when compared to the benefits received? Exhibit 15-1 displays a sampling of the up-front capital required to start a franchise for various companies. The franchisee receives a license to operate under an established business name in an assigned geographic area. Training frequently is offered initially and on an ongoing basis. In some instances, financial assistance may be provided in the form of enhanced access to bank loans, venture capitalists, or extended payment terms.

## LOWER FAILURE RATES

Many supporters of franchising point to a lower failure rate for franchises than for independent business ventures. That lower rate, they say, is a result of the marketing-management expertise and training offered by the franchisor. In reality, the lower failure rate of franchises is a result of the screening that takes place by the franchisors. Most of the larger, more successful franchising businesses closely screen applicants for franchise contracts. First, such applicants are required to have a minimum level of capital. This one requirement probably accounts for the major reduction in failures, because independent small businesses have no such requirement and almost universally go into business with inadequate capital. We will have more to say on this topic in a later chapter. Also, the franchisors require a knowledge base that must be demonstrated from business experience or developed in company training programs. Even if there were no capital limitations, this requirement would have a far-reaching impact on failures, as the stereotypical small business venturist knows little about managing a business. Clearly, the ongoing marketing and management assistance of successful franchisors is valuable, but it is not a panacea for all ills.

The rash of failures of Kentucky Fried Chicken outlets several years ago is a prime illustration. Several of the major franchisors have modified their strategies in the last few years to concentrate on more company-owned stores

**EXHIBIT 15-1** *Minimum Franchising Investment Costs, Excluding Real Estate*

| FRANCHISOR | BUSINESS | INVESTMENT |
|---|---|---|
| Aamco Transmissions, Inc. | Automotive transmission repair | $ 42,500 |
| Action Auto, Inc. | Retail auto parts, service, and gasoline | 125,000 |
| Midas International Corporation | Automotive exhaust system, brakes, shock absorbers, and front-end alignment | 170,000 |
| Hair Performers | Family hair care | 25,000 – 50,000 |
| Kampgrounds of America | Campgrounds for recreational vehicles | 80,000 |
| T-Shirts Plus | Retail of T-shirts and associated garments | 50,000 – 100,000 |
| Drug Emporium, Inc. | Retail drug store | 600,000 |
| Snelling and Snelling, Inc. | Employment agency | 40,000 – 80,000 |
| Dunkin' Donuts of America, Inc. | Coffee and donut shop | 27,000 – 40,000 |
| Hickory Farms of Ohio, Inc. | Retail specialty foods | 100,000 |
| Baskin-Robbins, Inc. | Retail ice cream store | 50,000 |
| McDonald's Corporation | Retail fast food | 160,000 nonborrowed plus 218,000 additional |
| Wendy's Old Fashioned Hamburgers | Retail fast food | 250,000 net worth 200,000 liquid assets |
| Roto-Rooter Corporation | Sewer and drain cleaning | 7,000 – 60,000 |
| Days Inns of America, Inc. | Hotels and motels | 500,000 |
| Sir Speedy, Inc. | Full-service printing | 92,500 |
| Electronic Realty Associates | Real estate brokerage | 12,900 |
| Mini-Golf, Inc. | Miniature golf courses | 4,900 |
| Computerland Corporation | Microcomputer retailer | 200,000 – 600,000 |
| Video Biz, Inc. | Video movies, equipment sales, and rentals | 55,000 |

*Source:* United States Department of Commerce, *Franchise Opportunities Handbook* (Washington, D.C.: U.S. Government Printing Office, 1988).

because of increasing problems with control over franchised stores. Whether this will become a trend, only time will tell. Currently, Department of Commerce statistics show a national trend toward less company ownership. It is true that there has been a tremendous growth in franchising in all sectors of the nation's economy and franchising constitutes a major force in the economy. Exhibit 15-2 shows the number of franchises and their sales for 1986, 1987, and 1988; Exhibit 15-3 displays national retail sales statistics for different types

**EXHIBIT 15-2** *Total Franchise Establishments and Sales*

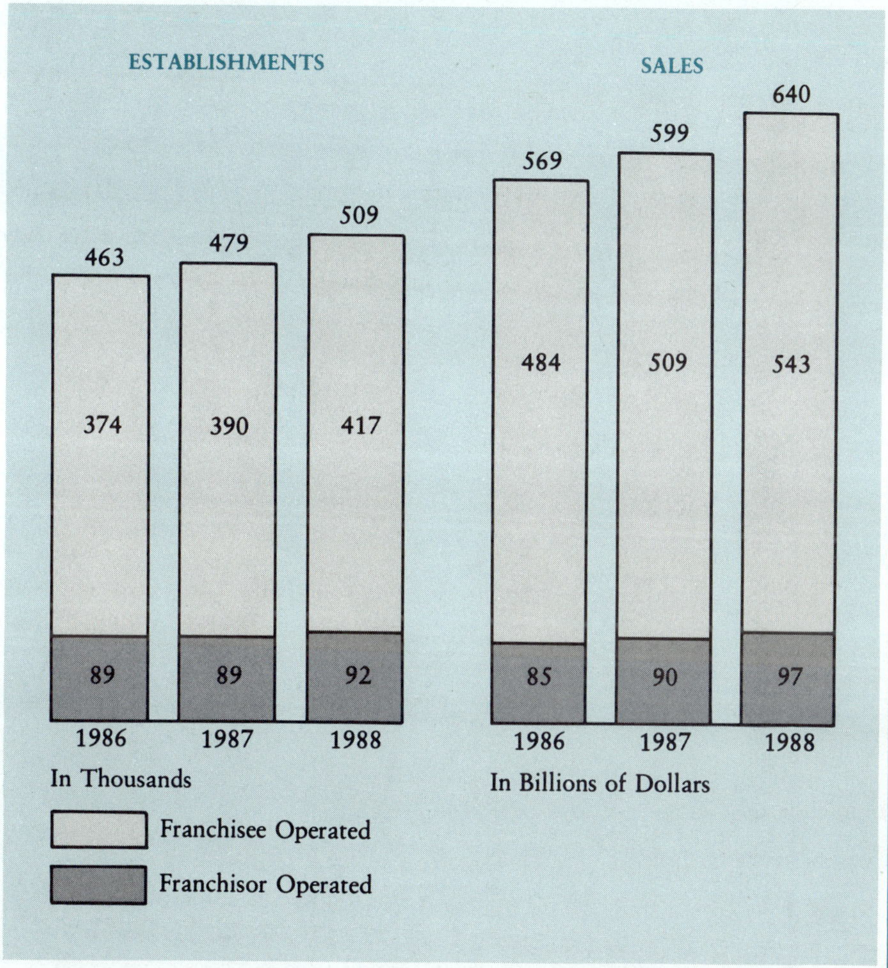


*Source:* U.S. Department of Commerce, *Franchising in the Economy, 1986–1988* (Washington, D.C.: U.S. Government Printing Office, 1988), p. 2

**EXHIBIT 15-3** *Retail Sales for Franchises in 1988, in Billions of Dollars*

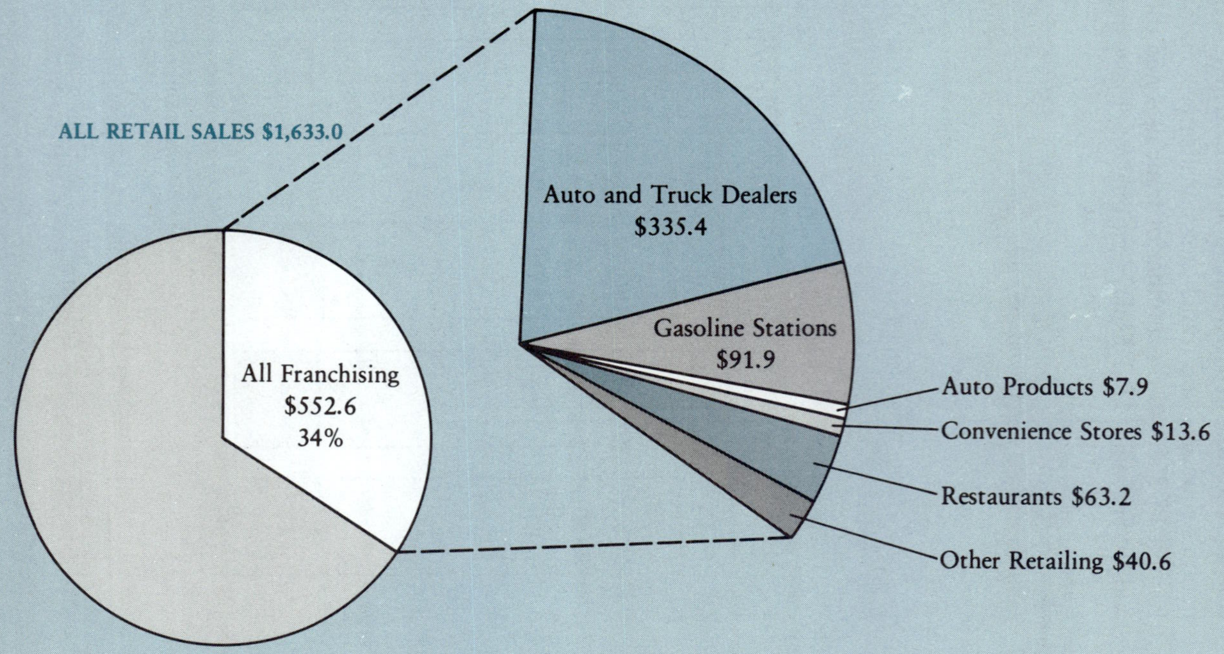


*Source:* U.S. Department of Commerce, *Franchising in the Economy, 1986–1988* (Washington, D.C.: U.S. Government Printing Office, 1988), p. 15.

of franchises in 1988. This rapid growth has also led to many cases of outright fraud and thousands of small investors have been lured into investment in small ventures that promise tremendous yields from franchising. Clearly, franchising can be a viable alternative in a new venture, but it is not guaranteed to be viable.

## EVALUATING FRANCHISE ALTERNATIVES

How do you decide whether a franchise is the right option for you? The first step should involve weighing the advantages and disadvantages for your particular situation. If you plan to open a fast food restaurant that will depend on one-time business from travelers for its sales, then the national marketing and advertising of a franchisor may be invaluable. If you plan to open a restaurant that will depend upon repeat business from an established clientele, then marketing support from a franchisor may be of limited value. If you have few management skills, then the management services provided by a franchisor may be more attractive than they would be if you were confident in your experience and abilities. In some industries you may have little choice. If you intend to open a soft drink bottling company or a new car sales lot, you may be forced to enter a franchise relationship to gain access to inventory. If there is a choice, then the relative value of franchising depends heavily on the strategy you intend to pursue in your business and the skills you will bring to the business. Completion of the business plan discussed in the prior chapters will help you determine the strategies and skills and will provide a basis for weighing the benefits of franchising for your particular situation.

At an early point in the consideration of a franchising relationship, the franchise contract should be scrutinized. We highly recommend using an attorney to evaluate any franchise contract. In addition, franchising arrangements frequently are accompanied by forecasts of sales and profits that really require expert analysis as well. A qualified CPA or accountant should be engaged to analyze any financial forecasts or cost estimates. Although the use of specialists will cost money that you might think could better be used to start the business, these expenditures could be invaluable in evaluating the franchise and could well assist in obtaining financing for the venture if the franchise agreement is accepted. This is especially true in the case of forecasts. People tend to be overly impressed by projections of sales and profits when they are formally presented and presumably based on the performance of similar firms. They should not be! Forecasts are simply that: guesses about what might happen. Every business is different, as is every market area. Therefore, projections based on the performance of other firms in an industry are not necessarily reliable. In fact, such forecasts tend to be slanted toward the upper end. Consider which firms are used to prepare averages for costs and sales. The firms that fail are not around to have their financial performance included in the averages. Therefore, the calculation of averages really is an exercise in examining those franchisees that were successful. How can the averages of those firms be expected to represent a new and untried venture?

---

The client managed a small hardware store that had been franchised by one of the national chains. He called us in because after a year and a half he was still losing money. He was behind in his payments to the bank, and he needed more cash to buy lawn care inventory for the spring season.

We looked the place over and examined the books. His sales had grown from about $150,000 the first year to what looked like a $180,000 pace for the second year, but his losses looked like they were going to be even greater in the second year. The owner was really upset because he said the franchisor had assured him that a store his size should do $250,000 easily. The worst part was that the franchisor had forecast a 40% gross profit level. He was actually getting a 27% gross.

We looked at the break-even analysis for his operation and found that he would be making money now if he had that 40% gross which he had expected. With a 27% gross his sales would have to exceed the $250,000 which the franchisor had indicated could be expected from his store. Because he had no control over the cost of the inventory, other than minor influences that would result from better inventory management, he would have to raise prices to drive the gross up. He felt, and we agreed, that raising prices would not be possible due to the competitive environment.

As a result the owner was faced with an impossible situation. There was no way he could drive sales up to break-even levels without a major infusion of cash to expand the operations, and there was no way to get the cash required from a lender due to his performance on the start-up loan. The only option was to find a private investor and give up a portion of ownership. He didn't find that a particularly attractive alternative nor did there seem to be time to find an investor given the pressure which the bank was bringing to bear.

The owner was able to find a buyer for the business, but at a much reduced price. The sell out covered the existing debts on the business, but did not recover any of the initial investment or recoup any of the losses he had sustained. It was really sad. We felt like the whole thing could have been avoided with a little attention devoted to planning up front and a careful analysis of the forecasts.

---

The story of the hardware store owner has been repeated countless times. The problem seems to be that everyone thinks of McDonald's when they think of franchises and assume that if there were a chance of failure, the franchisor would not approve the venture. This is just plain not true. Preventure planning is as important in a franchise as in an independent venture. The responsibility for success always rests with the owner of the business.

All this is not to say that franchising is a bad thing. If it were, there wouldn't be so many franchises in the country. It may well be that a franchise is the best option for you in your new venture. You should simply be sure to analyze the franchise opportunity carefully. The Federal Trade Commission requires all franchisors to disclose a wide variety of information to potential franchisees prior to the completion of a franchise contract. That information is displayed in Exhibit 15-4 and should be examined carefully, as should the financial statements of the franchisor. It would be a good idea to have your CPA analyze the data as well. Exhibit 15-5 is a list of questions and points to consider in any franchise contract. In addition, you should carefully examine the franchisor.

**EXHIBIT 15-4** *Federal Trade Commission Disclosure Requirements*

- The business experience of the franchisor and its affiliates.
- The business experience of the franchisor's officers, directors, and management personnel.
- The lawsuits involving the franchisor and its officers, directors, and managers.
- The bankruptcies involving the franchisor and its officers, directors, and managers.
- The initial franchise fee and other payments.
- The continuing payments required.
- The quality restrictions on goods and services and purchase restrictions.
- The financial assistance available.
- The restrictions on the sale of goods or services.
- The restrictions on the customers.
- The territorial protection.
- The conditions of repurchase, refusal of renewal, transference, and termination or modification by either party.
- The description of training programs.
- The involvement of celebrities and public figures.
- The assistance in site selection.
- The statistical data about the franchise, including present and future projections, terminations, nonrenewals, and repurchases.
- The financial statements.
- The personal participation in the operation by the franchisees.
- The statement of earnings and the basis for those claims.
- Listing of other franchisees.

**EXHIBIT 15-5** *Franchise Evaluation Considerations*

| | |
|---|---|
| **EXPIRATION** | What is the expiration date of the franchise contract? What happens when it expires? How are renewals handled? What aspects of the franchise agreement can be expected to change on renewal? |
| **THE FRANCHISOR** | How financially strong is the franchisor? How long has the franchisor been in business, and how many franchisees are there? Will you be given a list of franchisees to call? What happens if the franchisor should fail? What assets will belong to whom in that event? |
| **DISCLOSURE STATEMENT** | What information is contained in the disclosure statement? Remember that this statement is required by law. Consider having a professional evaluate the disclosure statement. |
| **TERMINATION AND TRANSFER** | What are the termination and transfer provisions of the contract? (There has probably been more litigation on this one aspect of franchising than any other. Courts have traditionally upheld the franchisor's rights to terminate contracts.) Do you have the right to sell the franchise to a third party? What are the restrictions on transfer? |
| **TERRITORIAL LIMITS** | What are the territorial limits of the franchise? Is the market within that territory adequate to support the projections of the venture? What is the competition within that territory? Can you expect to compete successfully with the established firms? |
| **PURCHASING RESTRICTIONS** | What are the purchase restrictions of the franchise? How much of the materials that you will use must be purchased from the franchisor? How do prices for these materials compare to other vendors? Are there restrictions on carrying competing lines of merchandise? Are these onerous? |
| **PRICING RESTRICTIONS** | Does the franchisor control pricing? If so, are prices competitive? Does the franchisor control hours of operation? Are they reasonable? Are other restrictions placed on operations? Are they reasonable? Do the expense estimates adequately consider operating restrictions? |
| **QUOTAS** | Does the franchise contract contain quotas? Are they reasonable? What happens if a quota is not met? Are there grace periods? Do quotas have escalation clauses for the future? |
| **RECORD KEEPING** | What record keeping is required? Do expense forecasts adequately cover the record keeping and reporting costs? Will any special equipment be required to comply? |
| **TRAINING** | What training is provided by the franchisor? Are there requirements for training of employees as well as management? Is the training ongoing? Are the costs included? What happens when employees turn over? Can new employees be trained? How much does that cost? |
| **IMAGE AND RECORD** | How well known is the franchisor? Is the name important to your venture? Is the image of the franchisor consistent with the image you intend to portray in your |

*continued*

**Exhibit 15-5 continued**

| | |
|---|---|
| | business? What is the track record of the franchise? How many failures occur, and why do they occur? |
| ADVERTISING | What advertising is provided by the franchisor? Will it be effective for your business? Will it reach your target market? |
| FINANCIAL SUPPORT | What financial assistance is provided by the franchisor? Will the franchisor cosign notes at banks? Will the franchisor permit deferred payments on franchise fees or other start-up costs? Will the franchisor aid in the establishment of credit lines with suppliers? If a new building is required, will the franchisor assist in the design and construction or the acquisition of fixtures and furniture? |
| AVAILABILITY OF SERVICES | What other services are provided by the franchisor? Are site analysis or location analysis services provided? What kind of market research data or services is provided? What kind of ongoing management assistance is provided? Are analytical reports on your financial statements available? If so, when? |
| FEES | What are the fees, up front and continuing? Are these consistent with the level of support you will be receiving? Are there any hidden costs, such as escalated prices for supplies that must be obtained from the franchisor? |
| REQUIREMENTS FOR THE FRANCHISEE | Do you meet the franchisor's requirements for a franchisee? Did they check you out fully? Do they have requirements beyond financial requirements to be a franchisee? If so, are they reasonable? Are you and the franchisor jointly satisfied with the probability of success for the venture? |
| OVERALL ASSESSMENT | Are you satisfied with the role you will play as a franchisee? Is the autonomy you are giving up acceptable to you? Will you have sufficient latitude in management to be able to adapt to local conditions as they develop? What aspects of business does the franchisor bring to you that you do not have and cannot obtain yourself? What does your attorney think of the contract? What does your CPA think of the financial aspects? Are you satisfied that the franchise will return real value? Will you be happy running this franchise? |

## THE FRANCHISOR

One final topic which we need to address concerning franchising is the perspective of the franchisor. Frequently, small business venturists are heard to say, "This is just our first store! Wait 'till this one is on the ground and we'll go national!" What they mean is, they will franchise the concept. Franchising contains benefits to the franchisor. Among these are speed of expansion, minimization of capital requirements, and reduction of labor and management requirements. There also are disadvantages to the franchisor. Profits tend to be greater with company-owned outlets than with franchises. In addition, control over company-owned stores is greater. If consistency is of great value in the successful approach to the customer, then company-owned stores are superior. Some analysts declare that Kentucky Fried Chicken problems came from a lack of consistency. It is clear that consistency is of prime importance in the fast food industry. Food doesn't have to taste good: the advertising will convince people that it does, so long as the food tastes the same in all of the restaurants. If it varies, all of the restaurants will suffer, not just the offending location. McDonald's has been more successful than most franchisors in enforcing consistency and all of the terms of its franchise contracts, but the firm works very hard at this and employs a staff of field inspectors to ensure compliance with service, production, and cleanliness requirements. This level of supervision is beyond a small franchisor. Nevertheless, franchising is an attractive alternative for a small business because of the reduced capital requirements of expansion. If you are considering this approach, be aware that the selection of the franchisees is of paramount importance. You can't simply give a franchise to anyone who has the money to buy it. You must try to select people who will portray the image you desire for the company or all of the outlets will suffer.

## SUMMARY

A franchise is a business that has a contractual relationship with another business in which marketing and management services are provided in return for initial and ongoing fees. The arrangement is spelled out in a franchise contract that establishes the rights and privileges of the franchisee (the independent business) and those of the franchisor (the sponsoring business). Franchise contracts are established between manufacturers, wholesalers, retailers, service, and other types of firms in all industries.

Franchises generally have a lower failure rate than independent businesses because of the screening of applicants by the franchisors. Generally, a minimum level of initial capital is required, which tends to deter undercapitalized firms from going into business. Ongoing marketing and managerial assistance may be provided. Such assistance can be of value but does not replace the need for planning and management by the franchisee.

The first step in determining whether a franchise is the right option for a new business start up is weighing the advantages and disadvantages for a particular situation. The franchise contract should be examined carefully by an experienced attorney, and a CPA should review financial forecasts or cost estimates provided by the franchisor. The business plan, described in the planning section, is applicable to a franchise decision and equally important as for an independent venture.

Exhibit 15-5, the essence of the chapter, displays questions and points that should be considered in addition to the normal planning steps when analyzing a franchise opportunity.

Franchising may be considered a strategy for any venture and embodies many benefits for the franchisor. Among these are speed of expansion, minimization of capital requirements, and reduction of labor and management costs. On the reverse side, profits tend to be greater with company-owned operations than with franchises. Control over franchises also is more difficult, making the choice of franchisees an important part of a successful franchising venture.

## QUESTIONS

1. What is the most popular method for starting a business in the United States?
2. Name several types of franchising opportunities.
3. Why is there a significantly lower failure rate among franchises than among independent start ups?
4. What are the problems and limitations of franchisor forecasts for income statement and balance sheet items?
5. Briefly list the considerations in evaluating a franchise relationship; choose the one you feel is of greatest concern to you in making that determination; and explain why.
6. Give some reasons why you might want to become a franchisor and also indicate some of the pitfalls.
7. Define the following terms:
   a. franchise
   b. franchise contract
   c. franchisee
   d. franchisor

## PROJECTS

1. Visit several franchises in your area. Then try to visit those same franchises in nearby communities and indicate whether you find consistency of product or service, location, and image in the different areas.
2. As a class project, investigate the possibility of purchasing a franchise. Decide on the one that interests you and then contact the franchisor for details of that contract.

Decide how you would improve upon the conditions of your chosen product or service, and find out what benefits you would receive from the franchise as opposed to becoming an independent competitor.

3. Go to your library and check the *Franchise Opportunities Handbook* published by the U.S. Department of Commerce. Make a list of the various franchise opportunities that might do well in your area and discuss those findings in class. Were you in agreement?

# Case

Several investors met at the home of one of the more prominent townspeople. They were interested in bringing some type of eatery to the area. Presently, the competition consisted of two restaurants: a Hardee's and an old inn, serving country-style meals that were rather expensive for everyday fare. The investors were friends who saw an opportunity in the town for some sort of franchise. They were not inclined to invest in another typical fast food place with hamburgers as the only fare, so they contemplated other possibilities.

Discussion ranged far and wide, and a committee was formed to investigate the availability of franchises. When the report came back, there was only one viable option — a steak house. Seafood was out because most such restaurants that allowed franchising also had bars, and the county prohibited liquor licenses. Other franchises either did not fit the bill or were too expensive for our investors.

Some planning was discussed, a site was selected, and several members consulted industry averages for steak houses. The decision was made. Someone had suggested a traffic count to ensure that there would be significant exposure to their facility at the chosen location. This, too, was undertaken. Counting cars that crossed the intersection seemed like a really good idea, and the result of the count was astounding. It seemed as if everyone in the county passed that spot every day of the week. What could be better?

The investors made their decision and purchased the franchise for the steak house. The facility was built in conformance with the terms of the contract, and they were almost in business. First, they had to hire a manager. All the investors held full-time jobs in the area and were not interested in the management duties themselves. A manager was hired and dreams of success followed.

Unfortunately, those dreams quickly turned sour. They found that they liked neither the food nor the service at their restaurant, and many of their friends were complaining. The manager was fired, and he took the help with him. So a simple fix was not possible. A replacement quickly was found, a new staff hired, and the quality of food and service seemed to improve. Then the kitchen caught on fire, and there were expenses to refurbish. The return on the investment planned for by the participants clearly was not going to materialize. In fact, the returns began to look negative. Also, there was no steady flow of traffic as indicated by their study. They learned that the corner at which the traffic count was made was a major intersection; one that many of the same cars passed repeatedly in a day's time. This explained the error in the count and suggested to the investors that other problems might exist that they did not know about. Consequently, the investors decided to hire a consultant to examine their operation and offer advice.

## Questions

1. If you were the consultant called in on this case, what would you do to discover any problems in the operation of the restaurant?
2. What problems might you foresee with the manager – investor relationship?
3. What should the franchisor have done before allowing this franchise to be bought?
4. What steps could be taken to improve the operation? What steps could be taken to improve the return on investment?

# PART V

# MANAGING FOR SUCCESS

# CHAPTER 16

# The Management Process

**LEARNING OBJECTIVES**

After completing this chapter, you should be able to

- Explain what management is and does.
- Distinguish between management of large and small businesses.
- Distinguish between the job descriptions of owners in each type of business.
- List the three functions of management.
- Explain the three levels of management and the function of each.
- Develop goals, objectives, and strategies.
- Know the reason for organization charts.
- Explain the why and how of time management.
- Explain the importance of planning your time.
- Know what consultants can do for you.

In 1748, Benjamin Franklin said to a young tradesman, "Remember, that time is money!" Old Ben's words of advice ring true down the centuries. Time is money because it is time that a manager uses to guide and direct a business. Such guidance is all important. The Introduction contained statistics from Dun & Bradstreet indicating that 90% of all business failures were a result of management problems.[1] Success in business largely is a result of success in management. Knowledge of a product or service is not sufficient to build a business based on that product or service. The Dun & Bradstreet figures demonstrate that! You also must have knowledge of how to run a business. This is what this chapter is all about. We explore what is involved in management and provide some guidelines for developing an effective approach to running your business.

## ISSUES IN MANAGEMENT

In simplest terms, **management** is a three-step process:

1. Deciding what tasks are to be done.
2. Assigning responsibility for those tasks to someone.
3. Checking that the tasks have been done satisfactorily.

It sounds quite simple when we talk about it in those terms, but in a small business setting the process of management is not simple at all. Consider the differences between small businesses and large businesses for a moment. The major difference between the two groups is not sales volume or number of employees or any of the more visible aspects. The major difference is in depth of management. In a large business the **Chief Executive Officer** (CEO), the individual with overall responsibility for the management of the firm, has a staff that can assist and advise in a large variety of functional areas. In addition, the CEO has managers at various levels in the organization who actually run the company on a day-to-day basis by carrying out the instructions of the CEO and other managers above them. In a small business, the owner is the CEO and frequently alone in the management ranks of the firm or at best has only limited assistance from other managers in the organization. Therefore, the small business owner faces a far-greater range of activities competing for time and attention and far-greater pressure from the day-to-day problems involved in running the business than the CEO in a large business. A CEO in a large firm has specialists in risk management, personnel, accounting, production, computer systems, marketing, and so on. In a small firm, the owner generally has no such specialists yet bears the same ultimate responsibility for managing these areas. In a large firm, the CEO does not meet with high schoolers selling ads in the annual, spend an hour with an unsatisfied customer, interview prospective employees, take telephone calls from people selling yellow pages ads and display counters, or fill in behind the cash register when the lines back up. In a small firm, the owner does all these things and more and still must retain responsibility for overall management of the firm. In a larger sense, the problem of management in a small business is an exercise in time management.

Perhaps you have read that the functions of management consist of planning, organizing, and controlling. That generally is a correct view and correlates with the simplistic process just outlined. **Planning** in an ongoing business means deciding where the business is going and how to get it there. This means setting goals and objectives for the business and deciding on strategies to advance the firm in the right direction. **Organizing** means structuring the people in the firm to perform what is necessary to carry out plans and delegating responsibility and authority. **Authority** to make decisions flows from the top levels of management. Individuals expected to carry out the strategies of the firm must have the authority required to permit that process. **Responsibility** means being held accountable for assigned tasks. Responsibility cannot be delegated, but rather flows from the delegation of authority. People who have been given power must be accountable for their use of that power and for the results of its exercise. **Controlling** means establishing a feedback system to keep the firm on track toward the established goals and objectives. How all of these things are done is the subject of the following sections.

## MANAGEMENT LEVELS

The management in a firm can be classified according to its focus and level of involvement with the functions of planning, organizing, and controlling. All managers are involved with all functions; however, managers at various levels must devote more time to one function than to another. We can say that a manager focuses on the function that demands the most time. The most senior level of management, frequently called **top management,** may consist of a single person or several people who are delegated authority to run the company by its owners. In the case of a corporation, this process is formalized along the lines of an election. Shareholders elect a board of directors to run the company for them, and the board of directors elects officers to run the company for the board. The single individual with overall authority is called the *Chief Executive Officer.* In some large organizations, the process of management has become so complex that an office of the CEO has developed with two or more occupants who share the authority. In other firms, a **Chief Operating Officer** (COO) is added to function as the number two person in the organization and relieves the CEO of some of the duties of running the firm. Frequently in a large firm, the board of directors will take an active role in managing the firm. In a small firm, the directors generally also are the officers of the firm. Regardless of the size of the firm, the top management has overall responsibility for the company. Top management is expected to do the planning for the firm and to develop **strategies** for running the organization. A military analogy can make the process more understandable. Top management consists of the general and the general staff of a military force. The goal of the force is to win a war or battle. The general staff decides what the objectives of the force will be: capturing a hill or town in enemy territory. The staff also decides the strategy: how to achieve that objective. This could involve air strikes to weaken the position, followed by an armored assault, supported by infantry to secure the objective.

The next level of management in a firm, called **middle management,** consists of those managers who are responsible for translating the plans and strategies of top management into actions. Following the military analogy, the middle managers are commanders of the units to be used in the attack. They decide the **tactics** to be used. The air commander will decide what kinds and numbers of aircraft will be used, the kinds of ordinance or bombs and missiles to be used, the specific targets of the strike such as artillery emplacements and other details of the strike. Commanders of the armor and infantry forces will coordinate the attack with the air commander and decide which forces will be used, the order and direction of the attack, and other details of that type. There may be multiple levels of middle managers, some of whom report to other middle managers, but the basic function of the group of middle managers is the development of tactics to carry out the strategies established by top management.

The very lowest level of management in a firm is the **supervisory level.** Managers at this level supervise the employees who actually do the work in the organization. These managers are hired and supervised in turn by managers above them in the organization. In the military analogy, supervisors are the junior officers who command the people involved in the attack. They are responsible for carrying out the tactics developed by the middle managers. They tell the people what to do, when and how to do it, and oversee the performance. Their primary focus is **operations.**

All of the officers in a military unit will be involved to some degree in all of the functions of the unit. That is, junior officers may attend strategy meetings with the general staff and may be asked to provide information on the state of readiness of troops under their command, suggestions as to strategies or tactics to pursue, and so forth. The general staff and senior officers also may become involved in the operations by suggesting or directing actions to junior officers. Nevertheless, the primary responsibility of each of the levels does not change. The general and the general staff must think primarily of objectives and strategies and not allow themselves to become overly involved with tactics or operations. Otherwise the development of strategies will suffer.

**EXHIBIT 16-1** *The Levels and Focus of Management*

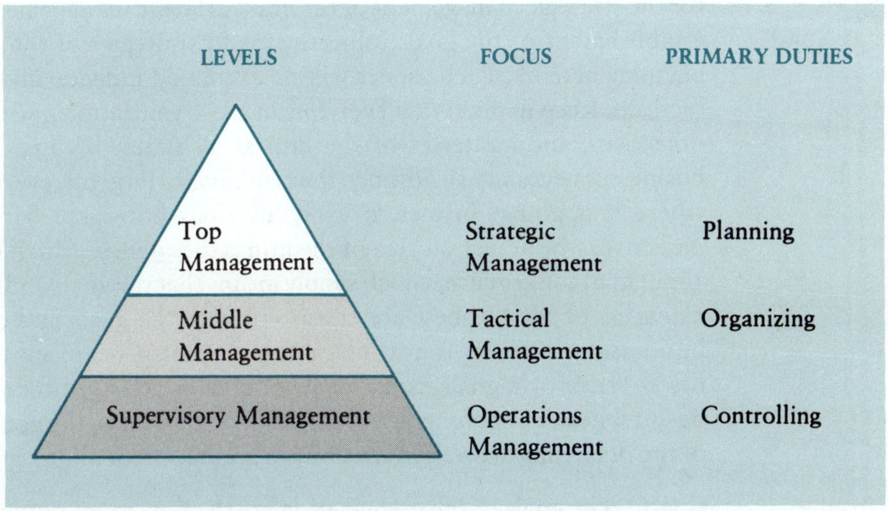


Exhibit 16-1 is a diagram of the levels and duties of management in an organization. The diagram makes it seem that there are clear-cut distinctions between the levels and functions, but this is not the case. As in the military analogy, the levels and actions of management frequently overlap. In fact, in a very small business, a single individual may be responsible for performing all aspects of management. Even in large organizations with many management people, the functions can overlap because managers can have multiple assignments. Finally, managers at every level have input to decisions made at every level.

## THE DUTIES OF MANAGEMENT

The duties of management spelled out in the exhibit can overlap tremendously, not only because the assignments of managers can overlap but because the duties influence each other. The influence runs up the scale, because top management must know what are the organization's resources and capabilities in order to form strategies. The influence also runs down the scale, because tactical and operations managers must react to rapidly changing conditions in carrying out their duties without having the time or opportunity to obtain decisions or involvement from higher levels. Nevertheless, the paradigm makes a convenient tool for the discussion of management, and each level will be discussed individually in the following sections.

## Strategic Management

Top management in a small firm is simply the owner. The owner is responsible for the strategic management of the firm. **Strategic management** consists of the establishment of the goals, objectives, and strategies of the firm; that is, the planning activity. Each aspect will be examined individually in the following sections. Keep in mind that everyone in the organization must know the goals, objectives, and strategies of the firm at all times. Because everyone in the business is necessary to advance the firm toward its goals, everyone must know where it is going. In fact, if everyone does not agree with the goals and objectives, the actual success of the firm is threatened. Much has been written about **goal congruence,** which simply means that the goals and objectives of the managers of the business are consistent with the goals and objectives of the business itself. If this is not the case, then managers are apt to guide the firm toward their own goals, consciously or unconsciously, rather than toward the business goals. Encouraging participation and input to the goals and objectives of the firm from all levels in the firm is a good tool for minimizing this problem.

**Goals.** The **goals** of the organization are the long range conditions the owner wishes to achieve. The goals may be such things as taking a business *public* (making it a publicly owned corporation), expanding its geographic territory, achieving preeminence in a particular market, diversifying the product or service offerings, or any of a host of other achievements the owner desires. **Goal setting** means deciding what you want the business to look like in five years, in ten years, or even longer into the future. Goals do not have to be financial or even quantifiable. A goal could be the development of a reputation for exceptional quality or service to the community. Goals may be quantifiable such as $1 million in sales in ten years, twenty-five outlets in five years, or operations in five states within five years. A firm may have as many or as few goals as the owner desires.

Goals must be obtainable in the environment in which the business must operate and sufficiently detailed to permit formulating objectives and strategies from them. For example, it would make little sense to develop the goal of becoming the world's largest company. Such a goal would not aid in guiding the company at all. It might very well make sense to develop a goal of becoming the major supplier of widgets in the United States market or obtaining the largest market share of gadget sales in the Southeast. The purpose of having goals for the company is to establish the direction in which the firm is to move and develop a measure of success. After all, what is success if it is not the achievement of established goals?

Goals should be reviewed constantly and modified or upgraded as conditions change. We mentioned the need for goals to make sense in the business environment. That environment is changing constantly. In the last few years there has been a major push from the federal government to deregulate various industries. A few years ago, interstate banking was not possible, airlines were heavily regulated, as was trucking and various types of freight. Changes in the laws and regulations governing these and other industries have changed the environment dramatically. Furthermore, there is a ripple effect on suppliers and firms that deal with deregulated firms so that regulatory change affects thousands of small businesses as well as the large ones. Such change will continue to be a fact of business life. Goals must be adjusted to take into consideration the changes as they occur.

Many changes have to do with consumer groups. Age, education, income, and other demographic factors of the consumer group for any product or service change constantly. Consumer tastes fluctuate widely, frequently reversing trends or directions. Markets appear, age, change, dry up, and reappear making established goals meaningless. In addition, major shifts in the competitive situation can be expected. New firms will come into existence; old firms will exit the market; established firms will change their marketing plans. In short, the competitive situation will be different every year. Goals must be changed to recognize all of these changing conditions in order to remain viable.

Many people overlook the impact that the regulatory changes can have on small business because they think of effects only in terms of giant corporations. This is a mistake! Consider the effect of the change in interstate banking laws. A few years ago small local banks had little to fear in competition from large out-of-state banks, because they were protected by regulations. This no longer is true! Even when the regulatory change affects only big firms, small businesses feel the impact as well. What happens if import restrictions on automobiles are eased? American automobile manufacturers will sell fewer cars. This means that they will buy fewer materials and components. Each automobile company purchases items from literally thousands of small businesses, all of whom will be affected. Regulatory changes also can have an indirect effect. If automobile workers make up a significant portion of the market for a small hardware store, then a layoff or cutback will have a dramatic effect on the hardware store as well.

Regulatory changes are not necessarily negative. Most regulations actually reduce competition. As regulations and restrictions are eased, competition tends to increase and many firms suffer. In the long run, however, the increased competition frequently will be good for the industry and increased opportunities will develop. Entrance barriers to industries can be lowered or eliminated by regulatory changes, making it possible for new firms to enter or small firms to grow.

Local, national, and international economic conditions also play a major role in determining the environment in which a business must exist. Everyone knows how recessions affect the general business condition in the United

States, but too few people understand how inflation in other countries can affect U.S. businesses. In addition to the impact on prices, inflation in a country affects the value of that country's currency in international exchange. For example, after enjoying a lengthy period of extreme success in U.S. sales, Japanese firms now are having problems because of the rising value of the yen in terms of the U.S. dollar. For the first time in recent memory, Japanese companies are no longer price leaders in the United States. In microcomputers and their components, automobiles, and a host of other manufactured products, Japanese imports are suffering when compared to domestic producers. Should the trend in yen/dollar exchange rate reverse itself, U.S. producers will find themselves suffering. As discussed earlier, the effect of imports on the U.S. economy will have a **trickle down** impact on thousands of small businesses. Consequently, the world economic condition affects small businesses in the United States just as the domestic economic conditions.

The U.S. economy is a **cyclic economy,** as are most economies in the world. This means that it is constantly going up and down. In the last 100 years, the United States has experienced more than forty recessions. Of course, each recession was followed by a recovery period. This works out to an average of one economic shift every two and a half years. This is only an average: the time between recessions has varied greatly over the years. Nevertheless, if you intend to be in business, you must be prepared to deal with economic shifts: they are virtually inevitable.

All of this talk about the environment should make it clear that a major requirement for effective goal setting is a good intelligence gathering process. To set goals, you must understand the environment in which you operate and what it can be expected to do over the short and long term. Both threats and opportunities will occur to a business as a result of environmental changes. Your goals should take both into consideration. You must stay abreast of the environment by reading business and trade journals and by listening and talking to other people in your market area. Constant awareness of what is going on and its potential effect on your business will make you better able to make and modify goals for your business.

**Objectives.** After goals are established for a business, objectives should be set. **Objectives** are simply intermediary goals; they provide a road map of how to get from here to there. If one of your goals is to become known for exceptionally high quality, then one of your objectives could be a quality control program that reduces defective output by 5% next year and by 10% within five years. Unlike goals, objectives need to be highly specific. The purpose of objectives is to establish **benchmarks** against which the firm's progress toward its goals can be measured. Therefore, objectives should be quantified whenever possible.

Multiple objectives and multiple levels of objectives are appropriate. Just as you can have many goals, you can have many objectives. As in the case of goals, the only rule is that objectives should be consistent with each other. You also can establish several levels for each objective. Like the example of reducing defective output, objectives can be established with higher performance levels required over time. Each objective should be obtainable and designed to provide progress toward one or more of the firm's goals. They should be reviewed and modified regularly. When the goals change, the objectives will probably need to be changed. Even when the goals do not change, objectives should be modified to take into consideration the company's progress. Each time we compare the firm to objectives all future objectives should be reviewed. Changes should be made in the levels desired or in the objectives themselves. It is a neverending process.

**Strategies.** Strategies are the plans for achieving objectives. Once we have determined where we want the company to be at a given point in time, we must decide how to get the company there. The most important strategy is the distinctive competency, discussed in the previous part. Needless to say, the distinctive competency must be consistent with the firm's goals and objectives. Other strategies aim at achieving objectives. So long as they are consistent with each other, a firm can have multiple strategies. A firm that has the objective of taking away market share from a class of competitors may establish a strategy of maintaining prices at or below those competitors at all times. A firm that wishes to increase the level of repeat business may have a strategy of contacting past customers with advertising data every six months.

Objectives are the desired ends or outcomes; strategies are what you intend to do to achieve the outcome. Objectives are *what*; strategies are *how*! The strategies can be highly specific like the ones just mentioned or they can be more general. For example, a general strategy could be "to grow through acquisitions." This would mean that the firm would focus on purchasing other businesses. Business policy textbooks talk about **generic** or general strategies that firms can pursue regardless of the industry in which they compete. Exhibit 16-2 is a list of the most frequently cited generic strategies. The exhibit also displays examples of more specific strategies that are applications of the broader thrust.

The list in Exhibit 16-2 is by no means complete. There are as many different strategies to pursue as there are businesses to pursue them. The only determination as to whether a strategy is appropriate for your business is whether it will help move the business closer to the objectives you have established. One word of caution is due here. In a small business, the owner frequently will be alone in the top management or will have very few assistants at that level. Consequently, the more strategies the company has, the more

**EXHIBIT 16-2** *Generic Strategies*

I. Concentration on a single business
   A. Create more uses for product or service
   B. Use advertising
      1. To stimulate demand
      2. To promote more uses for product/services
      3. To attract new groups of users to product/services
   C. Find new markets
   D. Find new channels of distribution

II. Vertical integration
   A. Backward: Acquire sources of supply
   B. Forward: Acquire distributors and vendors

III. Related diversification
   A. Acquire businesses in same industry
   B. Acquire businesses in related industries

IV. Unrelated diversification
   A. Acquire businesses in different industries
   B. Build a portfolio of businesses

V. Retrenchment, turnaround, and repositioning
   A. Retrenchment
      1. Raise prices to reduce demand or raise profits
      2. Reduce the scale of operations
   B. Turnaround
      1. Change the distinctive competency
      2. Change management personnel
   C. Repositioning
      1. Withdraw from some markets, products, or services
      2. Enter other markets, products, or services

VI. Abandonment, divestiture, and liquidation
   A. Sell off assets, divisions, or businesses
   B. Sell the business itself

VII. Combination strategies
   A. Mix strategies from the other groups
   B. Match strategies from the other groups

difficult it will be to manage them. It is wiser for a small business to select a small number of goals, objectives, and strategies and pursue them well than to develop large numbers and pursue them haphazardly.

## Tactical Management

The middle management levels of a firm are responsible for the **tactical management**. That is, middle managers must implement the strategies developed by top management. This is the organizing function of management. In general terms, it means telling people what to do. Top management ensures that middle management people know and understand business goals, objectives, and strategies. Top management then assigns appropriate middle management personnel responsibility for carrying out specific strategies. The middle managers then decide how best to carry out the strategies. They break the strategies down into specific tasks or tactics and assign people to carry out the tasks.

Of course, the top management, the owner in a small firm, also is involved in organizing. The owner engages in organizing when deciding which middle managers to employ for a task. The owner is organizing when deciding on the number and skill levels of employees to be hired. Middle managers must engage in planning, too. Not only do they have input into the planning process, they must plan how best to carry out strategies. Nevertheless, the primary focus, and consequently the primary time consumer, should be strategic management for the owner and tactical management for middle managers.

Tactics are specific actions and activities designed to further strategies. Consider a strategy to use advertising to stimulate demand. Tactics to enable that strategy to be implemented would include the determination of appropriate advertising media, the design of advertising messages and appeal, and the timing of the advertising. The marketing manager would have to develop a budget to be approved by top management and assign people to complete the various tasks. Note that successful completion will require gathering intelligence about the most effective media and the characteristics of the target market. Such knowledge would have to be continually updated through monitoring the effects of advertising and the changes in the target market composition and motivation. As you can see, it's simple to say "stimulate demand," but carrying out that charge is complex and time consuming.

## Operations Management

Operations managers are the direct supervisors of the people who carry out the work. We commonly think of assembly line workers in a manufacturing firm and the line supervisors when we think of **operations management.** Such supervisors indeed are operations managers, but other types of positions qualify as well. For example, the first level of management in an accounting firm supervises people. Frequently, middle managers also have operations responsibilities. For example, the marketing manager may be responsible for performing or overseeing the performance of much of the advertising work as well as developing the tactics to be used. In such a case, the advertising manager also would be an operations manager. Any person who must actually control the completion of a task is an operations manager. The key word is *control.*

Control is the management function used to keep employees on track as to the tasks they must accomplish. In a manufacturing firm, control of an assembly line means achieving the production levels required while maintaining the quality of output at acceptable levels. It also means containing costs to budgeted levels. A lot has been written about control, especially in the area of employee morale. Everyone knows that employees' morale is affected by their supervisory managers, and high morale means not only high worker satisfaction but high productivity and quality as well.

Every manager in an organization has control responsibilities in that people report to every manager. The owner manages people through the chain of command. Furthermore, the owner is responsible for control through setting up and enforcing the system that permits people to control others. In fact, this is the major problem small business owners face in day-to-day management of the enterprise. Far too many owners of small businesses get caught up in operations and fail to spend the necessary time on planning. It is easy to do because the outcome of planning is nebulous: hard to see and understand. The outcome of operations management is direct and immediate. Many people find operations management more enjoyable and more rewarding because of the immediate feedback and the ability to see a tangible result from the work.

Planning, on the other hand, tends to be dull, and the results are difficult to trace back to plans and frequently are delayed for months or years. In addition, in a small business, there is no one to oversee the planning function. There is no one to say, "you have not reviewed your goals, objectives, and strategies this week" or "you have not done your professional reading today." No one knows whether the planning is being done properly and in a timely fashion. No one knows, that is, until the business gets in trouble!

The lack of management depth in small firms frequently means that the owner is heavily involved in middle and supervisory management duties as well as top management duties. Because the organization and control functions have to be performed to get through the day, it is easy to let those functions take priority. This is a major mistake! It is like driving a car. You can concentrate on the road, on steering, braking, accelerating, and so on, but unless you know where you want to go, map out a route to get there, and monitor your progress toward the destination, you will never get there! You may enjoy the drive and you may control the car quite well; you may even make progress in that miles are put behind you; but you cannot achieve your destination.

## ORGANIZATION CHARTS

The most famous aspect of management is the **organization chart.** This is a series of boxes connected by lines that spell out how the various management positions in a firm relate to each other and establishes the chain of command. **Chain of command** simply means how the power of the owner is delegated throughout the organization, who should report to whom in the organization, and who supervises and evaluates whom in the firm. You should establish an organization chart for your business before it is started, evaluate the chart periodically, and change it when necessary. Exhibit 16-3 is an example of an organization chart. The chart shows only job titles, but in a real situation, names of managers holding those positions should be shown as well. The chart is not intended as a recommendation, simply an illustration. There is no such

**EXHIBIT 16-3** *Sample Organization Chart*

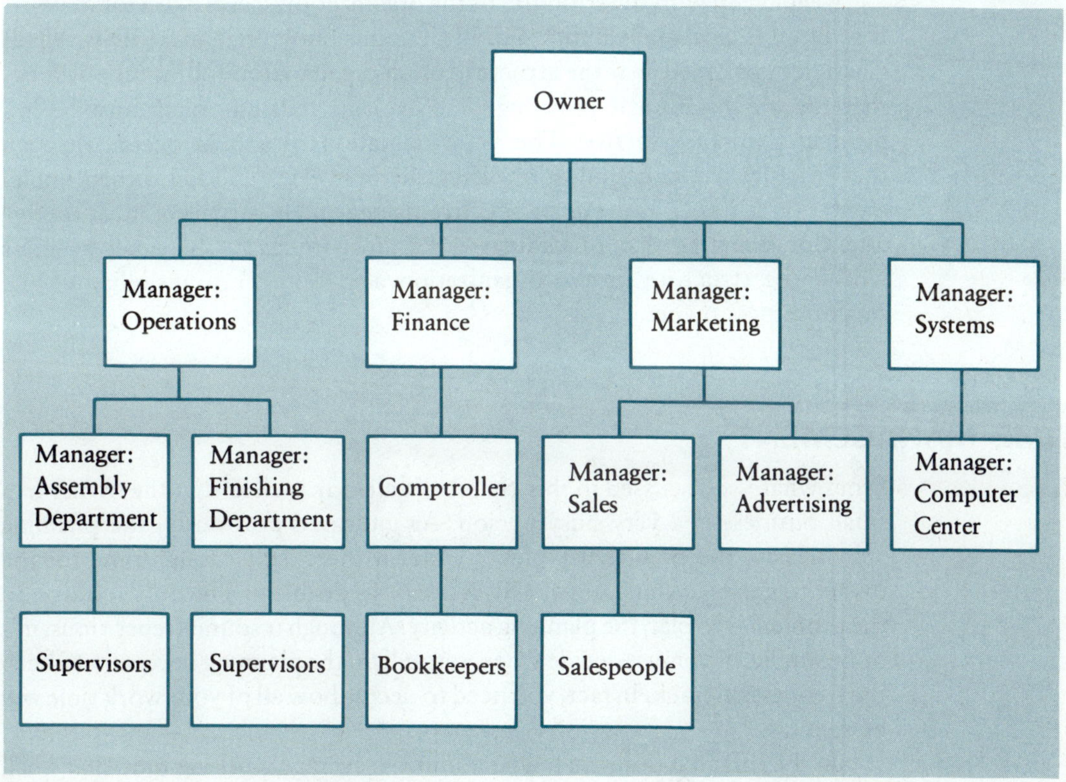

thing as a standard organization chart. What is appropriate for any business is a function of the owners and managers of that business and the environment in which it competes.

Every business must have an organization chart because if an official chain of command is not established, then an unofficial chain will develop. If people do not have a clear-cut idea of what they are responsible for, who they report to, and how they fit into the organization, then inefficiency will develop, jobs will be duplicated, and morale will suffer, as will the business itself. Just as everyone in the organization should know and understand the goals, objectives, and strategies of the firm, everyone should know and understand the organization chart.

The organization chart is simply a visual representation of the organizational structure of the business. In addition, a written job description should be developed for each position so that every manager understands the requirements of every position in the company. Just as the organization chart should change as the business changes, so should the job descriptions. This will permit the structure of the business to conform to the environment in which it operates.

Keeping up with the structure of the organization seems like a lot of work. It is! But it is also vitally important. In a famous book on management, Alfred Chandler explained that the structure of an organization follows the strategy that the organization is pursuing.[2] He explains that any plan must be implemented to be effective. The implementation of a plan occurs through the structure of the organization. Even the best plans will fail if their implementation is poor. To have an effective management, structure must receive attention equal to that of strategy. Like most things in the small business world, the structure of the organization also is the responsibility of the small business owner.

## TIME MANAGEMENT

From what we discussed in this chapter, it already is clear that the owner of a small business is a very busy person. As indicated previously, the planning activities are the ones that typically suffer if there isn't enough time for the owner to get everything done. This is a serious problem. The only solution to the problem is to plan the planning activity. Although it sounds repetitious, it is quite simple. You must decide when you will do the planning necessary to keep the business on track. In fact, you need to decide how all of your work time will be spent.

In the Introduction, we talked about the average working time that small business owners spend and indicated that a work week of 60 to 70 hours is not unusual. Usual or not, a work week that long presents problems. Everyone gets tired. When you are tired, your thinking and decision-making power are affected. Therefore, excessive working hours may get things done, but get them done poorly. The obvious solution is to reduce working hours to something closer to a normal work week and still get everything done. But how can that be accomplished? Consider what it is that consumes an owner's time.

Numerous surveys have been conducted to analyze how managers, especially CEOs, spend their time. All of the research indicates that most time is spent in oral communication. Everyone knows how ineffective meetings can be, but that doesn't seem to deter their use. The telephone also is a major time waster. How can you control this problem? The simple fact is that you must cut off discussion: limit conversations and discussions with employees, suppliers, customers, and other interested parties either individually on the telephone or in meetings. All individual and telephone discussions should be prefaced with a statement that "time only permits 10 minutes today." Then stick to the limit! When the time you have allocated expires, whether a resolution is achieved or not, you must end the conversation with a statement that time is now up! If further discussion is required, continue it another day. The secret is to enforce the time limit! Very few people will be offended by that so long as you tell them the time limit up front and so long as you are consistent in enforcing the limit. People will be offended if you are not evenhanded and consistent in limiting your time.

Meetings are a special problem. Not only do they waste owner time, they waste time for everyone in the meeting. A meeting with ten management people that lasts two hours has just used twenty hours of management time: half of a manager's work week! Because the managers tend to be the highest paid employees in a business, that twenty hours could be exceptionally expensive. Furthermore, the alternative uses to which that time could have been devoted may far outweigh the results of the meeting.

The first step is to reduce the number of meetings to the absolute minimum. Not all meetings can be eliminated, but those that can be, should be. Before it starts, a time limit for the meeting should be established as well as an agenda for the discussion. If it is important enough to have a meeting, then it is important enough to do it right! A chairperson for the meeting should be established in advance, either on a permanent or rotating basis. That individual should take responsibility for planning, organizing, and controlling the upcoming meeting. The subjects to be discussed at the meeting should be planned in advance and distributed in the form of an agenda. People expected to present information or arguments should be notified and a time limit for their presentations established in advance. Then the chairperson of the meeting should moderate all discussion by limiting each person to five minutes and by cutting off debate when it is unproductive. As in the case of limiting conversations, this will not cause a problem if everyone understands the rules up front and they are enforced consistently.

Some people have developed "cute" ploys to limiting meetings such as holding them at 4:00 on Friday afternoons, 7:00 on Monday mornings, over lunch, over breakfast or dinner. None of these ploys really work well: they simply result in animosity among the people at the meeting. There is no substitute for a professional approach and a no-nonsense management of the meeting itself.

One final point needs to be made about meetings. It is popular to establish a regular meeting to communicate, update, or inform people of current issues. This is a good idea only if the meetings are infrequent! Daily and weekly meetings largely are a waste of time. People just won't prepare for meetings when they occur that frequently.

Planning your work day is simply a matter of continuously scheduling your activities. A calendar with sufficient space to record activity reminders for a month at a time is a valuable tool as is a daily calendar with sufficient space to detail each day's activities. You should set aside time for planning, reading, and comparing results to objectives each week. Try to make those activities as important as attending meetings! When you are unable to complete the day's requirements — which will happen more frequently than anyone would like — be sure to carry those things that have not been completed to the next day.

Keeping a constant list of what you must accomplish is the key to never forgetting an important task. The first thing you should do each morning is review the activities planned for the day and assign priorities to the tasks. Work on completing them in the order of priority during the day. The last thing you should do each day is review the day's activities, mark off the tasks completed, and prepare a new list for tomorrow adding those things not finished today. Sound cumbersome? It really isn't. With a little practice you will find the process becoming second nature, and time management no longer will be a problem. Just remember, being a manager means managing yourself as well as the company. You cannot expect to be able to manage a company successfully if you cannot manage your own time. All it takes is a little foresight and a commitment to utilize your most important resource wisely. You wouldn't spend your money flippantly, so why spend your time that way? Your time is much more valuable than money!

## OUTSIDE ASSISTANCE

Throughout this chapter, we discussed the problem of the owner of a small firm having to cover a much broader range of activities than a CEO in a large firm and the lack of specialists and assistants to aid and advise. The limited financial resources of a small firm ensure that the problem will not go away. It is a recurring problem that will complicate management until the firm has grown sufficiently to employ the necessary staff. One approach taken by many small business owners to reduce the problem is the use of outside consultants. In previous chapters, we mentioned several sources of outside consulting services that could be used in structuring the start-up plan. We need to mention those sources again here, because they also are available to assist an ongoing business. Free assistance in a wide variety of areas is available from programs of the U.S. Small Business Administration (SBA). Those programs include the Small Business Institute (SBI), the Service Corps of Retired Executives (SCORE), and the Small Business Development Centers (SBDC).

The SBI has a program whereby students in a participating college or university guided by a business professor are assigned to work with a small business for a semester. The students gain college credit for the work, and the business gains fresh insight and assistance. Access to the SBI program can be obtained through the nearest office of the SBA, or you can investigate the business school of a college near you. The SBI program has recorded numerous successes.

SCORE perhaps is the most famous government assistance program for businesses. It has been around for a long time and has a long track record of successes. In essence, the SBA assigns a retired business executive to a small business seeking assistance. Access can be had through the nearest SBA office. The executive volunteers his or her time. Consulting engagements can be short lived or very long lived and are available in a variety of areas.

The SBDC program is one of the newest assistance avenues for small businesses. There are SBDCs established in almost every state. SBDCs are sponsored by the SBA but also receive funding at the state level. Offices are established at universities and many states have branch offices established across the state. Free consulting is available on a wide variety of topics and provided by students who receive assistantships within the SBDC under the supervision of permanent staff members. The SBDC program has established an excellent record. If one is available in your area, we highly recommend your exploration of services available.

All of the assistance programs described in the preceding sections can be reached through the local field office of the SBA. Generally, a telephone call will be sufficient to initiate the contact. If you do not know the location of the local office, a telephone call to the SBA home office in Washington, D.C., will result in that information.

In addition to the assistance programs, consulting can be obtained from individuals and firms on a fee basis. Numerous management consultants practice in the United States. These range from firms of one or two people to gigantic corporations. Many accounting firms also offer management consulting services. The fees these consultants charge vary greatly, from around $50 per hour to as much as $500 per hour. Fees also can be established by the day, the week, or the job. Annual retainer fees are offered by many consulting firms. The number of consultants has been growing in recent years, indicating that more and more businesses are utilizing their services. Small businesses can benefit from management consultants, as well as large companies, but frequently avoid them because of the expense involved. This could be a mistake. A good consultant, hired for the right reasons, can save the firm more money than the fees charged. Sometimes the savings will greatly outweigh the fees.

How do you determine whether a consultant is good? Unlike many other professionals, there are no licensing procedures for management consultants. This also is true for financial planners who are specialists in the consulting field, which means that virtually anyone can set up a consulting business. Consequently, there is a broad range of expertise and experience among practicing consultants. Explore the background and credentials of any person you consider hiring as a consultant to ensure that the person has experience and knowledge useful to your business.

This is true whether the individual is alone in a part-time consulting business or provided by one of the Big 8 accounting firms. Ask for references and check those references. If it is a large firm, ask who will be involved with your business either directly or indirectly and find out about their backgrounds. Remember, whether you are considering a large consulting business or a small one, only one individual or a few individuals will be looking at your business. The expertise of those individuals is the prime consideration. All the high-powered backup in the world won't help if the person in your shop is unable to find the pertinent facts to relay to that backup! Ask for the names of businesses similar to yours with which the consultant has worked, and call those businesses. Check with the Better Business Bureau in your town to see if anyone has registered a complaint about the consultant. Finally, talk to the individual. Does the person try to impress you by using professional jargon or by talking over your head? Does the person seem genuinely interested in your business and in making a contribution to your business? What does the consulting contract look like? Is the person willing to spell out in writing what will be done and when? Do you think you can work with this person? Remember, you will have to manage the consulting engagement just as you must manage the business.

How do you decide when you need a consultant? Consider the kinds of things a consultant can do for you. Exhibit 16-4 is a partial list; in reality, the list is almost endless. The list is provided to stimulate your imagination about useful applications of consultants.

As the exhibit makes clear, consultants can be used to do anything done by managers or other employees in a firm. They are especially useful in planning

**EXHIBIT 16-4** *Areas in Which Consultants Can Provide Assistance or Guidance*

- Start-up plans for new businesses, products, services, or markets.
- Expansion plans for existing businesses.
- Goals, objectives, strategies; short and long term.
- Organizational structure and job descriptions.
- Systems for accounting, record keeping, reporting, control of accounts receivable and payable, budgeting, pricing, cost control, internal control, computerizing, and so on.
- Human resources planning, training, recruiting, evaluating, reporting, supervision, fringe benefits planning and evaluation, pension plans, stock plans, and so on.
- Financial plans, capital budgets, cash flow forecasts and analysis, loan applications, cost analyses, profitability analyses, division or department effectiveness, financial analyses, pro forma statements, tax planning, bids preparation and evaluation, and so on.
- Marketing plans, advertising plans, promotional plans, evaluation of markets, target markets, market trends, customer satisfaction, new markets, products, or services, budgets and media for marketing activities, and so on.
- Production plans, plant layouts, workflow analysis, time and motion studies, distribution and storage analysis, equipment evaluation, automation plans, and so on.
- Training for managers, including the owner, in management, motivation, specialized areas, and so on.
- Risk management planning, evaluation, assessment, and so on.
- Inventory policy, purchasing, turnover evaluation, economic order quantity, control, and so on.

start ups and expansions and in assessing problems, but don't overlook their usefulness in day-to-day management. A long-term relationship with a competent management consultant can be a valuable aid to any small business owner.

## SUMMARY

Management is the process of deciding what tasks are to be done, assigning responsibilities for doing those tasks to someone, and checking to be sure that the tasks have been done satisfactorily. However, the process is not simple in small businesses because of the depth of management. The owner of a small business often is alone at the helm, must perform all the tasks, and accept all the responsibilities personally.

Management consists of planning, organizing, and controlling functions. These functions include the tasks of deciding where the business is going and how to get it there; structuring the people to perform their duties, delegating responsibility, and establishing a system of feedback for evaluation.

Management can be divided into three levels with appropriate responsibilities attached. Top management deals primarily with strategic issues and decisions that have far-reaching effects. This person is responsible for the life or death of the company and so must plan for and make decisions that will ensure its success. Middle management is involved primarily with tactical issues, which means that this level must translate the plans of top management into actions. The lower level of management is supervisory. Here the daily operations are overseen. All levels, functions, and duties of management overlap.

Strategic management consists of the establishment of goals, objectives, and strategies for the firm. The goals of the organization are its long-range goals. They should be specific, written, quantifiable, if possible, and reviewed and evaluated frequently.

Objectives are intermediary benchmarks used to measure progress toward goals. They, too, should be quantifiable. Strategies are plans for achieving the objectives. The most important strategy is that of a distinctive competency; that is, what the company does best and differently from its competitors.

Tactical management is concerned with carrying out the plans of top management. Tactics are specific actions or activities designed to further strategies.

Operations managers directly supervise the people who carry out the work and assure the completion of a task.

An organization chart is used by management to establish the chain of command in an organization. This chart shows the delegation of power to specific individuals and dictates who reports to whom. The assignment of responsibility is important, and job descriptions should be included to avoid later conflicts.

To effectively plan, organize, and control, management at all levels must be cognizant of time constraints. As emphasized earlier, management works long hours, but to be successful those long hours must be effective. Planning your time and staying with the time allocations is a must. Time truly waits for no one nor does your business thrive without constant surveillance.

Many assistance agencies, both for-profit and nonprofit, can help in a variety of ways. Several of those agencies are the SBI, SCORE, SBA, SBDC, or private firms. Exhibit 16-4 summarizes some of the consulting activities available to you from these sources. Don't be hesitant to ask for aid in any of these areas—your foresight will pay handsomely in the future.

## QUESTIONS

1. Define the following terms:
   a. planning
   b. organizing
   c. controlling
   d. organization chart
   e. goal
   f. objectives
   g. strategies
   h. tactics
   i. responsibility
2. What is the purpose of having a Chief Executive Officer and what does he or she do?
3. How is the CEO different from the COO?
4. What is *strategic management*?
5. Do all businesses use strategic management? Explain why or why not.
6. How do goals and objectives differ?
7. Why should goals change?
8. What is *tactical management*?
9. What is *operational management*?
10. Why is time management important?
11. What can consultants do for a business?

## PROJECTS

1. In a role play, have a member of the class act as a consultant to two or three others. Have that consultant discuss the goals, objectives, strategies, and tactics of the new venture being considered and have the consultant draw up an organization chart.
2. Investigate whether there are assistance agencies in your area and the types of assistance they can give.

# CASE

Eileen Johnson was hired as the secretary for the accounting department at ABC Associates. ABC Associates was a consulting and financial planning firm for area businesses. Johnson was hired by the manager as his secretary and the office secretary. There were five consultants in the department who would need different types of prospecti typed from time to time and various letters. Johnson was extremely efficient and everyone in the firm thought very highly of her skill and resourcefulness.

However, problems began to arise as the year continued. Letters went untyped and work was parceled out to the secretarial pool, whose members did not know the proper format or the deadlines. When the consultants would complain to Johnson that the work was not done in a timely fashion or properly, her response would be that she was sorry. However, as the manager's secretary, her time was his. She was glad to help the others when time permitted, as it had in the beginning, but now the other secretaries had to share the load. After all, it was not her job to do all the work.

Several of the consultants approached the manager about the attitude of the departmental secretary. He would only nod his head and continue on his way. Now, a new development caused more worry to the consultants: Ms. Johnson would come in very early, before the office opened, to get her day started because she was an early riser and liked to be at work early. The office was open from 9 to 5. However, because she had arrived at 7:30 and had taken no lunch, Johnson would leave at 3:30 or 4:00 when the manager was making his own calls on clients and not in the office. This meant that the consultants who were expecting late clients or needed paperwork prepared at a later time in the day would have to do it themselves or not get it done on time.

Because Johnson was such a personable woman, most of the consultants truly liked her, but their jobs were becoming impossible. Several of those close to her made suggestions as to what the problem might be. She claimed that she had no problem. She was hired as the manager's secretary and, so long as he had no complaints, everything was okay. If she was efficient enough to get her work done early, then she deserved the time off. What could be done?

### Questions

1. What is the real problem in this case and how could it easily be fixed?
2. What part does management play in the dilemma faced by the other consultants?
3. Is it a disservice for the manager to allow the secretary to labor under false impressions?
4. If you were the manager in this situation, how would you handle it? A consultant? A secretary?

# CHAPTER 17

# Human Resource Management

**LEARNING OBJECTIVES**

After completing this chapter, you should be able to

- Explain the importance of human resource management.
- Explain how to recruit the best people for the job.
- Specify the advantages and disadvantages of promoting from within.
- Evaluate the advantages and disadvantages of finding individuals outside the firm.
- Conduct an effective interview.
- Explain the value of on-the-job training programs.
- Distinguish between democratic and autocratic supervision and know where you stand in these typologies.
- Specify the why and wherefores of compensation policies.
- Explain how fringe benefits can be made to work for the employer as well as the employee.
- Understand the importance of good employee relations and how this relationship reflects upon the success of the company.
- Demonstrate the importance of performance evaluations of employees and how to go about them.
- Understand the legal restrictions involved with recruiting and promoting personnel.

The employer of people exercises power over those people. Benjamin Disraeli said, "all power is a trust—that we are accountable for its exercise." In Disraeli's words, with power comes a public trust and duty. It is well to heed his words, because people are the greatest asset of any business and the vehicle through which that business achieves success. Effective management of this asset is difficult, whether a business has 5 people or 50,000 people, but the kinds of problems that occur are different in small businesses.

The owner of a small firm frequently is the personnel officer as well and personally must oversee all aspects of human resource management. In addition, the impact of personnel problems is greater in a small business. If a large firm loses a skilled worker or a senior manager, little damage may occur, because other employees can step in. If a small firm loses even one employee, the business can suffer for weeks or months, because no one else in the firm can take over the duties without other duties suffering. Losing one manager in a small firm could mean that half the management staff is lost!

On the other hand, a small business has some advantages over large firms in personnel management. The employees of a small firm tend to feel a closer relationship to other employees and to the business, simply because of the scale of the operation. Many of the problems that occur in a large operation are a result of the employees feeling unimportant, like tiny cogs in a big wheel. In a small firm, such feelings are easily eliminated, and employees have no difficulty seeing the effect of their labor on the well-being of the business. Nevertheless, the owner of a small firm must be cognizant of the needs of the employees to take advantage of the potential value of the scale of operations. In this chapter, we discuss the management of people in all of its aspects from recruiting through training, to supervision, to compensation, to employee relations.

## RECRUITING

**Recruiting** is the process of locating and hiring people for positions within a firm. There are two places to look for people: inside the firm and outside the firm. We address each of these sources in turn, but first we need to discuss job specifications. You cannot recruit a person for a job unless you have a firm idea of what is required to perform that job.

### Job Descriptions

Most **job specifications** used in recruiting list the educational and work experience desired in a potential employee. How are such things determined? In some jobs, special training is required, which makes educational specifications easier. Most of the time, however, education is not that closely linked to job performance. Some large firms make it a habit to recruit MBAs for management positions and to require bachelors degrees for all other positions except unskilled labor. The theory is that, although there may be little of direct benefit to the firm from the education, the fact that the individual completed the education is valuable as a screening device. Consider, finding and hiring a person is difficult and time consuming. The situation is infinitely worse if you hire an individual who cannot do the job or who leaves shortly after having been hired. Then you have to start the hiring process over and live with the consequences of having had an incompetent person in the job. Therefore, any steps that will more effectively screen potential employees are worthwhile. Educational requirements frequently are used to fill that role.

Experience requirements largely serve the same purpose; that is, increasing the probability that an employee will be able to competently perform a job. The number of years of experience required is totally subjective. The theory is that the longer the experience, the greater is the level of knowledge in the field and the greater is the probability that the individual will be competent. Of course, it is entirely possible, and frequently happens, that neither education nor experience have anything to do with potential job performance. Nevertheless, education and experience requirements are used almost universally in job specifications. One frequently hears recent college graduates lamenting the experience requirements cited on job announcements. "How do they expect me to get experience if no one will hire me without experience?" they complain. Good point, and one you should keep in mind. Hiring a new graduate without experience may be a bit more risky than hiring someone older and with more experience, but giving a chance to a new grad could result in an exceptionally loyal, dedicated employee. Also, inexperienced people tend to be cheaper than old hands, at least, initially.

We consider the best approach to writing a job description is simply to use the internal job description talked about in the last chapter. If you recall, we indicated that part of the organizational structure planning was the development of organization charts and the writing of specifications for every position in the firm. If you have done this, then finding an employee is greatly simplified because you will have a firm understanding of what the individual must be able to do. If you are filling a vacancy, then the first step should be a review of the position description. It is easier to make changes in positions when they are vacant. Consequently, when replacing an employee, the first step should be to determine what the new job should look like. Once the written description is firmly established, an announcement of the position can be developed by simply summarizing the duties and requirements of the job. The only addition required in the announcement generally is working hours or arrangements and a salary range: minimum and maximum salaries, bonus or commission levels, overtime hours expected, or other indications of compensation. If you wish to add educational and experience requirements to the job announcement, we recommend that the wording indicate desired levels rather than required levels, so as not to unduly restrict potential applicants for the job. With the completed job announcement in hand, you are ready to begin searching for a person to fill the position.

There is just one more problem. The Equal Employment Opportunity laws make it illegal to discriminate against job applicants based on age, sex, color, race, national origin, religion, and so forth. If you are accused of discrimination, *you* must prove your innocence! Furthermore, you aren't even supposed to ask the kinds of questions that lead to discriminatory practices. For example, you can't ask about religion. But if you are accused of discrimination based on religion, it would be helpful to know whether any of the people you have hired held religious beliefs in common with the accusing party. You can't know that. So what do you do? In the first place, professional assistance may be required in planning the personnel activities and record keeping. In the second place, you should keep a record of why you hired the person you hired, and why you didn't hire other applicants. In other words, be able to prove that the person you hired met the job qualifications better than any of the other applicants. This generally means keeping notes based on interviews, reference checks, and so on, as well as specific job qualifications for each position.

## Promoting from Within

When we think about recruiting, we seldom think about looking inside the firm, but this really is the first place we should look. If there are people inside the firm who can do a job, then we should consider those people for the job. **Promoting from within** can be valuable because it encourages the other employees in the firm by demonstrating advancement possibilities. It also can be valuable because present employees have a track record; you have a better idea of how well they might work out in new positions. Hiring outsiders is always risky, because you can never be sure how capable they are until you have seen them work. Also, hiring from within can speed up the replacement process and shorten the training period. You don't have to waste time by searching for applicants and the insiders already have an understanding of the business and perhaps the job itself. There also are potential problems.

Hiring from within generally means that a second vacancy is created: the job that the person promoted originally held. Sometimes, people are not considered for promotion because their employers do not wish to search for their replacements or because they were doing exceptionally well in their present positions. An oversight like this is not good for morale in general. In a small firm everyone will know about it and be affected by it. If you intend to have a policy of promoting from within, it has to be evenhanded and you must accept the necessity of filling another position vacated by the promotion.

Hiring from inside will work only if the person selected to do a job is truly competent. Other employees will know how capable a person is and will feel betrayed if a job is given to an individual not competent to perform it. This means that seniority within the firm cannot be used as the basis for promotion. Problems also can develop if several people are capable of performing a job or believe that they are capable. The individuals not selected for a job may feel animosity toward the one promoted. Friends and supporters of those not selected can feel the same way. Consequently, the effectiveness of an insider can be damaged before that person starts the new job. Both of these possibilities can be alleviated to a large degree if the process of filling a position from within is formalized. Everyone should know about the job and its requirements and have the opportunity to be considered for it. Maximum input to the selection decision should be obtained from managerial people in the firm and those employees who will be directly affected by the new job. A list of potentially qualified people should be prepared, and those individuals should be interviewed. Selection of the one to be promoted should be made carefully. Then, everyone should know who was chosen for the job and why.

We must mention one major risk associated with promoting from within. Just because a person has done a good job in one position does not guarantee that he or she will do a good job in a more responsible position. This is called the **Peter Principle** and easiest to understand using a military example. In the old days in the military, an officer who had been a good captain was promoted to major. The promotion was not based on the ability to perform the duties of a major, but on past performance as a captain. The really damaging part of the Peter principle is what happens next. Now the person who does a poor job as a major is not promoted further, but that major is not demoted either! The person stays an incompetent major when he or she would be effective as a captain. This process also has been termed **promoted to the level of incompetence.** Fortunately, the military is more enlightened these days and seldom experiences such problems, but many businesses continue to practice a similar promotional policy. The difference in businesses is that an individual who is doing a poor job in a new position generally leaves the firm, voluntarily or otherwise, thereby leaving two positions to fill: the old position the person held and the new position as well. The moral is this: be careful when you promote from within because if you choose a good employee for a job that person cannot do, you will lose a valuable employee and gain an incompetent one at the same time. This is another reason why seniority with the firm should not be used as the sole criterion for promotion. Maximum emphasis should be placed on your evaluation of an employee's ability to do the job in question.

## Outside Sources

How do you go about finding an individual outside of the firm to fill a position? There are several ways to make contact with such people. The best known probably is through an employment agency. There are two types of employment agencies: private and public. **Public employment offices** are operated by the state government and are affiliated with the United States Employment Service. Branch offices are located in most of the larger cities in the nation. The services of the public offices are free. They maintain lists of people and summary data about their abilities and will furnish names of people with the particular job skills you specify. They also will keep an announcement of your position on file and compare it to new people as they come into the office. They will actively recruit for you in some situations. Public employment offices can be an excellent source of employees, but generally are more valuable in finding entry level or lower level employees and less valuable in finding senior level or more responsible employees. Nevertheless, you should always check with the local employment office whenever you have a vacancy. In fact, registering a job vacancy with the employment office is required in some states.

**Private employment agencies** perform the same kind of services as public agencies, but charge a fee. They will actively recruit for you based on the skills or experience you describe and prescreen applicants. The fees charged can be quite high, frequently a percentage of the starting salary of any person they find for you. These fees can be paid by the employee or by the employer. As you might expect, success generally is improved when you agree to pay the fees. Many applicants specify to the agency that they are interested only in seeking "fee-paid" jobs. Many employment agencies specialize in certain types of jobs and advertise in publications that appeal to selected groups of people. Such agencies are especially good at finding people who are already employed but unhappy with their employment or looking for a more responsible position because they tend to have a national scope. These firms, frequently called **headhunters,** will solicit applicants on a national basis. Because of their expense and the expense associated with bringing in an applicant from out of state for an interview, such agencies are generally valuable for senior level positions or highly skilled positions for which it is difficult to find qualified applicants.

If you are willing to recruit directly, excellent sources of employees are schools, colleges, and universities. Many institutions have placement offices that keep on file resumes of recent and potential graduates and arrange interviews between students and employers. Even if no placement office exists, contact with students interested in jobs is simplified and guidance counselors, teachers, and staff can be approached about prospective applicants. Schools also can be valuable sources of part-time or temporary employees as well as full-time employees. Many schools have cooperative education or internship programs, whereby students can obtain credit for a semester of work in a business and businesses can obtain low-cost temporary help and an opportunity to evaluate potential employees before they are actually hired. We highly recommend the use of coop programs both to students and to businesses.

The most obvious way to find job applicants is to advertise positions in the local newspaper. To that should be added advertisements in trade journals and publications that will appeal to the kind of people you are interested in hiring. This is a highly popular recruiting tool, but it is very time consuming. Such advertisements frequently result in large numbers of applicants. Someone must wade through the applications to select those who will be interviewed. The applications frequently are so sketchy that you must have the applicants fill out more complete forms or be interviewed to determine their relative skills and value. Consequently, if the owner of a small business lacks help in processing applications and time available to handle them personally, this form of recruiting should not be used.

Finally, applicants can be obtained for job positions by asking the present employees for recommendations. This simple process, frequently overlooked, can be highly successful. In addition, if files are kept on former employees and job applicants, then you may be able to fill a position from that source. All applications for employment should be kept, with those you think might be of value filed separately. Scanning those files could lead to a quick solution to a vacancy. Also, former employees who were valuable may be enticed to return, if not on a permanent basis, then on a temporary or part-time basis to take the pressure off finding a new employee. Temporary work may be especially attractive to retired employees.

Temporary help agencies, such as Kelly Services and Manpower, can provide people on a part-time or full-time temporary basis. Although such firms generally have a contract with a stiff penalty for hiring away temporary workers, the use of temporary help could smooth the process of looking for a new employee. Temporary employees generally are considered for covering vacation times of regular employees or short-term projects, but they can be valuable in other ways, too. If you can take more time for the search, then the probability of finding the right employee is increased. Temporary workers can give you that time.

## Evaluation of Applicants

Regardless of the source of applicants for your job, you will have to evaluate the people and choose the person you consider to be best for the job. Generally, the evaluation will be based on written documents and interviews.

Most employers require an **application form** to be completed. However, discrimination laws have made application forms dangerous. For example, Exhibit 17-1 displays the contents of an employment application actually in use by a small business five years ago. The form is filled with questions that are potentially dangerous to the employer. The rules make it clear that no questions may be asked unless **bona fide occupational qualifications requirements.** The use of standard forms with a standard group of questions makes it easy to violate that principle.

The solution to the problem is simply not to use a standardized application form. This would be extremely difficult for a large firm but presents little problem for a small business that does not hire very many people, very often. Using the job description talked about in the last section, draw up a series of questions that you will want answered by any applicants, based specifically on the job description. This not only will make the application form more valuable, it will be safer! Additional information about the applicant will be developed in the interview. That data, discussed in the following sections, should be added to the application form. Furthermore, you can always ask applicants to prepare a **resume.** This way, the applicant decides what information to give you, although you must still be careful not to allow any potentially illegal bias, such as age, sex, or dependents, to affect the decision.

Many texts criticize the use of resumes because they will not contain information applicable to a particular job. This is true; however, what the applicant chooses to include on a resume may well provide insight to the person's abilities in general.

The owner of a small business frequently is involved in all interviews. Other managers also may be involved or used to screen an initial group of applicants and narrow the field to a small number before involving the owner. In any case, every person who will be interviewing prospective employees should develop an outline to guide the interview. Remember, the ultimate purpose of the interview is the selection of an individual from a group of people who will be valuable to your firm. How can you fairly evaluate the applicants if you ask each of them different questions? Clearly, no two interviews will be exactly alike because the applicants' responses to questions will affect the flow of the discussion. Nevertheless, all interviews should cover the same basics and follow the same general pattern to maximize comparability between applicants.

An interview guide sheet should be developed that contains additional data about the applicant and basic questions to guide the interviewer. Here you must exercise extreme caution! Just as the questions asked on an application form can violate discrimination laws, so, too, can oral questions. You must not ask questions that are not related to the job under consideration. You also must be careful not to phrase questions or make remarks that could be considered discriminatory. For example, questions about previous job duties or responsibilities might be acceptable, but questions about the employment

**EXHIBIT 17-1** *Sample Application Form*

Firm Name: ______________________ Date: __________
Position Desired: ______________________
Salary Desired: ______________________

Personal Information:
Name: ______________ *Age: ______ *Sex: ______
Address: ______________ SSN: ______________
______________ Phone: ______________
*Marital Status: ______ *Dependents: ______ *Height: ______ *Wt.: ______
*Hobbies/Interests: ______________________

Educational Information:
List all schools attended, starting with the most recent.

| School Name/Address | Dates Attended | Degree Earned |
|---|---|---|
| | | |
| | | |
| | | |
| | | |

Work Experience:
List all jobs held, starting with the most recent.

| Employer Name/Address | Employed Dates | Duties |
|---|---|---|
| | | |
| | | |
| | | |
| | | |
| | | |
| | | |

References:
List three people whoe are knowledgeable about your abilities:

| Name/Address | Occupation | Phone |
|---|---|---|
| | | |
| | | |
| | | |

List below any information which you think may be important to your application.

* These are clearly illegal unless you can establish a bona fide reason for them related to the job.

status and record of a spouse are not! Nor should you use terms or job titles that are discriminatory. Busboy and girl friday are out, as are references to the girls in the office or the boys in the mail room. This is not really bad, because cleaning up words, references, and vocabulary will have an impact on the way you and those around you think about such things at the same time. One question you could ask during the interview is, Why did you leave your last job?

Notes concerning the applicant's answers to questions, appearance, questions asked, and so forth should be made either during the interview or immediately following it. Some people prefer to concentrate on the applicant during the interview and make notes as soon as it is over but before the information can be forgotten. Others prefer to tape record interviews. This last approach is seldom of real value from a practical perspective because no one ever gets an opportunity to listen to the tapes! The questions you intend to ask generally should be designed to put the applicant at ease initially, evaluate the quality of the applicant's background, and make a judgement as to how well the applicant will fit into the business and the position. Be sure to keep the entire interview short!

To start off the interview, many employers like to explain a few aspects of the company, its history, details of the job, policies of the firm concerning employment, promotion, fringe benefits, and so on. This "small talk" sets the applicant at ease, consequently, it should be very short: no longer than two or three minutes. Following the lead in, general questions can be asked as just discussed. Again, this section of the interview should be extremely short! Finally, questions of a more specific nature can be asked. These questions should deal with knowledge about the field, industry, or job; ability to relate to other people; take and follow instructions; or other information you deem pertinent to the position. Be sure that the questions are pertinent! The interview should close with the applicant being offered an opportunity to ask questions. During this part of the interview, you should pay very close attention to the applicant, because the kinds of questions asked can tell you as much about the person and his or her concerns as the answers to your own questions.

The notes from the interview should not only deal with the answers to questions, but also record your impressions of the applicant: the individual's dress, manner, carriage, posture, and so on. You should also note the way in which the applicant answered your questions: hesitantly, confidently, shyly, boldly. Did the responses indicate that the applicant had thought about the questions in advance? Did the applicant express himself or herself well? Did the applicant seem knowledgable about the work required? Do you believe that the applicant will be able to do the work? Will the applicant be able to fit into the company and get along well with other workers? What was your overall opinion of the applicant?

Armed with the information gathered from the application and the interview, you still are not ready to make a selection. You should discuss your findings with others who interviewed the applicants and form a consensus opinion about each. You should then narrow the field by eliminating those applicants who clearly are not qualified. Be sure to keep notes explaining why these people were eliminated from consideration. The references and former employers of the remaining applicants should be called or written. Education should be verified by transcripts directly from the schools. Police checks and credit checks may be appropriate, but be sure that the applicant knows you intend to make such checks and has given permission to make them. Many people fail to follow up on these simple checks because it's too much trouble. That is a mistake! Just a few telephone calls can help you make a more informed selection.

Former employers may be a problem. As will be discussed in Chapter 25, "Small Business Law," most employers are reluctant to reveal anything more than dates of employment. There is a good reason for this, and we will recommend in Chapter 25 that you follow the same procedure. Ours has become a **litigious** society, people are suing people right and left! Information given a prospective employer is potentially dangerous to the company giving that information. Consequently, you can expect little to come of calls to employers. Of course, you should still verify employment and dates, but to obtain further information by phone or letter will probably be fruitless.

You can and probably should ask those individuals who are in the final group of consideration to provide letters of recommendation from previous employers and supervisors. If the individual gives permission, then the legal aspects are safer. Be aware that no one will ask for a reference from an individual whom they expect to write a poor one! Nevertheless, the letters will at least demonstrate that someone at the previous employer thought highly of the applicant. Be sure to call the letter writers to ensure that they did indeed write the letter and did say what the letter contains.

Does all of this sound like a lot of work? It is! But the people you hire are the most important aspect of your business. They will make the difference between success and failure. That means that you should do it right!

## IMMIGRATION REFORM AND CONTROL ACT

There has been a change in legislation that has far-reaching implications for small business employers. The **Immigration Reform and Control Act of 1986** makes every employer, including small businesses, responsible for verifying that all people hired are either U.S. citizens or aliens legally authorized to work in this country. To comply with this law, you must complete a report on every person you hire within three days of employment. This report is a one-page document, called an **I-9 Form,** available from the Immigration and Naturalization Service (INS) offices around the country. The form also can be obtained from the U.S. Printing Office in Washington, D.C. The form has a section for the employee to fill out that indicates his or her citizenship status. You as the employer are required to examine documents or identification provided by the employee to see if they appear to be genuine. Then, you complete the bottom of the form, sign it, and keep it on file in case the INS or the Labor Department ever asks for it or comes by for an inspection. If they do decide to inspect you, they are required to give you three days advance notice. Nevertheless, it is wise to comply with the law even though you may never be called on to prove that you have.

The act also makes it illegal to discriminate against an applicant because of citizenship status or national origin. In this regard, it is one more aspect of potential discrimination that you must watch. Unlike the other aspects, this law will provide information for its own enforcement because you must keep the forms on file. Be sure to keep records on applicants whom you did not hire so that you can demonstrate that citizenship status had nothing to do with the hiring decision.

## TRAINING

Virtually all employees will require some kind of training after they are hired. In addition, most employees will require additional training as the business grows and changes to permit them to adapt to those changes. Training is as important as recruiting to a business. The most competent, capable employees in the world cannot be expected to perform a job they don't know how to do. All new employees should be given an orientation program, regardless of training planned. The orientation should involve explaining the business and its operations as well as personnel, compensation, and fringe benefit policies. Any working, safety, or production rules also should be carefully explained. Finally, the new employee should be given a tour of the operation and introduced to coworkers and managers. Then the training program can begin.

In small businesses, training generally is conducted in the form of on-the-job training (OJT), because of the expense involved in outside training. OJT can be formalized and a structured program developed to expose a worker to all aspects of a job. OJT can be completely informal in that another worker is assigned to help a new worker when necessary. Most frequently, OJT follows a middle path in which a new employee is assigned to observe other workers for a time, then is observed by others for a time. In manufacturing enterprises that use assembly line production, a new employee can disrupt the work flow. Consequently, training generally takes place on dummy equipment or at idle or off times to achieve a minimal level of competency before injecting the new person into the assembly line.

There are advantages to OJT. A major advantage is the opportunity for a new employee to develop familiarity with the people, the business, the customers, suppliers, the operation, and layout at the same time that job training takes place. Many people think that OJT is less expensive. This is not necessarily the case! The major expense associated with OJT is lost productivity on the part of workers involved in training a new employee. The cost of that loss can be high!

One word of caution is important concerning OJT. There are disadvantages. One of the foremost of these is the dilution effect of job turnover on training. For example, assume that a new microcomputer system is acquired and the vendor comes in to train the clerk who will be operating the system. Six months later, that clerk gives notice, and you have a new person trained by the old clerk before he or she can leave. The training cannot be as sound as the training the first clerk received because the clerk's level of understanding of the system cannot be as great as the understanding of the system trainers. Now, assume that six more months have passed, the second clerk decides to leave, and the process is repeated: a third clerk is trained by the second clerk. The third clerk's understanding of the system is even less than the second clerk's, which was less than the first clerk's. The knowledge is diluted with each turnover in the position.

Another disadvantage associated with OJT is that it can never advance employees beyond the levels of understanding or ability possessed by the employees doing the training. This means that, to introduce a new practice or work technique, you must introduce another training technique.

Training can take place inside or outside the workplace. It can be used for new employees or continuing employees, managers, or selected groups of people. You can bring in consultants or trainers to conduct seminars, short programs, in-depth programs, or demonstrations. These can be conducted during or after working hours. These same training opportunities can be offered outside the workplace if desired. Training can take place outside the workplace in the form of scheduled seminars, programs, short courses, or in-depth courses offered by schools, colleges, universities, trade associations, or consulting or training companies. The training can be related directly to a job, oriented toward developing superior working habits, and related to a job indirectly or not at all. Even programs unrelated to job performance can have an impact on that performance by increasing employee satisfaction and morale or by preparing employees for more responsible jobs.

Many companies have programs in which they pay the tuition and fees of employees who continue their education at local colleges and universities. Some firms even permit flexible working hours so that employees can take courses during the day instead of being limited to night courses. Other firms pay a portion of the tuition and fees for such students. Although such education frequently is not directly related to job performance, companies justify it by expecting employees to become better prepared for more responsible positions within the firm or to learn more logical, analytical, and decision-making skills. In fact, some employers simply use it to single out employees who are self-motivated, ambitious, and willing to work for advancement. Completing a college degree or a master's degree in night school while holding down a full-time job is a noteworthy achievement. It could be well worth the investment in education to single out employees who have the ability required for that accomplishment.

Training is well understood in large firms, where it frequently is formalized and continuous. Small firms all too often overlook its value, overestimate its cost, or simply fail to think about it at all. In a dynamic society, such as ours, training can be the key to translating competent, capable people into competent, capable employees and maintaining them as such.

## SUPERVISION

Perhaps you have had other courses in which supervision philosophies were discussed. A great deal has been written on the subject. Basically, the issues revolve around the degree of participation permitted to employees in the management process. At one end of the spectrum is the organization in which the owner makes all decisions individually and independently. That owner has a totally **autocratic** style. At the other end of the spectrum is the owner who delegates the maximum number of decisions to the lowest levels possible within the organization and solicits maximum input from the maximum number of people in the organization on those decisions that cannot be delegated. That owner has a totally **democratic** style. Of course, few managers actually fall at either end of the spectrum; rather, they are somewhere between the extremes. Like most aspects of business, there are pros and cons for both ends of the spectrum.

Autocratic managers typically can react faster to changes, problems, or opportunities in the environment but must expend great energies on obtaining intelligence about what is going on or structure the firm to provide maximum input. Most small businesses start out with an autocratic management simply because there are few managers and employees, and the owner must make all decisions personally. Democratic managers generally have higher employee morale because the people feel closer to the firm and more able to influence its development. Reaction time may be slowed, but the quality of decisions can be increased and the effectiveness of implementation of decisions is much greater.

People naturally work harder if they understand why they are doing something or if they can see the direct benefit of their labor. Larger firms typically develop a more democratic style simply because the span of control is such that one individual cannot keep up with everything going on in the business. There is a limit to the number of people or activities that any one person can oversee. When that point is passed, others must be brought into the process or the business suffers.

There is no best style of management. Businesses and their competitive environments vary so greatly and the quality and ability of managers vary so greatly that one approach cannot satisfy every situation. Nevertheless, in general, we can say that the more employees and managers a business has and the more complex are its operations, the more democratic its management should be. Many small business owners have difficulty with this transition. The stories about entrepreneurs who are forced out of their companies after the business has been successfully established and has grown, frequently overlook the problems developing because of the entrepreneur's inability to share management control with others. If a business intends to grow and become a major force in its industry, its management also must grow.

A factor complicating management is that different people prefer different levels of supervision. This means that some of your employees will work better in an atmosphere of freedom and will prefer maximum autonomy; others will prefer close supervision and little autonomy. To minimize the impact of personnel differences on the firm's effectiveness, you should be aware of the management style you have developed for the firm and discuss it with applicants during the interview process to determine whether they can accept that style. You also should make plans for the change in the management style by training people to accept higher levels of responsibility, and then establishing those levels as the business and the talents of its people grow.

The vehicle for establishing the management and supervision styles of your business is the organization chart and job descriptions. Everyone in the business should understand the chart and his or her place in it. Your plans for changing the structure also should be well established and well understood. In this fashion, employee supervision will be more effective.

## COMPENSATION

Employee compensation consists of two forms: direct and indirect. **Direct compensation** includes salary or wages, bonuses, commissions, and fees. Salary is a base pay rate that is not geared to hours worked. Wages generally are hourly based pay rates. The difference is that hourly employees are subject to minimum wage and overtime pay rules whereas salaried employees generally are exempt from those rules. Federal labor laws require all employees paid hourly to receive pay premiums for work beyond forty hours per week. The requirement, in general, is for a premium of one-half the pay rate; hence, the term **time and a half.** Wages also can be based on production. In a **piece-rate** shop, employees are paid a set amount for each item they complete. Such wages are still subject to minimum wage and overtime requirements; consequently, the record keeping system must permit wages to be calculated on an hourly basis as well as by production to ensure compliance with payroll regulations. Wages also can be based on a combination of hours and production. In manufacturing, production standards frequently are established. When the amount of output exceeds the production standard, employees receive a higher wage rate or an additional wage based on the number of units produced above the standard.

Other types of income include the bonuses, fees, and commissions. Bonuses generally are cash or property awards granted because the business has achieved a certain level of success or passed some benchmark. Bonuses are intended to reward employees for their role in making a business successful. Profit-sharing plans usually use a bonus based on the amount of profit the business produces. Other types of bonuses may be paid simply to enhance employee morale. Christmas bonuses generally are of this type and frequently consist of a gift of food in addition to, or in lieu of, a cash bonus. Fees can be paid for all kinds of activities. For example, a fee can be paid for each sales prospect developed by employees who are not employed as salespersons. Commissions generally are linked to sales and provide a vehicle for paying people based on the amount of business they create. Commissions can have steps so that percentage rates increase as the volume sold increases. Salaries and commissions can be linked so that a base rate is paid plus a commission for all sales or for all sales produced over a specified level. As you can see, the variety of calculation bases for direct compensation is almost unlimited. Of course, we must make one comment here; compensation from all sources must be based on work and must not be discriminatory. The rule is equal work for equal pay, despite the historic tendency to pay women less than men. Not only is this practice dangerous from a legal perspective, it is dumb from an employment perspective. Half the potential employees are women. If you discriminate against them, you will be denying yourself access to an extremely valuable pool of prospective people.

**Indirect compensation** consists of fringe benefits. Many small businesses fail to adequately explain fringe benefits offered to employees even though such benefits constitute a highly significant proportion of overall compensation. Fringe benefits consist of a variety of items like those listed in Exhibit 17-2. As you can see from the list, the variety of indirect compensation is limited only by imagination, as is the case with direct compensation.

**EXHIBIT 17-2** *Employee Fringe Benefits*

- Pay for vacations and holidays.
- Life and health insurance plans.
- Pension plans.
- Plans that result in financial incentives.
- Dental insurance plans.
- Education support for employees.
- Education plans for the children of employees.
- Stock option plans.
- Use of automobiles or reduced lease costs for automobiles.
- Use of vacation homes or facilities.
- Trips, vacations, or travel expenses.
- Housing or rental support.
- Moving expenses and home sales assistance.
- Credit union services and loans.
- Reduced-cost cafeterias.
- Gymnasium facilities.
- Recreation and leisure time activities and facilities.
- Employee discounts.

The purpose of compensation is to attract, satisfy, and keep competent and capable people. Consequently, the compensation policy a company pursues is a major component of human resource management. The problem is that if the compensation policy is not considered adequate by the employees, they will leave the firm; whereas, if the compensation policy is too liberal, the firm's profits and prospects for survival will be damaged. How do you determine how much is enough? Before we address this question, consider the value of the various forms of compensation.

Compensation can be monetary or nonmonetary. Frequently, compensation can be structured so that it is not taxed to the employee, or at least, taxation is delayed until some time in the future. This can be a valuable situation. Consider life and health insurance, for example. The premiums that the company pays for such insurance are tax deductible by the company, but the benefits are not taxable to the employee so long as certain conditions are met. If the employee is in a 30% marginal income tax bracket, then the insurance premiums paid by the company are worth 30% more because they are not taxable.

Another way of looking at it is to examine the alternative. Instead of paying insurance premiums, the company increases the employee's pay by the amount of the premiums. There is no difference to the company in this situation at all. The only change from the company's perspective is where the money is sent. There is a big difference to the employee! Suppose the company withholds the premiums from the employee's pay and uses it to purchase the same insurance coverage as before. Now the employee would have to pay 30% income taxes on the amount of the premiums and would really only have 70% of the money left. If you wanted to provide the same amount of after-tax income and benefits, the company would have to increase the amount of the payment. The increase would be more than 30%. If the insurance premiums were \$50, then the amount of pay that would result in having \$50 left after tax would be \$71.43 (\$50/.70 = \$71.43), which is almost 43%! The company-paid insurance benefits not only save the employee money, they can save the company money!

Many types of nonmonetary compensation can result in similar situations. For example, a company car can be provided. If personal use of the car is possible, a lease payment must be charged to the employee, but it is possible to structure such a payment far below the cost of leasing if the employee were to arrange it personally. The effect on after-tax benefits is the same as in the case of the insurance premiums.

Monetary compensation that also is delayed can have a beneficial income tax treatment. For example, pension benefits properly structured will not be taxable to the employee until after retirement. At that time, the individual's income tax rate and liability can be expected to be lower than during the working years making the after-tax benefits of the pension payments much higher. Now you can see why indirect compensation, nonmonetary compensation, and delayed compensation are so popular!

Obtaining favorable income tax treatment of the various forms of compensation is a complicated business. Professional help is mandatory to ensure that the desired results occur. Your CPA can help you in setting up what is needed and in monitoring rule changes by the Internal Revenue Service to make sure that the desired results will continue. The outcome of the compensation tax planning can be highly favorable results for both the company and the employees.

An added benefit of structuring compensation so that it receives favorable tax treatment is the effect on employee turnover. If employees understand the total compensation package, then they will think about the overall impact of changing to a new job with another firm rather than the more visible stated pay rate. This will reduce turnover. In addition, delayed compensation plans of all types can be made contingent on longevity with the company. This means that leaving the firm can result in the loss of accumulated benefits. It is common, for example, to make pension benefits subject to loss in the event of an employee's departure from the firm. There are rules governing this process as well, so you must obtain professional assistance in structuring the plan, but the result can be an encouragement to employees to stay with the company.

As in the case of nontaxable compensation, the key is in ensuring that employees understand the total compensation package, its true value in after-tax terms, and the effects of departure from the firm on that package. The initial orientation of new employees should cover this information, but constant reappraisal is necessary as well. At least once each year, every employee should be informed in writing of the total compensation package, its after-tax effects, and amounts held for future release. This communication could be prepared as part of the W-2 data at the end of the year or communicated in an annual employee performance appraisal, but it must be done or the impact of the compensation program on employee turnover will be damaged.

As you can see from the foregoing discussion, it is generally wise to structure a compensation program to maximize its after-tax benefits. But this still doesn't solve the problem of determining how much to pay employees. That determination requires a thorough understanding of the market for the services your people provide. Just as market forces affect the selling prices of the goods and services your company provides, market forces affect compensation programs. Skills that are in high demand cost more, whereas skills that are in high supply cost less. It's the old economic law of supply and demand applied to the labor force. If not enough people are qualified to operate a particular piece of machinery to meet the demand for such skills, then those people will be paid more than other types of employees. If far more people have clerical skills than are needed to fill the available jobs, then those people will be paid less than other types of employees.

You will be able to gain a great deal of insight into the relative supply and demand of the various types of labor you use in your company during the recruiting process. The number of applicants you receive for a particular job and the salary levels requested by those applicants will give you that insight. In addition, the compensation levels of your competitors can give you insight into what your levels should be. In general, the minimum compensation levels you will be able to offer and still attract and keep people will be those offered by your competition. It is just like your prices! You will have difficulty offering your products or services at higher than the prices offered by your competition: compensation works the same way. Just as you can manipulate prices by offering other benefits to customers, such as service levels, convenience, or higher quality, so you can affect compensation levels by offering added benefits to employees.

Determining the compensation levels of your competitors involves obtaining industry average data, joining industry and trade associations and asking people you meet at these gatherings, watching job advertisements in the newspaper and trade journals, asking your employees, and so forth. Because compensation levels are constantly changing in response to changing conditions, keeping up with the market for labor is an ongoing process.

One of the best ways of differentiating your compensation policies from those of your competitors is to tie a large portion of income to the performance of the company. This approach will permit the company to pay higher compensation amounts when it can afford to do so more easily while giving employee morale a boost by allowing employee performance to affect pay levels.

There are sound arguments to support such an approach. First, basic compensation levels can be set much lower than the competition normally would allow. This can help the firm's cash flow, especially during its early days. Second, employees feel closer to the firm and more a part of the operation and therefore tend to do a better job because they know that their paychecks will be directly affected by how well the company does. In such situations, the employees tend to make every effort to see that the firm does as well as is possible. If they are successful and the company is successful, they will make more than they would have with a competing firm, and their morale will be higher. Third, when the higher payroll costs occur, the money is available to cover them because the firm's profits have been leveraged up. It won't hurt the firm to pay higher than the going rate for compensation. In addition, those higher levels will attract and maintain better and better employees, which should facilitate the continued growth and success of the firm.

Of course, such a program has to be designed in such a fashion that the employees perceive it to be fair and equitable. You cannot assign the major share of profits to officers or managers of the company and expect the other employees to applaud the program. With careful planning, a sound program can be developed using fees, profit sharing, bonuses, commissions, and other devices tied to company benchmarks, which will result in the desired growth. Of course, the employees will have to be kept informed of the progress of the company toward the benchmarks. They also will have to have input into the development of those benchmarks so that they will consider them to be reasonable. The result will be a more participatory management overall. There is one potential problem.

Everyone is happy with a compensation plan tied to company performance so long as that performance is good. A major problem will develop if the company begins to falter as a result of shifts in the market, changes in competition, variations in demand, or any other factor the employees consider beyond their ability to influence. In this situation, the employees will leave. Their departure will be at exactly the wrong time for the firm because it will be fighting for survival. Consequently, good planning to keep the company out of such a situation and fast reaction to the development of such a situation is necessary to make the compensation plan work. In addition, the employees require knowledge about what is going on in order to encourage them to assist in combatting environmental problems.

The value of a compensation plan tied to performance generally is greater at higher levels of responsibility within the firm because such people feel more capable of influencing the performance. Nevertheless, it can have value at all levels if a conscientious effort is made to demonstrate to employees at all levels that their performance does reflect on the company. A good way to approach this is through involvement of employees in stock ownership. A portion of the compensation package can be devoted to stock purchase to facilitate the plan. The result can be employees who think more like owners of the company than like employees whose efforts are insignificant. In one firm, a janitor of some thirty years seniority was a major stockholder of a class of nonvoting stock. No one in the company was more concerned about the company or aware of its situation than that janitor. As you can guess, the offices of the company were among the cleanest in town!

A great deal is involved in establishing a compensation policy for a small business despite the small number of employees relative to other firms. If the business has a union, then the process involves negotiating a compensation plan with the union representatives, but little is really different. There are situations in which the relative power of a union is so great that it exceeds the power of the management of the firm, but even so an equitable compensation policy can be developed so long as an adversary relationship is avoided. Fear of unions frequently causes managers of small businesses to forget about employees until union contract renegotiation time comes around. A sound compensation program with genuine interest and concern for the employees of a company will eliminate virtually all union problems. In fact, such a program frequently will result in the absence of a union because workers will not feel the need for one.

Exhibit 17-3 lists the steps required to establish a compensation plan as outlined in the foregoing sections. Remember that there is no one way to approach compensation. What is right for a particular company is what works for that company.

A major portion of the time of the owner of a small business will be spent in managing people because people are the most important assets of any business. Consequently, it makes sense to spend the time and energy to develop and maintain a sound compensation policy. It will make the job of managing people easier and more rewarding.

**EXHIBIT 17-3** *Steps in Planning a Compensation Program*

STEP 1 Determine your competitors' going rate for compensation for each position in the company. Keep track of the information as it changes over time. Sources are industry averages, contacts in industry and trade associations, advertisements for positions in newspapers and journals, job applicants, and present employees.

STEP 2 Structure the compensation package with major portions of income tied to performance of the company. Fees, commissions, bonuses, profit sharing plans, and so on are vehicles for payment. Employees must understand the plan, have input to it, receive reports on its progress, and feel capable of influencing the performance of the company.

STEP 3 Structure a major portion of the compensation package with favorable tax treatment through the use of nonmonetary compensation, fringe benefits, and deferred compensation plans. A professional will be required to assist in completing such a plan.

STEP 4 Defer a portion of the compensation and tie its eventual receipt to continued employment with the company. A professional will be required to assist in completing such a plan.

STEP 5 Ensure that every employee understands the complete compensation package. Make a part of the orientation of new employees familiarization with the compensation plan. Make an annual report to all employees of the total compensation they are receiving, the after-tax benefits of the compensation, and the amounts deferred and contingent on continued employment with the company.

## EMPLOYEE RELATIONS

**Employee relations** refers to the interaction among the employees and managers of a firm and its owner. As in the preceding sections, a sound compensation program will go a long way toward establishing sound employee relations. Nevertheless, compensation is not the whole game. Consider what is at stake for a few minutes. The employees of the firm, including the managers other than the owner, are the people who make the firm function and carry out the strategies of the top management. Not only must those people be competent, capable, satisfied with the compensation plan, and knowledgeable of the company's needs and plans, they must want to work and see the company succeed. A desire to push the company forward is not automatic. In large measure, it comes from the interaction with other people and the owner.

The major component of a healthy interaction between people, regardless of what those people are doing, is communication. **Communication** is bidirectional; that is, communication requires both listening and speaking. Effective communication in a company takes effort on the part of the owner and every manager in the company. There must be a genuine desire to communicate on the part of every person in a position of responsibility in the firm. Most important, the owner must initiate and support effective communication. Without visible support on an ongoing basis from the owner, nothing will actually happen regardless of instructions or orders. Communication results from an attitude, and attitudes can be influenced only by example. It's a situation of leading versus directing. You can tell people where to go and what to do, but you cannot tell them what to think about the actions. There is an old adage about a man dragging a long chain down a dusty road. When asked why he was dragging the chain, the man responded, "Have you ever tried to push a chain?" His cryptic response works well in the arena of human emotions. You cannot push opinions and attitudes, but you can influence them by example.

Communication between managers and employees must take several forms. First, managers must direct employees to complete assigned tasks. This involves telling employees what to do, how and when to do it. For that communication to be effective, the employees must be willing to accept the direction and understand the instructions. This form of communication is well known and well practiced. However, the effectiveness of this form of communication is affected by the other forms.

Second, managers must inform employees of the quality of their performance. This includes both praise for tasks well done and criticism for poor performance. There should be more praise than criticism; and the praise should be specific, pointing out the situation of the business and the effects of the employee's actions on that situation. This is one of the difficult aspects of communication for managers, because they simply forget to offer the positive feedback. Negative feedback is easy to remember, but to remember to praise good performance, a manager's attitude toward employees must be one of constantly seeking positive feedback opportunities. This second aspect of communication is highly important because it will affect the first aspect. For employees to be willing to accept direction, they must feel that their efforts are recognized and appreciated. Otherwise, any compliance they make with assignments will be grudging, unenthusiastic, and uninspired.

The third form of communication involves managers listening to employees. For this form to be effective, the listening must be genuine, the atmosphere must be open and encouraging, and the manager must take action when valid points are raised. Employees all wish to have an opportunity to talk about the tasks they are to be assigned. They need to have input to the decision as to what those tasks will be, how and when they are to be completed. They need to feel that they are part of a team, led by the manager, but a team rather than a machine to accomplish some task. No manager can "fake" interest in and concern for employees. Such interest must be genuine or employees will sense the reluctance and withdraw into themselves. Without effective listening on the part of a manager, the effectiveness of the first form of communication is damaged. As in the last case, enthusiastic response to direction cannot be expected unless employees feel that they will be heard and understood when they communicate to their managers.

The final form of communication is communication between employees. People who work together form a social group. The overall effectiveness of the group largely is a function of the group dynamics, which is affected by the communication within the group. If one or more members of the group feel ostracized from the group, the effectiveness of the group will be damaged. Every member must feel valued and respected by the other members and must feel able to communicate with the other members for the group to be effective. This form of communication is extremely difficult for a manager to manipulate. You cannot tell the members of a working group to respect each other nor even to talk to each other. A manager can influence this form of communication by example. By ensuring that every member of the group is aware that the manager considers each member important and by encouraging each member to communicate with the manager freely, an atmosphere of mutual respect can be fostered. It takes genuine interest and concern on the part of the manager and constant attention to group interaction.

Our client was the manager of a branch office of a small bank. A serious personnel problem arose that he did not know how to handle. A young man, the manager had little experience in direct supervision, but he was concerned and aware that the internal strife in his branch was affecting its performance.

Two tellers, who worked side by side on the teller row, had gotten angry at each other. The manager had been unable to find out the cause of the conflict, but had been informed by another teller that the two had been friends for years prior to this argument. At any rate, the conflict seethed for a week or two then flared into the open on a day when the lobby was filled with customers. One teller threw a savings passbook at the other! In loud voices, each declaimed that she would never speak to the other again! The manager quieted them down, apologized to the customers, and somehow got through the day.

Repeated efforts at discussing the problem with the two tellers and reconciling them were fruitless. True to their words, each refused to speak to the other, despite the proximity of their work stations. Within a week, the entire office was suffering. The balancing rate of every teller in the branch went down. Tempers were short and arguments flared with no apparent reason. Several customers actually remarked to the manager that something was amiss. The manager discussed the situation with his boss, but got no help. ''These things happen, just ignore it,'' was the extent of the advice he received.

After three weeks a new head teller was brought into the branch. An experienced teller with ten years of experience with the bank, she had been on maternity leave during the time that the explosion took place. The day after she came back to work she went into the manager's office and asked him what had happened between the two feuding tellers. He explained.

The head teller waited until the lunch break, when the branch was closed and everyone was balancing their cash drawers, and loudly dressed down the two truants. She said that she was ashamed of both of them for acting like children rather than the capable, competent adults everyone knew them to be. She pointed out how their feud was affecting the rest of the tellers because everyone was afraid of taking sides and losing the respect of the other person.

It turns out that the head teller knew just what to do! The branch was back to normal within a day and the two former enemies were friends again. One of them even apologized to the manager, who just continued to feel helpless.

So far we have talked about communication as though it were between managers and employees. In reality the same conditions prevail for communication between managers and the owner and among managers. Like employees, managers are people and have the same needs and desires. Effective communication, in all its forms, must take place at every level within the organization in order for the firm to advance and succeed.

One aspect of human relations is unique to a small business. Only in a small firm can all of the employees develop a personal relationship with the owner. Such a relationship can be healthy, result in a more highly motivated staff, and foster the development of communication throughout the firm, but there is one danger. If employees feel able to "jump the chain of command" and bring problems or ideas directly to the owner rather than working through the organization chart, then the effectiveness of the managers can be undermined. It is important for employees to feel that they can come to the owner if a manager is unwilling to listen, but if employees are permitted to bypass managers, then an atmosphere will develop in which managers will have no power or authority.

By the same token, if one of the employees is a personal friend or family member of the owner, and consequently is perceived as enjoying special privileges, then the authority of managers over that person will be damaged, as will the morale of the business in general. If you intend to be the owner of a business, then you must be prepared to undertake a very special position with respect to the people who will work for you. The slightest sign of favoritism or special treatment toward one employee will affect the others tremendously. The slightest indication that a manager does not truly hold authority will result in damaging that manager's effectiveness. The owner must always be available when the need is genuine, must be evenhanded and fair with all employees and managers, must be seen to support the decisions and actions of managers, must lead by example, but must never appear to be used by any employee or manager for personal advancement. It is a difficult trust, but one that only the owner can undertake.

In the preceding sections, we talked about the need for both positive and negative feedback in maintaining effective employee relations. This need is critical in day-to-day supervision, but requires a more formalized system to solve the long-term needs. Every employee, regardless of the level of responsibility, should receive a formal evaluation of his or her performance at least once each year. The evaluation should be performed by the employee's immediate superior. If that supervisor should change during the course of the year, evaluations should be required on all people supervised before the change takes place. The evaluation should be discussed with the employee and the report and the results of its discussion with the employee made a permanent part of the employee's record.

The evaluation should consider the quantity and quality of work performed, dependability, cooperation, job attendance, achievement of objectives set for the employee, overall effectiveness of the employee, and suitability for pay raises, advancement, or promotion. As a part of the evaluation, objectives should be discussed for the employee for the coming year and those that both supervisor and employee agree upon made part of a work plan for the next year. Each evaluation should take into consideration the objectives established for the year and progress made toward those as well as the working record of the individual during the year. It will be difficult for managers to perform these evaluations initially, but with experience will come confidence. The formalized procedure is mandatory if you expect to recognize the strengths and weaknesses of the work force. Everyone, including managers, should be subjected to the process. The owner should perform an evaluation of himself or herself as well.

Should any employee disagree with the evaluation of his or her performance, he or she should have the opportunity to discuss the evaluation with the next highest level of supervision. If a resolution cannot be achieved after discussing the evaluation with the owner, then the employee should be offered the opportunity to make a written attachment to the evaluation form for inclusion in the personnel file. The discussion of the evaluation is as important as its preparation. Every employee is entitled to know what the supervisor thinks of his or her performance, good or bad, and to be informed of the specifics of actions that are considered positive or negative. The process of discussion also will be good for the supervisor. It will force the supervisor to think carefully about each employee and that person's performance and overall value to the firm. Supervisors will be more aware of employee performance on a daily basis if they know that at some point they will have to evaluate that performance and face the employee with the evaluation.

People have a natural tendency to avoid confrontations, so supervisors may be tempted to evaluate everyone highly. To counteract that tendency, the system should require each supervisor to rank the employees under his or her supervision in order of value to the firm. An alternative would be to establish a budget of pay raises to be distributed based on employee evaluations. Thus, supervisors will be more inclined to rank people fairly so that pay raises will be distributed fairly. A part of the evaluation of each supervisor should be an examination of the evaluations that supervisor has prepared. All management personnel should be constantly aware of the need to fairly and critically judge the performance of people they supervise at all times. If at all possible, the owner should personally review every employee evaluation before it goes into the personnel file. If any questions arise, the owner should discuss them with the supervisor and, if unsatisfied, with the employee. The evaluation forms should be used in all pay raise, advancement, and promotion decisions in the firm. In that way everyone will come to know the importance of the process. Remember, people are the primary asset of the business; therefore, employee performance appraisals are in large measure an appraisal of the business itself.

## SUMMARY

People are the greatest asset of any business and can influence its success or failure. They are even more important to a small business with fewer employees, because it will be affected more by the loss of a valued employee or the selection of incompetent personnel.

Promoting from within has advantages and disadvantages. Benefits may be derived by recognizing existing employees' skills and by demonstrating advancement possibilities to others in the firm. However, it also means creating an additional vacancy. The hiring must be fair, and the person in the new position must be competent, or friction will occur. Don't use seniority as the sole criterion or you may find yourself victim to the Peter Principle; that is, promoting someone to the level of his or her incompetence.

Be objective and fair in hiring. State the criteria and evaluate the applications according to qualifications and in the best interest of the company. Then after the selection process is complete, be sure that everyone is aware of who was chosen for the job and why. Keep records showing why every applicant was denied or hired to protect yourself from discrimination suits.

Outside sources for recruitment include both public and private employment agencies. Other sources are schools, colleges, and universities; professional conferences; advertisements; and cooperative education programs. Part-time employees from temporary employment agencies, your own previous employees, or other retired persons can help fill employment gaps.

Decide the jobs and the criteria for holding them before you begin the interview process. Make up a specific application form for the job that will garner you the desired information and comply with Equal Employment Opportunity laws.

Control the interview. Keep notes. Don't hire on the spot. Check references and verify information provided.

Almost every job requires some on-the-job training. Be aware of who is going to do the training so that the new employee does not receive fourth-hand knowledge. Training may occur both in the company on company time or outside in programs and seminars set up for that purpose.

Autocratic managers allow others little or no input to the decision-making process and so can react more quickly, whether positively or negatively, to situations. Democratic managers assure participation and, although the decision may be delayed, there typically is a consensus and therefore a rallying effect.

Compensation may be direct or indirect and its purpose is to attract, satisfy, and keep competent and capable people. It may be monetary or nonmonetary and with proper professional guidance often can be designed to benefit both employer and employee from a tax perspective. It can be tied to performance, which will not only boost employee morale but also attract other high achievers to your company.

Employee relations depend upon bidirectional communication. Just as employees need to receive reinforcement for a job well done or instructions for one poorly done, managers must receive feedback, too. They must listen to employees' suggestions and complaints and strive to do better. Communication between employees enhances the close ties that can result from a close working situation. Employees should be cognizant of the lines of communication through the chain of command and not disrupt that chain.

Performance must be evaluated according to a formal plan. The evaluation should cover all employees and managers and should consider the quantity and quality of the work performed, dependability, cooperation, job attendance, achievement of objectives, and eligibility for raises or promotions.

## QUESTIONS

1. Why are human resources so important to a company?
2. What are two methods for recruiting people?
3. What are the advantages and disadvantages of promoting from within?
4. How does one go about finding potential employees outside the firm? List several sources of applicants.

5. What are the key elements of a good interview?
6. Why is on-the-job training an important concept? What are the pros and cons of OJT?
7. Distinguish between an autocratic and democratic method of supervision. Which would you prefer if you were an employee?
8. What are direct and indirect compensation categories?
9. How can you establish fringe benefits that can benefit both employer and employee? Give an example.
10. How does a good employee relationship reflect upon a company? Give several examples.
11. How should you evaluate your employees?
12. What legal issues are involved in recruiting?
13. How do discrimination laws affect small businesses?
14. How do immigration laws affect small businesses?

## PROJECTS

1. Using role play, have a manager interview three prospective employees for the same job. Have two applicants be from within the company and the third from outside. Establish a format, evaluate the applicants, and make a selection. Be sure to include in the role play methods of compensation. The manager must give some thought to the role as must the applicants. This activity could be good practice for both future managers and employees.
2. Have two role play situations: one in which a manager is an autocratic supervisor and another in which the manager is democratic. The situation is as follows. A new company is starting up that markets the same product as you do. You had not previously heard of this company, and it will be operational within the month. What should your company do about the new competition and how would each type of supervisor handle the situation?

## CASE

John Davison sits at his desk long after hours and ponders the situation. He has been deluged all day with complaints about his long-time friend, Bob James. He knew Bob had not been doing his job well for some time, but he felt a certain amount of loyalty. After all, Bob had started with him when it was a two-man operation. John, as the president, and Bob, as the marketing vice-president, had run the company during the hard times of its start up. Bob was a super salesman with many years of experience. He really had brought in the sales for their fledgling company.

John had given him responsibility over the marketing department in fact as well as in title five years ago, when the company grew to the point that it had enough sales reps on staff to merit real supervision. He couldn't very well hire someone in over the head of his old buddy, so he had given the management post to Bob along with a well-earned raise. Things had gone smoothly for a couple of months while Bob was training his staff. He could demonstrate his sales techniques and explain why certain ploys worked and others didn't. But times were changing and the business was changing.

Meanwhile, Bob, too, sat mulling over how times had changed. Bob was still a cracker jack salesman. Now his duties were different. Bob had begun to change but not really. He was still a go-getter when he could teach or sell but supervising people was a different ballgame. Bob knew in his heart that he was making problems for the company. Not only had sales fallen off, the working environment of his department had the people in it walking on eggs. He knew the fault was largely his. He just couldn't get excited about someone else's successful closure of a difficult client. It was an ego thing, and he knew it. He knew that his staff could see through his false congratulations and felt that he was second-guessing their efforts. In reality, he envied them — out of the office and selling. He was a people person. He could sell fireplaces to the underworld, but he could not manage people.

Bob's dissatisfaction was revealed in the office. He could offer no managerial support to his staff. His people faced verbal warfare in the office. Just as it takes a special personality to be able to sell well and enjoy it, those same egos needed stroking for work well done. When no one would give them the attention they needed, those same egos tried to assert themselves with each other. Chaos was the result. Bob pulled himself out of his chair and decided that tomorrow he would try harder to enjoy pushing paper instead of pushing products. If only he could get some of that old excitement back. He hated to admit it, but he hated coming to work in the morning because it was the same old hassle. Oh well, he couldn't let down the friend who had given him this responsibility. So tomorrow would be another day.

John knew that he was going to have to do something. He had controlled the petty office jealousies himself for a while, but this was getting too big. Sales were falling off and in-fighting had made the office a battleground. He knew that deep down the fix involved a change for Bob, but could he do this to a friend? Perhaps if he hired a consultant to look at the situation, he could find a different solution to the problem. Maybe he wasn't being objective. Maybe he, too, was succumbing to the bickering within Bob's department. Maybe he wouldn't have to fire or demote his friend. Because he felt unable to make the decision, he called in a consultant.

### Questions

1. If you were the consultant, what would you do first?
2. What do you see as the real problem causing the ill health of the company? Could one person be responsible?
3. What several alternatives are available to John? To Bob?
4. Why do you suppose sales were falling off? How could that be remedied?
5. What do you think the consultant recommended?
6. What would be your recommendation and why?

# CHAPTER 18

# Marketing Management

**LEARNING OBJECTIVES**

After completing this chapter, you should be able to

- Understand the impact of marketing on an ongoing small business.
- Identify the factors that affect the purchasing decision.
- Distinguish between the three basic approaches to marketing.
- Know the value of a good image.
- Know the three basic approaches to setting the price for a product or service.
- Know the impact of advertising and pricing on the marketing effort.
- Distinguish between product or service advertising and image advertising.
- Identify and employ marketing techniques and evaluate their effectiveness.
- Understand how the marketing strategy makes everything in the small business come together.

Marketing frequently is confused with advertising. Since Shakespeare's day the focus of the sales effort has been on praising the goods or services held for sale. Marketing is much more than advertising. Although part of any marketing effort is the planning and execution of effective advertising, marketing must go far beyond advertising to be effective. The goal of **marketing** is to sell goods or services. These things actually are sold through a coordinated effort that includes every aspect of a business' operation. Effectiveness is determined more by the degree of coordination than by any advertising efforts undertaken.

We discussed marketing in a previous chapter in the start-up section of the text. This chapter begins with a brief overview of the key marketing aspects, discussed at length in Chapter 3, because those concepts are important to any marketing activity. In Chapter 3, we were concerned with marketing efforts for a new venture. Here we focus on how those factors are important in an ongoing business. This is followed with a discussion of advertising and pricing, and then marketing techniques, budgeting, and an overall strategy for ongoing businesses. Finally, we show how every aspect of a business must be coordinated to design an effective marketing approach.

## FACTORS THAT AFFECT THE PURCHASING DECISION

In Chapter 3, we talked about the difficulty in determining the factors that affect a person's decision to buy a product or service. We pointed out the need to examine the who, what, when, where, how, and why of purchasing decisions. *Who* refers to the **target market,** or the subgroup of the population to whom particular goods or services are sold. This group is selected in advance as part of the start-up marketing strategy based on socioeconomic and geographic factors as well as product or service appeal. We must continually monitor customers to determine the target market that actually purchases our offerings. We must know both who purchases and who uses our products and services on an ongoing basis to effectively market. This is because the buyer of a product or service frequently is not its ultimate consumer or user. Toys are a good example: bought by parents and grandparents; used by children.

Marketing efforts must appeal to both the purchaser and the consumer. A system must be developed to capture customer data or else marketing research will be required to identify the target market. For a small business, it is much easier and cheaper to capture data on customers in advance than to acquire data after the fact. Everyone in the firm needs to maintain a constant awareness of the need to keep records on customers and to gather information on the ultimate consumers of goods and services. Larger firms frequently engage in research and marketing surveys to identify the ultimate consumers of their products. Conducting such research is not only expensive, but requires considerable expertise in research methods. Consequently, research of this type frequently is not a viable alternative for a small business.

*What* refers to the product or service that a customer actually buys. This may be quite different from the products and services that a business sells. Convenience, speed, service, image, or other factors may be more important than the product or service being offered. It is important to know what people actually are buying because this is what must be promoted in marketing efforts. Learning what it is that customers buy largely is a function of careful observation of those customers, their response to advertising and marketing efforts, and their buying patterns and habits.

*When* includes the issue of the time of day when people buy things as well as the seasonality patterns of those purchases. It also addresses the frequency of purchase, highlighting differences between consumable items and durable items. Advertising and marketing efforts cannot function unless we understand the timing issue. The basis of appeal has much to do with the frequency of purchase. The timing of the advertising itself is a function of the purchasing when.

*Where* concerns store, outlet, branch, and warehouse location. This factor is difficult to change, but constant monitoring should take place to ensure that demographic or geographic shifts do not occur that render earlier location decisions invalid.

People buy with money, of course, but credit can play a significant role. *How* concerns the ongoing preference patterns of purchasers for various payment terms.

All of these factors are part of *why* people buy things but the primary aspects of the decision are psychological and sociological phenomena. **Advertising** is concerned more with this issue than with any other, because its purpose is to appeal to the buying trigger and move people to purchase products and services. The two basic approaches are to discover through marketing research what are the motivations and to appeal to those through advertising and to attempt to create a reason for people to want to buy. In essence, the first is a strategy of tapping an existing demand, whereas the second creates a demand for the goods and services. Creating demand frequently is an expensive operation and, therefore, often beyond the means of a small business. Falling back on the first strategy, identifying motivations, requires keeping constant and careful records on marketing efforts. The best way to identify motivations in a small business setting is to track various types of marketing strategies and identify those that work and those that don't. The strategies that work, in all probability, contain an appeal to one or more of the basic motivations for purchasing.

All the purchasing issues—who, what, when, where, how, and why—require constant, ongoing attention by everyone in the business. Everyone must be aware of the need to constantly monitor customer purchases and customer demographics as well as capture information about sales that are lost and the reasons for those losses. Successful marketing in a small business largely is a function of awareness of buying trends and patterns, target market characteristics, and historic marketing effects.

## MARKETING APPROACHES

In the start-up section, we talked about the three basic approaches to marketing: push, pull, and piggyback. *Push marketing* refers to an attempt to push an item through the market by persuading a retailer, distributor, or supplier to carry it. The method focuses on the vendor rather than on the ultimate consumer of the goods or services. The objective is to engage other firms in selling a product or service to its ultimate consumer. If businesses between our firm and the consumer can be encouraged to help persuade the consumer to buy, then the ultimate sale becomes more likely. Push marketing is popular among wholesalers but can apply to services as well as products. For example, a motel could appeal to travel agents rather than travelers in an attempt to push its services. The process of push marketing is a host of steps aimed at making the intermediary want to sell our wares. It tends to be a less expensive approach to marketing as it frequently employs pricing strategies, resupply agreements, premiums, gifts, and bonuses. This makes it an especially attractive marketing approach for a small business.

*Pull marketing* attempts to create a demand for an item in the ultimate consumer. The objective is to persuade intermediaries to carry our wares through consumer demand. The intermediaries will have to buy from us to satisfy their customers' needs. This also permits higher prices to the intermediaries and therefore enhances profit margins. Pull marketing is accomplished through a variety of techniques, all aimed at creating brand loyalty or consistent demand from the ultimate consumer for our products and services. This strategy is effective if the marketing is successful, but tends to be more expensive and time consuming. Consequently, it may not be a viable strategy for a small business.

*Piggyback marketing* is one of the most frequently encountered strategies among small businesses. The objective is to identify a successful competitor and piggyback that firm's marketing efforts. *Piggyback* means to copy and capitalize on the competitor's marketing in an effort to take market share away from the competitor. The competitor is allowed to build consumer demand through its marketing efforts while the customers are siphoned off through performing some aspect of the sales or distribution process more effectively. Low-cost motels built next to Holiday Inns are an example, as are discount department stores located near Sears stores. Clones or copies of IBM microcomputers are another example, as are firms who use alphabetic naming schemes that locate them first in the yellow pages of the telephone book. Piggyback marketing can be used in most industries and is one of the lowest-cost approaches available. It also is one of the most effective strategies and is one reason why many inventors and innovators do not do as well as the firms that follow them into new markets.

Combinations of these three basic approaches regularly are used. In fact, it is frequently difficult to determine by casual observation the dominant marketing approach used by a firm.

## MARKETING RESEARCH

We discussed marketing research at some length in Chapter 3, too. Basically, we described the techniques of library and field research. Marketing research can be a complex field, and entire curricula at universities are devoted to it. We identified one aspect of field research available for small firms but seldom used: footwork, or the personal investigation of a market and an area. To this technique we need to add record keeping and observation. If a small business can maintain a continuing awareness of who are its customers, what are their demographic and socioeconomic characteristics, where they come from, when and how they make their purchases, how they react to advertising and marketing campaigns, how they change over time — then the most important aspects of marketing research have been accomplished. The basic aim of marketing research is to learn those facts. An ongoing business has a major advantage over a start-up firm because it can have records available. Don't forget that capturing the information is a continuous battle! Everyone in the firm must understand the need for and use of information about customers and must be dedicated to obtaining it at all times.

## BUSINESS IMAGE

In Chapter 3 we emphasized that the image of the firm was the most important aspect in start-up marketing. We stressed that every aspect of the firm must be consistent with the selected image in order not to send conflicting signals to its customers. This also is true for marketing in an ongoing business.

*Business image* means the way customers perceive the business, what makes a business distinct from its competition, what a customer thinks of when seeing or patronizing a business. It is the personality of a business. Much of the marketing effort, in fact, is aimed at producing and maintaining a particular image in the minds of its customers. Changing an established image for a business can be extremely difficult—and dangerous as well. For a long time K Mart fostered an image of carrying everything that Sears did but at discount prices. Sears, of course, was fostering an image of quality and breadth of merchandise at the same time. Recently, K Mart has begun to try to shift its image to that of a high-quality department store. Development of a K Mart Best brand name and advertising directed toward merchandise quality and service is evidence of that shift. So far, consumers clearly continue to think of K Mart as a discount department store. Whether the ultimate change of image will be successful remains to be seen, but many major problems will resist the change including the location, design, and layout of stores. It is no accident that Sears has long preferred mall locations and invested significant dollars in the design and amenities of its stores, whereas K Mart has used shopping center sites and pursued a lower-cost store design. Changing the image may never be possible. There also is risk in making the effort to change. Should K Mart raise its prices across the board, it could well lose business because its customers would be confused by the conflict between price and the established discount image. Interestingly, Sears is currently trying to change its image to one of lower prices. Its mall locations and store investments will make this change difficult. The next few years will be interesting to watch as Sears and K Mart struggle with their images.

For these reasons, image is a pervasive concept, one that should be approached carefully and with great thought. Every aspect of the business must be consistent with the image, and changing it must be carefully managed. It generally is easier for a small business to change its image than a large one, because of the smaller number of people who will be affected. Nevertheless, it is difficult and filled with danger. This is a major factor that makes buying an existing business dangerous. If a business' image is poorly developed or negative, then new owners may not be able to make the conversion. Far too many businesses are sold because their owners are unable to make them successful. New owners of such firms are handicapped by the failure of the previous managers and frequently fail as a result. If you ever consider buying an existing business, keep this in mind and be sure you explore the image of that business in the minds of the target market.

## PRICING

If you ask an average person what is the main input to the price of an item, that person is likely to answer cost. As a matter of fact, the main inputs to price are demand and competition. Clearly, you cannot sell items for less than their variable costs, at least not for long, but you must keep in mind the purpose served by price. The **price** of an item is designed to sell that item, just like every other aspect of marketing. A *fair price* cannot be defined. You may have heard it said that a **fair price** is one in which both the seller and the buyer are happy. This is a rather simplistic view, but it recognizes that the buyer has no interest in the cost of the item to the seller. The buyer's sole interest is in acquiring a desired item at a price with which he or she is comfortable. The first part of that interest is demand. The buyer must first desire the item or there will be no purchase. The second part is price. What basis does a buyer have for judging prices? Only the price charged for similar items by competing firms. Consequently, demand and competition are the main ingredients in setting price.

## Supply and Demand

*Demand* can be a difficult concept. The demand for a particular item can go beyond the physical product itself. **Demand** can include such elements as entertainment in that the shopping experience can be as much a part of the customer's desire as ownership of the item itself. Many restaurants, especially those catering to young adults, sell entertainment in the form of opportunities to meet and mingle with friends and peers as well as food. Stores selling designer clothing for women may well be selling the opportunity to model various clothes as well as the clothes themselves. Demand also can include such aspects as convenience, both in location and hours of operation, service, advice and counseling, and a host of other factors, which can be far afield from the item being sold.

The economic theory of price and demand says that demand is affected by price in an inverse fashion. Further, they explain that the availability of an item is positively related to price and that the **market price** is set where supply and demand meet. The relationship is most easily seen graphically. Exhibit 18-1 displays a traditional supply and demand curve.

The exhibit shows that as price increases, the quantity of an item in demand decreases. The reverse also is true: as price decreases, the quantity demanded increases. **Supply** works opposite to demand. As the price an item will bring increases, the quantity supplied by firms increases. As the price declines, the quantity firms will supply also declines. Equilibrium is reached at the point of intersection of the two lines. For a true commodity item, one that does not differ between suppliers or manufacturers, the point of equilibrium is the market price. Not every item has a downward sloping demand curve, although most items do. Virtually everything has an upward sloping supply curve.

There are several problems with translating the economic theory into practice. First, it is extremely difficult to identify all of the elements of demand for most items. We have already talked about that problem. Further, even if we

**EXHIBIT 18-1** *Supply and Demand Relationship*

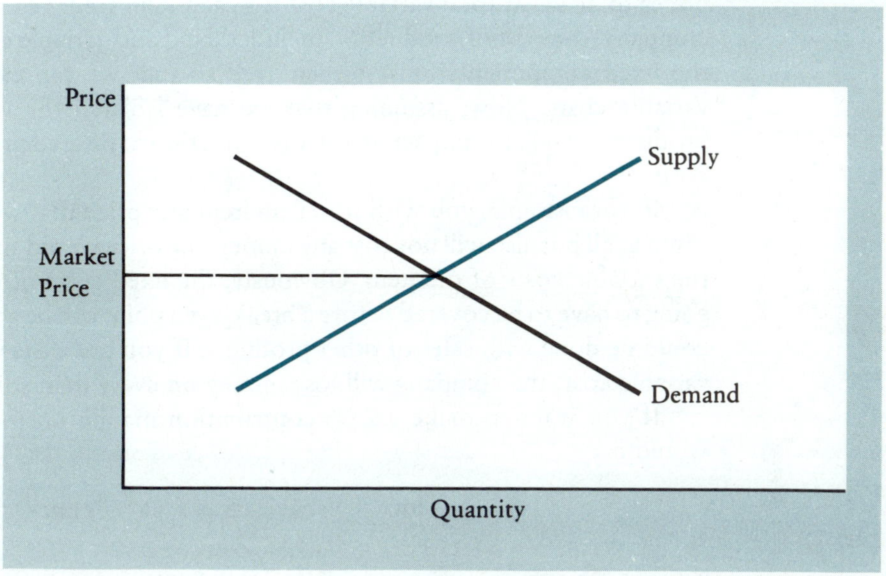


know that an item has a downward sloping demand curve, we seldom know how steep is the slope. The steeper the decline, the faster demand will fall off as price increases. It is difficult to identify how fast that trade-off will occur for any given item. Additionally, the theory assumes knowledge on the part of consumers and suppliers. From a practical perspective, few customers truly know what prices are available from various competitors at a given point in time, and few suppliers truly know what is the demand for an item at a given point in time. Nevertheless, the theory is quite valid and easily can be demonstrated to hold in the aggregate. This means that nationwide, over the entire range of the market for any given item, the price–demand trade-off can be expected to hold true. What it does not mean is that a small business should strive to offer the lowest possible prices.

## The Role of Cost

We mentioned earlier that you cannot sell products or services below the variable cost, at least not for long. In Chapter 5, fixed and variable costs were examined at great length. Review that section if you need to, because we are now going to examine the impact of cost on price.

For a retailer or wholesaler, the cost of acquiring inventory is a variable cost, and frequently no other significant costs are involved. If there are significant variable costs, like sales commissions, these must be added to purchase prices to arrive at total variable cost for each item sold. For a manufacturing company, the cost of production includes fixed and variable components, but the fixed components must be removed so that we can examine only the variable costs. Now, assuming that we have isolated the variable costs of products we sell, the impact on price is a function of desired profit plus variable costs.

If, for example, you wish to sell an item at a price that will not bring any profit at all but also will not cost any money, the price would simply be equal to the variable costs of the item. Obviously, the fixed costs of the business are going to have to be covered before a break-even point can be achieved, but that could be done with sales of other products. If you price the item at less than variable cost, the company will lose money on every item sold.

If you want to make a 25% contribution margin on the item, its price would be:

$$\text{Price} = \text{Variable costs} + 25\% \text{ of price}$$
$$1.25 \text{ Price} = \text{Variable costs}$$
$$\text{Price} = \text{Variable costs}/1.25$$

Contribution margins were discussed in Chapter 5. The *contribution margin* is the proportion of the price left over after variable costs are covered that contributes toward the coverage of fixed costs and, ultimately, profits. If there are no variable costs other than purchases, then the contribution margin is the same as the gross profit margin.

This procedure can be used to arrive at price estimates based on industry average margins or target margins established by the owner. For example, if the *Robert Morris Statement Studies* showed that hardware stores had an industry average margin of 30%, then the business might decide to establish prices for all items stocked by dividing their costs by 1.30. Of course, if competitive pricing disallowed such prices, some adjustments would have to be made. Nevertheless, the contribution margin approach can be used as a starting point for setting prices.

For service companies, the process is exactly the same, but the variable costs are those that result from delivering the service. In a TV repair shop, the variable costs will be labor and parts. A pricing policy probably will be established in which customers are charged the wholesale or retail price for parts used plus a set rate for each hour of labor. Deciding on the price to charge for parts would be handled in the same fashion as for a retail company because the repair shop is really selling these items. If the shop wanted to make a 20% margin on labor costs, the rate per hour would simply be the average wage rate divided by 1.20. The process of price/variable cost/profit trade-offs is the same whether products or services are involved.

Some service companies may think that they have no variable costs at all. For example, an accounting service company may have only salaried people who are paid the same whether or not they are posting client books. Here, the cost of employee time still is germane to the pricing decision. The salaries of clerks really is variable because they can handle only so many clients without increasing the size of the staff. Such a service company must establish an average wage rate per hour for its clerks and treat time posting records as variable and time doing other things as fixed cost. If the company truly has no variable costs, a dance studio in which the owner teaches all the classes, then pricing becomes a function of fixed costs and desired profits.

In Chapter 6, we spent a great deal of time discussing target profit levels for the business as a whole. We explained how the cost — volume — profit tools could be used to set prices that will achieve a desired level of profits for the business. These tools use the following relationship:

$$\text{Sales} = \text{Fixed costs} + \text{Variable costs} + \text{Desired profit}$$

Using this tool requires estimates for fixed costs, for variable costs as a function of sales, and for desired profits. If there are no variable costs, they drop out of the equation. For example, consider the dancing studio that has no variable costs and total fixed costs of rent, utilities, and so on of $19,000 per year. If the owner wants to make $35,000, then total sales must be

$$\text{Sales} = \$19{,}000 + \$35{,}000 = \$54{,}000$$

If the owner can teach three classes per week, each with ten students, then the total charge per student per lesson must be

$$\text{Price} = \$54{,}000/(3 \text{ classes} \times 10 \text{ students} \times 50 \text{ weeks})$$
$$\text{Price} = \$36 \text{ per student per class}$$

Obviously, $36 per class is going to be extremely high. Nevertheless, the calculation shows the owner that more classes or more students will be required to achieve the desired level of income. The minimum charge required to cover fixed costs with the projected enrollment is

$$\text{Price} = \$19{,}000/(3 \text{ classes} \times 10 \text{ students} \times 50 \text{ weeks})$$
$$\text{Price} = \$12.67 \text{ per student per class}$$

The CVP tools also can be used to find potential profit at established price levels. Assume that research shows that dance studios in the area charge $10.00 per student per lesson. With no other instructors except the owner, sales will have to be

$$\text{Sales} = \text{Fixed costs} + \text{Variable costs} + \text{Desired profit}$$
$$\text{Sales} = \$54{,}000$$
$$\text{Sales} = \text{Classes} \times \text{Students} \times \text{Weeks} \times \text{Price}$$
$$\text{Classes} \times \text{Students} \times 50 \text{ weeks} = \$54{,}000$$
$$\text{Classes} \times \text{Students} = \$1{,}080$$

This shows that three classes per week would require 360 students each to make the desired profit of $35,000. Again, that is impossible. If we decide to use other instructors who will be paid $25.00 to teach each class, then the equation will change. Assume that each class will be held to ten students. Then, at $10 each student, each class would produce $100 in sales and $75 in contribution margin after instructors are paid. The total number of classes required to achieve target profit would then be

$$\text{Classes} \times \$75 \times 50 \text{ weeks} = \$54{,}000$$
$$\text{Classes} = 14.4 \text{ or } 15 \text{ classes per week}$$

As you can see, CVP techniques can be valuable in pricing decisions, as well as in the break-even calculations where they are better known. Don't forget that cost is only one aspect of the pricing decision. By far the more important aspect is competition.

## Pricing Strategies

There are three basic approaches to setting the price for a product or service: pricing at competitive levels, below competitive levels, and above competitive levels. These also might be called *market levels.* Remember that when discussing the competitive or market price for an item, we are talking about near substitutes as well as exact substitutes. This means that the market for housing includes rental units as well as units for sale and the market for clothing includes discount houses as well as exclusive department stores. Food markets include convenience stores, grocery stores, and supermarkets. Accounting and tax services include CPA firms and noncertified accountants or bookkeepers, single practitioners and nationwide chains. The **market** simply means any source a consumer can utilize to satisfy the basic demand for an item.

**Pricing Above the Market.** Firms who consistently **price above competitive levels** must cultivate an image of providing a high level of quality and service and appeal to a target market that demands these things. For example, a men's clothing store that charged high prices would locate in an expensive area, such as a mall, would spend a great deal of money on store decor and amenities, would carry brands that had a reputation for high quality and the latest items in men's fashions. The store also would have to employ sales people who were well dressed and courteous and would need a large number of sales people to ensure that a customer never lacked assistance while shopping. Sales people would be trained to note and remember customers' names and to use them when possible. In addition, services such as store charge accounts and private sales might be offered, and a full range of clothing items might be offered. The key aspect is for such a store to cater to a target market that demands special treatment and high quality. Therefore, for such a store to be successful, a market in the area with those demands must exist. An exclusive men's store would not be successful in a small town or a rural setting in which the population had a low to middle socioeconomic level. It might very well be successful in a large city. The key point is that a firm that intends to pursue a strategy of higher prices than the competition must ensure that sufficient demand exists in the target area to support the firm. Second, the firm must ensure that all aspects of the operation are coordinated in fostering an image consistent with the pricing strategy.

Consider the consequences of inconsistency. If a store were to foster an image of high quality and high service but failed to charge higher prices, the customers probably would harbor beliefs that the merchandise was not of the expected quality or was made up of **factory seconds,** those items that failed quality control inspections at the factory. This is not to say that some people object to low prices. A sale in an expensive store can be just as successful as in any other store, but the long-term image of high quality cannot be maintained without a price differential. The reverse is also true: high prices alone will not create the desired image. If service levels and store decor are not consistent with the prices, then customers will feel that those prices are unjustified.

**Pricing Below the Market.** **Pricing below the market** refers to a consistent policy of offering prices below competitive levels. Sales or other short-term price reduction or discount plans are not part of this strategy. A firm that consistently prices its products or services below market levels is basically attempting to compete on the basis of price. This can be a lucrative strategy if an established demand exists for the products or services being offered. It is especially strong when used for items which consumers believe to be commodities. A **commodity** is any product or service that basically is indistinguishable from seller to seller. When consumers believe this to be the case, the primary difference between sellers becomes price. Items such as food, especially meat and produce, and other items that do not have a major brand image such as lumber, hardware and home repair items, or automobile accessories and repair parts have been successfully marketed on a commodity basis. Services, such as plumbing, appliance repair, and household maintenance also can be perceived as commodities. Any commodity item can be effectively sold using price as the principal vehicle of competition.

Goods and services are not permanently fixed as commodity items. Stock brokerage services were long considered to be above price competition and firms competed on the basis of advice, financial analyses, and other services provided to buyers. Recently, brokerage services have been successfully marketed on a commodity basis with low-cost or fixed-cost brokerage fees. A strong inroad has been made recently by generic drugs. Many firms have succeeded in using price as a competitive edge in the pharmaceuticals industry, which was long thought to be price insensitive. Of course, other firms have been successful in eliminating the commodity image. Chiquita brand bananas are the classic example of a commodity product endowed with a brand image. Sunkist oranges are another example; however, many such efforts have failed, ranging from attempts to establish brand images from lobsters to tomatoes.

If a firm decides to pursue a strategy of below market prices, that strategy must be effectively coordinated with all other aspects of the operation. Customers will simply refuse to believe that low prices are being offered in plush surroundings. It makes good sense to structure the firm on a low price image anyway, because the lower prices will create smaller contribution margins. This means that higher fixed costs will be more difficult to absorb.

**Pricing at Market Levels.** The most frequently observed practice among small businesses is **pricing at market levels.** Marketers call this strategy **follow-the-leader.** A firm pursuing this strategy attempts to price its goods and services at or near levels created by its competition. The objective is to remove price from the purchase decision so that the firm can compete on some other basis. This is somewhat of a middle ground to the above and below market pricing strategies discussed so far.

Pricing at the market has the advantage of flexibility over the other two approaches. This means that it is much easier to change the image of a firm when it is not an image keyed to price. Remember the difficulty in changing a firm's image. It can be done and sometimes must be done because of changes in demand, market area, demographics, competition, economics, or other factors. The most difficult image to change is that of a supplier priced above or below the market.

There are other advantages as well. Profit margins under market pricing can be attractive. Such a firm is plagued with neither the low contribution margins of a below market firm nor the high fixed cost levels of an above market firm. This also can translate into less risk. Remember that the higher the fixed costs in a firm, the higher is the risk, because break-even points will be leveraged higher. There also can be great risk to a below market firm, because there is less room to absorb sudden increases in costs due to the lower contribution margin.

## Price Competition

One of the most difficult aspects of a market price strategy is maintaining information about the state of the market. If you intend to use market pricing, then you must ensure that prices stay at market levels. Those levels change over time, sometimes rapidly. You must spend time gathering information about competitive prices in your area on an ongoing basis. Of course, the same should be done regardless of what pricing strategy you decide to use. It's just plain good sense to know what the competition's prices are at all times whether you plan to meet those prices or not.

Many firms constantly strive to avoid competing with other firms on the basis of price. They attempt to create situations in which customers will buy from them regardless of price. For a small business, this generally is not wise. Whether we understand the degree of its influence or not, the price of an item does affect demand. Further, price is never judged in a vacuum; it is a relative concept. A firm can have a 300% markup based on cost and still have its product or service perceived as low priced. Many items of jewelry fall into that category. A firm can also have a 10% markup based on cost and be perceived as having high prices. Many grocery items fall into that category. Because customers do not have knowledge of costs, they must make their evaluations based on prices at similar firms for similar items. This means that competition determines what is a high or low price.

The really important aspect of the pricing decision is to ensure that it is consistent with the image of the business as established by the rest of the operations. In order for that to happen, a firm must consciously decide what its image will be and what its prices will be simultaneously. This requires knowledge of prices charged by the competition at all times and constant attention to prices of individual items to ensure that they stay in the range dictated by the overall strategy of the firm. This does not mean that prices are changed every time costs change — frequently, this cannot be done. It means that prices are changed every time the market price changes.

If costs increase while market prices do not, profits will certainly suffer, but to key prices to costs only will result in customer dissatisfaction. Consider a situation in which costs are rising faster than market prices. Every firm in the industry will be affected. One firm must lead the others in raising prices before the market price can be set at a new and higher level. What will consumers think about the company who leads the price increase? Even if every other competitor follows suit with a price increase, the first firm to raise prices will experience negative reactions from consumers. Consider the problem that gasoline companies face. In 1989, when costs finally overbore competitive pressures and prices began to rise, consumers were outraged. Many accused the companies of using the catastrophic Alaskan oil spill as an excuse to increase prices without cause. It is possible to be placed in such a squeeze between costs and prices, that some ill will is to be preferred to a continuation of the situation. Nevertheless, you should always keep in mind the consequences of deviating from your established position relative to established market prices.

## ADVERTISING

Advertising is the most visible part of the marketing operation of a firm. The average person is bombarded with advertising every day. Television, radio, print media, direct mail, billboards—advertising is everywhere! Despite the broad range of media, there are really only two types of advertising a firm can do: product or service advertising and image advertising. Both are aimed at selling. That's all that advertising is—a sales pitch!

### Product or Service Advertising

Much of the advertising you see is aimed at promoting a particular product or service. It is easier to sell a specific item: you can talk about that item's features, its price, its desirability, and so forth. This can be broadened to advertising aimed at several items at once. For example, several items might be placed on sale and advertised to promote that fact. It can be highly specific. It may take several commercials or advertising spots to convey the entire message on a single product.

The outdoor advertising of Burma Shave is a classic example. Numerous signs located alongside the highway were used with each sign containing a few words of the overall message. These signs would appear sequentially some distance apart with the effect of drawing a traveler's attention to what were at first meaningless phrases in an attempt to find out the message. Regardless of how specific or general, regardless of the media used, advertising for a product or service is the easier approach because it deals with something tangible. As you will see in the next section, there can be some spillover between the two types of advertising, but the primary objective of **product or service advertising** is to create a desire in the minds of the customers for a specific item.

A risk also is associated with product or service advertising. If the advertising is successful and a demand for an item is created, there is no guarantee that the customers will use our business as the source of supply to satisfy their demand. Most large firms attempt to create a brand image that distinguishes their wares from competitors'. Most small businesses are unable to use such a strategy, as discussed in previous chapters, because of the cost and time required to create such an image. Consequently, for a small business, creating a demand for an item can carry great risk, because people may decide to buy the item from a competitor or to acquire a near substitute.

Frequently, price of an item is used as part of the advertising in an attempt to channel demand to a specific company. Consider a grocery store advertising its meat. If the advertising is effective, people seeing it will buy more meat, but not necessarily from the store doing the advertising. You can attempt to isolate the demand through a variety of techniques including reduced prices or sales, coupons, or trading stamps. Another device for isolating the demand is through image advertising either in conjunction with the product or service advertising or in separate efforts.

## Image Advertising

**Image advertising** promotes the reputation and image of the firm rather than its products or services. The two types of advertising often mingle in that some aspects of the products in general may be a part of the image promotion. For example, the image advertising could stress product or service quality, price, availability, and so on. Nevertheless, the primary objective of image advertising is the establishment of a specific set of beliefs about the company in the minds of its customers. The primary benefit is to isolate demand. This means that we wish the demand for items created through product or service advertising to benefit our firm rather than our competitors.

For image advertising to be effective, the strategic posture or competitive image of the firm must be established consistently throughout all phases of the operation. If the image we wish to portray is one of high quality and high service, then the firm must be structured so that this is always the case. If the image is one of low cost and no frills, then the firm must be consistent with that image in all of its phases. Some form of image advertising is valuable in any promotional activities, not only because it helps localize demand but because it forces a firm to analyze its image and consciously consider cultivating that image over time.

## Advertising Media

**Media** is the vehicle used to deliver an advertising message to customers. Television, radio, and newspaper advertising spring to mind immediately, but there are many other types of media. In fact, the array of advertising media available is staggering. Exhibit 18-2 lists some of the kinds of advertising outlets that exist. The list is by no means complete! In fact, the type of media that can be used is limited only by your imagination. Be sure to carefully think through any unusual steps. Recall the true story about an enterprising firm that promoted its sale of turkeys at Thanksgiving by dropping a number of live birds from a helicopter hovering over a shopping center parking lot. Unfortunately, the store owner failed to realize that only wild turkeys can fly! The domesticated variety plummeted straight down! No people were hurt, but several cars were damaged and the local chapter of the SPCA was enraged.

**EXHIBIT 18-2** *Advertising Media and Outlets*

- Television (including cable TV carriers)
- Radio
- Newspaper (including school papers)
- Outdoor
  - Billboards
  - Transit
    - Buses
    - Cabs
    - Trains
    - Personal automobiles
  - Houses
  - Barns and barn roofs
  - Fences
  - Flyers for car windshields
  - Handbills passed out to pedestrians and shoppers
  - Sandwich signs carried by individuals
  - Airplanes towing signs
- Indoor
  - Signs, placards, and posters
    - Grocery stores
    - Store windows
  - Card racks
    - Welcome centers and rest areas
    - Tourist bureaus and chambers of commerce
    - Hotels and restaurants
  - Point-of-sale displays
- Demonstrations
  - Product or service demonstrations
    - In your shop
    - On street corners
    - Other businesses
- Magazines
- Trade journals
- High school annuals
- Programs for ball games, plays, concerts
- Gifts, premiums, coupons (sold or given away)
  - Balloons
  - Pens

*continued*

**EXHIBIT 18-2 continued**

- Umbrellas
- Seat cushions
- T-shirts and sweatshirts
- Cups
- Hats
- Almost anything you can think of

Special events
- Radio shows
- Celebrities
- Ball games and competitions
  - Basketball played while riding donkeys
  - Our guys against their guys

Sponsoring
- Charity events
- Fund raising events
- School and amateur ball teams, clubs, groups

Yellow pages

The problem from a marketing perspective is the selection of a media that will provide maximum penetration of the target market for the dollars expended. It is not enough for a large number of people to be exposed to the advertising, the people exposed must be in your target market. For example, television generally is considered to have the broadest penetration of any advertising medium because so many people watch it. However, if your customers seldom watch TV, it may not be an appropriate medium.

The problem is complicated by timing and location. In TV and radio advertising, the time of day and day of week are factors in the effectiveness of the advertising. TV commercials during the middle of the day may be most effective if the target market is primarily homemakers, but commercials during sports games may be more appropriate for other products or services. Radio commercials during the 6:00 A.M. to 8:00 A.M. period and 4:00 P.M. to 6:00 P.M. period are best for catching people on the way to and from work, but may not be as effective as late night broadcasts, depending upon the target market. Of course, the variety of radio stations, rock to classical, complicate the issue even more. Most radio stations have viewer profiles that can aid in targeting your message, but that presupposes you know your target market.

With print media, location and timing still are issues. The Sunday newspaper gets a larger readership than any other day of the week, and location of the advertising within the paper can affect the likelihood of a member of the target market seeing it. With magazines and journals, location of the advertising also is a factor. It is no accident that the back cover of a magazine is the most expensive advertising spot. In addition, the size of the advertising and its location on the page, as well as its wording and layout, can affect its likelihood of being read.

Almost every type of media is affected by timing or location. Even flyers placed on car windshields can be more effective at certain times, such as on pay days of major employers in the area. In addition, all media is affected by the design of the advertising itself. Surely, you have noticed that some billboards draw your attention whereas you can drive by others without being aware that you have passed them.

The combinations of factors — timing, location, advertising design, and type of media — are almost limitless. How can you wade through all this to find the best way to spend your advertising dollars? Actually, you need more an understanding of your target market than of advertising. If you fully understand who are your customers, what are their habits and preferences, where and when they work, and where and when they play, then you can plan the best way to reach them. The more detailed your knowledge about your target market, the more effective your advertising can be. However, the less you know about your market, the less effective it will be. This also is true when applied to developing the proper image for your company. The more you know about a market to which you wish to appeal, the more effectively you can design a strategic posture or business image that will appeal to the market.

Be careful! The advertising and image selection and design must appeal to your target market, not to you! The biggest and most frequent mistake made by small businesses is confusing the owner's preferences with those of the customers. Put yourself in the shoes of your customers; develop a keen understanding of them and the people and businesses you wish to cultivate as customers.

How many times have you seen commercials in which the owner of a small business uses his or her children? What purpose can this serve? It serves self-satisfaction, not customer satisfaction. Advertising will not automatically attract customers. In fact, it can do the reverse. Poor advertising can discourage would-be customers and drive away existing ones. A recent election required a run off between two candidates vying for a position on the county school board. One candidate, who happened to be the incumbent in office, received about 49% of the vote in the first election, whereas his nearest competitor in a field of five people received about 20% of the votes cast. During the campaign for the run off, the leading candidate used a flyer with a photograph and covered virtually every car windshield in the county with those flyers. Unfortunately, the photograph was unflattering, to say the least. The quality of reproduction was poor and the candidate appeared haggard and unshaven. To top it off, the flyer carried virtually no message, no statement of position on any issue.

The flyer simply exhorted the reader to vote for the candidate because he had experience on the job. Can you guess what happened? On election day, the incumbent was soundly defeated. We'll never know whether he would have won if that flyer had not been circulated, but we can say that it certainly did not aid his campaign! The same thing happens to businesses. Poorly designed, poorly planned advertising can be worse than no advertising at all.

You must also be careful about what your advertising promises. Recently, a local grocery store displayed a special price on T-bone steaks. Several customers were heard to complain upon entering the store that the special price was for steaks that had turned dark, whereas fresher steaks displayed next to the sale meat looked better but were priced higher. The store probably lost many customers permanently as a result of that mistake.

Sometimes difficulties with promises can be more subtle. A local automobile dealer is well known for his television commercials in which he always displays several used cars with special prices. The dealer does the commercials personally and always ends the spot by saying, "Come and see me and let's make a deal."

After observing several years of highly successful operations using those commercials, another dealer in town decided to use the same approach. He began to air TV spots in which he displayed used cars with special prices and ended the commercial with an exhortation to "Come and see me for a real deal." After a few months of those spots, the dealer was reduced to the level that he could no longer afford TV commercials at all. A customer walking on his lot could never see the owner at all!

Every customer was met by sales people and the owner took no part in the sales at all. In the case of the successful car dealer, virtually every customer at least would see and speak to the owner, and a large number of them would be handled personally by the owner. The hidden promise in both of the commercials was an opportunity to bargain directly with the owner rather than a sales representative who lacked the power to "deal." Only one of the dealers was living up to that promise!

The image your business has and wishes to portray also must be clear in the advertising. If the advertising works and customers are attracted to the business, they must not be surprised. If they are led to develop one image of the business through the commercial and discover another image when buying from the firm, they will become confused and may cease to be a customer. The image is affected by the choice of media as much as it is by the design of the advertising itself. We cannot make absolute statements about the superiority of various media. It depends upon your target market. For some markets, flyers could be considered in poor taste and therefore never used by a "high-quality firm." To some markets, direct mail could be "high class" and to others it could be a nuisance.

So far, everything we've said about advertising seems to be negative. What can you do? You must choose the advertising media, timing, and location with care; you must approach the design and layout of the advertising with care; and you must get as many people involved in determining the advertising approach as you can. Sales people can be especially helpful because they deal with the customers you wish to persuade. Make sure that everything is consistent with the market you wish to reach and the image you wish to portray, then *keep records.*

Much of the knowledge about what kinds of media, timing, location, design, and so forth are effective for a particular business must be gained by trial and error. All advertising is aimed at increasing sales. If it works, sales should rise. If something works, keep doing it! If it doesn't work, stop doing it. If you are attempting something new, try to add a feature that will make the effectiveness more direct. For example, a new radio commercial might encourage listeners to mention a DJ's name to receive a free gift or a special discount. The gift can be a ballpoint pen with your firm's name on it. The point is that knowledge of the effectiveness, or lack of it, of a particular advertising approach is valuable. A small discount to a customer for clipping a coupon from a newspaper or magazine can be well worth the cost because it will tell you how well the advertisement worked.

With or without a direct measure or feedback of that type, you must have a feel for what the sales should be without advertising in order to judge its effectiveness. This means budgeting. Sales forecasting and budgeting were examined in an earlier chapter. Develop a history of sales and make forecasts of sales trends to determine whether your advertising is having any effect on those sales. Some sort of yardstick is necessary for measurement; otherwise, you will not be able to separate the forest from the trees! Remember the old tale about the security guard who suspected an employee of stealing something from the warehouse? The fellow appeared several times during the day at the gate with a wheelbarrow full of sand for use in the cement mixers and each time the guard carefully searched through the sand. He found nothing, but several days later discovered that several wheelbarrows had been stolen! The moral is that the more obvious a thing seems to be, the more it disappears. If you fail to keep careful records, fail to make sales forecasts, fail to use feedback devices, fail to monitor the results of advertising, you can never know whether your money is being wasted.

## Advertising Agencies

Advertising agencies exist because the selection of media, timing, location, design, and appeal is so complex that many firms prefer to employ professionals to handle the work. Should you consider using an advertising agency? The answer is maybe. Remember that the primary knowledge required for a successful advertising campaign is knowledge about your target market. No advertising agency has that knowledge. A good agency can have tremendous knowledge about advertising, the kinds and numbers of people who can be reached with various approaches and can have creative people who are capable of outstanding design and layouts. No agency can know your business image or your operations. This means that if you are willing to spend the time to make the people in an advertising agency knowledgeable about your firm's operation, its target market, and its image, and if you can find an agency willing to spend the time to learn the necessary information about your firm, that agency can be valuable. Without the investment of time on the part of both firms, no effective advertising can be expected. An agency can bring you knowledge of the advertising business and creativity, nothing more.

Most of the fees an agency earns are based on a percentage of media costs. This means that it is possible for an agency to overemphasize the standard approaches of television and radio, because those produce higher fees. Also, advertising agencies vary greatly in skill, knowledge, and creativity. Most agencies are small businesses and have the same problems as any small business. They are selling the advertising expertise and creativity of the staff. Consequently, the quality of the service is a function of the competency of the people. If you choose to use an advertising agency, be sure that you can develop a mutually satisfactory relationship with the people in the firm. You will need an agency that takes an active interest in your business and is willing to learn about it and its market. You will need an agency that will be open-minded about budgetary matters. You will need an agency that is willing to work within your budgetary restraints and to grow with you.

Hiring an agency does not absolve you of the record-keeping responsibility. You must still keep records to determine whether the advertising is effective. There is an added factor when an agency is involved. If the advertising is consistently ineffective, you should probably consider changing agencies. In short, it's even more important to keep records when you are using an agency to determine its effectiveness in addition to how well various advertising approaches work.

## MARKETING TECHNIQUES

**Marketing techniques** are plans or devices designed to sell products or services. Advertising is an example, but is not the only method of promoting sales. Marketing techniques can range far afield from advertising and may result from managerial actions and strategic plans. Virtually anything whose objective is increasing or obtaining sales can be thought of as a marketing technique.

## Sales Approach

The approach you take to the sale of goods and services is a marketing technique. Are your sales people commissioned or salaried? Do you sell through direct mail or a store? Is your telephone used for sales or personal calls? Almost an unlimited variety of **sales approaches** can be used. From door-to-door sales to warehouse showrooms, from part-time sales people to highly trained professionals, from independent sales representatives to salaried employees — the variety is limited only by your imagination.

How do you decide what sales approach to use? As in deciding on advertising media, it is based on knowledge of your target market and your business image. You must select an approach you believe will give you maximum coverage of the market and a competitive position. Frequently, an innovative approach can be valuable because it can make you stand out from your competitors. You must temper your approach with knowledge of the industry. In some industries, the sales approach is so thoroughly entrenched by tradition that change is virtually impossible. For example, college textbooks traditionally have been sold by providing "examination copies" to professors in the hopes that they will adopt the books for use in their classes. This can be a highly significant expense. Recently, several small firms in the textbook market have tried to change the sales approach. They require a professor to purchase or return examination copies within a certain time if the books are not adopted for use in a class. Many professors have reacted unfavorably to this change because it requires them to review a book quickly or be billed for it. This can be a problem due to other demands on their time. Consequently, the firms using the new sales approach are significantly less competitive. Whether the sales approach will shift over time cannot be predicted as yet. Many other industries have similar restrictions on the sales approach that has developed over time and that can limit the success of innovative approaches.

There is another aspect to the sales approach that the customer does not see: the compensation of employees. The sales people can be paid salaries, commissions, or some combination of the two. When deciding on the sales approach to use, you must also decide on the compensation approach to use for sales people. Generally, when sales people have the opportunity to increase their pay by increasing sales, they can be expected to produce more. Promotions that give away prizes, trips, and vacations for achieving established sales levels can be valuable in motivating sales people, as can be bonuses and other forms of recognition. The recognition need not be monetary. In the life insurance industry, for example, top sales people qualify for membership in the Million Dollar Round Table or some other "club" for high producers. This membership, which may be displayed on business cards, provides recognition and status for excellent performance. Recognition frequently can be worth more than money as an incentive. This is especially true for higher-paid people.

## Advertising

Many aspects of advertising have been discussed, but not its use as a marketing technique; that is, the coordination of advertising with operations, conditions, and other marketing techniques. How do you decide which items to advertise in product or service advertising? One approach is to select items you believe will appeal to the target market at a particular time: turkeys at Thanksgiving, toys at Christmas, swimsuits in the summer. Another approach is to choose items that are not selling well when compared to others. Still another approach is to choose items that make you stand out from your competition: items they do not carry or that are rare or difficult to find. You could choose some staple or basic item that has continuous appeal to the market. Or, you could choose items whose suppliers will provide co-op advertising support; that is, they will pay part of the cost of advertising. As you can see, there is a large number of approaches to deciding what is to be advertised!

In addition, you must coordinate advertising with the rest of the firm's operations. It makes no sense to promote an item that you do not have. If you are experiencing a strike or work slowdown, advertising may be wasted until the problems are settled. On the other hand, if you are expecting a major shipment of some item next week, advertising for that item could be most appropriate. In addition to internal factors, you also must coordinate advertising with conditions outside the firm that could affect it. For example, launching a major advertising campaign the week following large layoffs of people in your target market would be a waste of money. In a college town, advertising must take into consideration semester breaks and other times when students will not be in town if they are included in the target market. In a farming community, advertising would best be geared to harvest times and could be affected by extremes in weather.

Other marketing techniques need to be considered as well. Advertising efforts must be coordinated with sales people so that it will assist their sales efforts. In addition, everyone in the business needs to be aware of advertising campaigns so they can capitalize on those campaigns and so feedback information about the effectiveness of the campaign can be captured. Advertising must be coordinated with sales and take into consideration any premiums being offered.

One final word is necessary about advertising. Never overlook the value of the free advertising that comes from **word of mouth.** Customers who are pleased with you and satisfied with their purchases inevitably will talk about your firm to their friends, neighbors, and business associates. Customers who are displeased are even more inclined to talk about your firm. Therefore, always be aware of the satisfaction level of your customers and strive to keep it high. No advertising you can buy will be as effective as customer endorsement and nothing can be as damaging to your firm as customer criticism.

## Premiums

**Premiums** are gifts, discounts, or coupons given for purchasing an item. These can range from trading stamps given by a grocery store to dishes given by a bank for new savings deposits. If premiums of any type are used, the advertising should promote the premium offers and make sure that customers understand the premium program. Customers who do not understand the basis for the awarding of premiums can become angry, and the program can backfire, alienating customers rather than attracting them. In addition, premiums can be costly. Consequently, careful records should be kept concerning the effectiveness of premiums. Added costs of the premium program should be compared to increases in the contribution margin that result from the program. Increase in sales is not enough: the increase in contribution margin resulting from sales growth is the profit gained from the program, and this must be compared to the cost of the premiums and the cost of any advertising associated with them. Don't make the mistake of believing that all sales during a premium campaign result from the premium technique. As in all other advertising approaches, you must compare sales results to sales trends and forecasts to identify real new business that you would not have received without the premiums. It is even more important in this case because of the added costs.

## Sales

Everyone understands sales and how advertising is needed to promote sales. What is less obvious are the various reasons for a sale. Sales can be used to get rid of unsalable items. Have you noticed sales items marked **buy one, get one free**? This sales technique will get rid of more items than simply marking every item down to half price. Another reason for a sale is to attract people into the business. If some items are on sale and others are not, perhaps people can be encouraged to buy some of the regular items. This is the philosophy behind **loss leaders,** or items actually priced below cost. Sales also can be used to attract members of the target market who have not yet become customers or who are unfamiliar with the firm. Still another reason for a sale can be simply to make money. Have you noticed any firms that seem to have a perpetual sale? As soon as one promotion is over, another starts. Some firms, especially those that choose discount pricing strategies, use sales as their primary sales approach.

If a sale is used for any purpose other than disposing of stale or slow-moving merchandise, then you should be aware of its costs and benefits, as for any other marketing technique. The costs of the sale are reduced or lost contribution margins on the items marked down as well as any advertising associated with the sale. Gains from the sale arise from increases in the overall sales of the firm and the contribution margin from those gains. This means that you must compare sales to trends and forecasts, as discussed in the prior sections. You must be able to tell whether your sales are working. Careful record keeping is the only way to make that determination.

## BUDGETING

We have talked about budgeting for the firm as a whole and developing the budget for start-up marketing. Ongoing marketing also requires a budget. Because no firm has unlimited resources, you must plan how much you intend to spend on marketing. Some firms do this by designating a percentage of gross sales for marketing expenditures. Percentages from 1% to 5% are not uncommon under this approach. When the sales forecast and the expense forecast are prepared, the dollars budgeted for marketing will be a part of the overall budget. Other firms plan marketing campaigns and forecast the actual costs of those campaigns as part of the budgeting process. Still other firms, probably the majority of small firms, do no planning at all and simply spend money haphazardly. There is absolutely no way that a business can expect to maximize the yield from its marketing dollars if it does not budget those dollars and plan where and how they are to be spent.

Once a budget has been prepared, decide how the money is to be spent. This means apportioning the dollars to various advertising campaigns and media and to other marketing techniques. How you decide how much to apportion to each marketing effort on an ongoing basis depends largely on your record keeping. The most effective techniques should have the most dollars apportioned. Nevertheless, you should always strive to set aside part of the budget for continued experimentation. The marketing techniques that work are bound to change over time with the changing characteristics of your market, competition, and other factors. This means that you must always be trying new approaches. Because the changes generally will occur slowly, it makes sense to spend the majority of the budget on tried and true techniques. But because change is inevitable, some dollars must always be used to test new and potentially better techniques.

## STRATEGY

In this and all of the other chapters in the book, we stress planning and strategy development, because planning is the most important function of a successful management. The planning and strategy development must be done for the firm as a whole; it cannot be accomplished piecemeal. This means that the owner and top managers of a small business must be generalists and constantly strive to view the firm as a single functioning unit. The strategy development must include marketing strategies, of course, but those strategies must make sense in light of all other strategies in the firm. The long-term and short-term goals and objectives for the organization must drive the marketing strategy, just as they do every other aspect of the business.

There is a difference about marketing strategy, because this is the place where everything in the business must focus. Regardless of the kind of business or industry concerned, its long-term success in large measure will reflect the success of the marketing strategy. Every business must sell before anything else can happen. Consequently, every aspect of the business is directed to selling products and services. This is true regardless of the size of the business. Marketing is not something considered after everything else has been determined. It is an intricate part of the overall strategy development and planning of a firm. Marketing really is the place where everything in the business comes together.

## SUMMARY

Although the marketing effort at start up was discussed in another chapter, the subject merits continued investigation in an ongoing concern. Marketing is the effort used to sell goods or services. It is more than just advertising.

In developing an ongoing marketing strategy, we must continually monitor and adjust to the factors that affect the purchasing decision: the who, what, when, where, how, and why of marketing. *Who* refers to the target market; *what* refers to the product or service a customer actually buys; *when* includes not only the time of day but also the season in which particular purchases are made; *where* concerns store, outlet, branch, and warehouse location; *how* concerns payment patterns; and *why* is the sociological and psychological reasons behind a purchase. Successful marketing in a small business largely is a function of awareness of buying trends and patterns, target market characteristics, and historic marketing efforts.

The three basic approaches to marketing are push, pull, and piggyback. *Push marketing* refers to the attempt to persuade a retailer, distributor, or supplier to carry wares and is an attractive approach for small businesses. *Pull marketing* focuses on the ultimate consumer of an item and attempts to create a demand for the wares, which may not be viable for small businesses. *Piggyback marketing* probably is the approach most popular with small businesses because in it a business copies and capitalizes on a competitor's marketing efforts.

Marketing research is important to a small business in that it gives the owner tools to use for more effective marketing. A business that can identify its target market and the reactions of the market can better plan advertising and marketing campaigns to reach that market.

One of the most important areas affected by marketing but often overlooked by small businesses is image. Image is the way customers perceive the business: what makes it distinctive, its personality. Changing an established image is almost impossible, so decide on the image and work to maintain it.

Pricing is a very important marketing concept, which the novice quickly equates with cost. However, the main inputs to price are demand and competition, both of which are difficult concepts to measure. There are three basic approaches to setting the price for a product or service: pricing at competitive levels, below competitive levels, or above competitive levels. Firms that consistently price above competitive levels must cultivate an image of providing a high level of quality and service and appeal to a target market that demands those things. Pricing below the market means that a firm's prices consistently are less than its competitors'; for example, in the form of recurring sales or discounts. The most frequently observed practice among small businesses is pricing at market level; that is, the firm attempts to price its goods and services at or near levels created by its competition. Whatever the strategy, the strategy must remain consistent with the image portrayed for the firm to enjoy success.

Advertising is the most visible marketing operation of a business. Advertising may be done through many media and typically is aimed at promoting a particular product or service. The objective of product or service advertising is to create a desire in the minds of the customers for a specific item. However, the associated risk is that the customer will buy the advertised product or service from someone else.

Image advertising promotes the reputation and image of the firm rather than its products or services. As long as the image and advertising remain consistent, the element of risk is minimized.

Media is the vehicle used to deliver an advertising message to customers. The media used for advertising is limited only by the imagination; however, the problem comes in selecting the medium that will provide maximum penetration of the target market for the dollars expended. Yet the various combinations of the factors of timing, location, advertising design, and type of media are almost limitless.

Nevertheless, beware! Poor advertising can be worse than no advertising. Be sure that the advertising campaign will appeal to your customers, not to you personally. Your preferences may not be congruent. Also be careful about advertising promises and be sure that the advertising is consistent with the firm's image.

To help you to assess the effectiveness of the advertising, keep records. Know what works and what doesn't. An advertising agency may be beneficial if you are unsure about what will work for you. This approach is more expensive, yet it can be effective. If you choose to go this route, establish a good relationship with your agency, and keep records about the campaigns.

A business may pursue marketing techniques other than advertising. The approach you take to sales is one technique. Another technique is the use of premiums such as gifts, discounts, or coupons. Keep records to see what works. To learn why sales work is another marketing technique. The reasons for a sale may be to get rid of unsalable items, to attract new as well as regular customers, or to make money.

Just as budgeting was necessary in start-up planning, it is important in ongoing marketing efforts. Don't spend advertising dollars on whim, but plan for the expenditures. Many firms designate a percentage of gross sales for market expenses whereas others forecast the actual cost of marketing campaigns as part of the budgeting process. If you have kept careful records, you should know which marketing techniques are the best justified.

Because planning is the most important function of management, the development of effective marketing strategies should be of primary concern. Marketing is not something considered after everything else has been determined, but an intricate part of the overall strategy development and planning of the firm. Marketing really is the place where everything in the business comes together.

## QUESTIONS

1. How is advertising different from marketing?
2. What factors are involved in the purchasing decision?
3. What is the purpose of loss leaders and premiums in marketing?
4. Describe the supply-demand-price cycle.
5. What are the three approaches to marketing? Which is the best approach for small businesses? Explain why.
6. Why is image advertising less risky than product or service advertising? Explain why.
7. What are the various marketing techniques small businesses can use to enhance their marketing efforts?
8. Why is it better to plan and budget rather than react in marketing?
9. Is it better to use an advertising agency or do your own advertising? Explain why or why not.
10. Why is it said that the marketing effort brings together the planning and development function of a small business?

## PROJECTS

1. Make a list of all the commercials that occur during the television news on a weeknight. Identify each advertisement as a product or service ad or an image ad. Describe the basis of appeal each ad uses to encourage you to buy.
2. Repeat Project 1 using radio commercials that air between 7:00 A.M. and 8:00 A.M. on a weekday morning. What differences occur in types of firms advertising and types of ads? Did television or radio have a larger proportion of small businesses?
3. Visit a local radio station and ask for a listener profile and advertising rates. What kinds of businesses would find this particular station appropriate? What kinds of advertising do you think would be most appropriate on this station?
4. Visit a small business and ask the owner about marketing strategies and plans. Ask about the image the owner wants to convey. Do you think the image is consistent with the appearance and location of the business? What problems or weaknesses in marketing management do you see in the operation of the business?

# Case

Let's revisit the karate school of Chapter 14, prior to its sale—back to the reasonably good times in the beginning. Randy commented in passing that now things are really going to get hot. "What do you mean?" we asked.

Randy was excited. We had just passed a young man in the doorway and assumed that he was a supplier of some type, because he was just putting away a check and some papers. Randy was so pleased he had to share his good fortune.

"I just bought a listing in a directory that is going to be placed in hotels, resort areas, and rest areas in a 200-mile radius! Do you know how many resorts there are in this area? And think of the Blue Ridge Parkway! Business is going to boom now!"

Obviously he was thrilled. We didn't know what to say. We were his customers or at least our sons were. Although he knew that we were professors, he had never asked our opinion and seemed reluctant to do more than tell us what he had done. "Is that the only advertising you're doing?"

"Well, you know that the paper carries a special now and then. But it only comes out once a week and I haven't gotten much response from those ads. I have been offering a special, you know, the first two lessons free or a free gi with the introductory lessons. I've been alternating the ads. You know, that's a real deal. Those gis cost about $20 for the inexpensive ones."

Sensing our lack of enthusiasm, Randy quickly went to work out with the kids. What could we do? We wanted the dojo to be successful. Randy was a great young man. We wanted our boys to continue their studies, not just for the self-defense they were learning, but for the self-confidence and self-discipline that were already becoming obvious to us. Other parents had agreed with us. They were excited about the philosophy that was being taught. Many of us had gone to the karate tournaments and seen the violence taught by the other schools and felt truly indebted to Randy for not teaching that type of behavior.

Advertising can take a variety of forms as you have discovered in your reading. You can have the soft sell of McDonald's or the hard sell of some of the automobile manufacturers, but you don't need an advertising agency to tell you what appeals to you.

### Questions

1. Think about this business and the sort of image it wants to portray. What elements would appeal to the most people? Would it be appropriate to ask his students exactly why they had chosen to study with him rather than several other schools in the area?
2. Who is Randy's target market? Why were we not excited about the $150 he had just spent on the directory listing? What is the target market of the directory?
3. Because the newspaper comes out weekly rather than daily, what other advertising means might Randy have chosen?

4. What was Randy really selling? What is his distinctive competency? Do you think that he knows?
5. Develop a marketing plan for Randy's dojo. Refer back to the case in Chapter 14 and refer to the following note. In considering the market plan for this case, ignore the weight and exercise part of the business; focus only on the karate school aspects. Note that there are two locations for Randy's business: one in his home town and the other in a nearby college town.

*Note:* In the home town, about 50% of his students are from the local school systems, mostly junior high students. The other 50% are young men and women employed in the area. There are several police officers, a couple of postal carriers, some mill workers, and a few white-collar junior or middle managers. In the college town, almost 90% are from the university, and the other 10% from the local high school.

6. Would the same marketing efforts be appropriate for both locations? What would the difference in appeal be in the two locations? What types of marketing would be appropriate in each location? Is Randy adequately tapping the market at either place? What can he do?
7. You have been hired as a consultant and told that $250 maximum is available for the effort. What marketing plans can you come up with? Present your plans to the class.

# CHAPTER 19

# Risk Management

**LEARNING OBJECTIVES**

After completing this chapter, you should be able to

- Understand that financial planning includes consideration of risks to which firms will be exposed.
- Know the importance of risk management.
- Evaluate the four major risks in a business.
- Understand how to use insurance effectively and its limitations.
- Prepare a risk management contingency plan for a small business.

The financial planning required both in a new venture and in ongoing management includes consideration of the risks to which the firm will be exposed. Our society seems to be infatuated with the concept of risk. Far too many would-be business owners take Kipling's words to heart.

If you can make one heap of all your winnings
    And risk it all on one turn of pitch-and-toss,
And lose, and start again at your beginnings
    And never breathe a word about your loss.

. . .

Yours is the Earth and everything that's in it,
    And—which is more—you'll be a Man, my son!

"If"
Rudyard Kipling

In business, well-informed, capable managers never assume unexamined risk. It certainly is true that risk is involved in all business. What is not true is that owners of small businesses enjoy taking risks. In this chapter, we talk about business risks, insurance, and risk management. We explore the sources of risks and methods of minimizing the exposure of a firm to those risks.

## WHAT IS RISK MANAGEMENT?

When most people think about risk management, they think of **insurance.** Risk management is much more than just an insurance program. First, not everything can be insured. For a risk, or hazard, as insurance companies are fond of calling them, to be insurable, it must be possible to identify that risk, calculate the amount of loss that can occur, and spread the risk over a large number of people. Identifying a risk means an unambiguous statement of the potential loss. For example, a building can be insured against fire, but not against "everything." Calculating the potential loss requires knowledge about the dollar value of a loss. It would not be possible to insure a business against the revenues lost from a downturn in the economy.

**Spreading the risk** is a requirement of insurance companies for underwriting a risk. Insurance companies can exist only because they have a large enough base of policy holders that premiums received for coverage in the long term will exceed the amount of losses that will occur. This means that a circus high-wire walker or a daredevil who jumps motorcycles over buses will have trouble obtaining insurance coverage because there just aren't enough people doing those things to spread the risk.

Even if it were possible to insure against everything that could happen in a business, it still would not be feasible for a small business, due to the amount of insurance premiums that would have to be paid. **Risk management** is the science of identifying the risks inherent in a business venture, taking steps to minimize those risks as much as possible, insuring those risks that are appropriate to insure, and preparing a contingency plan to deal with potential losses. So you see, risk management is planning!

## IDENTIFYING RISKS

There are four major groups of risk in a business venture: risks associated with operations, property, customers, and employees. We address each of these independently and present some ideas for minimizing them.

### Operational Risks

**Operational risks** generally are not insurable. These risks include the risk of recession, changes in markets, product obsolescence, changes in competition, death or loss of key employees, and risks of that nature — in other words, the risks associated with the normal operations of a business. Effective operational risk management requires being aware of the kinds of environmental changes that can affect the business, structuring the business to avoid as many of these effects as possible, preparing a plan for dealing with those environmental changes that cannot be avoided, monitoring for the occurrence of those changes and reacting quickly to implement the plan when they do occur. This all sounds quite mystical, but really is simple and requires nothing more than common sense.

**Changes in Demand.** **Diversification** is probably the best protection against product obsolescence. If it is well planned, it also can protect against recessions and market and competition changes. Obviously, a company that has many products and markets is safer from environmental changes than a one product – one market company. Small business owners frequently fail to consider diversification because they think of it as something only large firms do. They think it means acquiring other companies, branching out into other countries, entering into new product or service markets, or strategies of that nature. All of these moves indeed are diversification strategies, but small businesses can diversify along more modest lines with a little planning.

A few years ago a small business started a cut-and-sew operation. The company started out bidding for contracts to make ladies' dresses. After a few months, the owner began to pursue contracts for other types of ladies' apparel. Then the company went after jeans and men's slacks. During this time, the company also was gaining experience cutting and handling various types of materials. After about three years, the company was cutting and sewing a wide variety of clothing items for men, women, children, and youth. The same company now makes covers from heavy canvas and rubberized materials for equipment and machinery, and the owner is looking into the possibility of surgical gowns.

This is clearly an example of small business diversification. The resulting company is not only larger and stronger than it would have been had it stayed with dresses, it avoided a problem many other small firms of this type experienced. Apparel can be manufactured much more inexpensively in Third World countries.

Our point is that small business, too, can pursue diversification and should do so, because it is sound business sense! It happens every day. A building contractor uses his crews to build dog and pet houses and prefabricated outbuildings when the weather is bad or the work is off. A real estate broker now sells property insurance. An accounting service company that began with a general purpose computerized accounting system now handles payrolls and has acquired several specialized systems, including one designed specifically for gas stations. A gas station operator handles fuel oil. Another has added a convenience store. A convenience store operator uses part of the store's land for a self-service car wash. Virtually all businesses can find opportunities to expand products, services, or markets with a little planning and effort.

**Loss of Key Employees.** Deciding in advance what to do if faced with the loss of a key employee is just common sense. Taking steps to minimize the risk of such a loss means paying attention to compensation policies and implementing pension and profit sharing plans. This will help ensure that you do not lose the employee to another company. These strategies were discussed at length in Chapter 17.

You should also take steps to minimize the impact of the death of a key employee through life insurance. Furthermore, you should plan for management succession by continually grooming new people for key positions. This way, if you lose a person to competition or to death, another employee will have been prepared to take over the duties. Needless to say, these last steps apply to yourself as well. What will happen to the business if you die or suddenly become incapacitated? Beyond the obvious effect on your family, there is the business to consider. Countless small businesses depend so heavily on the owner that even a brief loss of that person could destroy the business. More than one small business owner has recuperated from a heart attack to discover that the business did not survive! You owe it to yourself and to your business to ensure that it can weather the loss of any person, including yourself.

**General Risks.** How do you handle operational risks? You try to visualize all the things that might happen and make plans to avoid as many as possible and minimize the effects if the worst happens. Plans to deal with these risks should be made in writing and reviewed at least annually. Operational risks never go away and conditions never stay the same.

## Property Risks

**Property risks** are the type most people immediately think of when risk management is mentioned. Most of these risks can be covered by insurance. They include the potential destruction or loss of one or more of the physical assets of a business. This goes far beyond fire insurance. Risk management of property hazards requires taking steps to minimize the risk of loss, insuring against the loss, and planning for recovery.

To minimize the risks, you must first carefully identify them. For example, safe construction, the removal of fire hazards, and a fire prevention program can reduce the risk of fire; but how do you reduce the risk of shoplifting? The loss of inventory through shoplifting is a property risk. Natural disasters simply are the most obvious risks. Property risks include robbery and theft by employees as well.

**Theft of Goods.** Security systems, especially cameras, can help deter theft. Employee theft is especially vulnerable to camera security. One owner of a convenience store installed a camera system above the cash register to deter armed robbery. Even though there was never such an attempt, shoplifting losses went down by half in the first month! This made the owner suspicious, because the camera had only a limited field of vision and the film never captured any suspicious scenes. He installed other cameras including one in the storeroom that was off limits to customers. Shoplifting losses almost disappeared! Clearly, much of what he thought were shoplifting losses were really incidences of employee theft.

Other steps include sensible locations. Part of the site location process described in previous chapters should concentrate on avoiding areas subject to high crime rates or on making plans to minimize risks in areas subject to crime. Layout of the store, mirrors, and electronic sensing tags for merchandise are possible strategies.

**Theft of Cash.** An essential strategy is the protection of cash. Gas stations, convenience stores, and liquor stores now have signs that indicate that night staff do not have the combination to the safe. In addition, computerized price lookups built into the cash registers and product code sensors and light wands help protect against accidental and deliberate mistakes in merchandise sales.

Something as simple as requiring cash to be removed from the register whenever it exceeds a specific amount can be effective. Daily bank deposits of cash and additional deposits when cash exceeds a certain level are good ideas. Of course, procedures for handling that cash and the record keeping associated with it also are mandatory. Professional assistance from your CPA or accountant can be useful in this area. Internal controls can be designed to minimize cash risks and many other types of property risks as well.

**Computer Theft or Destruction.** An extremely disturbing form of property risk, born of the information age, is the risk to data files and automated equipment. Records may be the most valuable physical asset of a business. What would happen to a business if it suddenly lost all its records? How would it collect its accounts receivable or know which bills and statements it owed? How could it comply with statutory requirements to file sales tax returns, employee withholding statements, income tax returns? Some of the most spectacular losses businesses experience have come in the form of computer fraud. This area is so sensitive that sensible risk management requires a separate security and disaster plan just for computer based information systems. This subject was discussed at great length in Chapter 9, including a plan for computer security and disaster planning.

**Physical Destruction.** Safeguarding physical assets is an exercise in imagination. You must strive to identify potential hazards to the resources of your particular business, and plan for the reduction and minimization of those risks. Don't forget the ultimate risk: the loss of everything. Even if sufficient insurance coverage exists to permit the rebuilding of a business that has lost all of its physical assets, how does this take place? In an *Inc.* article, a small business owner detailed his efforts to rebuild a business that lost all its assets to a major fire. The effort was a success, but only due to the extraordinary perseverance of the owner. In hindsight he recommended that every business have a written contingency plan that outlines how rebuilding would take place.[1]

## Customer-Centered Risks

Most people think of customer-centered risks as involving suits for injuries received on the premises. This is a clear risk, but one that generally can be covered by insurance. Customer theft in the form of shoplifting is part of property risk. In reality, the greatest risk associated with customers is that of product or service liability. Originally, this risk was associated principally with products, but court precedents have moved its impact into the services field as well.

**Product Liability.** In general, the courts have held in **product liability suits** that a product must be fit for the purpose for which it was designed. This means that if a rope sold as clothesline breaks while the purchaser uses it for mountain climbing, the producer has no liability. But if the rope was sold for mountain climbing, then it must be able to stand up to reasonably anticipated rigors or the producer will be liable. Product liability suits frequently have attracted the news media in recent years because of the size of the awards and settlements and the tendency for class action suits to grow out of product liability claims. A **class action suit** is brought on the part of a group of customers or injured parties. In a broader sense, these actions can be brought by people who are not customers of a business. If a manufacturing plant explodes and the people living nearby are injured, then the business owning that plant may be found liable far in excess of its insurance coverage.

Services, like products, must be provided with reasonable competency. Medical malpractice suits have never been more common than now and services of all kinds increasingly are being brought under product liability expectations. Accounting firms are being sued by parties claiming injury from reliance on financial statements prepared by the firms. The trend shows every sign of intensifying.

Don't make the mistake of thinking that you are free from liability because you are a retailer or wholesaler. People in these businesses frequently think that product liability falls only on the manufacturer of the goods they carry. This is not true! Courts frequently have held that retailers are liable as well as manufacturers.

How do you reduce the risk of product or service liability claims? It requires a sincere and concerted effort to provide high-quality products and competent services. It requires restraint in advertising programs, and free communication with customers about product or service limitations. It requires an effective training program for employees about the way in which products and services are to be represented to the public, and training or education efforts aimed at customers to assure competent and proper use of the company's products or services. It requires constant vigilance on the part of the management of a business to ensure that short-term profits never become so important that short cuts or unacceptable risks may be taken. It requires planning on a continuing basis to ensure that risks are minimized and to prepare for actions if a disaster occurs. We have more to say on this subject in Chapter 25, "Small Business Law."

**Nonpayment of Accounts Receivable.** Another aspect of customer-related risk is the risk of nonpayment on accounts or notes receivable. If your business has accounts receivable, then it is inevitable that some loss will occur on those accounts. The difference in acceptable and unacceptable losses frequently is the result of planning. The business should develop lending and collection policies and set aside reserves to cover losses. A thin line must be walked in accounts receivable: a credit policy that is too tight will lose sales; a credit policy that is too loose will lose too many accounts. Finding where you should be in that continuum is challenging and difficult. Constant monitoring of the credit practices and experience and adjustment of the policy is the only plausible approach to solving the dilemma.

Adequate training of the people who will be extending credit and the people who will be collecting accounts is a must, as is a sound plan for how and when collection efforts will begin and end. **Trade credit** is by far the largest source of funding in the business world. It exceeds bank financing and bond and equity financing combined. Even large firms frequently are guilty of "riding" their accounts payable when times are tough. All the sales in an industry will not help a firm if it is unable to collect for those sales. Cash flow is infinitely more important than profits in the survival of a small business. Planning is crucial to determine how cash flow can be maximized through the credit practices of the business.

## Employee-Centered Risks

Many of the risks that revolve around employees also could be classified operational risks. For example, in a prior section, we talked about the risk of losing key people. Other types of employee risks involve property. Employee theft is something which is distasteful to consider, but a very real problem in the business world. Due to a reluctance to report employee theft, no one knows the true extent of the problem. Many experts believe it to be far greater than the sum of all shoplifting and burglary in the country! Internal control procedures are vital. We discussed such controls in general in Chapter 4 and described how your CPA can assist in designing them.

**Theft.** Specific controls to minimize employee risk include cash controls (discussed earlier), key controls, physical inventories, and trash control. Locks, strong effective locks, are an obvious control device but small business owners frequently make no effort to control the storage, location, or duplication of the keys themselves. Locks do no good if the keys or their duplicates are readily available. You need a system for checking out keys on an as-needed basis to responsible employees and a system for keeping those keys secure at other times. Physical inventories or counts of merchandise at unannounced times can be an effective device; this will be examined at more length in Chapter 20.

Trash control is an area easily overlooked. Two uses of trash have potentially damaging effects. First, the documents and papers thrown away present possible problems. Not only will documents containing your computer system passwords be dangerous, but so will papers that identify your suppliers, your customers, your employees, the location and arrangement of your business and warehouse, hours of operation, security arrangements, and so on. The list goes on! Clearly, you need to condition people not to throw away documents or papers; they should be shredded. Shredders are inexpensive and can be valuable additions to a security system.

Second, trash represents a tremendous opportunity for employee theft. An employee who takes an item of value may simply hide it in the trash! If it is discovered before the trash is thrown away, well it would be hard to link any individual to the item and it could have been an accident. More likely, no one looks through the trash, so the container is dumped outside for the trash collector to pick up. The employee comes back at night and retrieves the stolen item. What can you do about this? Don't make trash cans readily available. All the papers and documents should be shredded so one container can be set aside for this purpose. Other trash containers will be required in restrooms and lounges, of course, but don't put trash cans in other areas. Assign one person the job of emptying trash containers and make that person aware that trash can be used to conceal theft. Finally, don't leave trash outside for pick up. Store it inside the building and arrange to have the trash taken directly to the truck during working hours.

By far the most important and effective control for employee-centered risks is the careful selection, training, and supervision of employees. In Chapter 4, we indicated that the first rule of internal control is the hiring of honest, capable people. This puts more emphasis on the hiring process described at great length in Chapter 17. If honest people are hired in the first place, and they are well trained and well compensated, they are less likely to be a problem.

**Bonding** employees who are in sensitive positions can be accomplished through your insurance company. This will protect against their theft or fraud. Other employee risks affect the firm's records; and a major portion of the security planning for the computer-based information system must deal with protection from breaches of security or confidentiality by employees. This was discussed in Chapter 9. Also, employees and the work they do affect customer relations and have an impact on a business' ultimate liability for customer injuries or claims. Good supervision by competent managers will go a long way toward minimizing these risks.

Finally, employee risks involve loss of income through such devices as **sweetheart sales,** sales of items by cashiers at below price. This can be a serious problem, especially if you use young, inexperienced cashiers who frequently must ring sales for friends and peers. Mechanical devices, though expensive, and training and supervision can help to minimize the problem.

Before we leave the subject of employee risk, we must talk about polygraph testing. This is a popular and visible technique that many retail firms employ. However, polygraphs have come under attack because they have not always proven reliable. In fact, many states now have laws that prohibit their use. In many examples, employees have been discharged on the basis of polygraph tests and later won court suits as a result. Furthermore, reports about the effectiveness of polygraphs in preventing employee theft are mixed. In short, polygraphs are not a panacea! Their use does not guarantee employee honesty. Consequently, we strongly recommend against their use except in special industries and circumstances. For most small businesses, polygraphs are an expensive and not necessarily effective device that promises problems in the future. If you do intend to use polygraphs, be sure to obtain legal advice first and to follow careful procedures as outlined by professionals.

**Injury.** A business is responsible for providing a safe working environment for its employees. In some industries, such as mining and textiles, huge awards have been made by courts to employees who have sustained injuries related to their work. All states have enacted **workers' compensation insurance laws,** which provide for a schedule of payments to be made for employee injuries sustained in work-related activities. This means that the business is liable for employee injuries on the job.

Superficially, it seems that risks of employee injuries are easily covered by insurance, but courts have gone beyond workers' compensation coverage when they determined that the hazards reasonably should have been eliminated. For example, if a part of an underground mine was deemed unsafe and the owner took no action to correct the problems, then any employees injured could receive court-ordered compensation far beyond the level of workers' compensation. If a machine were improperly installed or security panels routinely were left open, an employee injured by that machine also could win an award in excess of insurance coverage. Don't make the mistake of minimizing these risks as associated only with dangerous occupations. If you run a bookstore that requires climbing a ladder to reach the top shelves, and that ladder is unsafe — watch out!

In essence, workers' compensation laws and court precedents say that an employer has an obligation to provide a workplace and working conditions that are reasonably safe. Part of the risk management planning should ensure that all reasonable safety precautions are taken and that safety is a continuing objective in all activities.

**Dissatisfied Employees.** Perhaps the strongest insurance against employee-centered risks in a business is an open relationship based on mutual respect between the owners and the employees of a firm. No one is in a better position to witness the development of problems of all types than the employees. If channels to management permit communication of developing problems and an atmosphere is established that recognizes the value of such communication, then potential problems can be headed off at an early stage. For example, the risk of loss of production through strikes and work stoppages can be greatly reduced by good employee relations. Such problems seldom develop when employees feel a sense of involvement in the business.

This concept is at the heart of the **quality circles** developed in many large organizations and so popular with the press. The quality circle approach organizes employees in small groups that meet periodically to discuss their work and ways to improve it, improve products, improve output, reduce costs, and so on. Many such programs have resulted in tremendous savings to the participating businesses, but more important, such programs can result in more concerned and caring employees and more rewarding work experiences. Whatever the method used, the fostering of an attitude of interest in the business and a belief that suggestions will be heard by management should be prime goals of any risk management program.

## INSURANCE

**Insurance** can be exceedingly complex as well as expensive. The kinds of coverage available and the variety of policies mandate the use of an expert to obtain a sensible insurance program. Many insurance companies specialize in particular hazards. This, and a natural desire to minimize policy premiums, means that an independent agent probably is the best source of insurance assistance and coverage. An independent agent does not work for one insurance company, but is licensed to write coverage with a variety of insurance companies.

### Independent Agents

At an early point in the establishment of a new venture, you should establish a relationship with an independent insurance agent and develop a comprehensive insurance plan to protect the business. Just as selecting an attorney and a CPA are important steps, so too is the selection of an insurance agent. Interview several agents, discuss your plans, and find out about the agents' backgrounds and areas of expertise. Your goal will be to develop a continuing relationship with an agent who is knowledgeable in the kinds of risks that exist in your industry and willing and competent to assist you in a comprehensive risk management program. The best deal is not necessarily the one with the lowest cost. For example, almost all fire insurance policies are written with a coinsurance clause.

## Coinsurance Clauses

If a policy specifies a coinsurance portion of 80% of the property value, then potential claims will be affected by that percentage. If you fail to insure property for its full value in an effort to reduce premiums, then that failure will affect coverage. A loss of $50,000 on a building valued at $100,000 but insured for $60,000 will be covered only at $30,000 (because the building was insured at 60% of its value, the loss will be covered only at 60%). Had the building been insured for $80,000, or 80% of its value, the loss of $50,000 would have been fully covered. With the variety of coverage available for any given hazard and the flexibility in underwriting, cost can be extremely misleading. You need a person with whom you can work, in whom you have confidence, and who takes a vital interest in your business.

## Types of Insurance

There are numerous types of insurance coverage beyond the life insurance we all think of when we hear the term. Among these are fire insurance and its related lines of coverage for natural disasters of all types. This type of coverage also can include business interruption protection, which will cover lost profits during the time that a business is unable to operate due to a covered hazard. **Casualty insurance** refers to protection against theft, protection for automobile collision and related liability, protection for glass breakage, and accident and health insurance. **Marine insurance,** so called from the days when virtually all shipping was conducted by water, provides protection for goods during shipment from place to place regardless of the method. There is a type of marine insurance that can protect goods and assets regardless of where they are located. Such coverage is especially valuable in an industry in which assets must be stored at unprotected sites, such as the construction industry. It is even possible to obtain **credit insurance,** which will provide protection against abnormal losses on accounts receivable. This coverage generally protects only against losses that result from a customer's failure to pay due to unusual circumstances such as a natural disaster. Finally, **fidelity** and **surety bonds** protect a business against dishonesty on the part of its employees or from breach of contractual responsibility on the part of another firm or individual with whom you have dealings. Exhibit 19-1 lists various types of insurance coverage available.

Any or all of these types of insurance may be necessary for a given business. As you can see, it is entirely too complex for anyone to handle without

**EXHIBIT 19-1** *Types of Insurance and Coverage*

- *Fire Insurance:* losses due to fire and lightning
- *Extended Coverage Insurance:* losses due to windstorm, hail, explosion, riot, aircraft, vehicle, and smoke
- *Business Interruption Insurance:* losses due to expenses incurred while rebuilding after a property loss
- *Casualty Insurance:* losses of automobiles and in automobile accidents
- *Liability Insurance:* losses from accidents suffered by people who come in contact with the business
- *Marine Insurance:* losses to goods in transit
- *Crime Insurance:* losses due to burglary, robbery, employee theft
- *Workers' Compensation Insurance or Employer's Liability Insurance:* losses due to employee injury
- *Life Insurance:* losses due to death
- *Health Insurance:* losses due to medical treatment
- *Disability Insurance:* losses due to inability to work
- *Fidelity Insurance:* losses due to employee theft or fraud
- *Surety Insurance:* losses due to failure of a business to properly complete a contract

professional assistance. This is why we do not recommend that you buy the cheapest policies available from various agents for various aspects of your insurance plan. You need one agent who can coordinate everything, who is an expert in small business insurance, and who will protect your interest. Your independent agent should be capable of assisting you in obtaining all the types of coverage as well as advising you as to the trade-offs between self-insuring and premium expense. Spend some time finding such a person. It will be time well spent.

**Self-insuring** refers to the assumption of a risk by a business without the involvement of an insurance company. Many large businesses decide to self-insure one or more aspects of their operations because they believe it to be justified by costs and benefits. The issue a small business owner should keep in mind is that an unrecognized or overlooked risk is a self-insured risk. Small businesses can seldom afford that!

## CONTINGENCY PLAN

The final outcome of the risk management planning process should be an insurance portfolio and a **contingency plan,** which identifies the risks of the business, the steps to be taken on a continuing basis to minimize those risks, and the actions to be taken in the event of a partial or total loss from any of the risks. The plan should be in writing and developed in conjunction with your insurance agent. The plan also should be reviewed periodically, at least annually, to ensure that as the business changes its contingency plan changes with it. Exhibit 19-2 lists areas to consider in a risk management contingency plan. Effective risk management is an extension of the planning process. For a small business with limited resources, it is an area that cannot be overlooked.

**EXHIBIT 19-2** *Considerations in a Risk Management Contingency Plan*

I. Identify all business risks
   A. Operational risks
      1. Economic downturns
      2. Change in market conditions
      3. Change in competition
      4. Change in product or service viability
      5. Death or loss of key people
      6. Your own death or incapacitation
      7. Loss or compromise of records (security and disaster plan for computer-based information systems)
   B. Property risks
      1. Natural disasters
      2. Theft or vandalism
      3. Shoplifting
      4. Obsolescence
   C. Customer-related risks
      1. Liability for injuries
      2. Product or service liability
      3. Credit losses (credit and collection policy and training for people)
   D. Employee-related risks
      1. Employee theft
      2. Employee injuries
      3. Work stoppages
      4. Internal control procedures
      5. Employee relations

*continued*

**EXHIBIT 19-2 continued**

II. Steps to minimize risk or exposure
  A. Operational risks
  B. Property risks
  C. Customer-related risks
  D. Employee-related risks

III. Insurance portfolio
  A. Independent agent
  B. Risks to be self-insured
  C. Risks to be insured
  D. Listing of all insurance policies and coverages
  E. Procedures to prevent lapse of coverage

IV. Contingency plan
  A. Actions to be taken in the event of a partial loss
  B. Actions to be taken in the event of a total loss

## SUMMARY

Risk management is the science of identifying the risks inherent in a business venture, taking steps to minimize those risks, insuring those risks appropriate to insure, and preparing a contingency plan to deal with potential losses.

There are four major groups of risk in a business: operations, property, customers, and employees. Operational risks generally are not insurable. They are managed by being aware of factors that can affect a business, structuring to avoid as many effects as possible, and preparing a plan for dealing with those that cannot be avoided.

Property risks generally can be insured. Be sure to consider the risk to data files and automated equipment. Sensible risk management requires a separate security and disaster plan for computer-based information systems.

Customer-centered risks involve suits for injuries (which can generally be covered by insurance), risks of nonpayment on accounts, and product or service liability. Reducing product or service liability requires a sincere and concerted effort to provide high-quality products and competent services. It requires planning on a continuing basis to ensure that risks are minimized and preparing actions to be taken if a disaster occurs.

Some employee-centered risks are covered under operational or property hazards. Others affect records, and a major portion of security planning for computer systems must deal with employees. Employees affect customer relations and liability for customer claims. Other employee risks involve loss of production through work stoppages and loss of income through "sweetheart sales," and so on. Insurance and bonding can cover some of these risks as can internal controls. But the strongest insurance against employee-centered risks is an open relationship based on mutual respect between owners and employees.

Insurance can be complex and expensive. The best approach is to establish a relationship with an independent insurance agent early in the life of a business and develop a comprehensive insurance plan.

The final outcome of the risk management planning process should be an insurance portfolio and a contingency plan that identifies the risks of the business, the steps to be taken on a continuing basis to minimize those risks, and the actions to be taken in the event of a partial or total loss.

## QUESTIONS

1. What are the elements of risk management?
2. Name the four major groups involving risk, and explain how the risks for each group can be minimized.
3. What are the elements in operational risks, and how might those risks be minimized?
4. What form of property risk has caused the greatest losses in recent years? How can those losses be avoided?
5. What is the greatest risk associated with customers?
6. Why are accounts receivable an area of risk?
7. Why is cash flow more important than profit in the survival of a company?
8. What are some of the elements of employee-centered risk?
9. What is the strongest insurance against employee-centered risk? Explain why.
10. Describe the concept of quality circles, and explain how this approach can help organizations.
11. Name the various types of insurance available, and explain why they are important to a small business.
12. What are the results of risk management planning?
13. What are the major steps in a contingency plan, and why is one important to small business owners?

14. Define the following terms:

a. risk
b. insurance
c. risk management
d. operational risks
e. property risk
f. customer risks
g. employee risks
h. product liability
i. trade credit
j. sweetheart sales
k. coinsurance
l. casualty insurance
m. marine insurance
n. credit insurance
o. fidelity and surety bonds
p. self-insured risk

## PROJECTS

1. Visit several independent insurance agents and decide on the best coverage and the most inexpensive coverage available to you. Write down the pros and cons of each program.
2. Develop a contingency plan for your business, using each of the steps outlined in the text.

# CASE

George was a genius when it came to computers and John was naive. George presented himself to John one day when John was at his wit's end. He had to take a financial statement to his bank that afternoon but his secretary was sick and he didn't know how to operate the computer. As John was busily swearing at the dumb machine and wondering why he had ever let himself be talked into automating his manual system, George walked in and saved the day.

George had heard that a new money order company was looking for employees. He had a partial degree in computer science; that is, he had dropped out of school before completing his degree. He still needed thirty hours of what he felt were silly requirements. After all, he was good and he knew it. He didn't need a degree to tell him how to program. He'd been doing that since he was fifteen.

George was able to give John his financial statements in time for the meeting with the bank. So John hired him on the spot. This was going to be great. Amy, John's secretary, had been trained on the accounting program, but she was not comfortable with it. Now George could take over those duties.

After several weeks George insisted that he could modify some of the existing programs to be more effective and give different reports. John, not really understanding the capabilities of the computer anyway, agreed to the modifications, whatever George wanted to do.

Six months later, the bank told John his account was overdrawn. According to John's record, he had $250,000 in his account; but according to the bank, John had −$50,000. John said that there must be some mistake.

John told George of his troubles. George said that he would check into the matter on the computer, while John tried to work with the bank. While John was gone, George erased several transactions that indicated money orders in the name of Jason George and implanted code that would erase all transactions if a listing of accounts were demanded.

Returning to his office, John found that George had gone out for a late lunch leaving a note that everything had been taken care of. When George did not return, John asked Amy to run a listing of all accounts, so the bank could trace the discrepancies, and she did. John never knew what hit him.

### Questions

1. What is the chief problem in this situation?
2. What kind of background check should have been done before turning over sensitive data to a stranger?
3. What should a manager do about security procedures?
4. Develop a contingency plan for this company.
5. What steps might have been taken to prevent this disaster?

# CHAPTER 20

# Inventory Management

**LEARNING OBJECTIVES**

After completing this chapter, you should be able to

- Explain the role that inventory plays in the determination of profit for a company.
- Understand the cash-to-cash cycle and its significance for inventory management.
- Explain the purchasing process and the effect of purchase discounts.
- List the various methods of inventory accounting.
- Understand and calculate economic ordering quantity.
- Demonstrate the role that computers can play in providing support for effective inventory management.
- Explain the principles of inventory budgeting and control.

After completing the appendix to this chapter, you should be able to state the various methods of inventory valuation and the role each plays in the financial statements under changing price conditions.

In a retail or wholesale business, few things can be more important than an effective management of the inventory. Plautus, a Roman scholar, understood the basics of the problem 2,000 years ago: "It is necessary to entice the buyer to unsalable wares; good merchandise easily finds a buyer." Today, we know that the merchandise must be desirable to the buyer in order to be salable. In the modern world, the problem has become infinitely more complex. Effective **inventory management** now must encompass not only stocking salable merchandise, but stocking proper amounts of merchandise, adequate controls over that merchandise, and its purchasing and control. Failure in any of these areas can be catastrophic to a small business because these factors dictate not only salability of inventory but its cost as well. A small business really exerts little control over the selling prices of its products. These are set by the competition. Consequently, profitability largely is a function of cost control. In this chapter, we address the aspects of inventory planning in a small retailer or wholesaler: from determining stock levels and order quantities to inventory accounting and control. The appendix to this chapter examines issues in inventory valuation and discusses the various methods.

## INVENTORY

**Inventory** consists of goods held for sale in a business. In a retail or wholesale business, the inventory typically is the largest asset representing the largest investment in the firm. Inventory is the major source of revenue for the business and the major expense in the business. Consequently, inventory management is the determinant of success or failure.

Inventory can take several forms. In a retail or wholesale business, inventory typically is finished goods; goods ready for use by the purchaser. In a manufacturing business, there typically are two additional forms of inventory: **raw materials,** which are products waiting to be converted into finished goods; and **work in process,** which represents those goods that have not yet been completed but are in the process of being converted from raw materials into salable form. In this chapter, we will focus on finished goods. Chapter 23 will concentrate on production management in small manufacturing firms.

Inventory can be displayed for customers to see and examine or it can be stored in a warehouse awaiting shipment to a buyer or movement to a display. We generally think of retailers as having inventory on display for customers and wholesalers as holding inventory in warehouses for shipment in larger quantities to purchasers that have bought from traveling sales representatives. Nevertheless, both retailers and wholesalers can, and frequently do, have inventory held in both display and storage. The display of inventory costs more than its storage because the location of the store or display site and the furnishings and fixtures used in the display create more expense. Warehouses can be located in less expensive areas and require no amenities beyond those required to protect the inventory; consequently, they cost less. This difference, plus the difference in sales quantities, results in higher prices for a retailer. Retailers typically expect to sell very small quantities of any single item, frequently single quantities, whereas wholesalers generally expect to sell in large quantities.

The difference is blurred by firms that specialize in wholesale situations but act as retailers. These firms sell to other businesses, which use the products to complete their own business, but sell in small quantities. Automobile parts houses are an example. Such firms generally have larger occupancy and display costs than those that use only warehouses, but less cost than those that seek out the ultimate users as customers. Other types of firms, such as mail order firms, appeal to consumers like retailers do, but use warehouse and low-cost sites like wholesalers. The only impact that the type of firm has on inventory management is in the quantities of inventory that must be stocked.

If the business does not depend on display of merchandise for sales and can obtain short shipping times for merchandise from suppliers, then the quantity of inventory stocked can be minimized. Mail order firms and catalog stores, as well as many wholesale firms, have such conditions. For stores of this type, inventory management is much simpler. In fact, most of the inventory planning will revolve around obtaining and maintaining dependable sources of supply, preparing sales materials such as brochures and catalogs, and the marketing effort itself. Some other types of firms are able to rely primarily on inventory that they do not own. Inventory owned by the supplier, but held for sale by the vendor is termed **consignment inventory**. Many retailers handling crafts are able to obtain inventory from the makers on a consignment basis, for example. Such firms are really conduits for the product and earn what really are sales commissions. The management of such firms has no aspects that are unique to inventory, consequently, we will not focus on such firms in this chapter. Here, we will be interested in those firms that must purchase and maintain major portions of the inventory that they will sell. Whether the sales effort is wholesale or retail, the inventory management is the same.

## THE CASH-TO-CASH CYCLE

Cash is required to purchase inventory and its sale produces cash. This is called the **cash-to-cash cycle** and is illustrated in Exhibit 20-1. As the exhibit shows, inventory is purchased, creating accounts payable that must be paid using cash. Then inventory is sold, creating accounts receivable that must be collected to yield cash. Part of that cash is profit: the portion that represents the markup or

**EXHIBIT 20-1** *The Cash-to-Cash Cycle*

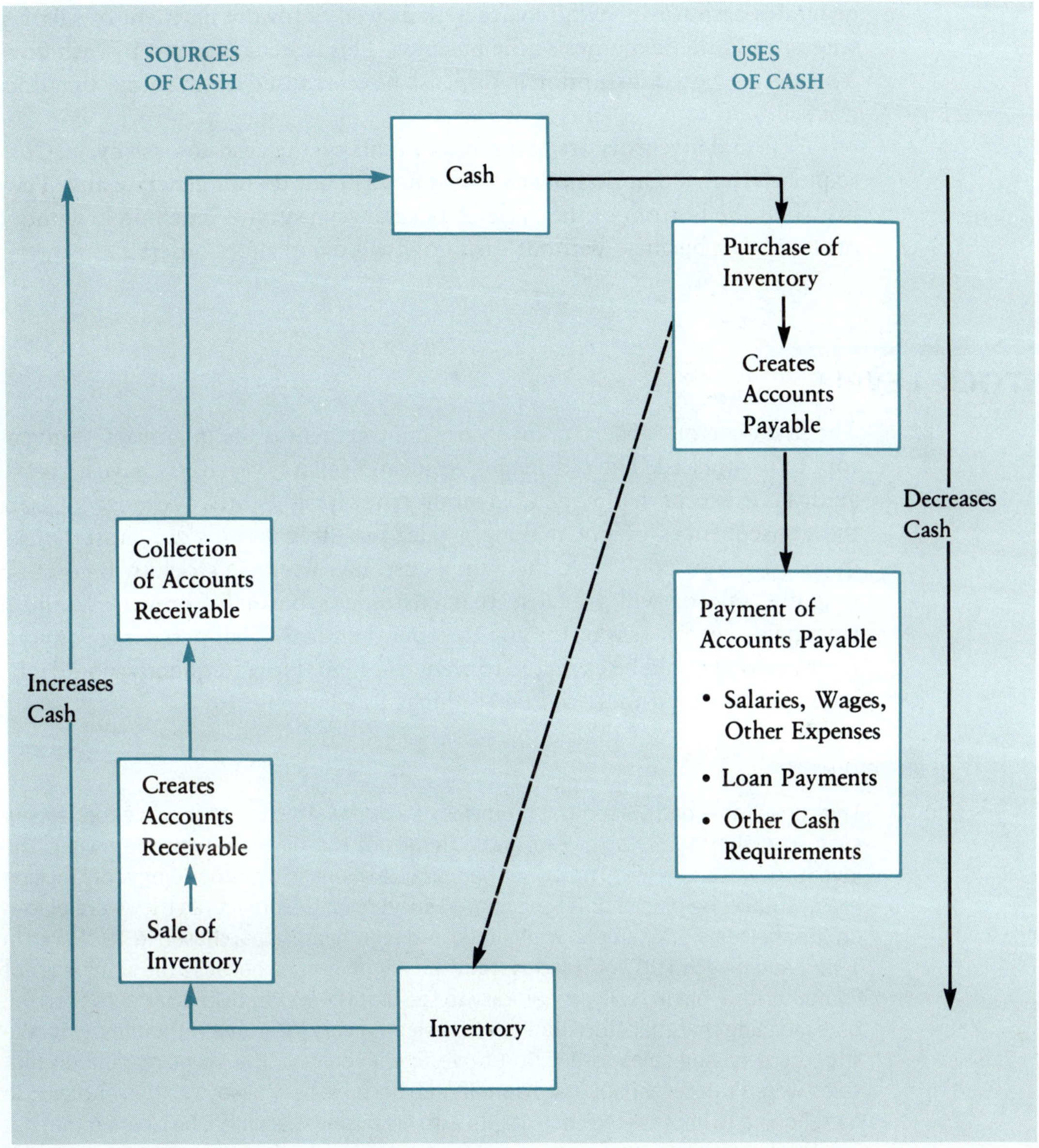

gross profit on the inventory items. Regardless, the resulting cash is available for use in the business. The primary need for cash in a retail or wholesale business is the acquisition of inventory. The sale of inventory, therefore, generates cash for its own replacement as well as for the payment of salaries, wages, and other expenses of the business. This is what is meant by **cash flow.** You can see how a disruption in this cash flow is caused by inventory that does not sell.

Cash and inventory are at opposite points on the cash-to-cash cycle. Consequently, items that do not sell consume cash but do not generate any. They just sit at the bottom of the cycle. A business can survive indefinitely without profits, but a business without cash flow will die in short order!

## STOCK LEVELS

The first issue of concern in inventory management is the quantities of inventory to be stocked. The old adage, "you can't sell it if you don't have it" is the guide here, except that we need to modify the saying slightly. We must consider the consequences of not making a sale. Just how serious are those consequences? If you don't have the item a customer wants in stock, will you lose that one sale or will you lose that customer's business forever? Would a reasonable customer wait for you to order the item? What percentage of your target market could be expected to want this item? How frequently would it be in demand? No business can be all things to all people.

The consultants had visited the premises of a hardware store that was experiencing cash flow shortages. In reviewing the details of the business with the owner, the inventory was assessed. The owner had picked an unusual methodology for tracking his inventory. He placed different colored stickers on the objects as they were placed on the shelves. For example, white indicated merchandise purchased in 1985, red in 1986, and blue in 1987. A good system one might assume because the store was not computerized, but in reality it was easy to see that the white stickers far exceeded the blue meaning that that stock had been there for a very long time without moving. We suggested having sales to get rid of overage inventory. The client responded that sales weren't necessary on hardware items, because they always sold eventually. In fact, hoping to impress the consultants with his business acumen, he claimed that not only did he not have sales on his regular inventory items, he often raised the price on that item when a new series came in at a higher price. He claimed that it helped the profit margin.

Another problem obviously overlooked by the store owner was when to reorder and what. When questioned about the basis for his reorder decisions, the owner indicated that he "eyeballed it." He also was influenced by the availability of discounts on quantity sales offered by his suppliers. If the inventory in the store was any indication, the suppliers were many and varied. Not only did he have almost any hardware item one might want, he had hand tools, power tools, gardening equipment, fertilizer, seeds of all types, and a large array of housewares. He even had chains available in twelve different link sizes.

The major problem in the hardware store was an attempt to stock any hardware item a customer conceivably could want. It costs too much money to do that. The problem is that unsold inventory must be paid for just like inventory that is sold, as is illustrated in the cash flow cycle in Exhibit 20-1. Now think about where the money comes from to pay for inventory that is not sold. It must come from cash injected into the business by the owner or by creditors. That is, the only sources of cash are sales of inventory or loans and investments by owners. If cash is not available from one of those sources, then one of the others must be used to provide the cash. If there is no more cash available from owners and if the business is unable to borrow any more money, then it will find itself unable to meet the payment obligations on payables, loans, and expenses. This is what is meant when people refer to **cash flow problems.** Such problems can destroy a business!

The issue for inventory management becomes balancing the need to stock inventory against the cash available to pay for it. The best approach is to establish a budget for inventory and stick to that budget. In Chapter 7, we talked about inventory budgets and tying them to sales forecasts. The first step is to calculate the inventory turnover rate. This is the ratio of cost of goods sold to inventory on hand. You can calculate the number for your business by dividing cost of goods sold by average inventory:

$$\frac{\text{Cost of goods}}{\left(\dfrac{\text{Beginning inventory} + \text{Ending inventory}}{2}\right)} = \text{Inventory turnover rate}$$

If the business does not have enough history for a calculation, the industry average for inventory turns can be used. The second step is the calculation of the cost of goods sold ratio. You can calculate this number by dividing cost of goods sold by sales (Cost of Goods/Sales). Again, an industry average can be used if the business has no history. Next, you must forecast sales, month by month, for the period of the budget, normally one year. Armed with this information, the preparation of an inventory budget is simplistic. Consider the following example:

**SALES FORECAST**

| | |
|---|---|
| January | $5,000 |
| February | 4,000 |
| March | 3,500 |
| April | 5,000 |
| Inventory turnover | 8.0 |
| Cost of goods sold | 65% |

**INVENTORY NEEDED AT DECEMBER 31 (OR JANUARY 1)**

| | *Cost of Goods* |
|---|---|
| January ($5,000 × .65) | $3,250 |
| February | 2,600 |
| March | 2,275 |
| April | 3,250 |

*Months in year/Inventory turnover*
*12 months/8.0 = 1.5 months*
*Desired inventory at any time should be the next 1.5 months of cost of goods sold*

**DECEMBER 31 INVENTORY**

| | *Cost of Goods* |
|---|---|
| January | $3,250 |
| 1/2 of February | 1,300 |
| Total | $4,550 |

**INVENTORY NEEDED AT JANUARY 31**

| | *Cost of Goods* |
|---|---|
| February | $2,600 |
| 1/2 of March | $1,138 |
| Total | $3,738 |

**INVENTORY NEEDED AT FEBRUARY 28**

| | *Cost of Goods* |
|---|---|
| March | $2,275 |
| 1/2 of April | 1,625 |
| Total | $3,900 |

The budget for inventory investment level can be used to determine the amount of inventory to be purchased, as will be discussed in the following sections, but the budget is for the total dollar amount to be invested in inventory. It takes considerable work and understanding to convert the information into quantities of the specific components of inventory. It would be simple if you carried a single product, because you would simply have to divide the budgeted amount by purchase price. Few companies carry a single product. In the early days of the business, you probably will have to rely heavily on advice from your suppliers and vendors. Proper records of sales will provide much better insight into the problem. Be sure always to subject the recommendations of suppliers to a healthy dose of common sense. Grits just do not sell as well in Michigan as they do in Georgia! If you deal with established, reputable suppliers, then chances are that the advice they give you will be sound. Such suppliers will be interested in obtaining your business over the long-term rather than for a single sale. Nevertheless, you should begin keeping records immediately so that you will be able to evaluate your inventory makeup without help from suppliers. This will be necessary, because the needs of each business are different. Your supplier cannot be expected to keep track of your individual inventory movement history. You must do that for yourself. Inventory record-keeping procedures will be explored later in this chapter.

The final topic we need to address in this section is desired minimum stock level. To facilitate purchasing and protect yourself from stock outs, you will need to establish a minimum number of items to be held in inventory for each component of inventory. This number is a function of the item's demand and its lead time or shipping time. Setting the desired stock level will be examined in more detail in the section for economic ordering quantities.

## PURCHASING

### Purchasing Budget

Once you have established the inventory budget, you must purchase the items necessary to maintain the budgeted levels. Determining the dollar amount of such purchases is simple. It requires that you remember the formula for calculating the cost of goods sold.

$$\text{Beginning inventory} + \text{Purchases} = \text{Cost of goods available for sale} - \text{Ending inventory} = \text{Cost of goods sold}$$

If we leave out the intermediary step, the formula simply is Beginning Inventory + Purchases − Ending Inventory = Cost of Goods Sold, or BI + P − EI = CofG. Using the data from the last example, we can calculate the amount of inventory which must be purchased during January:

**SALES FORECAST:**

| | |
|---|---|
| January | $5,000 |
| February | 4,000 |
| March | 3,500 |
| April | 5,000 |
| Inventory turnover | 8.0 |
| Cost of goods sold | 65% |
| Inventory needed at December 31: | $4,550 |
| Inventory needed at January 31: | 3,738 |

*January Purchases*

| | |
|---|---|
| Beginning inventory (December 31) | $4,550 |
| *Plus* purchases | ? |
| *Less* ending inventory (January 31) | $3,738 |
| Total cost of goods sold ($5,000 × .65) | $3,250 |
| Therefore purchases are | $2,438 |

*Solving for Purchases*

$$BI + P - EI = CofG$$
$$P = CofG + EI - BI$$

| | |
|---|---|
| Cost of goods sold | $3,250 |
| *Plus* ending inventory | 3,738 |
| *Less* beginning inventory | 4,550 |
| Total purchases | $2,438 |

*February Purchases*

| | |
|---|---|
| Cost of goods sold ($4,000 × .65) | $2,600 |
| *Plus* ending inventory (February 28) | 3,900 |
| *Less* beginning inventory (January 31) | 3,738 |
| Total purchases | $2,762 |

As in the case of the establishment of the inventory budget, the purchases budget is an indication of total dollars that can be used to acquire merchandise, but does not tell you how much of each item in inventory to buy. That information must come from your records on inventory movement. Nevertheless, the process yields a budget for inventory purchases, which can be an invaluable aid to preventing cash flow problems from developing. Of course, the budget must be adjusted each month as the sales forecast is adjusted. Each month you should compare the forecast to actual results, adjust the remaining months of the forecast and add another month to the end. Many managers have found automated spreadsheets like Lotus, Supercalc, Quattro, or any one of dozens of other fine programs to be a valuable aid to inventory and purchases budgeting as well as other types of budgeting. We will have more to say on this topic in a later section in the text.

## Purchase Discounts

When merchandise is purchased from a supplier, a discount for prompt payment often is extended. These discounts can represent major savings opportunities. **Trade credit** is one of the most frequently used forms of credit in business. The amounts extended each year by suppliers to their purchasers in the form of accounts payable easily exceed the total amounts borrowed from banks. Consequently, it is important for the long-term viability of a small business to maintain a healthy credit rating from suppliers. A small business that develops a reputation for slow payment on trade accounts can find itself with a highly limited number of suppliers willing to deal with it or saddled with cash-on-delivery terms for its inventory. Neither of these outcomes is desirable, consequently every small business should make it a practice always to pay accounts payable within the terms granted by the supplier.

Supplier terms are quoted with the percentage of any discount available and its time limit first and the ultimate due date quoted last. For example, 2/10 net 30, a common trade credit term, means that a 2 percent discount is available for payment made within ten days of the bill with the balance due in thirty days at the latest. Other terms could be 2/10, 1/20 net 60, which means a 2 percent discount is available for payment in ten days, a 1 percent discount for payment in twenty days, but the balance is due no later than sixty days. If terms are quoted net 30 or net 60, this means that no discounts are offered and the balance is due in thirty or sixty days.

As discussed earlier, failure to pay within the net period can damage the credit standing of the firm. With that in mind, if a firm fails to take advantage of a purchase discount, the cost could be extreme. Consider terms of 2/10 net 30. If you fail to pay within ten days, then you will lose a 2 percent discount. Because you gain only a twenty-day grace period (30 − 10), the effect is that you are paying 2 percent interest for a twenty-day loan. We can convert that to annual interest rates so that we can compare it to bank loan rates by examining how many twenty-day periods there are in a year. If we use 360 days for a year to make it simple, then there are eighteen periods (360/20 = 18). Consequently, the annual interest rate is 18 × 2 percent, or 36 percent—a high cost! If the terms were 1/10 net 60, then you would be paying 1 percent interest for a loan of fifty days' duration (60 − 10). The annual equivalent rate would be 7.2 percent (360/50 = 7.2; 7.2 × 1 percent = 7.2 percent). That's not a bad borrowing rate! The process of converting discount terms into annual interest rates always is the same: find the grace period built into the terms; divide that into

360 days; and multiply the result by the discount percentage. You need to keep the discount in mind and always calculate its true cost in annual terms so that you will know the real cost. In some situations, it could pay to arrange a bank line of credit to permit discounts to be taken on trade credit.

## INVENTORY ACCOUNTING

Three basic methods can be used for inventory accounting: the specific identification, the periodic method, and the perpetual method. As the words imply, the **periodic method** involves counting the inventory at various points in time, whereas the **perpetual method** involves keeping a running tally of inventory. **Specific identification** means recognizing each individual item in inventory and is suitable only for firms with a small number of inventory items. For many years, the periodic method was far and away the dominant procedure in small businesses because of the difficulty of keeping track of every inventory transaction. Recently, the reduced cost of microcomputers and inventory control systems have been changing that, but the periodic system is still popular with many small businesses because of its ease of use.

The inventory shrinkage problem can be severe for small firms. If a business depends heavily on part-time employees or has a high rate of employee turnover, carelessness, theft, sweetheart sales, and so on can be a real problem. For example, **sweetheart sales** occur when a cashier rings a price on an item for a friend that is less than the actual price or fails to ring the item up at all! The amount of inventory shrinkage cannot be determined without a physical count. Even then, it may be difficult if a firm has not kept good records. Any time the gross profit margin seems to be shrinking unduly and there have been no sales or markdowns to justify it, shrinkage may be the culprit.

### Physical Inventory

Regardless of which accounting method is used, the inventory must be subjected to a physical count, called a **physical inventory,** at least once each year. Tax rules require at least one physical count per year or some businesses might never count their goods. The tax requirement is not the basis for the need for a physical inventory. Inventory is subject to loss, damage, spoilage, theft, and a wide range of such problems that make it necessary to examine everything in inventory periodically to determine how much "shrinkage" has taken place. The inventory records then must be reconciled with the results of the count. The extension or pricing of the items in the count can be handled under several different methods, discussed in the appendix to this chapter.

Anyone who has worked for a retailer or wholesaler is familiar with the physical inventory and can tell stories about the problems involved in such a count. In recent years, equipment has been developed that makes the process a bit easier. Chief among these is a portable device that permits the inventory identification number to be keyed in and stores a running count of the items for each number. The device can then transfer the data to a microcomputer to produce a physical inventory report. Even with such devices, the physical inventory remains a major problem.

To most people, the physical inventory is a time when everything else is shut down and everyone pitches in to count. Actually, the requirement for a physical inventory can be accomplished piecemeal. That is, one department or division or category of inventory can be counted at one time and another category at another time. One good approach is to schedule a physical inventory for the end of every month with a portion of the inventory to be counted each month so that all will have been counted by year end. Exactly where and what is to be counted should be kept secret until the count starts to prevent employees from tampering with the merchandise. By the same token, a surprise inventory taken periodically is a good device to discourage employee pilfering or to uncover the source of problems that a division, department, or area is having.

When a physical inventory is conducted, the people making the count should not have access to records that indicate how many items are supposed to be on hand. The theory is the same as underlies the use of a blind copy of the purchase order for the receiving department to use in verifying the quantities of merchandise received. Not only does having a quantity available for an item make it possible for an employee not to count that item or to hide a shortage in that item, it can create errors in the count itself. Consider, if a person is asked to count a shelf that is supposed to contain 152 cans of black eyed peas, the probability is much greater that that person will come out with 152 cans. It is just human nature! A distraction during the count, a momentary mental lapse in concentration can easily be reconciled by comparing the results of the count to the number supposed to be there. If the person has no idea how many cans of black eyed peas are supposed to be on the shelf, then the chances are much greater that care will be taken to produce an accurate count. After all, if the count does not agree with the record when it is compared later on, that person might be asked to recount the peas!

## Goods in Transit

One thing that frequently gives people a problem in the physical inventory process is the handling of items in shipment. Both items that have been purchased, but not yet received, and items that have been sold, but not yet delivered present a problem. Should these items be included in the inventory count or not? The resolution is based on the shipping methodology. Are the items shipped **FOB destination**? This means that the purchaser does not own the items until they arrive at their destination. *FOB* is a term dating back to the days when everything was shipped by water. It stands for *Free on Board.* If items are shipped **FOB shipping point,** then the purchaser owns the items as soon as they leave the seller's place of business. It is an important distinction because the risk of loss goes with ownership. Whoever owns the items in transit assumes the risk of loss and must insure against such loss. A physical inventory must include all items that we own. Therefore, any items sold under FOB destination terms should be included in the count unless they have been received by the buyer. Any items purchased FOB shipping point should be included in the count whether or not they have been received.

## Specific Identification

Specific identification inventory accounting is a method used by firms with a small number of inventory items; for example, automobile dealers, mobile home dealers, heavy equipment dealers, recreational vehicle dealers, and similar firms. If the relative cost of each item of inventory is high, then specific identification is the best method to use in determining profits.

Under **specific identification,** each item in inventory has a separate record that shows the date acquired, cost, and any other pertinent information. Each car on a car dealer's lot has a file that contains that information. The cost of the item and the pricing policy of the firm is used to set a price for the item. In industries that use specific accounting, it is common for the sales price to be bargained, consequently, the actual price accepted for an item frequently is not the original price. As you can see, it is crucial in such a business to know the real cost of the item under negotiation so that it won't be sold at a loss. Also, profit margins vary item by item because of the bargaining. This means that the cost and price of the individual units sold must be accumulated to prepare a financial income and expense statement for the firm.

Some types of businesses mix specific identification with the other inventory accounting methods. For example, a jewelry store will probably want to keep separate records on diamonds or other expensive pieces, but will not need such detail on the lower priced costume jewelry items. Specific identification is a good choice for accounting for any inventory item that is costly relative to the rest of the items in inventory, or unique, or requires special handling or marketing such as price bargaining.

## Periodic Inventory Accounting

In periodic inventory accounting, records relating to purchases and sales of inventory are not kept on a unit basis. The dollar values of the transactions are stored in general ledger accounts, which periodically are reconciled against the physical count of inventory on hand. Frequently, this reconciliation is conducted annually as part of the fiscal year-end process of completing the company's tax return. Quite frequently the reconciliation is strictly financial with no effort made to reconcile quantities at all. The accounting is simplistic, but a major disadvantage is that you never know the true situation of your inventory until you count it. Interim financial statements at the end of each month or quarter must be prepared using an estimate of inventory costs. These can be, and frequently are, quite wide of the mark!

Purchasing decisions under a periodic inventory system are made using the **eyeball** or **bin** system, in which the manager periodically examines the inventory on display or in the warehouse. When the quantities look too low or the bins look too empty, more items are purchased. A more sophisticated approach is to establish a minimum stock level desired for each item in inventory. This information is either recorded for reference by the manager when considering purchases or posted on the shelves or bins where the inventory is kept. Frequently, the postings will be coded and located unobtrusively so as to prevent customers from noticing the information. Under the minimum stock level approach, the manager examines the inventory every day and reorders those items that have dropped below the desired stock level. Does this sound simple? The process is simplistic, but in practice it can be quite time consuming, laborious, and filled with error. Consider "eyeballing" 15,000 different items of inventory! The major problem with the process is the absence of any information that will aid in adjusting the established minimum stock levels. The manager can change stock minimums if they are too low and frequent stock outs occur. The process leaves much to be desired! Worse, the manager will seldom have occasion to notice when the minimum stock levels are too high, because this information is not available without deliberately searching for it. Consequently, the inventory frequently consists of too many slower moving items and too few rapidly moving items and changes only slowly as the demand for the various items changes.

## Gross Profit Method

One of the popular techniques for estimating the inventory, called the **gross profit method,** requires a historic estimate for gross profit ratios. Consider an example using the gross profit method. The general ledger account for Inventory will start the year off with the correct value of inventory at last year end because a physical count had to be performed. The general ledger account for purchases and for sales will start the year off with a zero balance as do all revenue and expense accounts. The total dollar value of all purchases during the year will be debited to the purchases account (the credit will go to accounts payable or cash). Let's assume that the year end is December 31st.

| INVENTORY | | PURCHASES | | SALES | |
|---|---|---|---|---|---|
| Jan. 1 | $5,000 | Jan. 5 | $ 250 | Jan. 3 | $ 750 |
| | | Jan. 9 | 325 | Jan. 10 | 1,200 |
| | | Jan. 15 | 475 | Jan. 17 | 925 |
| | | Jan. 21 | 150 | Jan. 24 | 575 |
| | | Jan. 30 | 300 | Jan. 31 | 550 |
| Balance | $5,000 | | $1,500 | | $4,000 |

*To estimate the financial results for January:*

| | | | |
|---|---|---|---|
| Average gross profit percentage historically | | 40% | |
| Sales | | $4,000 | (100%) |
| Cost of sales: | | | |
| Beginning inventory | $5,000 | | |
| *Plus* purchases | 1,500 | | |
| Cost of merchandise available | $6,500 | | |
| *Less* ending inventory | ? | | |
| Total cost of goods sold | | $2,400 | (60%) |
| Gross profit | | $1,600 | (40%) |

Ending inventory must be $6,500 − $2,400 = $4,100

| | | | |
|---|---|---|---|
| Sales | | $4,000 | (100%) |
| Cost of sales: | | | |
| Beginning inventory | $5,000 | | |
| *Plus* purchases | 1,500 | | |
| Cost of merchandise available | $6,500 | | |
| *Less* ending inventory | 4,100 | | |
| Total cost of goods sold | | $2,400 | (60%) |
| Gross profit | | $1,600 | (40%) |

As you can see, the method simply involves calculating gross profit as a percentage of sales using a historic average, then calculating back for cost of goods sold and ending inventory. The accuracy of the method depends on the accuracy of the average gross profit ratio. If a firm has few price changes during the year, either in inventory purchases or in sales prices, and few inventory items lost through theft, breakage, or spoilage, then the gross profit method will be close to the actual results. Unfortunately, few companies have such a stable situation. A more involved, but more accurate estimation device must be used when prices and costs vary; this is called the *retail method.*

## Retail Method

The **retail method** requires purchases to be captured both in terms of cost and in terms of retail sales value. In addition, price markups that occur when sales prices are increased for any reason must be captured, as must price markdowns for sales and so forth. If either price markups or markdowns are canceled during the month, the amount of the cancellations also is required. It sounds complex, but really is just more record keeping. With a computer system, it is not that difficult. When the debit is made to the purchases account, the bookkeeper must calculate the retail sales value of the merchandise purchased. This is not hard because the bookkeeper will know the markup policy of the store for each item purchased and what items were purchased. For example, if the store marks up everything 50 percent, then the retail value of purchases will simply be 50 percent more than cost. If markups vary by type of merchandise, which more often is the case, it is a little more work but still simply a process of calculating sales price item by item. Someone must do this anyway to put price tags on the merchandise!

The rest of the accounting revolves around markups and markdowns. Say the store decides to put a section of merchandise on sale. Then, as new price tags are placed on the merchandise, someone must keep track of the total amount of reduction in sales prices. Think about carrying a calculator with you while changing the price stickers on the merchandise. Every time you mark an item down, add up the amount of the price reduction. If you cancel any of the markdowns — for example, on items left over after the sale — just add the price increases as you put the old price stickers back in place. If you had a general price increase storewide, you would add up the additional price increases for each item as new price stickers were affixed. If any of those markups later were canceled, you would just add the amounts of price reductions. At the end of the month, you will have a total for inventory purchases at cost and at retail, a total for price markups and markup cancellations, a total for price markdowns and markdown cancellations, and of course the amount of sales.

You can find the net markups by subtracting markup cancellations from markups and the net markdowns by subtracting markdown cancellations from markdowns. You will also have the ending inventory value for last month both at cost and at retail. This will become the beginning inventory value for this month. To find the ending inventory value at retail is a straightforward reduction of the retail value of merchandise available for sale from the sales. This is converted to a cost basis using the ratio of inventory available for sale at cost to retail. An example will make the process easier to see. Walk through the following numbers carefully and the calculations will make more sense.

| | | *At Cost* | *At Retail* |
|---|---|---|---|
| Beginning inventory | | $5,000 | $12,600 |
| *Plus* purchases | | 7,500 | 10,575 |
| *Plus* net markups | | — | 425 |
| Total merchandise available for sale | | $12,500 | $23,600 |
| Sales | $9,950 | | |
| *Less* net markdowns | 450 | | |
| Total net sales | $9,500 | | |

*Ending inventory at retail must be:*

| | |
|---|---|
| Merchandise available for sale at retail | $23,600 |
| *Less* net sales | 9,500 |
| Total ending inventory at retail | $14,100 |

*To convert to cost basis:*

| | |
|---|---|
| Merchandise available for sale at cost | $12,500 |
| Merchandise available for sale at retail | 23,600 |
| Cost/retail ratio = $12,500/$23,600 = 53% | |
| Ending inventory at retail | $14,100 |
| Ending inventory at cost (53% of $14,100) | $ 7,473 |

*Now we can complete the income statement:*

| | | |
|---|---|---|
| Sales | | $9,500 |
| Cost of sales: | | |
| Beginning inventory | $5,000 | |
| *Plus* purchases | 7,500 | |
| Cost of merchandise available | $12,500 | |
| *Less* ending inventory | 7,473 | |
| Total cost of goods sold | | $5,027 |
| Gross profit | | $4,473 |

The retail method yields a more accurate estimate of the value of ending inventory, but it still is only an estimate. As in the case of the gross profit method, we cannot know the true results of operations until a physical count is taken and the value of the inventory is extended.

## Perpetual Inventory Accounting

In **perpetual inventory accounting,** a continuous running count of every item in inventory is maintained. If a manual system is used, a ledger card will be created for each item in inventory. As new items are purchased, the date, purchase price, and number of units will be recorded on the ledger card for each item purchased. As the items are received, the total number on hand is increased. As items are sold, the date and number of items sold are posted on the ledger card for each item sold and the total number on hand is decreased. As you can see, a manual system will work only if the number of inventory items is not too large. It is not uncommon for an auto parts house to carry 25,000 different items of inventory. A small hardware store can easily have 15,000 items in inventory. Manual systems just don't work with that many items! Fortunately, low cost microcomputer systems are available that perform the same function with no work beyond the normal requirement to count and record inventory receipts and to ring up on a cash register individual items sold.

Perpetual accounting does not eliminate the need for a physical inventory. Items must still be counted in order to determine inventory shrinkage, but under perpetual accounting, we can have a number for comparison to a count, which can help to identify and pinpoint problems. If, for example, we post broken, damaged, and spoiled items to the system as they are removed from inventory, then the only remaining source of shortages are errors in receiving, errors in selling, and theft, either by employees or by customers. If shortages are severe, then you have an idea where to focus efforts on correcting the problem. If any shortages are less likely than others due to control procedures, then the source of shrinkage can be pinpointed. This can be a significant advantage in inventory management over the periodic method.

Reordering information is available from the inventory records under perpetual accounting. The records will not only permit minimum stock levels to be pinpointed as they are reached item by item, but the records can show items that already have been ordered but not yet received. This can prevent duplicate ordering. Perhaps the greatest contribution to inventory purchasing that can accrue from a perpetual system is the ability to adjust minimum stock levels based on experience. The inventory records show not only the quantities on hand and on order at any given point in time, but inventory transactions item by item. As the volume of demand for an item increases, the transactions for that item will reflect the change, and stock levels can be increased. As the volume of demand for an item decreases, the transactions for that item will reflect that change as well so that the stock minimum can be decreased or the item eliminated completely. The transactions records can aid in determining which items would best benefit from sales or promotional pricing and marketing schemes. With a little imagination, there is almost no limit to the information available from perpetual inventory records! From cross-selling opportunities to effectiveness of sales and marketing campaigns; from the impact of commission levels to the effect of store display locations; from the relative value of individual sales people to the identification of target markets—all these and more can be determined from a good perpetual inventory accounting system. With the advent of affordable, automated inventory systems, we wonder why periodic accounting continues to exist!

## ECONOMIC ORDERING QUANTITY

One of the most talked about aspects of inventory management is the determination of the most economic quantity of inventory that can be ordered. Called the **EOQ,** the number is a function of the cost of placing inventory orders, the cost of holding items in inventory, and the demand for inventory. In essence, the EOQ model seeks to find an optimum relationship among these factors. Exhibit 20-2 displays a graph of costs. Note that the total cost curve simply is the result of adding the numbers on the other two cost curves together. This means that the low point on the total cost curve will occur at the intersection of the other two curves. Finding this point in terms of the number of units for an item of inventory is what EOQ is all about.

To be able to calculate an EOQ for your business, you must accumulate data to predict demand for an item. The sales forecasts already discussed must be converted to sales in numbers of units. A forecast is needed for every item on which you intend to calculate an EOQ. Not every item in inventory will require an EOQ because many will move very slowly. You will probably find that 20 percent or less of the items you stock will account for 80 percent or more of

**EXHIBIT 20-2** *Inventory Cost Curves*

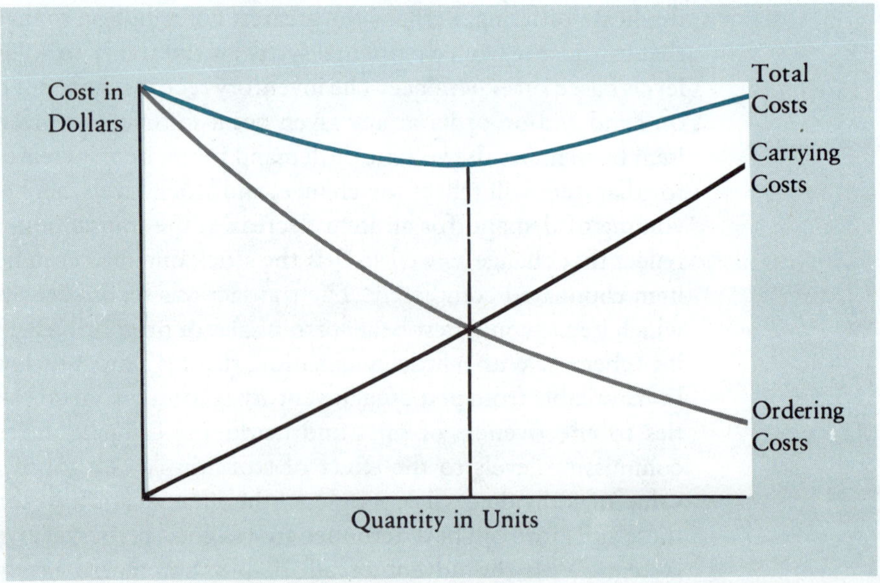

your sales volume. EOQs for those items can reduce costs significantly. The remaining items also should have EOQs, of course, but are not as critical and the calculations therefore can be postponed. Generally, EOQs are calculated for a year at a time, although shorter periods are possible. The demand figures should be for the period you intend to use. If that period is to be a year, then the demand should be for one year. We will assume that all numbers are for one year. If you have forecast sales, then cost of goods sold can be forecast as a percentage of sales and the number of items to be sold can be found by dividing the cost of goods sold by the expected unit price.

Carrying costs must also be calculated per unit. **Carrying costs** are the expenses created by inventory. These costs can be difficult to calculate, especially on a per unit basis, because they are so far reaching. Carrying costs include such things as storage costs, interest on loans used to purchase inventory, insurance costs, taxes on inventory and storage facilities, rental or lease costs for warehouses, and inventory shrinkage whether from loss, damage, theft, or other sources. Obsolescence could be a major cost of carrying inventory. If items become worthless due to changes in markets, competition, or demand, then the value of items that cannot be sold are carrying costs as well. In short, all the costs associated with the possession of inventory should be captured. It may be simpler for a small business to forecast expenses for the business and then aggregate those that relate to inventory and call these *carrying costs*. A large portion of the expenses of a retailer or wholesaler can be traced to inventory. The exclusion of salaries, wages, and other personnel costs, and the omission of costs of goods sold will leave a good starting point for the calculation of inventory carrying costs. Examination of the remaining expense items, line by line, should permit you to exclude costs not clearly associated with the holding of inventory. What remains can then be apportioned over the inventory items on the basis of the numbers of items, their dollar values, or their bulk or space requirements. We want an average carrying cost for each item in inventory.

The last cost to estimate is the cost of placing an order for inventory items. For manufacturing firms, this cost includes the cost of setting up an assembly or production line for producing the item. For retailers and wholesalers, this is mostly a personnel cost. The clerical, accounting, and managerial time spent in preparing and processing a purchase order is the major component. These costs can be difficult to estimate as well. A good approach is to track the preparation of several purchase orders for various items and allocate costs based on the results. For example, tracing the preparation of a purchase order might show one hour of clerical time, one hour of accounting time, and a half-hour of managerial time. Don't forget to include the time involved in receiving and paying the purchase order as well as its preparation. Once the time has been estimated, you can assign costs based on the average wage rates of the people involved. The resulting number should have a percentage added for the costs of paper, postage, computer time, and employee fringe benefits as well as a factor for those things that you forgot to capture. An average of the costs involved in several orders should yield a fair approximation of the ordering costs.

The EOQ can now be determined. We derived the cost and demand estimates used in the following formula from the cost curves relationships depicted in Exhibit 20-2

$$EOQ = \sqrt{\frac{2DO}{C}}$$

*where:*

D = Demand for the item for the entire period
C = Carrying cost for one unit for the entire period
O = Costs of placing and processing one order

To use the formula just plug in the numbers:

*Assume*

D = 5,000 units per year
C = \$1.50 per unit per year
O = \$10.00 per order

*then:*

$$EOQ = \sqrt{\frac{2DO}{C}} = \sqrt{\frac{2 \times 5{,}000 \times \$10.00}{\$1.50}}$$

$$EOQ = 258 \text{ units}$$

Once calculated, the EOQ indicates the optimum number of units to purchase in each order. Note that the EOQ must be calculated for each item in inventory because the demand will vary for each item. The order and carrying costs can be calculated for the inventory as a whole. Any error that results will be minimal because the dominant number in the calculation is the demand for the unit.

To put the EOQ into operation, as the desired minimum stock level for an item is reached, a purchase order should be prepared for the EOQ of that item. We talked about stock levels in an earlier section of the chapter, but the specifics were left until now. The actual numeric stock level decided for each item in inventory can be derived from the predicted demand for that item and the length of time it takes for resupply. In the preceding example, there was an annual demand for 5,000 units. If it takes ten days to receive merchandise after it has been ordered, then you could never let your stock drop below a ten-day supply. If the demand for the item were uniform throughout the year, we could find the amount of that supply by simply taking the annual demand, dividing by 360 days and multiplying by 10 days. This would yield 139 units (5,000/360 = 13.9 units per day; 13.9 × 10 days = 139 units). Of course, the demand for the item will not be uniform; almost everything has seasonal variations. Nevertheless, 139 units probably is a good starting point for choosing a safety stock level. We can adjust the amount to correspond to the experience from our record keeping. We could choose simply to increase the amount during the peak sales season each year. If one month of the year represents twice as much sales volume as the others, then we could double the safety stock number. Of course, if we had months with only half the normal sales volume, we could cut the safety stock level in half. **Safety stock levels,** or desired inventory levels, do not have to remain constant all year long. They can, and generally should be, adjusted to reflect seasonality.

The EOQ, in combination with a desired stock level, can make inventory management simpler and reduce the costs associated with inventory. Both require a sales forecast for the numbers of units to be sold for each item in inventory, as well as considerable additional calculations. Nevertheless, after the calculations have been prepared one time, future calculations will be simplified, and the time spent is easily justified. Not only will dollars be saved, managerial time spent in inventory management will be reduced overall! You will find that managers who do not use EOQs and safety stocks spend more time on inventory because they are drifting around in the dark!

## INVENTORY CONTROL

The elements of inventory management discussed so far are the technical aspects of inventory control. The more general aspects are decisions concerning what to stock and where to buy it. The initial decision about the extent of inventory, both which items to stock and their amounts, can be aided by advice from good suppliers. How do you find good suppliers?

### Suppliers

The reference librarian in the library can point you to directories of suppliers for virtually any item you can imagine. The yellow pages of the telephone book for your town or for the nearest large city can provide lists of suppliers for a surprising array of items. To select the actual suppliers you want to use from the lengthy lists that such research will yield, you need to look beyond price. A telephone call to any of the suppliers will yield catalogs and price lists as well as information about payment discounts, quantity purchase discounts, freight and shipping expenses, and delivery times. All of these factors are important, of course; and your first step should be to consider the costs of purchasing and obtaining inventory. Don't overlook freight and shipping expense. The actual cost of getting inventory items in place for sales purposes is the relevant cost. Be sure to examine quantity discounts for the volume levels you anticipate for your business initially and over the first year or two of operations. Such discounts can be a major factor in inventory costs. Lead time also is an important consideration. If the lowest cost supplier is located 2,000 miles away, not only could shipping costs make the supplier impractical, but delivery times could be so long as to make the supplier undesirable. If your business permits drop shipping to customers, be sure to explore this with the suppliers. **Drop shipping** means that orders are shipped directly to the customer from your supplier's warehouse.

A good system for evaluating potential suppliers is to prepare a list of suppliers from the yellow pages and library references that have acceptable price and shipping characteristics. The companies on this list should be asked to provide you with names of some of the companies with whom they deal in your industry. You should call some of their customers to determine whether they are satisfied with the supplier. Don't forget to call the Better Business Bureau in the cities in which those companies do business to see if anyone has lodged a complaint about the supplier. Pay particular attention to firms in your area and any of your direct competitors who will talk to you. This process should result in shortening your initial list somewhat. The second phase should involve talking to sales people in the remaining companies on your list. You are going to want a lasting relationship with your suppliers so you will need to be able to get along with the sales people and the office staffs of the suppliers. Also, the willingness of the sales people to help you in getting started and during the growth of your business will be important factors. Finally, the suppliers' credit policies will be an important factor. Many firms are unwilling to extend credit to new small businesses. An enlightened credit policy will be a tremendous asset to your firm.

Do not try to narrow the list to a single firm. Ideally, you will be able to find several suppliers who can meet your needs and with whom you can work. Make purchases from all of them and keep close track of the results. Any unsatisfactory experiences should be noted. Gradually, you will probably develop a relationship with one or two suppliers that is sound and satisfactory. As time goes on, you will be approached by the sales representatives of new suppliers. Remember the problems you had in start up and consider these new firms because new entrants and competitors can prove stronger, cheaper, and more helpful. The process of finding suppliers and establishing mutually agreeable relationships with them is a neverending job. For a firm with multiple products, use of multiple suppliers is almost always the rule. Constant attention and monitoring of the relationship with suppliers can be rewarded with a relationship that is invaluable. Because inventory is the source of revenue for a retailer or wholesaler, time spent on inventory supply is easily justified.

We need to make one more comment about suppliers. Many small firms have route suppliers call on them and replenish their inventory. The process usually is to allow the route driver to remove outdated merchandise and replenish the stock right there in the display area. This sounds like a really good deal, because the supplier does all the work! It's a fine process in general but it can present problems. You must remember that the supplier wants to sell and inevitably will have some items which sell better than others. The fast-moving items are easily disposed of, whereas slow-moving items take more work. There is a great temptation on the part of commissioned route sales people to stock your shelves heavily with slow-moving goods in the hopes that someone will buy them. You can't afford to let that happen. Too many small business owners turn over the inventory restocking entirely to route drivers. You must monitor sales for these items just as you do for any other inventory items.

## Inventory Selection

Early in the chapter, we talked about the mistake of trying to be all things to all people. No business, regardless of its size, can afford to stock items that appeal to everyone. One of the most important decisions a retailer or wholesaler can make is determining the inventory items to be stocked. This decision revolves around the target market to which the company appeals. Even then, trying to satisfy the entire market would mean stocking too large a range of items. After a little experience in business, if you have kept good records of inventory movement, you will find that a minority of the inventory items you stock constitute the majority of your sales. The rest of the items, which may well be 80 percent or more of the total number of items carried, are carried as a convenience to your customers. Exhibit 20-3 illustrates this concept; notice that 20 percent of the inventory yields 80 percent of the sales, and conversely, 80 percent of the inventory yields only 20 percent of the sales. You cannot eliminate all of these items because the goodwill of your customers is required for success. How do you make the final decision?

After a company has been in business for a while, unprofitable inventory items can be eliminated. A perpetual inventory accounting system will show clearly those items not carrying their own weight. With periodic accounting, this is more difficult; consequently, we recommend a perpetual inventory accounting system. The owner or manager should review the inventory movement data every month. When items appear sluggish, the safety stock levels used for reorder should be reduced, as should the EOQs for that item. If no complaints are received from customers and if sales performance does not suffer, then the levels of safety stock and EOQ can be reduced again. After several months of this kind of monitoring and adjusting, the item may be

**EXHIBIT 20-3** *Sales Volume Generated by Inventory Proportion*

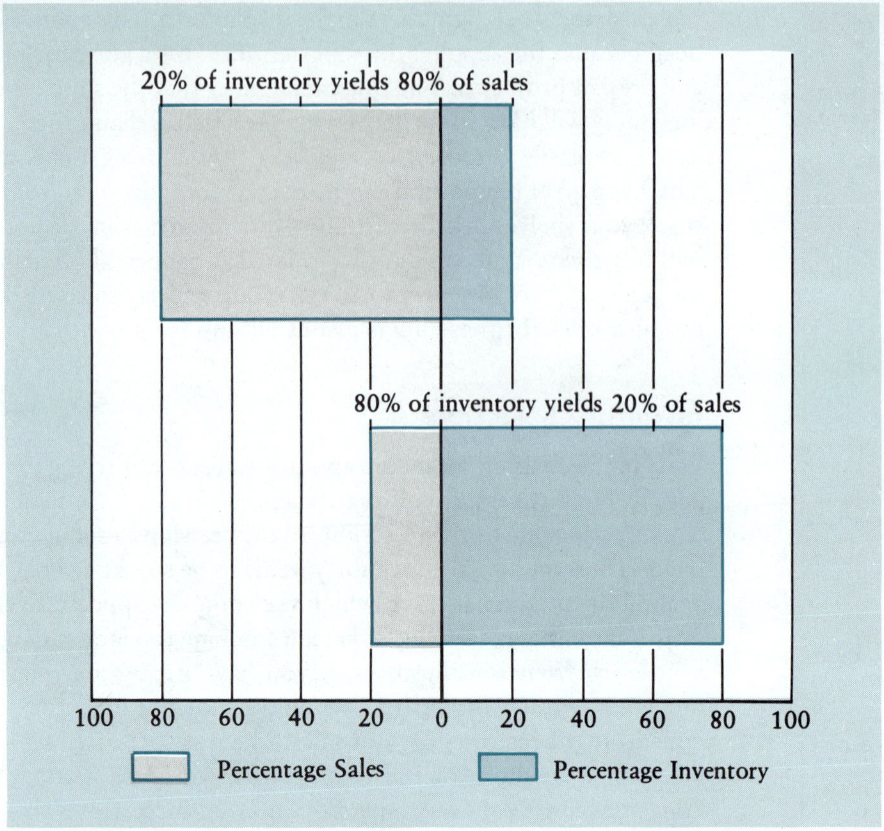


eliminated from inventory completely. No major shocks occur from this gradual process and if any unfavorable results begin to show, the process is easily reversed.

The decision about new products to stock comes from supplier recommendations, customer requests, and decisions about changes in the business or diversification plans. All of these should be approached in a reverse fashion from the elimination procedure. This means that new items should be added with small initial quantities and built to larger and larger quantities on hand as time goes by and experience warrants. As in the case of eliminations, this process will avoid major shocks to the business.

The process just described for inventory adjustment is recommended as a general approach to market changes over time. If there are major changes in markets, demand, or competition, then more dramatic and more rapid adjustment may be necessary. But you should be aware that rapid change in inventory makeup carries with it significantly more risk than slow, regulated adjustment.

None of this answers the question of establishing inventory makeup despite little or no experience. In such instances, the first step should be a detailed examination of the stocks of direct and indirect competitors. If possible, you should personally tour your competitors and make notes about the extent of their inventories. In addition, the advice of suppliers can be a valuable input to the decision. The tendency of most new ventures is to stock too much and too broad an array of inventory, assuming that later downward adjustment can be made. It is true that it is easier to adjust downward than upward, but far too many businesses expend too much capital on inventory that does not move to recover from the error. The best approach is to establish a budget for the dollar value of inventory based on expected sales and to stick to that budget. Tell your suppliers how much money you have available to spend and ask their advice as to the best way to spend it. Compare various inventories that your budget can support to those of your competitors. Make sure you stick to the budget. Customers will understand the growth and expansion of inventory in a new and growing business if you make an honest and sincere effort to respond to their needs. Don't be drawn into the all too frequent mistake of spending more than you can really afford!

## THE ROLE OF COMPUTERS

How many times in this chapter have you read about record keeping? Certainly enough times to give you the impression that you are going to be spending all your time keeping inventory records. Record keeping is important; virtually none of the procedures for inventory management discussed here could be accomplished without records. However, the physical maintenance of details you need on each item of inventory is probably beyond the capabilities of a manual system. Several times in the chapter microcomputer-based systems were mentioned and the possibility that they could help you. Many such systems have inventory and point of sale capabilities. If inventory is to be a significant aspect of your business, you will probably need a system.

Microcomputer-based systems can handle the inventory valuation, which is discussed in the appendix to this chapter, but that is of small value from a managerial perspective. You need a system that can provide the kind of detail discussed in the various sections of this chapter: a system that can produce information like that displayed in Exhibit 20-4 for each item in inventory. In addition to data on a per unit basis, the system should capture purchase

**EXHIBIT 20-4** *Inventory Data on Microcomputer Systems*

- Quantity on hand, on order by supplier, on backorder by supplier.
- Suppliers, addresses, payment terms, quantity discounts, delivery time.
- Preferred supplier, back-up supplier.
- Selling price, unit cost, minimum stock level, EOQ.
- Discounts available for various classes of customers.
- Quantity sold by month for current year and last year.
- Quantity lost in inventory shrinkage by month over two years.
- Date of last physical inventory.
- Location of items in storage or display.
- Special considerations: carried for customer convenience, delivered by route suppliers, exclusive rights, minimum sales requirement, and so on.

information that will permit the calculation of inventory values on various bases. Further, it should be able to produce reports on demand with user-designed contents and physical inventory sheets.

Exhibit 20-4 is not a complete list, but suggestive of the kinds of information that could be useful from a managerial perspective. Make a list of the kinds of information you consider valuable before beginning the search for an automated system.

**Point-of-sale inventory systems** are connected to, or based on, sales registers. A point-of-sale system is capable of updating inventory files using the sales register as part of the process. These systems also can be designed to look up and display prices based on stock numbers keyed in by clerks or read by light wands. Although more expensive than other types of inventory systems, point-of-sale systems are extremely valuable not only for inventory management, but to safeguard assets and ensure correct pricing. Don't forget that such a system creates more opportunities for theft or embezzlement, consequently, the files and the machines should be secured. In Chapter 9, we discussed an approach to computer security.

With the level of sophistication and ease of use that many modern microcomputer systems display, more and more small businesses are able to justify their purchase. For a firm whose success hinges on inventory management, automation may be the only viable method of generating adequate managerial information.

## SUMMARY

Inventory consists of goods held for sale in a business. In a retail or wholesale business, inventory represents the largest single investment and the major expense, therefore its effective management will affect the success of the business.

Inventory may be displayed or stored. If displayed, the cost is greater because of the necessity of creating an image that enhances the product and makes it more desirable. If stored, the concern is protection not enhancement, thus the cost is less.

The cash-to-cash cycle is so called because cash is required to purchase inventory and its sale ultimately produces cash not only for the replacement of inventory but for payment of salaries and other operating expenses.

The issue of how much inventory to stock involves balancing the need to stock inventory to support sales against the cash available to pay for it. The best approach is to establish a budget and stick to it. The budget will be in dollars rather than the actual numbers of each item to purchase. Experience is a good teacher and tracking sales will help you to become more proficient in detailing the purchases.

The three basic approaches to inventory accounting are the specific identification approach, the periodic method, and the perpetual method. *Specific identification* means recognizing each individual item, and it generally is suitable only for firms with a relatively small number of inventory items or items of a high value. The periodic method involves counting the inventory at various points in time, whereas the perpetual method involves keeping a running tally of inventory items. Regardless of which inventory accounting methodology is chosen, a physical count must be taken once a year. It is important not only from a tax perspective but to identify inventory shrinkage.

A problem of physical inventory is how to handle items in shipment. If the items are shipped FOB destination, then the purchaser does not own the items until they are received. If the inventory is shipped FOB shipping point, it belongs to the purchaser upon leaving the seller. Ownership determines how goods should be handled in inventory counts.

The specific identification method may be used for all or only some items, especially those with great value. Inventory replacement generally is simple because small numbers of items are involved. With periodic inventory accounting, the eyeball or bin approach may be used for replacement purposes. The best approach is a minimum stock level; however, this approach could be difficult without a computer, if the business handles large quantities of inventory. Perhaps the biggest contribution to inventory purchasing from a perpetual system is the ability to adjust minimum stock levels based on experience.

Because the inventory is counted only infrequently, monthly financial reports require an estimate of the inventory value. One of the most popular techniques for estimating the inventory is the gross profit method. This method involves calculating gross profit as a percentage of sales, then calculating back for the cost of goods sold and ending inventory. A more involved, accurate method used when prices and costs vary is the retail method. This method requires a record for inventory at both cost and retail.

The economic ordering quantity takes into account the cost of placing orders, the cost of carrying items in inventory, and the demand for inventory. Not every item needs to have an EOQ calculated, because 20 percent or less of the inventory items generally account for 80 percent or more of the sales volume.

Desired stock levels are a result of the EOQ evaluation. Once the number of units for a specified period is determined, the desired stock level is achieved by considering the demand for the item and the lag time for that order to be filled.

Inventory control involves all the decisions that affect inventory from the managers's perspective: what to stock and where to buy it. Suppliers are a good source of information. Reference librarians, telephone books, and traveling sales representatives are possible sources for suppliers.

Microcomputer-based inventory systems can tally items on a perpetual basis, provide data to support physical inventories, and establish values for inventory and costs of goods sold. Point-of-sale systems can handle price look-ups and update inventory records as items are sold.

## QUESTIONS

1. Define the following terms:
   a. inventory
   b. finished goods
   c. raw materials
   d. work in process
   e. consignment inventory
   f. cash flow
   g. economic ordering quantity
2. List the several forms of inventory.
3. Why is displayed inventory more costly?
4. What is the *cash-to-cash cycle* and why is it important?
5. What issues are involved in inventory management?
6. Why is cash flow an important concept in inventory management?
7. Why is lead time an important consideration in ordering inventory?
8. What is *trade credit* and how does it work?

9. List the three basic methods for inventory accounting and explain when is each type used.
10. Why should the physical count date be kept secret?
11. What role can a microcomputer system play in inventory management?
12. What are *point-of-sale systems* and what value do they have?

## PROJECTS

1. The most difficult task in computing the EOQ is gathering the values to go into the formula. The easiest task actually is calculating the value of the EOQ. Given the following data, what is the economic ordering quantity for this situation:
   - Demand is expected to be 7,500 units per year.
   - Carrying cost for one unit for one year is $2.25.
   - Costs of placing and processing one order are $15.00.
2. In your local area find a hardware store, an auto parts store, a microcomputer sales store, a shoe shop, a dress or clothing store, and a household appliance sales store. What inventory accounting and valuation methods would you expect each to use? Ask the owner or managers of each store what procedures are used to handle inventory, including physical counts. Do these stores manage inventory in the manner you would expect? Are there improvements that you can see in their inventory management? If so, what are they? Present your findings to the class.
3. As a class project, ask various members to choose one type of wholesaler or retailer to investigate with regard to inventory management. Report the results and discuss the differences and their bases.

# Case

Jeremy Blackstone was the owner of a small shop, RAX and TRAX, that sold records, CDs, and audio tapes. He had been in business a bit over five years, and the business was doing well. Jeremy had been so busy that he had had to hire two high school kids to work on Friday nights and Saturdays. Things were really popping! If business continued at this rate, he thought he might expand. A new, larger site was coming open in the mall later this year. With more room he could sell stereos, CD players, and the like. He needed to make a decision soon. But if the customers were any indication, this month's sales were going through the ceiling. Obviously, the two kids he hired had brought all their friends into the store.

When the month-end closeout for June was finished, Jeremy was in a quandary. As was his habit at this time of year, he had conducted his semi-annual physical inventory. At other times during the year he estimated inventory using the gross profit method. Now that he had a count, something was wrong. His gross profit margin was down significantly from its established level. Sales were up, but his profits were actually flat despite that rise! He had been experiencing a gross margin of about 30 percent except when he held a sale. There hadn't really been a sale since last Christmas, and he didn't remember making very many markdowns. Surely, he thought, there must be some mistake.

## Questions

1. What did the physical inventory tell Jeremy?
2. What is a possible explanation for the declining gross profit margin?
3. What calculations can he perform to determine the possible problem?
4. If sweetheart sales are taking place, how could they happen?
5. What precautions could Jeremy take to both discover the problem and prevent it from recurring?
6. If Jeremy were to institute a point-of-sale computer system, could sweetheart sales occur? Explain how.

# APPENDIX
# Inventory Valuation

Whether periodic or perpetual accounting methods are used for inventory accounting, when the physical inventory is taken, some methodology must be used to establish a value for the inventory. This would not be necessary if the purchase prices of inventory items were stable over time, but they are not. Consequently, determining how many dollars to apportion to cost of goods sold and how many to apportion to inventory on hand requires making some assumptions. Under specific identification, determining the cost of items on hand versus those sold is not a problem. Because records are kept on individual items, we know their value item by item. The other two methods do not take into account whether the items being sold were bought last week or the week before! The three basic approaches discussed in this appendix are the average method, the FIFO (first in–first out) method, and the LIFO (last in–first out) method.

Remember that two places in the financial statements are affected by the inventory: the **cost of goods sold account,** where the dollar value of the items sold will be subtracted from the sales; and the **inventory account,** which will show goods as an asset representing the value of the items that have not yet been sold. The problem will be to decide how much of the amount spent for inventory to apportion to each place. We want a method that presents a good picture of both income and assets. Note that, because the same dollars are involved, we are faced with a trade-off: the inventory must be shown in one place or the other, it cannot be shown in both places. We will talk about the effects of the trade-off in the following sections.

## FIFO INVENTORY VALUATION

**FIFO (first in–first out) valuation** techniques make more sense logically. Under this method, we assume that inventory is sold in the order in which it is received; that is, the first items sold are the first items received. This is the desired flow of inventory. In fact, this order of sales is crucial in many industries. For example, perishable goods of all kinds need to be sold before they can spoil. Try as you might, this order is never achieved perfectly. If you've ever watched people buying milk or produce at the grocery you know that! The customers, convinced that the grocery puts the fresh milk at the rear of the shelves, dig past the first containers to bring out one of the cartons in the rear. Shoppers paw through the produce sections to find the freshest looking items.

Consequently, the FIFO flow of inventory that is desired is never achieved totally.

It really doesn't matter what the actual flow of items is through the inventory, the method chosen to value the inventory is simply an assumption. Under FIFO, the costs for inventory simply are calculated as though a perfect FIFO flow had occurred. Thus, the oldest costs of inventory will be allocated to the income statement as cost of goods sold and the most recent costs will be allocated to the balance sheet as the inventory asset. In practice, we simply calculate the value of ending inventory and that takes care of both problems.

Consider an example. To simplify things we will assume that the business handles a single inventory item and all purchases and sales are of that item. In actuality, each item of inventory must be examined separately in preparing the financial statement and the totals for all items added up to get the final amounts.

---

DETAILS OF THE PURCHASES

| *Date* | *Transaction* | *No. of Units* | *Unit Cost* | *Total Cost* |
|---|---|---|---|---|
| Jan. 1 | Beginning inventory | 40 | $12.50 | $500 |
| Jan. 5 | Purchases | 19 | 13.00 | 247 |
| Jan. 9 | Purchases | 20 | 13.10 | 262 |
| Jan. 15 | Purchases | 30 | 13.00 | 390 |
| Jan. 21 | Purchases | 15 | 13.20 | 198 |
| Jan. 30 | Purchases | 20 | 13.25 | 265 |

Total purchases during the month = $1,362

Total sales during the month = $2,450

Physical inventory at January 31 shows 45 items on hand

FIFO value of ending inventory:

| | |
|---|---|
| 20 units at $13.25 | $265 |
| 15 units at $13.20 | 198 |
| 10 units at $13.00 | 130 |
| Total | $593 |

*Now we can complete the income statement*

| | | |
|---|---|---|
| Sales | | $2,450 |
| Cost of sales | | |
| Beginning inventory | $ 500 | |
| *Plus* purchases | 1,362 | |
| Cost of merchandise available | $1,862 | |
| *Less* ending inventory | 593 | |
| Total cost of goods sold | | $1,269 |
| Gross profit | | $1,181 |

---

The beginning inventory for February would be $593 and would consist of 20 units at $13.25, 15 units at $13.20, and 10 units at $13.00. Also, if required, it would be used to value the ending inventory in this order, because this is in order from most recent purchases to oldest. The FIFO method of valuing ending inventory always works this way: add the costs of the most recent purchases until enough units have been accumulated to account for the physical count. Just remember that first in – first out means that the last items in are still here! We call this **LISH.**

## LIFO INVENTORY VALUATION

**LIFO (last in – first out) valuation** assumes the exact opposite flow of inventory items from FIFO. The method assumes that the most recent acquisitions are the first to be sold and that the oldest purchases are still in inventory. This assumption probably is never valid in actuality, but the technique has value because of inflation in our economy. Because inflation means that replacement inventory items generally cost more than the items sold, the FIFO method really overstates profits. Consider this, we are not in business to sell off our inventory and quit; we are in business to sell inventory, replace it, sell that, replace it, sell that, and so on, into perpetuity. If this is the case, then matching older inventory costs to revenues, which is what the FIFO method does, does not truly represent the real profits our business is capable of generating over time. It is the replacement cost argument: in order to fairly represent profits, the replacement costs of inventory should be used to calculate cost of goods sold. The LIFO technique yields a lower profit level than FIFO if inventory costs are rising over time; consequently, LIFO can have a tangible benefit in that it can save income tax expenses! The arithmetic simply is reversed from the FIFO method. Let us use the same numbers as in the FIFO example for comparison purposes.

DETAILS OF THE PURCHASES

| *Date* | *Transaction* | *No. of Units* | *Unit Cost* | *Total Cost* |
|---|---|---|---|---|
| Jan. 1 | Beginning inventory | 40 | $12.50 | $500 |
| Jan. 5 | Purchases | 19 | 13.00 | 247 |
| Jan. 9 | Purchases | 20 | 13.10 | 262 |
| Jan. 15 | Purchases | 30 | 13.00 | 390 |
| Jan. 21 | Purchases | 15 | 13.20 | 198 |
| Jan. 30 | Purchases | 20 | 13.25 | 265 |

Total purchases during the month = $1,362

Total sales during the month = $2,450

Physical inventory at January 31 shows 45 items on hand

LIFO value of ending inventory:

| | |
|---|---|
| 40 units at $12.50 | $500 |
| 5 units at $13.00 | 65 |
| Total | $565 |

*Now we can complete the income statement*

| | | |
|---|---|---|
| Sales | | $2,450 |
| Cost of sales | | |
| Beginning inventory | $ 500 | |
| *Plus* purchases | 1,362 | |
| Cost of merchandise available | $1,862 | |
| *Less* ending inventory | 565 | |
| Total cost of goods sold | | $1,297 |
| Gross profit | | $1,153 |

Note that the gross profit is less under LIFO than it was under FIFO. The beginning inventory for February will be 40 units at $12.50 and 5 units at $13.00. It will be used to value ending inventory in that order because that is the order of oldest to most recent. The ending inventory under LIFO always is valued that way: the oldest purchases are added up until the number of items agrees with the physical count. Remember that last in, first out means that the first items in are still here. We call this **FISH!**

One note of caution is due: the LIFO technique should not be used by firms whose inventory costs are lower over time. Many firms in high technology industries have lower inventory replacement costs despite inflation. For such firms, FIFO is a better choice because LIFO will overstate profits just as FIFO does during inflation.

LIFO affects the balance sheet as well as the income statement. Remember that the value of ending inventory will show as an asset on the balance sheet. LIFO, if prices are rising, will show a lower value for that asset than does FIFO. Most people believe that the income statement is more important than the balance sheet when evaluating the results of operations, and so they think that an understatement of assets is better than an overstatement. Nevertheless, the assets will be understated and the inventory turnover calculations will be affected as well. In Chapter 8, we talked about evaluating the results of operations through ratio analysis and inventory turnovers.

## AVERAGE INVENTORY VALUATION

A third method of inventory valuation is to average unit costs. This method results in profits that fall between those generated by FIFO and LIFO. The logic behind the use of the average inventory valuation method is simply that it is a half-step between the other two methods. In industries in which inventory prices both rise and fall over time, the average method may be the most logical. The arithmetic is simplistic. To illustrate, let us use the numbers of the other two examples.

DETAILS OF THE PURCHASES

| *Date* | *Transaction* | *No. of Units* | *Unit Cost* | *Total Cost* |
|---|---|---|---|---|
| Jan. 1 | Beginning inventory | 40 | $12.50 | $ 500 |
| Jan. 5 | Purchases | 19 | 13.00 | 247 |
| Jan. 9 | Purchases | 20 | 13.10 | 262 |
| Jan. 15 | Purchases | 30 | 13.00 | 390 |
| Jan. 21 | Purchases | 15 | 13.20 | 198 |
| Jan. 30 | Purchases | 20 | 13.25 | 265 |
| Totals | | 144 | | $1,862 |

Total purchases during the month = $1,362

Total sales during the month = $2,450

Physical inventory at January 31 shows 45 items on hand

Average value of ending inventory:
1,862/144 units = $12.93 per unit
45 units @ $12.93 = $581.85 or $582

*Now we can complete the income statement*

| | | |
|---|---|---|
| Sales | | $2,450 |
| Cost of sales | | |
| Beginning inventory | $ 500 | |
| *Plus* purchases | 1,362 | |
| Cost of merchandise available | $1,862 | |
| *Less* ending inventory | 582 | |
| Total cost of goods sold | | $1,280 |
| Gross profit | | $1,170 |

Note that both the profit and the value of the ending inventory fall between those resulting from FIFO and LIFO valuation. The beginning inventory for February will be 45 units at $12.93, and it will be averaged in with the purchases during February to find a new average cost per unit for ending inventory. The average is a weighted average, with the number of units used as the weight factor. This is to prevent small purchase lots from unduly affecting the averages.

## LOWER OF COST OR MARKET

Regardless of which valuation method is used, the calculations should be subjected to the **lower of cost or market** considerations. This means that the unit prices should not be greater than the replacement cost. If the value of inventory falls greatly because of a change in demand, competition, technology, or other factors, then we need to be sure that our valuation calculations take this into consideration. From a practical perspective, this generally is not a problem. Nevertheless, it does happen that the cost of inventory falls so much that we could replace the inventory on hand and spend less than we did spend to acquire it in the first place. Industries that depend on commodities frequently have this happen. For example, the jewelry industry is affected by the market price of gold, which tends to fluctuate widely. The calculations are simple. We just look at the current prices of inventory, item by item. This amounts to looking at the current price lists of our suppliers. Now we simply compare the value of each inventory item — whether it was found under FIFO, LIFO, or average — to that current price. If the value we found is less than the current price, we make no changes. If the current price is less than the value we found, we adjust the inventory value. Actually, a bit more is involved: the average markup we use will have an effect on the comparison because retail selling price drops really concern us! We will not go into the actual calculations, because they are too technical for this book. They will be calculated by your accountant. We just want you to know the meaning of the *lower of cost or market* and understand that market conditions can affect the inventory valuation.

## PERPETUAL VALUATION

The preceding illustrations of inventory valuation were calculated under the periodic inventory accounting method. If perpetual accounting is used, the process has to be adjusted to reflect units sold as well as purchased. We will not go into the calculations here because it is needlessly complex for our purposes. In actuality, unless the price changes for inventory over the course of a year are extreme, there will be little difference in the valuation under the periodic or perpetual method. The perpetual process simply requires calculating the value of the cost of goods sold instead of the ending inventory. Each time items are sold, the costs for those items are calculated, just as in the illustrations, except that the beginning inventory will be that remaining after the last sale and the purchases used will be those since the last sale. The process is just more laborious! Incidentally, automated systems can make the calculations as part of a perpetual inventory system.

## QUESTIONS

1. What are the three methods for valuing inventory and how do you know when to use each?
2. What is *lower of cost or market* and what impact does it have on valuation?
3. What impact does perpetual inventory accounting have on the valuation process?

## PROJECT

The following sales, purchase, and inventory records were taken from the books of a small retailer.

| *Date* | *Transaction* | *No. of Units* | *Unit Cost* | *Total Cost* |
|---|---|---|---|---|
| Jan. 1 | Beginning inventory | 35 | $12.25 | ________ |
| Jan. 5 | Purchases | 13 | 13.75 | ________ |
| Jan. 9 | Purchases | 28 | 12.50 | ________ |
| Jan. 15 | Purchases | 45 | 13.10 | ________ |
| Jan. 21 | Purchases | 10 | 14.20 | ________ |
| Jan. 30 | Purchases | 25 | 14.25 | ________ |
| | Total purchases during the month | | | $________ |
| | Total sales during the month were | | | $ 2,050.00 |

A physical inventory at January 31 showed 40 items on hand.

Using these data, calculate the value of ending inventory and prepare an income statement down to the level of gross profit.

1. Perform the valuation on the basis of FIFO.
2. Perform the valuation on the basis of LIFO.
3. Perform the valuation on the basis of average.
4. Which method yields the highest ending inventory? The lowest?
5. Which method yields the highest gross profit? The lowest?
6. What causes the differences?

# CHAPTER 21

# Accounts Receivable Management

**LEARNING OBJECTIVES**

After completing this chapter, you should be able to

- Explain the importance of credit.
- Distinguish among the alternatives in credit sales.
- List the three different kinds of accounts that can be used to support credit sales and when each is used.
- Explain how the credit decision is evaluated.
- Understand the four *C*s of credit and how they affect the credit decision.
- Explain what information is captured on a credit history.
- Distinguish between the extension of credit to individuals and businesses.
- Know how to manage credit and delinquency.
- Understand the methods for accounting for bad debts.
- Know the methodology of collections for bad debts.

All business is based on trust. Nowhere is this more evident than in the practice of extending credit to the purchasers of goods and services. **Credit** is reversed savings. It permits people to acquire and enjoy things while they save the money to pay for them. In the absence of credit, we would have to save first, accumulate the cash necessary to purchase the items we desire, then buy them. Credit lets us buy first and pay later. Emerson said, "Trust men and they will be true to you; Trust them greatly and they will show themselves great." The experience of most businesses indicates that he was right. The vast majority of people retire their debts promptly and properly. This has been the case since credit was invented.

Some say that the first evidence of credit was the purchase of seeds to be repaid out of the harvest by Chinese farmers 4,000 years ago. Clearly, credit was well established by the time of the Phoenicians and had become a prime fact of business life by the time of the American Revolution. Originally, this credit was reserved for use between businesses. But, by the middle of the 1800s, credit began to change the lives of consumers. The Singer Company's well-known entry into consumer installment sales made it clear that business had changed for good. By the turn of this century, consumer credit was well established. In modern times, the use of credit has become so widespread that the use of cash is the exception rather than the norm. In many industries virtually all sales are made on credit, and the use of credit cards is making inroads into the traditionally cash-oriented industries of food service and consumables.

The growth of credit has brought special problems, especially for small businesses, who are more dependent on their cash flows for survival. Despite Emerson's encouraging words about trust, we know that some people will not pay their debts and others will have difficulty paying them. These people constitute a minority, but for a small business with limited capital, a loss of only a small percentage of credit accounts can be devastating. In this chapter we address the effective management of the credit granting and collecting process. We examine the hows and whys of credit extension as well as monitoring and collecting those credits.

## ACCOUNTS RECEIVABLE

**Accounts receivable** mean trade credit or extended payment terms for goods and services purchased from a vendor. But, increasingly, people use the term to describe sales on credit. There is a major difference between trade credit and other types of sales on credit. This difference is in the supporting documentation.

**Trade credit** generally is supported solely by a purchase order or invoice.

This is the most prevalent type of credit among businesses. Credit extended to consumers generally is not trade credit. Other types of credit sales have a note or contract of sale that specifies the payment terms, amounts, and so on. This practice is more common in credit extended to consumers. A **note** simply is a document that recognizes a specific debt and repayment obligations. This can make a difference if an account "goes bad." In the event of a bankruptcy, trade creditors will be treated as general unsecured creditors, which is not a desirable position because losses generally occur. Credit evidenced by notes can receive a more favorable position and may even be permitted a lien on assets. **Lien** simply means that a particular asset is pledged to secure a loan. In the event of nonpayment, the asset can be repossessed. Secured creditors generally are in a stronger position in a bankruptcy situation.

Frequently, industry practices make it impossible to avoid trade credit if you wish to be competitive. If a major purchase is made or a large item sold, then you should make every effort to handle such sales under contract. In all probability you will be unable to completely avoid trade credit. Consequently, at the first sign of delinquency on trade accounts, every effort should be made to convert the debt to one evidenced by a note and secured if possible. This is no guarantee of a stronger position because bankruptcy courts can set aside contracts that occur within 120 days of a bankruptcy under certain conditions. Nevertheless, an obligation spelled out by contract always puts the creditor in a stronger position.

## CREDIT SALES ALTERNATIVES

No one would sell on credit if it could be avoided because of the problems and risks involved. However, general business practices in most industries make sales on credit mandatory in order to be competitive. Credit cards are one alternative to credit sales but are not available to every industry. Other devices used to avoid problems with credit sales include financing through outside firms and factoring of accounts.

### Credit Cards

Many firms accept credit cards as a substitute for carrying their own accounts and in many industries this is an acceptable alternative. The advantage to **credit card sales** is that the risk of loss can be reduced greatly and the speed of collection can be increased greatly. If you follow proper procedures for credit card acceptance, checking stolen and lost card lists, requiring identification, and calling for authorization on larger purchases, then the risk of loss is reduced dramatically. Lists of stolen and lost card numbers is provided regularly by credit card firms and can even be obtained in machine readable format for use in a computerized checking scheme. The major credit card firms maintain twenty-four-hour telephone service for use in authorizing purchases. A call to the proper center will result in an authorization code number that guarantees that the store will collect its money when the charge is received by the company. With proper procedures, losses on credit card purchases can be lower than losses on bad checks. Of course, all this costs money, and the main disadvantage of credit card sales is that the card sponsors charge a fee for handling the transaction.

Credit card fees vary from 1 percent to 7 percent of the sales amount and generally are based on the volume of transactions that a firm generates. Small firms can never qualify for the volume discounts because of their size and so can generally expect to pay 4 percent to 5 percent fees. Because the fee comes off the top and simply is withheld from the amount of the purchase by the card sponsor, it is a direct reduction in the contribution margin. If the margin was 50 percent before the credit card charge, a 5 percent fee would make the margin 45 percent. We discussed the impact of a change in the contribution margin in the chapter on break-even analysis. It can be devastating! Some firms, especially gasoline stations that have a large volume of credit card sales, have begun to offer discounts for cash purchases. Consumer reaction to such discounts has been mixed, but the incentive for the discount clearly is to reduce the impact on the contribution margin. It is doubtful that discounts for cash purchases will become a viable solution to credit card fees for most industries. Consequently, most people will simply have to face the cost. Despite the magnitude of the fee, it could well be less expensive than running accounts receivable. Not only is the charge-off potential greatly reduced, but there is no need for a collection department, which can be extremely expensive. Therefore, credit cards frequently are a viable alternative to credit sales.

We indicated earlier that the collection period for credit cards could be much less than for accounts receivable. In a few industries, notably gasoline sales, credit card charge slips can be used as cash to pay for purchases, but most charge sales have to be handled through a collection procedure. Bank cards generally are handled through a special credit card account to which charge slips are deposited. A rapid collection process follows, after which the proceeds, net of charge fees, are available for use by the company. The collection period can range between one and seven days and in some instances can be handled as checks with the cash available upon deposit but with charge backs of bad charge slips a possibility. Nonbank cards generally require processing by mail. Charge slips are bundled by the company and a recap sheet prepared, after which the package is mailed to the collection center of the card issuer. A check, net of charge fees, is returned to the business by the card issuer. This collection period runs from seven days to thirty days from the date of receipt of the charge by the issuer. In either event, the collection period for credit card sales can be much more rapid than for ordinary accounts receivable.

## Financing Arrangements

Financing through outside firms frequently is used for large ticket items such as automobiles, but can be a viable alternative for many smaller purchases. A variety of products and services, from musical instruments to dental services, can be financed through local banks or finance companies. Arrangements can be made whereby the business receives cash from the lender in the amount of the purchase and the purchaser receives an installment loan from the lender. Most lenders have a minimum amount that they are willing to finance, but this minimum can be as low as $500. Lower limits sometimes can be arranged if a larger volume of transactions can be assured.

In outside financing arrangements, lenders frequently wish the business to take a recourse position. **Recourse** simply means that the business retains some form of liability for the performance of the purchaser on the loan. The level of liability can range from **full recourse,** which means that if a purchaser refuses to pay the business must pay off the lender, to **limited recourse,** which involves a dollar or percentage limit on the liability of the business. Where products are involved, such contracts also can be handled on a **full repurchase** basis, which means that the business must buy the collateral back from the bank in the event of repossession, or a **limited repurchase,** in which the business guarantees a minimum price for repossessed merchandise. The difference in repurchase and recourse is that, for the former, the lender handles repossession whereas, for the latter, the business handles repossession.

Even though outside financing arrangements may not reduce risk, they can speed up collections and reduce, if not eliminate, the need for a collection staff. Consequently, financing frequently can be a viable alternative to normal accounts receivable. A business interested in such arrangements should explore the possibility with its local bank. Even if the bank is not interested, it will be able to steer a business to a potential finance company.

## Factoring

**Factoring** is the sale of accounts receivable to a bank or finance company. Under a factoring arrangement, sales are made on accounts receivable in a normal fashion, then these accounts are sold to a lender under a prearranged contract of purchase. The accounts can be sold en masse, all of them, or selected accounts can be sold. The lender pays cash for the accounts upon receipt thereby speeding up the collection period. A charge is deducted from the amount of the accounts purchased to compensate the lender. This charge can range from 4 percent to 15 percent depending upon the volume of accounts a business sells and the quality of the accounts in terms of credit risk. As in the case of credit card sales, small businesses are at a disadvantage because of their size and can frequently pay 10 percent or 12 percent in factoring fees. In many instances, factoring can cost so much that it wipes out the profit! In addition, most factors are unwilling to purchase accounts on a nonrecourse basis. That means that some liability, in many cases full liability, for the collection of the accounts still rests with the business. Unless a favorable factoring fee can be arranged, this frequently is not a viable alternative for a small business. It can be useful for periods of extreme cash flow problems or as a tool for working a company out of financial problems. If you are interested in factoring, discussions with your local bank should reveal their interest, if any, or the names of finance companies who involve themselves with factoring.

## TYPES OF CREDIT

Three different kinds of accounts can be used to support credit sales: open accounts, revolving accounts, and installment accounts. We need to talk about each of these and how they function for a business. It is possible to use combinations of these credit accounts or to take various approaches to them, which results in a wide variety of possible credit accounts. We concentrate on the basic approaches that make up the various accounts.

### Open Accounts

An **open account** is the most frequently encountered form of sales credit. In an open account, a customer may or may not be reviewed for credit extension. If a review is performed, then a credit limit is established; otherwise, each sale is handled individually. An open account is simply an extended payment option for a single purchase. The terms of payment frequently include discounts for early payment and are expressed in standard terms that describe the discount and due date. Exhibit 21-1 displays some open account terms. Finance or service charges frequently are added to amounts not paid when due. If such penalties are assessed, then some indication generally will be made on the face of the invoice or bill sent to the customer.

As you can see from the lists, there can be an almost unlimited variety of payment terms on open accounts. Discounts may be offered to encourage early payment. Frequently, industry practices make offering payment discounts mandatory to be competitive. Nevertheless, payment discounts can be expensive and you should be aware of the impact they have on contribution margins. If you offer a 2-percent discount and all of your customers take advantage of it,

**EXHIBIT 21-1** *Open Account Payment Terms*

| TERMS | EXPLANATION |
|---|---|
| 2/10, net 30 | 2% discount if paid within 10 days of the date of the bill, balance due within 30 days |
| 2/10, 1/20, net 60 | 2% discount if paid within 10 days, 1% discount if paid within 20 days, balance due within 60 days |
| 2/10, net 30, ROG | 2% discount if paid within 10 days of the receipt of the goods, balance due within 30 days of the receipt of the goods |
| 2/10, net 30, MOM | 2% discount if paid within 10 days of the middle of the month, balance due within 30 days of the middle of the month |
| 2/10, net 30, EOM | 2% discount if paid within 10 days of the end of the month, balance due within 30 days of the end of the month |
| MOM | All purchases will be due on the 15th of the month |
| EOM | All purchases will be due on the last day of the month |
| COD | Payment will be collected at delivery |

the effect will be a 2-percent decrease in the contribution margin. If half of your customers take advantage of it, the effect will be approximately a 1-percent decrease in the contribution margin. Many companies are willing to forego the added margin to speed up the collection of accounts and thereby improve cash flow.

One problem that frequently develops associated with payment discounts is customers who take discounts but pay outside the discount period. Many small businesses are reluctant to risk angering customers by asking for the discount back when it has been taken improperly. Sometimes a discount is taken improperly by accident or oversight, but the consistent failure to observe payment terms should not be tolerated. A courteous but firm notification of the terms are expected to be honored followed by a consistent enforcement of those terms should not anger anyone.

## Revolving Accounts

A **revolving account** is a line of credit that permits purchases to be made on account up to the credit limit. Regular payments, usually on a monthly basis, are required. The payments generally are established as a percentage of the outstanding balance but have a minimum amount specified. For example, the account terms might require a monthly payment of 10 percent of the balance due or $25, whichever is greater. The percentage used is based on the maximum period that the business wishes to wait for payment. Credit cards are examples of revolving credit. For a business to offer revolving credit accounts to its customers, a formal credit policy must be established. Procedures to review applications for credit and establish credit limits are required. We talk about credit evaluation in the following section. After a credit line has been approved, the customer and the business establish a contract that spells out the terms of repayment, the way interest charges are calculated, and the interest rate used. This contract must be carefully prepared, because revolving charge accounts are governed by the Fair Credit Billing Act. Generally, an attorney will be required to prepare a contract that meets the requirements of the law and still protects the business. The maximum amount of interest that can be charged on these accounts is set by state usury laws, which is another reason for involving an attorney in the preparation of the contracts.

Revolving accounts can be a lucrative business if properly handled, because of the potential to produce profits from the interest charges. This is why so many large department stores offer their own credit cards. However, for a small business, revolving accounts generally should be avoided. To handle such accounts, a business will require a credit department to manage the credit granting process and oversee the use of credit. The business also will require a collection department to handle the billing and payment collection process and to control delinquency and manage slow-paying accounts. We talk about this process in a later section. Like any other function, revolving credit activities should be subjected to break-even analysis before a business decides to get involved. Most of the costs associated with maintaining a credit and collection department are fixed expenses. This means that the break-even point is higher in terms of volume, although profits accumulate faster once the break-even point is passed. Nevertheless, few small businesses can generate a sufficient volume of revolving charges to reach the break-even point. Consequently, revolving charges generally are not a viable option.

## Installment Accounts

The final type of credit account we discuss is **installment accounts.** These accounts generally are used for larger purchases. They function exactly like the outside financing discussed earlier, but the business holds the credit contracts and collects the payments itself. A single purchase is involved in an installment contract. A down payment of 10 percent to 30 percent is required on the purchase and the remainder is financed over a period of time. The balance financed is subject to finance charges, which must be spelled out on the face of a contract between the buyer and seller and is regulated by state usury laws. The disclosure of finance charges is required by the Truth in Lending Act. This generally requires a contract that has been approved by an attorney. The balance generally is payable in monthly installments, and the contract term can run from a few months to four or five years.

The contract usually provides the goods purchased as collateral to secure the future payments, although installment contracts frequently are used to finance the payment of services as well as goods. If goods are involved, the contract can take one of two forms: a conditional sales contract or a security agreement or chattel mortgage. The last two terms mean the same thing but are used in different states. A **security agreement** or **chattel mortgage** pledges a specific item or items as collateral. The purchaser owns the items, as title to the items is passed at the time of sale, but pledges that in the event of nonpayment of the contract, the items will be returned to the seller. If nonpayment occurs, a condition called **default,** and the buyer fails to return the property, the seller can take court action to repossess the goods. A **conditional sales contract** functions in exactly the same way except that title to the items purchased does not pass to the buyer until the contract has been paid. A seller has a stronger legal claim under a conditional sales contract and generally can take repossessive action without having to go to court. The selection of which form to use, as well as appropriate documents and contracts, is a legal matter and therefore requires the assistance of an attorney.

Like revolving credit accounts, installment accounts can be profitable given sufficient volume. They also require credit and collection efforts, which can be expensive. Most small businesses lack the volume to justify the use of such accounts. A break-even analysis examining the costs and income an installment credit activity can generate should be conducted before any business undertakes the task.

## THE CREDIT DECISION

To ensure that credit is extended only to customers who are honest and who can and will pay their bills, an evaluation must be made. This evaluation involves both the integrity and financial strength of the customer. Both are required for a satisfactory credit relationship. That is, a customer must be both willing and able to repay the debt before credit is extended. Judging a business rather than an individual is somewhat different. We will talk about extending credit to people first and then discuss credit for business customers.

### The Four *Cs* of Credit

The *four Cs of credit* refers to the evaluation of the customer and the risk of nonpayment that customer represents. The four Cs are **character,** which refers to the honesty and integrity of the customer; **capacity,** which refers to the customer's financial ability to repay the credit; **capital,** which also refers to financial strength but in regard to the ultimate collectability of the credit; and **conditions,** which refers to a host of factors that can affect the credit decision.

**Character.** The character of a customer is the single most important aspect of a credit decision. It also is the most difficult factor to assess. Most people fall back on the old saying about the difficulty a leopard has in changing its spots. In credit, this means that a customer that has handled credit well in the past is likely to do so in the future. Past credit payment habits can be learned through a review of the customer's credit history. We talk about sources of credit history in a moment. In a bank, credit officers are trained to use a personal interview to assess the character of a customer, but many people find that to be an art rather than a science.

We are reminded of a bank loan officer, Bob, who had the highest delinquency rate in the bank. This officer also had the highest production of loans, which is not remarkable when you compare that to his delinquency rate. He made more loans each month than any other loan officer in the bank, but more of his loans appeared on the delinquency reports each month than for any other officer. What is remarkable is that Bob had the lowest charge-off ratio in the bank. This means that fewer of his loans ultimately lost money for the bank than those of any other loan officer. **Charge offs** occur when a loan cannot be collected or when a repossession is required in which the collateral does not bring enough to pay off the loan. Furthermore, Bob's customers were extremely loyal. They would not deal with any other loan officer and, when called by a collection agent because of delinquency, they would reply that they would talk only to Bob about the problem. We asked Bob about his loans and their unusual characteristics. He simply replied that he made loans to honest people whether or not they had had problems in the past. He was sure that his people would pay him when they could. This is exactly what they did: they did not pay the bank, they paid Bob! Frequently when pressed by a collection agent, a customer would say, "Tell Bob I'll pay him when I can." The records clearly showed that Bob's customers did exactly that.

Few of us have Bob's sixth sense about people, and so credit history plays a major role in judging character. This is sad because it leads to the frequently heard complaint that "you can't borrow money if you never have borrowed any." People who have never used credit have no credit history. This makes it especially difficult for young people to obtain their first loans.

**Capacity.** The capacity to repay a debt means that a customer has enough income to be able to handle the payments. This is a function of available income, the income left after existing obligations are met. We must look at income after taxes are withheld, payments required on existing debts, and payments required for housing. The difference between these is the amount of income a person has to cover food, insurance, medical and other expenses, and repay a new debt. Rules of thumb have been developed to indicate that a person has the capacity to repay a debt if all payments, including those on a new debt, are no more than 30 percent to 45 percent of income. The exact percentage varies from firm to firm. This leaves the majority of income to cover living expenses. Living expenses surely can be expected to consume the majority of any person's income. Another method of judging capacity is to use credit history. If the customer has successfully handled a debt in the past with payments similar to those we are considering now, then chances are that the customer will be able to handle them again in the future.

A second aspect of capacity is judging its reliability. Because the debt we are considering will be paid out of future income, we are more interested in what that will be than what the past income has been. **Stability of income** generally is measured by the length of time a person has been employed and the reliability of that employment in the future. The longer an individual has held a job, the more likely he or she is to continue to keep that job in the future. The higher the skill level required in a person's job, the more likely are those skills to continue to be needed in the future.

**Capital.** The third of the four Cs of credit is capital: the financial strength of a customer. A personal financial statement will show the value of the assets that an individual owns and the amount of debts or liabilities that exist. The difference between these is called **net worth.** The larger the net worth, the stronger is a person financially. The make-up of net worth — that is, the assets owned — also is a factor, because some kinds of assets are more liquid than others. Stocks, bonds, and investments are more liquid than real estate. In addition, the appropriateness of the values set down for the assets is a factor. For most people, a home is the major asset. This also is a difficult asset to value without a professional appraisal, which usually is not possible in credit decisions because of the time and expense involved. Few people have the skill to be able to properly value their homes, consequently, dates of purchase and purchase costs as well as tax assessment values are frequently requested. This information can be used to determine whether the value an individual places on a home is realistic. Other questions can be asked on a financial statement for the same purpose: make and model of automobiles; specifics about investments; and so forth. Also, information about life insurance and wills can help to assure that capital will continue to exist even in the event of the death of the customer.

Some people substitute "collateral" for capital in the four Cs when a major asset is being acquired. For example, if an automobile is being purchased, its value can be used to secure the credit. If a sufficient down payment is obtained, then the asset will not depreciate in value faster than the debt is retired. Other items such as refrigerators, freezers, musical instruments, or other durable goods can be assessed in the same way.

**Conditions.** The fourth of the Cs of credit is conditions: any conditions that might affect credit and require anyone who is judging credit applications to be well informed. A condition that could affect a credit decision is an economic recession, which could affect a customer's income or employment, or a decline in an industry, which could result in layoffs in the company in which a customer works. Other conditions that affect a credit decision concern the business extending the credit. If our business is suffering a decline in sales, then we might be inclined to accept more risky credit accounts in an effort to increase sales. If our past experience in collecting credit accounts is poor, we might want to tighten our credit policies to reduce the problems. The reverse of these things also could occur. Almost anything can affect a credit decision from a new highway, which will claim the land on which an employer is located, to a change in import rules, which will affect the strength of an industry competing with foreign firms. Evaluating the conditions that affect a given credit decision is the job for a knowledgeable, well-informed, insightful person.

## Credit History

We indicated that credit history is an important part of evaluating the character and capacity of a customer. Sources of information about a person's history come from disclosures made on a credit application and from the merchant's association. The credit application should ask for the names of firms with which a customer has had credit dealings in the past as well as those to which money currently is owed. We can ask those firms how well a customer has handled his or her credit. In addition, there is a merchant's association or credit bureau in every major city in the country. These firms keep credit history information on file and provide it to members and customers for a fee. They also will undertake a current investigation of a customer and call the references that appear on the credit application, as well as credit bureaus in other cities in which a customer may have lived, to provide an up to date picture of the credit history. This level of information obviously costs more and takes longer than a simple check of the files of the bureau.

**Credit history** will show types of credit, *O* for open accounts, *R* for revolving accounts, *I* for installment accounts, high credit, amounts of payments, balances outstanding, and promptness of payments received. Promptness will be shown as a number from 1, meaning all payments received on time; to 2, meaning some minor slowness in payments occurred; up to 9, indicating a charge-off. We will want to place more emphasis on credit types and amounts that approximate the credit we are considering extending, but the overall history is important as well because it reveals the general approach a customer has taken in dealing with debts in the past.

### Extending Credit to Businesses

When we extend credit to businesses rather than individuals, the factors involved are the same, but assessment is somewhat different. For example, the character of a business is a more nebulous concept than for an individual. The character of a business actually is that of its management. A business does have credit history that we can examine, but if there has been a change in the top management of a firm, then we should keep this in mind, because it could signal a change in the character. Credit history for a business normally is not available from credit bureaus. The firm of Dun & Bradstreet functions as a credit bureau for businesses and can provide the same information about credit history as described for individuals. D & B also can provide information about the management of a firm and the backgrounds of its officers as well as financial statements for the firm. D & B services generally cost more than those of a local credit bureau.

The capacity and capital issues of a credit decision for a business come down to evaluating financial statements. Ratio analysis and interpretation of financial statements can be complex and generally require a high level of training in finance and accounting. Few small businesses possess the expertise to be able to handle in-depth financial analysis. A Dun & Bradstreet report will include some financial analysis but generally this takes up less of the report than the credit history. In Chapter 8, "Financial Analysis for Success," we talked about conducting ratio analysis on your own business to determine its financial well-being. The same techniques can be applied to the statements of a customer in a credit decision. If a major credit is being considered, one that could damage the company significantly if made incorrectly, consider having your CPA examine the statements of the business for you. Otherwise, the tools in the financial analysis chapter should be sufficient.

## CREDIT AND DELINQUENCY MANAGEMENT

We have made several references to credit and collection departments in this chapter. Any firm that intends to extend credit to its buyers needs an office or a person responsible for making credit decisions on customers, a process that will ensure the timely collection of accounts, and a policy that can be used to manage the credit activity. This generally is done by establishing credit and collection departments and by preparing a written credit policy.

## Credit Policy

A **credit policy** should be prepared by, or at least approved by, the owner of the business. The policy should spell out the information required to support credit applications, assign responsibility and authority for processing credit requests and monitoring and collecting credit accounts, and establish guidelines for the credit activity. Guidelines could include such things as minimum and maximum amounts of credit that will be considered, levels of financial strength and types of credit history that will be required, amounts of credit that a given person or manager will be authorized to extend, and timing and type of contact that will be made on delinquent accounts. Any major credits, those that could severely damage the company if a default occurs, should require the owner's approval. The credit policy should be in writing and should be reviewed periodically, at least annually, to ensure that it is appropriate in the changing environment of the business.

## Credit Extension

An application should be required on all credit accounts. The application can be prepared by sales people or by the customer, whichever is desired, but key information required in assessing the four *C*s of credit should be included. A sample application form for an individual is shown in Exhibit 21-2. After an application has been prepared and after we have a desired credit amount, an investigation should be undertaken. A basic investigation should be conducted, even on very small credit requests. For an individual, this should include verifying the employment, employment dates, position, and income levels by telephoning the employer. A basic check of the files of the credit bureau or of Dun & Bradstreet should be conducted. If the credit desired is a larger amount, then more up-to-date credit history should be required. This can be purchased or developed by telephoning credit accounts directly. For a business, a financial statement should always be required—several years worth of financial data if the credit is a large one. A large amount of credit to an individual should be accompanied by a personal financial statement. Exhibit 21-3 displays a sample personal financial statement form. Once the information has been gathered, a responsible person should evaluate it and make a credit decision.

A popular approach to evaluating credit is the use of a checklist. A customer is given so many points for holding the same job for a specified time, for living in the same place for a specified time, for owning rather than renting a home, and for holding a job with specified skill levels. These factors measure stability. Points can be awarded for the kind of credit history a customer has to measure character. Other points are awarded for amounts of income, for the

**EXHIBIT 21-2** *Credit Application for an Individual*

| | | | | |
|---|---|---|---|---|
| **Application** | | | | Reason Code ☐ Yes ☐ No |
| | Salesperson | Loan Officer | | Date |

**Applicant**

| | | | | | |
|---|---|---|---|---|---|
| First Name Middle Last | Social Security Number | | Age | | No. of Dependents |
| Present Address City State | Zip Code | | How Long Yrs. Mths. | | Telephone |
| Previous Address (If at present address less than three years) | | | | | How Long |
| ☐ Buying ☐ Renting | Payments $ | Mortgage Holder or Landlord | Cost $ | Value $ | Balance of Mtg. $ |
| Name and Address of Nearest Relative Not Living With You | | | | | Telephone |

**Employment**

| | | | |
|---|---|---|---|
| Name and Address of Present Employer | Supervisor | Time on Job Yrs. Mths. | Telephone |
| | Occupation | Gross Monthly Salary $ | |
| Name and Address of Previous Employer (If less than two years at present job) | | | How Long |
| Source of Other Income *(Alimony child support or seperate maintenance income need not be revealed if you do not wish to have it considered as a basis for repaying this obligation.)* | | | Other Income $ |

**Co-Applicant**

| | | | | |
|---|---|---|---|---|
| First Name Middle Last | Social Security Number | Age | | Telephone |
| Home Address | | Relationship to Applicant (if any) | | |
| Employer | Position | Years Employed | Business Phone | Monthly Salary $ |
| Source of Other Income *(Alimony child support or seperate maintenance income need not be revealed if you do not wish to have it considered as a basis for repaying this obligation.)* | | | | Other Income $ |

**Credit References**

| | | | | |
|---|---|---|---|---|
| Checking Account ☐ Yes<br>If Yes, List Name(s) of Bank ☐ No | Savings Account ☐ Yes ☐ No | Bank Loan ☐ Yes<br>If Yes, Give Name of Bank(s) ☐ No | | |
| | Name of Commercial Bank(s) | | Payment | Balance |
| | Name of Savings and Loan Assn.-Savings Account | | | |

| | | | | | |
|---|---|---|---|---|---|
| Other Credit References | | | Other Credit References | | |
| Last Car Financed | Payment | Balance | | Payment | Balance |

**Terms Of Sale**

| | | | |
|---|---|---|---|
| List Price | $ | PDI & Ad & D Ded. | $ |
| Selling Price | | (Use Chart) **Sub-Total** | |
| Trade-In | | Life Insurance | |
| Less: Amount Owing | | A&H Insurance | |
| Equity | | Unpaid Balance | |
| Cash Down | | **Finance Charge** | |
| Total Equity & cash | | Note Amount | |
| Amount To Be Financed | | No. Of Payments @ | |

**Credit Bureau Experience**

**Credit Bureau Name and Address**

Declaration Of Sound Health-Applicable where a charge for a credit life, accident and health, and/or accidental death and dismemberment insurance is proposed: Each of the undersigned Proposed Insured(s), does hereby declare that (1) Neither He nor She has consulted or been treated by a physician or other practitioner in the past six months for any of the following: Cancer or conditions of the heart, lungs, brain, liver, kidneys or back; (2) That He nor She has not attained age 65 or more on the date shown in the Application above and to the best of His or Her belief, He or She is now in sound health.

The undersigned certifies that all the statements made are true and have been made for the purpose of obtaining this loan.

is authorized to obtain such other information deemed necessary concerning the granting of this loan and give other creditors and credit reporting agencies information regarding its experience with the undersigned on this loan.

x
Signature

x
Signature

**EXHIBIT 21-3** *Personal Financial Statement Form*

Date of Statement ____________

| Name of Co-Borrower | Name of Applicant or Borrower |
|---|---|
| Address | Address |
| City | City |
| State Zip Code | State Zip Code |
| Occupation or Business | Occupation or Business |
| Social Security Number | Social Security Number |

**Assets** (Fill in all blanks)

| | | |
|---|---|---|
| Cash on hand in banks | $ | $ |
| Checking Acct # ____________ | ____________ | |
| Savings Acct # ____________ | ____________ | |
| Other depositories ____________ | ____________ | |
| Total Cash | | ____________ |
| Notes Receivable | | ____________ |
| Accounts Receivable | | ____________ |
| Investments | | |
| U.S. Government Securities | ____________ | |
| Marketable Securities | ____________ | |
| Other investments | ____________ | |
| Total investments | | ____________ |
| Real Estate (Schedule 1) | | ____________ |
| Cash Value of Life Insurance (not face value) | | ____________ |
| Other assets (fair market value) | | |
| Household furnishings | ____________ | |
| Auto (make and model) | ____________ | |
| ____________ | ____________ | |
| ____________ | ____________ | |
| Other (describe) | | |
| ____________ | ____________ | |
| ____________ | ____________ | |
| Total other assets | | ____________ |
| *Total Assets* | | ____________ |

*continued*

**Liabilities** (Fill in all blanks)

| | | |
|---|---|---|
| Notes Payable to Banks | $________ | $ |
| | ________ | |
| Total Notes Payable | | ________ |
| Accounts Payable | | |
| Installment Accounts | ________ | |
| Credit Cards | ________ | |
| Total Accounts Payable | | ________ |
| Taxes Due | | ________ |
| Mortgages Due | | ________ |
| Other liabilities (describe) | | |
| ________ | ________ | |
| ________ | ________ | |
| ________ | ________ | |
| Loans Against Life Insurance | ________ | |
| Total Other Liabilities | | ________ |
| *Total Liabilities* | | ________ |

**Net Worth**

| | | |
|---|---|---|
| Total assets | ________ | |
| —Total liabilities | ________ | |
| Net Worth | | ________ |
| Total Liabilities & Net Worth | | ________ |

Schedule 1 Real Estate

Location and Description

| (Size, Type Building, etc.) | Current Market Value | Mortgage Balance | Monthly Payment | Mortgage Holder |
|---|---|---|---|---|
| ________ | ________ | ________ | ________ | ________ |
| ________ | ________ | ________ | ________ | ________ |
| ________ | ________ | ________ | ________ | ________ |
| Totals | ________ | ________ | | |

**Contingent Liabilities** (letters of credit, endorser, guarantor, co-maker)

| Annual Income of Borrower | | Annual Income of Co-Borrower | |
|---|---|---|---|
| Source of Income | Amount | Source of Income | Amount |
| ________ | ________ | ________ | ________ |
| ________ | ________ | ________ | ________ |
| ________ | ________ | ________ | ________ |
| Total annual income | ________ | Total annual income | ________ |

*continued*

**EXHIBIT 21-3 continued**

I/We certify as a basis for credit that, to the best of My/Our knowledge and belief, the information furnished and all representations made herein constitute the true and correct statement of My/Our financial condition; that I/We have no assets or liabilities other than as shown on this statement; that all My/Our assets are free of lien assignment except as shown herein and that there are no judgments outstanding or suits pending against Me/Us.

| | |
|---|---|
| X ______________________ | X ______________________ |
| Witness | Signature |
| X ______________________ | X ______________________ |
| Witness | Signature |

percentage of income available to cover debts, and for the amount of financial net worth. These factors measure capacity and capital. Finally, points may be awarded for the amounts of down payment or any other factors desired. Exhibit 21-4 displays a sample credit checklist.

After all the points have been awarded and added up, the total is compared to one established as part of the credit policy. If the points are less than the policy level, then the credit is rejected. If the points are equal to or greater than the policy level, then the credit is approved. This process permits less skilled people to handle credit approvals, but can result in many good accounts being rejected if the point level established by policy is high. Consequently, many firms have rejections referred to a manager for a second look before the credit is turned down. This permits the checklist to be used for all strong credits thereby reducing the workload for the credit manager in credit approvals.

Another advantage of the checklist system is that it permits a stronger level of control over the credit extension process. Therefore, when credit experience or other factors indicate that policy needs to be changed, it can be done easily. A higher score can be indicated if you wish to tighten credit approvals, or a lower score can be required to loosen credit approval. You should be careful to keep in mind that any credit scoring system, regardless of its sophistication, is a poor substitute for human judgment. Consequently, careful and continuous monitoring of the application of such a system and human review of large credit and marginal applications is a must for the effective application of the system.

**EXHIBIT 21-4** *Credit Scoring Sheet*

| | | | SCORE |
|---|---|---|---|
| Applicant's age | Under 40 | 20 pts | |
| | 40 to 44 | 28 | |
| | Over 45 | 40 | Age: ______ |
| Years at address | Under $3\frac{1}{2}$ | 16 | |
| | $3\frac{1}{2}$ to $7\frac{1}{2}$ | 29 | |
| | Over $7\frac{1}{2}$ | 36 | Yrs: ______ |
| Time on job | Under $1\frac{1}{2}$ | 16 | |
| | $1\frac{1}{2}$ to $3\frac{1}{2}$ | 22 | |
| | $3\frac{1}{2}$ to $6\frac{1}{2}$ | 27 | |
| | Over $6\frac{1}{2}$ | 39 | |
| | Homemaker | 22 | Job: ______ |
| Home | Renting | 15 | |
| | Buying | 40 | Home: ______ |
| Banking | None | 16 | |
| | Checking/savings/loan | 22 | |
| | 2 of the 3 | 28 | |
| | All 3 | 40 | Bank: ______ |
| Credit card | None | 18 | |
| | Department store | 31 | |
| | Major card | 50 | Cards: ______ |
| Purchased auto | Less than 1 year | 55 | |
| | 1 year old | 42 | |
| | 2 years old | 30 | |
| | 3 years and over | 16 | Car: ______ |
| Income (weekly) | Under $500 | 16 | |
| | $500 to $599 | 22 | |
| | $600 to $1199 | 23 | |
| | Over $1200 | 28 | Income: ______ |
| Credit bureau report | No record | 8 | |
| | Slow | −23 | |
| | 1–2 Sat accounts | 13 | |
| | 3+ Sat accounts | 18 | Credit: ______ |
| | | | *Total Score:* ______ |

## Monitoring

**Monitoring** a credit activity means more than tracking delinquency. Of course, continuously monitoring delinquency is necessary, because some payment failure is inevitable. Reports of numbers of delinquent accounts and their dollar amounts should be prepared regularly: at least monthly. These reports should detail the numbers and percentages of delinquency by time. Accounts should be shown in 15-day accounts, 30-day accounts, 60-day accounts, 90-day accounts, and over 90-day accounts; that is, accounts that have payments late by 15 to 29 days, 30 to 59 days, 60 to 89 days, or 90 days and more. This is called **aging of the accounts.** In addition to showing the number and dollar value of accounts in each category and the percentage of accounts and percentage of the value of accounts in each category, the report should show the number and percentage of accounts contacted and those that have made promises to remedy the delinquency. It also should show charge-offs or actual amounts lost and any accounts referred to a collection agency as well as any amounts recovered on accounts charged off in the past.

Monitoring this information each month will reveal seasonal patterns within the collection of your receivables and provide trends that can be examined to evaluate the effectiveness of collection efforts. If, for example, delinquency percentages for December are higher than usual for a December, then credit extension or collection efforts are less effective than in the past. Don't forget that economic conditions or other environmental factors affect delinquency as well as the internal efforts of the staff. Also, remember that a decline in delinquency is not necessarily good. A certain amount of delinquency is normal, and the normal amount differs for each business. If your delinquency rate drops below a normal level for your business, your credit policy may be too tight and sales are lost. It also could signal a problem in the reporting.

One collection manager was fired after the internal auditor for the firm noticed an unexplained decline in delinquency over a period of two years. The manager had received great praise and several raises as a result of that decline, but the auditor became suspicious when his review of the collection department failed to turn up any significant changes in the collection practices. A thorough investigation and a careful monitoring of the manager's activities followed. It seems that the manager was extending the due dates of accounts in the computerized system so that they would not show as delinquent. The sad thing was that a recalculation of the true delinquency over the last two years showed that the manager really had been doing a fine job.

In addition to aging and delinquency reports, monitoring the credit activity requires examining the credit sales and their trends. Because receivables arise as a result of credit sales, the credit granting and approval process will affect both collection of accounts and amounts of sales recorded. Effective management of the credit activity means balancing the losses and expenses associated with receivables with the loss of sales. By minimizing delinquency and charge-offs, we may be damaging sales. If we lose more money in sales than we save in charge-offs and collection costs, then the business will be hurt. The comparison cannot be made directly with sales dollars because of the cost of goods sold and other variable expenses. The comparison must be made to contribution margin. The process requires the constant comparison of delinquency reports to credit and overall sales reports and contribution margins.

Finally, monitoring refers to the process of overseeing the collection effort itself. When an account defaults in payment, then the chances are that no money will be received on that account unless someone in the collection department contacts the customer and tries to arrange for payment. We will talk about collection efforts in just a minute, but the point here is that someone must monitor the collection activity itself. Records of all collection efforts must be made, and those records reviewed on a regular basis to ensure that timely, effective contact with delinquent accounts. Collecting accounts generally is considered to be one of the most unpleasant of duties in the business world. Nevertheless, it is necessary and critical to successful business operations. Consequently, the monitoring of the unpleasant task is vital.

## Bad Debts

Accounts that cannot be collected are called **bad debts** and must be removed from the books. This involves a reduction of revenues because the sales associated with the bad debts already have been recognized. The sales were recorded when the sale was made. If the account cannot be collected, then an expense or a decrease in sales must be recorded and the account must be removed from the books because it no longer is an asset. There are two methods of accounting for bad debt expense. The first and most popular method is called the **direct write-off method.** In this process, an account simply is charged off as an expense when it is determined that the account cannot be collected under ordinary means. The method is popular with small businesses because of its simplicity. Many firms simply write off bad debts at the end of the year. Many of these firms also write off only accounts that have declared bankruptcy or are very old. Bankrupts should be charged off, of course, because there will be little, if any, recovery on such accounts. It is a mistake to hold old accounts for an excessive period before charging them off because it distorts the true charge-off experience of the firm. Accounts should be removed regularly from the books, at the end of each month as they are determined to be uncollectible by ordinary means. They always can be reinstated if payment ultimately is received, but failure to remove them in a timely fashion will make the delinquency report incorrect in terms of both charge-offs and delinquency. Until the accounts are charged off, they will show as delinquent, thereby confusing two sections of the delinquency report.

The second method of accounting for bad debts, called the **reserve method,** is the method preferred by accountants and larger firms. In this method a percentage of credit sales or accounts receivable is set aside each year to cover bad debts. The percentage used is based on the experience of the individual firm and could range from $\frac{1}{2}$ percent to 3 percent of credit sales. If expressed in terms of a percentage of receivables, then the percentage could range from zero percent of the 30-day accounts at year-end to 50 percent of the 90-day accounts. Generally, the amount will be calculated using an aging of year-end receivables. Regardless of the method used to calculate the bad debt allowance, the amount determined is shown as an expense and as a reserve for uncollectible accounts on the balance sheet. The accounting entry is a debit to an expense account called *bad debt expense* and a credit to the reserve account. The reserve account will subtract from assets on the balance sheet and net receivables will show on that document much as accumulated depreciation is subtracted from long-lived assets to arrive at a net investment. Accounts determined to be uncollectible are removed from the asset account for receivables and charged against the reserve account, which means that the actual charge-off of an account does not affect expenses or sales. This process is preferred by accountants because the bad debt expense is recorded in the same year as the sale, thereby matching the two. Any error made in estimation of the amount of bad debts is taken care of at the end of the year by adjusting the amount of bad debt expense to be recognized for the next year.

Just because an account has been written off as a bad debt does not mean that collection efforts should not continue. Collection agencies will undertake to collect accounts you have failed to collect. Such firms charge a percentage of amounts recovered as a fee. These fees can range between 25 percent and 50 percent of the amount collected. This seems a high cost, but the alternative generally is the loss of the entire amount. The use of a collection agency generally is a last effort. However, waiting too long to turn an account over to an agency can result in the failure of the agency to recover any money. Consequently, the collection department should be constantly aware of **chronic accounts:** those that consistently break promises to pay and consistently are delinquent. When the collection effort on such accounts becomes extreme, consideration should be given to turning them over to a collection agency. The more typical pattern is for a firm to turn over accounts that are three to five months delinquent and have had no activity during that time. It may be too late to recover anything without litigation after that long a period of inactivity.

Litigation always is possible as a collection device, but it is an expensive and time-consuming process. It usually is practical only on larger accounts. Small claims court can be used without an attorney for small amounts. The fees for using this court are small, but it does require an investment of time. Many businesses feel that the time a small claims court will require cannot be justified by the amounts involved. Nevertheless, it is an option that always should be considered for accounts that refuse to pay.

When money is received on accounts that have been charged off, the handling of that money must be carefully monitored. Because no account is on the books to support the receipt of such payments, it is simple for a person to embezzle the funds. Consequently, careful controls must be set up to handle the processing of such transactions. The preferred method is to **reinstate the account.** This means putting the account back on the books as an asset. Then payments can be recorded against the accounts. Payments of this type commonly are received on bankrupts ordered by the court to pay a percentage of their obligations and accounts referred to collection agencies that have partial recovery.

## COLLECTION PROCEDURES

**Collection procedures** refer to the methods used to encourage customers who are delinquent or in default on their accounts to pay their debts. In general, these procedures simply require someone to ask for payment and then check that the payment is received. The customer can be contacted about payment by letter, by telephone, or in person. It is extremely expensive to employ collection agents to physically visit delinquent accounts; consequently, virtually no small businesses use such techniques. However, if sales agents or other employees of the business call on customers, then they should be made a part of the collection effort. When a sales representative calls on a business that is delinquent, the agent should know the situation and ask for payment as part of the sales call. If delinquency is consistent, then the agent should make the customer realize that future sales will be restricted or tighter payment terms enforced. In addition, sales agents and other traveling employees of the business should be used to call on delinquent accounts located along the route to be traveled. A firm, courteous discussion of a customer's delinquency in a face-to-face interview is the strongest possible collection effort. Involving the sales agents in the collection effort also makes it clear to those people that delinquency will damage sales commissions. It makes the sales agents more attentive to the overall operations of the firm.

### Letters

Letters to delinquent customers are the best known and most broadly used collection effort. Consequently, they tend to be less effective than other methods of contact. Nevertheless, they are useful for customers who honestly have forgotten about payments or due dates. This means that letters need to be sent early in the collection process. A computerized system with the capability of preparing delinquency letters is a must if there are large numbers of accounts, because letters should be sent no later than fifteen days after delinquency. Additional letters can be generated at other times, but the 15-day contact is important to head off serious problems. If a customer has forgotten to make a payment and is not reminded for thirty days, then two payments are now due and it becomes more difficult for the customer to handle the debt. Consequently, early contact is important. This first letter should be a courteous reminder of payment. Many good accounts, if not all accounts, can be expected to overlook a payment from time to time. If you are excessively harsh or rude in the reminder letter, you can do great damage to the long-term relationship with the customer.

Many books detail a series of collection letters, each more insistent and stronger than the last, to send over a period of time to delinquent accounts. We feel that such effort largely is wasted. A customer having payment problems on your account is probably having problems on other accounts as well. Consequently, a delinquent customer is frequently bombarded with collection letters from a variety of sources. Such letters frequently are ignored or even destroyed unopened. If a customer gets more than thirty days delinquent, someone needs to talk to that customer to find out what the problems are and what can be done to eliminate the delinquency.

## The Telephone

The telephone probably is the most efficient collection device ever invented. It permits the next best thing to a face-to-face interview with costs that approximate letters. A strong collection department will make telephone contact with every customer delinquent thirty days or more. This contact should be made earlier on accounts that have a history of delinquency. The collector should be trained to be courteous and helpful but firm. If customers cannot be reached during the day, then collectors should be employed to work evenings. If a customer cannot be reached by telephone, then immediate steps need to be taken to find the customer and protect the business.

Telephone collectors should not simply call people and ask for payment. If a reminder letter has been received, then the customer realizes that the account is delinquent. Mistakes happen, so it's always important to verify that the letter has been received. Continued failure to make payment must be the result of a financial problem. The telephone collector should make every effort to determine what is the problem and what can be done about it. This takes a genuine interest in the customer. A poorly trained collector simply will get promises that "the check is in the mail," that "it'll be mailed next week," or other statements made to terminate the conversation. A well-trained collector will never ask for payment but will ask what is wrong; will assure the customer that past business is appreciated and that future dealings are desired; that the business is willing and anxious to adjust payment schedules to meet temporary problems; that the customer is valued and that the delinquency is viewed as a joint problem that can be cured. Payment schedules can be adjusted to accept smaller amounts on a weekly or other basis until the delinquency can be eliminated. The telephone collector should strive to end every call with an understanding of exactly when and how much payment can be expected. Remember, many good customers experience temporary problems. A strike, job layoff, unexpected illness, breakdown of an automobile, dental expenses, or any one of an unlimited number of occurrences can disrupt income temporarily. When the problem is over, those firms that have displayed a helpful attitude toward the delinquency can expect to have a stronger, more loyal customer in the future.

### Follow-up

The secret to telephone collection, or any other collection effort, is follow-up. For specially arranged payment terms to be effective, a collection agent needs to check to see that payments have been made as agreed and call the customer as soon as a promise has been broken. The same collector needs to deal with a customer throughout the length of a delinquency so that a personal relationship can be developed. The assigned collector must make records of agreements and promise dates and must maintain a file of promises by date. Daily, the collector must check the date file against payment records and, as soon as a promise is broken, call the customer again. If the promise is kept, but the amount of payment is less than agreed, a second call should be made anyway. This second call should not wait! If a payment was to have been made on Tuesday, then the call should be made no later than Wednesday! Delinquent accounts must be encouraged to speak truthfully and honor commitments. If unexpected problems complicate a payment, then the customer should call the collector and make that information known. The only way that such a relationship can be cultivated is for a rapid and consistent follow-up to occur throughout the period of delinquency.

## THE IMPACT OF CREDIT ON SALES

We indicated at the beginning of this chapter that no one would extend credit to customers unless forced to do so by competitive pressure. It certainly is true that no business can expect to be successful if it is not competitive. Being competitive frequently means more than price: hours of operations, location, services, and credit terms frequently are requirements, too. Nevertheless, you should have a clear picture of the impact of credit on your sales and profits at all times. We discussed how too tight or too loose a credit policy can increase or reduce sales. We discussed how losses on credit accounts are to be expected, how they affect profits, and how the losses and collection costs need to be weighed against contribution margins to determine overall effectiveness. Considering all this, you also should examine the effect of credit on the firm's strategic posture. Many businesses survive and do well while refusing to handle any credit accounts. These businesses have developed a strategic posture that is consistent with cash sales. For example, many discount or factory warehouse retailers require cash or credit cards but have an image of being low-price stores. As a matter of fact, credit accounts were developed in exactly the same way. A growing number of businesses began to offer credit terms as part of a plan to gain a competitive edge and as part of their strategic postures. The pendulum has not swung back the other way, but it could. The important point to remember is that credit activities need to be consistent with your firm's image. If the image is low-cost, no frills sales, then credit may not be required. If the image is high-quality, high-service, exclusive products or services, then credit may be required. As in all other aspects of your business that affect customers, your credit policies must be consistent with your strategic posture.

## SUMMARY

Because all business is based on trust, nowhere is this more evident than in the extension of credit. Buy now and pay later is today's creed. Credit was first recorded as a practice 4,000 years ago but probably has been possible in some form since the advent of tribal living. Although traditionally credit was limited to business, the introduction of the credit card has made users of us all.

Yet, as with the growth of any element, the rapid growth of credit has brought with it special problems, especially for small businesses dependent on their cash flow for survival. These problems deal with the possible loss from those who cannot or will not pay and the costs of effective management of credit from granting credit to collecting delinquent accounts.

Accounts receivable, trade credit, and extended payment terms for goods and services purchased from a vendor have been discussed. Credit sales to consumers are another means of extending credit. Methods to limit the liability of your business when extending credit are the use of credit cards, financing through outside firms, and the factoring of accounts.

Three kinds of accounts can be used to support credit sales: open accounts, revolving accounts, and installment accounts. The advantages and disadvantages of each as it applies to small businesses have been examined.

Extending credit may be necessary to businesses as well as people. Judging their ability and desire to repay is a difficult process that requires some experience. There are four Cs of credit: character, which refers to the honesty and integrity of the customer; capacity, which refers to the financial strengths of the customer with regard to the ability to repay the credit; capital, which also refers to financial strength in regard to the ultimate collectibility of the credit; and conditions, which refers to a host of factors that can affect the credit decision.

Credit history is an important part of evaluating the character and capital of a customer. Information may be learned not only from the credit application but also from the merchants' associations or credit bureaus. Credit histories will show types of credit as well as promptness of payment.

Credit extension to businesses is similar to that of individuals but the assessment is different. The character of individuals is easier to assess than the character of a business. A business character reflects its management. Dun & Bradstreet functions as a credit bureau for businesses and provides information about credit history. The capacity and capital of a company is evaluated by its financial statement and its conditions are functions of its environment.

The management of credit and delinquency is important to the success of a small business. A credit policy should be prepared by and approved by the owner. The policy should spell out procedures and guidelines for processing applications, granting credit, and monitoring the collection of accounts.

Credit extension mandates a formal application, whether from an individual or business, with substantiating documents such as financial statements if a large amount of credit is desired. The credit may be evaluated according to a checklist with points assigned for various factors such as longevity in a particular situation.

Monitoring delinquency is necessary if credit is extended. Not only does monitoring credit activity show aging, delinquency, and the collection of accounts, it requires us to examine the credit sales and their trends. There are two methods of accounting for bad debt expense. The most popular is the direct write-off method. In this process an account simply is charged off as an expense after determining that it cannot be collected by ordinary means. The second method of accounting for bad debts, the reserve method, is preferred by accountants and large firms. In this method a percentage of credit sales or accounts receivable is set aside each year to cover bad debts.

After bad debts have been written off, the collection process may continue. Collection agents may be hired to pursue delinquent accounts or litigation may be initiated on large accounts. If the collection process is successful, the account should be reinstated and controlled for the period of time payments are received.

Collection procedures are methods used to encourage payment by customers who are delinquent or in default on their accounts. The collection effort may be aided by sales agents, a collection staff, or another employee who gets in touch with the delinquent account in person, by letter, or by telephone and then follows up on promises to pay.

The ability of a business to be competitive can dictate its survival. This includes its strategic posture. Remember that credit activities need to be consistent with the firm's image. If the image is of low-cost, no frills sales, then credit may not be required. If the image is of high-quality, high-service, exclusive products or services, then credit may be required. Therefore the effective management of a company's accounts receivable is necessary for its survival.

## QUESTIONS

1. Define the following terms:
   - a. accounts receivable
   - b. factoring
   - c. lien
   - d. note
   - e. recourse
   - f. trade credit
2. How could the extensive use of credit cards affect the survival of small businesses?
3. List three methods for limiting the risk in the extension of credit to consumers?
4. What problems are associated with trade credit?
5. Why is factoring generally not viable for a small business?
6. What three kinds of accounts can be used to support credit sales?
7. What are the four Cs of credit?
8. What is the single most important aspect of a credit decision?
9. What are the two methods of accounting for a bad debt?
10. What are the advantages of having a checklist in making the credit decision?

## PROJECTS

1. Using the checklist in the text, role play several loan applicants being interviewed by one or several bank officers concurrently. If concurrently, have a loan officer's meeting following the applications to discuss each application. How does the checklist make the decision easier? Under what conditions might it be essential that such checklists be used? Should any exceptions ever be made to the evaluation by checklist? What other considerations might there be in evaluating a credit application that may not be included on the checklist?

2. Several accounts have been delinquent for a period of thirty, sixty, or ninety days. Have the collection manager demonstrate the collection techniques to use in each situation. The collection manager may role play as if he or she were instructing new people in the collection department about how to do the job or as a collector with others playing the role of customers with delinquent accounts. Which techniques are most adequate in which instances? What attitude is important to the collection personnel? What could be the result of an abrasive personality in this situation? Would you do well in this job? Many bankers must go through a trial period in this position in the bank as training for their jobs as loan officers; why do you think that this is a good idea?

# Case 1

George Peabody is a local attorney specializing in real estate. He is well known in the community and has several loans with a very small local bank. The loans were for his house, his business, a business for his wife, leasehold improvements on his office, and his cars. In addition, his business accounts are at the same bank.

Like all busy people, George occasionally was late with a payment but never was really delinquent until the day the bottom dropped out. The bank was frantic because Mr. Peabody's trust account was overdrawn by $20,000. This couldn't happen. Trusts accounts are sacred. A real estate **trust account** is set up by attorneys to safeguard the money in real estate transactions prior to closing, at which time it is disbursed. It typically is a sizeable account.

Peabody was contacted immediately. He told a woeful tale about his trusted secretary forging his signature on a check on the account in that amount. It was a clear case of embezzlement according to Peabody. His secretary had stolen the money and run away. George Peabody had to make the money good. If he didn't come up with the $20,000 immediately, not only would he be in serious trouble but his professional reputation would be ruined. Because the bank was concerned about the situation, they loaned him the money to make up the deficit.

But Peabody's duplicity was not long in revealing itself. His other loans began defaulting and he was not available. His wife was filing for a divorce, and she was as interested as the bank in knowing his whereabouts. The office was closed and the bank started procedures to repossess the assets held as collateral for his many loans. What a nightmare for the bank! Discussion with Mrs. Peabody further clouded the issue of how guilty the bank may have been in covering the overdraft for his real estate account. They learned that Mrs. Peabody was naming Peabody's secretary as a corespondent in her divorce action. Of course, neither was available for questioning.

### Questions

1. Clearly, the bank was somewhat at fault in making a loan to cover an overdraft of this type rather than reporting it, but professional people usually are not examined quite as closely as other credit applicants by lenders. Also there was no clear accounting of the outstanding loans made to Mr. Peabody. With computerization, this is not as much of a problem, but what steps might the bank have taken in the loan process and credit history process that could have alleviated some of the later problems with this account?
2. What methods should have been taken to collect on the delinquent accounts?

3. If you had been involved with Mr. Peabody's credit decision, what would you have done and when?
4. What now can be done to enable the bank to recoup its losses?

# Case 2

Stephen Browne is a preacher from a very small church in the hills. He is very poor and had come to the attention of the collections department at the local bank. It seems that he had bought a used car to use to visit his parishioners and was having difficulty in meeting his payments.

Bob Jones, the collection agent assigned to his case, told Browne that he was sorry but without immediate payment, or at least some amount toward it, he would lose his car through repossession. This was on Friday. Browne solemnly promised that he would have the money on Monday, because he needed his car.

On Monday morning, Browne appeared at the bank and asked for Jones. Jones was delighted that Browne had kept his word and brought in the loan payment. Jones was even more surprised by the method of his payment. Browne handed Jones the amount of the loan payment in a shoe box. It contained nickels, dimes, quarters, and a few dollars amounting to the full payment of $175.23.

Jones was speechless and asked Browne why the money was mostly change. Browne proudly replied that on Sunday he had explained his predicament to his congregation. They all chipped in to help him retain his car.

## Questions

1. Browne's account was now current. Do you feel that his account was handled properly?
2. What method would you have used to collect on this account?
3. Why is the relationship between loan officer and borrower, as well as collection agent and borrower, so important and even fragile?
4. Do you think that Browne may have continued troubles meeting his future payments? If so, how should they be handled?

# CHAPTER 22

# Financial Management

**LEARNING OBJECTIVES**

After completing this chapter, you should be able to

- Explain the types and sources of financing for small businesses.
- Discuss the advantages and disadvantages of common and preferred stock.
- Distinguish among the different types of loans available to small businesses.
- Comprehend the role of debt in risk management.
- Explain the difference between long-term and short-term loans.
- Identify the two sources of cash flow in a small business.
- Understand the role of retained earnings in small businesses.
- Discuss the importance of maintaining a sound bank relationship.
- Comprehend fully the impact of growth on a small business.
- Know the importance of financial planning to a small business.

Most people think of finance in terms of loans and debts. **Finance,** however, consists of all sources of funding available to a business. There basically are only two such sources: debt and equity. The principal difference between the two is that **debt** must be repaid whereas **equity** does not have to be repaid. This means that debt presents greater operational problems for a small business than equity. Equity can create problems in control and be highly expensive, in that dividends or returns must be paid continually to equity holders, but the failure to repay debt can result in the bankruptcy of a business. In most states, as few as three unpaid creditors of a firm can force that firm into bankruptcy.

The United States economy truly is based on credit. Virtually every year new records are set for the highest debt levels by the nation, businesses, and consumers. Debt has become so thoroughly ingrained in the economy that virtually no small business can survive effectively without it.

Most of the focus in this chapter will be on debt because of its importance to a successful operation. Thomas Carlyle said, "There are but two ways of paying debt: increase of industry in raising income, increase of thrift in laying it out." Carlyle's words are of particular importance when we consider debt management. As he said, there are only two ways that debt can be repaid. One is through an increase in revenues and the other is through a reduction in costs. Therefore debt can be justified only when its use can result in one or the other circumstances for its repayment. Any other use of debt will cause problems because further actions will have to be taken for its repayment.

## TYPES AND SOURCES OF FINANCING

As we said earlier, financing can be obtained through debt or equity. *Equity* refers to funds invested in a business by its owners, regardless of whether the firm is a proprietorship, partnership, or corporation. In recent years new vehicles for equity investment have been developed to make raising money from investors easier.

### Equity Financing

**Limited Partnerships.** A **limited partnership** is a firm with two classes of owners: general partners and limited partners. A **limited partner** is closer to a shareholder in a corporation than a partner in a partnership. In fact, the SEC regulates limited partner shares as though they were stock certificates. A limited partner invests money in an enterprise by purchasing a certificate. Thereafter, the investor shares in profits or losses and cash distributions on a basis established by the partnership certificate. Because the firm generally is taxed as a partnership, it pays no tax, the limited partners must report on their personal income tax returns their share of profits or losses. Distributions of cash over and above profits reduce the tax basis of the partners' investment in the business. When that basis is reduced to zero, which means all of the partner's investment in the firm has been returned, any further distributions generally are taxed as capital gains. Consequently, a limited partnership can have favorable tax treatment. Nevertheless, limited partners have no control or participation in management in a firm. The general partners of the firm will exercise management control and make all decisions. For this reason, a limited partnership frequently is used as a device for raising equity capital rather than an organizational format.

For small businesses the limited partnership approach can be worthwhile. Many small ventures have used this vehicle successfully; however, the process can be complex because the area is highly regulated. Consequently, we recommend professional assistance in preparing limited partnership fund raising efforts. You will need an attorney who has experience in this area as well as a CPA firm to prepare a prospectus. Of course, the use of professionals will raise the cost, consequently, limited partnerships are probably not worthwhile unless you intend to raise substantial sums, say $250,000 or more.

**Stock.** In the corporate field, an unbelievable variety of investment instruments or securities have developed. These range from different classes of common stock to preferred stock, preference stock, stock rights, options and warrants, convertible bonds, and instruments of all kinds. To understand all these types of securities, we must recognize that the holders of **common stock** are the true owners of a corporation. These people share in the profits of the business through dividends or distributions of income and share in the management of the firm through election of a board of directors. The common shareholders generally are equal regardless of the cost of their stock. Each share of stock is entitled to one vote and a pro rata share of income based purely on the number of shares of stock outstanding.

A deviation from this one vote policy, called *cumulative voting,* exists in several states. Under cumulative voting, a shareholder has the right to cast one vote for each position on the board of directors or all votes for one candidate for the board. For example, if a corporation had fifteen members of the board, a shareholder could vote fifteen times: once for each position available on the board. Alternatively, the shareholder could cast fifteen votes for a single candidate for the board and give up the right to vote for the other fourteen positions. Originally, common stock was the only form of equity available for a corporation. Because people wanted to use equity for raising money but without losing control of the company, other forms were invented.

It is now possible to have more than one class of common stock: one class that has voting rights and one or more other classes that cannot vote but share in the income. In addition, there is **preferred stock** and **preference stock.** These securities generally take preference over common stock in terms of distributions of income but have no voting rights. The dividends paid to preferred and preference stockholders generally are stated in terms of an interest rate so that there is a guaranteed return. In the event of bankruptcy or liquidation of the firm, these shareholders take precedence over common shareholders for any capital left after creditors are paid. However, dividends are not paid above the specified rate if profits are high, as they would be on common stocks.

Common and preferred stocks of various types frequently are used as financing vehicles for small businesses. Family, friends, associates, and employees generally can be offered stocks as investments with good success for the business. If you wish to approach outsiders, you must be more careful because the Securities and Exchange Commission (SEC) regulates stock offerings. In Chapter 12, we talked about small offerings that avoid the requirement for registration with the SEC. These are the approaches small firms generally take, but they require professional assistance to ensure compliance with regulatory agencies.

**Rights, warrants,** and **options** are devices that entitle the holder to acquire stock in a corporation. Small business corporations seldom make any use of these securities because their value generally is based on the availability of a market for securities, such as a stock exchange. **Convertible securities** are generally types of debt that can be converted to equity under certain circumstances or at specified times. These, too, are seldom used in the small business world.

**Permanent Financing.** **Stock certificates** of all kinds and **limited partnership certificates** are considered **permanent** financing because the investment in the business never has to be repaid. Preferred and preference stock frequently carry **call options** that permit a business to repurchase the stock under certain conditions, thereby effectively repaying the investors, but those options are generally not mandatory. Because the investment does not have to be repaid, less risk is associated with equity financing. The other side of this coin is that the investors in equity have to be paid shares of income as long as the business exists. In addition, these payments, called **dividends,** are not tax deductible. This means that equity financing can be quite expensive in terms of the amount of cash that must be invested in the financing each year and over the long term. You frequently hear of large corporations that pay no dividends on their stock thereby avoiding this cash drain, but this normally is not possible for a small business. Holders of stock in large businesses have the stock markets in which to buy and sell stock certificates. Profits can be made in the markets through those sales. Such markets generally are not available for a small business; consequently, stockholders in small firms look to dividends for the returns on their investments.

**Going Public.** Finally, the absence of stock markets for small businesses and the complexity of SEC rules governing stock and equity sales makes finding equity investors difficult for a small business. You frequently hear about small businesses **going public.** Such firms have made the jump from small, closely held corporations with a small number of shareholders, to corporations whose stock will be traded on some stock market and therefore available to anyone who wishes to buy it. This is a dream for many small business owners because it marks the entry of a business into markets that make equity financing a viable option. Unfortunately, very few small firms ever make the jump. It requires a tremendous amount of capital to pay the professional fees to CPAs and attorneys for the development of the initial stock offering and for the necessary filings with the SEC. Nevertheless, going public remains the only really effective approach to consistently obtaining equity financing.

If you have dreams of taking your operation public, you should plan carefully for that event. Professional advice will be required not only to structure the offering in accordance with legal guidelines, but to protect yourself and the interest of other owners in the firm.

## Trade Credit

People frequently overlook trade credit when they talk about sources of financing. Perhaps, this is because it is so obvious. Nevertheless, **trade credit** is a tremendous source of financing for a firm, regardless of its size. In reality, the amount of trade credit issued each year by businesses in this country exceeds the amount of all other types of borrowing. Trade credit, as discussed in previous chapters, arises by purchasing inventory, merchandise, supplies or other goods on account from a vendor. The terms of trade credit range from a few days to several months and generally are established by industry practices. If trade credit were not available, then cash would have to be used for all purchases. Such a requirement would put tremendous numbers of small firms out of business!

Trade credit frequently is issued with discount terms for early payment of the obligation. In a previous chapter, we explained how those cash discounts could be converted to annual percentage rates. The method was to divide the grace period or extended payment period into 360 days and multiplying the result by the amount of the discount. For example, 2/10, net 30-day terms means a 2-percent discount is available if paid within ten days, but the balance is due in thirty days at the most. For these terms a 20-day extended payment period exists (30 – 10) and there are eighteen such periods in a year (360/20). This means that the annual percentage rate that would result from not taking the discount is 36 percent (18 × 2%). The other side of the coin is that the ten-day payment period amounts to free credit. The cost of not taking cash discounts may be too high to afford, although this is not always the case. If a firm gets into trouble and is unable to obtain other types of financing, then the cost becomes less important. Under normal circumstances, the discount period may be all that is available, but it still is a source of credit.

## Loans

Most people think about financing as loans. A tremendous variety of loan arrangements can be made; prominent among these are revolving credits and term loans. **Revolving credits** are amounts set aside by a bank or other lender that can be used on an as needed basis by a business, repaid, and then used again.

### Lines of Credit.

A **credit card** is a line of credit for an individual. A specified amount is established as the maximum that can be borrowed. Thereafter, the borrower can use the credit whenever desired. Payments must be made regularly, but when the line is reduced below the maximum, more funds are available for borrowing.

For businesses, **lines of credit** generally are issued for a year at a time. A firm will request a specified amount of credit that usually is supported by a cash budget. The line is intended to cover timing problems in the cash flow of a firm, not for expansion or other purposes. Needs of this type are called **working capital requirements.** The approved line generally can be drawn by simply writing a check or by telephoning the bank to ask for an advance deposited to the checking account. At the end of a year, the line generally is required to be completely repaid before it is extended for another year. This last requirement is to ensure that the funds are used strictly for temporary cash needs. Total repayment of the line would be difficult or impossible if the funds were used to finance anything other than short-term cash flow requirements.

Lines of credit may be secured or unsecured; that is, collateral may or may not be pledged. Owners of small businesses frequently are asked to **endorse, cosign,** or **guarantee** the line. Any of these actions simply makes the owner personally responsible for the repayment of the debt. This precaution frequently is required by lenders because a small business often is totally dependent upon its owner for success.

A revolving line of credit can be an extremely valuable type of financing if properly managed. Almost every company will experience cash flow variations that can cause extreme problems in the short run. Lines of credit are ideal solutions for such problems. It is virtually impossible for a small business to obtain such a line, however, unless good budgeting techniques are used by the business. All banks prefer, and most demand, that lines of credit be supported by cash flow budgets that show when and how much will be needed as well as when and how much will be repaid. One word of caution is due here. Never use a line of credit for anything other than short-term cash flow deficits. If you follow that rule, a line of credit can make managing a business easier and more pleasant.

Many small businesses do not use revolving lines. Instead, they use 30-, 60-, or 90-day notes. These may be unsecured or secured and may require owner guarantees, just like other loans. These short-term loans can serve the same purpose as a revolving line. However, the bank has total control over each transaction and whether the note must be paid at maturity or will be renewed. Should the bank become disturbed over economic or other conditions, an interim financial statement, or any other change in a business, it probably will not be willing to renew notes or advance any further amounts. Consequently, these short-term notes are not a viable vehicle for financing. Their popularity is due to the absence of budgeting activities among small businesses. Banks will make 90-day loans supported only by a financial statement and a verbal description of need. A line of credit generally needs more. We highly recommend that you avoid short-term notes payable. Do the budgeting necessary and use lines of credit. The results will be much more desirable.

**Term Loans.** For needs other than those of a cash flow nature, **term loans** of all types can be used. These loans have maturities from one to ten years although banks tend to prefer the shorter periods. Anything over five years is unusual. Term loans generally are secured. This means that some of a firm's assets are pledged as collateral. Accounts receivable, inventory, furniture, fixtures, machinery, equipment, and vehicles can be used as collateral. Term loans are paid in installments; that is, a specified amount of payment is required each month during the life of the loan. Because the loan repayment is fixed, budgeting the cash to cover the requirements is possible.

Term loans are used for a variety of purposes, most frequently for financing purchases of long-lived assets. They are one of the most frequently used financing vehicles for small businesses. They frequently have higher interest rates than short-term notes because the risk factor for the lender is greater with a longer period for repayment. Guarantees from the owner are frequently required as well.

**Commercial mortgages** are term loans secured by real estate or buildings. These loans generally have maturities from ten to twenty years. Owner guarantees frequently are required for these loans as well as the other types. Mortgages generally are used to acquire land, build buildings, make renovations or major repairs, and so on. A mortgage can be acquired on a building alone when the land under it has a long-term lease. Frequently, a business will be able to obtain lease terms for urban land of ten, twenty, or thirty years, but will be unable to buy that land. In such cases, a mortgage can be acquired to finance the construction of a building with the lease assigned and a lien on the building conveyed to the lender.

**Bonds.** **Bonds** are debt securities sold to investors just like stock certificates or limited partnership certificates. Large firms use bonds, which are generally secured by assets of the business, or **debentures,** which generally are not secured, to raise debt capital. These securities will have specified interest rates and maturity dates and will be sold in financial markets. This approach generally is not feasible for a small business because it really requires access to a financial market to be effective. Firms that make the leap to public corporations can use bonds and debentures, but most other small firms cannot.

**Sources of Financing.** **Loans** can be acquired from banks, finance companies, insurance companies, mortgage companies, savings and loan associations, venture capitalists, private investors, and individuals. Loans can be obtained from federal, state, and local governments and agencies or can be partially or fully guaranteed by such agencies. These sources were explored at length in Chapter 12. For a small business, access to future credit frequently can be as important as good terms and rates on a loan. This means that obtaining a loan, of any sort, is not simply a matter of choosing the lender with the longest maturity and the lowest interest rate. It may be worth a little higher rate and a shorter term if a borrowing relationship develops that can help the firm in the future. Building a good relationship with a lender is vital. Taking some business away and bringing some business to a lender normally is not a good way to cultivate such a relationship. This is discussed further in a later section on bank relations.

Exhibit 22-1 recaps the sources of funding and their typical uses in small businesses. We examined the start-up capital issue in Chapter 12. In this chapter, focus is on expansion and working capital, commercial mortgages, and equipment financing. Expansion loans indicated in the exhibit generally are a combination of working capital and purchases of equipment or fixtures. That is, some portion of the loan is expected to be used to handle the short-term needs associated with growth of the business. In the next section, we examine the differences and roles of short-term, long-term, and permanent financing.

**EXHIBIT 22-1** *Sources and Uses of Capital*

| SOURCES OF CAPITAL | USES OF CAPITAL | FORM OF CAPITAL |
|---|---|---|
| Personal funds and savings | Start-up capital | Equity<br>Long-term debt |
| Family and friends | Start-up capital | Equity<br>Long-term debt |
| Partners, friends and business associates | Start-up capital<br>Expansion capital | Equity<br>Long-term debt |
| Private investors (need professional assistance) | Start-up capital<br>Expansion capital | Equity<br>Long-term debt |
| Venture capitalists (more than 500 appear in published lists) | Start-up capital<br>Expansion capital | Equity<br>Long-term debt |
| Small business investment companies (SBICs), minority enterprise SBICs, SBICs and MESBICs chartered by the SBA | Start-up capital<br>Expansion capital | Long-term debt |
| State sources (check with state business assistance office) | Start-up capital<br>Expansion capital | Long-term debt |
| Local development companies | Expansion capital | Long-term debt |
| Industrial development and business development agencies | Expansion capital | Long-term debt |
| Federal sources: Small Business Administration, Department of HUD, Department of Commerce, Economic Development Administration, Farmers Home Administration (350 assistance programs directory available from printing office) | Start-up capital<br>Expansion capital | Long-term debt |
| Banks: independent, SBA certified, SBA participating | Start-up capital<br>Expansion capital<br>Working capital<br>Commercial mortgage<br>Equipment purchase | Long-term debt<br>Short-term debt<br>Lines of credit |
| Savings and loans, mortgage companies | Start-up capital<br>Expansion capital<br>Commercial mortgage<br>Equipment purchase | Long-term debt |

*continued*

**EXHIBIT 22-1 continued**

| | | |
|---|---|---|
| Insurance companies | Start-up capital<br>Commercial mortgage<br>Equipment purchase | Long-term debt |
| Finance companies | Start-up capital<br>Equipment purchase<br>Working capital | Long-term debt<br>Short-term debt |
| Stock offerings (public or private; need professional assistance) | Start-up capital<br>Expansion capital | Equity |

## THE ROLE OF DEBT IN RISK MANAGEMENT

How much debt should a business have? Which is better: short-term debt or long-term debt? These are difficult questions because there is no one answer. Like most things in business, it depends on the industry, conditions, competition, and the desires and preferences of the owner of a business.

### Debt Versus Equity

Three factors should be considered about debt or equity financing: risk, cost, and availability. The availability issue frequently makes the decision for a small firm; that is, equity financing frequently is not a viable option for a small firm outside its start-up period, as discussed in the previous section. Consequently, small firms may depend totally on debt for their financing needs. Even if equity financing is not available, you need to be aware of the impact of debt on a firm's risk.

The greater the debt level in a firm, the higher is the risk to which that firm is exposed. This is simply because the more money a firm is obligated to repay, the harder it is for that firm to handle the repayment. Failure to honor debt obligations will destroy a firm. Like all risk issues, however, there is a return trade-off. Exhibit 22-2 displays abbreviated financial data for three firms that are identical in every way except the proportion of debt financing they use. Note how the debt leverages up the return on the owner's investment in the firms. Because of this leveraging effect, debt levels are termed **leverage.** We say that a firm is highly leveraged, meaning that it has high levels of debt. **Leverage** refers to the relative amount of debt a firm has versus the amount of equity.

The higher the leverage is in a firm, the lower its equity; consequently, the higher its return on investment. This is true so long as the interest rate for the debt is less than the profit margins. If interest rates exceed profit margins, then

**EXHIBIT 22-2** *Debt Versus Equity Financing Examples*

| | FIRM A | FIRM B | FIRM C |
|---|---|---|---|
| Total assets | $100,000 | $100,000 | $100,000 |
| Total debt | 25,000 | 50,000 | 75,000 |
| Total equity | 75,000 | 50,000 | 25,000 |
| Profit before interest | 15,000 | 15,000 | 15,000 |
| Interest on debt (10%) | 2,500 | 5,000 | 7,500 |
| Profit before taxes | 12,500 | 10,000 | 7,500 |
| Taxes (30%) | 3,750 | 3,000 | 2,250 |
| Net profit | $ 8,750 | $ 7,000 | $ 5,250 |
| Return on equity: | | | |
| Net profit/total equity | 12% | 14% | 21% |

undesirable results will follow. Of course, the risk also goes up with the returns. Judging how much debt is too much is largely a function of a firm's ability to repay the debt or its **debt servicing** capacity. In Chapter 8, "Financial Analysis for Success," we talked about financial analysis and discussed ratios that can be calculated to evaluate a firm's debt capacity. We also discussed how comparisons of various ratios, including the debt ratio, could be made to industry averages to determine how a firm compares with its peers.

The cost of the debt/equity trade-off is complicated by income taxes. The interest paid on debt is tax deductible. This means that a profitable firm in a 30-percent income tax bracket will actually pay only 70 percent of the interest charges on a loan because the remaining 30 percent of the interest will be saved in income tax reductions. All of the dividends paid on equity must be paid after tax, as discussed, so there is no corresponding reduction. In addition, debt eventually is repaid in full, whereas equity investments generally are permanent. Consequently, the after-tax cost of debt generally is less than the cost of equity.

This is not the whole picture. In previous chapters, we stressed that cash flow really is more important to a firm than profits. Dividends on equity do not have to be paid when there are no profits or when cash is not attainable, but loan payments must be made regardless of profitability or cash levels. In addition, the principal must be repaid along with the interest on a loan. Principal repayments do not show as an expense, but constitute a cash drain. This is the real reason that the risk level increases with the debt level. The impact of debt on cash flows must be assessed, and this impact is the real cost of debt.

## Short-Term Versus Long-Term Debt

Another factor in the management of debt is the mix between short-term debt and long-term debt. Revolving credit, trade credit, and notes payable all are short-term credit obligations. Term loans and commercial mortgages are long-term debts, although the portion of the loan that must be paid during the next fiscal year actually is a short-term obligation as well. It shows on the balance sheet as current maturities of long-term debt. The issue of which is better, short- or long-term debt, revolves around the source of funds for repayment.

A business really has two sources of cash flow: the liquidation of current assets and profits. *Profits* are funds left over after expenses have been paid and can be used for debt repayment, distribution to the owners, or any other purpose a firm desires. But if we take a short-term perspective, the collection of accounts receivable will produce cash. This cash could be used to repay debt. You could argue that both sources of cash flow really are the same and, strictly speaking, this is true. However, if we view them as distinct sources, we can better balance short-term and long-term debt levels in the business. From a different perspective, we can say that long-term debts are never actually repaid but reclassified as short-term debts or current maturities, which are then repaid. This sounds like a circular argument—and it is. Viewing the sources and types of debt as distinct simplifies everything and permits evaluating the firm's debt level and debt mix.

Short-term debts should be repaid from the liquidation of current assets. Therefore, if the level of current assets goes up, the amount of short-term debt that can be handled also goes up. This is a working capital concept. In Chapter 8, **working capital** was defined as the difference between current assets and current liabilities, and it indicates the resources a firm has to support its day-to-day operations. So long as an appropriate balance between current assets and short-term debt is maintained, the firm can handle its obligations. Long-term debt should be repaid from profits. So long as the relationship between profits generated and long-term debt is appropriate, the firm can handle its obligations.

The trade-off between short-term and long-term debt comes about because of the fluctuating nature of short-term assets. Exhibit 22-3 displays a growth curve for short-term or current assets and long-lived or fixed assets such as plant, property, and equipment. The growth curve demonstrates how the assets must grow to support sales growth, but current assets behave in a "sine wave" fashion. We saw this same up and down pattern in the cash budget in Chapter 7, and it was the cause of the fluctuating cash flows.

Fixed-asset growth follows a step function, as discussed in Chapter 6. You cannot acquire half of a machine. Consequently, when sales grow beyond the firm's capacity, another block of fixed assets must be acquired.

**EXHIBIT 22-3** *Current and Fixed Asset Growth*

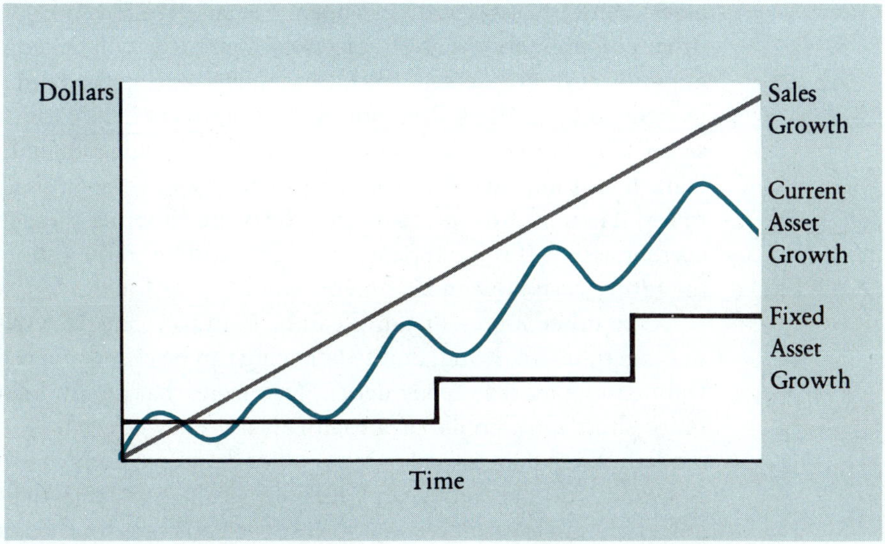


The graph shows current assets going up and down with the seasonality of the business. As those assets go up, short-term debt is needed to finance that growth. As those assets go down, cash is generated that should be used to repay the short-term debt. The growth in fixed assets, on the other hand, is more constant and these assets do not generate cash directly, although they support sales. The building a firm occupies or the machines it uses in its business do not generate cash but they make it possible for sales to be made. Consequently, it would be foolish to acquire fixed assets with short-term debt because no cash will be generated by those assets for repayment. Long-term debt should be used to finance the fixed assets and the source of funds for its repayment is profit or cash flow from current asset liquidations that is not required to cover short-term debt.

It is possible to finance short-term assets with long-term debt, but this also usually is not wise, because the debt will remain after the assets have been liquidated. A drain on future profits will result even though the firm's life was improved by the debt for only a very short period. To finance a major expansion of a firm usually requires financing some short-term assets with long-term debt, because the firm wants to achieve a higher level of sales without having working capital problems restrict the growth.

For normal financing needs, working capital, equipment acquisitions, and such needs, it makes more sense to balance the use of debt: short-term debt for short-lived assets; long-term debt for long-lived assets. A portion of the current assets can be considered permanent because the inventory, receivables, and other components of current assets never actually will be reduced to zero. The graph of current assets clearly shows this. Treating the permanent portion of current assets as long-lived and using long-term debt to finance it can make sense. This is the justification for including working capital in an expansion loan. It can improve the operating cash flows of the business and make life easier. There is a danger, however, in overestimating the permanent level of current assets. If this happens, we simply will be trading short-term cash flow for future cash flow and problems will develop for the firm in the future.

One other source of funds can be used to repay debt that deserves mentioning: other financing. Equity financing can be raised and used to repay debt. Debt can be used to repay debt. This means that a term loan can be used to retire short-term credit or a loan can be renewed; that is, the maturity extended. When debt is used to repay older debts, we simply postpone a problem. Individuals do this frequently when they get into financial difficulties with loan consolidation loans. It can make sense for a business for the same purposes, but careful management of the debt in the first place will go a long way toward avoiding a repayment problem.

## RETAINED EARNINGS

Many people are confused by the role of retained earnings in small business finance. They show as an entry in the capital section and so are considered as equity. Consequently, many people talk about retained earnings as a source of financing. This is true, strictly speaking; however, the financing is hidden. **Retained earnings** come from profits. Any profit not distributed to shareholders or owners of a firm will be credited to the retained earnings account. If we use a proprietorship as an example, it will become clearer. A proprietorship does not have an account for retained earnings. Instead all monies invested in a firm are credited or added to the owner's capital account. In addition all profits of the firm are added to that account as well. Whatever the owner takes out of the business is deducted from the capital account. The balance is the amount of the owner's investment in the firm. This money *already has been invested* in the business, which means that it already has been spent. It is a type of financing because it has been used to acquire assets or repay debts, but it is not a future source of financing. It is much like trade credit in that it arises on a daily basis as part of the business operations, is used on a daily basis, and is spent on a daily basis. Retained earnings in a corporation are exactly the same. They do not constitute a source of unused capital or future financing, but simply evidence of the amounts of money the owners have left in the firm and have used in the firm in the past.

## MAINTAINING BANK RELATIONS

Any business that experiences seasonality or that is growing rapidly will require frequent access to credit. We have discussed how the fluctuations in current assets resulting from seasonality will create short-term borrowing needs. The long-term growth of sales also will create borrowing needs to finance the fixed assets that must be acquired to support the growth. Before the sales can grow, the capacity of the firm must be expanded. If we are operating at capacity in the present facilities, then no more sales can be made until capacity is expanded. It takes cash to finance the expansion. The money cannot come from operations, because sales have not yet expanded. Consequently, the funds must come from debt or equity financing. Because equity frequently is not viable, the conclusion is that term loans will be needed to support the growth.

Despite all the various sources of financing that exist, your local bank remains the most important single source because of the speed of possible response to credit needs. When a strong relationship has been established, no sources of credit can react as fast as a bank. Consequently, developing and maintaining a strong relationship is important.

Banks actually make most of their money on businesses through deposits not through loans. This sounds strange because interest is charged on loans, but numerous studies have demonstrated its truth. All of the loans and other investments a bank makes are supported by its customers' deposits; therefore, no income is possible without those deposits. In reality, this is the primary reason for the difficulties small businesses frequently encounter in bank relations: they simply do not have large enough account deposits to make them as valuable to the bank as larger firms.

There are two schools of thought about developing bank relations. One school says, "Don't put all your eggs in one basket, develop relations with at least two banks." Another school says, "Banks don't like to share business with other banks so be loyal." Both have some validity. It is true that banks prefer not to share a banking relationship with other banks. This means that you will have a stronger relationship if you do all of your business with a single bank, which includes all checking accounts, credit card accounts, investments, and loans for both the business and its owners. However, if the banking officer you come to know leaves the bank or transfers to another town or if any changes occur inside the bank, it is possible for you to experience problems with loan requests. People who ascribe to the two bank approach often have experienced such problems in the past and sought to avoid such problems in the future. However, because deposit balances are so important to a bank relationship, using two banks will inevitably lower your value to each bank. What can you do?

We recommend that you use a single bank until the business grows to a point that it generates deposits that can support multiple banking relationships. This means that to avoid potential problems, you need to choose the bank carefully and strive to keep current with what is going on inside the bank. Far too many people make the choice of a bank based solely on convenience. The bank with the branch closest to their business is selected. It is wiser to visit every bank in town, talk to the lending officers, find out if there is experience in your industry in the bank, develop a relationship with the banking officers who will be supporting your accounts. If a bank has no lending experience with firms in your industry, it is going to be less supportive of your needs. Banks tend to specialize and lending officers employed by banks tend to specialize even more. Find an individual with whom you can talk, who is responsive to your needs, understands your business, and is willing to take the time to become acquainted with your operation.

Your banker needs to have a sufficient lending authority to handle your needs. Bankers are assigned a lending limit based on experience and longevity. If the officer you cultivate cannot approve your loan requests, then much of your efforts will be wasted. This frequently happens to small firms. They develop a strong relationship with the branch manager of the closest branch, never realizing that all of their loan requests will be approved in the main office downtown.

Determining whether a bank officer has a loan authority that can cover your needs can be difficult. Bankers frequently avoid such inquiries by saying that the loan committee makes the actual decisions. The **loan committee** is a group of loan officers who meet periodically to approve very large loans and loans beyond the credit limit of an officer. In some very small banks, virtually all loans must be approved by the loan committee, but in most banks the majority of small business loans are small enough, relatively speaking, that individual officers can approve them.

As a general rule, if your loans have to be approved by committee, you are in trouble. There is no way that all the members of a committee can know you personally. This means that the decision will be based on cold, hard facts, like your financial statements and the bank's assessment of economic conditions. Your lending officer generally will be able to make a presentation to the committee in your behalf and can support your needs, but the value of that support is a function of the internal politics of the bank. This means that the relative power and prestige of your loan officer will affect the committee's reaction to his or her support. Not only that, it is much easier to make a negative decision in a group. It's just human nature to want to avoid unpleasant situations. When a group makes a decision, then the lending officer who has to tell you about it is absolved of responsibility.

This is one major reason why it is so hard for an individual to obtain the loan necessary to start a business. No relationship has been established with an individual, and the amount of such loans frequently are so large that they require committee action. What this means to you is that you should avoid a bank if it is going to shuffle all of your loan requests to a committee for action. Go somewhere else! If you cannot find a bank in which an individual can handle your needs, then at least make sure that the person you cultivate inside the bank is a permanent member of the loan committee.

How do you learn all this information about a bank? It takes patience and persistence in visiting and interviewing bankers. Don't concentrate on branch managers. Go to the main office and ask to see people in the commercial or business lending area. Pick up a copy of the bank's financial statement—they will be lying on almost everyone's desk—and read the names and positions of the officers. Pick out someone in commercial lending. Ask people direct questions. Make them understand that these are issues that will influence whether you do business with the bank. Make them understand that once you settle on a bank you will bring all of your personal and business accounts to them and deal with them exclusively. Find out how the loan committee works. If the individual you're talking to cannot handle your needs, ask who can, and then see that person. In short, pay as much attention to choosing and developing a banking relationship as to the selection of any other professional with whom you deal.

You need a banker who will visit your business, spend time getting to know you and your managers, and understanding your markets, suppliers, problems, and so forth. After you have found such a person, keep the contact alive! This means providing monthly financial statements to the bank, whether or not they request them; visiting with your banker regularly, whether or not you need something. You want to develop such a sense of loyalty that your banker will keep you informed of pending changes within the bank that could affect your firm. You also want the banker to develop such a feel for your operation that he or she will know when and how you need money as soon as you do. This means being open with the banker. The monthly financial statements will help, but you should make it a point to discuss potential changes and developments in your business even when those are not positive. One of the strongest actions you can take is to institute a budgeting process and send copies of the monthly budget to the bank. This not only will keep the banker informed as to projected developments but force you to do a better job of budgeting.

## THE IMPACT OF GROWTH

We talk about growth in businesses as if it were the primary objective of every firm. In fact, growth that is not planned and too rapid can kill a firm.

We were called in to assist a client in obtaining a loan. We were to help prepare an SBA loan package because the firm had been turned down by every bank in town. There were two owners, young men in their late twenties, who shared the business 50/50. They had been together for about a year and a half. Their sales growth was phenomenal. In the first year of operations, sales were $40,000. The second year sales were $170,000, and sales for the first two months of the third year were $70,000. This was really the problem.

The business had sold strictly retail for most of its first year. They sold pottery, baskets, macrame, and craft items; supplies, wicker, and rattan items; and a large assortment of imported gifts and novelties. The retail store seemed to do well. They had started the business with an SBA-guaranteed loan through a local bank, and they made money the first year.

Then one of the partners discovered selling wholesale. Dan was approached by several small dealers at a show. His wicker and rattan items were popular and hard to find. He agreed to sell some of it wholesale. In less than four months he had become known nationwide. His were the best prices in the country. When we arrived, the business had $60,000 of wholesale orders it couldn't fill because it didn't have the money to buy the merchandise. They needed a loan, quick!

Burt wasn't too happy with his partner. They had been friends since high school, but Burt had doubts about how much profit they actually were making on these sales. They had to rent a warehouse to process the stuff and hired two or three more people to try to keep up with it. We wondered about profits, too. Dan was too popular. During our first visit with him, he was interrupted by telephone calls from buyers six times in one hour. He sold each of them something.

The accounting system was a mess. They had hired an accountant to prepare the year-end statement and intended to do that again. A clerk posted records in-house, but no one had any idea what the inventory looked like. The sales weren't even separated between wholesale and retail. The P&L statements they were preparing showed a profit, but only Dan believed it was true.

We tried to talk them out of a loan application. We said that a loan would only postpone the problem. Things had to be brought under control before they got entirely out of hand. Dan wouldn't listen. We prepared a loan application, but it was turned down after four months of trying. Dan continued to sell. Things got worse.

They hired a bookkeeper. We set up the books, but it didn't seem to work. The bookkeeper couldn't get the transactions down. Dan was too busy to tell her what he had done. He was buying and selling by phone with no records. Bills and invoices would come in and no one knew where the stuff was. Some of the goods were drop shipped. The warehouse was a mess. It wasn't safe to go in the place. Rattan furniture was stacked so high that it looked ready to fall over. Dan kept selling.

We tried to get him to slow down, but he wouldn't listen. There was no money to meet the payroll. Burt had quit coming in. He wanted Dan to buy his stock. We said it's easy to slow down, just raise prices! Not only will your growth slow down but you'll generate more money with each sale. Dan wouldn't listen. A bank lent him $8,000 using some accounts receivable as collateral. This got him through the end of the year.

We tried to rush the year-end financial statement so that Dan would see the real problems. The accountant couldn't figure out the books. We never did see the actual statement for the third year. The internal records still showed a profit, but the inventory levels were ridiculous. Dan kept selling.

People started suing. Actually, we discovered that they had been suing for some time. Dan finally told us that he had some suppliers who hadn't been paid in a year. When they cut off his source of supply, he just found another one and kept right on. These guys were in Spain and all over the world. We couldn't believe they would sell on credit to someone they never heard of, but Dan was a born salesman.

Things got so bad that Dan began to listen. He laid off most of the people. Burt wasn't talking to him anymore. It looked like it was too late to save much. We told him either to stop selling or face bankruptcy. He listened. Then the phone rang and Dan sold $20,000 worth of stuff he didn't have. When he got off, he told his bookkeeper to write checks to pay off three of the suppliers. He wanted to buy from them again to fill this order. She said there was no money in the bank. He said, "Yeah, but it'll get me a couple weeks." We walked out. We heard a few months later that he had gone bankrupt. We weren't surprised. We never saw anyone who worked harder at failing.

The problem with growth is that you must back it up with people, systems, and resources to handle the increased volume. Otherwise, it becomes a constant battle of trying to keep up—a battle that's hard to win. The larger a firm becomes, the more important it is to have good systems for handling sales, record keeping, merchandise, and so on. The systems are as important as the people. If there are no established ways of doing things and keeping track of things, then no one will know what is happening or be able to keep up with what is required. Systems require planning. People and resources require money. The time and money must be planned and managed as well as the added sales, or the firm will lose. Our client lost what promised to be a strong, healthy business because he would not or could not do anything but sell. The owner of a business must be a manager. There is no one else to worry about organization or planning.

How can you avoid these problems? The answer is to plan. Use the budgeting processes we discussed. Make arrangements for the financing to support the growth in additional resources and people. Set up systems to handle the growth. Don't let the growth get out of hand! If it starts going faster than you can handle, raise prices. If this doesn't work, raise prices again. You always can drop back the prices when you get a handle on things. Don't be afraid of losing out permanently because of higher prices. Losing some accounts is preferable to losing the business.

## FINANCIAL PLANNING

**Financial planning** has gained popularity in recent years. From a narrow perspective, it is the process of arranging the financial support for a company's needs. The tools are budgeting and financial analysis. From a broad perspective, much of what has been discussed in this book could be considered financial planning. Almost everything done in a business has a financial impact: from determining salary levels for employees to deciding how much capacity is required in our fixed assets; from establishing minimum cash levels to determining prices. The important part of the phrase is *planning*. Throughout the text, we have stressed the need to plan. In an article, Bruce Posner called planning just another word for good management.[1] The success stories of entrepreneurs who made a fortune with "seat of the pants" management are examples of "pure, dumb luck," Posner says. In truth, the failure to plan can doom a firm to a mediocre existence if not absolute failure.

In the realm of finances, planning requires attention to the sources and uses of financing alternatives, and the maintenance and cultivation of financing relationships that can be used in the future. There are no mysteries or magic formulas. Planning simply is work—a manager's work. It is the one thing an owner must do and the thing that separates weak businesses from strong ones. All the talk about firms that fail due to cash flow problems, inadequate capital, and all the rest are really stories about firms that did not plan. The primary message of this book—and all the literature about successful small business management—is: to **plan** is to *succeed.*

## SUMMARY

Finance consists of all sources of funding available to a business. There are two such sources: debt and equity. The principal difference between the two is that debt must be repaid whereas equity need not. Therefore, debt creates greater operational problems for a small business. Although equity can cause control problems and can be expensive in terms of dividends, debt can bankrupt a business.

How much debt a business should have depends on the industry, conditions, competition, and the desires and preferences of the owner. However, three factors have an impact on debt: risk, cost, and availability. Nevertheless, availability frequently makes the decision for a small business.

The cost factor involved in debt and equity is complicated by income taxes. The after-tax cost of debt generally is less than the cost of equity, but its real cost is the impact on cash flow. Dividends do not have to be paid when there is no profit, but repayment of debt must be made regardless.

A major factor in the management of debt is the mix between short-term and long-term debt. The issue of which is better revolves around the source of funds for repayment. There are two sources of cash flow in a business: the liquidation of current assets and profits. In general, the most sensible policy is to use short-term debt to acquire short-lived assets and long-term debt to acquire long-lived assets. Short-term debt is repaid from liquidations, whereas long-term debt is paid from profits.

Retained earnings often mistakenly are considered sources of funds. However, they simply are evidence of the amounts of money the owners have left in the firm and used in the firm in the past.

Any business that experiences seasonality or rapid growth will require frequent access to credit. Consequently, it is important to develop a relationship with the right bank and the right person in the bank to meet your needs.

Growth typically is a primary goal for small businesses and to be admired for the success it reveals. However, unplanned and too rapid growth can and will kill a business. The solution is planning, which is the ultimate task of the manager.

## QUESTIONS

1. What two sources of funding are available to a small business?
2. What is the difference between these two sources?
3. In what two ways may debt be repaid?
4. How does a limited partnership work?
5. What are some of the investment instruments available to a corporation?
6. How do dividends work in preferred stock investments?
7. What is the difference between common stock and preferred stock?
8. Why is it difficult for small businesses to find equity investors?
9. Why is trade credit such a good source of funding for small businesses?
10. What various loans are available to small businesses?
11. What are the three factors to consider about debt or equity financing?
12. Explain the relationship between debt and risk.
13. What are the two sources of cash flow in a business?
14. For what should long-term and short-term loans be used?

15. What is the role of retained earnings in small business finance?
16. How does one establish a good bank relationship?
17. Why is it necessary to investigate the bank and loan officer before deciding who should handle your loan requests rather than just adhering to the policy of convenience of location?
18. With how many banks should you establish a relationship and why?
19. Why can unplanned and too rapid growth kill a small business?
20. What is the primary illness that kills small businesses?

## PROJECTS

1. Make an appointment with a local bank loan officer, preferably in the main office, and ask questions about evaluating a small business that wants to make a loan. Are different guidelines used for long-term loans and short-term loans? How does the banker feel about small businesses in general? Does the banker make client calls? Upon whom? Evaluate your impression of the visit for the class. Would you consider this banker for your own if you were involved in a small business?
2. Visit a small business owner and ask how that person chose a banking situation and why. Don't be surprised if the owner tells you that the firm uses more than one bank. Ask why, if such is the case. Also, ask if the firm has ever considered a different banking relationship and why?
3. Have you ever watched a seemingly thriving business suddenly close its doors? Do you know why? If you can question someone involved with the business perhaps you can discover what caused the failure? Was it growth? What could you have specifically recommended to the owners given the chance?

# Case

Trey Ensley and Jason Fairchild were asked to help a local business. They were surprised by the call because, all around town, the scuttlebutt was that Strips and Straw was astoundingly successful. Jane and George Cleveland opened their doors five years ago when they decided to turn a hobby into a business. They had been making baskets, chairs, and anything wooden for a number of years. George learned the craft from his father and grandfather, who had used the skill to get them through bad times when they were laid off at the mill. George learned by being their errand boy and picked up the trade quickly. He had a way with wood really that the others envied. He could see a plan in his mind and transform that image into reality.

As was the custom in the mountains, George married just out of high school, and both Jane and he had gone to work at the local plant. Jane was employed in the bookkeeping area and George was on the loading dock. For relaxation, George still worked on baskets and wooden furniture. Jane found that she had a talent for painting designs and embroidery, so many evenings found them in front of the fire making things for their friends and family.

They went into business by happenstance. George hurt his back on the job and had to leave on disability. His injury meant that he no longer could lift heavy burdens, but he wasn't qualified to do anything else. Jane's job also was in jeopardy. The mill where she worked was being forced to relocate and her job was running out. What could they do?

During George's convalescence, he had worked on weaving baskets, because that kept him occupied while he was unable to be up and around. Friends hit upon a perfect way to help them out—they asked George to make baskets for them for gifts. This brought in some income and the demand increased.

When Jane's job finally was phased out, she began helping George with the woodwork while she looked for another job. Everyone liked the Clevelands, but jobs were scarce. So more and more time was spent in what they perceived as a hobby.

One evening, after a frustrating day of looking for nonexistent jobs, they decided that they already were working and making an income. A friend of theirs had asked them to make some baskets and wooden products on consignment for his craft shop and everything sold quickly. He asked for more. In fact, he had asked for 100 more over the next three months.

Jane and George gave their business the name Strips and Straws. The next few years were busy but happy; then their work really caught on. They had shown their wares at several craft shows and the orders were really coming in. In fact, they had more orders than supplies or time. They were working out of their house. Already, there was no room to walk and work was becoming impossible. Yet the demands on their time were incredible. They decided to open a store, but they needed a loan and they needed advice. Things were getting out of control. They were six months behind in orders and even though their expenses had been reasonably low, they were finding it hard to actually ship their finished products. They had purchased a large supply of materials because they needed it to finish up their last order. They had not received payment for the order because the contract called for payment on delivery, yet they had to pay for the material on receipt. At the rate they were going, they weren't going to be able to make the delivery. So they called Trey and Jason for help.

### Questions

1. List several problems Strips and Straw currently is facing or soon will face. What kinds of decisions will they be forced to make?
2. What advice can the consultants give Jane and George?
3. What do you suppose are their prospects for getting a bank loan to tide them over? What must they prepare to show to a lender?
4. What kinds of things should the Clevelands have done in prior planning for such an occasion?
5. List some possible sources of funding for the Clevelands.
6. Discuss how the business can be saved.

# CHAPTER 23

# Production Management

**LEARNING OBJECTIVES**

After completing this chapter, you should be able to

- Explain what manufacturing is.
- List the types of production.
- Understand the concept of risk and return.
- Explain the steps in production planning.
- Understand the concept of just-in-time inventory policies and when it will apply.
- Understand the concept of product control and to what it refers.
- Know management's role in control and production.
- Differentiate between engineering standards and attainable standards.
- Calculate and explain variances.

Thomas Carlyle said, "Man is a tool using animal . . ., without tools he is nothing, with tools he is all." When he distinguished humans from animals through tool use, Carlyle probably was thinking about the use of hand tools and simple machines. During his day, sophisticated machinery was virtually unknown. Nevertheless, machines are tools and the modern application of machines has been the dominant factor in the rise of civilization. The Industrial Revolution largely was brought about by the development of machines and manufacturing processes. Today, only a tiny fraction of the world's population is untouched by manufacturing and that percentage shrinks each year. The first step emerging nations must take to make themselves part of the world community is the development of their manufacturing processes. You have probably read about the decline of manufacturing in the United States and the rise of service industries; how we are shifting away from a production orientation. It is true that the number of manufacturing and blue collar jobs is shrinking and the number of clerical and white collar jobs is growing. Firms in the services industries are making great strides and many such firms now are named in the *Fortune* list of the 100 largest firms in America when once that list was dominated totally by manufacturing firms. Nevertheless, the production of goods is and always will be a mainstay of business. No economy can exist without manufacturing; no business can survive without products, tools, and machines produced by manufacturers; no standard of living can be maintained without the products and goods produced by manufacturing. The only thing that has truly changed is that manufacturing has become an increasingly complex and competitive business. The management of manufacturing firms must become increasingly sophisticated for its firms to remain competitive.

None of this means that small businesses cannot enter and succeed in manufacturing. Although the majority of small business ventures are in fields other than manufacturing, this is predominantly due to entry barriers. It takes a great deal more capital to start a manufacturing operation than any other type of venture because of the initial investment required in plant assets. Because small businesses almost universally are plagued by capital shortages, it follows that fewer small firms venture into manufacturing. Nevertheless, many highly successful small firms engage in production. In fact, some of the greatest opportunities for new ventures exist in the area of manufacturing. Such firms frequently are the site of the development of new products, new methods of production, and innovative operations. Like their counterparts in other industries, small manufacturers are a mainstay of the United States economy and a vibrant part of American business. In this chapter, we address the key aspects of production planning and control required for a small manufacturing operation to succeed.

## MANUFACTURING

In general terms, **manufacturing** is the process of converting raw materials into usable products. To raw materials are added labor and capital to transform them into salable units. Success in such an operation involves the effective management of the resources of money and people and effective control of their combination through a production process. Human resources management was discussed in Chapter 17 and financial management in Chapter 22, consequently, we focus here on the management of the production process itself.

There are many types of production. The type most people think of when they think of manufacturing is a process system. In a **process system,** a homogeneous product is produced in a continuous operation. **Homogeneous** means that the individual units of product cannot be distinguished from each other. A good example is a cement manufacturing plant. Raw materials go in one end in a continuous stream and cement comes out the other end, also in a continuous stream. Special problems are associated with the management of a process system, as is the case with other types of systems. **Job order systems** are polar opposites of process systems. In this type of production, no two units of output are the same. A manufacturer that produces a unique product to customer specifications is an example; such as a producer of custom designed machine tools. Of course, few firms ever are clearly one type or the other. There are differences in cement! It may take a chemist to identify different types of cement, but engineers specify characteristics of cement that they require for their projects. In addition, one of a kind orders frequently develop into repeat opportunities. The first order for a space shuttle was custom designed, but the second shuttle was not!

One of the main differences among manufacturing operations is the use of **subassemblies.** Many manufacturing firms really are assemblers because they purchase everything they need in the form of completed subassemblies from other manufacturers and then assemble the parts into a finished product. Many computer manufacturers operate in this fashion. Other firms start with totally raw materials and carry through to a finished product. Oil refining frequently is done like this. Still other firms stop at various points along the way. These are the companies that produce the subassemblies used by other manufacturers. Still other firms purchase completed products and modify them. Firms that produce custom vans, automobiles, and the like generally buy a completed vehicle and then convert it in their plants. As you can see, the combinations possible among these approaches are limitless!

Before we talk about the management of production, we need to say a few words about the risks and returns associated with production. Because specialized machinery and plants are required to manufacture a product, the impact of failure is high. If a retailer fails to make a go of one of its products, it simply drops that product. If a manufacturer fails to succeed with one of its products, the equipment and facilities may not be usable for other purposes. The market for used, special purpose equipment is small! The manufacturer stands to lose a great deal. This is why assembly has become so popular in high technology businesses. If subassemblies are bought from other manufacturers, then conversion to another product is simplified should the market for our product change. The risk is shifted back to the firm producing our subassemblies. Of course, we won't make as much money, because the subassembly manufacturers are charging us the cost of production plus a profit margin for themselves. Risk and return almost always are commensurate with each other. The point to keep in mind is that your manufacturing business can manipulate its risk–return trade-offs by subcontracting parts of the production process or by buying more and larger subassemblies. The choice should not be made blindly, but only after a careful evaluation of the alternatives.

## PRODUCTION PLANNING

**Production planning** consists of the designation of raw materials required for production, the selection of machines and labor skills to be used in production, the specification of volume of output, the acquisition of material and labor required to achieve that output, and the timing required for each phase of the operation. The first part of planning is the design phase. Here you decide how you will build each product, what raw materials are required, what subassemblies will be used, and how the fabrication will take place. The outcome of the design planning will be a bill of materials and a work layout. The bill of materials is a list of the specific items and quantities required to produce one unit of output. It is the basis for raw materials inventory management, which will be conducted in much the same way as retail inventory management, discussed earlier.

The **work layout** details the fabrication steps: what must be done to convert the raw materials to finished goods; whether the step will be done by machine or by hand; the order in which steps must be completed; and how the work will flow through the fabrication process. The work layout can be a lengthy document if the fabrication process is complex. Each stage in manufacturing must be detailed and described. This is where you say "part A is attached to part B" and describe how they are attached: by hand, by machine, welded, bolted. In addition, the work layout must specify how all the steps in fabrication fit together. If two parts must be put together to form a subassembly that will be added just before the fabrication is finished, then the work flow must be planned to ensure that the needed subassembly is ready when the rest of the production has been completed.

## Design Planning

To visualize design planning, think about the manufacture of automobiles. Thousands of parts are involved in the bill of materials, and hundreds of subassemblies will be used in production. If an assembly line approach is used, then multiple assembly lines are required so that a continuous stream of subassemblies are ready to be added to the units in process at the correct time. The main assembly line starts out with the construction of the frame of the automobile, but simultaneously another assembly line must be preparing the engines to be attached to the frame at the correct point. The same is true for the fabrication of the automobile bodies. Still other items from the bill of materials must be provided in a continuous stream to the correct point in the work flow: seats, windows, tires, batteries, and a host of other items. The efficiency of the operation, in large measure, is a result of the planning that has been done. Whether you are building a product as complex as a car or not, the process is the same for your operation.

The best approach to the work layout is to start with the finished product and disassemble it on paper and in detail. Use graph paper and design the working space to scale at the same time. The space requirements will be a function of the number of people required to perform the operation, and the size and number of machines required. Be careful to properly locate sources of supply of raw materials and subassemblies. Place storage bins or tables or storerooms so that parts required will be close to the operation in which they will be used. Locate assembly areas for phases of the operation that can be carried out simultaneously so that the subassemblies will flow into the main production smoothly. Make access to the storage areas easy for stocking purposes. Be sure to include inspection stations for quality review and control. This process is outlined in Exhibit 23-1. Your finished plan will be a plant layout diagram and a written description of each operation in the fabrication process. Exhibit 23-2 is an example of such a plant layout.

The result looks like a big flowchart. That's exactly what it is! It will not only show the work flow, but will show the size and layout for the building you will need. As you can see from Exhibit 23-2, raw material is off-loaded at the dock and goes into the receiving area where it is checked against invoices. Raw materials not yet ready for the fabrication process are stored in the area marked raw material until such time as they are needed. If just in time inventory is used, material stocks can be minimized, saving time, money, and space. (Just-in-time inventories are discussed later in this chapter.) Nevertheless, when storage of raw material is required, the control of those materials is essential. They must

**EXHIBIT 23-1** *Work Layout Procedures*

I. Begin with a finished product, dissembled on paper
  A. List all subassemblies
  B. List all materials (include subassemblies)
  C. List all supplies (glue, lubricants, etc.)
  D. Describe the labor procedures
    1. Number of people
    2. Duration of labor procedure
  E. Describe the machine procedures
    1. Number and size of machines
    2. Duration of machine process
  F. Draw a graph or diagram of the manufacturing steps

II. Layout the production process
  A. Determine the space requirements for each step
    1. Space required for machines
    2. Space required for people
    3. Space required for materials
    4. Space required for supplies
  B. For each step in the graph or diagram
    1. Draw a floorplan to scale using graph paper
    2. Locate machines and people on the floor plan
    3. Indicate points at which materials and supplies must be injected into the process
    4. Determine what materials and supplies are needed at each point
  C. Determine the material and supply similarities among steps

III. Lay out the plant
  A. Draw a floor plan that aligns production steps so that common material and supply input points are located close to each other
  B. Locate subassembly steps so that they appropriately feed into assembly steps
  C. Locate storage bins or table or storerooms so that materials and supplies feed into appropriate steps
  D. Arrange access to assembly process and storage areas to ease the transfer of goods and restocking of materials and supplies
  E. Locate inspection points for quality control

not be lost, stolen, or broken prior to use. The materials are checked out of storage and are placed in the raw material storage bins at the beginning of each subassembly process as required. The supervisor handles this transfer of materials on an as required basis.

**EXHIBIT 23-2** *Plant Layout*

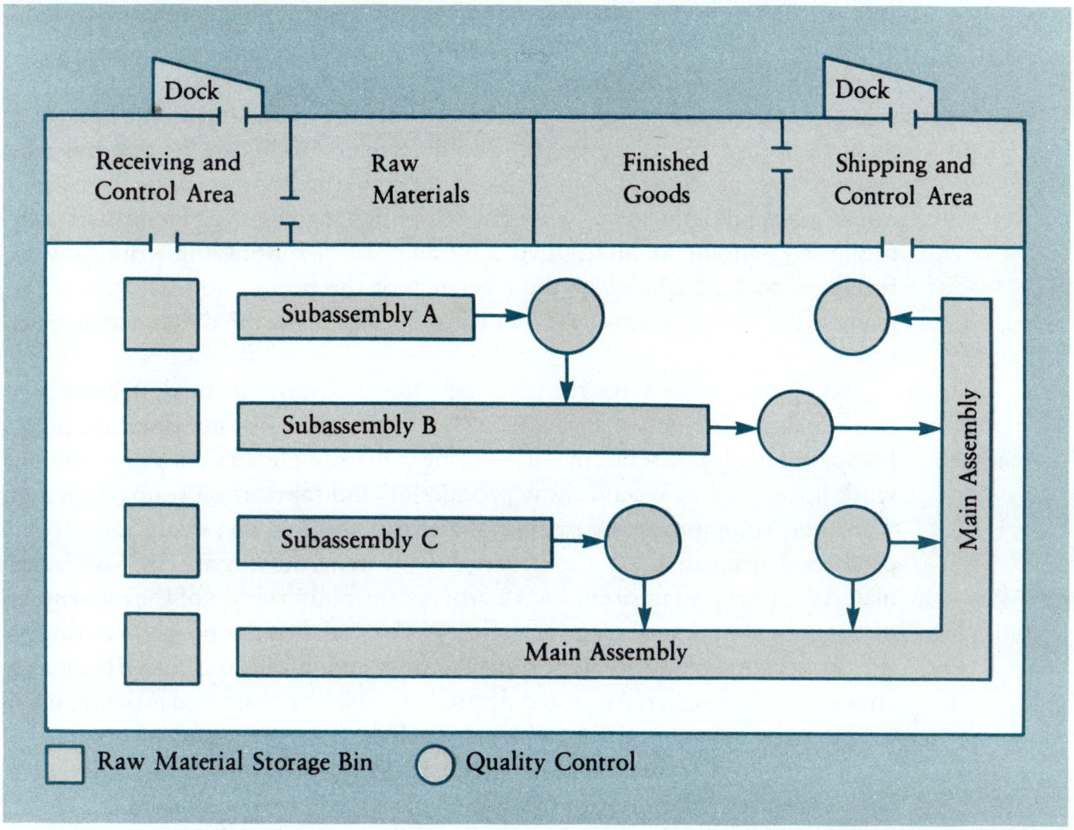


As the exhibit shows, subassembly B is impacted by the completion of subassembly A. That means that a part completed in process A is used in process B. Both parts produced in process B and C are introduced into the main assembly. There is a quality control checkpoint at the end of process A and at the ends of the other subassembly processes. This prevents inferior parts from being introduced into the assembly process. Other checkpoints may be established as desired. Notice that such a checkpoint occurs in the main assembly process prior to the introduction of subassembly B. There is always a final check after assembly before shipping.

Finished goods may be stored until the required shipping date or shipped directly upon completion. The shipping area serves as a control point for shipments and control of finished goods. Raw materials and finished goods must never commingle, and checks must be maintained to prevent loss, damage, or theft. The two dock and storage areas in the diagram serve to limit access and maintain separation and control.

Once the layout has been completed, any restraints, such as the size and shape of a particular building you wish to use, can be adjusted on the flowchart to fit the process into the facility and determine modifications that must be made or special requirements such as wiring or water connections. Be careful not to allow adjustments to snarl the work flow. If an existing facility is totally unsuitable, finding an alternative is better than disrupting the work flow by forcing it to fit. Remember, the efficiency of the production will reflect the planning of the work flow, and that efficiency can make the difference in profit or loss.

So far we assumed that the units in process will move through stages where work is done. In some manufacturing processes, the product does not move because of its size. Aircraft manufacturing is an example. In such a situation the work flow diagram should show production and fabrication teams, together with their equipment, raw materials, and supplies, moving in and out of the product. The result is still a flowchart, but the items moving are employees and materials. The key factors in such a process are minimization of the movement of equipment and arranging for delivery of material to the proper location at the proper time. Another important factor is minimization of interference of crews with each other. An added detail that must be considered is the removal or relocation of equipment no longer needed.

The description of each block in the work flowchart should explain what is done in that cell. This not only will provide a guide for supervising the work, but a basis for specifications of skills and training required for the people to be employed. You should also devote some attention to estimating the amount of time required to complete each step. This will be an ongoing problem, because the labor times will vary with skill levels and experience, but the initial estimates should be made at the time the work flow is laid out so that labor cost estimates can be prepared.

The design work is not completed when the flowchart is done. It will be difficult and expensive to change the work flow once it has been established, so you need to be as careful as possible. Nevertheless, the actual flow of work through the plant should be monitored constantly and, if changes need to be made to streamline the process, they should be. Involve the people working on the production line and first line supervisors. Make sure that the layout is effective and efficient. Attention to the work flow will pay off in profit margins!

## Production Scheduling

The second phase of production planning consists of volume scheduling, an ongoing need. The desired objective is to produce the correct number of items to meet the demand for those items. If you produce less than is needed, then the demand for higher levels of production can result in overtime wages or excessive errors, too much rework, and poor quality as people try to find short cuts and push for higher output—all these factors increase your expense. In addition, if quality falls, the firm's image can be permanently damaged. If you produce more than is needed, excessive inventories of finished goods develop, which creates problems in storing and handling and raises inventory carrying costs. The answer, it seems, is to prepare a sales forecast and produce the correct amount of product to cover the forecast.

There are two problems. The first is the difficulty of preparing a sales forecast. As discussed previously, the sales forecast is less accurate, the farther in advance it is prepared. This means constantly adjusting the sales forecast to reflect changing conditions. This is less of a problem for a manufacturer that has a short production time, but can be a major problem for a firm that has a lengthy production phase. The second problem is in varying the production process itself. The skill and training levels required for manufacturing workers makes them expensive and difficult to replace. This means that you will not be able to afford large amounts of idle or unproductive time in the work force, but neither will you be able to lay off workers for short periods as demand fluctuates. Changing the pace of production normally is not feasible either, because of problems in maintaining quality and controlling rejects. If the pace of production is constantly going up and down, then errors, mistakes, and oversights will be magnified. The workers won't be very happy either, especially if the compensation plan includes production incentives.

One approach to production scheduling is to determine the desired pace of production and then forecast sales. Now the inventory of finished goods is used to balance the two numbers. For example, assume that desired production is 10,000 units per month and sales forecasts are for 9,000 units per month over the next three months with an increase to 12,000 units for the fourth month. If you produce 10,000 units per month over the entire four months, you will satisfy the forecast because 1,000 units will be added to inventory each of the first three months. The extra 2,000 units needed in the fourth month can come from inventory, leaving it with 1,000 units left to carry forward to the fifth month. Most manufacturers make more than one item, consequently, the production planning is a matter of juggling the fabrication process between products. Because a new set up of the production line is required to change products and this is a time consuming, expensive proposition, the production runs for each product need to be as long as possible without creating unreasonable inventory levels. Major changes in production volume beyond that possible at desired capacity are achieved by shifting workers from one task to another, by changing the number of shifts working, by scheduling overtime production, and by buying larger quantities of subassemblies or contracting portions of the work out to other firms. All these alternatives are expensive, consequently, the planning strives to minimize them. Of course, storing inventory is expensive, too, but generally less costly than the alternatives for production increases. The main concern will be to prevent inventory levels from becoming excessive.

This was a major problem for Chrysler before the coming of Lee Iaccoca. Chrysler regularly built up large inventories of the various models of cars it manufactured before it retooled to produce different models. The other major car manufacturers had abandoned this practice, but Chrysler continued it. As Murphy's law predicts, when the market for large, high gasoline consumption cars dried up, Chrysler was left with thousands of unsalable vehicles. It actually had to rent vacant lots on which to store automobiles dealers would not buy. Iaccoca not only changed the company's strategic competency by focusing on smaller, more efficient cars, he changed its production scheduling policies to protect it from excessive inventories in the future. The turnaround of Chrysler, hampered as it was by a myriad of other problems and inadequate capital, was a milestone in management history.

## Just-in-Time Inventory Management

In some industries, the problems of production scheduling are reduced by the willingness of purchasers to wait for products. In such industries, a **just-in-time** scheduling system is possible. Just-in-time (JIT) inventory policies have been gaining popularity in recent years because of the increasing use of automated scheduling and production control systems. Under JIT, inventories are eliminated. Production output is scheduled to coincide with projected shipping dates so that items are shipped directly to purchasers as they roll off the assembly line. Under conditions of stable demand or industry acceptance of longer lead times for shipment of purchases, JIT is a viable tool for reducing the cost of production. If demand fluctuates widely so that forecast of sales is difficult or if purchasers demand immediate delivery of their purchases, then JIT cannot work for production scheduling, although it can function for raw materials acquisition. If your company is a producer of consumer goods, then the demand characteristics are less likely to be as predictable as desired. If you sell to other manufacturers, who use your products in their own manufacturing, then stability of demand is more likely to occur. In fact, your customers may want to use a JIT approach in their purchases from you!

A manufacturer must manage raw materials inventory as well as finished goods inventory. An alternative to the practice of inventory management discussed in an earlier chapter is the application of just-in-time inventory control to raw materials. The objective of the process is to have sufficient raw materials arrive at the factory to support the production taking place, thereby eliminating the need to store large quantities of raw materials. For JIT to work for raw materials, the sources of supply must be dependable, and lead times for the receipt of purchases must be predictable. If the industry is subject to problems in supply or to undependable shipping and transportation of goods, then JIT cannot work. Remember that both the **source of supply,** which depends on the firms from which you purchase goods, must be dependable, and the **lead time,** which depends on the firms that transport the goods from suppliers to your factory, must be predictable. If your raw materials are acquired from manufacturers in Third World companies, where political and economic conditions make suppliers undependable, or if your goods are shipped by ocean freight, in which arrival times are undependable, then you will probably have to accumulate at least basic levels of raw materials to prevent disruption of the production. If JIT is possible, then it is vastly preferable to the other alternatives.

The bill of materials provides a listing of raw materials and subassemblies that must be acquired outside the company. The production schedule predicts the volume and rate of manufacturing. This information can be combined with lead time information on each item to be purchased to produce a series of orders for raw materials that will arrive at the plant in time to support manufacturing without a build up of inventory. If the bill of materials is lengthy, if lead times vary greatly by item, or if there are multiple raw material injection points into production, then the purchasing of raw materials can be extremely complex. From a practical perspective, it is extremely difficult to conduct a just-in-time inventory policy for raw materials without a sophisticated computer-based system. Such a system frequently can be justified in the cost savings that can result. Just as economic ordering quantities, EOQs, were a step in reducing inventory costs, JIT is a larger step. Most suppliers who are dependable enough to permit JIT will cooperate in the implementation of the process. Although more orders occur under JIT, the overall supply of items by vendors takes on desirable characteristics for their companies as well. Remember that the vendors are manufacturers, too. They are plagued with the same problems in production scheduling as you! Shipments under a JIT plan to your factory from their factories can provide the stability required to improve efficiency of their production. Therefore other pricing concessions can equal or exceed the old quantity discount you would have received under EOQ inventory management. The cost reduction, combined with the virtual elimination of inventory carrying costs, and the minimization of inventory handling costs add up to great savings.

If JIT policies can be applied to production scheduling, then additional savings can occur in the form of more efficient production methods, higher quality of output, reduced set-up costs, and the virtual elimination of finished goods inventory carrying and handling costs. As in the case of JIT raw materials inventory policies, JIT for production requires a dependable forecast of the demand for items and the dates such items must be shipped. Again, balancing the shipment times or lead times for delivery, the production time for fabrication, and the units required by various purchasers is an extremely complex process. An automated system really is required.

## PRODUCTION CONTROL

**Production control** consists of the management of the flow of raw materials through the plant, the application of labor and machinery to the raw material, the flow of finished units and units in process through the plant, and monitoring the quality of production. Much of the problem of handling raw materials and finished goods is eliminated with a just-in-time inventory policy. Under JIT, the management is limited to receiving raw materials and shipping finished goods. If a JIT system is not used, then you must address the flow of raw materials from the receiving station to the storage locations, and the movement of those inputs from storage to the production line at the time required for use. Finished goods must be removed from the production line at completion and transferred to a storage location from which they will be removed for shipping when sold. Raw materials really follow the control patterns for inventory management. In the case of a manufacturer, the production schedule and the bill of materials dictates the quantities of items required over time. This takes the place of converting sales forecasts to numbers of units of inventory. Using inventory monitoring procedures, minimum stock levels, and economic ordering quantities, the raw materials must be kept flowing to production. As in the case of retailers, the raw materials can be tracked on a periodic or perpetual basis. They must be subjected to physical inventory at least once each year, and the ending inventory must be valued using FIFO, LIFO, or average techniques. Exactly the same things are true for a finished goods inventory. In addition to controlling production, a manufacturer has two complete inventory systems that must be monitored! All this is another strong argument for JIT inventory policies whenever they can be used.

The other aspect of production control is the management of the fabrication process. There are two aspects to this management: controlling the flow of physical units and work; and monitoring costs associated with that flow. The **physical flow** refers to the introduction of raw materials into the fabrication process, the application of labor to the production, the movement of units in process from work station to work station, and the maintenance of desired quality levels.

## The Flow of Physical Units

The design planning produced a flowchart of the work stations, a description of the work to be completed at each station, and an outline of the flow of raw materials and subassemblies into the production process. All that was just a plan. For it to work, it has to be implemented. The supervisors of the production process must oversee the actual work and ensure that the plan is carried out. The two inputs to production are labor and raw materials. Control over the raw materials flow is shared by the people who handle the purchasing of raw materials and those who manage the use of raw materials. If either falls down, production will suffer. Purchasing control has been discussed previously, so we will concentrate on the control over the use of raw materials.

The design plan will show how raw materials should flow into production. One of the production supervisor's duties will be to see that the flow occurs. The individual should constantly monitor the bins, storage tables, shelves, or storerooms in which raw materials begin their journey down the production line to ensure that the flow is not disrupted. Generally, the supervisor should take custody of the raw materials at the injection point. This custody should take the form of a signature of release for the raw materials from storage or from receiving. A document, generally called a **requisition form,** shows the quantities and description of items that have passed to the control of the production supervisor. Thereafter, the supervisor will be concerned with observing the use of raw materials to ensure that the items are handled properly and that excessive breakage, waste, or damage do not occur.

Control over the people doing the work is an exercise in human resource management. This was discussed at length in an earlier chapter. The production supervisor is responsible for maintaining desired production levels and monitoring the hours worked by the various people under supervision. If production incentives are incorporated into the payroll plan, then the supervisor must capture the information necessary to make the incentive plan work. Of course, all this must be done while maintaining high levels of morale and quality of work. No easy job! Good first line supervision is crucial to effective production control.

The supervisor is responsible only for quantities of inputs. The costs of inputs are beyond the ability of the supervisor to control. Costs of raw materials are affected by purchasing, and wage rates are set by management levels above the supervisor, although both of these costs can be influenced by the supervisor. Recommendations concerning quality levels of raw materials and performance levels of employees will have an effect on the ultimate costs of the inputs. Ultimate responsibility, however, rests with other management people. When we discuss standards and variances in the appendix to this chapter, we will show you how to partition deviations from plans into cost and quantity variances.

## Quality Control

The supervisor also is responsible for the quantity and quality of output. He or she is charged with achieving the production goals and must accomplish this without sacrificing quality. Both quantity and quality of output is influenced by the quantity and quality of inputs. If inferior raw materials are purchased, inferior products will result. If poorly trained or incompetent people are used on the production line, inferior products will result. A first line supervisor will have little control over either of these occurrences, consequently, we must be careful to ensure that problems with output are within the ability of the supervisor to control before placing blame or taking corrective actions.

**Quality control** is not well understood. Most people tend to think of it as a technique for ensuring that no errors occur in production or assuring that all items produced are perfect. In reality, it is a management process devoted to the maintenance of an established level of product performance. Perfect products can never be produced consistently. Even if it were possible, it might not be desirable because of the costs of production. There are two aspects of quality control. One is the proper completion and construction of the product. Quality control procedures must be designed to totally prevent improper construction or fabrication. Defective items cannot be sold. If quality control procedures allow an excessive number of defective units to slip through, then the company will be damaged. It will have to replace defective units sold or refund purchase prices. It also may suffer damage to its reputation that could affect sales in the long term. The second aspect of quality has to do with product performance: how well a product stands up under its intended use. This aspect of quality is subject to determination.

Control over defective units requires inspection stations set up along the production line so that items can be examined at crucial points. The location of the inspection station will have a major impact on its effectiveness. If fabrication results in interior components enclosed in a shell, engine, or body, then it will be impossible to inspect those components after they have been enclosed. Inspectors can check every item in production or take a sampling of items. It obviously will cost more to check every item than to check every twenty-fifth item. The decision about frequency of inspection is a function of the impact of errors. If we are filling 5-pound bags of dog food, then the impact of an error that results in putting 4.75 pounds in a bag is much less than the impact of putting 3 screws in a package that needs 4 screws for use in assembling a bicycle. In the former case, the error would probably go unnoticed by the consumer. In the latter case, we might get called by an irate consumer at midnight on Christmas Eve!

Quality control inspectors normally should not work for the line supervisor so that they are less likely to be influenced in their reports. Because they evaluate the work of the supervisor, they should report to a different manager or to the manager above the supervisor. Of course, defective units should be pointed out to the supervisor as they are found for repair or rework.

The owner of a manufacturing firm must decide what level of performance quality is acceptable. This generally is a function of demand. For example, in the pharmaceuticals industry, an exceptionally high quality of output is required because the purchasers of the drugs and chemicals will be using them to treat human illnesses. On the other hand, a company manufacturing umbrellas will require a much lower quality level. In fact, the relative sales value of the umbrellas will affect the quality control. For umbrellas intended to retail for $5.00, a much lower level of performance quality is required than for umbrellas intended to retail for $40.00! Performance quality is affected by inputs as well as fabrication. If lower-quality raw materials are acquired, or less-skilled employees are utilized, lower-quality products can be expected. Of course, those products will cost less to produce! Errors in fabrication also can affect performance. To consider the umbrella example again, if the fabrication process results in an inferior job of attaching ribs to cloth, then the item may not be caught as a defective item because it does work at the point the item is completed. Nevertheless, the umbrella will be inferior in that it will survive only a small number of uses before coming apart.

Performance quality cannot be measured by inspectors on the production line. Instead, products must be subjected to performance tests. The general approach is to select a sample of units and subject those to a variety of tests designed to monitor performance under simulated conditions. Sometimes commercials for products are designed to show performance testing as a way of building consumer confidence. In one such commercial a car door was opened and closed by a mechanical hand while the announcer was saying that the door was subjected to 50,000 openings. We just hoped that the car in the commercial was not the one that we had bought! Like quality inspectors, the performance testers must not report to the people who are responsible for production. In the case of inspectors, they could report to the supervisor's boss because the supervisor has control over defectives. In the case of performance, the purchasing manager, the supervisor, the manager responsible for employee training, and a host of other people can have an impact on the product. Consequently, performance checkers generally report to a high level of management such as the plant manager or the owner.

Quality control is an important part of the production process because purchasers demand products that perform as their cost indicates they should. If a gap is perceived in that matchup, then over the long term, the producer will suffer. Effective quality control is not just a function of production. It requires attention from every manager in the organization on a continuing basis.

## SUMMARY

Machines are tools and the modern application of machines has been the dominant factor in the rise of civilization. Although service companies are proliferating in the United States today, remember that the production of goods is and always will be the mainstay of business. No economy can exist without manufacturing; no business can survive without products, tools, and machines produced by manufacturing; no standard of living can be maintained without the products and goods produced by manufacturing. Although most small businesses are not in manufacturing, it does not mean that they won't succeed there. The only real limitation is the necessity for a large amount of operating capital required at start up.

Manufacturing is the process of converting raw materials into usable products. To raw materials are added labor and capital to transform them into salable units.

There are several types of production. One type is the process system, whereby a homogeneous product is produced in a continuous operation. Another type of production is the job order system, where no two units of output are the same. A main difference among manufacturing operations is in the use of subassemblies, which can speed up the process of production considerably. Some concerns use no subassemblies and begin with the raw materials whereas others use partial assemblies in various phases of the operation.

Inherent to the manufacturing firm, as to other businesses, is the concept of risk and return. Manufacturing companies are especially susceptible to risk because of the size of the operation. Also, the greater the use of subassemblies in a manufacturing operation, the lower is the risk.

Production planning consists of the designation of raw materials required for production, the selection of machines and labor skills to be used in production, the specification of volume of output, the acquisition of material and labor to achieve that output, and the timing required for each phase of the operation.

Production control concerns managing the flow of raw materials through the plant, the application of labor and machinery to the raw materials, the flow of finished units and the units in process through the plant, and monitoring the quality of production. Control is especially important if JIT inventory management is not possible. The other aspect of production control is the management of the fabrication process. This involves control of the flow of physical units and work and monitoring the costs associated with that flow.

Another important control is quality control. Both quantity and quality of output are influenced by the quantity and quality of input, and this should be kept in mind by the manufacturer. Those charged with the task of quality control should be autonomous and free of the production process so that the temptation to pass certain imperfect items will not be a problem. The owner must decide what level of performance or quality is acceptable and ensure that those guidelines are maintained.

## QUESTIONS

1. What do the terms *manufacturing* and *production* mean, and to what do they apply?
2. What are the two types of production?
3. How do risk and return trade off?
4. Explain the steps in production planning.
5. Why are just-in-time inventory policies not always possible?
6. What are the various functions involved in production control?

## PROJECTS

1. Assume that you have been hired as a consultant to help with the plant layout requirements for a furniture manufacturer. How would you design the plant for such a company, if fifteen pieces have to be assembled and then shipped? What other considerations might arise or what questions might you be asked when presenting your design?
2. If any small, or even not so small, manufacturing companies are in your area, perhaps with the help of your instructor you could tour their facilities, note the plant layout, and evaluate their operation.

# CASE

Ralph and Virginia Hobbs ran a small manufacturing firm. They employed thirty part-time employees to cut and sew garments. There were ten sewing machines and twenty long tables equipped with patterns, shears, pins, needles, and thread. Ralph was not only the supervisor of the operation but also the one who laid out the work for each station and tracked inventory. Having part-time employees, he saved on fringe benefits, but the employees worked at very different times. However, the workers were encouraged to make production and were paid on that basis. For example, the cutting of sleeves might be worth \$.20 a sleeve with production being twenty-five sleeves per hour. When the task was finished, the same employee might move to cutting legs or even to sewing sleeves. Operating the machines earned more money and so was frequently a source of contention among those employed there. Ralph had tried an equal time-sharing technique for the machines, but some of the workers did not do well on the sewing machines. The same was true for the pressing machine, which was not as popular because of the heat.

Payroll was a nightmare handled by Virginia Hobbs. It took her a whole

HOBBS' GARMENTS

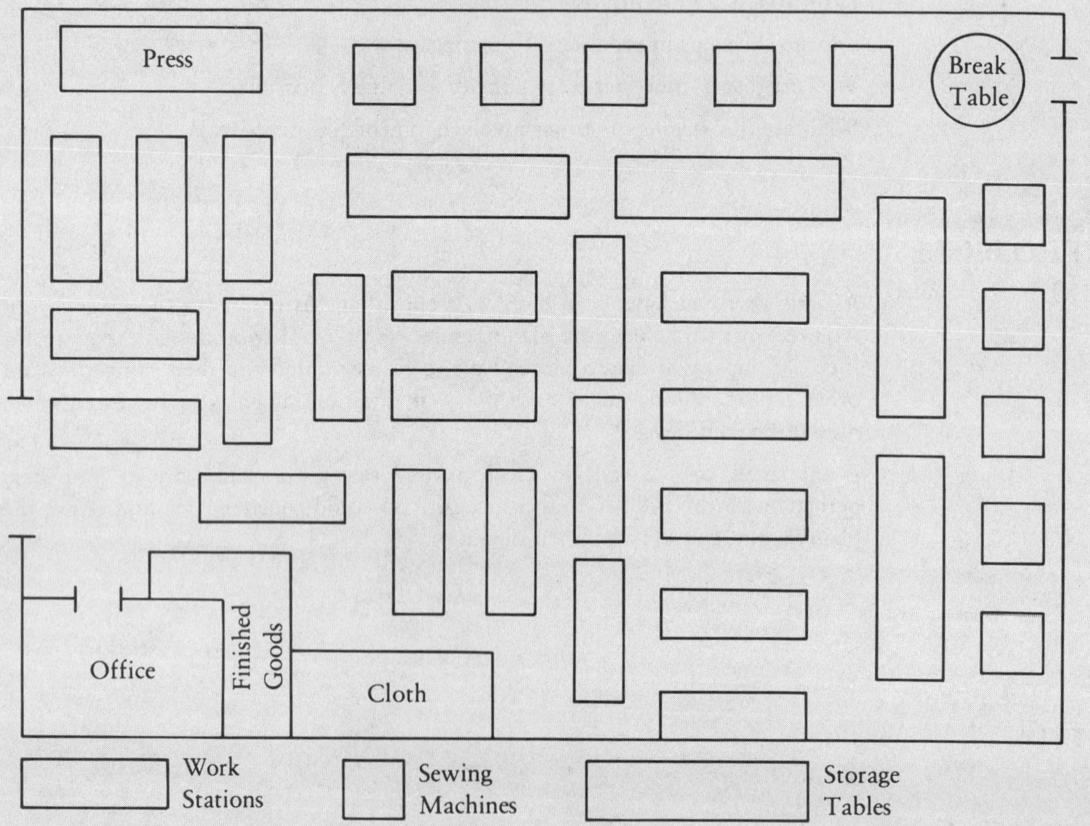

day to figure the production and write the checks. At the end of each day, the workers would turn in the stubs that showed the amount of work done at which cost. The bookkeeper would then enter those stubs on a giant spreadsheet listing the employee's name, the day of the week, and what had been done by that person on that day.

Because work was part time for the employees, production varied from week to week, but Ralph tried very hard to finish the orders as they came in and to ship them out on or before their due date. Because he wanted to increase his business, he knew he had to accept more orders, but this would require more part-time workers or working some of his existing staff full time. Most of his employees were middle-aged women who seemed reluctant to give up their free time unless the full-time position paid much more.

Ralph and Virginia had talked about how they could expand their business and take in some of the contracts they had let pass because of the size of their operation. If they really wanted to be successful, they would have to expand their operation. They had started out small doing much of the work themselves and with family help, until even they could not do all the work. But the growth had been sporadic with a large turnover in employees. Those employees who had wanted to earn a good living left to work at a mill in the next town and those others who weren't as qualified stayed on.

## Questions

1. As you can see, the Hobbs have several problems they need to overcome if they are to expand their business. Take each problem and discuss what can be done to help the Hobbs become very successful through expansion. Note also the plant layout chart on page 602 to see how their present plant looks. What would you do differently?
2. Assume that temporarily a new site is out of the question. How could you take the Hobbs from a marginally successful company to a very strong company?

## APPENDIX
# Production Costs

The second aspect of production control is monitoring and controlling costs. Three categories of costs are involved in production: costs of raw materials, costs of labor, and overhead costs. The first two, called **direct costs,** are easily understandable. The last one is a bit more difficult to see because it consists of costs that cannot be traced directly to any units being manufactured. **Overhead costs** consist of the salaries of supervisors, quality control inspectors, performance quality monitors, and managers and staff who support the production process. Even the accounting clerk's salary is part of the overhead, because the clerk prepares financial reports that deal with production and cost control. Other types of overhead expenses include the rent on the factory or depreciation on the factory if it is owned, insurance on the building and equipment, depreciation on the machinery, repairs and maintenance on the building and equipment, utility expenses for the factory, and a host of similar expenses. Overhead costs also include the salaries and other expenses associated with acquiring, handling, and storing raw materials inventory and handling and carrying finished goods inventory. Manufacturing supplies, such as lubricants, abrasives, glues, and such items must be included as well as information systems, and computer costs associated with production systems. In short, everything but selling and administrative expenses could well be considered overhead. Where you draw the line and what you determine to be overhead frequently is a process of deciding how you want to treat the costs. The difference is when the costs will be expensed or shown on the income and expense statement. Direct costs and overhead costs are considered as inventory costs and carried as assets in the form of work-in-process inventory or as part of finished-goods inventory until the items actually are sold, when they show as costs of goods sold. Other costs are considered period expenses and therefore show on the income statement as expenses in the period in which they occur. Exhibit 23-3 illustrates the flow of costs through a manufacturing business.

The expenses will be shown on the income statement at the time they occur. The cost of goods sold will be shown when the items in finished goods are sold. This is called **matching expenses to revenues.** It is an important concept because it permits the gross profit, or profit after cost of goods sold, to be compared to historic levels. If the matching were not carried out, then the costs that would be traced to the income statement would vary with the production level. As production went up, the costs would go up; as production went down, the costs would go down. This would make it impossible to evaluate the firm's performance over time because its profits would go up and

**EXHIBIT 23-3** *Cost Flow in a Manufacturing Business*

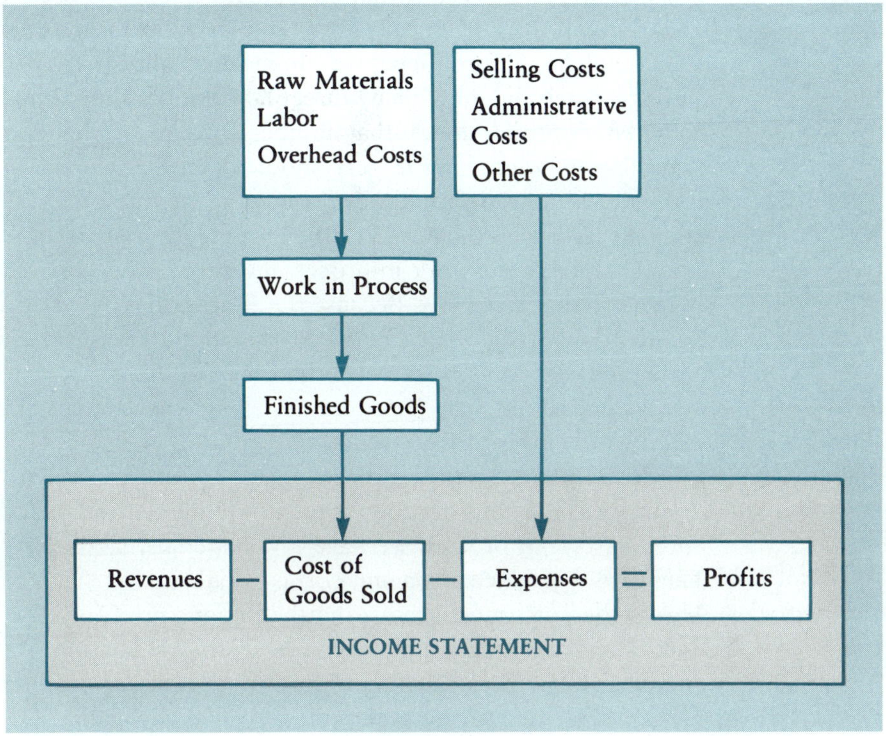


down with production rather than sales. Problems like these were discussed in the chapter on financial analysis.

As Exhibit 23-3 indicates, the costs of raw materials, labor, and overhead are captured in the work-in-process inventory account. The raw materials cost is captured at the time that the requisition slip is completed by the line supervisor. As goods are drawn from the raw materials inventory, the cost of those materials is removed from that inventory and transferred to the work-in-process inventory. Labor also is a direct cost. As the payroll costs are accumulated, they are posted to the work-in-process inventory as well. Overhead is not so straightforward. Because many different categories of costs make up overhead and these costs cannot be traced directly to the production of specific units, the transfer of costs is made on a budgeted basis. This means that the business will decide how much overhead it expects to occur each year, when it makes up the budget for that year. The business also decides the production for the year. The next step is to decide on an allocation basis for overhead. This usually represents direct labor hours, direct labor costs, or machine hours; the objective is to choose a basis related to the actual flow of overhead expenses. To illustrate, let us assume that direct labor hours is chosen for the allocation basis. Now if the budget calls for $120,000 in overhead for the next year and 40,000 units to be produced, we can make an allocation. We check the standards to determine how many direct labor hours should be used to produce each item of production. If that number is 2.5 hours, then the total budget for direct labor hours for the year should be 100,000 hours (40,000 × 2.5 = 100,000). Overhead should be allocated at the rate of $1.20 per direct labor hour ($120,000/100,000 = $1.20). This means that for every hour of direct labor charged to the work-in-process inventory, $1.20 in overhead also will be charged to that inventory. Because the allocation is based on a budget, there is bound to be a difference between the actual overhead expenses incurred during the year and its forecast. Whatever that difference is, we will dispose of it at the end of the year. We either will charge the variance off as an expense or add it to the inventory accounts.

Costs in the work-in-process inventory are charged to finished goods inventory as the units of production are completed and roll off the production line. In **work in process,** we have raw materials, labor, and overhead costs. These are aggregated and a unit cost is calculated for each item of production. This is the cost transferred to finished-goods inventory for each completed unit. The actual accounting involved in the calculation of the unit costs is complex. It involves calculating equivalent units of production and using a FIFO, LIFO, or average technique to value each unit. This is the kind of calculation covered in a cost accounting course. We will not go into the accounting process here. The important thing to remember is that the dollar value calculated for each unit completed is made up of raw materials, labor, and overhead costs incurred to produce that unit.

As units are sold, the costs for those items are transferred from the finished-goods inventory to the cost-of-goods-sold account. This is an expense account that is subtracted from sales to arrive at gross profit. None of the costs associated with production are expensed until this point. This means that production changes, up or down, will not affect profits. The inventory accounts will be affected by production changes, but those are asset accounts. This is important because it permits a company to compare its performance from month to month and year to year.

How can all of these costs be controlled? The raw materials and labor costs have quantity and price components. The overhead costs include fixed and variable components. The people who can control the various aspects of the costs are widely scattered throughout the company. So how can we control them? The answer is a standard cost system.

## STANDARD COSTS

In a **standard cost system,** a manufacturer establishes costs for labor, materials, and overhead for each unit manufactured. The costs are determined from both past costs and budgets for future costs. These costs simultaneously serve as devices for monitoring cost control and a budget for achieving cost objectives. The standards can be established as **absolute perfection standards,** which means that the cost can be achieved only if everything is performed exactly right. Standards of this type are called **engineering standards.** Not only must labor and material be used with no waste or error, capacity must be used perfectly as well. Such conditions can never prevail in practice, consequently, the use of engineering standards will not work well as objectives. People will object to the use of a budget they can never achieve. A looser standard is needed.

**Currently attainable standards** are costs that can be achieved under existing conditions. These standards permit a reasonable level of errors, rework, and idle time and are based on capacity levels in the plant expected during the coming year. Currently attainable standards are much more popular in budgets because they permit people to achieve the cost containment required. This is an important concept for any tool intended for establishing objectives for people. Other standards exist, but the various approaches possible in setting standards are too complex to discuss here. However, it is important to remember that the standards you choose will affect the performance of the people who must achieve them as well as providing a yard stick to measure the effectiveness of cost control. The remainder of the discussion of standards will revolve around their use in evaluation.

Once standards have been set, deviations from them are called **variances.** These variances are the principal tool for use in evaluating cost control. We must capture the actual costs incurred during production as well as the standard costs that should be incurred. The difference between these two numbers is the variance, but must be decomposed into quantity and price components to pinpoint problem areas.

## MATERIAL AND LABOR VARIANCES

**Direct labor** and **raw material variances** are the simplest to deal with and the most direct to capture. The process is to capture the actual quantities of labor and material used and the actual cost per unit for labor and material. These are then compared to standard quantities and prices for labor and material. Exhibit 23-4 displays a diagram for the calculation of the variances.

**EXHIBIT 23-4** *Labor and Material Variances*

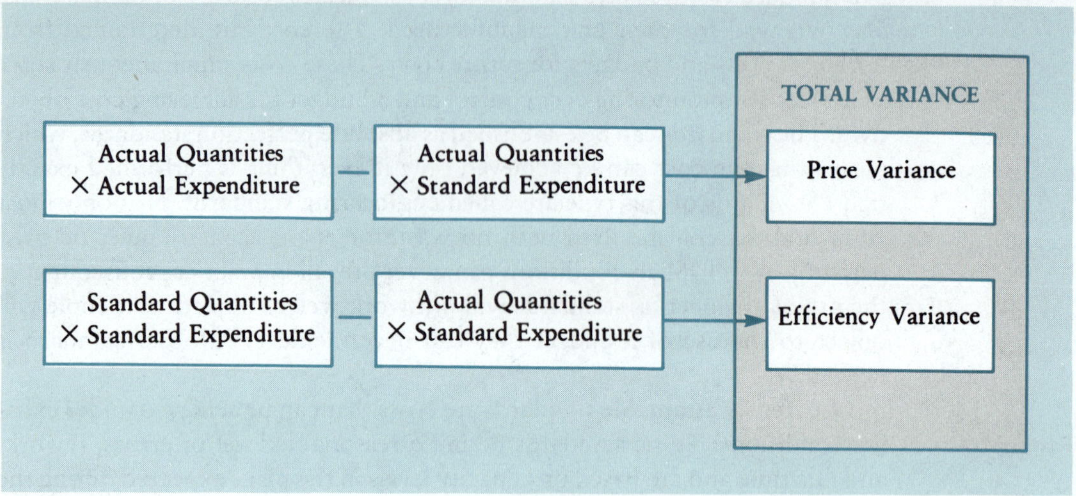


As the exhibit shows, the process is to multiply actual units used by the actual price paid and then subtract actual units used multiplied by the standard price. The result is a **cost or price variance.** Subtracting actual quantities multiplied by standard prices from standard quantities multiplied by standard prices will yield a quantity variance, called the **efficiency variance.** The sum of these is the **total variance,** which can also be calculated by subtracting the items in column 1 of the table.

The variances are called *unfavorable* if they show more being spent than should have been and *favorable* if the reverse is true. For example, if column 1 of the table is less than column 2, then the price variance is favorable. If column 2 is larger than column 1, the price variance is unfavorable. The same pattern holds true for efficiency variance. If column 1 is less than column 2, then the efficiency variance is favorable. If column 1 is larger than column 2, the efficiency variance is unfavorable. Of course, the two variances should be subtracted to arrive at the total variance if they are of different types.

The actual costs used in column 1 can be obtained directly from the general ledger without the need for multiplication. We show the calculations to make it clear that the price variance is calculated by holding quantity constant and allowing price to vary. The efficiency variance is calculated by holding price constant and allowing quantity to vary. Consider some actual numbers in an example to make the process clear. Assume that labor during the month consisted of 4,500 hours and aggregated $22,050; 8,000 units of direct material were used at a total cost of $14,000. The standards are for 2.5 hours of direct labor for each unit produced; the standard rate for direct labor is $5.00 per hour; the raw material standards are for 5 units of material for each unit produced; the standard cost is $1.50 per unit of raw material. A total of 1,640 units of finished goods were produced during the month. The variances for these numbers are shown in Exhibit 23-5.

The variances in the calculations show that labor usage was greater than budgeted, consequently the efficiency variance was unfavorable; but the cost of labor was less than budgeted causing a favorable price variance. Material cost was more than was budgeted, but fewer units were used than the standard allowed giving a favorable price variance but an unfavorable efficiency variance. Both overall variances were unfavorable, however. If the variances had not been decomposed, we would never have known that some aspects of good control had been exercised!

The interpretation of variances must be done carefully. Variances simply point out areas that require management's attention, they do not indicate that a mistake or error has been made or that someone has done something wrong. Remember that the variances simply show a deviation from the standards. This means that the standards have an effect on variances as well as the actual use of material and labor. If the standards have been set too high, then unfavorable variances can result. If the standards have been set too loosely, then favorable variances can occur. This means that you must always be aware of the effect that standards have on the variances. Not only that, favorable variances are not automatically good! Consider the case of raw materials that are cheaper because of lower quality. This would result in a favorable price variance for material, but could be a problem for the company because it results in poorer performance of the product. It also could affect efficiency variances. If the raw materials are inferior, then more of them might be used in production because of excessive breakage. It also could affect labor variances. Poor quality materials could cause excessive reworking time thereby resulting in an unfavorable efficiency variance for labor. What good are variances?

Variances point out areas that merit management attention. More effective cost control can result from investigating variances to determine their true cause. In addition, variances can be compared to each other over time to yield a picture of production cost control. If positive management action is taken to correct the underlying causes of variances, then variance trends should show that happening. You must be very careful not to try to "fix blame" for variances and to ensure that everyone in the company understands what they are and how they are used. Many variances actually may be the fault of the owner/manager! Who sets the compensation policy? If wage rates exceed the standards for labor, then unfavorable variances will result. If the work flow design is

**EXHIBIT 23-5** *Labor and Material Variances Illustrated*

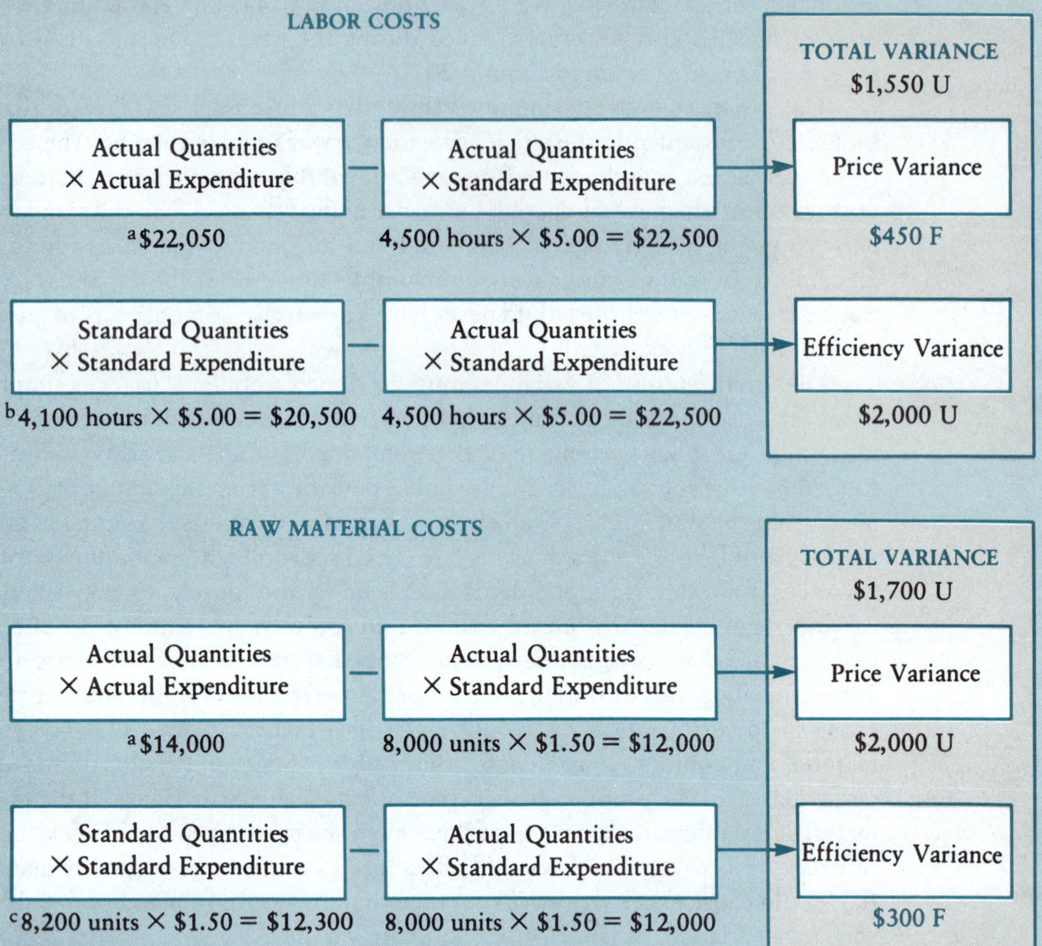


[a] From the General Ledger
[b] 1,640 units of production × 2.5 hours each = 4,100 hours
[c] 1,640 units of production × 5 units of material = 8,200 units

U = unfavorable
F = favorable

poor, then efficiency variances can result in both material and labor. Who is responsible for the work design? The key issue is not who is to blame for variances, but who is in a position to minimize problems. Variance investigation should be undertaken with this in mind and with the intent that the most appropriate people in the company will be made aware of potential problems before they can damage the firm. In this way an atmosphere can be developed in which everyone strives to achieve more effective cost control.

## OVERHEAD VARIANCES

Variances can be calculated for overhead costs, too. Because the variable component of overhead costs will fluctuate with production whereas the fixed components will not, the overhead factor must be separated. This is simple to accomplish. At the time that the overhead budget is being prepared and the application factors for overhead are being calculated, we just separate the overhead costs into fixed and variable portions and calculate two application rates. All mixed costs have to be dealt with as indicated in prior chapters. The result will be a **variable-overhead application rate** and a **fixed-overhead application rate.** The application rates are standard costs for the two types of overhead. The discussion that follows has been greatly simplified from the normal treatment of overhead variances in cost accounting for purposes of illustration. The important points include what overhead variances are, their sources, and their uses in small business management.

For variable overhead the difference between the actual spending recorded in the general ledger accounts and the amount of overhead applied to work in process inventory is called a **spending variance.** The **efficiency variance** is a bit more confusing. The problem is that overhead is applied based on direct labor hours or some other factor, but the original budget for overhead was based on the units of production to be completed during the year. This means that a difference in the application basis will cause a variance in overhead because it is tied to that base. This difference is called an *efficiency variance.* Exhibit 23-6 displays the decomposition of the variable overhead variance.

Consider an example to clarify the situation. Using the numbers from the example in Exhibit 23-5, assume that the variable overhead application rate was determined to be $2.50 per hour of direct labor. Remember that 4,500 hours of direct labor were used and that the standard was 2.5 hours per unit produced and that 1,640 units were produced. Checking the general ledger shows actual spending for variable overhead items of $12,000. Exhibit 23-7 displays the variable overhead variances.

**EXHIBIT 23-6** *Variable-Overhead Variances*

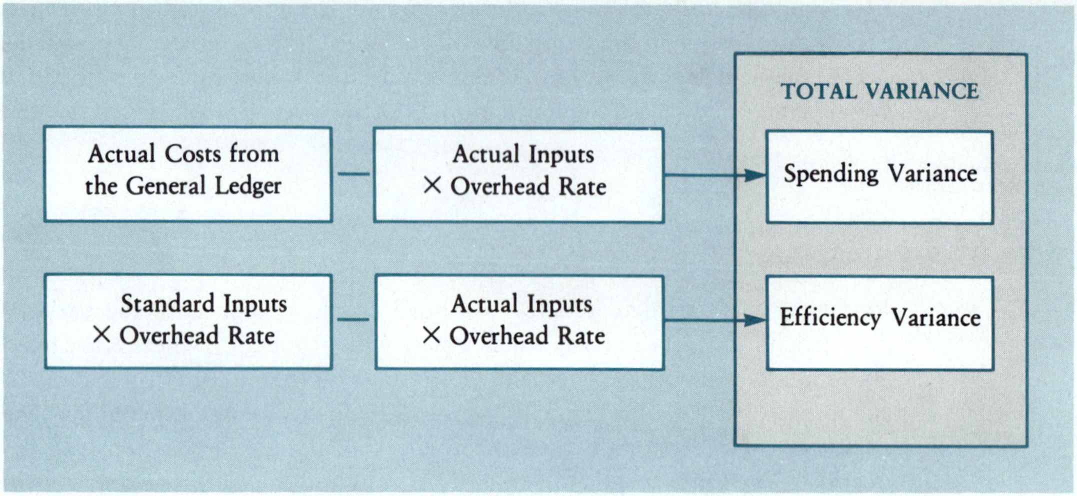


**EXHIBIT 23-7** *Variable-Overhead Variances Illustrated*

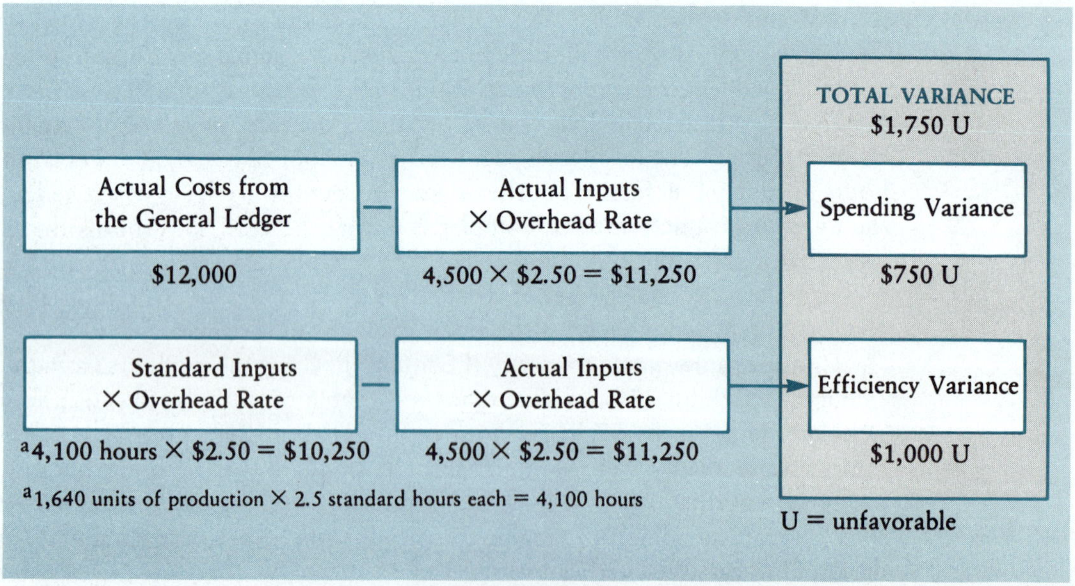

The exhibit shows an unfavorable spending variance of $750 and an unfavorable efficiency variance of $1,000 for a total variance of $1,750. Variance calculations are especially important for overhead costs because part of the variance is hidden. In the case of labor and material, the total variance shows as a difference between numbers in the general ledger. In the case of overhead, actual costs and applications can be found in the general ledger, but the efficiency variance will never be known without a special calculation.

**Fixed-overhead variances** look similar when the spending variance is considered, but there can be no efficiency variance. Fixed overhead does not fluctuate with production levels, therefore efficiency is not a concept that has value. The total dollar amount of fixed overhead budgeted at the beginning of the period simply is compared to actual spending as recorded in the general ledger. This difference is the spending variance. There will be a variance that results from production volume because we will probably never achieve exactly the production levels forecast as part of the budget. This difference between budgeted costs and costs for actual output is called a **volume variance.** Exhibit 23-8 displays the variance calculations for fixed overhead.

As in the case of variable overhead, the actual costs come directly from general ledger accounts. The standard is a calculation based on the standard inputs for the output achieved. Budgeted costs come from the forecast made at the beginning of the period. For example, using the same company as pre-

**EXHIBIT 23-8** *Fixed-Overhead Variances*

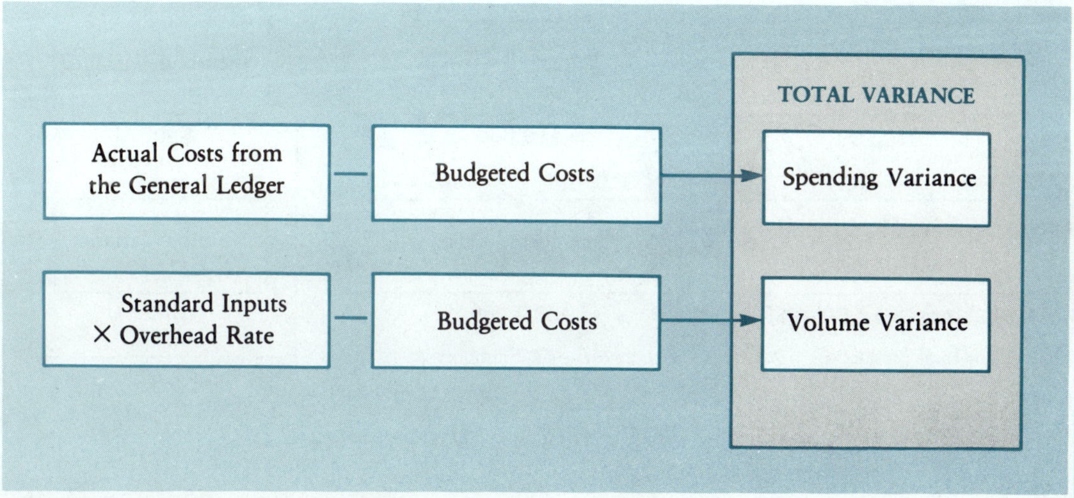

viously, assume that budgeted fixed costs for the year were to be $10,000 and actual fixed costs shown in the general ledger were $10,500. Now, if the overhead application rate was $2.00 per direct labor hour then the variances shown in Exhibit 23-9 would result.

In the case of fixed overhead as for variable overhead, the variance calculations show much more information than can be found in the general ledger accounts. The actual costs will be in the accounts, but the amounts charged to production will be based on actual inputs rather than the standard inputs required to isolate volume variances. In the example cited, the fixed overhead would have been charged to production in the amount of $2.00 per actual direct labor hour. There were 4,500 actual hours rather than the 4,100 standard hours shown in Exhibit 23-9. Consequently, the variance calculations added much detail.

As in the case of labor and material variances, the interpretation of overhead variances must be approached with care. The variances do not pinpoint problems, rather they indicate areas that merit management attention. If you approach all variances in this fashion, then they will prove to be an invaluable tool in the production cost management of the business.

**EXHIBIT 23-9** *Fixed-Overhead Variances Illustrated*

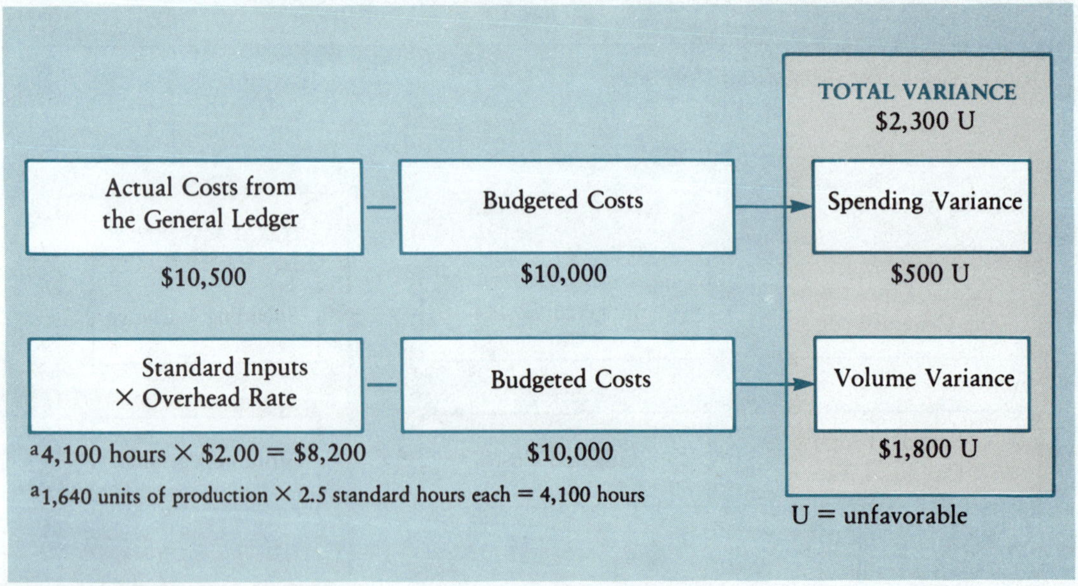

## QUESTIONS

1. What is the difference between engineering standards and attainable standards?
2. What should management do when the standard and variance procedure indicates that efficiency or pricing variances are unfavorable?
3. Using the following diagrams, calculate the variances on labor, material, and overhead and evaluate the result with possible suggestions.

### LABOR VARIANCES
(Labor Costs)

| | | | |
|---|---|---|---|
| Actual Quantities × Actual Expenditure | — | Actual Quantities × Standard Expenditure | → Price Variance |
| $47,050 | | 6,000 hours × $6.00 = $____ | $______ |
| Standard Quantities × Standard Expenditure | — | Actual Quantities × Standard Expenditure | → Efficiency Variance |
| [a]_____hours × $6.00 = $_____ | | 6,000 hours × $6.00 = $_____ | $______ |

TOTAL VARIANCE
$______

[a]1,750 units of production × 3.0 hours each =_____ hours

### MATERIAL VARIANCES
(Raw Material Costs)

| | | | |
|---|---|---|---|
| Actual Quantities × Actual Expenditure | — | Actual Quantities × Standard Expenditure | → Price Variance |
| $21,500 | | 8,500 units × $2.50 = $____ | $______ |
| Standard Quantities × Standard Expenditure | — | Actual Quantities × Standard Expenditure | → Efficiency Variance |
| [b]_____units × $2.50 = $_____ | | 8,500 units × $2.50 = $_____ | $______ |

TOTAL VARIANCE
$______

[b]1,750 units of production × 5 units of material =_____units

*continued*

## VARIABLE OVERHEAD VARIANCES

**TOTAL VARIANCE**
$______

| Actual Costs from the General Ledger | — | Actual Inputs × Overhead Rate | → | Spending Variance |
|---|---|---|---|---|
| $11,000 | | 4,500 hours × $2.50 = $____ | | $______ |

| Standard Inputs × Overhead Rate | — | Actual Inputs × Overhead Rate | → | Efficiency Variance |
|---|---|---|---|---|
| [c]____ hours × $2.50 = $_____ | | 4,500 hours × $2.50 = $_____ | | $______ |

[c]1,750 units of production × 3.0 standard hours each = _____ hours

# PART VI

# SPECIAL TOPICS

# CHAPTER 24

# International Small Business Opportunities

**LEARNING OBJECTIVES**

After completing this chapter, you should be able to

- Understand international markets and how a small business can gain access to them.
- Understand exporting and importing and the special problems involved in such businesses.
- Understand how to make contacts with potential markets and buyers for your products internationally.
- Plan and manage an international marketing effort.

International marketing is one of the oldest aspects of business. In the age of the Phoenicians, 3000 B.C., international trade was well established. In fact, much of the exploration of the world was a direct result of the search for new markets and new sources of supply. Small businesses have been leaders in international trade as they have been in business since those earliest days. The Phoenician traders were family businesses intent more on profits than the spread of culture. Columbus, himself a merchant and small business owner, sailed to America in hopes of finding a shorter route to the Indies, which were a major source of spices and trade items. His discovery of America was just an accident! In a large sense, then, America is a product of small business!

The role of small business in **international trade** is not just a foreign phenomenon. In fact, when this nation was founded, 200 years ago, Yankee traders were well established in foreign trade. U.S. small businesses were sending ships to Europe and to the Far East to trade American products for local goods. These international small business operators drove the country to second place behind the already well established empire of Great Britain in trade with China![1]

Beyond discovering countries, small businesses have driven modern improvements in transportation and communication because they have been trying to improve access to markets and sources of supply. International areas long have been prize specimens of both markets and sources of supply. In addition, tensions have been easing between the United States and other powers, providing a more open environment for trade. As a result of these improvements, international access and trade opportunity is greater today than at any time in history. We've already got Kentucky Fried Chicken in China and Pizza Huts in Russia! It is logical and proper that small business should take its share of these new markets.

## MISCONCEPTIONS IN FOREIGN TRADE

Far too many owners of small businesses view international business as the playground for large firms. They don't even consider the possibility of doing business across national borders because they think it too complex, too expensive, or too difficult. Nothing could be farther from the truth. As mentioned in prior chapters, the overwhelming majority of firms in the United States and throughout the world are small businesses. Just as they dominate business in their own countries, these firms have the potential to dominate international trade. Many of the firms involved in such trading are small businesses. It is true that within the United States, most of the firms involved in international business are larger firms. This is a result of interest, not any barriers to trade.

The small business owners who have taken the time to learn about international trading opportunities have reaped rich rewards for their efforts. Consider a case from our files.

The fellow asked our help in preparing an application for insurance on an international trade. He wanted to insure against the default of his customer in the event of a political problem in the country. We set up an appointment to meet with him and go over the particulars.

When we got to his place we were surprised to find the man and his wife alone in a rather run-down warehouse half filled with lumpy looking bags. They were located in a small town in central Georgia. There were no employees other than the owners. They had a couple of desks and a filing cabinet in one corner, a coffee pot, and a telephone. It was not a very impressive place.

When we began to look at the application for insurance, we were really impressed by how sharp these people were. Their records were in order, they understood what was needed, and they were ready to go. Actually they didn't need us!

Naturally we had to know what kinds of products were being sold in order to complete the package. We were amazed to find out that they were selling rags! We said, "What do you mean, you're selling rags!"

They said, "They're rags. Just rags. We discovered that a lot of countries in South America and in Asia don't have enough textiles to be able to provide clothing requirements and so there is a need for rags. They need them for cleaning and wiping up in manufacturing plants, they're really in demand. All we had to do was find out how much they were willing to pay, what it would cost to ship them, and then find a supply cheap enough to make a profit. It was easy! We sure couldn't do this domestically, because there must be 1,000 firms selling rags by mail order and every other way! Over there, we're all alone."

At first we couldn't believe it, but there was a half warehouse full of laundry bags of rags just waiting to be shipped. When they were sold, they were trucked out to a port on the Atlantic and then went by ship to the country of destination. They had all kinds of suppliers and they were certainly making money. They didn't have any employees because they didn't need any, and they didn't see any sense in wasting rent on a better facility. We had to admit that it was a first class operation!

Were you surprised to find that the business was selling rags? The range of products in demand in countries around the world is absolutely staggering. In reality, every product in demand in the United States also is in demand elsewhere. All that is required is the foresight to look for a market.

More and more small businesses are doing exactly this. In fact, a survey published in *Inc.* magazine reported that exports are growing four times as fast as the gross domestic product, which is a general measure of economic expansion in the United States. Even more exciting is the fact that only half of that phenomenal growth in exporting came from the nation's largest firms.[2]

One of the most pervasive myths about foreign trade is that it takes a long time to establish sales and develop profitability. Although the performance of an individual company cannot be predicted, a survey conducted by *Inc.* indicated that over 60 percent of respondents were profitable within one year of beginning international operations.[3]

## INTERNATIONAL MARKETS

Markets exist around the world for every conceivable product and service. In fact, the vast majority of the potential market are small businesses themselves. This means that a U.S. small business owner actually has an advantage because foreign firms will prefer to deal with businesses of their own size who can better understand their problems and needs.

A great deal is heard about the problems of international finance, the instability of foreign governments, and culture and language barriers. The reality is that such problems are not barriers to doing business. Clearly, international customers are going to want credit terms on their purchases just as domestic firms do. Clearly, there will be differences in monetary exchange rates, which have the potential to wipe out profits. It may even be that a political climate is such that business is jeopardized by the instability. All of this can be handled by insurance. Language problems can be handled by using intermediaries who will buy and resell. All that is really required is the interest and a bit of research. The federal government is keenly interested in fostering international trade and has a tremendous range of assistance services available.

## GOVERNMENT ASSISTANCE PROGRAMS

In 1987, the **Interagency Task Force on Trade** was created to better serve small businesses in the area of international trade. The task force was established as a response to the 1986 White House Conference on Small Business. The conference found that there was a bewildering array of federal programs that were not well known, but that could provide valuable assistance to small firms that wanted to get involved in international trade. The conference recommended that a central office be created to act as a clearing house for information.

The federal government was anxious to get more small firms involved because of the tremendous potential that these firms have for alleviating the international trade deficit. Because our nation is dominated by small businesses, large firms cannot be expected to produce enough exports to balance the huge imports that other countries are selling so successfully to American consumers. Small businesses could easily wipe out the trade imbalance if they could be persuaded to get involved. Consequently, with thoughts of the original Yankee traders, the government created the task force to encourage, aid, and support small firms who wish to export.

The task force, run by the Export-Import Bank of the United States, is headquartered in Washington, D.C. The first step that the task force took after its creation was the publication of the *Exporter's Guide to Federal Resources for Small Business*. This was its initial response to the call for a central clearing house of information. The publication is an excellent resource for small firms. Exhibit 24-1, developed from the guide, lists some of the sources of information it contains.

The guide can be obtained by calling the U.S. Small Business Administration office at the number indicated in the exhibit. In addition to the information sources listed in the exhibit, the guide includes contact offices and people all over the United States and the world. It also includes a bibliography of publications available from various federal sources and where the publications can be obtained. Exhibit 24-2 is a partial list of those publications.

In addition to the guide, information about these and other publications can be obtained from the local office of the Small Business Administration. Contact the Washington office at the number listed in Exhibit 24-1 to find the local office.

Most small business owners think that credit and insurance are the major stumbling blocks to international trade. The Export-Import Bank of the United States has a variety of programs that can alleviate this problem. The Export-Import Bank can lend at competitive rates to small businesses to finance export sales. It also can guarantee loans made by local banks to firms involved in exporting. The bank will guarantee loans made to foreign firms who are buying U.S. goods and services. It also has an insurance plan. The Foreign Credit Insurance Association, a subsidiary of the bank, offers insurance policies that protect U.S. firms from nonpayment by foreign customers. Special policies are available for small businesses to guarantee that the business will not lose in the event of nonpayment by a foreign customer due to commercial or political problems.

Federal agencies offer a tremendous range of financial services to small businesses. Any firm interested in pursuing international trade has available programs that can alleviate most of the problems and fears of default and nonpayment. The programs also provide assistance in protecting against loss due to currency trading fluctuations. The Export-Import Bank, listed in Exhibit 24-1, can provide information on all of its programs with a simple telephone call.

In addition to federal efforts to aid small firms, some states have estab-

**EXHIBIT 24-1** *Federal Assistance Programs for International Trade*

| AGENCY | CONTACT PERSON |
|---|---|
| Agency for International Development | Betty L. Briscoe, Office of Small Business Utilization<br>(703) 875-1551 |
| U.S. Department of Agriculture | Dugger Harris<br>Foreign Agricultural Service<br>(202) 382-9498 |
| U.S. Department of Commerce | Gordon Studebaker<br>Foreign Commercial Service<br>(202) 377-1289<br>Helen Burroughs<br>Trade Development<br>(202) 377-2829 |
| U.S. Department of Education | Susanna C. Easton, Center for International Education<br>(202) 732-3302 |
| Export-Import Bank of the United States | Gerald Solomon, Marketing and Program Development<br>(202) 566-8818<br>Business Advisory Service<br>(800) 424-5201<br>Foreign Credit Insurance Association<br>(212) 227-7020 |
| Overseas Private Investment Corporation | Cassandra Pulley<br>Director for Small Business<br>(202) 457-7200 |
| U.S. Small Business Administration | Sheryl J. Swed, Office of International Trade<br>(202) 653-7794 |
| U.S. Department of State | Office of Commercial and Public Affairs<br>(202) 647-8988 |
| U.S. Trade and Development Program | Percy Reynolds<br>Regional Director<br>(703) 235-3657 |
| U.S. Trade Representative | Barbara North<br>Private Sector Liaison<br>(202) 395-6120 |

**EXHIBIT 24-2** *Partial List of International Publications*

- *A Basic Guide to Exporting*
- *Business America*
- *Foreign Trade Statistics*
- *Is Exporting for You?*
- *Market Overseas with U.S. Help*
- *Country Market Surveys*
- *U.S. Export Sales*
- *Agricultural Trade Leads*
- *International Marketing Profiles*
- *Export Credit Insurance*
- *Financing and Insuring Exports*
- *A Guide to Financing Exports*
- *Official Sources of Export Assistance for Small Business*

lished offices and programs. Many of these provide much more than simply information—they provide money! For example, the Minnesota Export Finance Authority obtains credit and provides bank guarantees for loans to support exporting by small businesses. Its program has been so successful that it was copied by more than thirteen states, and more join the ranks of small business supporters every day. Other states actually make direct loans to small businesses. Indiana has one of the most aggressive direct lending programs. There are a tremendous variety of state programs. In fact, *Inc.* published a list of state agencies and resources available to help small businesses in the international arena. It is must reading for small firms.[4]

## MAKING CONTACTS AND FINDING MARKETS

The final barrier to international trade is finding a market and a buyer in a foreign country. Federal assistance programs and some of the state programs can help in this area as well. The United States and Foreign Commercial Service (US&FCS), a division of the U.S. Department of Commerce, offers a host of assistance programs. Among these are market surveys and identification of foreign distributors who will buy and distribute your products. Many services are free, others are available for a small fee. The fees are truly small! For about $90, the US&FCS will investigate any country you choose for any product you choose and provide you with a list of as many as six qualified agents and distributors interested in your products. The agency also will put you in contact with those people and help you to begin working with them. For about $10, you can get an in-depth study on the best foreign markets for a product or a group of products for an entire country. Exhibit 24-3 is a partial list of US&FCS services available to small businesses. As Exhibit 24-3 indicates, the US&FCS is a goldmine of information and assistance to any firm interested in selling its products or services overseas. Like all other agencies, it makes a special effort to assist small businesses and first-time exporters.

## GETTING INVOLVED IN INTERNATIONAL TRADE

As the preceding sections show, the federal government has numerous programs and agencies ready and willing to help any small business become involved in international trade. The reasons for this are self-serving. The Export-Import Bank has estimated that each billion dollars of exports is worth 30,000 jobs in the United States. They also believe that at least 18,000 more small businesses could produce $4.5 billion in exports within the first year through simple education. The potential for the long run is absolutely staggering. Small businesses really do have the potential to dominate the international markets. All that is really required is interest!

**EXHIBIT 24-3** *United States and Foreign Commercial Services*

- Analyze foreign markets.
- Find representatives and buyers overseas.
- Gather data on specific export opportunities.
- Identify foreign prospects who want to represent a product.
- Provide sales leads from overseas firms.
- Prepare custom background reports on potential trading partners.
- Provide personal counseling to exporters.

*Inc.* recommends that one way to break into exporting is to begin selling to American operations of foreign firms. It is only one short step from there to selling to their domestic operations.[5] Of course, one of the most popular approaches to selling overseas is the use of another firm specializing in exporting. Exporters are firms who use their contacts to find markets for your products. These firms charge a commission for the sales they produce but can provide a variety of services, from fax machines to translation to advice about product modification. **Facsimile machines** can be a very important aspect of international trade because they permit written communications in languages foreign to the parties, and written communications are more comfortable for people dealing in foreign languages. Most exporters also are engaged in importing so they can be good sources of supply as well. You can attend international trade shows and conferences. Many of these are held in the United States each year. Not only can you find contacts, you can find exporters at these shows as well.

We highly recommend that every small business owner explore the possibilities of international sales. You might just find that it is easier than doing business in the United States because the competition is lower! Large firms are not interested in pursuing what they consider to be small markets, yet such a market can be quite large to a small business. In addition, most small business owners in the United States have not yet had the interest to get involved. This provides a tremendous opportunity for aggressive, forward-thinking small firms. Yet, as in all enterprises, the key to success in international trade is **planning.**

## SUMMARY

It is popularly believed that international business is complex, difficult, and filled with risk of nonpayment and other problems resulting from political and commercial instability. Consequently, a small business cannot hope to get involved in it. In reality, this is not the case. Many small businesses are successfully running international operations.

The White House Conference on Small Business held in 1986 recognized that many more small businesses had international prospects. They also recognized that many federal assistance programs existed but were not well known. Consequently, they recommended that the Interagency Task Force on Trade be developed. The task force has published a guide for exporters, which is invaluable to any small business wishing to pursue international trade.

A tremendous variety of federal assistance programs exists, designed to aid small businesses in international trade. These agencies are summarized in Exhibit 24-1. They can provide assistance in financing and credit; insurance to protect against nonpayment from commercial or political sources; locating markets, customers, buyers, and representatives; and advice and counseling to a small business. Services from these agencies are often free or have an extremely low cost. In addition, a tremendous number of publications are available that spell out how to get involved in international trade and support an international operation.

Any small business can get involved in international trade if its owner has the interest to investigate possibilities. A small business can find itself in a superior position internationally because most of the firms it deals with also will be small firms. In addition, the level of competition may well be lower.

## QUESTIONS

1. Why have small businesses felt that only large companies could experience international trade?
2. How might the high tech industry have facilitated the possibility of international trade for small businesses?
3. Would you consider entering an international market for your product or service? Why or why not?

## PROJECTS

1. Visit the Small Business Development Center closest to you and gather any pertinent information regarding the international market or write or call the agencies listed in the text to further your knowledge of the international prospects for small businesses. In a business plan, include the opportunity for internationalizing your business if your product or service lends itself to such an expansion. Don't limit yourself.
2. After reading the chapter on ethics, discuss what limitations might be imposed on international trade in the interest of foreign relations, national security, and ethical considerations.

# Case

Guy Rambois was an interesting individual. He had asked us to advise him about starting a small business. Guy had worked in Nigeria for a number of years as a missionary on a training mission for his church and developed many friendships while there. He presently was working part time at a local technical college teaching various classes. Yet, he wasn't satisfied. He wanted to do something more exciting and more profitable.

Although he had been back in the United States for three years, he had maintained his friendships with the people of Nigeria and had even tried his hand at trade on a small scale. On each of his trips, he brought back several types of souvenirs representing the African culture and his friends had asked to purchase them. He had sold his souvenirs and contacted his friends in Nigeria to send him more. They did and he sold those items quickly as well.

His African friends had now asked him to return the favor by sending them goods such as books, paper supplies, tapes, records, and a variety of American products. The demand was growing to the point that Guy had decided to use this export prospect as a means of livelihood. The demand for American products was growing among his acquaintances in Africa, and no one seemed to be responding to their needs.

### Questions

1. Where could Guy go for real start-up information for his new venture?
2. What types of goods might he export?
3. What political unrest in neighboring countries might give him pause?
4. Develop a plan for Guy for marketing, finance, and inventory.
5. Would any ethical considerations arise from the difference in culture, environment, or attitudes?

# CHAPTER 25

# Small Business Law

**LEARNING OBJECTIVES**

After completing this chapter, you should be able to

- Know what the Uniform Commercial Code is and understand its significance.
- Understand torts and how claims are brought and settled.
- Understand the intentional torts of defamation, assault and battery, false imprisonment, and fraud and how to avoid potential claims for intentional torts.
- Understand the tort of negligence and how claims are brought and settled.
- Understand duty and due care and how to plan for minimization of liability under claims of negligence.
- Understand warranties, express and implied.
- Understand contract law and agency law and know the elements required for an enforceable contract.
- Understand the importance of copyrights, patents, trademarks, and trade secrets and the levels of protection they provide.
- Understand the contents and differences among Chapters 7, 9, 11, and 13 of the Federal Bankruptcy Act.

A full and complete treatment of **business law** is beyond the scope of this book; however, certain aspects of the law affect all prospective small business owners. We have termed these aspects *small business law,* although the law does not actually make special dispensation for small businesses. Because it is a pervasive issue and one that affects every small business owner in the country every day, we would be remiss if we failed to present an overview of the more basic aspects of business law. All serious people planning a career in small business should pursue a more detailed study of this topic because every aspect of the operation of a business is affected by the law. Businesses, like people, are subject to the law and are responsible for their actions. This means that a small business owner not only is responsible for obeying the law personally, he or she is also responsible for ensuring that the business obeys the law as well.

Please be aware that this entire discussion is general in nature. Not only are legal issues exceedingly complex, they are frequently specific to a particular situation. This means that the law takes into consideration all circumstances surrounding an event. To be well advised, a small business owner must consult with an attorney in establishing business policies and practices. Such a consultation goes beyond using an attorney in establishing the business. Legal advice will be needed on an ongoing basis. A wise business owner establishes a relationship with an attorney early and consults that attorney frequently.

## THE UNIFORM COMMERCIAL CODE

The principal body of law that all small business owners are expected to know is the **Uniform Commercial Code** (UCC). Developed in the 1940s, as an approach to standardize the way various states dealt with merchants, the code has been adopted by every state, although there are minor differences among the states on some issues. The most important aspect of the code is the requirement that all merchants be familiar with its contents. Under the code, every small business owner in the country who sells a product is a **merchant.** Furthermore, a seller of services can be a merchant in some instances. Even if not classified as a merchant, a small business owner will be affected by code provisions because they cover negotiable instruments—which includes most personal and business checks, letters of credit, documents of title, bank deposits, and collections—and a host of factors that occur every business day. The result is that you must become familiar with the code if you intend to go into business.

The code covers sales and contracts for sale of goods in general. The important aspect about this component of the code is that it has the capability of overriding some aspects of common law. For example, under normal contract law, which we discuss later, an offer and its acceptance must be exactly alike in terms of their provisions. Under the UCC, changes and conditions to the original contract usually can be made freely and without concern for contract validity. The code also requires that sales contracts in excess of $500 be written to be enforceable.

Obviously, a full discussion of the code is beyond the scope of this book. Fortunately, the code is readable and understandable without a legal education. We highly recommend that you obtain a copy, read it, and become familiar with it. The code can be obtained in many bookstores. In fact, books and texts are available that contain the code, comments and explanations of aspects of the code, and differences among the states, when those occur. Refer to the *Books in Print,* carried by your local bookstore or library, if they do not carry copies.

## TORTS

Laws designed for the protection of an individual's rights to person and property are called **tort laws. A tort** is a civil or private wrong, other than breach of contract. We examine contracts later. Torts are important in small business management because a court will grant an action for damages when a tort has been proven. This action, called a **remedy,** usually is monetary in form. Torts are different from crimes. Exhibit 25-1 displays the primary legal differences.

As the exhibit indicates, a **crime** is a violation of a law that affects society. Prosecution of such violations is the responsibility of a **district, city,** or **county**

**EXHIBIT 25-1** *The Differences in Torts and Crimes*

| | CRIMES | TORTS |
|---|---|---|
| WHO IS WRONGED | Society | An individual |
| WHO BRINGS SUIT | The people, action by the district attorney | An individual, action through litigation |
| BURDEN OF PROOF | To a moral certainty, "beyond reasonable doubt" | Preponderance of evidence, 51% |
| PUNISHMENT | Incarceration, fines, etc. | Restitution, monetary damages |

**attorney;** a person appointed in a city or county for the purpose of pursuing people suspected of wrongdoing. The burden of proof in a court action involving a crime is **to a moral certainty.** This means that a jury or judge must be convinced of guilt beyond a reasonable doubt. The punishment for crimes can include prison terms, fines, assignments to perform public service, and so on.

Torts are violations of laws that affect an individual. Court actions in tort cases are brought by the individual who has been wronged in the form of litigation. Juries or judges in these cases need only be convinced that the **preponderance of the evidence,** or the majority of the evidence, supports the claim of wrongdoing. Punishment in such cases is usually restitution in the form of monetary awards for damages.

Torts can result from an intentional act. These will be addressed in the following section. Torts can also result from negligence, which is a far more serious problem for small business owners.

## INTENTIONAL TORTS

The most common **intentional torts** are defamation, assault and battery, false imprisonment, and fraud. We will examine each of these individually and will focus on the best way to avoid problems for your business and yourself.

### Defamation

**Defamation** means falsely and maliciously attacking an individual's name or reputation. The word **malicious** in this context implies that the attack on the individual is intended to cause harm to that person. Oral or spoken defamation is called **slander. Libel,** the other form of defamation, is written, published, broadcast, or in a movie or play.

As is always the case, the best defense against defamation is to avoid it in the first place. You should be careful about making statements about your competitors, suppliers, customers, employees, or other people. The best advice is simply to never say anything negative about others, even if you are convinced that they have wronged you. This is just good business sense. In the first place, you should never reveal any personal information you might have access to because it violates a person's privacy. It also will brand you as a gossip. In addition, revealing information of a negative nature will not improve your position. Negative statements do not win customers or enhance your own reputation. You can only improve your position through performance, not by attacking others. The rule to follow is simple: if you can't say something positive about a person or a business, don't say anything at all.

## Personnel References

Giving personnel references can be a problem if the individual in question has not performed well. If a prospective employer of a former employee calls for a reference, you clearly cannot lie. This would be an unethical act. However, if you go into any detail with respect to unsatisfactory performance, you may be opening yourself to a defamation claim. The best practice is to simply say, "It is against our policy to make any statements about employees. We will verify only length and time of employment and positions held." There is nothing wrong with verifying that kind of factual information, but you should verify it only to a legitimate party, not volunteer information. You should ensure that neither you nor any other employee reveal any information of a personal nature or give any negative information about any person who is or who has ever been associated with your business. Most employers will not even verify salary data and we recommend that course of action for you. Say nothing beyond a verification of employment term.

If you have an employee that you really would like to support in obtaining a new position, it is best to handle that through a personal letter of recommendation. You can make it clear to all employees that the company's policy is not to reveal or verify any information beyond employment dates and positions. Then, if an individual wishes to ask you for a recommendation, you can handle that with a personal letter, or you can refuse to write such a letter if you do not feel that you can in good conscience recommend the person.

## Assault and Battery

**Assault** is placing an individual in fear of immediate bodily harm. The fear must be reasonable, and this reasonableness must be proven in court. The use of threatening words or actions can constitute assault; pointing a loaded gun clearly is assault. **Battery** is the intentional touching of another person without that person's consent. Battery is the actualization of assault. We normally think of battery as striking a person, but the contact need not be that violent. Simply shoving a person or other less violent contact can be battery.

Obviously, the best defense is to avoid conflict. Be wary of losing your temper and walk away from potential arguments and conflicts. Nothing is ever settled in a shouting match, anyway! Cultivate this attitude among the people in your business. If you lead, they will follow, so you need to set the example in this as well as all the other areas of concern.

## False Imprisonment

Individuals have a right to freedom and movement. Holding someone without their permission or without "just cause" constitutes false imprisonment. This can be a real problem for small businesses when an act of theft, embezzlement, or bad check writing occurs. Some states allow reasonable detainment of suspected shoplifters or lawbreakers; however, determining what is reasonable is difficult. Furthermore, there is the possibility of assault or battery as well as false imprisonment if you or your employees attempt to take action in a case of suspected theft or other wrongdoing.

What can be done to protect the business? You should discuss the issue with your attorney and establish a policy and procedure for the business to cover incidents of suspected shoplifting, theft, or other wrongdoing. You need to establish that policy in writing, be specific with respect to actions that will be taken, and have your attorney review and approve it. Then you must ensure that all employees are familiar with the policy and know what to do when they suspect someone of a crime. The policy should be reviewed by your attorney periodically, to ensure that it remains current. It should be discussed with your employees on a regular basis, especially those who come into contact with customers, to ensure that they understand and comply with the policy.

## Fraud

Perhaps the best-known tort is **fraud;** however, it generally is not well understood among small business owners. The tort of fraud is complicated and an incident of fraud is difficult to prove in court. Legally, six elements are involved in the demonstration of an incident of fraud. In other words, a court must be convinced that each of six different actions occurred to accept an allegation of fraud. These six factors are listed in Exhibit 25-2. The exhibit discusses the parties to a claim of fraud using legal terms. The individual who brings a claim of fraud or other legal wrongdoing in a court action is called the **plaintiff.** The individual accused of the wrongdoing is called the **accused.**

**EXHIBIT 25-2** *The Elements of Fraud*

1. There was intent to deceive.
2. There was misrepresentation of a "material fact," or an important factor in the plaintiff's action.
3. The accused knew the representation was false.
4. There was intent that the plaintiff would act in reliance on the false fact.
5. The plaintiff did rely on the false fact, and it was reasonable to do so.
6. The plaintiff suffered personal or financial injury and can prove that loss.

As the exhibit indicates, fraud requires the intent to deceive a person. It can be difficult to prove intent. Nevertheless, careful attention to the claims made in writing or verbally by sales personnel or other employees is a must for effective avoidance.

The concept of a material fact is more straightforward. In essence, any information that a reasonable person might be expected to consider in reaching a decision is material. In business, material facts or information are used all the time. Every statement made by a sales person or other individual representing your business to a customer could be a material fact.

Avoidance of potential fraud makes sound business sense, even though it is difficult to prove in court. Even if a customer or other person dealing with your business does not bring a claim of fraud against you, your reputation will be damaged if that individual feels that you or your people misrepresented a product or service. Misrepresentation need not actually occur for there to be a problem. If a customer perceives that a product or service has been misrepresented, or even poorly represented, the damage to the company will be done.

Careful attention to training the people who will represent the firm to customers and others is the best strategy to avoid misrepresentation. Whenever possible, especially in the case of services to be rendered, a contract between your firm and its customers is a sound procedure. Spell out everything in writing and there is less likelihood of misunderstanding. Be sure to have your attorney review all contracts.

## NEGLIGENCE

As indicated earlier, a tort can occur from negligence. This is an extremely important aspect of law for a small business owner because of the contact with so many people inside and outside the business. The concept of negligence is not easily understood. To demonstrate what is involved, consider a claim of negligence. In a successful action for **negligence** four things must be proven: the duty, the breach of the duty, causation from the breach, and the actual injury. What this means is that a plaintiff must have incurred an injury as a result of a failure of the accused to behave properly.

In defining *duty,* courts traditionally have used the actions of a fictitious person—a reasonable, prudent person—to determine if an individual's behavior in a certain set of circumstances were acceptable. A reasonable, prudent person owes a duty of "due care" to others, particularly to those who are foreseeably in risk of some danger. *Due care* means taking reasonable precautions to protect others.

People visiting the premises of a business are divided into three categories: invitees, licensees, and trespassers. A different standard of duty is owed to each of these three classes. **Invitees** are persons present through the express or implied request of the owner for social or business-related purposes. The business and its owners have a duty to provide reasonably safe premises to all invitees. **Licensees** are those persons allowed to frequent premises for reasons relating to their own businesses, purposes, or conveniences. The owner owes a lesser degree of duty to licensees. That duty is to refrain from being actively negligent. **Trespassers** are people who enter without permission from the owner. Trespassers are owed no duty except to refrain from their willful injury. These levels of duty and the determination of due care are complex to establish and understand. The simplest approach is probably to examine how a **breach of duty** is established.

To prove a breach of duty, a plaintiff must show that the accused failed to execute the due care of a reasonable, prudent person. Some cases that appear inherently negligent do not require comprehensive proof.

**Proof** often is aided by the doctrine of **res ipsa loquitur,** meaning "the thing (or act of negligence) speaks for itself." If an individual sustains an injury that would not ordinarily occur unless some other person was negligent, this doctrine can be applicable. The only other tests that must be met are that the injured party did not contribute to his or her own injury and that the injury was caused by a device within the control of the accused.

**Injury** is the simpler concept. Simply put, if no physical or financial harm results from an individual's actions, no matter how reckless those actions are, he or she may not be sued for negligence. **Causation** is the more complex and crucial element of proving a breach of duty and, therefore, supporting a claim of negligence.

There are two types of causation: actual cause and proximate cause. **Actual cause** is an obvious cause; an automobile strikes a pedestrian. **Proximate cause** is cause from a natural, continued sequence that is unbroken by any efficient, independent, or intervening cause. This is an extremely difficult concept. It is really decided on a case-by-case basis after consideration of all factors leading up to an injury. In essence, the law attempts to decide whether it is reasonable for an accused to be held liable for an injury.

Negligence claims all revolve around whether a business owner has provided reasonably safe premises for the various parties who will come into contact with the business. Consequently, the best preventative measure is to practice concerned management of the premises. Consider what possible dangers may exist on the company's premises and the best way to protect people from those dangers. Posting signs will frequently *not* be adequate. Proper use of barriers, shielding, safety equipment, security precautions, and so on is a wiser course. If you have a business in which potentially dangerous or harmful conditions can exist, you will be well advised to discuss the situation with your attorney and take precautions.

Proof of negligence can be difficult or impossible if the defendant can prove that the plaintiff assumed the risk. Assumption of the risk applies in cases where the plaintiff realized the risk involved but proceeded to act anyway. A potential problem with this philosophy is children!

Children represent a special case in potential negligence claims because they are not capable of understanding and assuming risk. Everyone is aware that if a child falls into a swimming pool that has no fence or barrier around it or crawls into an abandoned refrigerator that has its door intact, the owner can be sued for negligence. Businesses must be especially careful: their premises may be attractive to children because of the premises, equipment, inventory, or machinery. The law expects a reasonable, prudent person to anticipate the actions of children. This can sometimes be difficult to do!

Our earlier comments about making the premises reasonably safe can be echoed here with a stronger need for caution in some circumstances. If there is any aspect of the premises that might be interesting or attractive to children, then you will need to make an heroic effort to make the place secure. Signs clearly will not be acceptable! In fact, some aspects of normal security can themselves be attractive to children. Consider the case of guard dogs used to patrol inside a fence at night. Children are frequently attracted to animals, consequently, you should anticipate that a child might reach through a fence to pet a dog. If that child were injured, you could be liable. Furthermore, blocking access to a dangerous area with a fence might not be adequate. A fence that represents a barrier to an adult may not be a barrier to a child. In fact, the fence itself could be an attractive nuisance!

It should be clear that security precautions themselves must be reviewed to protect yourself. Be sure to consult your attorney before you install any type of security and pay particular attention to blocking access to little people and safeguarding people who might have no concept of danger.

## WARRANTIES

The function of a warranty is to establish the characteristics and level of quality the purchaser can expect of the goods or services being acquired. **Warranties** are part of a contract for the sale of goods. There are two basic types of warranties: expressed and implied.

An **expressed warranty** is communicated from the seller to the buyer in writing or orally. Two legal buzzwords are applicable to expressed warranties: quantifiable and relative. Quantifiable statements will be treated as facts. For example, if a real estate broker says the roof doesn't leak, the statement would be treated as a warranty. Relative statements are treated as opinion or supposition. A statement such as "good roof" would not constitute an expressed warranty. The wording is extremely important. Many small business owners frequently make statements that could be warranties without realizing what they are doing.

**Implied warranties** are a part of the Uniform Commercial Code. Under the code, there are four types of implied warranties. These are displayed in Exhibit 25-3, along with their meanings.

Fitness for purpose and merchantability pose potential problems for small businesses. Far too many retailers and wholesalers think that implied warranties are applicable only to manufacturers. This is not the case! You must make sure that you are familiar with the products you sell, establish their quality, understand their uses and purposes, and advise your customers as to those uses as well as the quality of the item.

## PRODUCT LIABILITY

**Product liability** deals with situations where no warranty protects an injured buyer. In this case, remedies are available through the negligence or liability aspects of tort law and liability of a business will be established in accordance with tort requirements. In essence, manufacturers or sellers or both may be held accountable because of negligence in the manufacturing, designing, or packaging of products. This takes us back to the exercise of "due care,"

**EXHIBIT 25-3** *Implied Warranties*

| TYPE | MEANING |
|---|---|
| Title | • Requires the goods to be of clear title<br>• No liens or claims against the goods |
| Infringement | • The seller must protect the buyer from claims by third parties (usually applies to patents or copyrights) |
| Merchantability | • Goods sold must be fit for the customary purpose for which they are used<br>• They must be safe for that use<br>• They must be adequately contained, packaged, and labeled, and conform to any facts or promises on the label |
| Fitness for purpose | • The goods must be fit for the purpose for which they are intended<br>• The buyer is entitled to rely on the seller's skill or judgement to select or furnish suitable goods |

discussed in an earlier section. Strong quality controls are the best defense against product liability, as well as attention to fitness of purpose and proper use and care of the item.

There is even stronger concern for makers and sellers of goods that are imminently or inherently dangerous. Businesses involved with these items are subject to strict liability even though there was no lack of due care in the manufacture or sale of the item. If you make or carry such products, be sure to consult with your attorney early and on a regular basis!

## CONTRACT LAW

A **contract** is a legally binding agreement made by two or more competent parties containing a promise or set of promises to perform or refrain from performing some act or acts. In other words, a contract is a set of promises that can be enforced by a court. It must have been made between two or more people who are legally capable of handling their own affairs. This means that none of the parties is a minor or a mental incompetent.

Contracts can be written or oral. To be legally binding a contract must fulfill six elements, which are displayed in Exhibit 25-4. As the exhibit shows, any attempt to contract is not effective in the absence of consideration. Consideration is the element usually lacking in quasi-contracts. Some things cannot be consideration; the more common ones are gifts, acts that are duty bound, past considerations, and moral obligations. Employers often promise raises on the basis of "faithful service in years past." These promises are not real because past service cannot be a stipulation of an agreement.

Several types of contracts are thought to affect such a vital thing to the parties that a written form is required to show evidence of contractual intent: estates, bonding or surety, and marriage contracts, for example. Several other types affect small businesses every day. These are contracts which cannot be performed in one year, that is, a long-term contract; an agreement for the purchase or sale of an interest in land; or an agreement for the sale of personal property over a certain amount, $500 in most cases. For contracts involving these situations, oral agreements are not enforceable. Further, a written contract must be in proper form and contain proper information for it to be enforceable. This requires legal advice. You should refer the development and review of all written contracts to your attorney.

Contracts can be classified from several perspectives. Exhibit 25-5 illustrates a classification of contracts and their characteristics. Note that the categories are not mutually exclusive. This means that a contract does not necessarily have to be one or another of the types indicated. A contract may have characteristics of one or more types.

**EXHIBIT 25-4** *The Elements of a Contract*

1. *Offer:* A proposal must be made by one party to another to enter into a contract. An offer may be oral, written, or implied from the facts but it *must* be made with intent to enter into a contract.
2. *Acceptance:* Another party, the offeree, must accept the terms of the offer in the manner requested by the offeror. Unilateral acceptance is constituted by an act of substantial performance of the contract. Bilateral acceptance can be made orally or in writing and specifies how the offer can be accepted.
3. *Consideration:* Something is given in exchange for a promise in the contract. In short, the offeror bargains for and receives something in exchange for his or her promise. In bilateral agreements, the mutual promises can serve as consideration. In a unilateral agreement the act performed can be the consideration.
4. *Capacity of the Parties:* The individuals must be able to enter into a contract. In general, mentally incompetent or intoxicated persons or minors lack contractual capacity. Although they may enter into and fulfill contracts, a person without capacity may avoid or discharge any contract to which he or she is a party.
5. *Legal Objective:* The contract must be based on a legal act or promise. Contracts made with an illegal objective are void.
6. *Proper Form:* Oral contracts may be acceptable, but written form may be required for some categories of contracts.

Note that a quasi-contract is not a contract but may be enforceable. Generally, a quasi-contract can be enforced if the four elements listed in Exhibit 25-6 exist. Clearly, the strongest situation is to utilize contracts appropriately rather than depend on the enforceability of a quasi-contract. Many small business owners fail to make and use contracts, even for purchases or sales that are large enough to require them. This failure results from a lack of understanding of the legal ramifications. We cannot overstress the necessity for a close working relationship with an attorney and attention to legal issues. Businesses, including small firms, are being sued on an ever increasing basis.

## AGENCY LAW

An **agent** is a person who represents another person in a business transaction. This means that your employees generally will be agents for you. This is a serious matter because of the potential liability that exists. The general rule is that you will be responsible for any damages or injury an employee causes so

**EXHIBIT 25-5** *Classifications of Contracts*

| CATEGORY | CONTRACT TYPE AND CHARACTERISTICS |
|---|---|
| Formality | • *Formal:* Formal contracts must be in a specified format to be enforceable. Two examples of formal contracts are checks and promissory notes. Wording is important.<br>• *Informal:* Generally referred to as simple contracts, they require no particular format or wording. |
| Parties | • *Unilateral:* A promise in exchange for a specific act, such as an agreement to pay a specified amount for a specified job. Performance of the act constitutes acceptance of the offer.<br>• *Bilateral:* A promise in exchange for a promise or mutual promises. Each party promises to perform an act contingent upon other factors. |
| Compliance | • *Executed:* A promise that already has been performed; that is, both promises have been met. If one of the promises has been satisfied, the contract is partially executed.<br>• *Executory:* Promises yet to be performed. If one promise has been satisfied, the contract is partially executory. |
| Intent | • *Express:* The parties set forth their intentions and promises specifically and definitely. The contract may be written or oral.<br>• *Implied:* Its existence must be inferred from the actions and conduct of the parties. |
| Validity | • *Valid:* Contains all the necessary elements of a contract and therefore is easily enforced by the courts.<br>• *Void:* Not a contract because it lacks one or more of the legal requirements. A void contract is a contradiction in terms, but is frequently used.<br>• *Voidable:* A contract that can be cancelled by one or both of the contracting parties. Contracts made under duress or fraud are voidable. A contract with a minor is voidable at the minor's option.<br>• *Unenforceable:* A valid contract that cannot be enforced due to the operation of the law; for example, immunity from collection as a result of bankruptcy or statute of limitations. |
| Quasi-contracts | • *A Legal Fiction:* It lacks one or more of the elements of contracts. A legal fiction that courts will sometimes enforce as a contract to prevent the undue enrichment of one party at another party's expense. |

long as that person is performing his or her duties. In fact, a temporary employee, a part-time worker, a delivery agent, or even a friend who volunteers to perform some service for you can be your agent. The impact of this aspect of agency law makes the internal control aspect of hiring competent people and training them for their jobs even more important.

**EXHIBIT 25-6** *Elements of Enforceable Quasi-Contracts*

1. Plaintiff conferred a benefit on the defendant.
2. Plaintiff expected to be paid.
3. Plaintiff was not meddling in another's affairs.
4. To allow the defendant to retain the benefit would result in undue or unjust enrichment.

## Liability for Contracts

Another aspect of agency law is the ability of an agent to bind the company. An agent can enter into contracts with other parties on behalf of the company. This means that you can be forced to comply with an oral or written contract established by an employee. In general, you will be liable for contracts of employees in any of the situations outlined in Exhibit 25-7. The owner of the business will be the principal and the employee will be the agent described in the exhibit.

As you can see from Exhibit 25-7, you must be extremely careful to avoid the appearance of authority that does not exist if you wish to protect the business. Ostensible and apparent authority are the most dangerous aspects. You should develop personnel and supervision policies and practices to ensure that employees who are authorized to perform tasks can be identified as such by third parties. You will need the assistance of your attorney to accomplish this.

## Independent Contractors

**Independent contractors** are not employees and, therefore, are not agents. In general, the difference between an independent contractor and an employee is the degree of control you have over their actions. If you have the right to direct a person to perform a task *and* the right to control how the task is done, that person is an employee. You don't actually have to control how the task is done, it is enough simply to have the *right* to control how it is done.

If you have the right to direct a person to perform a task and you do *not* have the right to control how the task is done, that person is an independent contractor. These people are expected to rely on their own expertise to determine how to accomplish a task. It is an important distinction not only because an independent contractor cannot be an agent, but because they are not employees for tax purposes. This means that payroll taxes and social security taxes are not required for independent contractors.

**EXHIBIT 25-7** *Agent Authority*

| | |
|---|---|
| EXPRESS AUTHORITY | Principal authorizes agent to perform a task or enter into a particular contract. |
| | An agent has the power to enter into a contract for the purchase of an item when directed by the principal to do so. |
| RATIFICATION | Principal approves an unauthorized act of an agent at a later date. |
| | An agent enters into an unauthorized contract, but the principal decides to accept the terms of that contract, anyway. |
| INCIDENTAL AUTHORITY | An agent is authorized to perform tasks or enter contracts necessary to carry out his or her assigned duties. |
| | A department manager has the power to enter into a contract of employment with an individual needed to work in the manager's department. |
| IMPLIED AUTHORITY | An agent has authority based on his or her assigned position in the business or based on past dealings with a third party. |
| | A purchasing agent has the power to enter into contracts with established suppliers of the business for the purchase of items normally acquired. |
| EMERGENCY AUTHORITY | An agent has the authority to respond to emergencies. |
| | An agent supervising the construction of a building has the power to enter into a contract for the purchase of equipment required to respond to an emergency situation. |
| APPARENT AUTHORITY | A principal implies that an agent has the power to enter into a contract by his or her conduct toward a third party. |
| | An employee is undergoing a trial period of employment before being granted express authority to enter into sales contracts. The principal accompanies the agent and implies to a customer that the agent has the power to enter into a sales contract by introducing the agent as a sales representative of the company. The agent later returns to the customer and enters into a sales contract. That contract can be binding on the principal. |
| OSTENSIBLE AUTHORITY | A principal permits an agent to represent to a third party that contract power exists. |
| | A sales agent calls on the principal who allows an employee to represent himself as an agent authorized to make purchases for the business. A contract between the sales representative and the employee can be binding on the principal. |

## COPYRIGHTS, PATENTS, TRADEMARKS, AND TRADE SECRETS

Small businesses are frequently involved with creative processes and consequently need protection for their ideas. Although limited in scope and effectiveness, there are several areas of protection available under federal law. These include copyrights, patents, and trademarks. We will examine each of these in turn and close with a discussion of state and common laws that protect trade secrets.

### Copyrights

A **copyright** grants an exclusive right to sell, publish, or reproduce a book, computer program, catalog or directory, song, work of art, or similar item. Even such items as advertising copy may be copyrighted. Protection generally lasts for the lifetime of the creator plus fifty years. Copyright is held either by the author of the work or by an entity (such as a publisher) that the author has agreed may assume the copyright. In the case of works made for hire and certain other works, the duration of the copyright is 75 years from publication or 100 years from creation, whichever is shorter. In order to obtain a copyright, one must complete an application, pay a small fee, currently $10.00, and deposit copies of the material with the Library of Congress. Copyrights and applications are handled by the U.S. Copyright Office, Library of Congress, Washington, D.C. 20559. Applications and explanatory material may be obtained by writing to that office.

Copyrights provide passive protection. That is, the holder of a copyright must bring a claim of copyright violation in federal court and must demonstrate to the court's satisfaction that a violation of copyright has occurred. For most small businesses, this self policing is not feasible. Furthermore, copyrights protect the expression of ideas, not the ideas themselves. Neither the Copyright Act of 1976 nor the Computer Software Copyright Act of 1980 has effectively dealt with the expression versus idea problem. Consequently, sound legal advice is a must in order to maintain copyright protection.

### Patents

A **patent** is a protected monopoly given to the inventor of a device or process. The monopoly lasts for seventeen years, although design patents can be granted for shorter periods at an inventor's discretion in order to protect the development phase of a patentable product. Patents and their regulation are handled by the U.S. Patent and Trademark Office and the Court of Customs and Patent Appeals.

Patentable matter must consist of (1) a process or method, (2) a machine, (3) a manufacturing technique, (4) a composition of matter, or (5) a new and useful improvement on any of the other aspects. If a device or process meets the definitional requirement, there are three conditions which must be met to obtain a patent. The object must be useful, novel, and not obvious to a person of ordinary skill in the industry in which the patent exists. Obtaining a patent is a lengthy and complex process often requiring two or more years of work. In addition, a registered patent agent or attorney is a must. A list of the 11,000-plus registered agents can be obtained from the U.S. Patent Office in Washington, D.C. Although the filing fees are not extreme, the legal fees can be. Not only is the application complex, a search of existing patents is required. Expert assistance is generally required to handle the search and to analyze the findings.

As in the case of a copyright, the holder of a patent must bring action against others who infringe upon the invention. This can often be a lengthy and expensive process and requires legal assistance throughout. However, the protection can be stronger than that provided by a copyright. If the patent has been properly prepared, imitators will not be able to make minor modifications to avoid liability. Clearly, the field of patents is complex. Anyone considering a patent should seek legal advice early about the viability of the idea and the level and cost of protection it affords. If the decision is made to proceed with a patent application, a registered agent or attorney should be consulted.

## Trademarks

A **trademark** is a protected mark or symbol that identifies a particular product, brand, or company. Such marks can be registered with the U.S. Patent and Trademark Office in order to prevent others from using the same mark. Trademark protection can even extend to packaging or "trade dress." That is, imitators will not be able to offer competing products in similarly shaped, sized, or colored packages to try to mislead consumers.

As in the case of patents, the application for a trademark must demonstrate that the mark is unique. Phonetic, deviate, or unusual spellings of common terms cannot be registered, nor can generic names. A variety of registrations are available. In addition to the trademark, a service mark symbolizes the services offered by a business; a logotype is simply an identifying symbol.

The owner of a registered trademark or service mark must protect the symbol through litigation aimed at violators to prevent losing the protection. Our language today is filled with generic terms that were once trademarks:

escalator, cellophane, and thermos, to name a few. If the owner fails to protect the symbol it can become a generic name and no longer subject to protection. The responsibility for protection and enforcement rests with the owner.

## Trade Secrets

Unlike the previous types of protection, **trade secrets** are governed by state and common law. In fact, a series of doctrines including trade secrets, unfair competition, and misappropriation can serve to protect a small business. No public registration is required, however, strict secrecy must be maintained to insure that a claim can be successful.

In general, any device, process, or knowledge that has the potential of competitive advantage for its holder can be a trade secret. The courts consider the following facts in determining whether a trade secret exists:

1. The value of the information to the business and its competitors.
2. How broadly the information is known outside the business.
3. How broadly the information is known inside the business.
4. Steps taken by the business to ensure secrecy.
5. The cost or effort of developing the information.
6. How easily the information could be duplicated or acquired by other businesses.

If a trade secret exists legally, then it can continue into perpetuity. That is, it can last as long as the information continues to afford a competitive advantage.

Clearly, legal advice is required in order to develop and establish procedures that will enable a firm to protect its trade secrets. Some of the steps an attorney may recommend could include:

1. Nondisclosure, noncompete, or confidentiality agreements with employees.
2. Physical segregation of employees and limited access to development and storage areas and records of the business.
3. Licensing agreements to accompany sales.
4. Proprietary labels for records and products.
5. Entry and exit interviews with employees and agents.

Even if a trade secret has not been established, some actions are flagrant enough to be covered under unfair competition or misappropriation doctrines. For example, if an employee takes a customer list, quits the company, and begins to call upon those customers for a new employer selling similar goods, legal action may be available. As in the case of the other types of protection, legal advice is required when you think a violation has occurred.

## BANKRUPTCY

**Bankruptcy** is not a pleasant topic for consideration. Nevertheless, thousands of small businesses file for or are forced into bankruptcy each year. In fact, the number of bankruptcies has been growing annually and shows no signs of slowing in the near future. It is wise to understand something of how the law functions in this area.

When America was colonized, many of the immigrants were fleeing debtors' prisons. The nation's founders wanted to avoid the possibility of such treatment, consequently, the Constitution includes an authorization for Congress to establish uniform laws on bankruptcies. Several laws have existed throughout the nation's history, but the **Bankruptcy Reform Act,** established in 1978 and amended in 1984, establishes the legal aspects of bankruptcy in the United States.

The law established a separate court system to hear and handle bankruptcy cases. The act has four major sections, which are called chapters: Chapters 7, 9, 11, and 13. They dictate how liquidations, municipal debt adjustments, reorganizations, and individual debt adjustments must be handled. Chapter 9, municipal debt adjustments, is relevant only to incorporated cities and towns.

### Chapter 7

**Chapter** 7 proceedings involve a straight liquidation. That means that an individual or a business has its assets sold off and the proceeds paid over to its creditors. If any residual funds remain they are the property of the debtor, but any unpaid debts are discharged by the court. Contrary to popular belief, the law does not require a debtor to be insolvent. In other words, you do not have to be in a position of inability to pay debts to file bankruptcy. In practice, this led to some misuses, consequently, the 1984 amendment gave courts the power to assess the need of a debtor to seek relief from creditors. If the court decides that the filing would result in abuse, the bankruptcy will not proceed.

A business or individual can voluntarily file for bankruptcy or can be forced into bankruptcy by creditors. If a debtor has twelve or more creditors, then three of them together can force a trial. If a debtor has less than twelve creditors, only one creditor is required to force a trial. The creditors must have an aggregate claim against the debtor of at least $5,000, and those debts must not be secured by collateral. Farmers are specifically exempt from an involuntary proceeding, but most other types of small businesses have no such protection. Of course, an involuntary petition simply forces a trial, not a bankruptcy. The court will decide whether a debtor is bankrupt.

The possibility of an involuntary petition for bankruptcy can be especially dangerous for a small business that is not a corporation, because personal assets of the owner may be available to creditors. This issue was discussed in Chapter 13, and it is one reason we recommend the corporate form.

In the event of a Chapter 7 bankruptcy the debtor is permitted to keep some property. The surprising thing is that the amount of property that can be protected is determined by state laws even though the bankruptcy laws are federal. There are wide differences in the amounts of property protected in the various states. Consult with your attorney for more relevant information.

## Chapters 11 and 13

**Chapter 11** of the bankruptcy code is designed to support the reorganization of a corporation so that it can continue to exist; **Chapter 13** is the counterpart for individuals. Both chapters establish a payment plan for creditors with the anticipation that the debtor eventually will be able to pay creditors in full. The advantage of these chapters over Chapter 7 is that they permit the business to continue to exist and they force creditors to cooperate. The same rules about involuntary petitions for bankruptcy apply to these chapters as for Chapter 7.

Chapters 11 and 13 proceedings require that a debtor prepare a plan that will permit the debtor to avoid a liquidation and at the same time satisfy the claims of creditors. When the bankruptcy proceeding is first filed, the court will issue an order of relief that will stop creditors from attempting to collect from the debtor. The debtor will now have 120 days to propose a plan. If the debtor fails to do so, any interested party — a creditor, a stockholder, a trustee — can propose a plan. Further, the court must be satisfied that the plan is feasible and fair to all parties. Otherwise, a new plan may be considered or the debtor may be forced into a Chapter 7 liquidation.

Obviously, the details of a reorganization or payout plan and the factors involved in handling a bankruptcy petition or response require legal advice. This is particularly true for small firms, because of the difficulty in separating business assets from personal assets. Even if a business is incorporated, the owner generally will be asked to personally guarantee loans from banks and most other lenders. Trade credit generally will be limited to a corporate liability, but those guarantees make personal assets, as well as corporate assets, available to the lenders. Small business owners generally have no choice in the matter of guarantees because they are such an established practice among lenders.

The result is that a business experiencing difficulties should seek legal counsel early and explore possible options. Bankruptcy may be a last resort, but if it becomes necessary, early planning with the aid of an experienced attorney can make the difference between survival and a disastrous outcome.

## SUMMARY

A full treatment of business law is beyond our scope, but everyone planning a career in small business should become familiar with business law because it affects every aspect of business. You should consult with an attorney to establish business policies and practices on an ongoing basis.

The principal body of relevant law is the Uniform Commercial Code, adopted by every state with minor differences. The code requires that all merchants be familiar with its contents. It governs negotiable instruments, sales, and contracts for sale of goods.

Laws protecting an individual's rights to person and property are called tort laws. A tort is a civil or private wrong and can result from an intentional act or negligence. The most common intentional torts are defamation, assault and battery, false imprisonment, and fraud.

Defamation is maliciously attacking an individual's name or reputation; in oral form it is slander, in written form, libel. The best defense is avoidance: be careful about making statements about competitors, suppliers, customers, employees, or others.

Giving personnel references can be a problem. The best practice is to simply say, "It is against our policy to make any statements about employees." Do not verify salary data. Say nothing beyond a verification of employment term.

Assault is placing an individual in fear of immediate bodily harm. The use of threatening words or actions can be assault. Battery is the intentional touching of another person without consent. The contact need not be violent. The best defense is avoidance: walk away from potential arguments.

Holding someone without their permission or "just cause" constitutes false imprisonment. With your attorney you should establish a specific, written policy and procedure to cover suspected shoplifting, theft or wrongdoing, and ensure that employees know what to do if they suspect someone of a crime.

The best known tort is fraud, but it is complicated and difficult to prove in court. Among other things there must be an intent to deceive, a misrepresentation, and actual personal or financial injury. Avoidance of misrepresentation makes sound business sense because of its potential impact. If a customer has even the perception of misrepresentation, it will be damaging. Careful attention to training of people is the best defense.

A tort can occur from negligence. In general, a plaintiff must have incurred an injury as a result of a failure of the accused to behave as a reasonable and prudent person. The best preventative is concerned management of the premises. Consider possible dangers and the best way to protect people from those dangers. Children present a special case. The law expects a reasonable, prudent person to anticipate the actions of children.

An expressed warranty is communicated in writing or orally. Many small business owners frequently make statements that could be warranties without realizing it. Implied warranties exist under the Uniform Commercial Code. In general, a product must be salable and fit for the purposes for which it is intended. You must be familiar with the products you sell, know their quality, uses, and purposes, and advise your customers accordingly.

Product liability deals with situations where no warranty exists. Manufacturers and sellers may be held accountable for negligence in manufacturing, designing, or packaging. Strong quality controls are the best defense.

A contract is a legally binding agreement between competent parties. It can be written or oral and must include an offer and an acceptance, and consideration must be given. Some contracts must be written: estates, bonding or surety and marriage contracts, long term contracts, an agreement for the purchase of land or personal property over $500.

An agent is a person who represents another in a business transaction. You will generally be responsible for any damage an employee causes as long as that person is performing his or her duties. Hiring competent people and training them for their jobs is important.

An agent can enter into contracts on behalf of the company. You can be forced to comply with an oral or written contract made by an employee. You must be careful to avoid the appearance of authority that does not exist. You should develop personnel and supervision policies and practices to ensure that employees who are authorized to perform tasks are identifiable by third parties.

Independent contractors are not employees or agents. If you do not have the right to direct a person to perform a task and the right to control how the task is done, that person is not an employee. Aside from agency considerations, it is an important distinction because an independent contractor is not an employee for tax purposes.

Small businesses frequently need protection for their ideas. A copyright grants exclusive rights to a book, computer program, catalog or directory, song, work of art, or similar item for the lifetime of the creator plus fifty years. A copyright holder must bring a claim of infringement in federal court and demonstrate to the court's satisfaction that a violation has occurred.

A patent is a monopoly given to the inventor of a device or process that is useful, novel, and not obvious to a person of ordinary skill in the industry. The patent lasts for seventeen years, although design patents can be granted for shorter periods. The holder of a patent must bring action against others who infringe upon the invention.

A trademark is a protected mark or symbol that identifies a particular product, brand, or company. The owner must protect the symbol through litigation to prevent losing the protection.

Trade secrets are governed by state and common law. In general, any device, process, or knowledge that has the potential of competitive advantage for its holder can be a trade secret. Trade secrets can continue as long as the information continues to afford a competitive advantage.

The Bankruptcy Reform Act of 1978, amended in 1984, established a separate court system to hear and handle bankruptcy cases. The act has four major sections: Chapters 7, 9, 11, and 13. Chapter 9 covers municipal debt adjustments. Chapter 7 covers a straight liquidation: the assets are sold off and the proceeds paid over to the creditors. Chapter 11 covers the reorganization of a corporation. Chapter 13 is the counterpart for individuals. These chapters establish a payment plan for creditors with the anticipation that the debtor will eventually pay creditors in full.

A business or individual can voluntarily file for bankruptcy or can be forced into bankruptcy by creditors, although farmers are specifically exempt from an involuntary proceeding. An involuntary petition simply forces a trial, not a bankruptcy. The court must always decide whether a debtor is bankrupt.

## QUESTIONS

1. Define the following terms:
   a. tort
   b. defamation
   c. negligence
   d. fraud
   e. attractive nuisance
   f. quasi-contracts
   g. ostensible authority
   h. bankruptcy
   i. agency law
   j. apparent authority
   k. warranty
2. Why is the Uniform Commercial Code important to small businesses?
3. In what ways are torts different from crimes?
4. Why is it important not to give references, either good or bad, about previous employees?
5. What would happen if the employee was dismissed from a firm and that firm was called for a reference? What should the owner-manager do? Why?
6. What laws might apply in a case of shoplifting? Why must the business be especially careful?
7. What is fraud? What are some examples of fraud?
8. What would happen if a microwave purchased in your store gave off radiation? Under what legality would this apply?
9. What is a quasi-contract and when would one be used?
10. What is the difference between a contractor and an employee?

11. Why is the concept of agency so important to small businesses?
12. What are the four chapters of bankruptcies and which ones apply to small businesses?
13. What are the five types of authority given an agent?
14. Which authorities are the most dangerous to a small business?
15. Why could it be said that copyrights are easy to get but difficult to sustain for small business owners?
16. How are patents and copyrights different?
17. Is a copyright or a patent more likely for a small business owner to acquire and why?
18. What is a trademark? Name a few that have become household words. What trademark would you like to protect?
19. What trade secrets might a small business have?
20. What can be done to protect small businesses from losing their trade secrets?
21. Under what conditions may a business or individual be forced into bankruptcy under Chapter 7?
22. Why should small business owners be aware of bankruptcies laws?
23. Which bankruptcy chapters would cover each of the small business organizational types?

## PROJECTS

1. Check out the Uniform Commercial Code from a library. Read about the particular rules and report back to the class.
2. Ask a local attorney who deals with small business or a business law professor to talk to your class or group about the laws that can apply specifically to small business.

# Case 1

Jacob Zell is a born salesman. He was hired to sell commercial spots on the local cable channel. He has had many years of experience, selling everything from shoes to computers. He could sell snow to Eskimos and tickets for the River Styx. Tom Bradley was delighted to have the opportunity to hire Jacob away from his last employer. He was selling microcomputers and was doing extremely well according to all accounts.

Tom was amazed! Jacob had sold fifty slots in his first month and yet his closest competitor had only sold twenty. If Tom could only find a few more salespersons like Jake, he could expand into other areas.

Three months later, however, Tom was bewildered. Jake was still making fantastic sales, but they weren't sticking. Tom had just hung up the phone from his last frustrated customer, who had said that Jake had promised him a spot during the nightly news and it still had not appeared. Tom tried to explain to the unhappy client that only a few slots were available for those times and previous customers already had bought those spots and retained them.

In an effort to appease the customer, Tom suggested that as soon as the present contract for one of the current customers was complete, he personally would put the client into that time slot. What else could he do? Frustrated, he answered the phone again and listened to a similar complaint.

### Questions

1. What has Jake done to harm the business?
2. What can Tom do about it? In what manner is he accountable?
3. Why do you suppose that Jake has been in so many different jobs over the years?
4. What should Tom do about Jake?
5. What are the potential legal implications in the case?

# Case 2

It was nearly 7 P.M. and sirens were screaming into the work site on Vine and Elm. A child had fallen under a subflooring in the building being constructed. Several children had been chasing each other around the fence surrounding the site, when they discovered that the earth had fallen away from the base in back of the construction following several days of rain. They had great fun slipping back and forth under the fence for about an hour, then two children got rather adventuresome and decided to explore the site. When they left for the day, the workers had pulled away the plank used to cross the threshold into the main approach to the building. The kids, eager to see inside, found a plank and laid it across the doorway. But, they did not seat it securely. As a young boy was edging across the plank to the doorway, his weight caused the board to sag and fall, dropping him onto the subflooring below. He was trapped and shaken up by the fall. Frightened, his friend ran for help.

### Questions

1. What legal situation is presented here?
2. Of what is the company guilty? Why?
3. What can be done now?
4. What should have been done previously?

## Case 3

Mark Wheelen has just been fired from the RYC Loan Company. Fred Hankamer, the owner, discovered that Mark has been embezzling funds through a computerized accounting scheme over which he had been given control three years ago. Fred is devastated, not just by the amount of money he lost but even more by the thought that Mark, whom he had come to treat as a family member, had written himself $250,000 worth of checks over the last six months.

Mark was dismissed, but no charges were filed against him when he claimed hardship had made him do it and he promised to pay Fred back. Fred wanted to believe Mark and hated to see him convicted. Even more, Fred hated to have everyone know of the lack of internal controls that had allowed the embezzlement to occur. Fred truly felt that in large measure he was to blame for Mark's behavior.

Three weeks later, Fred receives a call from ZYT Credit Company. Mark has applied for a job in their computerized accounting area and listed RYC Loan Company as the name of his last employer. What should Fred do?

### Questions

1. Why is Fred correct in feeling that he was to blame for Mark's behavior?
2. What should Fred do about the reference call by ZYT Credit concerning Mark?
3. What would you have done in this situation had you been Fred and why?

# CHAPTER 26

# Ethical Considerations in Small Business

**LEARNING OBJECTIVES**

After completing this chapter, you should be able to

- Understand the concept of ethics as it applies to small business.
- Distinguish between legal and ethical issues.
- Have a social awareness of ethics in the small business arena.
- Design a formal development plan for your business with an ethical base.

The term *ethics* seems to create an avoidance syndrome. Just as many of us have very deep feelings about what is right and what is wrong, many of us dislike discussing issues very close to our hearts with other than our closest friends and family. Yet such avoidance has tended to prevent resolution of issues in society that can have a major impact on our lives and the success of our businesses. Can ethics be taught? Or, is it a birthright that is unchanged? No matter what your attitude, the important issue is to share with your employees your expectations and your perception of theirs.

## WHAT IS AN ETHICAL SITUATION?

Just because a business is small does not mean that it is free from ethical issues. What happens, for example, if a small business has ten microcomputers and one copy of a software package that claims no copies can be made except for backup copies? Yet the business quickly discovers that several people need access to the software. The manager chose not to purchase a site license because he wasn't even sure the package would be used, and indeed it wasn't for some time. Once the employees became familiar with the package and its capabilities, they all found uses for it. Technically, it is illegal to violate the copyright, yet how many businesses have rationalized that the one copy was purchased by the business, and it is the same business after all, so why buy additional copies? Does this then become an ethical as well as a legal issue?

Jim came breezing into the office whistling a merry tune on Monday morning. He had played golf on Saturday with the parts supplier for the office equipment and was thrilled with his play. Mary Anne was delighted that her boss was happy because Mondays usually were bad days, catching up on the weekend orders. Also today was the day that the owner came in to touch base, and she was never sure what he would ask to see.

ABC Office Services sold not only office supply materials but computer components and software. Mary Anne liked her job, but she often was frustrated with Jim who seemed never to be able to make up his mind about purchases from the suppliers. One minute, he was making out a large purchase order for one supplier and the next telling her to cancel that order and go with another supplier. His indecision made constant paperwork for her, and record keeping was a nightmare. Also she had to answer the telephone, which brought complaints from frustrated suppliers when the order changed.

She was thinking seriously about quitting her job when Jim arrived in such a good mood. Yet, she wondered how he could be so cheerful when Mr. Durant was due at any time, so she asked about his weekend.

Jim was so thrilled with himself that he told her about the new set of golf clubs Hagmore Supplies had given him for his last two orders of ribbons and carbon paper. He also claimed that they had promised him a weekend in Las Vegas if he would bring them a larger order for their machines. Mary Anne was amazed. They had always used Dunbar Services for their machines because of the quality of Dunbar's machines and their reputation for service. The change-over would cause some problems.

Later in the day, Mr. Durant stopped by Mary Anne's desk and said that he would be opening another branch office in the nearby town. He wanted a list of the suppliers and copies of all purchase orders for the last year. He was going to use the information to find out what sort of start-up inventory he could expect and who would give them the best deal. Mary Anne gave him the information, and he studied it that week. On Friday he came back and was furious. "Why have we changed suppliers constantly? Why haven't we developed a relationship with any particular one? And why, when I tried to call Dunbar yesterday to get estimates, were they so unfriendly? We have always had a good working relationship with Dunbar and now they act as if they don't want our business. Do you know why?" Durant demanded.

Mary Anne was in a quandary. She had caught on to the fact that Jim was vying for the highest personal premium in his decision about suppliers. After all, it wasn't his money, but it was his trip, his golf clubs, his portable bar, his tickets for the plays, and so on. "How much difference could there be in paper or ribbons? So it cost the company a few dollars more on each order," Jim thought, "but they could afford it and this was a great method for improving his perquisites."

Mary Anne was concerned because she had worked for the company longer than Jim and felt that she always had been treated well. What should she tell Mr. Durant about the premiums paid by the suppliers to Jim for their orders?

This situation may or may not be common, but it is possible. On the surface this is not a legal issue but an ethical one, and it is damaging not only employee morale but the company's image. If no one really is hurt, does that make it right? This brings us to the question of ethics and the role it plays in small businesses.

## WHAT IS ETHICS?

Ethics has an ambiguous meaning. Webster defines it as "the study of the standards of conduct and moral judgment." Many organizations have their own ethical codes, which in effect outline the acceptable conduct for their professions, such as the Association of Accountants (AICPA) and the Association of Computing Professionals (ICCP). These associations also rescind membership in situations when individuals have been found not to comply, and those individuals may be subject to imprisonment or fines from a legal perspective as well. Yet, what is ethics to the general populace? Do they have written guidelines for behavior? Of course not—and yet should they?

Everyone can understand and accept the ethical issue relating to the standards of conduct because they are written, acknowledged, and accepted by those who join professions requiring such compliance. But how does one define *moral judgement?* Again Webster claims that **moral judgement** deals with the ability to make the distinction between right and wrong. If everybody does it, does that make it right?

The fast pace, constant competition, global quality, and diversification of today's business arena has seemed to blur those distinctions between right and wrong. Today it seems that the world and its concepts are in various shades of gray rather than the black and white of the past. Can we blame our ability to communicate and trade internationally? When we were isolated and lacked sufficient technology for rapid communication, we didn't know what our competition was doing until we saw it. We were not able to have a small business in Kansas with international outlets. But high tech has brought with it changes in the psyche of the business owner. To compete and survive, some have turned ruthless, not illegal. But what does this do to the moral fiber of our country? Remember that small businesses and the men and women who own them are the backbone of our nation, the reason for its survival. What happens when issues important to us as individuals start becoming ethical issues in various shades of gray?

Each time a person does one small thing with which he or she is uncomfortable, it becomes easier to rationalize the next uncomfortable act that presents itself. Very soon, that person is hardly the same individual as a few years earlier. Has this change been prompted by endeavors in nations that have different standards of conduct or have we been steadily eroding our values in the name of competition? This may not be true for you or many others, but more and more the news tells us of fraud, embezzlement, illegal transfer of technology to the Russians, and so on. These items make headlines, but each of us may be faced with dilemmas of smaller scale every day. What should we tell our bosses about using the computers for personal accounts; using office supplies for our children's homework; doing our own work on company time and with company resources; implying company support for personal promises; using the petty cash for lunch without repaying; filling up with gas at the company pump and not leaving a record?

## SOCIAL AWARENESS OF ETHICS

Morrie Helitzer, publisher of *New Accountant,* in a Publisher's Memo asked the question, "Does Mr./Ms. Clean Exist?"

> A great foe of sound, ethical business practice, or of sound behavior in general, is indifference. The notion that our actions, or inactions, don't much matter, paves the road to disastrous outcomes. What we do and how we do it does matter. As an employee, an employer, a shareholder or a member of the public, you and I are cheated—or cheat the others—when we break the rules.[1]

Much of his discussion was prompted by the fact that firms that have been given a seal of approval by auditors subsequently were found guilty of various infractions, some major and some minor. He also notes that the cleanest of us may have areas in which we are not 100 percent pure.

Ethical considerations quickly are becoming an issue for us today as we see cases of insider trading, malicious hacking, and viruses let loose on the nation's computer networks. Longnecker, McKinney, and Moore surveyed large and small businesses and presented them with ethical vignettes concerning such issues as padded expense accounts, environmental pollution, faulty investment advice, foreign business pay-offs, hiring a key employee of a competitor, collusion in bidding, gifts to purchasing agents, favoritism, discrimination, and misleading advertising. They discovered that, in some areas, small firms appeared more tolerant than larger firms. The researchers found that this was true in areas where there was more involvement on the employees' part and where there was less rigor in the controls of the firm. Longnecker et al. remarked that small businesses have a less formal structure and may have looser controls than larger firms, which might account for some of the differences recorded.[2] Perception indeed seems to be a factor in ethical decisions.

## DISTINCTION BETWEEN ETHICAL AND LEGAL ISSUES

What is the difference between legal and ethical issues? Legal issues are very much like the codes of conduct mentioned earlier. **Legal** means that an action is in conformity with the law. Laws mandate what is constituted as right or wrong and punishments are described for enforcement of those laws. Because breaking legal codes can lead to specified punishments of the person, most people try to conform and see that others do likewise. But what about ethical issues that may mark only the soul and have no outward appearance? Ethical issues may relate to legal ones, but this is not a given. Codes of right and wrong that have been mandated by laws typically are enforced, but moral judgement calls are not so well delineated. Bribes or "greasing palms" may be an accepted practice in other parts of the globe, but it is not an accepted, legal practice in the United States. Do companies who deal internationally forget where they are at times? We don't think so. Accepted practices can be both ethical and legal.

## ETHICAL ISSUES

If indeed social awareness of ethical misconduct is an issue, it probably is the result of the coverage given to companies who allow their sense of profit to outdistance their sense of right. How can computer companies knowingly allow high tech products to find their way to the Soviets? How can we produce software viruses that can destroy companies' records? How can we produce cheaper imitations of products for sale? How can we ban the sale of certain products in the United States and then sell them abroad? Has our sense of fair play been replaced by our lust for the dollar? Surely not!

Quality and competency are other issues with ethical overtones. How can we be content with substandard products or services? Why are cars scheduled to disintegrate with the last payment? Where is our pride of workmanship? Should we not be able to expect a day's work for a day's pay? Should we not expect our doctors, our lawyers, our accountants, our consultants, and our managers to be competent? These issues are important to our discussion of the ethics of small business. Many of our professional people are beginning to realize that they are in small businesses, too. They must promote a service to a particular number of clients or find that they can no longer stay in business. Many professionals are going back to school to learn business topics, so they see a need for competency not only in their chosen fields but in business as well.

## MORAL OBLIGATIONS

Small businesses are increasingly confronted with the moral obligations that relate to their chosen industry. Because the ethical attitudes of the business are a reflection of those held by the owner, the owner also feels the onus when an employee steps out of line. The owner has a moral obligation to provide a safe, comfortable working environment for the employees, which may soon mean enforcing restrictions on smoking; providing for the employee safety; providing good, reliable services or products; assuring a high-quality environment and the maintenance of an ethical image for the company.

Perhaps our legal system has had to replace our consciences in recent years. Why else would companies be forced to go to court for manufacturing faulty and dangerous products; for giving erroneous and harmful advice; for causing harm through neglect or ignorance; for endangering the environment by polluting it; for trading secrets for money; for taking products that are not theirs? Small business owners need not sell their souls to Mephistopheles to succeed. Success in the business arena means creating the best product or service for the best price and making it available to the people. This is done through **planning**, not through scheming.

## DEVELOPING AN ETHICAL PLAN

What can you do? You have pressures. You have felt the twinges or witnessed the results of pseudo-ethical practices and have had to handle them as they arose. What can you do? The best solution is to plan. Many organizations that have struggled with these issues feel that the best approach is to set down standards of conduct. You can, too. When you work out your business plan, think about possible problems that could arise and address them in a written format. Decide on your use of company resources: what is acceptable and what is not? Decide on how you deal with suppliers. Decide who has access to sensitive data on the computer. Decide on a job description for each employee. Decide how you are going to handle and credit innovations. Define ownership of products. Reward "watch dogging," don't punish it. Explain that this is not carrying tales but working for everyone's success. Most of all, write down your standards and have them read as a part of the employment contract. And, be the first to obey the rules! Granting exceptions is the fastest road to disaster, because then inequities are perceived and the edges get blurred.

There is a misconception that a business cannot be successful without condoning some unethical practices, but this is not true. Successful businesses cannot sustain profit without acting ethically, according to Duane Kullberg, because of the link among owners, employees, and customers.[3] As long as there is a recourse or an alternative, the customer will opt for fair treatment or fair product at a fair price.

Ethical issues are felt by some to be a personal assessment of right and wrong, so it becomes a subject taboo for discussion. Today we need open discussions about what is ethical, legal, and moral. We can no longer hide our heads in the sand and pretend indifference. Our business, our life, and our country have a stake in our ethical decision making. Let's make the right decisions.

## SUMMARY

Ethics are a standard of conduct that all must come to terms with individually and for their own enterprises. The standards of conduct must be written down and passed to the employees as guidelines for acceptable behavior. Written rules of conduct can eliminate judgements that often are painful on the part of the owner.

Often the issues faced by a company have legal as well as ethical overtones. Be aware of the consequences of actions and ponder your decisions in light of how well you can live with yourself as the result of such an action. Let this serve as a guideline to ethical behavior. Just because an action is legal does not necessarily make it ethical.

The key to ethical consideration is awareness. Don't refuse to think about or decide upon possible courses of actions, because you feel that ethics are too personal. Be willing to delineate your expectations for yourself as well as others. Develop a written code of conduct to be applied in given situations and there can be no misunderstandings of what is right or what will be condoned by you or your company.

## QUESTIONS

1. What is Webster's definition of *ethics?* What is your definition of *ethics?* Do the two definitions differ in any substantive way?
2. Can ethics be taught? Why or why not?
3. What is the difference between ethical and legal behavior? Can you give some examples of legal but not ethical behavior?
4. Why should there be social awareness of ethical attitudes? How does social awareness make ethical decisions easier?
5. Why is it necessary to have a written plan agreed to by the employees of a small business?
6. Is Jim's behavior, in the situation presented at the start of the chapter, ethical or unethical? What should Mary Anne do? What should Mr. Durant do? How would you solve the problem?
7. Define the following terms:
   a. ethics
   b. moral
   c. legal
   d. pseudo-ethical

## PROJECT

The following situations have legal or ethical overtones. In some cases the problems have not been delineated, because problem identification may be more important to success than problem solution. Define the potential problem and decide what you would do in each situation.

*Situation 1:* Take both sides of the issue or divide into opponents and proponents within your groups. You are a computer information systems professional. What is your stance on hacking and copying applications? What is your stance on those issues as a manager?

*Situation 2:* You have just been given the position as principal buyer for the office supplies for your company. There appears to be no difference among several suppliers except that one carries a special catalog with premiums that could be earned by purchasing from his company. A set of golf clubs could be yours if the company purchases only 200 boxes of paper.

*Situation 3:* Your chief competitor has come out with a new product just six weeks before yours was due to be released, and it has many similarities.

*Situation 4:* As a computer professional, you are asked to erase the record of a transaction for a charitable contribution so the company does not exceed the cap on its income tax deduction for such contributions. This means underreporting income in the same amount.

# Case

Norman was concerned that his company was losing money. The usual cash flow was not there, and yet business seemed to go on as usual. He ran a sheltered workshop that employed handicapped individuals. The workshop used company vans to provide transportation to its employees.

The orders had not changed, the number of employees had not changed, and none of the expenses seemed out of line. So Norman called in a consultant to help him find the difficulty.

The consultant received the financial records of the organization and, at first, seemed unable to find any points of discrepancy. Hal, the consultant, took his lack of findings to his supervisor and explained the difficulties at the workshop and his lack of findings. Hal's supervisor suggested that he try some reasonableness testing in various areas.

Hal performed his reasonableness checks and found nothing out of line, until he looked at gasoline expenses: company vans were getting one mile to the gallon. This item previously had been overlooked, because the vans were used to provide transportation for the handicapped clients and large gas consumption was expected. Could any vehicle still be on the road if it got only one mile per gallon?

When told of the findings, Norman could not explain it and truly did not believe it. Hal then proceeded to observe the facility for several days. He discovered that the employees who drove their personal automobiles were topping off their tanks at the facility's gas pump periodically and leaving no record of the transaction. Hal again reported his findings to Norman. Norman was appalled. He called his employees together and explained the situation to them. He discovered that the practice had started when some of the company vans were in the shop and the employees had to use their own cars for transportation of clients. They had been reimbursed for their gas. Then a couple of times, employees would find that they were low and would give themselves enough to get to the station for a fillup.

What had started as a legitimate practice had become an abusive and unethical one. As new employees saw these practices taking place in the company, they perceived this as a job perquisite to which they, too, were entitled, and so the financial impact on the company was not considered. When the employees were confronted with their behavior, they were not contrite! Rather, they reacted as if a fringe benefit that was their due had been removed.

### Questions

1. Why was it difficult to find the cause for the financial losses?
2. What do you suppose prompted this behavior?
3. Why do you think the employees did not react well to the disclosure?
4. What would you have done in this situation?

# CHAPTER 27

# Small Business Succession

**LEARNING OBJECTIVES**

After completing this chapter, you should be able to

- Understand the importance of planning for succession.
- Know the various contingencies for which the owner must plan to ensure successful succession.
- Identify the problems that could result from divorce.
- Understand the impact a change in management can have on a small business.
- List problems created even when succession is planned.
- Understand that contingency plans should be made for the disability of the CEO in a small business.
- Know how to deal with the problems that will arise when taking over a business.

Like the Walrus in Lewis Carroll's famous poem said, "the time has come to talk of many things." We find ourselves come to a time to talk of different topics. What concluding topics could be more important than the recognition of mortality. It has been said that the human race owes its speed of development and its pace of invention and innovation to the shortness of the lives of its members. A passage in Homer's *Iliad* says it best:

> Like leaves on trees the race of man is found,
> Now green in youth, now withering on the ground,
> Another race the following spring supplies;
> They fall successive; and successive rise.
>
> Homer
> *The Iliad,* Book 6

Like the leaves of Homer's tree each spring brings a new generation and each generation is filled with drive and ambition. That shortness of life drove humankind to develop writing so that knowledge might be preserved; and the invention of writing freed each succeeding generation to blaze new trails building on the wisdom accumulated over the ages. It behooves each of us to make plans for passing the torch to the next generation so that our creations and knowledge can live on. This is the primary subject of this chapter.

There are special problems in small businesses both with passing a business along and with managing a business after its passing. How do you plan for **management succession?** How do you leave a business to your heirs? How can second-generation management succeed? A special stage of this passing is involved in planning for the continuance of a business despite the failure of human institutions or the incapacitation of its management. This refers to the problems and effects of divorce and of disability. What happens to the business when a marriage fails? What happens when the owner becomes disabled?

## DIVORCE

The cover story of the March 1986 *Inc.* magazine was "Divorce, Entrepreneurial Style." The author concluded that to plan for it could ruin your marriage but not to plan for it could destroy your company.[1] The reporter detailed several accounts of people so distraught about the potential loss of a business that they lost everything. One man was convicted of hiring a killer to murder his wife. Another was killed in an altercation with his wife about the division of a business. Many entered into dubious schemes involving salaries and under-the-table deals in an attempt to influence the valuation of a business during a divorce settlement. Others, both men and women, lost their firms to bankruptcy after a divorce. With the rising rate of divorces in the United States, a serious problem has emerged for small business owners.

Nine states have community property laws that, in general, treat a business as a marital asset, in which case it is likely to be divided 50/50. Forty states have equitable property distribution laws that consider economic contribution toward assets in deciding on settlements (Mississippi is a title property state). However, Wisconsin has passed the Uniform Marital Property Act and four other states are presently considering that act, which treats marriage as a partnership. Under that treatment, a business is likely to be divided on a 50/50 basis.[2]

Even if ownership of the business is not an issue, the emotional trauma of a divorce can destroy a small business owner's ability to concentrate and make decisions. Some owners have worked out divisions of businesses only to have the company fail during the transition period. In some companies in which both spouses were active, the parties have attempted to continue their business relationship in the interests of the company. It takes a very unusual couple to make this work!

Until a divorce occurs most people do not think about such things as who owns what and how stock certificates are registered. Of course, it sounds heartless to arrange for the possible distribution of business assets and ownership while a marriage is healthy. Few people are willing to consider that a marriage might fail until it actually happens—then it's too late! The best approach seems an honest appraisal of business ownership and planning for the best interests of both spouses and the business in the event of a breakup. After all, the parties to a divorce are not the only people affected when a business is involved. Employees, other owners or partners, lenders, suppliers, and customers also are affected by a business that is hurt or destroyed by a divorce. Consequently, distasteful as it may seem, the wisest course is to discuss with your attorney the effect of various stock ownership options in the event of a divorce before that stock is distributed. As usually is the case, planning can prevent a host of ills, but it requires careful consideration of all of the contingencies.

## CHANGE

It has become almost a cliche that small business owners can't let go of their companies. In fact, it has become so prevalent for small business owners to sell their stock to their children and stay on as manager, that the IRS has special rules governing such sales. The IRS doesn't like the fact that the proceeds from the sale are taxed at capital gains rates, which tend to be lower than income tax rates, while nothing really changes. These "sham" sales are discouraged by IRS rules, which can require that a small business owner sell 100 percent of his or her investment in the company and then never set foot on the premises again. An article in *Inc.* details one family's successful efforts to get around IRS rules that would prevent the first generation management from continuing to be involved in the company.[3] Color Art, Inc., was successfully passed to the sons of the founders while the founders stayed on as consultants to the business. However, the founders did give up control—a hard thing for many owners to do.

Actually, companies go through a life cycle just like people. A problem frequently develops because, during the start-up phase of a business, which can last from one year to ten years, the skills required for success are entrepreneurial. This means that penetration of a market for a new firm requires innovative approaches. After a firm has passed start up, it enters a growth and consolidation phase, during which time it must establish itself as a permanent member of the competitive community. The skills required to consolidate gains and see a firm through to its maturity stage are administrative skills. Many entrepreneurs do not possess such skills and consequently are forced out of their businesses by other shareholders, venture capitalists, or lenders. The solution to the problem is self-evaluation. A small business owner must recognize personal strengths and weaknesses and be prepared to acquire personnel with the skills necessary to handle the company as its needs change. Cultivate the expertise and share power and authority with the people who have it. This means sharing control.

Frequently, small business owners look to their children for such expertise. At least they say they do! Sons and, with increasing frequency in recent years, daughters are sent off to school and then brought into the firm at lower management levels. These young people are then brought up through the company with the purpose of giving them a broad-based understanding of the business and its needs. In effect, they are being groomed to take over the firm. Unfortunately, the old hands are reluctant and frequently unable to turn over the reins of control. Billye Ericksen-Desaigoudar is an exception.[4] She is grooming five managers, including her three children, to take over her business and has taken pains to keep bankers, customers, suppliers, and employees up to date on her plans. She has even set up a new board of directors to assist in the training the next generation will need. In a few years, she plans to sell the business to the next generation using the customary leveraged buy-out.

(A leveraged buy-out is a process by which the business funds its own purchase. That is, funds are borrowed from the business by the new owners and given to the old owners. Repayment of the debt to the company will come from future salaries and bonuses paid to the new owners. If necessary, the company can borrow the funds and pass them along to the new owners, who repay the loan from salaries and bonuses. Alternatively, the stock of the business is pledged as collateral to secure a loan made by the new owners to fund the purchase from the old owners. The key in every variation is the funding of the payment from future business profits.)

Billye is able to carefully plan this transition because she has other activities that she wishes to pursue, including two other businesses she owns. Perhaps the problem with other owners is that they have no such activities and fear retirement and inactivity. Small business owners tend to be workaholics, as discussed in the introduction to this text. It is much more difficult for someone like that to contemplate retirement. Perhaps, the problem is with the degree of involvement many owners have in their businesses. Starting a business is a creative act and people can be fiercely protective and possessive about their creations. Many have difficulty even thinking about someone else making decisions that will affect the company. You don't have to totally give up a company to bring along a successor.

How about staying involved with the business as long as your health permits? This can be done, but even then problems can arise because of the next generation's desire to "do something important." The successors quite naturally become impatient, want to try out new ideas, and want to change things. The old hands frequently fear such change, fear the mistakes that could be made and the damage that could be done to their creations. But new ideas are the hallmark of small businesses and should be encouraged. Of course, there is risk, but new ideas can rejuvenate a company. Consider the case of M. Jacob & Sons, a hundred-year-old family business.[5] Max Jacob, a Russian immigrant, started the business in 1882. Bottles were hand-blown and expensive and Max saw an opportunity to make money by collecting used bottles door to door in Detroit and then selling them to local breweries and other businesses. Despite stiff competition, the business grew and prospered. Max became the king of the used-bottle business in Detroit.

He brought his sons into the business in 1915. William became a salesman, Ben was the bookkeeper, and Sam drove the horse-drawn delivery wagon. In the 1920s, new technology made mass production of bottles possible. The Jacob brothers saw that the business had to change or die. They developed relationships with bottle manufacturers and became a distributor linking manufacturers with breweries and other users of bottles. They built a strong statewide business. Sales were $1 million in 1940 when Marty, Ben's son, came into the business. It continued to grow until the 1950s when breweries began to consolidate and turn to cans. Sales dropped from $6 million to $3 million, and the brothers were lost. Marty put the company into plastics. By 1977, the company was selling $20 million of plastic bottles each year to Michigan businesses.

Then the businesses started to move south and plants started closing. Sales slumped and Marty tried a host of ideas but nothing worked. His son, Joel, had come into the business in 1982, fresh out of college. Marty had made it clear that Joel would have to prove his worth or he would never take over the business, and that nothing special was going to happen just because he was the boss' son. Joel hit the road selling. One day he noticed that the plastic spray bottles in a K Mart store had poor lettering and wondered about changing the company's emphasis to mass merchandisers. Marty was skeptical; the company had never sold to retailers before, but he told Joel to give it a try. Joel did. He landed the K Mart account, then Frank's Nursery. They set up a division of the company to specialize in spray bottles, and Joel ran it. He started using sales representatives instead of sales people. By 1985, the firm was selling bottles nationwide through a network of representatives. It had been rejuvenated again. Marty is pleased and proud, of course, but not totally comfortable. He sometimes feels that he has lost control and gets upset with Joel's constant ideas for change. He finds the enthusiasm draining sometimes. This is perfectly understandable. Marty was probably like that himself once upon a time, he just doesn't remember it.

The moral of the story is that, if you want to stay involved with your business while bringing along a successor, do so! Just don't be afraid of new ideas, and let your candidate have some freedom to learn to fly. Some things won't work, of course. Mistakes are inevitable. However, think back to the mistakes you made and how much you learned from them. Don't become so arrogant as to think that you will always be able to judge what will and will not succeed. The best thing you can do is ensure that any moves you consider dangerous are always **hedged.** This means that you never bet the entire firm on a new idea. Be sure that the firm will survive even under the worst possible results. This way, the losses won't hurt as badly and the winnings may well rejuvenate the company. It also will allow you to get used to the idea of sharing control and eventually giving it up. It is a great way to evaluate a successor, too!

## MANAGEMENT SUCCESSION

You may remember reading in an introduction to management book that the first responsibility of management is to provide for succession. Large firms do this as a matter of course. The multiple levels of management provide opportunities for new people to be trained and groomed for advancement. As their experience and knowledge grow, their responsibilities grow so that there always are individuals who can be tapped to fill vacancies in management resulting from death, departure, or retirement. The difference in small businesses is that there are fewer levels of management and control typically is vested in a single person or, at most, in a very small number of people. To groom a person for leadership in a small business means that the manager and any other owners must give up part of their control so the new managers can gain the necessary experience to be able to take over the operation one day.

How do you do that? Like most things in business, it is done by planning. If a son or daughter or any other individual is selected as the **heir apparent,** then you must plan for the education and training of that individual. Your candidate for ownership or control must be identified and a willing participant in the grooming process. What role will college play? Are some fields of study more important than others? What jobs and positions within the company are important for understanding the operation? How long should a person be apprenticed in those positions? How can you bring them into more responsible positions? How can you avoid problems with employees who might resent the "fair-haired child"? These and a host of other issues must be dealt with and planned.

There are no absolute answers because the needs of every business and every candidate will be different. One thing is constant, however: the need to bring your successor into top level management activities. The candidate should be exposed to the planning process itself at an early point and encouraged to help with the planning, budgeting, and financial review. Ideas must be encouraged, and the candidate must be allowed to develop and demonstrate competency. At some point, authority must be delegated and the candidate must be allowed to make and follow up on decisions. A sound approach is to provide experience in running the business by having your candidate take over for you during vacations, sales trips, conventions, and so on. These periods gradually can be lengthened as the candidate gains maturity and experience.

One word of caution is due at this point. The individual whom you choose to succeed you must want to succeed you. If you attempt to force a son or daughter into the business, both your child and the business will suffer. The one will be unhappy and, consequently, a poor manager, which can destroy the other. Being a small business owner is hard work and requires long hours. It is filled with risk and diversity. It can be rewarding, but only to a person who enjoys the job. A candidate who does not truly want the job will not do the job well. If your candidate discovers, for whatever reason, that he or she really doesn't want the job after the training and grooming has begun, then change candidates.

The person you choose to groom for your successor need not be a relative. Many small business owners cultivate a promising employee. You must choose someone, however, in your own self-interest. Even if you care nothing for the prospects of the business surviving you, you must be concerned about it providing for your retirement and surviving a disability. You won't feel comfortable about retirement if you don't have capable hands in which to leave the business. In fact, you can't even take a vacation, spend time with your family, or find time away from the business unless someone can be trusted to take care of it during your absence. You will be like the independent dairy farmer who could never take a day off because the cows had to be milked every day. You must find someone who can milk the cows, at least occasionally, and you must plan for the candidate and the cows to get used to each other.

## DISABILITY

A large firm simply moves another manager into a slot if a person becomes disabled. A small firm may be able to do that with employees but not with the owner, unless someone has been groomed for the job. It makes good business sense to cross-train people so that they can cover for each other in the event of an emergency. You should do the same for yourself. You can cover your financial risks of disability with insurance, but you cannot prepare your business to survive your disability without planning.

Even a short period of disability can destroy a small business. If, through accident or disease, you should be unable to function as the manager for only a few months, what would the business do? Who would make decisions? Who would do the planning? Would you have a business to come back to after you recovered? A small business can never rest on its laurels. No matter how strong it has been in the past, no matter what its position now, a small business depends on its future management for survival. The market, competition, and conditions are constantly changing. The business must be constantly changing also. Even a business in a stable industry with an established customer base will suffer from the absence of the owner/manager. Not only are there numerous decisions which must be made daily, but the planning must be done by that person.

This means that you must train and prepare people to be able to take over your functions to protect yourself. What if no one in the business can do the job? What if there is someone, but it will be years before that person is sufficiently trained to do the job? You can provide income to hire a competent manager through insurance. You can obtain disability protection insurance, which will pay the firm money to be used for the salary of a good manager. It may be hard for the firm to find such an individual and you must appoint people to do the hiring in the event that you are unable to participate, but it is the only option available outside simply hoping that nothing bad will happen. At least you can be assured that your planning and budgeting records will be a valuable asset for anyone coming in to take over the operation. They will provide a sound foundation in where the company is, what it does, the strategic image it portrays as well as the goals and objectives you had established. We all hope, but statistics show that many of us hope in vain. It makes more sense to plan and prepare, then hope!

## PLANNING FOR SUCCESSION

The first step in planning for succession is grooming a replacement for yourself as manager. However, several other questions must be answered. Principally, who will own the business in the event of your death? Who will manage it? What role will your spouse play? Do you plan to leave the business to someone who cannot manage it? If so, have you discussed the management of the firm with that person and made plans for that need? Do you have a will? What about life insurance? What will the estate taxes do to your business? More than a few people have had to sell businesses to pay the inheritance taxes because there was not enough cash in the estate to cover them.

It is vital that these factors be considered and contingency plans made. Not only is the survival of the business at stake, but the welfare of your family as well. A business acquaintance had built a strong, healthy chain of automotive service firms specializing in automatic transmission and brake repair. The business was doing several million dollars per year in volume in some nine shops and was well established, when he was killed in an automobile accident. Like most small business owners, he had never faced his own mortality; consequently, he had made no plans for that contingency. His will simply left all assets to his wife, because his two children were of preschool age. Unfortunately, she had neither the business knowledge nor the time to run the firm. What we all had thought was healthy life insurance coverage disappeared quickly in business expenses and payments to suppliers, while the operation began to rapidly decline. She hired a manager, but it was several months before one could be found. In the interim, several employees tried to help, but their knowledge of the operation was less than optimum. Bankers and other lenders began to press for payment when several substantial 90-day notes matured and there was no money to pay them. She was forced to sell the business, but because of its size and condition was unable to find a buyer for the operation as a whole. Each location finally was disposed of in separate deals. As you might imagine, the business did not bring anywhere near its value at the time of the accident. Most of the proceeds of the sale were consumed by bank notes, little actually was left when it was finally over. All this could have been avoided with a little planning.

There are special problems to consider if there are other owners in the business. Are there family members or investors who have a stake in the operation but are inactive in management? In the event of a problem in your estate, such people are likely to exert influence in appointing a manager. Is this what you want? If you have a partner, do you agree on what will happen in the event of the death or disability of one of you? If you have a partner or co-owner who will take over the firm, what will happen to your family? Is there key person life insurance that can be used to buy out your family's interest? Does your partner have the same situation?

Have you done any estate planning? Even though you may not consider yourself to be wealthy, estate and inheritance taxes can be a significant burden on your family. One of the great needs of the estate will be cash or highly liquid assets. If these are inadequate, then the business or part of its assets may have to be sold under distressed conditions. It surely won't bring much that way. Do you know how much your business is worth? Its value will be part of your estate and you can be sure that the IRS will determine a value for it if you haven't. That value will have a major impact on the amount of cash the estate will require. You should talk to an attorney or estate planning specialist to protect your family and your business. This is not a one-time action. You must regularly update your estate plans as the value of your business grows and other circumstances change. A yearly review of your estate plans is good practice.

## TAKING OVER A BUSINESS

There are special problems for a person being groomed to take over a business and for the new CEO of a business. If you wish a smooth transition and a healthy business, you need to be aware of these. Many of the problems can be minimized by the right approach on the part of the old management.

The heir apparent, the person being groomed to take over a business, can be resented by the other employees and managers of the firm. Phrases such as "that's the boss's idiot son," or "here comes our future boss" frequently may be heard in the employee lounge. If the staff of a small firm has no confidence in your candidate, then his or her effectiveness, both on the present job and later as owner/manager, can be greatly harmed. These feelings of resentment spring from a natural feeling of superiority that most people have. They consider themselves to be more knowledgeable and capable than your successor and so they resent being forced into a subordinate position. They may dislike the prospects your successor has for advancement. After all, that person is assured of rapid movement through the company and choice job assignments whereas everyone else has to work for those things. They also may resent the idea of a successor. It establishes a limit to their own ambitions. How do you fight these problems?

First of all, your candidate as well as the staff and employees need to know that nothing is guaranteed. No one will be permitted to succeed to the office of owner/manager without first demonstrating the capability to handle the job. You need to dispel the idea of choice jobs and rapid promotion by requiring that your candidate work harder than anyone else in the firm. The one overriding quality that your successor is bound to need is a capacity for hard work. You know that; your candidate should know it as well. Promotions may be rapid in terms of time, but if they are always based solely on merit and demonstrated competence, then the resentment will be less. The competence must be real. Your candidate rapidly must become knowledgeable. You need it; the company needs it; and the candidate needs it to forestall problems with the employees of the firm.

A good part of the problem with other employees can spring from the attitude of your candidate. If that person is arrogant in speech, mannerism, or action, then your staff and employees will react unfavorably. Your training must make it clear to your candidate that the future management of the enterprise means the management of its people and that their trust and confidence, or lack of it, will limit the effectiveness of such management. Your successor must win the trust and confidence through hard work, study, and concern for the company and its employees. This sounds a little like a sermon, doesn't it? What it truly is, is psychology. People are managed by maneuvering them into *wanting* to perform for the company. They cannot be *made* to choose the company's goals and objectives as their own. They must want to do so. They also must want to help bring along your successor. To accomplish this, both you and the candidate must work together. Skills and knowledge must be developed, but leadership ability must be cultivated, too. As the old saying goes, "You lead from the front. You can't push a chain, it must be pulled to get it anywhere."

Even if you have the perfect candidate, an outstanding training and educational program, and an enthusiastic and supportive staff, your successor will never be able to succeed if you personally do not let go. At the end of Chapter 9, we described a second-generation manager who was unable to establish an effective inventory control program because of his father's continued involvement in the firm. Control had been relinquished; the son was the owner/manager and made most decisions. The problem was that the founder of the company made decisions as well; decisions that frequently were at odds with those of his son. This happens more often than most would believe. It is one thing to give up control of a company you founded and fought to establish, it is quite another thing to give up all power in that company.

We talked earlier about maintaining an involvement in a company after turning it over to a successor. There is nothing wrong with this action; however, both you and your successor should understand the limits of that involvement. It cannot be at odds with the role of your successor. The most valuable role you can play in a company after passing it on is as a senior advisor and consultant on policy matters. This is also the most rewarding role you can play from your perspective. The place to maintain an involvement is in the planning activities. You can truly make a continued contribution to the firm and its growth and development in this fashion. Nothing is more important than setting goals and objectives; strategic posture development; budgeting, forecasting, and financial analysis; in short, the planning process. This is where a firm is made or broken, the future molded. It is the most difficult and challenging aspect of management and the hardest skill to develop. A new owner/manager who has an old hand to guide this effort is twice blessed. Not only will that involvement help guard against counterproductive actions, planning will be stronger and more effective.

As any small business owner who has practiced planning activities will testify, planning can consume as much time as you will devote to it. In a typical firm, the owner/manager never has enough time for planning. This means that you can devote as much or as little time to planning assistance as you desire. Your continued involvement in the firm can be full time, half time, or one weekend per month. Not only will that effort be useful to the firm, it can continue the training of your successor as you participate in the planning activities together. A more rewarding solution to the problem of continued involvement cannot be found!

One word of caution is due here. The new ideas talked about earlier must be encouraged in the planning process. You must allow your successor full input. Only in this way can the firm benefit both from your accumulated wisdom and experience and the fresh insight and enthusiasm of your successor. If you have done your job well, if you have cultivated a strong successor, then the give and take of the planning sessions can be the most fun you have ever had in managing the company. This truly is the secret of family businesses that succeed from generation to generation: the mingling of fresh ideas and approaches with the wisdom and insight of experience. It also can be the secret of a happy and long-lasting career.

## SUMMARY

No one likes to think of death or plan for its contingencies. But planning for such an event is a very unselfish act. Even without having to contend with a business's survival, a spouse has to shoulder a large burden when a loved one dies. With the added stress of grief, why compound the suffering by precipitating financial insecurity in the form of business decisions? Plan for your loved ones as well as your business. If you have dreams of building a successful business for your family, don't allow it to be taken away from them by failure to plan.

The loss of a business is not predicated only on death. It also could result from divorce or disability. An owner-manager who becomes ill or survives a debilitating accident may not be able to run the business for long periods of time. Can it survive your absence, even temporarily? It can if you have planned wisely.

Divorce also is not a popular contingency for which to plan. But, in an age when almost three out of four marriages end in divorce, it is a contingency for which plans must be made. Then pray that it doesn't happen to you. Working closely together in a business sometimes is hazardous to a marriage. Partners often are heard to say that they have no breathing space away from each other or they bring the stresses found in the business home with them. Just as it takes effort to have a successful business, so, too, effort is required for a successful marriage. Perhaps planning for the contingency of divorce will strengthen a marital relationship by causing you to examine what could happen if the marriage were not successful. Planning again is an unselfish act. Not only is the business in jeopardy from a divorce, but so, too, are the employees, other partners or owners, and the customers.

Change in management from first to second generation also is an area for which plans should be made. Many founders find that they cannot really leave the business to those for whom it was intended. Children are sent to school or employed by the business in anticipation of coming into their own, only to find that the owner won't let them make any decisions.

Successful businesses that are not family oriented also have problems in the same area. If a business is to grow over time, the owner/manager must relinquish some of the control to others. Many founders discover that they cannot grow in their management skills as the company grows, with the result that the company does not achieve its potential or others take it away through stock manipulation. The solution is to plan for growth and succession and to stick to your plans. Because start up of a new business is a creative venture and many small business owners put their very souls into its success, they find it difficult to watch others take over and do things differently. The best solution when you pass the company on to your successor is to take over the aspects of the company for which operational management has no time. Be a consultant for the firm. Give it the benefit of your wisdom, experience, and expertise and help with the strategic planning of the company. In this way, the company remains successful under second-generation leadership, and you continue to be useful.

Large businesses plan for succession naturally. However, when small businesses do likewise, problems can develop. Naming a successor can lead to jealousy and frustration if that successor is unwilling or incompetent. So be sure that you choose wisely and train well your successor. On the other side of the succession coin are the problems related to how well your successor will fare when the plan is known. The attitude of the successor is vital to the success of the company. How well he or she can relate to the other employees is important. Your successor's competency should be without question.

Yet as in all else the emphasis has been on planning. Here, too, it is imperative. The life of your company depends upon it.

## QUESTIONS

1. What problems are associated with succession?
2. How can the problems of succession be eliminated?
3. Why do you suppose so many states are looking at the issue of property rights when a business is at stake in a divorce proceeding?
4. Why does the owner have difficulty in turning over his or her company to a successor?
5. What problems do the successors have even when chosen early and groomed for the take-over?

## PROJECTS

1. Contact several business owners and broach the topic of succession with them. Have they considered it? Are they planning to turn the company over to a son or daughter? What makes the son or daughter qualified to take over the business? Is there someone else who plans to take over? If so, when and how?
2. Talk to a local attorney about the divorce laws that relate to a small business in your state. Perhaps, the attorney can give you examples of the types of actions to beware of in making your contingency plans. What are the estate laws for your state? What happens if the owner does not leave a will?
3. Share with your class or group any examples of how business succession was treated in the case of a death, divorce, or disability with which you may be familiar. What would you do if you were a small business owner to cover these contingencies?

# Case 1

Betty Lynn and Dan Roberts were co-owners of a moderately successful book store in the northern section of Atlanta, Georgia. They had been married for six years and in business for five years. The marriage failed and they decided to divorce. The problem is what to do with the business. The business is incorporated with each spouse owning 50 percent of the stock. Both want to keep the business and continue to operate it under its established name: Roberts' Books.

Betty Lynn and Dan have discussed the possibility of continuing their business association after the divorce is final, but both of them are concerned that there will be too much strain for that to succeed. They could sell the business, but neither really wants to do that.

Each has offered to buy the other out using a leveraged buy-out arrangement. Neither wants to sell, because they both want to continue in the business. Both have been advised by their attorneys that they must reach an agreement soon or else the court is likely to force the sale of the business.

### Questions

1. What would you recommend to the Roberts?
2. Could prior planning have eased this problem?
3. What kind of prior agreement would you have recommended?

# Case 2

Arnold Brackett, twenty-six years old, was the proud owner of a roofing company in a medium-sized city in eastern North Carolina. Arnold's father had retired a year and a half ago after setting him up as the owner and manager of the family business. Arnold's father founded the firm more than twenty years ago and built it into a strong, reputable, local contracting business, specializing in roofing for commercial buildings.

Arnold called in a consultant because the firm had not been performing well over the last couple of years. The consultant examined the books and the financial statements and determined that the business had lost sales and profits since the change in management. The business had done well for many years prior to that change.

Arnold explained that the problem was the economic conditions: housing starts were down and that affected commercial construction as well. He needed some way to make the permanent staff more productive.

A core of employees were employed full time, year round, because of their skills. The bulk of the employees were hired on a job-by-job basis. The core employees handled the supervision of the temporary staff and all the details of completing a roofing job. One of the older men had been with the firm fifteen years and handled most of the job bidding for Arnold. Because this core of people basically was not productive when the weather was bad or a job was not underway, it created a great drain on the business.

Arnold had grown up in the business. He worked summers during high school for his dad. He went to college after high school, but in his words, "That didn't work." After a year and a half, he returned to work in the business. His dad immediately made Arnold a supervisor and set out to teach him the roofing business. That was six years ago. Arnold had worked at every job in the firm and learned them all. All of the employees liked him.

During the interview, Arnold frequently became defensive. He was especially sensitive about the decline in the firm's performance since he had taken over control. His dad had retired for real and was unaware of the decline in the business.

The consultant developed a series of ideas to make the permanent staff more productive. These ranged from fabricating a variety of wooden products that could be sold in the local area to diversifying the business into related lines of construction. Arnold didn't like any of them.

On the third visit, the consultant began to ask personal questions. What did Arnold really want to do with this company? What were his goals and objectives? Where would he like to be in five years, etc.? He replied, "I dunno, fishin' I guess."

The consultant asked Arnold if he enjoyed his job. Arnold replied, "No one likes roofing. It's a hot, dirty job and mighty hard work." The second consultant asked why he was in the business if he felt that way about it. "My Dad always wanted me to take over the business some day. Everyone knew I would."

## Questions

1. If you were the consultant in this case, what advice would you give Arnold?
2. Do you think Arnold's father did a good job of preparing him to take over the business?
3. What mistake do you think Arnold's father made in making his succession plans?

# References

## Chapter 1


1. Megginson, L. C., Trueblood, L. R., and Ross, G. M. *Business* (Lexington, Mass: D. C. Heath & Co.), 1985, p. 4.
2. Bursk, C. B. *The World of Business* (New York: Macmillan, 1963), p. 2.
3. Driver, G. R., and Miles, J. C. *The Babylonian Laws* (Oxford: The Clarendon Press, 1955), p. 83.
4. U.S. Small Business Administration. *SBA Rules and Regulations* (Washington, D.C.: U.S. Government Printing Office, 1978), p. 121.
5. *The State of Small Business: A Report of the President* (Washington, D.C.: U.S. Government Printing Office, 1987).
6. "Small Business Keeps America Working," *Nation's Business* (June 1979).
7. *Business Loans from the SBA* (Washington, D.C.: Small Business Administration, September 1984), p. 3.
8. U.S. Department of Commerce. *Enterprise Statistics* (Washington, D.C.: U.S. Government Printing Office, 1977).
9. The President's Task Force on International Private Enterprise. *Report to the President* (Washington, D.C.: Agency for International Development, 1984), p. 161.
10. Chandler A. D. *Strategy and Structure: Chapters in the History of the American Industrial Enterprise* (Cambridge, Mass.: MIT Press, 1962).
11. *The State of Small Business.*
12. *Small Business and Innovation* (Washington, D.C.: U.S. Government Printing Office, 1979).
13. Chandler, *Strategy and Structure,* pp. 114–18.
14. Cocks, J. "The Updated Books of Jobs," *Time* (January 3, 1983), p. 26.
15. Richman, T. "The Entrepreneurial Mystique: An Interview with Peter Drucker," *Inc.* (October 1985), p. 36.
16. Kroc, R. A., with Anderson, A. *Grinding It Out* (Chicago: Henry Regnery Co., 1977).
17. Carland, J. W., Hoy, F., Boulton, W. R., and Carland, J. A. "Differentiating Entrepreneurs from Small Business Owners: A Conceptualization," *Academy of Management Review* (April 1984), p. 358.
18. *Ibid.*
19. Brockhaus, R. H. "Risk Taking Propensity of Entrepreneurs," *Academy of Management Journal* (September 1980), pp. 509–520.


## Chapter 2


1. Kilby, P. "Hunting the Heffalump," *Entrepreneurship and Economic Development* (New York: Free Press, 1971).
2. McClelland, D. *The Achieving Society* (Princeton, N.J.: Van Nostrand, 1961); McClelland, D. "Achievement Motivation Can Be Developed," *Harvard Business Review* (November–December 1965), pp. 6–24, 178; McClelland, D., and Winter, D. G. *Motivating Economic Achievement* (New York: Free Press, 1969).
3. Hull, D. L., Bosley, J. J., and Udell, G. G. "Renewing the Hunt for the Heffalump: Identifying

Potential Entrepreneurs by Personality Characteristics," *Journal of Small Business Management* (January 1980), pp. 11–18.

4. Liles, P. R. *New Business Ventures and the Entrepreneur* (Homewood, Ill.: Irwin, 1974).
5. Rotter J. B. "Generalized Expectancies for Internal Versus External Control of Reinforcement," *Psychological Monographs* 80, no. 609 (1966).
6. Liles, *New Business Ventures.*
7. Hull, Bosley, and Udell, "Renewing the Hunt for the Heffalump"; Brockhaus, R. H., and Nord, W. R. "An Exploration of Factors Affecting the Entrepreneurial Decision: Personal Characteristics Versus Environmental Conditions," *Proceedings of the Academy of Management* (August 1979).
8. Hornaday, J. A., and Aboud, J. "Characteristics of Successful Entrepreneurs," *Personnel Psychology* (Summer 1971), pp. 141–153.
9. Shapero, A., and Sokol, L. "The Social Dimensions of Entrepreneurship," in C. A. Kent, D. L. Sexton, and K. H. Vesper (eds.), *Encyclopedia of Entrepreneurship* (Englewood Cliffs, N.J.: Prentice-Hall, 1982), pp. 72–90.
10. Hornaday, J. A., and Tieken, N. B. "Capturing Twenty-One Heffalumps," in J. A. Hornaday, J. A. Timmons, and K. H. Vesper (eds.), *Frontiers of Entrepreneurship Research* (Wellesley, MA: Babson College Center for Entrepreneurial Research, 1983), pp. 23–50. Reprinted by permission.
11. Shapero and Sokol, "Social Dimensions of Entrepreneurship."
12. *Ibid.*
13. Peterson, W. "Chinese Americans and Japanese Americans," in T. Sowell (ed.), *American Ethnic Groups* (Washington, D.C.: Urban Institute, 1978); Light, I. H. *Ethnic Enterprise in America* (Berkeley: University of California, 1972).
14. Shapero and Sokol, "Social Dimensions of Entrepreneurship."
15. Richman, T. "The Entrepreneurial Mystique: An Interview with Peter Drucker," *Inc.* (October 1985), p. 34.
16. Hornaday and Aboud, "Characteristics of Successful Entrepreneurs."
17. Collins, D. F., and Moore, D. G. "The Enterprising Man," *MSU Business Studies* (1964), pp. 19–33.
18. Cooper, A. C., "Technical Entrepreneurship: What Do We Know?" in C. M. Baumback and J. R. Mancuso (eds.), *Entrepreneurship and Venture Management* (Englewood Cliffs, N.J.: Prentice-Hall, 1975), pp. 42–53.
19. Hornaday and Tieken, "Capturing Twenty-One Heffalumps."
20. *Failure Rates of New Business Ventures* (New York: Dun and Bradstreet, 1977).
21. *The Business Failure Record* (New York: Dun and Bradstreet, 1981).
22. *Ford at Fifty* (New York: Simon and Schuster, 1953).
23. "Chief Executives Typically Work 60 Hour Weeks, Put Careers First," *Wall Street Journal* (August 19, 1980), p. 31.
24. Wozniak, S. "Chips and Dips," *InfoWorld* (October 8, 1984), pp. 50–51; "To Each His Own Computer," *Newsweek* (February 22, 1982), pp. 50–56.

## Chapter 3

1. Lynn, R. (ed.). *The Entrepreneur* (London: George Allen & Urwin, 1973), p. 50.
2. Emerson, R. W., lecture in 1871.

3. Wall Street Journal (eds.). *The New Millionaires and How They Made Their Fortunes* (New York: Bernard Geis Associates, 1961).
4. *News Front* (eds.). *The 50 Great Pioneers of American Industry* (Maplewood, N.J.: Hamond, 1964).


## Chapter 4


1. Previts, G. J. "The Accountant in Our History: A Bicentennial Overview," *Journal of Accountancy* (July 1976), p. 46.
2. Winkler, J. *John D., A Portrait in Oils* (New York: Vanguard Press, 1929), p. 67.


## Chapter 9


1. McLellan, V. "The Assassins: Off Line Computer Crime Points up the Widespread Carelessness of Serious Micro Users," *Digital Review* (February 1985), p. 15.
2. McLellan, V. "Of Trojan Horses, Data Diddling, and Logic Bombs: How Computer Thieves Are Exploiting Companies' Hidden Vulnerabilities," *Inc.* (June 1984), p. 104 ff.
3. Keown, T. "Disaster Plan Worked Despite Unforeseen Loopholes," *MIS Week* (July 28, 1982), p. 22.
4. Stair, R. M. "Computer Disaster Planning for the Small Business," *Journal of Small Business Management* (July 1983), pp. 13–18.
5. Black, B. C. "Rooting out Security Mania," *Infoworld* (April 8, 1985), p. 7.


## Chapter 10


1. Wojahn, E. "Divorce," *Inc.* (March, 1986), pp. 55–64.
2. Linden, E. "Frederick W. Smith of Federal Express: He Didn't Get There Overnight," *Inc.* (April, 1984), p. 89; Jenster, P. V. with Chevion, D., Gardner, J., and Rinehart, D. "Federal Express: Is There Any Zip Left in Zap Mail?" in J. A. Pierce, and R. B. Robinson (eds). *Strategic Management* (Homewood, Ill: Richard D. Irwin, 1988), pp. 510–520; "Overnight Wonder," *Time* (February 15, 1982), p. 43.
3. Merwin, J. "Nike's Fast Track," *Forbes* (November 23, 1981), pp. 59–62; "Fitting the World in Sport Shoes," *Business Week* (January 25, 1982), pp. 73–74; "Fast Track," *Time* (February 15, 1982), p. 43; Magnet, M. "Nike Starts the Second Mile," *Fortune* (November 1, 1982), pp. 158–166.
4. "Dealing in Discounts," *Time* (February 15, 1982), p. 44.
5. Richman, T. "How Do You Sell a Light Bulb that Never Burns Out?" Reprinted with permissions, *Inc.* magazine, (March 1986). Copyright © 1986 by Goldhirsh Group, Inc., 38 Commercial Wharf, Boston, MA 02110.


## Chapter 12


1. Dahl, J. "Opening the Financial Door," *Wall Street Journal* (May 19, 1986), pp. 1D ff.
2. *Ibid.*
3. *Ibid*, p. 40.


## Chapter 13


1. Hand, L. *Commissioner v. Newman*, 159 F. 2d 848 (2d Cir., 1947).

## Chapter 14

1. Carland, J. W., and White, L. R. "Valuing the Small Business," *Journal of Small Business Management* (October 1980), pp. 40–48.
2. Gomes, G. M. "Excess Earnings, Competitive Advantage and Goodwill Value," *Journal of Small Business Management* (July 1988), pp. 22–31.
3. Coyne, K. P. "Sustainable Competitive Advantage—What It Is, What It Isn't," *Business Horizons* (January–February 1986), pp. 54–61.
4. Stoner, C. R. "Distinctive Competence and Competitive Advantage," *Journal of Small Business Management* (April 1987), pp. 33–39.
5. Stoner, "Distinctive Competence and Competitive Advantage."

## Chapter 15

1. *The Business Failure Record* (New York: Dun and Bradstreet, 1981).
2. Chandler, A. D. *Strategy and Structure* (Cambridge, MA: MIT Press, 1962).

## Chapter 19

1. "Joe Larson's Trial by Fire," *Inc.* (December 1981), pp. 61–64.

## Chapter 22

1. Posner, B. G. "Real Entrepreneurs Don't Plan," *Inc.* (November 1985), pp. 129–135.

## Chapter 24

1. "The American Opportunity," *Inc.'s Guide to International Business,* Special Edition (Fall 1988), p. 5.
2. *Ibid.*
3. Plotkin, H. "Going International," *Inc.'s Guide to International Business,* pp. 6–12.
4. Finegan, J. "State Capital," *Inc.'s Guide to International Business,* pp. 31–34.
5. Egan, T., "Home Court Advantage," *Inc.'s Guide to International Business,* pp. 37–39.

## Chapter 25

1. Davidson, D. V., Knowles, B. E., Forsythe, L. M., and Jesperson, R. R. *Business Law: Principles and Cases,* Third Edition (Boston: PWS-KENT, 1989), p. 1008.

## Chapter 26

1. Helitzer, M. "Does Mr./Ms. Clean Exist?" *New Accountant* (September 1988), p. 2.
2. Longnecker, J. G., McKinney, J. A., and Moore, C. W. "Ethics in Small Business," *Journal of Small Business Management* (January 1989), pp. 27–31.
3. Kullberg, D. "Right and Wrong: How Easy to Decide?" *New Accountant* (September 1988), pp. 16–20, 37.

## Chapter 27


1. Wojahn, E. "Divorce, Entrepreneurial Style," *Inc.* (March 1986), pp. 55–64.
2. Freed, D. J. and Walker, T. B. "Family Law in the Fifty States: An Overview," *Family Law Quarterly* (Winter 1985).
3. Kahn, J. P. "A Perfect Pass," *Inc.* (June 1985), pp. 68–71.
4. Fenn, D. "The Family Plan," *Inc.* (April 1986), pp. 119–120.
5. Posner, B. G. "The 100 Year Old Start-Up." Reprinted with permission, *Inc.* magazine, (September 1985). Copyright © 1985 by Goldhirsh Group, Inc., 38 Commercial Wharf, Boston, MA 02110.

# Index